CW01668768

European Company Law

Second edition

Taking a text, cases and materials approach, de Luca's successful textbook remains the only offering for students of European company law, and has been thoroughly updated in this new edition. Chapters have been expanded to cover the latest legislation and directives on cross-border mergers, the use of digital tools, and cross-border insolvency, while figures and graphs have been introduced to help illustrate complex processes and relationships. Clearly differentiated explanatory textboxes from the first edition have been revised, and allow students to quickly identify sources such as EU legislation, official documents and excerpts from scholarly papers. The book explores a diverse range of topics, from what European company law is, to the structure of the Societas Europaea Statute, capital markets and takeover law. It continues to be an essential resource for the growing number of graduate courses in European company law, European business law, and comparative corporate law.

Nicola de Luca is Full Professor of Law at Vanvitelli University, Naples and Luiss Guido Carli, Rome. His research and teaching interests include company law, insurance law, mergers and acquisitions, shareholders' relations and comparative corporate governance. He has previously been a visiting scholar at Yale University, the University of Heidelberg and Goethe University of Frankfurt. He has authored four monographs, a handbook on company law, a treatise, and numerous articles and case notes.

European Company Law

Second edition

NICOLA DE LUCA
Vanvitelli University, Naples & Luiss Guido Carli, Rome

CAMBRIDGE
UNIVERSITY PRESS

CAMBRIDGE
UNIVERSITY PRESS

University Printing House, Cambridge CB2 8BS, United Kingdom

One Liberty Plaza, 20th Floor, New York, NY 10006, USA

477 Williamstown Road, Port Melbourne, VIC 3207, Australia

314–321, 3rd Floor, Plot 3, Splendor Forum, Jasola District Centre, New Delhi – 110025, India

79 Anson Road, #06–04/06, Singapore 079906

Cambridge University Press is part of the University of Cambridge.

It furthers the University's mission by disseminating knowledge in the pursuit of education, learning, and research at the highest international levels of excellence.

www.cambridge.org
Information on this title: www.cambridge.org/9781108843522
DOI: 10.1017/9781108918992

First edition published 2017
Second edition published 2021

Printed in the United Kingdom by TJ Books Limited, Padstow Cornwall

A catalogue record for this publication is available from the British Library.

ISBN 978-1-108-84352-2 Hardback
ISBN 978-1-108-82565-8 Paperback

To Grazia, and to all my students.

Contents

Part III Formation

Part IV Finance and Accounts

Part VII Merger, Division, Conversion, Dissolution, and Insolvency

Table of Cases

Acronyms and Abbreviations

Text

AG	Aktiengesellschaft
BBG	Undesbeschaffung GmbH (Austrian Federal Procurement Agency)
BGHZ	Bundesgerichtshof in Zivilsachen
CESR	Committee of European Securities Regulators (now ESMA)
CFO	Chief Financial Officer
CJEU	Court of Justice of the European Union
CLD	Company Law Directive
COMI	Centre Of Main Interests
CRD	Capital Requirements Directive
DG ENTR	Directorate-General for Enterprise and Industry
d. lgs.	Decreto legislativo
EEA	European Economic Area
EEC	European Economic Community
EC	European Community
ECGI	European Corporate Governance Institute
ECHR	Convention for the Protection of Human Rights and Fundamental Freedoms
ECL	European Company Law ECOFIN/Ecofin Economic and Social Affairs Council
EEC	European Economic Community
EEIG	European Economic Interest Grouping
EESC	European Economic and Social Committee
EMCA	European Model Company Act
ESMA	European Securities and Markets Authority
EU	European Union
FC	Foreign company
FE	*Fundatio Europaea* (European Foundation)
FSAP	Financial Services Action Plan
GAAP	Generally Accepted Accounting Principles (US)

GmbHG	Gesellschaft mit beschränkter Haftung (Law on limited-liability companies, Germany)
I+R	Interest and Royalty
IAS	International Accounting Standard
IASB	International Accounting Standards Board
IASC	International Accounting Standards Committee
IFRIC	International Financial Reporting Interpretations Committee
IFRS	International Financial Reporting Standards
IFSC	International Financial Services Centre
IMI	Internal Market Information System
IPO	Initial Public Offering
ISA	International Standards on Auditing
LLP	limited-liability partnership
LSA	Ley de Sociedades Anónimas (now LSC)
LSC	Ley de Sociedades Comerciales
MAD	Market Abuse Directive
MBCA	Model Business Corporation Act
ME	*Mutua Europaea* (European Mutual Society)
MEP	Member of the European Parliament
MiFID	Markets in Financial Instruments Directive
MTF	Multilateral Trading Facility
NA	National Association (Bank of America)
NYSE	New York Stock Exchange
OECD	Organisation for Economic Cooperation and Development
OTC	Over-The-Counter (transaction)
OTF	Organised Trading Facilities
PLC	Public Limited Company
RGDN	Dirección General de los Registros y del Notariado (Spanish General Direction of Register)
ROL	recapitalise or liquidate
SBA	Small Business Act
SBI	Social Business Initiative
SCE	*Societas Cooperativa Europaea* (European Cooperative Society)
SE	*Societas Europaea* (European Private Company)
SEC	Securities and Exchange Commission (US)
SIC	Standards Interpretation Committee
SLIM	Simpler Legislation for the Internal Market
SME	Small and Medium-Sized Enterprise
SPE	*Societas Privata Europaea* (European Private Company)

SUP	*Societas Unius Personae* (European Single-Member Company)
TFEU	Treaty on the Functioning of the European Union
UCIT	Undertakings for the Collective Investment in Transferable securities
UGB	Unternehmensgesetzbuch (Austrian commercial code)
UK	United Kingdom
UmwG	Law on Company Transformations (Germany)
UNCITRAL	United Nations Commission on International Trade Law
US	United States
VAT	value-added tax
WFBV	Law on Formally Foreign Countries (Netherlands)

Law Journals

Brook. J. Int'l L.	Brooklyn Journal of International Law
Bus. Law.	Business Lawyer
Cal. L. Rev.	University of California Law Review
Cardozo J. Int'l & Comp. L.	Cardozo Journal of International and Comparative Law
Cardozo L. Rev.	Cardozo Law Review
Colum. J. Eur. L.	Columbia Journal of European Law
Colum. L. Rev.	Columbia Law Review
Comm. Mkt L. Rev.	Common Market Law Review
Cornell L. Rev.	Cornell Law Review
Del. J. Corp. L.	Delaware Journal of Corporate Law
EBL	European Business Law
EBLR	European Business Law Review
EBOR	European Business Organization Law Review
ECFR	European Company and Financial Law Review
ECL	European Company Law
EC Tax Rev.	EC Tax Review
Geo. L.J.	Georgetown Law Journal
Harv. Int'l L.J.	Harvard International Law Journal
Harv. L. Rev.	Harvard Law Review
Hous. J. Int'l L.	Houston Journal of International Law
Indus. L.J.	Industrial Law Journal
InterEULawEast: J. Int'l & Eur. L., Econ. & Market Integrations	Journal for International and European Law, Economics and Market Integrations

Int'l & Comp. L.Q.	International and Comparative Law Quarterly
Int'l L. & Mgmt Rev.	International Law & Management Review
J. Comp. L.	Journal of Comparative Law
J. Corp. Fin.	Journal of Corporation Finance
JFE	Journal of Financial Economics
J. Int'l L.	Journal of International Law
JLEO	Journal of Law, Economics, & Organization
Maastricht J. Eur. & Comp. L.	Maastricht Journal of European and Comparative Law
Mich. L. Rev.	Michigan Law Review
MLR	Modern Law Review
Nw. J. Int'l L. & Bus.	Northwestern Journal of International Law & Business
QJE	Quarterly Journal of Economics
Richmond J. Global L. & B.	Richmond Journal of Global Law and Business
So. Cal. L. Rev.	Southern California Law Review
Texas Int'l L.J.	Texas International Law Journal
UCLA L. Rev.	University of California at Los Angeles Law Review
U. Pa Int'l Econ. L.J.	University of Pennsylvania International Economic Law Journal
U. Pa L. Rev.	University of Pennsylvania Law Review
Va J. of Int'l L.	Virginia Journal of International Law
Va L. Rev.	Virginia Law Review
Yale L.J.	Yale Law Journal

Preface

This book deals with European Company Law. Whilst many are (more or less) aware of what a company is, and of the fields that company law covers, a clarification of the adjective 'European' is required.

Similarly to the US or other federal systems, companies established and/or operating in any of the Member States of the European Union (hereafter EU) are regulated by the company laws of the Member States. However, on the one hand, the company laws of the Member States must comply with some rules and principles which constitute the body of a supranational set of laws delivered by the EU institutions, binding as either hard or soft law. On the other hand, notwithstanding that the EU is neither sovereign State nor a federation of States, its institutions may issue acts directly binding all citizens and companies established and/or operating in the EU, thereby prevailing over the company laws of the Member States.

Therefore, the adjective 'European' qualifying company law here is intended to make direct reference to the legal rules and principles of company law enshrined in the sources of law of the EU. In turn, this book is not intended to deal with the individual/domestic company laws of EU Member States, unless it is necessary for a better understanding of EU law.

Since European Company Law has become an important study matter for lawyers of EU Member States, many European (and not only European) universities offer courses in European Company Law, or broader courses including European Company Law (such as European Business Law or Comparative Company Law). Therefore, this book aims to give an insight into the existing European Company Law and shed some light on its foreseeable future development. It includes seven Parts. Part I explains what European Company Law is, where it comes from and where it is potentially going. Part II illustrates how companies formed under EU Member States' laws may enjoy the freedom of establishment and the freedom to provide services. Parts III–IV describe the common rules for establishing, financing and accounting in a company. Part V concerns corporate governance, including management and control, shareholders' rights and general meeting issues. Parts III–V reflect the structure of the SE (*Societas Europaea*) Statute, whilst also discussing the EU Company Law Directives. Part VI gives a brief overview of capital markets and takeover law. Part VII deals with merger and division, as well as with winding-up, liquidation and insolvency of companies (based on the Regulation on Insolvency Proceedings and on the Directive on Restructuring and Insolvency). Each Part is further divided into chapters and paragraphs. The book is designed so that the reader may easily recognise explanatory commentary, cases and materials (EU legislation, European Court of Justice cases, official documents or excerpts from scholarly papers) as well as references for further reading (scholarly papers or other cases and materials): these references are mainly designed to support more in-depth study (papers or final dissertations).

Indeed, this book is expressly designed to support law students – both in residence and those visiting on exchange programme basis, undergraduate as well as postgraduate ones – and to help familiarise them with European Company Law. The book itself is the outcome of many years teaching this subject at Luiss University – Guido Carli in Rome, and is dedicated to my wife Grazia and to all my (past and future) students. I wish to thank those who gave me their class notes, read earlier drafts and provided me with valuable comments from a 'consumer perspective'. For the second edition, I have also benefited from the book reviews and comments of academics and students of many European universities who read the first edition as an adopted textbook or having chosen to read it for their studies. This book would have not come to fruition without their support. The usual disclaimers apply.

Part I

The Origins and Future of European Company Law

1

TFEU Provisions on Company Law

1.1 European Company Law: An Introduction

Action Plan: European Company Law and Corporate Governance – A Modern Legal Framework for More Engaged Shareholders and Sustainable Companies (2012)(COM/2012/0740 final)

European company law is a cornerstone of the internal market. It facilitates freedom of establishment of companies while enhancing transparency, legal certainty and control of their operations.

The scope of EU company law covers the protection of interests of shareholders and others, the constitution and maintenance of public limited-liability companies' capital, branches disclosure, mergers and divisions, minimum rules for single-member private limited-liability companies and shareholders' rights as well as legal forms such as the European Company (SE), the European Economic Interest Grouping (EEIG) and the European Cooperative Society (SCE).

This definition is a good starting point. However, for the purposes of this book, it needs some further clarification. Indeed, the expression European Company Law (hereafter 'ECL') requires one to focus on the meaning of both 'company' and 'company law', on the one hand, and on the qualification 'European', on the other.

What is a company or – as it would be put in the US – a corporation? Let's take advantage of two authoritative definitions, one of which is provided for by the Court of Justice of the European Union (hereafter 'CJEU').

C-81/87, The Queen v. H.M. Treasury and Commissioners of Inland Revenue, ex parte Daily Mail and General Trust plc., [1988] ECR I-5483, § 20

it should be borne in mind that, unlike natural persons, companies are creatures of the law and, in the present state of Community law, creatures of national law. They exist only by virtue of the varying national legislation which determines their incorporation and functioning.

Melvin A. Eisenberg, 'The Structure of Corporation Law', 89 Colum. L. Rev. 1461–1525, at 1461 (1989)

A corporation is a profit-seeking enterprise of persons and assets organized by rules. Most of these rules are determined by the unilateral action of corporate organs or officials. Some of these rules are determined by market forces. Some are determined by contract or other forms of agreement. Some are determined by law.

As companies are creatures of the law, and more specifically enterprises of persons and assets organised by rules, including the law, there is an unbreakable link between companies and company law.

What, then, is company (or corporate) law? Prominent legal scholars, both European and non-European, have investigated how this question should be answered. The reading of their introductory paragraph is a very useful tool to discuss the issues considered in this book.

John Armour, Henry Hansmann, Reinier Kraakman and Marianna Pargendler, 'What is Corporate Law?', in John Armour, Luca Enriques et al., *The Anatomy of Corporate Law: A Comparative and Functional Approach* 1–28, at 1–3 (Oxford University Press, 3rd ed., 2017)

What is the common structure of corporate (or company) law across different national jurisdictions? Although this question is rarely asked by corporate law scholars, it is critically important for the comparative investigation of the subject. Existing scholarship often emphasizes the divergence among European, American, Japanese, and emerging market corporations in term of corporate governance, share ownership, capital markets, and business culture. But, despite the very real differences across jurisdictions along these dimensions, the underlying uniformity of the corporate form is at least as impressive. Business corporations have a fundamentally similar set of legal characteristics – and face a fundamentally similar set of legal problems – in all jurisdictions.

Consider, in this regard, the basic legal characteristics of the business corporation. To anticipate our discussion below, there are five of these characteristics, most of which will be easily recognizable to anyone familiar with business affairs. They are: legal personality, limited liability, transferable shares, delegated management under a board structure, and investor ownership. These characteristics respond – in ways we will explore – to the economic exigencies of the large modern business enterprise. Thus, corporate law everywhere must, of necessity, provide for them. To be sure, there are other forms of business enterprise that lack one or more of these characteristics. But the remarkable fact – and the fact that we wish to stress – is that, in market economies, almost all large-scale business firms adopt a legal form that possesses all five of the basic characteristics of the business corporation. Indeed, most small jointly-owned firms adopt this corporate form as well, although sometimes with deviations from one or more of the five basic characteristics to fit their special needs.

It follows that a principal function of corporate law is to provide business enterprises with a legal form that possesses these five core attributes. By making this form widely available and user-friendly, corporate law enables entrepreneurs to transact easily through the medium of the corporate entity, and thus lowers the costs of conducting business. Of course, the number of provisions that the typical corporation statute devotes to defining the corporate form is likely to be only a small part of the statute as a whole. Nevertheless, these are the provisions that comprise the legal core of corporate law that is shared by every jurisdiction ... we briefly explore the contracting efficiencies that accompany these five features of the corporate form, and that, we believe, have helped to propel the worldwide diffusion of the corporate form.

However, our principal focus in this book is not on the basic attributes that define the corporate form. Rather, it is on a second, equally important function of corporate law: namely, reducing the ongoing costs of organizing business through the corporate form. Corporate law does this by facilitating coordination between participants in corporate enterprise, and by reducing the scope for value-reducing forms of opportunism among different constituencies. ... Corporate laws everywhere share core features which can be understood as serving to reduce the costs for participants of organizing their activities in business firms.

Much of corporate law can be understood as responding to three principal sources of opportunism that are endemic to such organization: conflicts between managers and shareholders, conflicts between controlling and non-controlling shareholders, and conflicts between shareholders and the corporation's other contractual counterparties, including particularly creditors and employees. All three of these generic conflicts may usefully be characterized as what economists call 'agency problems.' Consequently, [we examine] these three agency problems, both in general and as they arise in the corporate context, and survey the range of legal strategies that can be employed to tackle those problems.

The reader might object that these three types of coordination costs and agency conflicts are not uniquely 'corporate.' After all, *any* form of jointly-owned enterprise faces coordination costs and engenders conflicts among its owners, managers, and third-party contractors. We agree; insofar as the corporation is only one of several legal forms for the jointly owned firm, it faces the same generic functional challenges that confront all jointly owned firms. Nevertheless, the particular characteristics of the corporate form matter a great deal, since it is the form that is chosen by most large-scale enterprises – and, as a practical matter, the only form that firms with widely dispersed ownership can choose in many jurisdictions. In our view, this is because its particular characteristics make it uniquely effective at minimizing coordination costs. Moreover, these same features determine the particular contours of its agency problems. To take an obvious example, the fact that shareholders enjoy limited liability – while, say, general partners in a partnership do not – has traditionally made creditor protection far more salient in corporate law than it is in partnership law. Similarly, the fact that corporate investors may trade their shares is the foundation of the anonymous trading stock market – an institution that has encouraged the separation of ownership from control, and so has sharpened the management-shareholder agency problem.

> ... [We] explore the role of corporate law in minimizing coordination and agency problems – and thus, making the corporate form practicable – in the most important categories of corporate actions and decisions. More particularly, ... [we] address seven categories of transactions and decisions that involve the corporation, its owners, its managers, and the other parties with whom it deals. Most of these categories of firm activity are, again, generic, rather than uniquely corporate. For example, ... [we] address governance mechanisms that operate over the firm's ordinary business decisions, while ... [we later turn] to the checks that operate on the corporation's transactions with creditors. As before, however, although similar agency problems arise in similar contexts across all forms of jointly-owned enterprise, the response of corporate law turns in part on the unique legal features that characterize the corporate form.
>
> Taken together, ... [we] cover nearly all of the important problems in corporate law. ... [W]e describe how the basic coordination costs and agency problems of the corporate form manifest themselves in the given category of corporate activity, and then explore the range of alternative legal responses that are available. We illustrate these alternative approaches with examples from the corporate law of various prominent jurisdictions. We explore the patterns of homogeneity and heterogeneity that appear. Where there are significant differences across jurisdictions, we seek to address both the sources and the consequences of those differences. Our examples are drawn principally from a handful of major representative jurisdictions, which we label our 'core jurisdictions'. These are Brazil, France, Germany, Italy, Japan, the UK, and the U.S., though we sometimes make incidental reference to the laws of other jurisdictions to make particular points.

After having benefited from this comprehensive explanation, we shall turn to the qualification of company law as 'European'.

One might argue that European Company Law is something comparable to – let's say – Norwegian, Japanese or Swiss company law: as Norwegian, Japanese or Swiss company law is the law applicable to companies established and/or operated in Norway, Japan or Switzerland, one might reckon that European Company Law is the law applicable to companies established and/or operated in the EU. This reasoning, however, would be misleading as the EU is neither a sovereign State, as Norway or Japan, nor a federation of States, as Switzerland.

In some aspects, European Company Law may be profitably compared to the company law of the US federation. Each of the fifty States of the US federation has its own company law: whilst twenty-four States have adopted the so-called Model Business Corporation Act (the Revised MBCA dates from 1964), which is a model set of law prepared by the Committee on Corporate Laws of the Section of Business Law of the American Bar Association, other States including Delaware have drafted their own company laws. As is well known, Delaware is the State of incorporation of the majority of publicly traded corporations listed in the New York Stock Exchange (NYSE) and the NASDAQ:

hence, Delaware company law – including the Delaware General Corporation Code and the vast case law of the Delaware Supreme Court – is applicable to these and many other American companies. Federal law also plays a role in the American system of company law as it creates minimum standards for trade in company shares and governance rights, found mostly in the Securities Act of 1933 and the Securities and Exchange Act of 1934, as amended by laws like the Sarbanes–Oxley Act of 2002 and the d-Frank Act of 2010. However, federal and State law operate in different fields of company law and do not overlap. Therefore, in an American company law textbook the reader would find references to Delaware law (as the most representative State company law), the Revised MBCA, and – where appropriate – to federal acts.

Quite similarly to US company law, companies established and/or operated in any of the EU Member States are regulated by the company laws of the Member States. However, on the one hand, in contrast to the US legal system, where adoption of the Revised MBCA is merely voluntary, the company laws of the Member States must comply with the rules and principles that constitute the body of ECL. On the other hand, notwithstanding the EU is neither a sovereign State nor a federation of States, its institutions may issue acts that directly bind all citizens and companies established and/or operating in the EU, thereby prevailing over the company laws of the Member States.

There is no doubt, however, that US company law largely influences EU institutions and academia. It is worth mentioning that, in 2017, a group of company law experts – working together for more than ten years and based in Aarhus University (DK) – drafted a European Model Company Act (EMCA), with the aim of providing a free-standing general company statute that can be enacted by Member States either substantially in its entirety or by the adoption of selected provisions. As it is made clear in its introduction, the EMCA – as the Revised MBCA – is not a mandatory harmonisation instrument, as Member States are not bound to follow the Model Act. Thus, the EMCA can promote regulatory competition, but can also act as a tool for a harmonisation of, and convergence between, Member States' company laws.

This rough comparison clearly shows that in the expression 'European Company Law', reference is made to the legal rules and principles of company law enshrined in the sources of law of the EU, either binding EU Member States as lawmakers or courts, or directly applicable to citizens or to companies or firms established under the laws of any EU Member State and/or operating in the EU. However, unlike US company law, that also includes State law, ECL does not include the company law of EU Member States.

Therefore, before going into the core of ECL, it is appropriate to recall how the EU creates its sources of law. Under Article 288 of the Treaty on the Functioning of the European Union (hereafter 'TFEU'):

Article 288 TFEU

To exercise the Union's competences, the institutions shall adopt regulations, directives, decisions, recommendations and opinions.

A regulation shall have general application. It shall be binding in its entirety and directly applicable in all Member States.

A directive shall be binding, as to the result to be achieved, upon each Member State to which it is addressed, but shall leave to the national authorities the choice of form and methods.

A decision shall be binding in its entirety. A decision which specifies those to whom it is addressed shall be binding only on them.

Recommendations and opinions shall have no binding force.

There are ECL 'rules' – binding either as hard law (treaty, regulations, directives or decisions), or soft law (recommendations, opinions) – and ECL 'principles', emerging from decisions of the CJEU. All such rules and principles constitute the so-called *acquis communautaire* (a French expression meaning 'that which has been acquired or obtained'), or simply the *aquis* in the field of ECL.

The object matter of this textbook is the ECL *acquis*. Conversely, this book does not address the company law of Member States, nor the implementation in those laws of ECL directives: reference is made to the company law of Member States only in the case where it is necessary to explain choices at Union level or to assess its validity in respect of the ECL *acquis*.

In this respect, it is useful to recall that questions of validity of national company law are solved by the CJEU and may be raised before it in two ways: *either* by a European Commission complaint that a Member State has failed to fulfil an obligation under the TFEU or ECL directives, *or* by preliminary rulings in the case where a question is raised before any court or tribunal of a Member State.

Article 258 TFEU

If the Commission considers that a Member State has failed to fulfil an obligation under the Treaties, it shall deliver a reasoned opinion on the matter after giving the State concerned the opportunity to submit its observations.

If the State concerned does not comply with the opinion within the period laid down by the Commission, the latter may bring the matter before the Court of Justice of the European Union.

Article 267 TFEU

The Court of Justice of the European Union shall have jurisdiction to give preliminary rulings concerning:

(a) the interpretation of the Treaties;
(b) the validity and interpretation of acts of the institutions, bodies, offices or agencies of the Union.

Where such a question is raised before any court or tribunal of a Member State, that court or tribunal may, if it considers that a decision on the question is necessary to enable it to give judgment, request the Court to give a ruling thereon.

Where any such question is raised in a case pending before a court or tribunal of a Member State against whose decisions there is no judicial remedy under national law, that court or tribunal shall bring the matter before the Court.

If such a question is raised in a case pending before a court or tribunal of a Member State with regard to a person in custody, the Court of Justice of the European Union shall act with the minimum of delay.

FURTHER READING

Dominique Carreau and William L. Lee, 'Towards a European Company Law', 9 *Nw. J. Int'l L. & Bus.* 501–512 (1989).

Jan Wouters, 'European Company Law: Quo Vadis', 37 *Comm. Mkt L. Rev.* 257–308 (2000).

Friedrich Kübler, 'A Shifting Paradigm of European Company Law', 11 *Colum. J. Eur. L.* 219–240 (2005).

Luca Enriques, 'A Harmonized European Company Law: Are We There Already?', 66 *Int'l & Comp. L.Q.* 763 (2017).

See also:

Mads Andenas and Frank Wooldridge, *European Comparative Company Law* 1–6 (Cambridge University Press, 2012).

Paul Krüger Andersen, 'The European Model Company Act (EMCA) – a tool for European integration', 19 *ERA Forum* 77–85 (2018).

José Engrácia Antunes and Mónica Fuentes Naharro, 'Director's' Duties and Conflicts of Interest in the EMCA', 13 *ECFR* 269–276 (2016).

John Armour, Henry Hansmann, Reinier Kraakman, and Marianna Pargendler, 'What is Corporate Law?', in John Armour, Luca Enriques et al., *The Anatomy of Corporate Law: A Comparative and Functional Approach* 1–35 (Oxford University Press, 3rd ed., 2017).

Pierre-Henri Conac, 'The Chapter on Groups of Companies of the European Model Company Act (EMCA)', 13 *ECFR* 301–321 (2016).

Ronald J. Gilson, 'A Model Company Act and A Model Company Court', 13 *ECFR* 351–362 (2016).

Evanghelos Perakis, 'The EMCA: General Principles and Main Content', 13 *ECFR* 200–214 (2016).

1.2 Freedom of Establishment and Freedom to Provide Services

The roots of ECL can be found among early provisions of the Treaty of Rome on the European Economic Community (EEC) of 1957, concerning the freedom of establishment and the freedom to provide services. The same provisions are now incorporated in the TFEU.

As it is well known, one of the major goals of the Treaty of Rome was that of creating a European single market.

Article 26(2) TFEU

The internal market shall comprise an area without internal frontiers in which the free movement of goods, persons, services and capital is ensured in accordance with the provisions of the Treaties.

The cornerstones of the single market are often said to be the 'four freedoms'. Two of these fundamental freedoms – i.e., the freedom of establishment and the freedom to provide services – are especially set out to ensure the free movement of people and services. More specifically, the principle of *freedom of establishment* enables an economic operator to carry on an economic activity in a stable and continuous way in one or more Member States. The principle of the *freedom to provide services* enables an economic operator providing services in one Member State to offer services on a temporary basis in another Member State, without having to be established.

Granting those fundamental freedoms, the Treaty of Rome referred not only to national individuals, but also to business organisations. For the time being, two fundamental rules – included in Articles 49 and 56 TFEU – shall be considered.

Article 49 TFEU

Restrictions on freedom to provide services within the Union shall be prohibited in respect of nationals of Member States who are established in a Member State other than that of the person for whom the services are intended.

Article 56 TFEU

Restrictions on the freedom of establishment of nationals of a Member State in the territory of another Member State shall be prohibited. Such prohibition shall also apply to restrictions on the setting-up of agencies, branches or subsidiaries by nationals of any Member State established in the territory of any Member State.

Article 49(2) TFEU further clarifies the concept of freedom of establishment for business activities, in that it specifies that this includes the right *to set up and manage undertakings, in particular companies or firms.*

Article 49(2) TFEU

Freedom of establishment shall include the right to take up and pursue activities as self-employed persons and to set up and manage undertakings, in particular companies or firms, under the conditions laid down by Member States where such establishment is effected for their own nationals.

FURTHER READING

Jesper Lau Hansen, 'Full Circle: Is There a Difference between the Freedom of Establishment and the Freedom to Provide Services?', 11 *EBL* (2000) 83–90.

Alexandros Roussos, 'Realising the Free Movement of Companies', 12 *EBLR* 7–25(2001).

Alberto Santamaria, *European Economic Law* 9–53 (Alphen aan den Rijn, Kluwer Law International, 3rd ed., 2014).

Erik Werlauff, *EU Company Law* 57–61 (Copenhagen, DJØF Publishing, 2nd ed., 2003).

See also:

Mads Andenas and Frank Wooldridge, *European Comparative Company Law* 7–14 (Cambridge University Press, 2012).

1.3 Companies and Firms

Companies and firms referred to in Article 49 TFEU are defined in Article 54 (2) TFEU.

Article 54(2) TFEU

'companies or firms' … constituted under civil or commercial law, including cooperative societies, and other legal persons governed by public or private law, save for those which are non-profit-making.

To understand such a provision, we shall consider that national laws regulate business organisations in various ways. Some EU Member States (such as France, Belgium, Germany, and Spain) have a civil and a commercial code, along with special acts, providing a legal framework governing firms and companies (including partnerships). Some other EU Member States (such as Italy and the Netherlands) only have a civil code, some (such as Portugal and Poland) have a civil code and a company code, some (such as Ireland and the UK) have no civil or commercial codes, but the common law and special acts for partnerships and companies. Those countries having both a civil and a commercial code differentiate firms or companies (and partnerships) constituted under civil or commercial law.

Diego Corapi and Barbara De Donno, 'European Corporate Law', in Mauro Bussani and Franz Werro (eds.), *European Private Law: A Handbook*, Volume II 209–260, at 216–217 (Durham, NC, Carolina Academic Press and Stämpfli Publishers, 2014)

Companies and partnerships are commercial entities, which in the Roman legal tradition are treated differently than other associations (sociétés civiles, associations). The latter are less structured entities, whose purpose is not considered as belonging to the realm of commerce. The distinction was for a long time reflected in the fact that companies and partnerships were made subject to commercial codes, while other associations were governed by the provisions of civil codes.

French law has opened new operational areas to sociétés civiles, making the regulation of the latter in many respects similar to that of commercial entities, not only in the domains of agriculture, mining and real estate, but also in the liberal professions.

Today some countries (including France, Belgium, Germany and Spain) maintain separate civil and commercial codes. In others (such as Italy, the Netherlands and Switzerland) there is a unified civil code, which also covers the matters traditionally dealt with in commercial codes. Even in those countries in which the distinction between commercial and civil companies has been formally eliminated, however, it continues to play a role doctrinally. This is similar to the situation under English law where, since the eighteenth century, commercial law has been incorporated into the common law. In the United Kingdom, therefore, both agricultural and professional activities exercised in association are governed by the Partnership Act, which applies to entities whose nature is similar to that of what the civil law calls 'civil companies'.

In civil law countries (even where a separate commercial code exists) the definition of a company, as shared by all incorporate associations, as a rule in the civil code: art. 1832 of the French civil code, BGB § 705, art. 2247 of the Italian Civil Code.

The regulation of commercial companies, including public limited companies, is contained either in unified civil codes (as in Italy and Switzerland), commercial codes (in France and Belgium) or special laws. In Germany and Spain, for example, partnerships are governed by the commercial code, public limited companies and limited liability companies are subject to special legislation.

In the United Kingdom, because the notion of contract is narrower than in the civil law countries and is thus unable to comprise within it the phenomenon of incorporation, partnerships and companies are regulated separately, in special acts, which often give legislative expression to principles that were developed in case law.

Notwithstanding these differences in the law of the Member States, all these firms and companies (including partnerships) are regarded identically from an EU perspective, as all enjoy the freedom of establishment and to provide services.

Companies and firms, both civil and commercial ones, are generally set up to pursue business activities for the profit of their members, hence these are profit-making and engage in economic activity. Non-profit-making societies do not benefit from the right of establishment. This rule may be understood because non-profit-making societies do not engage in economic activity and are not considered undertakings in the light of the TFEU. Indeed only undertakings (and Member States) are the addressees of the European common rules on competition, taxation and approximation of laws, ensuring along with the right of establishment and to provide services the creation of an economic single market.

Cooperative societies do not pursue the aim of making profits for distribution to their members. Rather, they are set up for the purpose of providing services on a non-profit basis either to, or in the interest of, their members. However, in the light of TFEU, they are not regarded as non-profit-making entities as they are considered undertakings, thereby also contributing to the formation of the single market. Therefore, as undertakings, they must comply with the EU rules on competition, whilst enjoying of the freedom of establishment. In this respect it is useful to recall two leading cases before the CJEU, in which the qualification of a cooperative society as an undertaking was disputed. Both cases concerned mutual societies providing pension schemes in France (for either farmers or craftsmen). Membership and, therefore, contributions to such mutual societies were mandatory by law. Some members, however, objected that such legal rules violated the prohibition of an abuse of dominant position (Article 102 TFEU), as they precluded the possibility to freely choose other (better performing) pension schemes offered by undertakings providing similar services. Notwithstanding the facts and the complaints were very similar, the CJEU resolved the two cases in different ways: in so doing, the Court clarified the concept of non-profit-making organisation.

In the older case (Joined cases C-159/91 and C-160/91, *Poucet et Pistre*, [1993] ECR I-00637), the EJC stated that the notion of undertaking encompasses all entities engaged in an economic activity. However, it does not include organisations involved in the management of the public social security system, although qualifying as cooperative or mutual societies, which fulfil an exclusively social function and perform an activity based on the principle of national solidarity that is entirely non-profit-making.

In a subsequent case (Case C-244/94, *Caisse d'Assurance et de Prévoyance Mutuelle des Agriculteurs et al.*, [1995] ECR I-04013), the CJEU distinguished its precedent. On this occasion, it clarified that a non-profit-making organisation (i.e., a mutual society) which manages an old-age insurance scheme intended to supplement a basic compulsory scheme, established by law as an optional scheme and operating according to the principle of capitalisation, engages in an economic activity, thus qualifying as undertaking for the purposes of Article 101 et seq. TFEU. Even if such an organisation is non-profit-making, and the scheme it administers exhibits certain limited features of solidarity that are not comparable with the features that characterise compulsory social security schemes, it nevertheless carries on an economic activity in competition with life assurance companies.

FURTHER READING

Diego Corapi and Barbara De Donno, 'European Corporate Law', in Mauro Bussani and Franz Werro (eds.), *European Private Law: A Handbook*, Volume II 209–260 (Durham, NC, Carolina Academic Press and Stämpfli Publishers, 2014).

Bartlomiej Kurcz and Athanasios Paizis, 'Company Law, Connecting Factors and the Digital Age – a New Outlook', 16 *ECFR* 434–456 (2019).

Joined cases C-159/91 and C-160/91, *Poucet et Pistre*, [1993] ECR I-00637; Case C-244/94, *Caisse d'Assurance et de Prévoyance Mutuelle des Agriculteurs et al.*, [1995] ECR I-04013.

See also:

Mads Andenas and Frank Wooldridge, *European Comparative Company Law* 99–168 (Cambridge University Press, 2012).

Stefano Lombardo, 'Some Reflections on Freedom of Establishment of Non-profit Entities in the European Union', 14 *EBOR* 225–263 (2013).

1.4 European 'Citizenship' for Companies or Firms

As with individual nationals, one may discuss a European 'citizenship' for companies and firms. European citizenship for both individuals and companies or firms depends on the existence of a connecting factor – i.e., the circumstances that make a linkage between a person and a country – with one of the EU Member States.

Individuals are considered citizens of the EU based on the connecting factor referred to by the laws of the single Member States. Common Law Member States (along with Denmark) rely on the *domicile*. There are three forms of domicile for individuals:

(a) *domicile of origin*, acquired at birth, and depending on the parents' domicile, not on the place of birth nor on the parents' residence at that time;
(b) *domicile of dependence*, conferred on legally dependent persons by operation of law (such as for underage children or mentally incapable persons);
(c) *domicile of choice*, acquired by an independent person residing in a country with the intention to settle indefinitely.

Civil law Member States generally rely on *nationality*: apart from cases of naturalisation, nationality depends essentially on the place of birth and/or on parentage, and is independent from the place of residence (ordinary or habitual).

Legal entities, such as companies or firms, also enjoy EU citizenship based on a connecting factor with one Member State. Common law EU Member States, along with some others (such as the Netherlands and, basically, Italy) adopt the *incorporation theory*, similar to the place of birth, as the connecting factor for individuals. Civil law Member States (such as Germany, France, and

Hungary) generally adopt the *real seat theory*, similar to the domicile of choice as the connecting factor for individuals. Under the incorporation theory, a company is governed by the law of the place of incorporation. Under the real seat theory, a company is governed by the law of the place where the central management and control is located.

The TFEU has made no choice as to whether the incorporation theory or the real seat theory should prevail. As the CJEU puts it:

C-81/87, The Queen v. H.M. Treasury and Commissioners of Inland Revenue, ex parte Daily Mail and General Trust plc., [1988] ECR I-5483, § 21

The legislation of the Member States varies widely in regard to both the factor providing a connection to the national territory required for the incorporation of a company and the question whether a company incorporated under the legislation of a Member State may subsequently modify that connecting factor ... The Treaty has taken account of that variety in national legislation.

Indeed:

Article 54 TFEU

companies or firms formed in accordance with the law of a Member State and having their registered office, central administration or principal place of business within the Union shall be treated ... in the same way as natural persons who are nationals of Member States.

Given the above, the CJEU concludes that:

C-81/87, The Queen v. H.M. Treasury and Commissioners of Inland Revenue, ex parte Daily Mail and General Trust plc., [1988] ECR I-5483, § 21

the Treaty places on the same footing, as connecting factors, the registered office, central administration and principal place of business of a company.

In further decisions on the right of establishment for companies and firms, the CJEU has frequently dealt with the consequences of the choice made by the EU founders. We will later examine in detail several cases concerning the so-called right of primary establishment, such as *Daily Mail* (*see*, Chapter 5, § 5.3) and the so-called right of secondary establishment (*see*, Chapter 6), as well as cases involving the insolvency of companies having their registered office or principal place of business spread across different EU Member States (the cross-border insolvency): in these cases, reference is made to a company's centre of main interests or COMI, under Article 3 Regulation 2015/848/EU (*see*, Chapter 20, §§ 20.4ff.).

FURTHER READING

Paschalis Paschalidis, *Freedom of Establishment and Private International Law for Corporations* 1–11 (Oxford University Press, 2012).

See also:
Dan Prentice, 'The Incorporation Theory – The United Kingdom', 14 *EBLR* 631–641 (2003).

1.5 Participation in the Capital of Companies or Firms and Free Movement of Capital

It is not only Member States that may not put restrictions on the freedom for companies or firms to provide services and to establish within the Union, but also:

Article 55 TFEU

Member States shall accord nationals of the other Member States the same treatment as their own nationals as regards participation in the capital of companies or firms.

This provision is strictly linked to that granting the free movement of capital.

Article 63(1) TFEU

All restrictions on the movement of capital between Member States and between Member States and third countries shall be prohibited.

The combination of the two principles – that of equal treatment of shareholders being nationals of other Member States and that of free movement of capital – led the CJEU to deliver many important decisions assessing the validity of laws, granting special powers to Member States themselves or other public bodies, as shareholders of companies operating in strategic sectors, such as gas and power or telecommunication. As we will see later (Chapter 16, §§ 16.6ff.), minority holdings, called *golden shares*, often grant to Member States or other public bodies the right to elect additional board members, or to compulsorily repurchase the majority stake at will, or to express a majority in a meeting regardless of the stake. The EC and the CJEU generally consider the special powers granted by golden shares contrary to the free movement of capital as they often restrain or compromise the market for corporate control.

FURTHER READING

Guido Ferrarini, 'One Share – One Vote: A European Rule?', 3 *ECFR* 147–177 (2006).

See also:

Mads Andenas and Frank Wooldridge, *European Comparative Company Law* 14–20 (Cambridge University Press, 2012).

1.6 Approximation of Company Laws

Companies or firms formed under the laws of Member States could not effectively enjoy the freedom of establishment and provide services granted by the TFEU in the absence of a common legal framework on company law applicable throughout all EU Member States.

The establishment of such a common legal framework does not necessarily imply unification of the Member States' legislations in a single uniform law. Rather, it suffices that the national legislations share common basic principles. This end may be reached by way of approximation of laws or harmonisation.

In order to attain freedom of establishment as regards a particular activity, and in particular in respect to that of companies and firms, the TFEU authorises:

Article 50(1) TFEU

the European Parliament and the Council, acting in accordance with the ordinary legislative procedure and after consulting the Economic and Social Committee, [to] act by means of directives.

As regards companies and firms, the European Parliament and the Council may issue directives aiming at granting the freedom of establishment or, under a different procedure, other goals.

Article 50(2) TFEU

...

(f) by effecting the progressive abolition of restrictions on freedom of establishment in every branch of activity under consideration, both as regards the conditions for setting up agencies, branches or subsidiaries in the territory of a Member State and as regards the subsidiaries in the territory of a Member State and as regards the conditions governing the entry of personnel belonging to the main establishment into managerial or supervisory posts in such agencies, branches or subsidiaries;

(g) by coordinating to the necessary extent the safeguards which, for the protection of the interests of members and others, are required by Member States of companies or firms within the meaning of the second paragraph of Article 54 with a view to making such safeguards equivalent throughout the Union.

Article 115 TFEU

Without prejudice to Article 114, the Council shall, acting unanimously in accordance with a special legislative procedure and after consulting the European Parliament and the Economic and Social Committee, issue directives for the approximation of such laws, regulations or administrative provisions of the Member States as directly affect the establishment or functioning of the internal market.

As we will see (Chapter 2), the European Parliament and the Council have jointly delivered (or cooperated in the delivery of) many directives in the field of the law of companies and firms.

FURTHER READING

Bartlomiej Kurcz, 'Harmonisation by Means of Directives: A Never Ending Story', 12 *EBLR* 287–307 (2001).

Luca Enriques, 'EU Company Law Directives and Regulations: How Trivial Are They?', 27 *U. Pa Int'l Econ. L.J.* 1–72 (2006).

Gerard Hertig and Joseph A. McCahery, 'Optional Rather than Mandatory EU Company Law: Framework and Specific Proposals', 3 *ECFR* 341–362 (2006).

Luca Enriques, 'A Harmonized European Company Law: Are We There Already?', 66 *Int'l & Comp. L.Q.* 763 (2017).

See also:

Erik Werlauff, *EU Company Law* 61–71 (Copenhagen, DJØF Publishing, 2nd ed., 2003).

Mads Andenas and Frank Wooldridge, *European Comparative Company Law* 20–28 (Cambridge University Press, 2012).

1.7 Uniform Company Law

As the provisions included in the TFEU constitute the body of a uniform ECL of which Member States' nationals, companies, or firms directly enjoy, so the EU institutions may also create uniform company law and EU types of companies or firms, entirely or partially regulated by EU sources of law, acting by means of regulations.

Action by means of regulations sometimes requires a high degree of convergence, depending on whether Article 114(1) or 352 TFEU apply.

Article 114(1) TFEU

Save where otherwise provided in the Treaties, the following provisions shall apply for the achievement of the objectives set out in Article 26 [thus, in case measures are adopted with the aim of establishing or ensuring the functioning of the internal market]. The European Parliament and the Council shall, acting in accordance with the ordinary legislative procedure and after consulting the Economic and Social Committee, adopt the measures for the approximation of the provisions laid down by law, regulation or administrative action in Member States which have as their object the establishment and functioning of the internal market.

The EU institution may act following the ordinary legislative procedure set out in Article 294 TFEU, or – where appropriate – a special procedure set out in Article 352 TFEU.

Article 352 TFEU

1. If action by the Union should prove necessary, within the framework of the policies defined in the Treaties, to attain one of the objectives set out in the Treaties, and the Treaties have not provided the necessary powers, the Council, acting unanimously on a proposal from the Commission and after obtaining the consent of the European Parliament, shall adopt the appropriate measures. Where the measures in question are adopted by the Council in accordance with a special legislative procedure, it shall also act unanimously on a proposal from the Commission and after obtaining the consent of the European Parliament.
2. Using the procedure for monitoring the subsidiarity principle referred to in Article 5(3) of the Treaty on European Union, the Commission shall draw national Parliaments' attention to proposals based on this Article.
3. Measures based on this Article shall not entail harmonisation of Member States' laws or regulations in cases where the Treaties exclude such harmonisation.
4. This Article cannot serve as a basis for attaining objectives pertaining to the common foreign and security policy and any acts adopted pursuant to this Article shall respect the limits set out in Article 40, second paragraph, of the Treaty on European Union.

Either on an ordinary or special legislative procedure, the European Parliament and the Council have jointly delivered (or cooperated in the delivery of) various regulations over time, both establishing common rules directly applicable to companies or firms established under the laws of Member States (e.g., the adoption of IAS/IFRS accounting standards, or the regulation of cross-border insolvency proceedings) and European types of companies or firms. As we will later see in more detail (Chapter 3, §§ 3.1–3.3), regulations establishing three models of EU business organisation already exist: on the European Economic Interest Grouping (EEIG), on the *Societas Europaea* (SE), and on the *Societas Cooperativa Europaea* (SCE).

The adoption of some other regulations is currently under discussion, in particular that on the *Mutua Europaea* (ME) and on the *Fundatio Europaea* (FE). Moreover, whilst the one on the *Societas Privata Europaea* (SPE) has been dropped, another project – the *Societas Unius Personae* (SUP) – has replaced it: as we will see (Chapter 3, § 3.7), however, this new project is supposed to take the form of a Directive.

1.8 European Company Law, European Union, European Economic Area (EEA), and Brexit

As of 31 January 2020, after the United Kingdom withdrew from the European Union (so-called Brexit), the Union currently consists of twenty-seven countries. Figure 1.1 shows the current territories of the European Union after Brexit.

However, ECL applies to an area of the European continent larger than the territories of the EU Member States, corresponding to that of the European Economic Area (EEA).

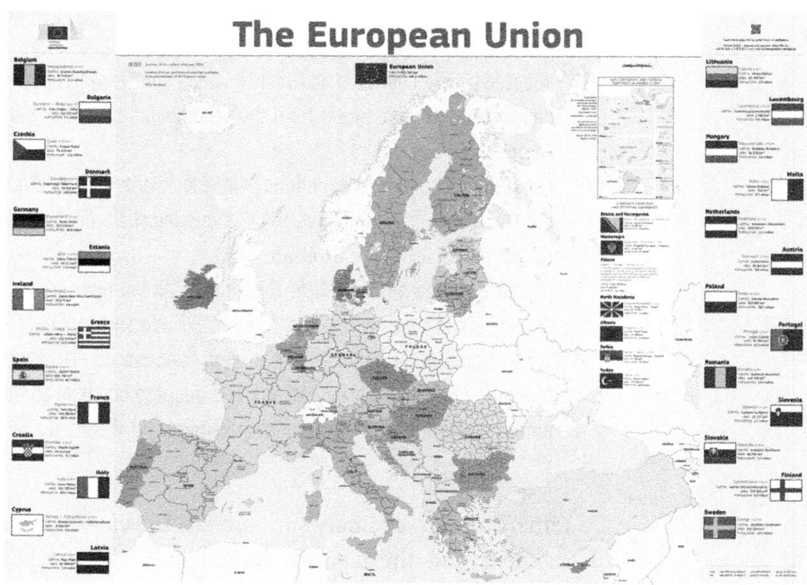

Figure 1.1 Map of the European Union after Brexit. Used with permission from Peter Hermes Furian / Alamy Stock Photo.

The EEA Agreement was signed in 1992 and the EEA was established on 1 January 1994 upon entry into force of the Agreement. The contracting parties were the EU, its member states, and three European Free Trade Association (EFTA) member states, i.e., Iceland, Liechtenstein, and Norway. One EFTA member, Switzerland, has not joined the EEA, but has a set of bilateral agreements with the EU.

The EEA enables the extension of the European Union's single market to EFTA member states establishing an internal market governed by the same basic rules. These rules aim to enable free movement of labour, goods, services, and capital, including the freedom to choose residence in any country within this area. EFTA states that are party to the EEA adopt most EU legislation concerning the single market, including ECL.

The UK ceased to be an EEA member after it withdrew from the EU on 31 January 2020, and entered into a transition period ending 31 December 2020. During the transition, the EEA agreement remained unchanged, and continued to apply as before, to both the remaining EEA members and the UK, as the UK will continue to be treated as if an EEA state.

There were three basic options for the UK: (i) to continue to be part of the EEA, as Iceland, Liechtenstein, and Norway; (ii) to sign a set of bilateral agreements, as Switzerland; (iii) or to terminate the EEA Agreement with a 'no deal'. On 30 December 2020, after a long negotiation, the UK and the EU signed an extensive bilateral agreement establishing a free trade area, under WTO rules.

FURTHER READING

Pavlos Masouros and Thomas Papadopoulos, 'The Impact of Brexit on UK Company Law', 13 *ECL* 208–209 (2016).

John Armour, Holger Fleischer, Vanessa Knapp, and Martin Winner, 'Brexit and Corporate Citizenship', 18 *EBOR* 225–249 (2017).

Ovidiu Ioan Dumitru, 'The European Company, Perspectives after Brexit', 7 *Juridical Tribune* 134–146 (2017).

Hans-Jürgen Hellwig, 'The Effects of Brexit on the Law of Companies and Financial and Legal Services in Europe: A Summary Overview', 14 *ECFR* 252–268 (2017).

Julia Told, '(BR)EXIT from the EU: A Legal Perspective', 14 *ECFR* 490–567 (2017).

Eilìs Ferran, 'Revisiting Legal Capital', 20 *EBOR* 521–545 (2019).

2

The Company Law Directives

2.1 General

Acting under Article 50(2) TFEU, the European Parliament and the Council have delivered many company law directives, aiming at harmonising the Member States' company law.

On 18 December 1961, the Council of the EEC adopted a General Programme for the abolition of restrictions on freedom of establishment within the EEC, which aimed *inter alia* at the coordination of safeguards required for companies and firms (Part VI).

General Programme for the Abolition of Restrictions on Freedom of Establishment within the European Economic Community

It is intended that the safeguards required by Member States of companies and firms for the protection of the interests of members and others should, to the extent necessary and with a view to making such safeguards equivalent, be coordinated before the end of the second year of the second stage of the transitional period [i.e. by 31 December 1963].

In execution of the General Programme, the EEC Commission submitted on 19 February 1964 a Proposal for a Council Directive to coordinate and render equivalent the guarantees required in the Member States of companies as defined in Article 58, second paragraph, of the Treaty, to protect the interests of the members of such companies and third parties. This draft was later amended and renamed as 'First' company law draft directive. The addition 'First' made it clear that the Commission already had in mind other proposals, or rather the full plot of the series of twelve company law directives, later delivered with this numbering.

The first Recital to the First Directive gives a clue on the choice of having a series of directives, instead of only one: basically, there was a matter of urgency suggesting the need to have some provisions immediately at work and to set aside all other provisions not considered similarly urgent and on which, presumably, the Council would not reach the necessary degree of convergence in the short term.

Over time, ten out of twelve proposals of the original plan have been approved, whilst two – the Fifth and the Ninth – are still (and, probably, will always remain) at the stage of draft proposals. Later on, all of the approved company law directives have been amended and some of them have been replaced by consolidated new acts: in this case they have lost their original numbering (in practice, however, some new directives are still addressed as, for example, the new Eighth Directive).

In addition, acting under the provisions of the Treaty now corresponding to Articles 50 and 114 TFEU, other directives on relevant fields of company law and capital markets have been drafted and approved, for example, the series of directives concerning financial markets (such as the Admission to Listing, the Prospectus (now regulation), the Transparency, the Market Abuse and the Market in Financial Instruments directives), the Takeover Bids directive (also referred to as the Thirteenth Directive), the Shareholder Rights directive and others.

The major part of the series of twelve directives aimed at harmonising the laws of all companies limited by shares or otherwise having limited liability, thus, both private and public companies. An updated list of such Member States' business models may be found in Annex I to Directive 2013/34/ EU (the new Fourth and Seventh Directives, on annual and consolidated accounts).

Types of Undertaking Referred to in Point (A) of Article 1(1)

- Belgium: la société anonyme/de naamloze vennootschap, la société en commandite par actions/de commanditaire vennootschap op aandelen, la société privée à responsabilité limitée/de besloten vennootschap met beperkte aansprakelijkheid, la société coopérative à responsabilité limitée/de coöperatieve vennootschap met beperkte aansprakelijkheid;
- Bulgaria: акционерно дружество, дружество с ограничена отговорност, командитно дружество с акции;
- Czech Republic: společnost s ručením omezeným, akciová společnost;
- Denmark: aktieselskaber, kommanditaktieselskaber, anpartsselskaber;
- Germany: die Aktiengesellschaft, die Kommanditgesellschaft auf Aktien, die Gesellschaft mit beschränkter Haftung;
- Estonia: aktsiaselts, osaühing;
- Ireland: public companies limited by shares or by guarantee, private companies limited by shares or by guarantee;
- Greece: η ανώνυμη εταιρία, η εταιρία περιορισμένης ευθύνης, η ετερόρρυθμη κατά μετοχές εταιρία;
- Spain: la sociedad anónima, la sociedad comanditaria por acciones, la sociedad de responsabilidad limitada;
- France: la société anonyme, la société en commandite par actions, la société à responsabilité limitée, la société par actions simplifiée;

- Italy: la società per azioni, la società in accomandita per azioni, la società a responsabilità limitata;
- Cyprus: Δημόσιες εταιρείες περιορισμένης ευθύνης με μετοχές ή με εγγύηση, ιδιωτικές εταιρείες περιορισμένης ευθύνης με μετοχές ή με εγγύηση;
- Latvia: akciju sabiedrība, sabiedrība ar ierobežotu atbildību;
- Lithuania: akcinės bendrovės, uždarosios akcinės bendrovės;
- Luxembourg: la société anonyme, la société en commandite par actions, la société à responsabilité limitée;
- Hungary: részvénytársaság, korlátolt felelősségű társaság;
- Malta: kumpanija pubblika – public limited-liability company, kumpannija privata – private limited liability company, so-jeta in akkomandita bil-kapital maqsum f'azzjonijiet – partnership en commandite with the capital divided into shares;
- Netherlands: de naamloze vennootschap, de besloten vennootschap met beperkte aansprakelijkheid;
- Austria: die Aktiengesellschaft, die Gesellschaft mit beschränkter Haftung;
- Poland: spółka akcyjna, spółka z ograniczoną odpowiedzialnością, spółka komandytowo-akcyjna;
- Portugal: a sociedade anónima, de responsabilidade limitada, a sociedade em comandita por ações, a sociedade por quotas de responsabilidade limitada;
- Romania: societate pe acțiuni, societate cu răspundere limitată, societate în comandită pe acțiuni;
- Slovenia: delniška družba, družba z omejeno odgovornostjo, komanditna delniška družba;
- Slovakia: akciová spoločnosť, spoločnosť s ručením obmedzeným;
- Finland: yksityinen osakeyhtiö/privat aktiebolag, julkinen osakeyhtiö/publikt aktiebolag;
- Sweden: aktiebolag;
- UK: public companies limited by shares or by guarantee, private companies limited by shares or by guarantee

Some directives from the series of twelve (e.g., the Second) were aimed at applying to only public limited companies, on the grounds that their activities predominated in the economy of the Member States and frequently extended beyond their national boundaries (Recital 1 Second Directive). An updated list of such business models may be found in Annex I to Directive 2017/1132/EU (including the original Second Directive, on capital formation and maintenance).

Types of Companies Referred to in the First Subparagraph of Article 1(1)

- Belgium: société anonyme/naamloze vennootschap;
- Bulgaria: акционерно дружество;
- Czech Republic: akciováspolečnost;
- Denmark: aktieselskab;

- Germany: Aktiengesellschaft;
- Estonia: aktsiaselts;
- Ireland: public company limited by shares, public company limited by guarantee and having a share capital;
- Greece: ανώνυμη εταιρία;
- Spain: sociedad anónima;
- France: société anonyme;
- Italy: società per azioni;
- Cyprus: δημόσιες εταιρείες περιορισμένης ευθύνης με μετοχές, δημόσιες εταιρείες περιορισμένης ευθύνης με εγγύηση που διαθέτουν μετοχικό κεφάλαιο;
- Latvia: akciju sabiedrība;
- Lithuania: akcinė bendrovė;
- Luxembourg: société anonyme;
- Hungary: nyilvánosan működő részvénytársaság;
- Malta: kumpanija pubblika/public limited-liability company;
- Netherlands: naamloze vennootschap;
- Austria: Aktiengesellschaft;
- Poland: spółka akcyjna;
- Portugal: sociedade anónima;
- Romania: societate pe acţiuni;
- Slovenia: delniška družba;
- Slovakia: akciová spoločnosť;
- Finland: julkinen osakeyhtiö/publikt aktiebolag;
- Sweden: aktiebolag;
- UK: public company limited by shares, public company limited by guarantee and having a share capital.

One directive of the series of twelve (the Twelfth, now replaced by Directive 2009/102/EC) is aimed at harmonising the law of only the private limited-liability company.

It must be added that, notwithstanding that the TFEU applies to all companies and firms, including partnerships, these business forms are not specifically addressed by directives. However, since 2013, some provisions of Directive 2013/34/EU have been applicable also to partnerships and, therefore, a useful list of such business models is now available as Annex II of Directive 2013/34/EU.

Types of Undertaking Referred to in Point (B) of Article 1(1)

- Belgium: la société en nom collectif/de vennootschap onder firma, la société en commandite simple/de gewone commanditaire vennootschap, la société coopérative à responsabilité illimitée/de coöperatieve vennootschap met onbeperkte aansprakelijkheid;
- Bulgaria: събирателно дружество, командитно дружество;

- Czech Republic: veřejná obchodní společnost, komanditní společnost;
- Denmark: interessentskaber, kommanditselskaber;
- Germany: die offene Handelsgesellschaft, die Kommanditgesellschaft;
- Estonia: täisühing, usaldusühing;
- Ireland: partnerships, limited partnerships, unlimited companies;
- Greece: η ομόρρυθμος εταιρία, η ετερόρρυθμος εταιρία;
- Spain: sociedad colectiva, sociedad en comandita simple;
- France: la société en nom collectif, la société en commandite simple;
- Italy: la società in nome collettivo, la società in accomandita semplice;
- Cyprus: Ομόρρυθμες και ετερόρρυθμες εταιρείες (συνεταιρισμοί);
- Latvia: pilnsabiedrība, komandītsabiedrība;
- Lithuania: tikrosios ūkinės bendrijos, komanditinės ūkinės bendrijos;
- Luxembourg: la société en nom collectif, la société en commandite simple;
- Hungary: közkereseti társaság, betéti társaság, közös vállalat, egyesülés, egyéni cég;
- Malta: so·jeta f'isem kollettiv jew so·jeta in akkomandita, bil-kapital li mhux maqsum f'azzjonijiet meta s-so·ji kollha li għandhom responsabbilita' llimitata huma so·jetajiet in akkomandita bil-kapital maqsum f'azzjonijiet – partnership en nom collectif or partnership en commandite with capital that is not divided into shares, when all the partners with unlimited liability are partnership en commandite with the capital divided into shares;
- Netherlands: de vennootschap onder firma, de commanditaire vennootschap;
- Austria: die offene Gesellschaft, die Kommanditgesellschaft;
- Poland: spółka jawna, spółka komandytowa;
- Portugal: sociedade em nome colectivo, sociedade em comandita simples;
- Romania: societate în nume colectiv, societate în comandită simplă;
- Slovenia: družba z neomejeno odgovornostjo, komanditna družba;
- Slovakia: verejná obchodná spoločnosť, komanditná spoločnosť;
- Finland: avoin yhtiö/ öppet bolag, kommandiittiyhtiö/kommanditbolag;
- Sweden: handelsbolag, kommanditbolag;
- UK: partnerships, limited partnerships, unlimited companies.

Some legal scholars have criticised ECL and in particular EU Directives, maintaining that they have a trivial influence on the Member States' company law. Ultimately, they argue that European company laws have indeed been harmonised: European Member States company laws fit together, which may well be what harmonisation, not only etymologically, is all about.

Luca Enriques, 'EU Company Law Directives and Regulations: How Trivial Are They?', 27 *U. Pa Int'l Econ. L.J.* 1–78, at 1–2 (2006)

What role does European Community ('EC') legislation in the corporate law area play within the EU? How much does it shape Members States' corporate laws? And how relevant is it for the corporate governance of EU companies and their management? At first sight, the EC appears to have played and to be playing a central role in shaping EC corporate law, with the high number of directives and regulations covering a wide range of corporate law issues. One might think that EC institutions have a strong influence upon Member States' corporate laws, whether because they have intervened in the area or because they may do so. Quite the opposite: EC company law directives and regulations appear to have had very little impact on national company law thus far and, more to the point, little impact on EU businesses' governance and management. First, EC corporate law does not cover core corporate law areas such as fiduciary duties and shareholder remedies. Second, EC corporate law rules are underenforced. Third, in the presence of very sporadic judiciary interpretation by the European Court of Justice, EC corporate law tends to be implemented and construed differently in each Member State, according to local legal culture and consistently with prior corporate law provisions. Fourth, when the EC has introduced new rules, it has done so with respect to issues on which Member States would have probably legislated in the absence of an EC mandate. Last but not least, most EC corporate law rules can be categorized as optional, market-mimicking, unimportant or avoidable. National corporate laws, on the other hand, contain core corporate rules, which do have an impact upon EU companies' governance and management. There are, of course, due qualifications to the triviality thesis. First, a few rules or sets of rules indeed have had or are bound to have a meaningful impact upon companies and their operations. Second, EC corporate law has increased the regulatory burden of corporate laws across the EU, correspondingly securing more benefits in favour of certain interest groups. Third, secondary EC corporate law has had and will continue to have an impact on the evolution of European corporate laws and the dynamics of regulatory competition. Finally, its production has become an industry itself, employing many EC and national functionaries and lobbyists, and creating occasions for rent extraction by politicians.

Luca Enriques, 'A Harmonized European Company Law: Are We There Already?', 66 *Int'l & Comp. L.Q.* 763–777, at 777 (2017)

EU Member States' company laws are not uniform, despite half a century of harmonization measures, and will most likely never be. Yet, they do fit together well, if that means that private parties may set up companies that will be recognized as such across the EU to do business anywhere within the EU, reincorporate midstream in a different Member State at reasonable cost (possibly with the exception of the few countries of destination that adopt the real seat doctrine), reorganize their business across EU Member States' borders without the need for reincorporating (again, with the exception of companies set up in real state doctrine Member States) and do business with companies from other Member States without facing unreasonable company-law related transaction costs.

In a less ambitious meaning, thus, the long quest for a harmonized European company law has been successful. More, of course, can be done to make diverse national company laws fit even better together, such as by simplifying the tools for mid-stream reincorporations, namely the rules on cross-border mergers. It goes without saying that attempts to make European company laws more uniform and more 'beautiful' will never stop. And no attempt has been made here to argue that the present landscape is already one that provides the right degree of protection for the interests of members and others across the EU. But it is comforting to think that, if those attempts fail, much has already been achieved in the field of company law that is instrumental to the TFEU's goal of market integration.

Also, authors of the EMCA are of the opinion that it is time to replace the approximation approach to ECL with a regulatory competition approach. As already mentioned, the EMCA is inspired by the MBCA, as a free-standing general company statute that can be enacted by Member States either substantially in its entirety or by the adoption of selected provisions. Instead of requiring compulsory harmonisation, a model act is suitable for stimulating spontaneous convergence. As a non-legislative piece, the EMCA is subject to be continuously developed in response to the changing environment and market conditions that modern businesses face.

1 The Aims of the EMCA

While harmonization or convergence of European Company Law can be achieved by a toolbox of measures, until now the tools have been confined largely to Regulations, Directives, Recommendations, and Corporate Governance Codes. It is submitted that there is a need to provide new measures to develop future European company law and that a European Model Act (EMCA) would be a useful tool for European integration in this area. The objective of the EMCA project thus is to establish, on a solid scientific foundation, a new way forward in European company law inspired by the US Model Business Corporation Act (MBCA).

The EMCA is designed as a free-standing general company statute that can be enacted by Member States either substantially in its entirety or by the adoption of selected provisions.

This approach differs from previous European company law initiatives, as it is a general settlement of the debate on which of the two regulatory approaches is superior – regulatory competition or harmonization. The EMCA offers the Member States a harmonized company law, but leaves it to each Member State to decide whether it will offer its businesses the advantages given by harmonization. The major benefit from an integrated company law framework is that it establishes similar conditions for company shareholders and third parties all over the EU, thus facilitating cross-border investment and trading by ensuring shareholder rights and rebuilding investor confidence. The EMCA is not a mandatory harmonization instrument, as Member States are not bound to follow the Model Act. Thus the EMCA can promote regulatory competition, but can also act as a tool for a harmonization of, and convergence between, Member States' company laws.

At the same time the EMCA allows for special local considerations and for experimentation with new or different ideas, as Member States are free to opt out of parts of the Model Act in order to implement national company law innovations.

The EMCA can be regarded as a tool for better regulation in the EU since it provides a coherent, dynamic and responsive European legislative framework. Member States can benefit from using the Model Act as a company law paradigm, as it will be a modern competitive Companies Act. Moreover, the project allows the EU Commission the opportunity to take part in, or to support, a continuous modernization of the Model Act, without forcing legislation on the Member States.

The EMCA may be viewed as a dynamic piece of legislation capable of being continuously developed in response to the changing environment and market conditions that modern businesses face. The EMCA may thus overcome some of the criticism of traditional inflexible law-making, as it will offer a more informal and organic convergence of European company law.

A very interesting piece is the part of the EMCA Introduction dedicated to Theory and Methodology. This takes into account not only the opportunity to set provisions both at hard and soft law levels, but also considers the advantages of a comparative and functional approach to company law and recognizes the relevance of law and economics in many parts of ECL (corporate governance, directors remuneration, shareholders' engagement, optimal capital structure, and so on).

3 Theory and Methodology

3.1 Legal Theory on Different Legal Tools for Regulation

In its 2003 Action Plan, the European Commission called for "alternative tools for regulation", in other words, alternatives to EU Directives implemented in national company laws. One alternative is "soft law", such as corporate governance codes and other self-regulatory measures.

Usual Companies Acts and soft law are sources of law placed in the hierarchy of national sources of law. Companies Acts as well as soft law are both aimed at the authorities applying the law and at the persons, legal or otherwise, applying them. Model Acts are different, but it is not quite clear how to categorize them. They may contain "principles" in the way used, for example, in the Definitions and Model Rules of European Private Law (DCFR), defined as "principles [...] intended to be applied as general rules (on contract law) in the European Union." As such, principles can have a normative function in the Member States. Partly the EMCA conforms with such a view: The EMCA seeks to promote basic principles of European company law, such as equal rights for shareholders, and other rules on minority protection, principles on directors' duties of loyalty and care and principles of creditor protection. A number of basic principles are defined in the EMCA Chapter 1 on General Company Law Principles.

However, the EMCA also seeks to provide a model for a full text Companies Act, which can be used as a model for future or partial legislation in Member States, for candidate countries to the European Union (especially currently in the Balkan area) and, if interested, to other European or neighbouring countries (Norway, Russia, Switzerland, Ukraine...).

As mentioned above, the purpose of the EMCA is to offer Member States and all European countries, at a low cost, a tool for the convergence of European company legislation that is simultaneously flexible and capable of allowing Member States and all European countries to deal with new developments in the economy. Being inspired by the best solutions in each Member States, the EMCA should contribute to the circulation of models and legal transplants in the EU.

Beyond this goal, the purpose of the EMCA is also to offer a source of inspiration to all countries in the world that are looking to modernize their company law. The EMCA represents an European vision of company law and offers an alternative to countries who do not wish to only refer or be influenced by the United States approach to corporate law, whether the MBCA (Model Business Corporation Act), the Delaware General Corporate Law (DGCL) or the ALI Principles of Corporate Governance: Analysis and Recommendations.

3.2 Some Fundamental Problems and Approaches

When analysing company regulation in Member States and developing the EMCA, a number of fundamental problems appeared and a number of approaches had to be clearly defined.

As a superior criterion for the choice of the regulatory method, the Group has accepted that the EMCA should be based on an appreciation of the following policies:

- Simplification of regulation,
- Flexibility of regulation,
- Reducing agency and transaction costs.

These same policies have also been accepted by the EU Commission as part of its 2006 Strategic Review of Better Regulation.

In recent years, the Commission has worked on assessing initiatives within the area of Company Law. Among others, this has resulted in a report of the Reflection Group "On the Future of EU Company Law" (April 5 2011), the Commission's Green Paper (COM(2011) 164 final), and the Commission's 2012 Action Plan (COM(2012) 740 final).

In the Commission's 2012 Action Plan, three main lines of action are identified; enhancing transparency, engaging shareholders and supporting companies' growth and their competitiveness.

The Commission's work and plans have been taken into account by the EMCA Group's assessment and design of the Model Act. Thus, for example, the Group has emphasized recommendations stating that regulation should promote the company's long term planning and an increased weighting of the management's observation of risk management. Dealing with national differences in company regulation and legal traditions, the EMCA takes a functional approach, meaning that the starting point for the analysis is company problems regardless of whether a problem is, for example, dealt with in the national Companies Act or the national insolvency act. For example, the duty of a director to ensure that a company does not continue to operate once it is foreseeable that the company cannot survive is regulated in the Insolvency Act 1986 as wrongful trading in the UK and in the Companies Act 2009 under the law of liability in Denmark. Further, the regulation of private companies (AG/SA/Plc. etc.) vs. public companies (GmbH/Sarl, Ltd. etc.)/traded companies is based on how typical companies of each type function. Among other things, this is reflected in the Chapter on management which allows different management structures.

In line with the principles on simplification, flexibility and reduced agency costs, there are some necessary considerations on

- the choice between mandatory and non-mandatory (default) rules,
- the use of disclosure rules vs. substantive rules,
- the choice between codes/self-regulation and substantive (Model Act) rules.

In general, prior to the 2008 financial crisis, non-mandatory rules, EU Recommendations and codes/self-regulation were considered preferable, but the Group examined in detail, if and how these general principles should be used in the EMCA, and whether the 2008 financial crisis has altered the formerly preferred general view on this question.

With respect to simplification, the Group took the view that the EMCA needs to contain rules on all relevant company law matters. The various Companies Acts of the EU Members States vary in size. For example, large and detailed regulation can be found in France, Germany, Sweden and the UK, while shorter and less detailed regulation can be found in Denmark, Greece, Luxembourg and Poland. The EMCA aims to reach a balance between general and detailed regulation. In reaching this balance, the Group has taken into consideration the Member States' practical experience of their domestic legislation as well as the huge theoretical work, history and cultural influence behind the different Companies Acts. However, those aspects of the Acts which were too closely related to national traditions (and not of widespread application) were not considered. The intention thus was to avoid overly detailed regulation in the EMCA.

The Group gave particular consideration to the choice between mandatory and non-mandatory (default) rules. The EMCA proceeds on the accepted European tradition in company law that an important goal of the EMCA is the protection not only of outside shareholders but also of creditors. This remains the case even if this goal is supplemented with new goals, such as the use of company law as a tool for economic efficiency and competitiveness or a tool to promote other societal goals (see Section 3.4 below). Thus, rules on creditor and shareholder protection are mandatory rules. These include for example a large number of the rules on capital protection which are contained in the Chapters on formation, companies' capital, general meeting and minority protection. However, the approach of the Group is to avoid drafting overly burdensome and costly rules.

Other rules, in particular with respect to the organization of the company, take the approach of non-mandatory rules allowing companies to organize themselves with flexibility according to their actual needs, within the framework provided by the EMCA.

Generally, there is a need for a proper mix of mandatory, default and soft (i.e. comply or explain) rules with more room for default rules applicable to private companies. Corporate scandals and the recent financial crisis neither justify a radical deregulation nor a hastily adoption of burdensome and untested formalities.

Special consideration is taken with respect to the division between private and public companies (see Section 6 below).

In determining whether an issue should be regulated in the EMCA or dealt with by Member States in the form of self-regulation, a number of issues were considered. An examination of national corporate governance codes indicated that the codes differ in many ways. Some are very detailed and others are shorter and focus primarily on principles. Also, standards of what is considered as good corporate governance vary. Furthermore, EU Recommendations, such as the Recommendation on Directors' Remuneration in Listed Companies (2009/385/EC), have been implemented differently in the various Member States. There is no short answer or formula as to how to deal with these issues. In the EMCA the approach is considered Chapter-by-Chapter and Section-by-Section, see below Section 3.4.

Finally, the EMCA, as a model Companies Act, does not purport to deal with securities regulation/capital markets law, nor with all kinds of regulatory rules that can be seen as flanking measures of corporate law and that are often intended to combat abuses in the area of tax or social security or economic crime.

3.3 Use of Comparative Method

The most important working method to be used during the preparation of the EMCA was the comparative method. Since the members of the Group have solid knowledge – both as academics and in practice – of the Companies Acts of the various Member State, it was possible to use a combination of the "Länderbericht" (national report) method and the analytic method.

The comparative process started with questionnaires on each topic in order to gain a general view of similarities, differences, new ways to deal with problems and recent issues. At the same time, a collection of Companies Acts was established for specific analyses of problems and solutions. The analyses were carried out by working groups, chaired by one member, and representing more than one Member State (old/new Member States, common law/civil law countries etc.). The chair and members of each working group was also chosen considering that their national law, could serve as references for the EMCA on this topic. The reasons were the success of the national Member State law in this area, or its modernity. However, all national Companies Acts were analysed when drafting the chapters in order to have a blend of national traditions (civil law countries/Nordic countries etc.). It was considered also that using national law on certain issues would allow courts and practitioners in Member States adopting parts or the whole of the EMCA, to easily refer to the case law developed under the provisions which served as inspiration.

In certain circumstances, external company law experts were invited by the Group.

The working groups prepared the first drafts of the respective Chapters. The drafts were discussed, revised, and agreed on in meetings (at least twice a year) by the entire Group.

3.4 Use of Law and Economic Theories

Over the last decade or two there has been a paradigm shift in European company law. In short, under the influence of the US, the aim of company legislation/regulation has shifted from being exclusively shareholder and creditor protection to explicitly including the promotion of economic efficiency. The former is reflected primarily, but not exclusively, in the maximization of profits for shareholders (see further below). Use of economic theory and law and economy studies have become a natural part of the development of company regulation particularly in the areas of corporate governance, financing of companies and takeovers.

The project aims to ensure that the contribution, which law and economics have made to company law and corporate governance in recent years, is incorporated and exploited in the EMCA.

As noted earlier, traditional company law is aimed at protecting a company's shareholders and creditors. The shareholders must be ensured influence and profit, and creditors must be protected against losses which are not a result of taking reasonable commercial risks. These goals remain important for any Companies Act.

In order to ensure that the shareholders are able to play an active role in the company's decision-making process, a growing number of measures have been adopted both at national and EU levels. For example, the EU Shareholders' Rights Directive (2007/36/EC) provides new rights for shareholders of listed companies to attend and vote at general meetings remotely, to raise questions and to gain access to relevant information. The amendments to the shareholders' rights directive adopted in 2017 reinforce this approach, for instance on the issue of compensation of directors and managers ("say on pay"). Similarly, the Directive on Takeover Bids (2004/25/EC) regulates takeovers of public listed companies and provides for the protection of minority shareholders by implementing a mandatory bid rule as well as requiring the disclosure of adequate information to the shareholders of the target companies. The purpose of these measures is to ensure an improvement of the corporate governance system. In its 2011 Corporate Governance Green Paper, the Commission stated that shareholders need to take a more active role and concludes "It therefore seems useful to consider whether more shareholders can be encouraged to take an interest in sustainable returns and longer term performance, and how to encourage them to be more active on corporate governance issues". To underline that the Group shares this view, Chapter 1 of the EMCA contains a provision on the principle of shareholder democracy.

The debate has dealt with the possibility of constructing company law rules that encompass incentives for more active involvement by shareholders. In particular, recent experience of the lack of control of directors' remuneration in the form of share options and bonus schemes has illustrated the importance of shareholders' activism. According to Recommendation (2009/385/EC), the structure of directors' remuneration should promote the long-term sustainability of the company and ensure that remuneration is based on performance. As this Recommendation can be implemented into national Companies Acts or corporate governance codes building on the experiences in the Member States, the Group considered whether the Recommendation should be implemented legally in the EMCA or if it is sufficient to deal with the problem in the national corporate governance codes. Some basic principles of the Recommendations are implemented in Chapter 8 of the EMCA on management of the company.

The economic theory which arguably has had, and still has, the largest impact on company law is the principal/agent theory. The main focus of this theory is on the company's organization. The theory concerns the interaction between owners and managers and, in particular, how the owners can control the managers. The shareholders must expend time and resources to control the managers and defray the so-called "agency costs". The EMCA seeks to improve shareholders' opportunities to control managers and to reduce agency costs. (see Chapter 9 on directors' duties and Chapter 11 on general meetings.)

The traditional principal/agent theory focuses on shareholders as principals; however, especially in continental Europe it is recognized that there are additional principals such as employees, creditors and the society as a whole. Following that trend, the EMCA also encompasses the relationship between companies and such stakeholders.17 (see Chapter 9 on directors' duties).

Another economic theory, which has had a great impact on the regulation of takeovers, is the theory on "market for corporate control". This theory suggests that takeovers, and the threat of a takeover, have a disciplinary effect on managers and thus incentivize them to operate their companies more efficiently. The EU's Takeover Bid Directive (Directive 2004/25/EC) is based in part on an acceptance of this theory. While the theory is not without its weaknesses, the EMCA also acknowledges the importance of this theory. While the Takeover Bid Directive (the 13th Directive) was considered as a part of company law directives it is now considered as a part of securities regulation. Thus, the EMCA only considers issues that are of importance with respect to company law matters (see Chapter 13).

Recently, questions have been asked about the economic foundation of takeover regulation and, in a broader sense, on the fundamental objectives of European company law. It has been argued that European companies should have further legal obligations such as taking into account human and environmental interests, corporate social responsibilities and sustainable development.

Many of these interests have been safeguarded by Member States in their own domestic legislation. An example of this would be the "enlightened shareholder value" perspective of directors' fiduciary duties in Section 172 of the UK Companies Act 2006. The Group has further examined in which way these objectives should be implemented in the EMCA. Generally, the Group agreed that companies must take developments in society and changes in society's goals into account. Securing environment, sustainable development (CSR) is not considered as the fundamental and mandatory objective of company law but should primarily be considered by special regulation in the various fields. However, there is a clear tendency that such goals are also recognized in company law, accounting law and corporate governance codes. See in particular Chapter 8 on directors' duties and Chapter 13 on reorganization of companies.

Corporate finance theorists have since the 1960's developed a series of models, the aim of which is to develop an optimal capital structure of companies. This theory has also had a considerable influence on company law. These theories have also been considered and taken into account by the EMCA Group. Company law rules must facilitate a flexible adjustment of the company's capital. The Group shares the view that companies should be allowed wide discretion in deciding how to organize the capital structure of the company. Such rules must at the same time secure shareholder influence and control without ignoring the interests of creditors. (see Chapter 6 on financing the company and Chapter 7 on companies' capital.)

Economic theories represent a necessary foundation for the configuration of single provisions of the EMCA. A main theme of the EMCA project is to consider the effect which the 2008 financial crisis has had on the aforementioned theories. For example, the financial crisis gives rise to questions as to whether the previous trend to "optimize" the optimal capital structure needs to be corrected. The trend in the ten or so years before the financial crisis was to operate companies with less equity capital and more debt. A predominant view held by economic theorists has justified that approach. In some Member States thus company law as well as accounting regulation is built on economic theory which has underlined the advantage of a high debt ratio. However, it is appropriate to re-examine this balance between risk and return on the one hand, and the protection of creditors and other constituencies in company law and accounting rules on the other. Risk management, focusing on directors' duties, provides for an example of this view (see Chapter 8).

The group is aware of the fact that particular types of conflicts may arise within private companies. A private company usually is composed by a small number of shareholders. Agency problems in relation to the directors are thereby reduced, in most cases there is no clear separation between ownership and management. Instead, conflicts amongst shareholders become more important with particular attention to be paid to the conflict between minority and majority shareholders. The EMCA is following the one-law model (see Section 8 below) aiming at both public and private companies thereby taking into account the particular needs of typical private companies (see Section 7 below).

FURTHER READING

Luca Enriques, 'EU Company Law Directives and Regulations: How Trivial Are They?', 27 *U. Pa Int'l Econ. L.J.* 1–78 (2006).

Nikolaos D. Tellis, 'Expansion of the Applicability of EU Company Law Directives via Analogy? – A Study Based on the Example of Greek Sea Trading Companies', 5 *ECFR* 353–377 (2008).

Luca Enriques, 'A Harmonized European Company Law: Are We There Already?', 66 *Int'l & Comp. L.Q.* 763–777, at 777 (2017).

See also:

Mads Andenas and Frank Wooldridge, *European Comparative Company Law* 33–40 (Cambridge University Press, 2012).

Alberto Santamaria, *European Economic Law* 119–149 (Alphen aan den Rijn, Kluwer Law International, 3rd ed., 2014).

2.2 Formation of a Company and Disclosure of Information

The First (along with the Second) Company Law Directive laid down general rules on setting up limited-liability companies, capital, and disclosure requirements.

The First Company Law Directive – First Council Directive 68/151/EEC, of 9 March 1968 on coordination of safeguards which, for the protection of the interests of members and others, are required by Member States of companies within the meaning of the second paragraph of Article 58 of the Treaty, with a view to making such safeguards equivalent throughout the Community, now replaced by Directive 2017/1132/EU, of 14 June 2017, relating to certain aspects of company law – covers the disclosure of company documents, the validity of obligations entered into by a company, and nullity. As mentioned, it applies to all public and private limited-liability companies.

The reasons behind this piece of legislation are clearly expressed in the Recitals to the Directive.

Recitals 7–8 Directive 2017/1132/EU

The coordination of national provisions concerning disclosure, the validity of obligations entered into by, and the nullity of, companies limited by shares or otherwise having limited liability is of special importance, particularly for the purpose of protecting the interests of third parties.

The basic documents of the company should be disclosed in order that third parties may be able to ascertain their contents and other information concerning the company, especially particulars of the persons who are authorised to bind the company.

This information is made available for all interested parties, who may obtain from the register a copy of such documents and particulars by paper means as well as by electronic means. In particular:

Recital 12 Directive 2017/1132/EU

Cross-border access to company information should be facilitated by allowing, in addition to the mandatory disclosure made in one of the languages permitted in the company's Member State, voluntary registration in additional languages of the required documents and particulars. Third parties acting in good faith should be able to rely on the translations thereof.

Furthermore, the protection of third parties is ensured by provisions that restrict to the greatest possible extent the grounds on which the obligations entered into in the name of the company are not valid. Also, in order to ensure certainty in the law as regards relations between the company and third parties, and also between members, the cases in which nullity can arise and the retroactive effect of a declaration of nullity must be restricted.

The provisions related to the mentioned issues concerned by the First and the Second Company Law Directive, now carried by Directive 2017/1132/EU will be discussed in Chapter 8.

The Eleventh Company Law Directive later complemented the First Directive. The Eleventh Council Directive 89/666/EEC of 21 December 1989 on *disclosure requirements in respect of branches opened in a Member State by certain types of company governed by the law of another State* introduces disclosure requirements for foreign branches of companies. It covers EU companies that set up branches in another EU country or companies from non-EU countries setting up branches in the EU. Also, the Eleventh Company Law Directive is now replaced by Directive 2017/1132/EU.

The grounds for extending disclosure requirements also to branches are expressed as follows:

Recitals 14–15 Directive 2017/1132/EU

The opening of a branch, like the creation of a subsidiary, is one of the possibilities currently open to companies in the exercise of their right of establishment in another Member State.

In respect of branches, the lack of coordination, in particular concerning disclosure, gives rise to some disparities, in the protection of shareholders and third parties, between companies which operate in other Member States by opening branches and those which operate there by creating subsidiaries

Some of the provisions of Directive 2017/1132/EU concerning the establishment of branches will be discussed in Chapter 6.

FURTHER READING

Silvia Nashenveng, 'Companies' Liabilities under The First EC Directive', 12 *EBLR* 89–96 (2001).

Oliver Vossius, 'The Innoventif Case of the ECJ 1.6.2006, C-453/0', 3 *ECFR* 475–482 (2006).

Karsten Engsig Sørensen, 'Branches of Companies in the EU: Balancing the Eleventh Company Law Directive, National Company Law and the Right of Establishment', 11 *ECFR* 53–96 (2014).

See also:

Erik Werlauff, *EU Company Law* 90 (Copenhagen, DJØF Publishing, 2nd ed., 2003).

Alberto Santamaria, *European Economic Law* 168–169 (Alphen aan den Rijn, Kluwer Law International, 3rd ed., 2014).

2.3 Formation by a Single Member

Under the First Company Law Directive, the nullity of a company may be ordered on the grounds:

Article 12 First Company Law Directive

(vi) that, contrary to the national law governing the company, the number of founder members is less than two.

However, the Twelfth Company Law Directive – Twelfth Council Company Law Directive 89/667/EEC of 21 December 1989 *on single-member private limited-liability companies*, now replaced by Directive 2009/102/EC of 16 September 2009 – provides a framework for setting up a single-member company, in which all shares are held by a single shareholder. As mentioned, this directive covers only private limited-liability companies, but EU countries may decide to extend it to public limited-liability companies. The grounds for permitting a single-member private limited company are clarified as follows:

Recital 4 Directive 2009/102/EC

A legal instrument is required allowing the limitation of liability of the individual entrepreneur throughout the Community, without prejudice to the laws of the Member States, which, in exceptional circumstances, require that entrepreneur to be liable for the obligations of his undertaking.

The provisions of Directive 2009/102/EC will be discussed in Chapter 8, § 8.1. It must be added that in April 2014, the European Commission, as part of its package on corporate governance and company law (*see*, Chapter 4, § 4.5), published a *proposal for a directive on single-member private companies with limited liability* (COM/2014/0212 final – 2014/0120 (COD)), called the *Societas Unius Personae* (SUP). The new directive, whilst replacing Directive 2009/102/EC, aims at facilitating the establishing of companies across the EU.

Some more details on this proposal will be discussed in Chapter 3, § 3.7.

FURTHER READING

Edwina Dunn, 'Single Member Private Limited Companies: 12th Company Law Directive', 1 *EBLR* 6–7 (1990).

Barbara De Donno, 'From Simplified Companies to One-man Limited Enterprises', 11 *ECL* 155–156 (2014).

Iris Wuisman, 'The Societas Unius Personae (SUP)', 12 *ECL* 34–44 (2015).

Pierre-Henri Conac, 'The Societas Unius Personae (SUP): A "Passport" for Job Creation and Growth', 12 *ECFR* 139–176 (2015).

Jesper Lau Hansen, 'The SUP Proposal: Registration and Capital (Articles 13–17)', 12 *ECFR* 177–190 (2015).

Vanessa Knapp, 'Directive on Single-Member Private Limited Liability Companies: Distributions', 12 *ECFR* 191–201 (2015).

Christoph Teichmann, 'Corporate Groups within the Legal Framework of the European Union: The Group-related Aspects of the SUP Proposal and the EU Freedom of Establishment', 12 *ECFR* 202–229 (2015).

Stephan Harbarth, 'From SPE to SMC: The German Political Debate on the Reform of the "Small Company"', 12 *ECFR* 230–237 (2015).

Corrado Malberti, 'The Relationship between the Societas Unius Personae Proposal and the acquis: Creeping Toward an Abrogation of EU Company Law?', 12 *ECFR* 238–279 (2015).

See also:

Erik Werlauff, *EU Company Law* 91 (Copenhagen, DJØF Publishing, 2nd ed., 2003).

2.4 Capital Formation and Maintenance

The Second Company Law Directive – Second Council Directive 77/91/EEC of 13 December 1976 on coordination of safeguards which, for the protection of the interests of members and others, are required by Member States of companies within the meaning of the second paragraph of Article 58 of the Treaty, in respect of the formation of public limited-liability companies and the maintenance and alteration of their capital, with a view to making such safeguards equivalent, now also replaced by Directive 2017/1132/EU – covers the formation of public limited-liability companies and the rules on maintaining and altering their capital. In particular, it sets the minimum capital requirement for EU public limited-liability companies at €25,000, regulates the acquisition and the financial assistance on a company's own shares, and expresses a principle of equal treatment for all shareholders who are in the same position.

The grounds for harmonising company law as regards the formation and maintenance of a share capital are expressed as follows:

Recitals 3–5, 47 Directive 2017/1132/EU

(3) In order to ensure minimum equivalent protection for both shareholders and creditors of public limited liability companies, the coordination of national provisions relating to their formation and to the maintenance, increase or reduction of their capital is particularly important.

(4) In the Union, the statutes or instrument of incorporation of a public limited liability company must make it possible for any interested person to acquaint himself with the basic particulars of the company, including the exact composition of its capital.

(5) Union provisions are necessary for maintaining the capital, which constitutes the creditors' security, in particular by prohibiting any reduction thereof by distribution to shareholders where the latter are not entitled to it and by imposing limits on the company's right to acquire its own shares.

…

(47) In order to enhance standardised creditor protection in all Member States, creditors should be able to resort, under certain conditions, to judicial or administrative proceedings where their claims are at stake as a consequence of a reduction in the capital of a public limited liability company.

The protection of shareholders and creditors requires not only restrictions on the company's right to acquire its own shares, but a comprehensive regulation of all transactions on a company's own shares, such as the subscription, the acquisition, and the financial assistance, either directly or indirectly enacted by the company's directors. This point is clarified as follows:

Recitals 41–42 Directive 2017/1132/EU

(41) The restrictions on a company's acquisition of its own shares should apply not only to acquisitions made by a company itself but also to those made by any person acting in his own name but on the company's behalf.

(42) In order to prevent a public limited liability company from using another company in which it holds a majority of the voting rights or on which it can exercise a dominant influence to make such acquisitions without complying with the restrictions imposed in that respect, the arrangements governing a company's acquisition of its own shares should be extended to cover the most important and most frequent cases of the acquisition of shares by such other companies. Those arrangements should be extended to cover subscription for shares in the public limited liability company.

As regards the protection of shareholders, the principle of equal treatment of shareholders is worth mentioning: originally linked to decisions on the increase and reduction of capital, this principle later acquired general application to all transactions regarded in the directive. Further on, in 2006, the principle was expressly reiterated for the acquisition of a company's own shares. Recital 46 of Directive 2017/1132/EU – similar to the original one expressed within the Second Directive – reads as follows:

Recital 46 Directive 2017/1132/EU

(46) It is necessary, having regard to the objectives of Article 50(2) (g) of the Treaty, that the Member States' laws relating to the increase or reduction of capital ensure that the principles of equal treatment of shareholders in the same position and of protection of creditors whose claims exist prior to the decision on reduction are observed and harmonised.

The provisions related to the mentioned issues concerned by the Second Company Law Directive, now carried by Directive 2017/1132/EU, will be discussed in Chapters 10, 11, and 16.

FURTHER READING

See the references included in Chapters 10, 11, and 16.

2.5 Merger and Division

The Third Company Law Directive – Third Company Law Directive 78/855/EEC, *on mergers of public limited liability companies*, now also replaced by Directive 2017/1132/EU – deals with mergers between public limited-liability companies in a single EU country. It covers protection for shareholders, creditors, and employees. The Third Company Law Directive was later complemented by the Tenth Company Law Directive – Tenth Company Law Directive 2005/56/EC of 26 October 2005, *on cross-border mergers of limited liability companies* – setting out rules to facilitate mergers of limited-liability companies involving more than one country (cross-border mergers).

In some aspects, the Third Directive was also complemented by the Sixth Company Law Directive – Sixth Company Law Directive 82/891/EEC, *on division of public companies*, now also replaced by Directive 2017/1132/EU – dealing with the division of public limited-liability companies in a single EU country. The Sixth Directive also covers protection for shareholders, creditors, and employees.

The grounds for a harmonisation in the field of mergers (and divisions) are expressed in Recitals 49–51 of Directive 2017/1132/EU (and similarly in Recitals 61–70 of Directive 2017/1132/EU), as follows:

Recitals 49–51 Directive 2017/1132/EU

(49) The protection of the interests of members and third parties requires that the laws of the Member States relating to mergers of public limited liability companies be coordinated and that provision for mergers should be made in the laws of all the Member States.

(50) In the context of such coordination it is particularly important that the shareholders of merging companies be kept adequately informed in as objective a manner as possible and that their rights be suitably protected. However, there is no reason to require an examination of the draft terms of a merger by an independent expert for the shareholders if all the shareholders agree that it may be dispensed with.

(51) Creditors, including debenture holders, and persons having other claims on the merging companies should be protected so that the merger does not adversely affect their interests.

Similarly to the provision of the First Directive, the Third and the Sixth Directives also put restrictions on the possibility to declare the nullity of a merger or division transactions. Recital 54 of Directive 2017/1132/EU (and similarly Recital 73 of Directive 2017/1132/EU) reads as follows:

Recital 54 Directive 2017/1132/EU

(54) To ensure certainty in the law as regards relations between the companies concerned, between them and third parties, and between the members, it is necessary to limit the cases in which nullity can arise by providing that defects be remedied wherever that is possible and by restricting the period within which nullification proceedings may be commenced.

The provisions concerning domestic mergers and those concerning divisions under Directive 2017/1132/EU will be discussed in Chapter 19.

Harmonisation of EU legislations regarding mergers and divisions of companies was a first step towards an EU regulation on cross-border mergers. The cross-border merger is a matter of the utmost importance for the realisation of the right of primary establishment set out by the TFEU. As will be explained later, the possibility of a cross-border merger of EU companies was already declared by the CJEU in *Sevic*, a case decided in 2005 in the absence of the Tenth Directive on cross-border mergers. This makes clear that the aim of having a cross-border merger directive was not only that of declaring the validity of the transaction in itself, but also that of having a common framework on how the merger between two companies formed under the laws of different Member States should be realised.

Indeed, the grounds for delivering the Tenth Directive – now included in Directive 2017/1132/EU – are expressed as follows:

Recital 55 Directive 2017/1132/EU

(55) This Directive also facilitates the cross-border merger of limited liability companies. The laws of the Member States should allow the cross-border merger of a national limited liability company with a limited liability company from another Member State if the national law of the relevant Member States permits mergers between such types of company.

Given the above, the Tenth Directive, and now Directive 2017/1132/EU aimed at facilitating cross-border mergers of EU companies by coordinating the relevant national provisions on mergers. In particular:

Recitals 56–61 Directive 2017/1132/EU

(56) In order to facilitate cross-border merger operations, it should be specified that, unless this Directive provides otherwise, each company

taking part in a cross-border merger, and each third party concerned, remains subject to the provisions and formalities of the national law which would be applicable in the case of a national merger. None of the provisions and formalities of national law, to which reference is made in this Directive, should introduce restrictions on freedom of establishment or on the free movement of capital, save where these can be justified in accordance with the case-law of the Court of Justice of the European Union and in particular, by requirements of the general interest and are both necessary for, and proportionate to, the attainment of such overriding requirements.

(57) The common draft terms of a cross-border merger should be drawn up in the same terms for each of the companies concerned in the various Member States. The minimum content of such common draft terms should therefore be specified, while leaving the companies free to agree on other terms.

(58) In order to protect the interests of members and others, both the common draft terms of cross-border mergers and the completion of the cross-border merger should be publicised for each merging company via an entry in the appropriate public register.

(59) The laws of all the Member States should provide for the drawing-up at national level of a report on the common draft terms of the cross-border merger by one or more experts on behalf of each of the companies that are merging. In order to limit experts' costs connected with cross-border mergers, provision should be made for the possibility of drawing up a single report intended for all members of companies taking part in a cross-border merger operation. The common draft terms of the cross-border merger are to be approved by the general meeting of each of those companies.

(60) In order to facilitate cross-border merger operations, it should be provided that monitoring of the completion and legality of the decision-making process in each merging company should be carried out by the national authority having jurisdiction over each of those companies, whereas monitoring of the completion and legality of the cross-border merger should be carried out by the national authority having jurisdiction over the company resulting from the cross-border merger. The national authority in question may be a court, a notary or any other competent authority appointed by the Member State concerned. The national law determining the date on which the cross-border merger takes effect, this being the law to which the company resulting from the cross-border merger is subject, should also be specified.

(61) In order to protect the interests of members and others, the legal effects of the cross-border merger, distinguishing as to whether the company resulting from the cross-border merger is an acquiring company or a new company, should be specified. In the interests of legal certainty, it should no longer be possible, after the date on which a cross-border merger takes effect, to declare the merger null and void.

The provisions concerning cross-border mergers carried by Directive 2017/1132/EU will be discussed in Chapter 7, § 7.1.

FURTHER READING

James Kirkbride, 'The Merger Regulation - An Acceptable Compromise?', 2 *EBLR* 55–57 (1991).

Allan F.T. Tatham, 'Merger and Division of Companies in Italy', 3 *EBLR* 52–54 (1992).

Cedric Guyot, 'New Regulations on the Merger and Split-up of Belgian Companies', 4 *EBLR* 287–289 (1993).

Marieke Wyckaert and Koen Geens, 'Cross-border Mergers and Minority Protection: An Open-ended Harmonization', 5 *ECL* 288–296 (2008).

Geert T.M.J. Raaijmakers and Thijs P.H. Olthoff, 'Creditor Protection in Cross-border Mergers: Unfinished Business', 5 *ECL* 305–308 (2008).

See also:

Erik Werlauff, *EU Company Law* 83, 87 (Copenhagen, DJØF Publishing, 2nd ed., 2003).

Alberto Santamaria, *European Economic Law* 159–164 (Alphen aan den Rijn, Kluwer Law International, 3rd ed., 2014).

2.6 Annual and Consolidated Accounts

An important chapter of EU company law includes annual and consolidated accounts. The Fourth and Seventh Company Law Directives originally carried provisions in these fields. Both these directives have been replaced by new acts. The Fourth Directive – Fourth Council Directive 78/660/EEC, of 25 July 1978 based on Article 54(3)(g) of the Treaty *on the annual accounts of certain types of companies* – and the Seventh Directive – Seventh Council Directive 83/349/EEC of 13 June 1983 based on Article 54(3)(g) of the Treaty *on consolidated accounts* – basically aimed at harmonising the mandatory information that both public and private limited companies give to shareholders and third parties via their annual and consolidated accounts, these documents being the main source of information. Both directives were later replaced by Directive 2013/34/EU of the European Parliament and of the Council of 26 June 2013 *on the annual financial statements, consolidated financial statements and related reports of certain types of undertakings, amending Directive 2006/43/EC of the European Parliament and of the Council and repealing Council Directives 78/660/EEC and 83/349/EEC* (hereafter also referred to as the new Fourth and Seventh Directives).

The grounds for delivering a directive on annual accounts are expressed as follows:

Recitals 3–4 Directive 2013/34/EU

(3) The coordination of national provisions concerning the presentation and content of annual financial statements and management reports, the measurement bases used

therein and their publication in respect of certain types of undertakings with limited liability is of special importance for the protection of shareholders, members and third parties. Simultaneous coordination is necessary in those fields for such types of undertakings because, on the one hand, some undertakings operate in more than one Member State and, on the other hand, such undertakings offer no safeguards to third parties beyond the amounts of their net assets.

(4) Annual financial statements pursue various objectives and do not merely provide information for investors in capital markets but also give an account of past transactions and enhance corporate governance. Union accounting legislation needs to strike an appropriate balance between the interests of the addressees of financial statements and the interest of undertakings in not being unduly burdened with reporting requirements.

The grounds for delivering a directive on consolidated accounts are expressed as follows:

Recitals 29 and 31 Directive 2013/34/EU

(29) Many undertakings own other undertakings and the aim of coordinating the legislation governing consolidated financial statements is to protect the interests subsisting in companies with share capital. Consolidated financial statements should be drawn up so that financial information concerning such undertakings may be conveyed to members and third parties. National law governing consolidated financial statements should therefore be coordinated in order to achieve the objectives of comparability and equivalence in the information which undertakings should publish within the Union. However, given the lack of an arm's-length transaction price, Member States should be allowed to permit intra-group transfers of participating interests, so-called common control transactions, to be accounted for using the pooling of interests method of accounting, in which the book value of shares held in an undertaking included in a consolidation is set off against the corresponding percentage of capital only …

(31) Consolidated financial statements should present the activities of a parent undertaking and its subsidiaries as a single economic entity (a group). Undertakings controlled by the parent undertaking should be considered as subsidiary undertakings. Control should be based on holding a majority of voting rights, but control may also exist where there are agreements with fellow shareholders or members. In certain circumstances control may be effectively exercised where the parent holds a minority or none of the shares in the subsidiary. Member States should be entitled to require that undertakings not subject to control, but which are managed on a unified basis or have a common administrative, managerial or supervisory body, be included in consolidated financial statements.

More details on Directive 2013/34/EU will be given in Chapter 12.

It must be added that, in the field of consolidated accounts, the EU institutions have delivered additional regulations in order to have a uniform legislation for listed companies formed under the legislations of EU Member States. This uniform legislation includes Regulation 2002/1606/EC of the European Parliament and of the Council of 19 July 2002 *on the application of international accounting standards* (hereafter referred to as IAS/IFRS) and Commission Regulation 2008/1126/EC of 3 November 2008 *adopting certain international accounting standards* (replacing Commission Regulation 2003/1725/EC of 29 September 2003).

The grounds for adopting these regulations are expressed as follows:

Recitals 2–4 Regulation 2002/1606/EC

(2) In order to contribute to a better functioning of the internal market, publicly traded companies must be required to apply a single set of high quality international accounting standards for the preparation of their consolidated financial statements. Furthermore, it is important that the financial reporting standards applied by Community companies participating in financial markets are accepted internationally and are truly global standards. This implies an increasing convergence of accounting standards currently used internationally with the ultimate objective of achieving a single set of global accounting standards.

(3) Council Directive 78/660/EEC of 25 July 1978 on the annual accounts of certain types of companies, Council Directive 83/349/EEC of 13 June 1983 on consolidated accounts, Council Directive 86/635/EEC of 8 December 1986 on the annual accounts and consolidated accounts of banks and other financial institutions and Council Directive 91/674/EEC of 19 December 1991 on the annual accounts and consolidated accounts of insurance companies are also addressed to publicly traded Community companies. The reporting requirements set out in these Directives cannot ensure the high level of transparency and comparability of financial reporting from all publicly traded Community companies which is a necessary condition for building an integrated capital market which operates effectively, smoothly and efficiently. It is therefore necessary to supplement the legal framework applicable to publicly traded companies.

(4) This Regulation aims at contributing to the efficient and cost-effective functioning of the capital market. The protection of investors and the maintenance of confidence in the financial markets is also an important aspect of the completion of the internal market in this area. This Regulation reinforces the freedom of movement of capital in the internal market and helps to enable Community companies to compete on an equal footing for financial resources available in the Community capital markets, as well as in world capital markets.

More details on Regulation 2002/1606/EC and Commission Regulation 2008/1126/EC will be given in Chapter 12, § 12.7.

FURTHER READING

David Monciardini, 'Regulating Accounting for Sustainable Companies: Some Considerations on the Forthcoming EU Directive', 11 *ECL* 2 (2014), 121–124.

See also:
Erik Werlauff, *EU Company Law* 83–85, 87 (Copenhagen, DJØF Publishing, 2nd ed., 2003).

2.7 The Statutory Audits

Statutory audits are also related to the fields covered by Directive 2013/34/EU: indeed, 'statutory audit' means an audit of annual financial statements or consolidated financial statements. However, statutory audits have a much broader relevance in the corporate governance of companies.

The Eighth Directive – Eighth Council Directive 84/253/EEC of 10 April 1984 *on the approval of persons responsible for carrying out the statutory audits of accounting documents* – (only) aimed at laying down the conditions for the approval of persons responsible for carrying out the statutory audit. Over time, the Eighth Directive has been replaced by Directive 2006/43/EC of the European Parliament and of the Council of 17 May 2006 *on statutory audits of annual accounts and consolidated accounts*, amending Council Directives 78/660/EEC and 83/349/EEC and repealing Council Directive 84/253/EEC: the so-called new Eighth Directive – lastly amended by Directive 2014/56/EU of 16 April 2014 – lays down (in addition to the conditions for the approval and registration of persons that carry out statutory audits) the rules on independence, objectivity, and professional ethics applying to those persons, and the framework for their public oversight.

In addition Regulation 2014/537/EU of the European Parliament and of the Council of 16 April 2014 *on specific requirements regarding statutory audit of public-interest entities* and repealing Commission Decision 2005/909/EC, provided uniform legislation on statutory audits of public-interest entities.

Further details on the Directives and Regulations on statutory audits will be given in Chapter 12, § 12.8 and Chapter 14, § 14.11.

2.8 The Fifth Draft Directive on Corporate Governance

Originally submitted to the Council on 9 October 1972 (the 'Original Proposal') – but later revised in 1983 (the 'Amended Proposal') and 1991 (the 'Third Draft') – the Fifth Company Law Draft Proposal concerned the structure of public limited companies and the powers and obligations of their organs. In other words, this draft directive aimed to harmonise the corporate governance of public limited companies.

The grounds for such a harmonisation are expressed as follows:

Preamble Fifth Company Law Directive (Original Proposal)

Whereas, so that the protection afforded to the interests of members and others is made equivalent, the laws of the Member States relating to the structure of public limited companies and to the powers and obligations of their organs must also be coordinated;

Whereas, in the fields aforesaid, equivalent legal conditions must be created in the Community for competing public limited companies.

The Original Proposal approached this task by suggesting the mandatory adoption of the two-tier board structure, consisting of a management organ and a supervisory organ, following the German model of corporate governance. The mandatory nature of this structure is also coupled with the requirement of employee participation in the supervisory board, which is another typical feature of the German model of corporate governance, generally referred to as workers' co-determination (*Mitbestimmung*).

The grounds for adopting a mandatory two-tier board structure are expressed as follows:

Preamble Fifth Company Law Directive (Original Proposal)

Whereas, so far as concerns the organisation of the administration of this type of company [i.e., the public limited companies], two different sets of arrangements at present obtain in the Community; whereas one of these provides for one administrative organ only while the other provides for two, namely a management organ responsible for managing the business of the company and an organ responsible for controlling the management body; whereas, in practice, even under the arrangement which provides for only one administrative organ, a de facto distinction is often made between executive members who manage the business of the company and non-executive members who confine themselves to supervision.

Therefore, the Commission maintained that in order to clearly differentiate the responsibilities of executive and non-executive directors it was preferable to vest separate organs with the management and supervisory functions. The adoption of a mandatory two-tier board structure would also facilitate the involvement of workers, as – where the company employs more than 500 workers – they would be allowed to elect up to one third of the members sitting in the supervisory board.

The grounds for suggesting an involvement of workers, however, are not clearly expressed.

Preamble Fifth Company Law Directive (Original Proposal)

Whereas the laws of certain Member States provide for employee participation within the supervisory or administrative organ but no such provision exists in other Member States;

Whereas provision should be made for such participation in all Member States ...

The proposal to adopt a mandatory two-tier board structure including workers' co-determination provisions led to a long discussion within the Council and, as the UK joined the EEC in 1973, it became clear that the Original Proposal would not be adopted, unless a basic revision was made.

In 1983, the Commission delivered an Amended Proposal and, in 1991, a Third Draft. Notwithstanding a clear preference for a two-tier board structure, the Commission proposed an option for Member States and/or for founders to adopt a one-tier or a two-tier structure.

Preamble Fifth Company Law Directive (Third Draft)

Whereas in both systems a clear delimitation is desirable between the responsibilities of the persons charged with one or other of these duties; whereas the general introduction of such a distinction will facilitate the formation of public limited companies by members or groups of members from different Member States and, thereby, interpenetration of undertakings within the Community; whereas the general introduction of the two-tier system on a compulsory basis is for the time being impracticable though such systems should be made generally available at least as an option for public limited companies;

Whereas one-tier systems may therefore be maintained provided that they are endowed with certain characteristics designed to harmonise their functioning with that of two-tier structures;

With regards to workers' participation, both the Amended Proposal and the Third Draft significantly changed the EU approach.

Preamble Fifth Company Law Directive (Third Draft)

Whereas in order to make provision for employee participation, the Directive does not make rules uniform for all the Member States but leaves them to choose between a number of equivalent arrangements;

Whereas certain common principles are nevertheless necessary in particular as to the appointment of employee representatives;

In brief, co-determination of workers became mandatory only where the company employs more than 1,000 workers, whilst the Original Proposal identified the threshold at 500 workers. Second, instead of a mandatory participation of members in the supervisory board, the Third Draft expressed the principle that workers' participation could be assured by one of several means. For both companies adopting a one-tier or two-tier structure, workers' participation would be assured by direct appointment, co-optation, or collective agreement. Additionally, companies could assure employee participation by processes that do not entail membership on the supervisory organ: such processes shall provide access to both the management and the supervisory board's decisions and extensive information.

In addition, the proposal aimed at harmonising provisions with regards to the civil liability of the members of the management and supervisory organs.

Preamble Fifth Company Law Directive (Third Draft)

Whereas the members of the management and supervisory organs must be made subject to special rules relating to civil liability which provide for joint and several liability, reverse the burden of proof in respect of liability for wrongful acts and ensure that the bringing of proceedings on behalf of the company for the purpose of making those persons liable is not improperly prevented;

Also, all the proposals included comprehensive provisions on the general meeting and shareholders' powers, with a view to enhancing shareholders' powers of control and preventing conflicts of interests. The grounds for such a harmonisation are expressed as follows:

Preamble Fifth Company Law Directive (Third Draft)

Whereas, as regards the preparation and holding of general meetings, the shareholders must be protected by equivalent provisions relating to the form, content and period of notice, the right to attend and to be represented at meetings, written or oral information, exercise the right to vote, the majorities required for the passing of resolutions and, finally, the right to bring proceedings in respect of void or voidable resolutions;

Whereas certain rights of shareholders should be capable of being exercised by a minority of them;

Whereas the position of shareholders regarding the exercise of their voting rights should be strengthened in order to endure a wide measure of participation in the life of the company; whereas voting rights should accordingly be proportionate to the shareholder's stake in the company capital, and limits should be imposed on the issue of preference shares without voting rights;

Whereas the freedom of the general meeting to appoint members of the organs of the company should not be reduced by giving particular categories of shareholders an exclusive right to put forward nominations; whereas the majority required for such resolutions on the part of the general meeting should be no greater than the absolute majority;

Neither the Original, nor the Amended nor the Third Draft Proposal of the Fifth Company Law Directive has been approved. However, they have had a significant influence in the debate on corporate governance in Europe and have ultimately led to the adoption of the Regulation on the SE and its complementing directives on workers' participation: this will be discussed in Chapter 14. Many of the provisions of the Fifth Directive regarding shareholders' meetings and shareholders' powers have also been introduced in the Shareholder Rights Directive – Directive 2007/36/EC of the European Parliament and of the Council of 11 July 2007 *on the exercise of certain rights of shareholders in listed companies* (as amended by Directive 2017/828/EU, of the European Parliament and of the Council of 20 May 2017 *as regards the encouragement of long-term shareholder engagement*), as we will see in Chapter 15; however, this only addresses listed companies.

FURTHER READING

Daniel T. Murphy, 'The Amended Proposal for a Fifth Company Law Directive – Nihil Novum', 7 *Hous. J. Int'l L.* 215–235 (1985).

See also:
Erik Werlauff, *EU Company Law* 85–87 (Copenhagen, DJØF Publishing, 2nd ed., 2003).

Mads Andenas and Frank Wooldridge, *European Comparative Company Law* 28–29 (Cambridge University Press, 2012).

2.9 The Ninth Draft Directive on Groups of Companies

Based on a pre-draft dated 1974, in December 1984 the EEC Commission submitted to the Council a Draft Proposal for a Ninth Council Directive, relating to the links between undertakings and in particular to groups. This Draft Proposal focused on the conduct of groups containing a public limited company (hereafter PLC) as a subsidiary. According to its Explanatory Memorandum, the directive was intended to provide a framework in which groups can be managed on a sound basis whilst ensuring that interests affected by group operations are adequately protected. Such a legal framework, adapted to the special circumstances of groups, was considered to be lacking in the legal system of most Member States. Apart from its provisions dealing with the notification and disclosure of shareholdings in PLCs, which covered all PLCs, the directive otherwise applied only when a PLC was the subsidiary of another undertaking (which could itself be a PLC, but could also be a natural person or a legal person).

The grounds for a harmonisation in the field of groups of companies are expressed as follows:

Preamble Ninth Company Law Directive (Draft Proposal)

A growing number of public limited liability companies are linked with each other and with other undertakings through capital holdings. Having regard to the economic importance of such companies, it is necessary in the interest not only of shareholders, creditors and employees but also for the general public that clear insight be afforded into their ownership and power structures by means of the extensive disclosure measures possible. The national laws of Member States concerning notification and disclosure of holdings must therefore be coordinated to guarantee a minimum degree of equivalence in this respect in the Community.

Many public limited liability companies are linked with other undertakings in such a way that they are all subject to unified control by a single undertaking and are managed collectively as a single entity.

In our modern economy, based as it is on the division of labour, such arrangements, known as groups, are the most important means of cooperation available to undertakings at the national as well as international level.

It is essential that the economic and financial relationships within such groups should be transparent. This is why by virtue of Directive 83/349/EEC of 13 June 1983 the annual accounts of the various participant companies must be consolidated in order to give a true and fair view of the group's assets and liabilities, financial position and profit and loss.

The EEC Commission acknowledged that the legislation of various Member States contained (and still contains) no provisions on the structure of groups. Considering that coordination of national provisions on the structure of groups of companies is necessary to ensure a minimum degree of equivalence and considering also that coordination by stages was appropriate, the EEC Commission proposed some actions to be undertaken. It is worth mentioning that provisions included in the Draft Proposal of the Ninth Directive are basically taken from the German legislation on groups of companies, carried by the joint-stock corporation act of 1965 (*Aktiengesetz*).

Preamble Ninth Company Law Directive (Draft Proposal)

The first stage of such coordination should be the incorporation into the Law of Member States of provisions concerning groups formed by means of a control contract. This will give legal status to the power to manage the group. Interested parties will be properly protected.

Member States will also be given an opportunity to enact provisions for groups to be based on other criteria. Such methods of constituting groups must however provide guarantees identical to those laid down for contract based groups.

Where an undertaking has directly or indirectly acquired 90 per cent or more of a company's capital a special situation exists on account of the shareholding. The creation of a group relationship in law ought therefore to be facilitated by taking the actual situation into account and avoiding excessive formalism. A unilateral declaration by the undertaking constitutes the most appropriate means to that end.

It must not be possible to make a public limited liability company economically subservient to a parent undertaking except within the legal framework of one of these group structures. In such a framework the interests of a subsidiary company which is part of the group should be subordinate to those of the group. Even detrimental measures should be legally permissible in so far as they are in the interests of the group.

The shareholders, creditors and employees of public limited liability companies dependent on a group must, moreover, be suitably protected. Shareholders must be afforded the choice of remaining in the company or of receiving a consideration in respect of their shares. If they remain in the company, the guarantees granted to them must be independent of the financial results of their company.

Where 90 per cent or more of the capital of a company has been acquired by an undertaking, the outside shareholders must be entitled to withdraw from the company. This right appears to be the counterpart of the right enjoyed by the undertaking to compel such shareholders to dispose of their shares.

Creditors of the subsidiary company in a group must be protected against any detriment by the imposition of a secondary liability on the undertaking.

Notwithstanding that the Commission has withdrawn the Ninth Directive Draft Proposal, the project of a harmonisation in the field of groups and pyramids is still under discussion. The current debate is part of the Action Plans that we will discuss in Chapter 4, § 4.5. Also, groups of companies are considered in the regulation concerning cross-border insolvency, as we will see in Chapter 20, § 20.11.

FURTHER READING

Klaus Bohlhoff and Julius Budde, 'Company Groups – The EEC Proposal for a Ninth Directive in the Light of the Legal Situation in the Federal Republic of Germany', 6 *J. Int'l L.* 163–197 (1984).

Stephan Rammeloo, 'The Judgment in CJEU C-186/12 (Impacto Azul): Company Law, Parental Liability and Article 49 TfEU – A Plea for a "Soft Law" Oriented EU Law Approach on Company Groups', 11 *ECL* 20–29 (2014).

Gitte Søgaard, 'Introduction of a Group Definition in the New Accounting Directive: The Impact on Future Accounting Regulation', 11 *ECL* 232–236 (2014).

See also:

Erik Werlauff, *EU Company Law* 89–90 (Copenhagen, DJØF Publishing, 2nd ed., 2003).

Alberto Santamaria, *European Economic Law* 164–168 (Alphen aan den Rijn, Kluwer Law International, 3rd ed., 2014).

3

Uniform Company Law

3.1 The European Economic Interest Grouping Regulation (EEIG)

As mentioned previously, the European Parliament and the Council have jointly delivered (or cooperated in the delivery of) various regulations on company law, including comprehensive statutes for establishing European types of companies or firms. The first approved regulation establishing a European supernational type of business organisation is that on the European Economic Interest Grouping (EEIG).

The grounds for adopting Council Regulation 1985/2137/EEC of 25 July 1985 on *the European Economic Interest Grouping (EEIG)* are expressed as follows:

Preamble Regulation 1985/2137/EEC

Whereas a harmonious development of economic activities and a continuous and balanced expansion throughout the Community depend on the establishment and smooth functioning of a common market offering conditions analogous to those of a national market; whereas to bring about this single market and to increase its unity a legal framework which facilitates the adaptation of their activities to the economic conditions of the Community should be created for natural persons, companies, firms and other legal bodies in particular; whereas to that end it is necessary that those natural persons, companies, firms and other legal bodies should be able to cooperate effectively across frontiers;

Whereas cooperation of this nature can encounter legal, fiscal or psychological difficulties; whereas the creation of an appropriate Community legal instrument in the form of a European Economic Interest Grouping would contribute to the achievement of the above-mentioned objectives and therefore proves necessary;

The difference between a company or a firm and a grouping is clarified as follows:

Preamble Regulation 1985/2137/EEC

Whereas a grouping differs from a firm or company principally in its purpose, which is only to facilitate or develop the economic activities of its members to enable them to improve their own results; whereas, by reason of that ancillary nature, a grouping's activities must be related to the economic activities of its members but not replace them so that, to that extent, for example, a grouping may not itself, with regard to third parties, practise a profession, the concept of economic activities being interpreted in the widest sense;

Notwithstanding that a grouping shall not replace its members in carrying out their respective activities, and notwithstanding that it is left to the Member States to decide whether the grouping shall enjoy of a legal personality (as companies),

Preamble Regulation 1985/2137/EEC

to enable a grouping to achieve its purpose, it should be endowed with legal capacity and provision should be made for it to be represented vis-à-vis third parties by an organ legally separate from its membership;

Whereas the protection of third parties requires widespread publicity; whereas the members of a grouping have unlimited joint and several liability for the grouping's debts and other liabilities, including those relating to tax or social security, without, however, that principle's affecting the freedom to exclude or restrict the liability of one or more of its members in respect of a particular debt or other liability by means of a specific contract between the grouping and a third party;

Whereas matters relating to the status or capacity of natural persons and to the capacity of legal persons are governed by national law;

Given all the above, an EEIG is a business organisation created by contract (Article 1 Regulation 1985/2137/EEC), entered between at least two natural persons who carry on any industrial, commercial, craft or agricultural activity or who provide professional or other services, or between at least two companies or firms (or a combination of natural persons and a company or firm) of at least two different Member States (Article 4 Regulation 1985/2137/EEC).

The contract for the formation of an EEIG must include its name, its official address and objects, the name, registration number and place of registration, if any, of each member of the grouping and the duration of the grouping, except where this is indefinite (Article 5 Regulation 1985/2137/EEC).

The contract shall be subject to the internal law of the State in which the official address is situated, as laid down in the contract itself (Article 2 Regulation 1985/2137/EEC). The official address referred to in the contract for the formation of a grouping must be situated in the European Union and must correspond with the place (a) where the grouping has its central administration, or (b) where one of the members of the grouping has its central administration or, in the case of a natural person, his principal activity, provided that the grouping carries on an activity there (Article 12 Regulation 1985/2137/EEC).

Once registered with the registry designated by Member States (Articles 6, 7 and 39 Regulation 1985/2137/EEC), the EEIG shall have the capacity, in its own name, to have rights and obligations of all kinds, to make contracts or accomplish other legal acts, and to sue and be sued; however, the EEIG shall only enjoy legal personality where the legislation of the Member State where the grouping is formed so provides (Article 1(2–3) Regulation 1985/2137/EEC). Similarly to the law of partnerships, notwithstanding the legal capacity, the members of a grouping shall have unlimited joint and several liability for its debts and other liabilities of whatever nature. However, creditors may not proceed against a member for payment in respect of debts and other liabilities, before the liquidation of a grouping is concluded, unless they have first requested the grouping to pay and payment has not been made within an appropriate period (Article 24 Regulation 1985/2137/EEC).

As clarified in the Preamble, the purpose of a grouping is to facilitate or develop the economic activities of its members by a pooling of resources, activities or skills and to improve or increase the results of those activities. This will produce better results than the members acting alone. It is not intended that the grouping should make profits for itself. If it does make any profits, they will be apportioned among the members and taxed accordingly.

The activity of the EEIG shall be related to the economic activities of its members and must not be more than ancillary to those activities (Article 3 Regulation 1985/2137/EEC). Therefore, the profits resulting from a grouping's activities shall be deemed to be the profits of the members and shall be apportioned among them in the proportions laid down in the contract for the formation of the grouping or, in the absence of any such provision, in equal shares. Similarly, the members of a grouping shall contribute to the payment of the amount by which expenditure exceeds income in the proportions laid down in the contract for the formation of the grouping or, in the absence of any such provision, in equal shares (Article 21 Regulation 1985/2137/EEC).

An EEIG cannot employ more than 500 persons and may not invite investment by the public.

Governance of a grouping is similar to that of a partnership. The organs of a grouping shall be the members acting collectively and the manager or managers (Article 16 Regulation 1985/2137/EEC). In meetings, each member has one vote (the contract may give more than one vote to certain members, provided that no one member holds a majority of the votes) and the meeting shall decide on a majority basis, except in the following matters, requiring unanimous decision: (a) alter the objects of a grouping; (b) alter the number of votes allotted to each member; (c) alter the conditions for the taking of decisions; (d) extend the duration of a grouping beyond any period fixed in the contract for the formation of the grouping; (e) alter the contribution by every member or by some members to the grouping's financing; (f) alter any other obligation of a member, unless otherwise provided by the contract for the formation of the grouping; (g) make any alteration to the contract for the formation of the grouping not covered by the Regulation, unless otherwise provided by that contract (Article 17 Regulation 1985/2137/EEC).

One of the matters for the meeting to decide, in the absence of a provision in the contract, is the appointment of one or more managers, who must be natural persons, unless the legislation of the Member State of registration provides for a legal person to become manager (Article 18(2) Regulation 1985/2137/EEC). Managers are entrusted with the power to engage in obligations on behalf of the EEIG *vis-à-vis* third parties.

Once more similarly to the law of partnerships, interests in an EEIG may be assigned to third parties only with unanimous consent of the other members (Article 24 Regulation 1985/2137/EEC). New members may be admitted by decision of the members, whilst any existing member may withdraw or otherwise cease to be a member (Articles 26–27 Regulation 1985/2137/EEC).

An EEIG may be wound up by a decision of its members ordering its winding-up (Article 31 Regulation 1985/2137/EEC). The winding-up of a grouping shall entail its liquidation, under the laws of the Member States of registration (Article 35 Regulation 1985/2137/EEC). In addition, groupings shall be subject to national laws governing insolvency and cessation of payments (Article 36 Regulation 1985/2137/EEC).

FURTHER READING

Howard Linnane, 'Forming an EEIG', 1 *EBLR, Issue 2* (1990) 38–38.

Stephen Weatherill, 'The Perils of an Anti-Competitive EEIG', 2 *EBLR* 195–197 (1991).

See also:

Erik Werlauff, *EU Company Law* 95 (Copenhagen, DJØF Publishing, 2nd ed., 2003).

Alberto Santamaria, *European Economic Law* (Alphen aan den Rijn, Kluwer Law International, 3rd ed., 2014) 173–180.

3.2 The *Societas Europaea* Regulation (SE)

The second approved regulation establishing a European type of business organisation is that of the *Societas Europaea* (SE). Regulation 2001/2157/EC of 8 October 2001 *on the Statute for a European Company (SE)* entered into force in 2004, some thirty years after it was first proposed to the Commission. The process of adopting the SE Statute was parallel to that of the Fifth Directive, as they both included provision on the two-tier structure and worker co-determination. As anticipated in Chapter 2, § 2.8, the SE Statute is supplemented by Directive 2001/86/EC of 8 October 2001 *supplementing the Statute for a European company with regard to the involvement of employees*, thereby recognising their place and role in the business, whilst leaving a greater room to manoeuvre for the legislations of Member States.

Similarly to the EEIG, the SE is a legal structure that allows a company to operate in different EU countries under a single statute, as defined by the law of the Union and common to all EU countries.

Details on the SE Statute will be given in the following parts of the book discussing the formation, operation and dissolution of companies in the EU (*see*, Parts III–V and VII). Indeed, the SE Statute provides a complete framework of EU rules on many aspects of an EU established company. It goes without saying that the SE Statute, being an act of the EU having direct binding effect in all EU Member States, complies (and must be deemed to comply) with all the principles expressed in the EU company law directives: therefore, discussion on topics brought to our attention by company law directives will follow the outline of the SE Statute. For the time being, it suffices to give an overview of the main features of an SE. A useful summary is provided for by the EU institutions on their official website (http://www.eur-lex.europa.eu), as follows:

An SE with its headquarters in an EU country is governed:

- by the provisions of the regulation; and
- for those aspects not covered by the regulation, by the national provisions adopted in application of European measures targeting the SE specifically and those applicable to public limited-liability companies. As a guide, winding-up, liquidation, insolvency and suspension of payments are in large measure governed by the applicable national law.

A European company is established with at least two companies originating in different EU countries, which means especially that it can only be created from an existing base. It must have a minimum capital of €120,000 and it can be created in the following ways:

Type of constitution	Type of company	Criteria to be met
Merger (to establish a European company)	Public limited-liability companies	At least two of the companies must originate in different EU countries
Establishment of a European holding company	Public limited-liability company or a limited-liability company	At least two of the companies must originate in different EU countries or they must have had a subsidiary or branch in another EU country for at least 2 years
Establishment of a European subsidiary	Companies, enterprises or other legal entities	At least two of the companies must originate in different EU countries or they must have had a subsidiary or branch in another EU country for at least 2 years
Conversion	Public limited-liability company	The company must have had a subsidiary in another EU country for at least 2 years

In addition, a European company can create one (or more) subsidiaries that are also European companies [i.e., an SE 'incubator'].

The registered office of the SE must be the place where it has its central administration, that is to say, its true centre of operations. The SE may, however, transfer its registered office within the EU without having to dissolve the original company to form a new one.

The registration and completion of liquidation of an SE is published for information in the *Official Journal of the European Union.*

The statutes of the European company can relate to two different systems:

- the two-tier system that provides for a management board and a supervisory board in addition to the general meeting of shareholders; and
- the single-tier system that provides simply for the general meeting and an administrative board.

The SE are subject to taxes and charges in all EU countries where their administrative centres are situated.

No SE may be established without a model of employee involvement being selected by agreement between the management and the employees themselves. This agreement must of necessity include information and consultation procedures and, where appropriate, employee involvement in the management bodies of the SE. This involvement is nevertheless only mandatory if the employees already benefited from it before the creation of the SE. Where the two parties are unable to reach a satisfactory arrangement, a series of standard principles listed in an annex to the directive then apply.

It should be added, that a survey by the European Commission dated 31 December 2017 (available at www.worker-participation.eu/European-Company-SE/Facts-Figures) acknowledged that between 2004 and 2017 a total number of 2,943 SEs had been formed (the total number grew to 3,000 in 2018 and to 3,280 in 2020). These data are shown in Figure 3.1 below. Notwithstanding the good pace, these numbers are trivial compared with those of companies established under EU Member States' domestic types. More data of this survey – concerning forms of foundation, states of incorporation, systems of governance, participation of workers, and so on – will be analysed later, as the discussion of such topics is involved.

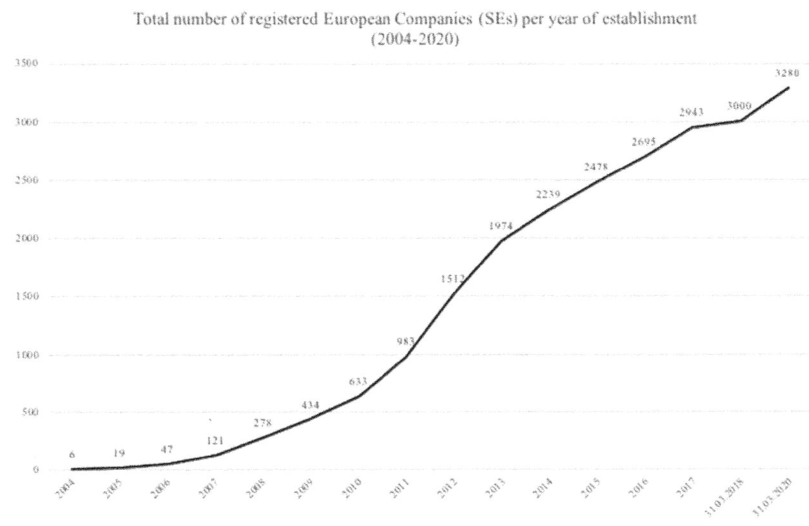

Figure 3.1 Total number of registered European Companies (SEs) per year of establishment (2004–2020)

FURTHER READING

Nicholas Bourne, 'The European Company – Societas Europea', 1 *EBLR* 8–8 (1990).
Erik Werlauff, 'Common European Company Law Status 1998 Part III: Group, Company Structure, New Company Forms', 9 *EBLR* 274–280 (1998).
Erik Werlauff, 'The SE Company – A New Common European Company from 8 October 2004', 14 *EBLR* 85–103 (2003).
Sabine Ebert, 'The European Company on the Level Playing Field of the Community', 14 *EBLR* 183–192 (2003).
Mike Edbury, 'The European Company Statute: A Practical Working Model for the Future of European Company Law Making?', 15 *EBLR* 1283–1293 (2004).
Stefano Lombardo and Piero Pasotti, 'The Societas Europaea: A Network Economics Approach', 1 *ECFR* 169–205 (2004).
Camilla Skøie Mørkve, 'The European Company in Scandinavia: Nordea's Transformation to an SE', 16 *EBLR* 353–358 (2005).
Noëlle Lenoir, 'The SE or Societas Europaea – A European Citizenship for Corporations', 4 *ECL* 116–117 (2007).
Horst Eidenmüller et al., 'How Does the Market React to the Societas Europaea?', 11 *EBOR* 35–50 (2010).

See also:
Erik Werlauff, *EU Company Law* 99–100, 135–158 (Copenhagen, DJØF Publishing, 2nd ed., 2003).
Erik Werlauff, *SE – the Law of the European Company* (Copenhagen, DJØF Publishing, 2003).
Alberto Santamaria, *European Economic Law* 169–173 (Alphen aan den Rijn, Kluwer Law International, 3rd ed., 2014).

3.3 The *Societas Cooperativa Europaea* Regulation (SCE)

Two years after the adoption of the SE Statute and of its complementing directive on workers' participation, the EU institutions also approved Council Regulation 2003/143/EC of 22 July 2003 *on the Statute for a European Cooperative Society (Societas Cooperativa Europaea – SCE)* and Council Directive 2003/72/EC of 22 July 2003 *supplementing the Statute for a European Cooperative Society with regard to the involvement of employees.*

By making legislative provision that takes account of their specific features, the EU aimed at facilitating cooperatives wishing to engage in cross-border business. Similarly to the EEIG and the SE Statutes, the SCE Statute allows the creation of new cooperative enterprises by natural or legal persons at the European level. The complementing directive ensures the rights of information, consultation and participation of employees.

A summary of the SCE Statute and of the complementing directive is provided for by the EU institutions in their official website (www.eur-lex.europa.eu), as follows:

Formation of the SCE

An SCE may be formed:

- by five or more natural and/or legal persons resident in at least two Member States of the European Economic Area (EEA), formed under the law of a Member State of the European Union (EU), and governed by the law of at least two different EU Member States;
- by a merger between cooperatives formed under the law of an EU Member State with registered offices and head offices in that Member State, provided that at least two of them are governed by the law of different Member States;
- by conversion of a cooperative formed under the law of an EU Member State, which has its registered office and head office within the EEA if the cooperative has had for at least two years an establishment or subsidiary governed by the law of another EU Member State.

A Member State may provide that a legal body the head office of which is not in the EEA may participate in the formation of an SCE provided that the legal body:

- is formed under the law of a Member State;
- has its registered office in that Member State;
- has a real and continuous link with the Member State's economy.

Capital of the SCE

The capital of an SCE shall be represented by its members' shares. It must be a minimum amount of EUR 30,000. The laws of a Member State requiring a greater subscribed capital for legal bodies carrying on certain types of activity (such as banking, insurance activities, etc.) shall apply to SCEs with registered offices in that Member State.

The general meeting is to pass a resolution each year recording the amount of the capital at the end of the financial year and the variation by reference to the preceding financial year. If the legislation of the Member State where the registered office is located allows it, the SCE may have cooperative investor members with limited voting rights.

Statutes of the SCE

The founder members shall draw up the statutes of the SCE in accordance with the provisions for the formation of national cooperative societies. The statutes shall be in writing and signed by the founder members.

Transfer of Registered Office

The registered office of an SCE may be transferred to another Member State without resulting in the winding-up of the SCE or in the creation of a new legal person. The registered office, as established in the statutes, must be located within the Community and must correspond with the location of the head office.

Principle of Non-discrimination

Subject to this Regulation, an SCE shall be treated in every Member State as if it were a national cooperative.

Registration and Disclosure

Every SCE shall be registered in the Member State in which it has its registered office in a register designated by the law of that Member State. Notice of registration and of the deletion of such a registration shall be published for information purposes in the Official Journal of the European Union.

Structure of the SCE

The SCE structure is made up of a general meeting on the one hand, and on the other hand:

- either a management board with a supervisory board (the two-tier system);
- or an administrative board (the one-tier system), depending on which option is chosen in the SCE statutes.

At the general meeting, members have in principle an equal right to vote. Exceptions may be made in favour of large cooperative investors in certain financial cooperatives.

The management board or the administrative board, depending on the type of structure chosen, is responsible for managing the SCE and may represent it in legal proceedings and in dealings with third parties.

The statutes of the SCE shall list the categories of transactions that require authorisation. This may be granted by the supervisory organ or the general meeting to the management organ or the administrative organ.

Auditing and Disclosure of Accounts

As regards the drawing-up, auditing and disclosure of its annual accounts, and its consolidated accounts if any, the SCE is to be subject to the law of the State.

Winding-up, Liquidation, Insolvency and Suspension of Payments

An SCE may be wound up either by:

- a decision of the general meeting, in particular where the period fixed in the rules has expired or where the subscribed capital has been reduced below the minimum capital laid down in the rules;
- or by the courts, for example where the registered office has been transferred outside the EEA.

As regards liquidation, insolvency or suspension of payments, the SCE is to be subject to the laws of the State in which it has its registered office.

Involvement of Employees

The arrangements for the involvement of employees (information, consultation and participation) shall be established in every SCE.

As a general rule, a special negotiating body is set up. It brings together representatives of the legal entities' employees who participate in the formation of the SCE or its subsidiaries.

This body negotiates an agreement with the competent organs of the participating legal entities in order to lay down the arrangements for the involvement of employees within the future SCE. The standard rules apply in the absence of an agreement.

However, in defining the arrangements for the involvement of employees in the SCE, the national rules of the State where the head office is located apply to SCEs established:

- exclusively by natural persons or by a single legal entity and natural persons; and
- which together employ fewer than 50 employees, or employ 50 or more employees in only one Member State.

In its 2012 Action Plan (*see*, Chapter 4, § 4.5) the EU Commission acknowledged only the twenty-five SCEs incorporated until July 2012. These data, confirmed by the 31 March 2017 survey, correspond to the widely accepted opinion that the SCE Statute is not successful, as many cooperatives engaging in cross-border business prefer to maintain a national form of incorporation.

With the Communication from the Commission to the Council and the European Parliament, the European Economic and Social Committee (hereafter EESC) and the Committee of the Regions of 23 February 2004 on the promotion of co-operative societies in Europe (COM(2004) 18 final), the Commission considers that the potential of cooperatives has not been fully utilised and that their image should be improved at national and European levels. In this context, it sets out steps that may encourage the wider use of cooperatives across Europe. These focus on increased visibility, further improvement of national laws on cooperatives, and enhancement of cooperatives' contribution to community policy. The main issues dealt with in the Communication are:

- promoting greater use of cooperatives across Europe by improving the visibility, characteristics and understanding of the sector;
- further improving the legislation governing cooperatives in Europe;
- maintaining and improving the account taken of cooperatives in Community objectives and their contribution to those objectives.

FURTHER READING

Ruud Galle, 'The Societas Cooperativa Europea (SCE) and National Cooperatives in Comparative Perspective', 3 *ECL* 255–260 (2006).

Irene Escuin Ibáñez, 'Law Applicable to the European Cooperative Society: Special Reference to the European Cooperative Established in Spain', 8 *ECFR* 30–46 (2011).

Antonio Fici, 'Cooperative Identity and the Law', 24 *EBLR* 37–64 (2013).

Antonio Fici, 'The European Cooperative Society Regulation', in Dante Cracogna et al. (eds.), *International Handbook of Cooperative Law* 115–153 (Berlin and Heidelberg, Springer Verlag, 2013).

See also:

Erik Werlauff, *EU Company Law* 100, 158–160 (Copenhagen, DJØF Publishing, 2nd ed., 2003).

3.4 The *Societas Privata Europaea* (SPE) Draft Regulation

Along with the three already approved statutes – the EEIG, the SE, and the SCE – the Commission has submitted to the Council various other proposals for the adoption of regulations establishing other types of EU business organisation.

On the grounds that progress must be made to improve access for small and medium-sized enterprises (SMEs) to the Single Market and to promote their development in the EU, the Commission submitted the Proposal for a Council Regulation of 25 June 2008 *on the Statute for a European Private Company*, enabling companies to be set up across the Community, under simplified conditions.

A summary of the SPE Statute is provided for by the EU institutions on their official website (www.eur-lex.europa.eu), as follows:

This Proposal aims to establish a European Private Company Statute (SPE) with limited liability, in order to create a simplified legal form to encourage the setting up and running of small and medium-sized enterprises (SMEs) in the Single Market.

Formation

The SPE can be formed ex nihilo by one or several natural persons and/or legal entities. It may also be formed by transforming, merging or dividing existing companies. The latter can have a statute governed by national or Community law, such as those recorded as being a European Company (Societas Europaea) or SE.

Capital and Shareholders

The minimum capital of an SPE can be 1 euro. It is divided into unquoted shares, which cannot be offered to the public or negotiated on a regulated market. Each shareholder is only liable up to the amount for which they have subscribed or agreed to subscribe.

The management body establishes a list of shareholders, which constitutes proof of ownership for the shares. All shareholdings must be notified to the management body which registers them in the list of shareholders. The procedure of excluding a shareholder is subject to a resolution of the shareholders which then leads to a request made by the SPE to the court having jurisdiction. Similarly, shareholders can withdraw from the SPE in order to protect their interests.

Registration

The registered office and the central administration or main establishment of the SPE are established in the European Community. The company is registered in the Member State in which the statutory registered office is located. Its subsidiaries are governed by the national law where they are established. An SPE is not bound to establish its central administration or main establishment in the Member State in which the registered office is located. Administrative formalities and registration costs must be reduced as much as possible.

The registered office of the SPE may be transferred to another Member State, without having any consequences on the legal personality or on the rights and obligations created by contracts concluded previously. The transfer takes effect on the date of registration in the host Member State.

Organisation

The shareholders determine the Articles of Association of the SPE, according to the matters listed in Annex I of the Proposal. Matters not covered by the Articles of Association are subject to the national law of the Member State in which the SPE has its registered office.

The management body is responsible for the management of the SPE, and exercises all prerogatives that are not held by shareholders.

Shareholders are responsible for the organisation of the SPE. They adopt resolutions that are binding upon shareholders, the management body and the supervisory body of the SPE and on third parties.

Accounts

Accounts management and the preparation, filing, auditing and publication of accounts shall be subject to national law.

Employee Participation

Methods for participation are subject to the regulations of the Member State where the SPE has its registered office. Directive 2005/56/EC shall apply in the case of cross-border mergers. In addition, the Proposal for the Regulation provides for a series of specific regulations on this subject if the registered office of a SPE is transferred to another Member State. This is to avoid pre-existing rights concerning employee participation being circumvented.

Context

The existing forms of Community companies are adapted to large enterprises. European SMEs and individuals must therefore benefit from a new form of simplified private company. The Proposal is part of the Commission initiative called the 'Small Business Act' (SBA) to encourage the development of SMEs in Europe.

In 2008, SMEs represented 99% of enterprises in the EU, whereas only 8% of them carried out cross-border commercial activities and 5% have subsidiaries or joint companies abroad.

The SPE proposal was withdrawn in 2014, when a new proposal on the *Societas Unius Personae* (SUP) was made: on this proposal *see* Chapter 3, § 3.7.

FURTHER READING

Christoph Teichmann, 'The European Private Company', 1 *ECL* 162–165 (2004).

Arkadiusz Radwan, 'European Private Company and the Regulatory Landscape in the EU –An Introductory Note', 18 *EBLR* 769–780 (2007).

Harm-Jan de Kluiver, '(Re)Considering the SPE', 5 *ECL* 112–113 (2008).

Adriaan F.M. Dorresteijn and Odeaya Uziahu-Santcroos, 'The Societas Privata Europaea under the Magnifying Glass (Part 1-2)', 5 *ECL* 277–283 (2008).

Mathias M. Siems et al., 'The Protection of Creditors of a European Private Company (SPE)', 12 *EBOR* 147–172 (2011).

Lars-Göran Sund et al., 'A European Private Company and Share Transfer Restrictions' 23 *EBLR* 483–496 (2012).

See also:

Erik Werlauff, *EU Company Law* 100 (Copenhagen, DJØF Publishing, 2nd ed., 2003).

3.5 The *European Mutual Society* (ME) Draft Regulation

In 1992, the EC Commission submitted a proposal for a Regulation of the European Parliament and of the Council on the statute for a European Mutual Society. The proposal has developed similarly to the SE and SCE statutes.

A mutual society is a business entity engaging in an insurance activity or in a provident, health assistance or credit assistance activity; a mutual society shall, in return for a subscription, guarantee its members the full settlement of contractual undertakings entered into in the course of the activities authorised by its statutes. In other words, the insured of a mutual society are its members and, in general, members of a mutual society are also insured. This differentiates mutual societies from both companies and cooperatives operating in the field of insurance. Similarly to cooperatives and groupings, the activity of a mutual society is not intended to make profits for the mutual itself. Nevertheless, as clarified by the CJEU, mutual societies shall not be considered not-for-profit as they engage in business activities in competition with all other companies of firms (*see*, Joined cases C-159/91 and C-160/91, *Poucet et Pistre* [1993], ECR I-00637; Case C-244/94, *CNAVMA* [1995], ECR I-04013).

Notwithstanding attempts to bring it forward, the proposal of a mutual society statute never got beyond the discussion stage. A consultation document on 'Mutuals in an Enlarged Europe' was launched in 2003. In the feedback summary, the Commission states that (with one exception) 'all replies to the question on the need for a European statute for mutual societies … consider that such a statute is necessary'. Despite this, in September 2005 the draft Regulation on a European Mutual Society Statute, whose legislative process was seen by the European Commission as lacking substantial progress, was removed from the European agenda.

In 2010, the European Parliament's Committee for Employment and Social Affairs commissioned a study *The role of mutual societies in the 21st century*. The researchers concluded that 'mutuals should be better recognised as a distinct and important actor within the European economy and society' and that '[f]or this purpose, an appropriate instrument could be a statute for

European mutuals.' Following and based on this study, the same research team was asked by the European Commission's Directorate-General for Enterprise and Industry (DG ENTR) to produce an in-depth *Study on the situation and prospects of mutuals in Europe*, which was published in November 2012. The study recognises that a Statute for European Mutuals 'could help mutual-type organisations to gain recognition, to increase the understanding concerning mutual-type organisations in the countries and to better respect mutual-type organisations' interests at European level'.

In March 2011, the European Parliament adopted a written declaration, calling on the Commission 'to take the necessary steps to introduce (a) proposal(s) for (a) European statute(s) for ... mutual societies'. In the autumn of 2012, the same European Parliament decided to produce its own-initiative report with recommendations to the Commission on the Statute for a European Mutual Society. As a consequence, in spring 2013, the Commission started a consultation on the results of the study and on possible follow-up. In an impact assessment completed at the end of 2013, Commission services recommended the creation of the legal framework for the European Mutual Society through a recast of the European Cooperative Statute. A draft of this Regulation was sent into inter-services consultation in April 2014.

FURTHER READING

https://ec.europa.eu/growth/sectors/social-economy/mutual-societies_en; http://www.amice-eu.org/ems.aspx.

3.6 The European Foundation (FE) Draft Regulation

On 8 February 2012, the EU Commission submitted a Proposal for a Council Regulation *on the Statute for a European Foundation* (FE).

As the EU Commission puts it,

Explanatory Memorandum to the Proposal for a Council Regulation on the Statute for a European Foundation

Foundations play an important role in the EU, particularly in civil society. Through their various activities in numerous areas, they contribute to the fundamental values and objectives of the Union, such as respect for human rights, the protection of minorities, employment and social progress, protection and improvement of the environment or the promotion of scientific and technological advances. In this context, they make a substantial contribution to achieving the ambitious goals of smart, sustainable and inclusive growth set by the Europe 2020 strategy. They also enhance and facilitate a more active involvement of citizens and civil society in the European project. Nonetheless, the exercise of their activities encounters various obstacles across the EU.

The Single Market Act Communication adopted in April 2011 highlighted the need to put an end to market fragmentation and to eliminate barriers and obstacles to the movement of services, innovation and creativity in order to deliver growth and employment, and promote competitiveness. It stressed the importance of strengthening citizens' confidence in the single market and of ensuring that its benefits are passed on to citizens. In the context of foundations' contribution to the social economy and to financing innovative initiatives of public benefit, the Single Market Act called for action to remove obstacles that foundations face in operating on a cross-border basis. The same call was made in the EU Citizenship report 2010 'Dismantling the obstacles to EU citizens' rights', which stressed the importance of enhancing the European dimension of the activities of public benefit purpose foundations with a view to promoting citizen action at EU level.

The Commission also underlined the importance of developing European legal forms for entities in the social economy sector (e.g. foundations, cooperatives or mutuals) in its 'Social Business Initiative' (SBI) Communication of 25 October 2011. The SBI aims to support the development of businesses which primarily focus on creating social impact through their activities and its actions also address and benefit those social economy entities (including foundations) that meet the general criteria for a 'social business' set out in the Communication. The European Parliament called for an appropriate legal framework for foundations (as well as for mutual societies and associations) in its resolution responding to the Commission's Single Market Act; it argued in favour of introducing Statutes for these legal entities in its written declaration 84/2010 of March 2011; and it urged the Commission to work towards this objective in its previous resolutions of 2009 and 2006. The European Economic and Social Committee advocated a Statute in its 2010 own initiative opinion, which set out its reflections on how such a Statute should be developed, and the Committee of the Regions supported the Commission's announcement of the initiative on foundations in the Single Market Act.

Given this general context, the EU Commission identifies the grounds for and objectives of the proposal, as follows:

Explanatory Memorandum to the Proposal for a Council Regulation on the Statute for a European Foundation

Foundations cannot channel funds efficiently on a cross-border basis in the EU. When they decide to operate across borders, foundations have to spend part of the resources they collect on legal advice and fulfilling legal and administrative requirements laid down by the different national laws.

The present initiative creates a new European legal form intended to facilitate foundations' establishment and operation in the single market. It will allow foundations to more efficiently channel private funds to public benefit purposes on a cross-border basis in the EU. This, in turn, should result – for instance, due to lower costs for foundations – in more funding being available for public benefit purpose activities and therefore, should have a positive impact on European citizens' public good and the EU economy as a whole.

This proposal does not aim to deal with the particular situation of political foundations affiliated to political parties at European level ...

This proposal is currently under discussion.

3.7 The *Societas Unius Personae* (SUP): A Hybrid?

As already mentioned, in April 2014, the European Commission published a *proposal for a directive on single-member private companies with limited liability* (COM/2014/0212 final – 2014/0120 (COD)), called the *Societas Unius Personae* (SUP). The new directive aims at facilitating the establishment of companies across the EU.

The SUP proposal takes into account the existence of a new Twelfth Directive on single-member private companies and aims at replacing it on the following grounds:

Explanatory Memorandum to the Proposal for a Directive on Single-member Private Companies with Limited Liability

Part 1: General Rules for Single-member Private Limited Liability Companies

The general rules for single-member private limited liability companies apply to all companies listed in Annex I, including the companies referred to in the second part of this Directive (Articles 1–5). The Twelfth Council Company Law Directive 89/667/EEC, which was codified by Directive 2009/102/EC, has introduced a legal instrument allowing for the limitation of liability of a company with a single-member throughout the EU. Furthermore, the provisions of the first part of this Directive require disclosure of information about a single-member company in a register accessible to the public and regulate both decisions taken by the single-member and contracts between the single-member and the company. If a Member State also grants public limited liability companies the possibility of having a single shareholder, the rules of the first part of the Directive apply to those companies as well.

... *The Directive repeals Directive 2009/102/EC which is replaced by this Directive and amends Regulation 1024/2012 in order to allow for the use of the Internal Market Information System (IMI) (Articles 29 and 30).*

In addition, the SUP proposal provides for specific rules on a new 'uniform' type of single-member private limited company, named *Societas Unius Personae* (SUP). A summary of such provision is provided below.

Explanatory Memorandum to the Proposal for a Directive on Single-member Private Companies with Limited Liability

Part 2: Specific rules for the Societas Unius Personae (SUP)

Chapter 1: General Provisions

The provisions of the second part of this Directive apply to single-member private limited liability companies established in the form of an SUP (Article 6).

Where a matter is not covered by this Directive, relevant national law should apply.

Chapter 2: Formation of an SUP

The Directive restricts the possible ways of founding an SUP to either establishing a company ex nihilo (founding an entirely new company) or converting a company which already exists under another company law form. Certain provisions for each of these two methods are made in the Directive (Articles 8 and 9) and the process of forming an SUP is also governed by national rules for private limited liability companies.

An SUP can be formed ex nihilo by any natural or legal person, even if the latter is a single-member limited liability company. Member States should not prevent SUPs from being single-members in other companies.

Only private limited liability companies listed in Annex I are allowed to form an SUP by conversion. A company which converts to an SUP preserves its legal personality. The Directive refers to national law with regard to conversion procedures.

According to this Directive, an SUP must have its registered office and either its central administration or its principal place of business in the EU (Article 10).

Chapter 3: Articles of Association

The Directive provides for the standard template for the articles of association, the use of which is obligatory in the case of on-line registration. It further sets out the minimum content of the template, as will be included in the implementing act to be adopted by the Commission (Article 11).

The articles of association can be changed after registration, but the changes must comply with the provisions of the Directive and national law (Article 12).

Chapter 4: Registration of an SUP

Provisions relating to the registration procedure form the main part of this Directive being a critical issue in facilitating the establishment of subsidiaries in EU countries other than the home country of the company. The Directive requires Member States to offer a registration procedure that can be fully completed electronically at a distance without requiring the need of a physical presence of the founder before the authorities of Member State of registration. It must therefore also be possible for all communication between the body responsible for registration and the founder to be carried out electronically. The registration of the SUP must be completed within three working days in order to allow companies to be formed quickly (Article 14).

Moreover, the Directive contains an exhaustive list of documents and details which Member States may require for the registration of an SUP. After registration, the SUP may change the documents and details in accordance with the procedure specified by national law (Article 13).

Chapter 5: Single Share

As an SUP has only one shareholder, it is only allowed to issue one share that cannot be split (Article 15).

Chapter 6: Share Capital

The Directive prescribes that the share capital shall be at least EUR 1, or at least one unit of the national currency in [the] Member State in which this is not the euro. Member States should not impose any maximum limits on the value of the single-share or the paid-up capital and should not require an SUP to build legal reserves. However, the Directive allows SUPs to build voluntary reserves (Article 16).

The Directive also contains rules regarding distributions (e.g., dividends) to the single member of the SUP. A distribution may take place if the SUP satisfies a balance-sheet test, demonstrating that after the distribution the remaining assets of the SUP will be sufficient to fully cover its liabilities. In addition, a solvency statement must be provided to the single-member by the management body before any distribution is made. The inclusion of the two requirements in the Directive ensures a high level of protection of creditors, which should help the label 'SUP' to develop a good reputation (Article 18).

Chapter 7: Structure and Operational Procedures of an SUP

The Directive covers the decision-making powers of the single-member, the workings of the management body and the representation of the SUP in relation to third parties (Article 21). In order to facilitate [the] cross-border activities of SMEs and other companies, the Directive grants the single-member the right to take decisions without the need to organise a general meeting and lists subjects that must be decided by the single-member. The single-member should be able to take other decisions than mentioned by this Directive, including the delegation of its powers to the management body, if it is permitted by national law.

Only natural persons can become directors of SUPs, unless the law of the Member State of registration allows legal persons to do so. The Directive includes certain provisions on the appointment and removal of directors. The directors are responsible for managing the SUP, and also represent the SUP in its dealings with third parties. It is envisaged that the SUP may be an attractive model for groups of companies and the Directive therefore allows the single-member to give instructions to the management body. However, these instructions must comply with national laws protecting the interest or of other parties (Article 22).

The SUP can be converted into another national legal form. In case the requirements of this Directive are no longer fulfilled, the SUP is required to either transform into another company law form or to dissolve. If it fails to do so, national authorities must have the power to dissolve the company (Article 25).

Part 3: Final Provisions ...

The European Economic and Social Committee has vigorously criticised the SUP proposal.

Opinion of the European Economic and Social Committee on the 'Proposal for a Directive of the European Parliament and of the Council on Single-member Private Limited Liability Companies' (COM/2014/0212 final – 2014/0120 (COD))

1 Conclusions and Recommendations

1.1. The European Commission's proposal for a directive on single-member private limited liability companies (Societas Unius Personae – SUP) is designed to make it easier for SMEs to operate on a cross-border basis. The EESC believes that, as it stands, the proposal is in need of further development, since many of its provisions entail (serious) potential risks to the proper conduct of trade on the internal market and to the interests of creditors, consumers and employees. Therefore, the EESC strongly urges the Commission to take account of the recommendations set out in this opinion and to apply them.

1.2. The choice of legal basis (Article 50 TFEU) is unconvincing, and appears to be primarily aimed at circumventing the requirement for unanimity in the Council and ensuring that this initiative does not fail as the European private company (SPE) has. The intention may be for SUPs to be formally enshrined in national law as an alternative company form, their essential characteristics are nonetheless clearly defined in supranational law. The legal basis should therefore be Article 352 TFEU.

1.3. The EESC endorses the objective of making it as easy as possible for SMEs, in particular, to set up companies. However, the minimum capital requirement for SUPs of EUR 1, and the prohibition on requiring them to build reserves, effectively constitute a 'free' limitation of liability. They may cause market parties to require personal guarantees from the business owner to reassure third parties (consumers, suppliers, creditors) which will nullify the advantages of the limited liability.

1.4. The EESC stresses the need to encourage the creation of healthy companies and therefore recommends requiring a substantial minimum share capital appropriate to the company's purpose, in the form of a 'credibility threshold' for SUPs, in order to protect the interests of creditors, consumers, employees and the general public and to avoid any risk to business. This could be based on the experience of certain Member States where a reduction in the initial share capital requirement has been counterbalanced by a 'saving' scheme whereby the company has to build reserves in subsequent years, to avoid long-term undercapitalisation. For the sake of 'company clarity', a reference to limitation of liability and the country of registration should be added to the name of a SUP.

1.5. The EESC believes that a SUP should not be registered in a place where it carries out no business activities whatsoever (letter boxes). The proposed distinction between a company's registered office and its administrative headquarters, which is a first for [a] European company form, therefore sets a precedent, which has raised concerns at the EESC. In conjunction with the provision that SUPs are subject to the law of the State in which they are registered, it could jeopardise employees' participation rights, but also enable circumvention of national tax law.

1.6. It is possible that the formal transfer of a company's registered office, and the resulting change of company statute, could undermine the right to participate in company decision-making bodies (supervisory board or management board). The EESC therefore explicitly calls for SUPs to have a single registered office and administrative headquarters, as is the case for other supranational legal forms such as the European company (SE) or European cooperative society (SCE). Furthermore, the EESC calls for employee participation rights in a Member State where a SUP carries out its main business activities to be guaranteed and for unfair competition to be resolutely tackled. The EESC therefore feels that uniform rules on SUPs in relation to employee participation are also needed.

1.7. The EESC believes that, in the interests of company founders, it is important to ensure that a company can be established quickly within an appropriate time frame. However, the use of a purely online procedure for registering SUPs can raise problems and risks if the identity of the company founder is not checked. The omission of identity checks would reduce transparency concerning business partners, undermines the integrity of legal transactions, and harms consumer interests. It would encourage and facilitate the creation of 'letterbox companies' and bogus self-employment. Nevertheless, in order to take account of the desire for online registration, the Member States should be free to provide for this type of registration on a voluntary basis. In this case, however, there should be a preliminary identity check, as well as measures by the competent authority and/or notaries to provide the founder of the company with information and advice.

1.8. The EESC approves the intention to introduce a new form of company making it easier for SMEs (including start-ups and micro-enterprises) in particular, to operate in the single market. To ensure the proposed directive is favourable for SMEs, its scope should be restricted to such companies. This instrument is not intended to give internationally operating groups of companies the option of running subsidiaries that may have hundreds or thousands of employees as SUPs. The EESC therefore proposes that the SUP should only be available to companies which meet the criteria set out in Article 3 (2) of the Accounting Directive (2013/34/EU). This would mean that when the SUP reaches a certain size, the company has to be turned into another legal form.

1.9. To sum up, it should be noted that adoption of the draft directive would result in national principles of company law for limited companies being called into question in a number of Member States. In view of the choice of legal basis, the EESC questions whether the proposal is compatible with the subsidiarity principle.

It therefore calls for the status of SUP to be available only to companies that are active internationally and are operating in at least two Member States at the time of registration or can credibly demonstrate that they will be doing so at the latest within a specified time (two years, for example) of their registration. The Proposal for [a] European Foundation (EF) and the European Parliament's interim report on this could serve as a model here.

1.10. For the reasons given, although the EESC welcomes the Commission's efforts to support SMEs in the area of company law, it still sees a considerable need to discuss the directive's actual content. The EESC can only endorse the proposal if the recommendations set out in this opinion are followed. In particular, a balanced solution now needs to be found in close cooperation with the stakeholders, which unfortunately were not consulted on an equal basis by the Commission beforehand.

FURTHER READING

Barbara De Donno, 'From Simplified Companies to One-man Limited Enterprises', *ECL* 155–156 (2014).

Iris Wuisman, 'The Societas Unius Personae (SUP)', 12 *ECL* 34–44 (2015).

Pierre-Henri Conac, 'The Societas Unius Personae (SUP): A "Passport" for Job Creation and Growth', 12 *ECFR* 139–176 (2015).

Jesper Lau Hansen, 'The SUP Proposal: Registration and Capital (Articles 13–17)', 12 *ECFR* 177–190 (2015).

Vanessa Knapp, 'Directive on Single-member Private Limited Liability Companies: Distributions', 12 *ECFR* 191–201 (2015).

Christoph Teichmann, 'Corporate Groups within the Legal Framework of the European Union: The Group-related Aspects of the SUP Proposal and the EU Freedom of Establishment', 12 *ECFR* 202–229 (2015).

Stephan Harbarth, 'From SPE to SMC: The German Political Debate on the Reform of the "Small Company"', 12 *ECFR* 230–237 (2015).

Corrado Malberti, 'The Relationship between the Societas Unius Personae Proposal and the acquis: Creeping Toward an Abrogation of EU Company Law?', 12 *ECFR* 238–279 (2015).

4

Simplifying and Modernising European Company Law

4.1 General

As previously mentioned, all of the company law directives have been revised or recast over time, with a view to coping with the needs of a more engaged economic environment in Europe. Before proposing amendments or replacements of existing acts, the Commission has entrusted groups of company law experts to recommend proposals for either simplifying or modernising European Company Law.

A first group of company law experts, chaired by Professor Eddy Wymeersch (University of Ghent), was created in 1999 as part of the fourth phase of the Simpler Legislation for the Internal Market initiative. The SLIM Group was entrusted with the task of simplifying the First and Second Company Law Directives. A final document named *Recommendations by the company law SLIM Working Group on the simplification of the First and Second Company Law Directives* was delivered in September 1999.

A second group of company law experts, chaired by Professor Jaap Winter (Duisenberg School of Finance, Amsterdam) was later created in 2001 as the High Level Group of Company Law Experts. This group was entrusted with the broader task of making recommendations for a modern regulatory European company law framework designed to be sufficiently flexible and up to date to meet companies' needs, taking into account fully the impact of modern technology. A First Report of 10 January 2002 (*Report of the High Level Group of Company Law Experts on Issues Related to Takeover Bids*) only dealt with issues related to the Takeover Bids Directive. A *Final Report of the High Level Group of Company Law Experts on a Modern Regulatory Framework for Company Law in Europe* was delivered on 4 November 2002.

All necessary information on the formation, works and proposals of these groups are included in the Explanatory Memorandum of each final document (*see*, §§ 4.2–4.3).

The Commission has thoroughly considered all the proposals and recommendations made by the two groups and has consequently drafted action plans for the Council. A first Action Plan, named *Modernising Company Law and Enhancing Corporate Governance in the European Union – A Plan to*

Move Forward was presented on 21 May 2003. A second Action Plan named *European Company Law and Corporate Governance – A Modern Legal Framework for More Engaged Shareholders and Sustainable Companies* was submitted on 12 December 2012.

These documents draft the current and future plans of the EU institution in the field of company law, shaping its future. Excerpts of the most relevant parts of these action plans are reported in §§ 4.2–4.3.

FURTHER READING

'Report of the High Level Group of Company Law Experts on Issues Related to Takeover Bids', in Guido Ferrarini, Klaus J. Hopt, Jaap Winter, and Eddy Wymeersch (eds.), *Reforming Company and Takeover Law in Europe* 825–925 (Oxford University Press, 2004).

'High Level Group of Company Law Experts on a Modern Regulatory Framework for Company Law in Europe', in Guido Ferrarini, Klaus J. Hopt, Jaap Winter, and Eddy Wymeersch (eds.), *Reforming Company and Takeover Law in Europe* 925–1091 (Oxford University Press, 2004).

4.2 The Company Law SLIM Working Group

Explanatory Memorandum to the Recommendations by the Company Law SLIM Working Group on the Simplification of the First and Second Company Law Directives

The simplification of the First and Second Company Law Directives is part of the fourth phase of the SLIM initiative. It is important to note that the purpose of SLIM is not to further harmonise, but to slim regulation.

A small working group, called the Company Law Slim Working Group (hereafter: the 'Working Group'), was created with a view to identifying where simpler legislation could replace the existing legislation in the field of the First and Second Company Law Directive.

The Working Group was composed of Member States' representatives (namely from Austria, Finland, Italy, Luxembourg and Spain) and experts in and users of company law.

It was chaired by Eddy Wymeersch, professor at the University of Ghent. The names of the members of the Working Group are listed in the annex to this document.

The Company Law Slim Exercise was defined as a 'deregulation exercise' aimed at indicating certain matters within the scope of the First and Second Company Law Directives with respect to which the Single Market legislation could be simplified and to make appropriate proposals with respect to them. Certain links to the Eleventh Company Law Directive where thereby considered indispensable.

The Working Group worked out its proposals during three meetings, held on 12 February 1999, 26 March 1999 and 17 July 1999.

Given the limited working time table of its exercise, the Working Group did not aim to cover all possible areas susceptible to simplification in a comprehensive manner. It could only focus on certain selected substantial matters that could be the subject of simplification.

It recognises, however, that a more in-depth review of the two directives would certainly reveal additional areas for simplification.

With respect to the subject matters it examined, the Working Group worked out a number of proposals for simplification. The implementation of these proposals into coherent legislation is left to the competency of the European Commission (see, Explanatory Memorandum with regard to the Recommendations by the Company Law SLIM Working Group on the Simplification of the First and Second Company Law Directives).

The SLIM Group made four proposals concerning the First Directive and six proposals concerning the Second Directive. These are discussed in the action plan named *Modernising Company Law and Enhancing Corporate Governance in the European Union – A Plan to Move Forward* (*see*, § 4.4).

4.3 The High Level Group of Company Law Experts

Letter from the Chairman, Jaap Winter, of the High Level Group of Company Law Experts (October 2002)

The High Level Group of Company Law Experts was set up by the European Commission in September 2001 to make recommendations on a modern regulatory framework in the EU for company law. In our First Report of January 2002, we dealt with issues related to the Takeover Bids Directive, which was rejected by the European Parliament in July 2001. Our original mandate was further extended in April 2002 by the Commission following the ECOFIN Council meeting in Oviedo to deal specifically with a number of corporate governance issues. Our Final Report is presented here.

A fundamental review of company law in Europe was certainly due. Many agree that EU company law has not kept up with developments which shape its role and application, in particular the creation of a single EU market which companies and their investors wish to use to the optimum, the development of European securities markets and their regulation, the development of modern information and communication technologies which should be facilitated and could be used to improve company law arrangements and the development of corporate governance practices and standards.

Indeed, we believe company law in Europe must catch up with these developments. We hope that our Report will stimulate this process, which will require [the] concerted actions of many in the EU.

The High Level Group has made six recommendations concerning general themes, sixteen recommendations concerning corporate governance, fourteen recommendations concerning capital formation and maintenance, four recommendations concerning groups and pyramids, nine recommendations concerning corporate restructuring and mobility, three recommendations concerning the European private company, and six recommendations concerning cooperatives and other forms of enterprises. The Final Report concludes with two final recommendations worth mentioning.

Company Law Action Plan – Recommendation IX.1 (see, p. 125)

The Commission should prepare a Company Law Action Plan which sets the EU agenda, with priorities, for regulatory initiatives in the area of company law and agree such an action plan with the Council and the European Parliament.

Permanent Advisory Structure – Recommendation IX.2 (see, p. 127)

The setting up of a permanent structure to provide the Commission with independent advice on future regulatory initiatives in the area of EU company law should be duly considered.

FURTHER READING

Jaap Winter, 'EU Company Law at the Crossroads', in Guido Ferrarini, Klaus J. Hopt, Jaap Winter, and Eddy Wymeersch (eds.), *Reforming Company and Takeover Law in Europe* 3–21 (Oxford University Press, 2004).

Gérard Hertig and Joseph A. McCahery, 'An Agenda for Reform: Company and Takeover Law in Europe', in Guido Ferrarini, Klaus J. Hopt, Jaap Winter, and Eddy Wymeersch (eds.), *Reforming Company and Takeover Law in Europe* 21–51 (Oxford University Press, 2004).

Jonathan Rickford (ed.), 'Reforming Capital: Report of the Interdisciplinary Group on Capital Maintenance', 15 *EBLR* 919–1027 (2004).

Jonathan Rickford, 'Reforming Capital: An Introductory Note', 15 *EBLR* 1029–1030 (2004).

Friedrich Kübler, 'A Comparative Approach to Capital Maintenance: Germany', 15 *EBLR* 1031–1035 (2004).

Hanno Merkt, 'Creditor Protection and Capital Maintenance from a German Perspective', 15 *EBLR* 1045–1057 (2004).

Hanno Merkt, 'European Company Law Reform: Struggling for a More Liberal Approach', 1 *ECFR* 3–35 (2004).

4.4 Modernising Company Law and Enhancing Corporate Governance in the European Union – A Plan to Move Forward

Based on both the results of the SLIM Group work and the High Level Group's Report, on 21 May 2003, the Commission published a communication to the Council and the European Parliament, named *Modernising Company Law and*

Enhancing Corporate Governance in the European Union – A Plan to Move Forward.

Modernising Company Law and Enhancing Corporate Governance in the European Union – A Plan to Move Forward (2003)

Introduction

A dynamic and flexible company law and corporate governance framework is essential for a modern, dynamic, interconnected industrialised society. Essential for millions of investors. Essential for deepening the internal market and building an integrated European capital market. Essential for maximising the benefits of enlargement for all the Member States, new and existing.

Good company law, good corporate governance practices throughout the EU will enhance the real economy:

- An effective approach will foster the global efficiency and competitiveness of businesses in the EU. Well managed companies, with strong corporate governance records and sensitive social and environmental performance, outperform their competitors. Europe needs more of them to generate employment and higher long term sustainable growth.
- An effective approach will help to strengthen shareholders' rights and third parties' protection. In particular, it will contribute to rebuilding European investor confidence in the wake of a wave of recent corporate governance scandals. The livelihood of millions of Europeans, their pensions, their investments are tied up in the proper, responsible performance and governance of listed companies in which they invest.

Scope

This Communication outlines the approach that the Commission intends to follow specifically in the area of company law and corporate governance.

Achieving the objectives pursued (fostering efficiency and competitiveness of business, and strengthening shareholders rights and third parties' protection) requires a fully integrated approach.

Related initiatives, forming part of this integrated approach but not part of this Action Plan, include:

- The Financial Services Action Plan of 1999, which confirmed the overall objectives which should guide the financial services policy at EU level and set out a framework for an integrated capital market by 2005;
- The Financial Reporting Strategy of 2000, which seeks to achieve high quality financial reporting through the adoption of a common set of accounting standards and the development of a proper enforcement system, which led to the adoption in 2002 of the Regulation on the application of the international accounting standards;
- The Communication on Corporate Social Responsibility of 2002, which addresses the social and environmental dimension of business in a global economy and led to the setting up of

a European Multi-Stakeholder Forum with a view to promoting voluntary social and environmental practices of business, linked to their core activities, which go beyond their existing legal obligations;
- The Communication on Industrial Policy in an Enlarged Europe of 2002, which addresses the need for EU industry to achieve a more sustainable production structure as a driver of growth and productivity;
- The Communication on the priorities for the statutory audit in the EU, which is published together with the present Communication and which covers an EU policy approach aimed at ensuring audit quality and public confidence in the audit profession. It covers issues like the use of ISA's (International Standards on Auditing), public oversight of auditors, and the modernisation of the Eighth Company Law Directive into a comprehensive principles-based approach.

Responding to the High Level Group's Report

On 4 November 2002, a High Level Group of Company Law Experts appointed by Commissioner Bolkestein in September 2001 and chaired by Jaap Winter presented its Final Report on 'A modern regulatory framework for company law in Europe'. This report focused on corporate governance in the EU and the modernisation of European Company Law. The Competitiveness Council (30 September 2002) invited the Commission to organise an in-depth discussion on the forthcoming report and to develop – in coordination with Member States – an Action Plan for Company Law, including Corporate Governance, as soon as is feasible, declaring its intention to deal with the Action Plan as a matter of priority. The Ecofin Council has also shown a major interest in this work.

This Communication is the Commission's response. It explains why the European regulatory framework for company law and corporate governance needs to be modernised. It defines the key policy objectives which should inspire any future action to be taken at EU level in these areas. It includes an action plan, prioritised, over the short, medium and long term. It indicates which type of regulatory instrument should be used, and by when.

Guiding Political Criteria

In developing this Action Plan, the Commission has paid particular attention to the need for any regulatory response at European level to respect a number of guiding criteria:

- It should fully respect the subsidiarity and proportionality principles of the Treaty and the diversity of many different approaches to the same questions in the Member States, while at the same time pursuing clear ambitions (strengthening the single market and enhancing the rights of shareholders and third parties);
- It should be flexible in application, but firm in the principles. It should concentrate on priorities; be transparent; and subject to proper due process and consultation;
- It should help shape international regulatory developments. The EU must define its own European corporate governance approach, tailored to its own cultural and business traditions. Indeed, this is an opportunity for the Union to strengthen its influence in the world with good, sensible corporate governance rules. Corporate governance is indeed an area where standards are increasingly being set at international level, as evidenced by the

recent developments observed in the United States. The Sarbanes-Oxley Act, adopted on 30 July 2002 in the wake of a series of scandals, delivered a rapid response. The Act unfortunately creates a series of problems due to its outreach effects on European companies and auditors, and the Commission is engaged in an intense regulatory dialogue with a view to negotiating acceptable solutions with the US authorities (in particular the Securities and Exchange Commission). In many areas, the EU shares the same broad objectives and principles of the Sarbanes-Oxley Act and in some areas robust, equivalent regulatory approaches already exist in the EU. In some other areas, new initiatives are necessary. Earning the right to be recognised as at least 'equivalent' alongside other national and international rules is a legitimate and useful end in itself.

...

Conclusion

The present Communication explains why the European regulatory framework for company law and corporate governance needs to be modernised. It defines the key policy objectives which should inspire any future action to be taken at EU level in these areas. It includes an action plan, prioritised, to plan the various actions which appear necessary over the short, medium and long term. It determines which type of regulatory instrument should be used, and approximately by when.

Further to the conclusions adopted by the Brussels European Council of 20 and 21 March 2003, which requested the adoption of an Action Plan on Company Law and Corporate Governance, the Commission addresses this Communication to the European Parliament and the Council, and transmits it also to the European Economic and Social Committee and the Committee of the Regions ...

In Annex I to the Action Plan, the Commission proposed a list of actions for the short (2003–2005), the medium (2006–2008), and the long term (2009 onwards).

Modernising Company Law and Enhancing Corporate Governance in the European Union – A Plan to Move Forward

List of Actions
SHORT TERM (2003–2005)

	Description of action	Preferred type of initiative
Corporate Governance	Enhanced corporate governance disclosure requirements (including confirmation of collective responsibility of board members for key non-financial statements)	Legislative (Directive amending existing legislation)
	Integrated legal framework to facilitate efficient shareholder communication and decision-making (participation in meetings, exercise of voting rights, cross-border voting)	Legislative (Directive)
	Strengthening the role of independent non-executive and supervisory directors	Non-legislative (Recommendation)

(*cont.*)

Modernising Company Law and Enhancing Corporate Governance in the European Union – A Plan to Move Forward		
	List of Actions SHORT TERM (2003–2005)	
	Description of action	Preferred type of initiative
	Fostering an appropriate regime for directors' remuneration	Non-legislative (Recommendation)
	Confirming at EU level the collective responsibility of board members for financial statements	Legislative (Directive amending existing legislation)
	Convening a European Corporate Governance Forum to coordinate corporate governance efforts of Member States	Non-legislative (Commission initiative)
Capital Maintenance	Simplification of the Second Directive, on the basis of the SLIM recommendations as supplemented in the HLG Report (SLIM-Plus)	Legislative (Directive amending existing legislation)
Groups of companies	Increased disclosure of group structure and relations, both financial and non-financial	Legislative (Directive amending existing legislation)
Restructuring	Proposal for a Tenth Directive on cross-border mergers	Legislative (Directive)
	Proposal for a Fourteenth Directive on cross-border transfer of the seat	Legislative (Directive)
European Private Company	Feasibility study in order to assess the practical needs for – and problems of – a European Private Company	Non-legislative (Study)
EU legal forms	Active progress on current proposals (European Association, European Mutual Society)	Legislative (existing proposals)
	MEDIUM TERM (2006–2008)	
	Description of action	Preferred type of initiative
Corporate Governance	Enhanced disclosure by institutional investors of their investment and voting policies	Legislative (Directive)
	Choice for all listed companies between the two types (monistic/dualistic) of board structures	Legislative (Directive)
	Enhancing the responsibilities of board members (special investigation right, wrongful trading rule, directors' disqualification)	Legislative (Directive or Directive amending existing legislation)
	Examination of the consequences of an approach aiming at achieving a full shareholder democracy (one share/one vote), at least for listed companies	Non-legislative (Study)
Maintenance	Review of the feasibility of an alternative to the capital maintenance regime	Non-legislative (Study)
Groups of companies	Framework rule for groups, allowing the adoption at subsidiary level of a coordinated group policy	Legislative (Directive)
Pyramids	Prohibition of stock exchange listing for abusive pyramids, if appropriate, following further examination and expert input	Legislative (possible Directive amending existing legislation)

(*cont.*)

Modernising Company Law and Enhancing Corporate Governance in the European Union – A Plan to Move Forward		
	MEDIUM TERM (2006–2008)	
	Description of action	Preferred type of initiative
Restructuring	Simplification of the Third Directive (legal mergers) and Sixth Directive (legal divisions)	Legislative (Directive amending existing legislation)
European Private Company	Possible proposal for a Statute for a European Private Company (depending on the outcome of the feasibility study)	Legislative
EU legal forms	Assess the need for the creation of other EU legal forms (e.g., European Foundation)	Non-legislative (Study)
Transparency of national legal forms	Introduce basic disclosure rules for all legal entities with limited liability, subject to further examination	Legislative (Directive or Directive amending existing legislation)
	LONG TERM (2009 onwards)	
	Description of action	Preferred type of initiative
Capital Maintenance	Possible introduction in the Second Company Law Directive of an alternative regime (depending on the outcome of the feasibility study)	Legislative (Directive amending existing legislation)

Although not all proposed actions have been undertaken, significant goals have been achieved. Worthy of special mention are: (i) the recasting of the First, Second, Third, Sixth, Eighth, and Twelfth Directives; (ii) the delivery of the Tenth Company Law Directive on Cross-border Mergers and the Shareholder Rights Directive on Listed Companies; (iii) Recommendations on directors' independence and remuneration policies (as well as rules on the 'say on pay'), and on civil liability of auditors.

FURTHER READING

Dominique Thienpont, 'Corporate Governance in the EU: The Commission's Approach', 1 *ECL* 19–23 (2004).

Massimo Miola, 'Legal Capital and Limited Liability Companies: The European Perspective', 2 *ECFR* 413–486 (2005).

Eilís Ferran, 'The Place for Creditor Protection on the Agenda for Modernisation of Company Law in the European Union', 3 *ECFR* 179–221 (2006).

Kristina A. Sadlak, 'The European Commission's Action Plan to Modernize European Company Law: How Far Should the SEC Go in Exempting European Issuers from Complying with the Sarbanes–Oxley Act?', 3 *Int'l L. & Mgmt Rev.* 1–42 (2006).

Dario Latella, 'Shareholder Derivative Suits: A Comparative Analysis and the Implications of the European Shareholders' Rights Directive', 6 *ECFR* 307–323 (2009).

Susanne Kalss, 'Shareholder Suits: Common Problems, Different Solutions and First Steps towards a Possible Harmonisation by Means of a European Model Code', 6 *ECFR* 324–347 (2009).

James D. Cox and Randall S. Thomas, 'Common Challenges Facing Shareholder Suits in Europe and the United States', 6 *ECFR* 348–357 (2009).

4.5 European Company Law and Corporate Governance – A Modern Legal Framework for More Engaged Shareholders and Sustainable Companies

On 12 December 2012, the Commission sent a new communication to the European Parliament, the Council, the European Economic and Social Committee and the Committee of the Regions, proposing an *Action Plan: European company law and corporate governance – a modern legal framework for more engaged shareholders and sustainable companies.* Whilst it is appropriate to postpone the discussion to issues related to corporate governance to a later stage, it is useful to read those parts of the new Action Plan defining the current issues on which the European institutions propose to deliver new legislation.

1 Introduction

The Commission's 'Europe 2020' Communication calls for improvement of the business environment in Europe. A modern and efficient company law and corporate governance framework for European undertakings, investors and employees must be adapted to the needs of today's society and to the changing economic environment. The latest comprehensive review in this policy area stemmed from the 2003 Action Plan on Modernising Company Law and Enhancing Corporate Governance in the European Union and the subsequent consultation on future priorities for this Action Plan carried out in 2005 and 2006. A large number of initiatives announced in the 2003 Action Plan have been adopted. In particular rules on corporate governance statements have been introduced in the Accounting Directive, a Directive on the exercise of shareholders' rights and the Tenth Company Law Directive on Cross-border mergers have been adopted. Moreover, the Commission adopted two Recommendations regarding the role of independent non-executive directors and remuneration. Besides, the Second Company Law Directive on formation of public limited-liability companies and the maintenance and alteration of their capital and the Third and Sixth Company Law Directive on mergers and divisions have been simplified. Nevertheless, new developments have taken place since that require in the Commission's view further action.

Corporate governance defines relationships between a company's management, its board, its shareholders and its other stakeholders. It determines the way companies are managed and controlled. An effective corporate governance framework is of crucial importance because well-run companies are likely to be more competitive and more sustainable in the long term. Good corporate governance is first and foremost the responsibility of the company concerned, and rules at European and national level are in place to ensure that certain standards are respected. The EU corporate governance framework is a combination of legislation and soft law, namely national corporate governance codes applied on a 'comply or explain' basis which gives companies and their shareholders an important degree of flexibility. Shareholders have a crucial role to play in promoting better governance of companies. By doing this they act in both the interest of the company and their own interest.

However, the past few years have highlighted shortcomings in this area. The financial crisis has revealed that significant weaknesses in corporate governance of financial institutions played a role in the crisis. In order to respond rapidly to the problem of excessive risk-taking in credit institutions and ultimately the accumulation of excessive risk in the financial system, the Commission launched in 2010 a Green Paper on corporate governance in financial institutions and, in 2011, it proposed stricter rules on corporate governance in financial institutions in the framework of the CRD IV package. Although corporate governance in listed companies outside the financial sector did not give rise to the same concern, certain weaknesses have also been observed. In particular, there is a perceived lack of shareholder interest in holding management accountable for their decisions and actions, compounded by the fact that many shareholders appear to hold their shares for only a short period of time. There is also evidence of shortcomings in the application of the corporate governance codes when reporting on a 'comply or explain' basis. Against this backdrop the Commission adopted its Green Paper on the EU corporate governance framework (hereafter 'the 2011 Green Paper'), which launched a discussion on how to improve the effectiveness of the current rules. While respondents were divided as to the need for further regulation at EU level, there was strong support for EU measures in some specific fields. The European Parliament also expressed its view on the questions raised by the 2011 Green Paper in a Resolution adopted on 29 March 2012 highlighting the importance of corporate governance to society at large.

European company law is a cornerstone of the internal market. It facilitates freedom of establishment of companies while enhancing transparency, legal certainty and control of their operations. In recent times, however, it has become more difficult to reach agreement at EU level on the adoption of company law initiatives. These difficulties are, for example, illustrated by the lack of progress on some simplification initiatives and on the proposed statute of the European Private Company (SPE). Nevertheless, at the same time, the cross-border dimension of business has grown tremendously from both a company and a consumer perspective. The Commission services have therefore launched a process of reflection on the future of European company law, beginning with the publication of a report prepared by an ad hoc reflection group and a public conference held in Brussels on 16 and 17 May 2011. In order to gather views across a broad spectrum of stakeholders, an on-line consultation was launched on 20 February 2012 (hereafter 'the 2012 public consultation'). The European Parliament also expressed its view on the way forward for European company law in a Resolution adopted on 14 June 2012. A majority of respondents to the 2012 public consultation were in favour of new measures to modernise the existing company law framework. This Action Plan outlines the initiatives that the Commission intends to take in order to modernise the company law and corporate governance framework. It identifies three main lines of action:

- Enhancing transparency – companies need to provide better information about their corporate governance to their investors and society at large. At the same time companies should be allowed to know who their shareholders are and institutional investors should be more transparent about their voting policies so that a more fruitful dialogue on corporate governance matters can take place.
- Engaging shareholders – shareholders should be encouraged to engage more in corporate governance. They should be offered more possibilities to oversee remuneration policy and related party transactions, and shareholder cooperation to this end should be made easier. In addition, a limited number of obligations will need to be imposed on institutional investors, asset managers and proxy advisors to bring about effective engagement.
- Supporting companies' growth and their competitiveness – there is a need to simplify cross-border operations of European businesses, particularly in the case of small and medium-sized companies.

Besides supporting these three key objectives, the Commission will launch an overarching codification exercise in order to make the regulatory framework more user-friendly.

This Action Plan is the fruit of the 2012 public consultation, of various discussions with many stakeholders and of the Commission's own analysis. It sets out the initiatives which the Commission intends to take in the areas of company law and corporate governance. The different measures in the Action Plan will not all have the same scope. EU corporate governance rules only apply to companies listed on a stock exchange. On the other hand EU company law applies in principle to all EU public limited-liability companies. The Commission will ensure that the initiatives will not create unnecessary burdens for companies, and will in particular take into account the specific situation of SMEs.

All the initiatives will be subject to ex-ante impact assessments. The Action Plan cannot pre-empt the results of these impact assessments. The Commission may therefore have to modify its planning, as regards either its content or timing, if need be. New issues may subsequently arise and need to be pursued in addition to the initiatives set out in this Action Plan. New elements might arise from the responses to the planned consultation on the long-term financing of the European economy. The forthcoming Green Paper on this issue will launch a broad debate on how to strengthen the capacity of the financial sector in the EU to provide long-term financing for productive investment needed to drive sustainable growth. It will address issues such as the need to ensure there is access to diverse sources of finance; the importance of avoiding too much focus on short-term horizons only; and the need to enhance capacity and develop new products conducive to long-term financing. The scope of the Green Paper is therefore broader than corporate governance issues; but it may also provide further input on how long-term shareholder engagement can be encouraged and how appropriate corporate governance arrangements might support long-term financing.

...

4 Improving the Framework for Cross-border Operations of EU Companies

European company law is an integral part of the internal market. It facilitates freedom of establishment of companies while enhancing legal certainty for their operations. It can thereby support companies' growth and competitiveness.

4.1 Transfer of Seat

Apart from the rules contained in the Statutes for the European Company (SE), for the European Cooperative Society (SCE) and for the European Economic Interest Grouping (EEIG), there are no EU rules enabling companies to transfer their registered office across borders in a way which would preserve the company's legal personality. Currently, only a few Member States allow for a seat transfer without winding up and subsequent re-incorporation. Companies can also use the cross-border mergers Directive or the SE as a tool for changing their home Member State. The responses to the 2012 public consultation revealed considerable interest in EU rules on cross-border transfers of seats. The Commission acknowledges the importance of this issue. However, it considers that any future initiative in this matter needs to be underpinned by robust economic data and a thorough assessment of a practical and genuine need for and use made of European rules on transfer of seat. This is also in the light of the recent case law of the European Court of Justice as well as of the developments in Member States' legal frameworks. For this purpose, the Commission will conduct public and targeted consultations on the outcome of which it will report.

Throughout 2013, the Commission will conduct public and targeted consultations to update its impact assessment on a possible initiative on cross-border transfer of registered office. Subsequently, the Commission will consider the appropriateness of a legislative initiative.

4.2 Improving the Mechanism for Cross-border Mergers

Directive 2005/56/EC on cross-border mergers of limited-liability companies was a big step forward for cross-border mobility of companies in the EU. The framework thus created should now be adjusted to meet the changing needs of the Single Market. The Commission will analyse the conclusions of a forthcoming study on the application of the Directive which will be available in the second half of 2013, taking into account both the experience gained and future needs in this field. There seems to be a particular case for enhancing the procedural rules, given that a number of issues have been identified as a potential source of uncertainty and complexity, in particular a lack of harmonisation as regards methods for valuation of assets, the duration of the protection period for creditors' rights, and the consequences for creditors' rights on completion of the merger. The 2012 public consultation shows strong support for improvement of the cross-border mergers framework. The study that is being conducted will assist the Commission in preparing the necessary follow-up steps.

In 2013 the Commission aims to report on the outcome of the study and subsequently it will consider the appropriateness of amendments to the Directive on cross-border mergers.

4.3 Enabling Cross-border Divisions

Divisions at national level have for some years been harmonised by Directive 82/891/EEC. However, this has not yet been reflected in the EU legislation on cross-border transactions, under which only cross-border mergers have been explicitly enabled. Currently, companies wishing to undertake a cross-border division have to perform several operations, such as creation of a subsidiary and a subsequent transfer of assets or a domestic division followed by a transfer of seat. Moreover, a clear legal framework setting out the conditions under which cross-border divisions can be made directly would help to reduce costs significantly. There is in fact considerable demand for a clear legal framework for cross-border divisions, as demonstrated by the results of the 2012 public consultation.

In 2013, following the results of the study on the application of the Directive on cross-border mergers, the Commission will consider an initiative to provide a framework for cross-border divisions, possibly though an amendment of the cross-border mergers' Directive, as the latter is well known to stakeholders and it provides a tested framework for cross-border restructurings.

4.4 Smart Legal Forms for European SMEs

European SMEs (small and medium-sized enterprises) have an essential role to play in strengthening the EU economy, especially in the face of the economic crisis. Significant work has already been done to make life easier for SMEs in a number of areas in which they seem to have problems, including actions following the 2011 review of the Small Business Act. As regards company law in particular, the Commission believes that SMEs need simpler and less burdensome conditions for doing business across the EU and it remains a clear priority for the Commission to take concrete measures in this regard.

In view of the lack of progress in the negotiations of the proposal of the European Private Company (SPE) Statute, the 2012 public consultation demonstrated stakeholders' hesitation about continuing the negotiations on this proposal. At the same time the stakeholders were keen to explore alternative measures. The Commission will continue to explore means to improve the administrative and regulatory framework in which SMEs operate in order to facilitate SMEs' cross-border activities, provide them with simple, flexible and well-known rules across the EU and reduce the costs they are currently facing.

The Commission will continue to work on the follow-up to the SPE proposal with a view to enhancing cross-border opportunities for SMEs.

4.5 Promoting and Improving Awareness of the European Company (SE) and the European Cooperative (SCE) Statutes

The SE Statute brought a number of advantages for companies with a European dimension and, with 1,426 SEs registered as of October 2012, interest in this legal form continues to grow. According to the 2010 report on the application of the Statute, companies have opted for this legal form because of its European image and the possibility to transfer the registered office and to restructure more effectively on a cross-border basis. At the same time, stakeholders complain about high set-up costs, complex procedures and legal uncertainty, often stemming from the many references to national law, lack of sufficient awareness and practical experience with the Statute, and some reportedly strict requirements in the Statute that must be fulfilled to create an SE. Similarly, as far as the SCE is concerned, the Commission takes note of the fact that, following extended consultation, the complexity of the Regulation is considered to be one factor explaining the weak use of this instrument (only 25 SCEs incorporated until July 2012), the other being the lack of awareness of the existence of this instrument and of understanding of its benefits for SMEs.

The respondents to the 2012 consultation were supportive of revising EU legal forms in general. However, as the expected benefits of a revision, in terms of simplification and improvement of both Statutes, would not outweigh the potential challenges involved in reopening the discussions, the Commission does not plan to revise them in the short term. Instead, the Commission will focus on improving the awareness of companies and their legal advisers about the SE and the SCE Statutes (including the aspects related to employee involvement) in order to encourage them to opt for these legal forms more often.

The Commission will, in 2013, launch an information campaign to increase awareness of the European Company (SE) Statute through a comprehensive website bringing together practical advice and relevant documents on the Statute and will examine how a similar action can be undertaken for the promotion of the European Cooperative (SCE) Statute.

4.6 Groups of Companies

The 2012 public consultation has shown that the public is in favour of well-targeted EU initiatives on groups of companies. In particular two items have been previously identified on the basis of the reflection group report and other material submitted to the Commission before or during the consultation. Simplified communication of a group's structure to investors and an EU-wide move towards recognition of the concept of 'group interest' would be welcomed by stakeholders. On the other hand the idea of a comprehensive legal EU framework covering groups of companies was met with caution.

The Commission will, in 2014, come with an initiative to improve both the information available on groups and recognition of the concept of 'group interest'.

5 Codification of EU Company Law

European company law provisions are spread across many different legal acts. This makes it difficult for users to have a clear overview of applicable law in this policy area. The large number of Directives dealing with company law also carries the risk of unintended gaps or overlaps. The 2012 public consultation shows that there is strong support for the idea of merging existing company law Directives. More than 75% of respondents asked for either the creation of a single EU company law instrument absorbing the existing Directives or several mergers of groups of Directives with a similar scope. The European Parliament also supports this approach. The Commission considers it important to make EU company law more reader-friendly and to reduce the risk of future inconsistencies. It will therefore prepare the codification of major company law Directives and their merger into a single instrument. This exercise will encompass Directives covering mergers and divisions, the formation of public limited companies and the alteration and maintenance of their capital, single-member private limited companies, foreign branches and certain rules on disclosure, validity and nullity. It will also include the changes introduced by the recent Directive on the interconnection of business registers. Progress on the work will to some extent depend on the conclusion of parallel initiatives such as the crisis management framework, which involves minor amendments to existing company law Directives.

The Commission plans to adopt, in 2013, a proposal codifying and merging major company law Directives.

6 Conclusion

The Commission has identified in this Action Plan a number of concrete lines of action in the area of company law and corporate governance to ensure further improvements in these areas. These include in particular initiatives increasing the level of transparency between companies and their shareholders, initiatives aimed at encouraging and facilitating long-term shareholder engagement and initiatives in the field of company law supporting European businesses and their growth and competitiveness. The initiatives in the area of corporate governance do not aim at altering the current approach, but ensure, by encouraging proper interaction between companies, their shareholders and other stakeholders, that this approach becomes more efficient. As regards company law, the initiatives proposed focus in particular on providing companies [with] more legal certainty, in particular as regards cross-border operations. The Commission will continue to explore with stakeholders possible further actions to ensure that the EU framework for company law and corporate governance contributes to the objective of smart, sustainable and inclusive growth ...

FURTHER READING

Francesco Chiappetta and Umberto Tombari, 'Perspectives on Group Corporate Governance and European Company Law', 9 *ECFR* 261–274 (2012).

Pierre-Henri Conac, 'Director's Duties in Groups of Companies – Legalizing the Interest of the Group at the European Level', 10 *ECFR* 194–226 (2013).

Reflection Group on the Future of EU Company Law, 'Response to the European Commission's Action Plan on Company Law and Corporate Governance', 10 *ECFR* 304–327 (2013).

Part II
The Right of Establishment

5

Primary Establishment in CJEU Case Law

5.1 Freedom (and Freedoms) of Establishment

As briefly discussed earlier (Chapter 1, § 1.2), intimately linked to the so-called 'four freedoms' granted under the TFEU is the freedom of establishment. This freedom, therefore, lies at the very heart of both EU law and, more specifically, ECL.

Despite this fundamental importance within the European legal framework, the liberty that an economic operator enjoys in deciding *where* to carry out its economic activity is not an exclusive feature of the European Internal Market. Indeed, its importance in fostering a beneficial competition among States and, ultimately, economic growth, has long been acknowledged in the US as well.

In this regard, it is of particular interest to take a look at the way US legal scholarship has traditionally dealt with the issue since, with due proportion, the US institutional architecture somewhat resembles the European one (*see*, Chapter 1, § 1.1 for the differences between the EU and the federal systems). The debate over the best system to grant this competition, and therefore the freedom of establishment for both individuals and business entities, has in fact been posed in similar terms.

Roberta Romano, 'The State Competition Debate in Corporate Law', 8 *Cardozo L. Rev.* 709-757, at 709-723 (1987)

A perennial issue in corporate law reform is the desirability of a federal system. For notwithstanding the invasive growth of regulation by the national government, principally through the federal securities laws, corporate law is still the domain of the states. While no two corporation codes are identical, there is substantial uniformity across the states. Provisions typically spread in a discernible S-shaped pattern, as one state amends its code in response to another state's innovation. The revision process is often analogized in the academic literature to market competition, in which states compete to provide firms with a product, corporate charters, in order to obtain franchise tax revenues. This characterization is the centrepiece of the federalism debate in corporate law whether competition, and hence a federal system, benefits shareholders. The hero – or culprit – in the debate is Delaware, the most successful state in the market for corporate charters ...

The State Competition Literature

The Classic Positions Revisited

The foundation of the federalism debate in corporate law is that revenues derived from franchise taxes provide a powerful incentive for state legislatures to implement corporation codes that will maintain the number of domiciled corporations, if not lure new firms to incorporate in their state. All participants in the debate believe that the income produced by the chartering business spurs states to enact laws that firms desire. This behavioral assumption is plausible: There is a positive linear relation between the percentage of total revenues that states obtain from franchise taxes and states' responsiveness to firms in their corporate codes. The more dependent a state is on income from franchise tax revenues, the more responsible is its corporation code. The potential revenue from this tax source can be substantial for a small state. Delaware's franchise tax revenue averaged 15.8 percent of its total revenue from 1960 to 1980, and while it is impossible to generate a precise figure, this income considerably outdistances the cost of operating its chartering business.

Given the shared assertion that revenues compel states to be responsive to firms' demands for legislation, the crux of the dispute is, therefore, whether this responsiveness is for the better. Because of the separation of ownership and control in the management of many large public corporations, when a firm's managers propose a reincorporation or urge the enactment of a statute, no less the adoption of a charter provision, we are concerned about whether they are maximizing the value of the firm. This is the classic agency problem, which goes to the heart of corporation law ...: How do principals – the shareholders – ensure that their agents – the managers – behave faithfully?

Advocates of a national corporation law have termed state competition a race for the bottom because they believe that managers' discretion is unfettered, enabling them to promote laws that are detrimental to shareholders' welfare. They base this conclusion on a characterization of the statutes and case law of Delaware – which is the most frequent location for a reincorporation – as excessively permissive, by which they mean titled toward management. Proponents of the current federal system, however, question this phrasing of the issue, typically viewing the agency problem as trivial. They maintain that the many markets in which firms operate – the product, capital, and labor markets – constrain managers to further the shareholders' interests. Accordingly, in their view, conflict between investors and managers over the content of state laws is largely illusory, and the laws that are promulgated can best be explained as mechanisms for maximizing equity share prices ...

A Transaction Cost Explanation of the Market for Corporate Charters

Why is Delaware the Destination State of Choice? The transaction cost explanation of the corporate charter market provides a different perspective on state competition. Delaware's persistent large market share is maintained by a first-mover advantage created by the reciprocal relation that develops between the chartering state and firms due to their substantial investment in assets that are specific to the chartering transaction ...

Of all the states, Delaware is best positioned to credibly commit itself to responsiveness. First, its very success in the incorporation business serves, ironically, to constrain its behavior: The high proportion of total revenue it derives from franchise taxes guarantees continued responsiveness because it has so much to lose. For unlike states less dependent on franchise revenues, Delaware has no readily available alternative source to which it can turn in order to maintain expenditures. It cannot afford to lose firms to other states by failing to keep its code up-to-date. In this way, Delaware offers itself as a hostage by its reliance on franchise taxes to finance its expenditures.

Second, an additional institutional mechanism warranting responsiveness is Delaware's constitutional provision mandating that all changes in the corporation code be adopted by a two-thirds vote of both houses of the state legislature. This makes it difficult to renege on provisions already in the code and, correspondingly, on the overall policy of being responsive to firms. While the provision would appear to make future changes equally difficult, if firms are risk averse when it comes to corporation codes, they might favor a miximin strategy in which the constitutional provision would be desirable, since it helps to ensure that the legal regime will never be worse that it is at the time of incorporation. This provision thus complements Delaware's high proportionate franchise tax, for while the constitution is backward-looking, limiting radical revamping of the code, the incentives provided by the franchise tax revenue are forward-looking, as the state reacts to the high proportion of franchise tax revenues in the past by maintaining its responsiveness to incremental change in the future.

Third, Delaware has invested in assets that have no use outside of the chartering business. These assets, which can best be characterized as legal capital, consist of a store of legal precedents forming a comprehensive body of case law, judicial expertise in corporate law, and administrative expertise in the rapid processing of corporate filings. These features are not as easily duplicated by other states as the provisions of a corporation code because [of] the start-up costs in developing expertise and the dynamic precedent-based nature of adjudication by courts.

The combination of these factors – the high proportion of franchise tax revenue, the constitutional supermajority requirement, and the investments in legal capital – create an intangible asset with hostage-like qualities, a reputation for responsiveness, that firms weigh in their incorporation decision. The large number of firms already incorporated in Delaware further solidifies its commanding position in the market by giving it a first-mover advantage. There is safety in numbers – the more firms there are the higher the level of franchise tax paid and the more the state relies on its incorporation business for revenue, which provides the incentive to behave responsively. In addition, the large number of firms makes it more likely that any particular issue will be litigated and decided in Delaware, providing a sound basis for corporate planning. This attracts even more firms for the more responsive a state and the more settled its law, the cheaper it is for a firm to operate under that legal regime. The first-mover advantage is self-sustaining because the more firms there are paying a franchise tax, the greater the return Delaware earns on its reputation for responsiveness, and the stronger its incentive to not engage in an end-game strategy of exploiting firms that would damage, if not destroy, its investment in a reputation.

In the preceding excerpt, Professor Romano examines the interplay between federal and local government in providing a legal framework for corporate law, and focuses in particular on the reasons why Delaware is so successful in attracting new companies or existing ones willing to operate there. More recently, similar analyses on the major role played by Delaware in the US context have led legal scholars to highlight other policy considerations that might underlie the development of Delaware corporate law.

Lawrence A. Hamermesh, 'The Policy Foundations of Delaware Corporate Law', 106 *Colum. L. Rev.* 1749–1792, at 1752 (2006)

What emerges is a picture in which the policymakers are attentive to, and respond to, interstate competitive threats as well as potential federal expansion in the field of corporate law. Within those very broad limits, however, these policymakers act on conventional notions of (1) enhancing flexibility to engage in private ordering; (2) deferring to case-by-case development of the law, and avoiding legislation that is prescriptive and proscriptive; (3) avoiding impairment of pre-existing contractual relationships and expectations; and (4) most importantly, avoiding legislative change in the absence of clear and specific practical benefits. Above all, Delaware corporate law is conservative.

This inherent conservatism will significantly affect the course of federal and state roles in regulating corporate governance. Delaware is unlikely to expand materially the regulation of corporate actors by means of either statutory or common law change. Additional federal regulation will emerge sporadically in response to political crises in which matters of corporate governance take on political salience beyond the management and shareholder groups that are ordinarily involved in such matters. Delaware can do and will do little if anything to stand in the way of such responses. Any effort by Delaware to head off such additional federal regulation of corporate governance will involve small steps that will not significantly alter the existing allocation of power and authority among corporate constituencies.

At the EU level, there exists no such distinction between federal and local government; however, like the American one, EU company law is (still) mostly regulated by Member States. As in the US, too, the freedom of establishment stimulates a competition amongst Member States to create the best economic and legal conditions for companies or individuals to operate.

At present, no Member State has asserted itself as 'the European Delaware'; none seems to have a clear competitive advantage over the others. In addition, the absence of real profitable incentives such as high franchise taxes and legal fees weakens the enthusiasm and the subsequent effort in the race to Delaware's imitation.

This being said, there is no doubt that the aspiration to play a prominent role within the EU corporate law context has been pursued more thoroughly (and more successfully) by two Member States in particular. Traditionally, such a major position has been taken by the UK. Its attractiveness – for smaller enterprises in particular – was due to a number of factors, among which were a special attention to shareholders, the widespread usage of the English language, the absence of minimum legal capital requirements for private limited-liability companies and low start-up costs. This trend has declined over time, as many other EU Member States – such as Germany (2008), Italy (2012), Spain (2013), and France (2016) – have passed laws permitting, like in the UK, the formation of so-called One-Euro limited companies. The process of legislative imitation – which is reported to be unsuccessful in the US (e.g., Maryland mimicking Delaware) – has caused two main effects: on the one side, having the option to set up a One-Euro company regulated by the law of the Member State of origin, founders of new businesses have less interest in the use of UK limited, as it implies agency costs; on the other side, some already established UK limited companies have decided to 'convert'. The conversion process is, however, complicated, as it requires either to wind up and reincorporate, or to perform a cross-border merger – into limited companies of other Member States (generally those where the shareholders are resident). This last phenomenon developed after the UK government notified the EU Commission of its decision to withdraw from the Union: as UK companies no longer enjoy the freedom of establishment across the EU, Brexit makes the UK an unattractive legal environment for business to be carried out in the EU.

Nowadays – and with regard to bigger companies in particular – the most competitive and favourable legal regime seems to be found in the Netherlands rather than in the UK. Put simply, such a shift can be attributed to the adoption of some particularly business-friendly policies enacted in the last few years, such as that of not going further than the minimal requirements defined by company law directives and, in some cases, even abolishing existing rules deemed to be too strict (e.g., in the field of financial disclosure). Besides the skilled legal services offered, a number of pro-managerial rules on share ownership and mergers (e.g., the rule allowing double voting rights to stable shareholders that facilitates the maintenance of control) also contributed to making the Netherlands a jurisdiction attractive enough to be (rightfully) likened to Delaware.

David A. Charny, 'Competition Among Jurisdictions in Formulating Corporate Law Rules: An American Perspective on the "Race to the Bottom" in the European Communities', 32 *Harv. Int'l L.J.* 423–456, at 429 (1991)

Dutch corporate law permits managers to control large blocks of voting stock by placing such stock in the hands of [a] company-owned trust – an arrangement generally forbidden in most jurisdictions' corporate law, and only recently available, de facto, to US managers with the emergence of the employee stock ownership trust, whose trustees may be effectively controlled by management.

As a matter of fact, Fiat–Chrysler Group's decision in 2013 to register the newly formed Fiat–Chrysler Automobiles N.V. in the Netherlands rather than in Italy or the UK (notwithstanding its fiscal domicile and centre of administration was originally located in the UK) is a significant example of the shift that has occurred and of the prominent role acquired by the Netherlands. This choice has been later confirmed when Fiat–Chrysler Automobiles and Peugeot Société Anonyme agreed a merger of equals, the resulting company of which is incorporated in the Netherlands.

FURTHER READING

Roberta Romano, 'The State Competition Debate in Corporate Law', 8 *Cardozo L. Rev.* 709–757 (1987).

Lawrence A. Hamermesh, 'The Policy Foundations of Delaware Corporate Law', 106 *Colum. L. Rev.* 1749–1792 (2006).

David A. Charny, 'Competition Among Jurisdictions in Formulating Corporate Law Rules: An American Perspective on the "Race to the Bottom" in the European Communities', 32 *Harv. Int'l L.J.* 423–456 (1991).

Federico Pernazza, 'Fiat Chrysler Automobiles and the New Face of the Corporate Mobility in Europe', 14 *ECFR* 37–72 (2017).

Alessio Bartolacelli, 'Almost Capital-less Companies in Europe: Trends, Variations, Competition', 14 *ECFR* 187–233 (2017).

Andrea Zorzi, 'A European Nevada? Bad Enforcement as an Edge in State Competition for Incorporations', 18 *EBOR* 251–272 (2017).

Riccardo Ghetti, 'Unification, Harmonisation and Competition in European Company Forms', 29 *EBLR* 813–842 (2018).

5.2 General: Freedom of Establishment under European Company Law

Under ECL, as already briefly explained (Chapter 1, § 1.2), the freedom of establishment includes both

- the right to set up and manage companies or firms in any Member States, under the same conditions laid down for their own nationals (Article 49(2) TFEU) (*primary establishment*); and
- the right to set up agencies, branches or subsidiaries in any Member States, under the same conditions laid down for their own nationals (Article 49(1) and Article 56 TFEU) (*secondary establishment*).

In the following paragraphs, we will deal with the right of primary establishment, and in particular with the interpretation of Article 49(2) TFEU given by the CJEU in several cases. After the case study, it will be possible to state the EU *acquis* on the matter.

FURTHER READING

Erik Werlauff, 'Common European Company Law: Status 1998 (1): Equal Treatment of Companies, Domicile under Company Law and Related Concepts', 9 *EBLR* 169–175 (1998).

Ulrich Klinke, 'European Company Law and the ECJ: The Court's Judgements in the Years 2001 to 2004', 2 *ECFR* 270–321 (2005).

Wolf-Georg Ringe, 'No Freedom of Emigration for Companies?', 16 *EBLR* 621–642 (2005).

Nadja Kubat Erk, 'The Cross-border Transfer of Seat in European Company Law: A Deliberation about the Status Quo and the Fate of the Real Seat Doctrine', 21 *EBLR* 413–450 (2010).

Wolf-Georg Ringe, 'Corporate Mobility in the European Union – A Flash in the Pan? An Empirical Study on the Success of Lawmaking and Regulatory Competition', 10 *ECFR* 230–267 (2013).

Aaron Khan, 'Corporate Mobility under Article 49 TFEU: A Question of Means, not Ends', 22 *EBLR* 847–870 (2011).

Eilis Ferran, 'Corporate Mobility and Company Law', 79 *Modern Law Review*, 813–839 (2016).

5.3 *Daily Mail* Case

In *Daily Mail* (C-81/87, *The Queen* v. *H.M. Treasury and Commissioners of Inland Revenue, ex parte Daily Mail and General Trust plc.*, [1988] ECR I-5483), the question referred to the CJEU arose in proceedings between Daily Mail and General Trust PLC, the applicant in the main proceedings (*'Daily Mail')*, and HM Treasury for a declaration, *inter alia*, that 3.4. is not required to obtain consent under UK tax legislation in order to cease to be resident in the UK for the purpose of establishing its residence in the Netherlands.

In 1984, Daily Mail, which is an investment holding company, applied for consent under the relevant national provision in order to transfer its central management and control to the Netherlands, whose legislation does not prevent foreign companies from establishing their central management there; the company proposed, in particular, to hold board meetings and to rent offices for its management in the Netherlands. Without waiting for that consent, it subsequently decided to open an investment management office in the Netherlands with a view to providing services to third parties.

It was common ground that the principal reason for the proposed transfer of central management and control was to enable Daily Mail, after establishing its residence for tax purposes in the Netherlands, to sell a significant part of its non-permanent assets and to use the proceeds of that sale to buy its own shares, without having to pay the tax to which such transactions would make it liable under UK tax law, with particular regard to the substantial capital gains on the assets which the applicant proposed to sell. After establishing its central management and control in the Netherlands the applicant would be subject to the Netherlands' corporation tax, but the transactions envisaged would be taxed only on the basis of any capital gains that accrued after the transfer of its residence for tax purposes.

After a long period of negotiations with the Treasury, which proposed that it should sell at least part of the assets before transferring its residence for tax purposes out of the UK, the applicant initiated proceedings before the High Court of Justice, Queen's Bench Division, in 1986. Before that court, it claimed that Articles 52 and 58 of the EEC Treaty gave it the right to transfer its central management and control to another Member State without prior consent or the right to obtain such consent unconditionally.

In order to resolve that dispute, the national court stayed the proceedings and referred the following questions to the Court of Justice:

C-81/87, The Queen v. H.M. Treasury and Commissioners of Inland Revenue, ex parte Daily Mail and General Trust plc., [1988] ECR I-5483, §§ 6–9

(1) Do Articles 52 and 58 of the EEC Treaty [current Articles 49 and 54 TFEU] preclude a Member State from prohibiting a body corporate with its central management and control in that Member State from transferring without prior consent or approval that central management and control to another Member State in one or both of the following circumstances, namely where:
   a. payment of tax upon profits or gains which have already arisen may be avoided;
   b. were the company to transfer its central management and control, tax that might have become chargeable had the company retained its central management and control in that Member State would be avoided?

(2) Does Council Directive 73/148/EEC give a right to a corporate body with its central management and control in a Member State to transfer without prior consent or approval its central management and control to another Member State in the conditions set out in Question 1? If so, are the relevant provisions directly applicable in this case?

(3) If such prior consent or approval may be required, is a Member State entitled to refuse consent on the grounds set out in Question 1?

(4) What difference does it make, if any, that under the relevant law of the Member State no consent is required in the case of a change of residence to another Member State of an individual or firm?

The CJEU resolved the above-mentioned questions as follows:

C-81/87, The Queen v. H.M. Treasury and Commissioners of Inland Revenue, ex parte Daily Mail and General Trust plc., [1988] ECR I-5483, §§ 23, 25, Operative Part 1, §§ 28–29, Operative Part 2

The Treaty regards the differences in national legislation concerning the connecting factor required of companies incorporated thereunder and the question whether – and if so how – the registered office or real head office of a company incorporated under national law may be transferred from one Member State to another as problems which are not resolved by the rules concerning the right of establishment but must be dealt with by future legislation or conventions, which have not yet been adopted or concluded. Therefore, in the present state of Community law, Articles 52 and 58 of the Treaty [current Articles 49 and 54 TFEU], properly construed, confer no right on a company incorporated under the legislation of a Member State and having its registered office there to transfer its central management and control to another Member State.

The title and provisions of Council Directive 73/148 of 21 May 1973 on the abolition of restrictions on movement and residence within the Community for nationals of Member States with regard to establishment and the provision of services refer solely to the movement and residence of natural persons, and the provisions of the directive cannot, by their nature, be applied by analogy to legal persons. Therefore, Directive 73/148, properly construed, confers no right on a company to transfer its central management and control to another Member State.

FURTHER READING

Alberto Santamaria, *European Economic Law* 53–58 (Alphen aan den Rijn, Kluwer Law International, 3rd ed., 2014).

5.4 *Überseering* Case

In *Überseering* (C-208/00, *Überseering BV* v. *Nordic Construction Company Baumanagement GmbH (NCC)*, [2002] ECR I-09919), the questions referred to the CJEU were raised in proceedings between Überseering BV ('*Überseering*'), a company incorporated under Dutch law and registered on 22 August 1990 in the register of companies of Amsterdam and Haarlem, and Nordic Construction Company Baumanagement GmbH ('*NCC*'), a company established in the Federal Republic of Germany, concerning damages for defective work carried out in Germany by NCC on behalf of Überseering.

In October 1990, Überseering acquired a piece of land in Düsseldorf (Germany), which it used for business purposes. By a project-management contract dated 27 November 1992, Überseering engaged NCC to refurbish a garage and a motel on the site. The contractual obligations were performed but Überseering claimed that the paintwork was defective.

In December 1994, two German nationals residing in Düsseldorf acquired all the shares in Überseering.

Überseering unsuccessfully sought compensation from NCC for the defective work and in 1996 it brought an action before the Landgericht (Regional Court), Düsseldorf, on the basis of its project-management contract with NCC. It claimed the sum of DEM 1,163,657.77, plus interest, in respect of the costs incurred in remedying the alleged defects and consequential damage.

The Landgericht dismissed the action. The Oberlandesgericht (Higher Regional Court), Düsseldorf, upheld the decision to dismiss the action. It found that Überseering had transferred its actual centre of administration to Düsseldorf once its shares had been acquired by two German nationals. The Oberlandesgericht found that, as a company incorporated under Netherlands law, Überseering did not have legal capacity in Germany and, consequently, could not bring legal proceedings there.

Therefore, the Oberlandesgericht held that Überseering's action was inadmissible.

Überseering appealed to the Bundesgerichtshof (High Court) against the judgment of the Oberlandesgericht.

The Bundesgerichtshof decided to stay proceedings and to refer the following questions to the Court for a preliminary ruling:

C-208/00, Überseering BV v. Nordic Construction Company Baumanagement GmbH (NCC), [2002] ECR I-09919, § 21

1. Are Articles 43 EC and 48 EC [current Articles 49 and 54 TFEU] to be interpreted as meaning that the freedom of establishment of companies precludes the legal capacity, and capacity to be a party to legal proceedings, of a company validly incorporated under the law of one Member State from being determined according to the law of another State to which the company has moved its actual centre of administration, where, under the law of that second State, the company may no longer bring legal proceedings there in respect of claims under a contract?
2. If the Court's answer to that question is affirmative:

Does the freedom of establishment of companies (Articles 43 EC and 48 EC [current Articles 49 and 54 TFEU]) require that a company's legal capacity and capacity to be a party to legal proceedings is to be determined according to the law of the State where the company is incorporated?

The CJEU decided the referred questions as follows:

C-208/00, Überseering BV v. Nordic Construction Company Baumanagement GmbH (NCC), [2002] ECR I-09919, § 52, Operative Part 1, § 95, Operative Part 2

Where a company formed in accordance with the law of a Member State ('A') in which it has its registered office is deemed, under the law of another Member State ('B'), to have moved its actual centre of administration to Member State B, Articles 43 EC and 48 EC [current Articles 49 and 54 TFEU] preclude Member State B from denying the company legal capacity and, consequently, the capacity to bring legal proceedings before its national courts for the purpose of enforcing rights under a contract with a company established in Member State B.

Where a company formed in accordance with the law of a Member State ('A') in which it has its registered office exercises its freedom of establishment in another Member State ('B'), Articles 43 EC and 48 EC [current Articles 49 and 54 TFEU] require Member State B to recognise the legal capacity and, consequently, the capacity to be a party to legal proceedings which the company enjoys under the law of its State of incorporation ('A').

FURTHER READING

Frank Wooldridge, 'Überseering: Freedom of Establishment of Companies Affirmed', 14 *EBLR* 227–235 (2003).

Werner F. Ebke, 'The European Conflict-of-corporate-laws Revolution: Überseering, Inspire Art and Beyond', 16 *EBLR* 9–54 (2005).

Andrea J. Gildea, 'Uberseering: A European Company Passport', 30 *Brook. J. Int'l L.* 257–292 (2004).

See also:

Marco Ventoruzzo, Pierre-Henry Conac, Gen Goto, Sebastan Mock, Mario Notari, and Arad Reisberg, *Comparative Corporate Governance* 74–89 (St Paul MN, West Academic Publishing, 2015).

5.5 *Sevic* Case

In *Sevic* (C-411/03, *SEVIC Systems AG*, [2005] ECR I-10805), the reference was made in the context of an action brought by SEVIC Systems AG ('*SEVIC*'), a company established in Neuwied (Germany), against a decision of the Amtsgericht (Local Court) Neuwied rejecting its application for registration in the national commercial register of the merger between itself and Security Vision Concept SA ('*Security Vision*'), a company established in Luxembourg, on the ground that the Umwandlungsgesetz (UmwG, German law on company transformations) provides only for mergers between companies established in Germany.

Sevic had applied for registration in the commercial register, in accordance with the UmwG, of the merger with Security Vision, the relevant contract providing for the absorption of the latter company and its dissolution without liquidation.

That application was rejected by the Amtsgericht Neuwied on the ground that, in Paragraph 1(1)(1), the UmwG provides that only legal entities established in national territory may be the subject of transformation by merger ('internal mergers') and that, therefore, that law does not apply to transformations resulting from cross-border mergers.

In Germany, there are no general rules, analogous to those laid down by that law, which apply to cross-border mergers.

There is therefore a difference in treatment in Germany between internal and cross-border mergers.

The question referred by the national court to the CJEU was understood as

C-411/03, SEVIC Systems AG, [2005] ECR I-10805, §§ 11–15

asking essentially whether Articles 43 EC and 48 EC [current Articles 49 and 54 TFEU] preclude registration in the national commercial register of the merger by dissolution without liquidation of one company and transfer of the whole of its assets to another company from being refused in general in a Member State where one of the two companies is established in another Member State, whereas such registration is possible, on compliance with certain conditions, where the two companies participating in the merger are both established in the territory of the first Member State.

The CJEU decided the referred question as follows:

C-411/03, SEVIC Systems AG, [2005] ECR I-10805, §§ 18–19, §§ 23, 28, 31, Operative Part

The right of establishment covers all measures which permit or even merely facilitate access to another Member State and the pursuit of an economic activity in that State by allowing the persons concerned to participate in the economic life of the country effectively and under the same conditions as national operators.

Cross-border merger operations, like other company transformation operations, respond to the needs for cooperation and consolidation between companies established in different Member States. They constitute particular methods of exercise of the freedom of establishment, important for the proper functioning of the internal market, and are therefore amongst those economic activities in respect of which Member States are required to comply with the freedom of establishment laid down by Article 43 EC [current Article 49 TFEU]. Articles 43 EC and 48 EC [current Articles 49 and 54 TFEU] preclude registration in the national commercial register of the merger by dissolution without liquidation of one company and transfer of the whole of its assets to another company from being refused in general in a Member State where one of the two companies is established in another Member State, whereas such registration is possible, on compliance with certain conditions, where the two companies participating in the merger are both established in the territory of the first Member State.

Such a difference in treatment can be permitted only if it pursues a legitimate objective compatible with the Treaty and is justified by imperative reasons in the public interest, such as protection of the interests of creditors, minority shareholders and employees, and the preservation of the effectiveness of fiscal supervision and the fairness of commercial transactions. Furthermore, application of such a difference in treatment must be appropriate for ensuring the attainment of the objectives pursued and not go beyond what is necessary to attain them.

FURTHER READING

Clemens Philipp Schindler, 'Cross-border Mergers in Europe – Company Law is Catching Up! – Commentary on the ECJ's Decision in SEVIC Systems AG', 3 *ECFR* 109–119 (2006).

Thomas Rønfeldt and Erik Werlauff, 'Merger as a Method of Establishment: On Cross-border Mergers, Transfer of Domicile and Divisions, Directly Applicable under the EC Treaty's Freedom of Establishment', 3 *ECL* 125–129 (2006).

Paul Storm, 'Cross-border Mergers, the Rule of Reason and Employee Participation', 3 *ECL* 130–138 (2006).

Gert-Jan Vossestein, 'Companies' Freedom of Establishment after Sevic', 3 *ECL* 177–182 (2006).

Harald Gesell and Pieter Riemer, '"Outbound" Cross-border Mergers Protected by Freedom of Establishment: Annotation to the Decision of the Amsterdam District Court (Kantongerecht) 29 January 2007, EA 06-3338 166', 4 *ECFR* 308–316 (2007).

Lone L. Hansen, 'Merger, Moving and Division Across National Borders – When Case Law Breaks through Barriers and Overtakes Directives', 18 *EBLR* 181–204 (2007).

See also:

Alberto Santamaria, *European Economic Law* 58–65 (Alphen aan den Rijn, Kluwer Law International, 3rd ed., 2014).

Federico M. Mucciarelli, 'E pluribus unum? Language diversity and the harmonization of company law in the European Union', 26 *Maastricht J. Eur. & Comp. L.* 669 (2019).

5.6 *Cartesio* Case

In *Cartesio* (C-210/06, CARTESIO Oktató és Szolgáltató bt., [2008] ECR I-09641), the reference was made in the context of proceedings brought by CARTESIO Oktató és Szolgáltató bt. ('*Cartesio*'), against the decision rejecting its application for registration in the commercial register of the transfer of its company seat to Italy.

Cartesio was formed on 20 May 2004 as a 'betéti társaság' (limited partnership) under Hungarian law and was registered in the commercial register on 11 June 2004. Its seat was established in Baja (Hungary). Cartesio had two partners both of whom were natural persons resident in Hungary and holding Hungarian nationality: a limited partner, whose only commitment is to invest capital, and an unlimited partner, with unlimited liability for the company's debts. Cartesio was active, *inter alia*, in the field of human resources, secretarial activities, translation, teaching and training.

On 11 November 2005, Cartesio filed an application with the Bács-Kiskun Megyei Bíróság (Regional Court, Bács-Kiskun), sitting as a Cégbíróság (Commercial Court), for registration of the transfer of its seat to Gallarate (Italy) and, in consequence, for amendment of the entry regarding Cartesio's company seat in the commercial register. By decision of 24 January 2006, that application was rejected on the ground that the Hungarian law in force did not allow a company incorporated in Hungary to transfer its seat abroad while continuing to be subject to Hungarian law as its personal law. Cartesio lodged an appeal against that decision with the Szegedi Ítélőtábla (Regional Court of Appeal, Szeged).

On the view that resolution of the dispute depended on the interpretation of Community law, the Szegedi Ítélőtábla decided to stay proceedings and to refer the following questions to the Court for a preliminary ruling:

C-210/06, CARTESIO Oktató és Szolgáltató bt., [2008] ECR I-09641, § 40

(4) (a) If a company, [incorporated] in Hungary under Hungarian company law and entered in the Hungarian commercial register, wishes to transfer its seat to another Member State of the European Union, is the regulation of this field within the scope of Community law or, in the absence of the harmonisation of laws, is national law exclusively applicable?

(b) May a Hungarian company request transfer of its seat to another Member State of the European Union relying directly on Community law (Articles 43 [EC] and 48 [EC] [current Articles 49 and 54 TFEU])? If the answer is affirmative, may the transfer of the seat be made subject to any kind of condition or authorisation by the Member State of origin or the host Member State?

(c) May Articles 43 [EC] and 48 [EC] [current Articles 49 and 54 TFEU] be interpreted as meaning that national rules or national practices which differentiate between commercial companies with respect to the exercise of their rights, according to the Member State in which their seat is situated, are incompatible with Community law?

[(d)] May Articles 43 [EC] and 48 [EC] [current Articles 49 and 54 TFEU] be interpreted as meaning that, in accordance with those articles, national rules or practices which prevent a Hungarian company from transferring its seat to another Member State of the European Union are incompatible with Community law?

The CJEU resolved the above-mentioned question as follows:

C-210/06, CARTESIO Oktató és Szolgáltató bt., [2008] ECR I-09641, §§ 109–110, 114–115, 117, 119, Operative Part 4

As Community law now stands, Articles 43 EC and 48 EC [current Articles 49 and 54 TFEU] are to be interpreted as not precluding legislation of a Member State under which a company incorporated under the law of that Member State may not transfer its seat to another Member State whilst retaining its status as a company governed by the law of the Member State of incorporation.

In accordance with Article 48 EC [current Article 54 TFEU], in the absence of a uniform Community law definition of the companies which may enjoy the right of establishment on the basis of a single connecting factor determining the national law applicable to a company, the question whether Article 43 EC [current Article 49 TFEU] applies to a company which seeks to rely on the fundamental freedom enshrined in that article – like the question whether a natural person is a national of a Member State, and hence entitled to enjoy that freedom – is a preliminary matter which, as Community law now stands, can only be resolved by the applicable national law. In consequence, the question whether the company is faced with a restriction on the freedom of establishment, within the meaning of Article 43 EC [current Article 49 TFEU], can arise only if it has been established, in the light of the conditions laid down in Article 48 EC [current Article 54 TFEU], that the company actually has a right to that freedom.

Thus a Member State has the power to define both the connecting factor required of a company if it is to be regarded as incorporated under the law of that Member State and, as such, capable of enjoying the right of establishment, and that required if the company is to be able subsequently to maintain that status. That power includes the possibility for that Member State not to permit a company governed by its law to retain that status if the company intends to reorganise itself in another Member State by moving its seat to the territory of the latter, thereby breaking the connecting factor required under the national law of the Member State of incorporation.

Moreover, the legislation and agreements in the field of company law envisaged in Articles 44(2)(g) EC [current Article 50 TFEU] and 293 EC [abrogated by the Treaty of Lisbon] have not as yet addressed the differences between the legislation of the various Member States concerning the place of connection of the companies and thus have not yet brought an end to them. Although certain regulations, such as Regulation No 2137/85 on the European Economic Interest Grouping, Regulation No 2157/2001 on the Statute for a European company and Regulation No 1435/2003 on the Statute for a European Cooperative Society, adopted on the basis of Article 308 EC, in fact lay down a set of rules under which it is possible for the new legal entities which they establish to transfer their registered office (siège statutaire) and, accordingly, also their real seat (siège réel) – both of which must, in effect, be situated in the same Member State – to another Member State without it being compulsory to wind up the original legal person or to create a new legal person, such a transfer nevertheless necessarily entails a change as regards the national law applicable to the entity making such a transfer.

Where the company merely wishes to transfer its real seat from one Member State to another, while remaining a company governed by national law, hence without any change as to the national law applicable, the application mutatis mutandis of those regulations cannot in any event lead to the predicted result in such circumstances.

FURTHER READING

Veronika Korom and Peter Metzinger, 'Freedom of Establishment for Companies: The European Court of Justice Confirms and Refines its Daily Mail Decision in the Cartesio Case C-210/06', 6 *ECFR* 125–160 (2009).

Gert-Jan Vossestein, 'Cross-border Transfer of Seat and Conversion of Companies under the EC Treaty Provisions on Freedom of Establishment', 6 *ECL* 115–123 (2009).

Vittoria Petronella, 'The Cross-border Transfer of the Seat after Cartesio and the Non-portable Nationality of the Company', 21 *EBLR* 245–265 (2010).

Marek Szydło, 'The Right of Companies to Crossborder Conversion under the TFEU Rules on Freedom of Establishment', 7 *ECFR* 414–443 (2010).

5.7 *Vale* Case

In *Vale* (C-378/10, VALE Építési kft., [2012] ECR *on-line*), the reference has been made in proceedings concerning a cross-border conversion of a company governed by Italian law into a company governed by Hungarian law.

VALE Costruzioni Srl (a limited-liability company governed by Italian law) ('*VALE Costruzioni*'), established on 27 September 2000, was registered in the Rome (Italy) commercial register on 16 November 2000. On 3 February 2006, VALE Costruzioni asked to be removed from that register on the ground that it intended to transfer its seat and its business to Hungary, and to discontinue business in Italy. In accordance with that request, the authority responsible for the commercial register in Rome deleted the entry relating to VALE Costruzioni from the register on 13 February 2006. An entry was made in the register under the heading 'Removal and transfer of seat', stating that 'the company had moved to Hungary'.

Given that the company established originally in Italy under Italian law had decided to transfer its seat to Hungary and to operate there in accordance with Hungarian law, on 14 November 2006, the director of VALE Costruzioni and another natural person adopted, in Rome, the articles of association of VALE Építési kft. (a limited-liability company governed by Hungarian law) ('VALE Építési'), with a view to registration in the Hungarian commercial register.

Moreover, the share capital was paid up to the extent required under Hungarian law for registration.

On 19 January 2007, the representative of VALE Építési applied to the Fővárosi Bíróság (Budapest Metropolitan Court), acting as the Cégbíróság (Commercial Court), to register the company in accordance with Hungarian law. In the application, the representative stated that VALE Costruzioni was the predecessor-in-law to VALE Építési.

The Fővárosi Bíróság, acting as a commercial court at first instance, rejected the application for registration. VALE Építési lodged an appeal before the Fővárosi Ítélőtábla (Regional Court of Appeal of Budapest), which upheld the order rejecting the registration. According to that court, a company which was incorporated and registered in Italy cannot, by virtue of Hungarian company law, transfer its seat to Hungary and cannot obtain registration there in the form requested. According to that court, under the Hungarian law in force, the only particulars which can be shown in the commercial register are those listed in Paragraphs 24 to 29 of Law V of 2006 and, consequently, a company which is not Hungarian cannot be listed as a predecessor in law.

VALE Építési brought an appeal on a point of law before the Legfelsőbb Bíróság (Supreme Court), seeking the annulment of the order rejecting registration and an order that the company be entered in the commercial register. It submits that the contested order infringes Articles 49 TFEU and 54 TFEU, which are directly applicable.

The Legfelsőbb Bíróság decided to stay the proceedings and to refer the following questions to the Court of Justice for a preliminary ruling:

C-378/10, VALE Építési kft., [2012] ECR On-line, §§ 9–13

(1) Must the host Member State pay due regard to Articles [49 TFEU and 54 TFEU] when a company established in another Member State (the Member State of origin) transfers its seat to that host Member State and, at the same time and for this purpose, deletes the entry regarding it in the commercial register in the Member State of origin, and the company's owners adopt a new instrument of constitution under the laws of the host Member State, and the company applies for registration in the commercial register of the host Member State under the laws of the host Member State?

(2) If the answer to the first question is yes, must Articles [49 TFEU and 54 TFEU] be interpreted in such a case as meaning that they preclude legislation or practices of such a (host) Member State which prohibit a company established lawfully in any other Member State (the Member State of origin) from transferring its seat to the host Member State and continuing to operate under the laws of that State?

(3) With regard to the response to the second question, is the basis on which the host Member State prohibits the company from registration of any relevance, specifically:

- if, in its instrument of constitution adopted in the host Member State, the company designates as its predecessor the company established and deleted from the commercial register in the Member State of origin, and applies for the predecessor to be registered as its own predecessor in the commercial register of the host Member State?
- in the event of international conversion within the Community, when deciding on the company's application for registration, must the host Member State take into consideration the instrument recording the fact of the transfer of company seat in the commercial register of the Member State of origin, and, if so, to what extent?

(4) Is the host Member State entitled to decide on the application for company registration lodged in the host Member State by the company carrying out international conversion within the Community in accordance with the rules of company law of the host Member State as they relate to the conversion of domestic companies, and to require the company to fulfil all the conditions (e.g. drawing up lists of assets and liabilities and property inventories) laid down by the company law of the host Member State in respect of domestic conversion, or is the host Member State obliged under Articles [49 TFEU and 54 TFEU] to distinguish international conversion within the Community from domestic conversion and, if so, to what extent?

The CJEU decided the referred questions as follows:

C-378/10, VALE Építési kft., [2012] ECR On-line, § 41, Operative Part 1, § 62, Operative Part 2

Articles 49 TFEU and 54 TFEU must be interpreted as precluding national legislation which enables companies established under national law to convert, but does not allow, in a general manner, companies governed by the law of another Member State to convert to companies governed by national law by incorporating such a company.

Articles 49 TFEU and 54 TFEU must be interpreted, in the context of cross-border company conversions, as meaning that the host Member State is entitled to determine the national law applicable to such operations and thus to apply the provisions of its national law on the conversion of national companies governing the incorporation and functioning of companies, such as the requirements relating to the drawing-up of lists of assets and liabilities and property inventories. However, the principles of equivalence and effectiveness, respectively, preclude the host Member State from

- refusing, in relation to cross-border conversions, to record the company which has applied to convert as the 'predecessor in law', if such a record is made of the predecessor company in the commercial register for domestic conversions, and
- refusing to take due account, when examining a company's application for registration, of documents obtained from the authorities of the Member State of origin.

FURTHER READING

Gerco C. Van Eck and Erwin R. Roelofs, 'Vale: Increasing Corporate Mobility from Outbound to Inbound Cross-border Conversion?', 9 *ECL* 319–324 (2012).

Jesper Lau Hansen, 'The Vale Decision and the Court's Case Law on the Nationality of Companies', 10 *ECFR* 1–17 (2013).

Mathias Krarup, 'VALE: Determining the Need for Amended Regulation Regarding Free Movement of Companies within The EU', 24 *EBLR* 691–698 (2013).

5.8 *Kornhaas* Case (Preview)

In *Kornhaas* (C-594/14, *Simona Kornhaas* v. *Thomas Dithmar*, [2015], ECLI: EU:C:2015:806), the CJEU has dealt with the freedom of establishment in conjunction with issues of cross-border insolvency. They answered the question of whether a national provision allowing a liquidator to bring an action for reimbursement of payments which occurred prior to the declaration of bankruptcy *vis-à-vis* a director of a company registered in another Member State can be deemed to violate the freedom of establishment.

Since the understanding of the reasoning of the Court requires a preliminary study of the framework regulating cross-border insolvency situations at EU level, the case will be examined in Chapter 20.

5.9 *Polbud* Case

In *Polbud* (C106/16, *Polbud – Wykonawstwo sp. z o.o., in liquidation*, [ECLI:EU: C:2017:804]), the questions referred to the CJEU have been made in the context of an action brought by Polbud – Wykonawstwo sp. z o.o. ('Polbud') against the decision to refuse its request that it be removed from the Polish commercial register, made following the transfer of its registered office to Luxembourg.

Polbud is a limited company established in Łąck (Poland). By a resolution of 30 September 2011, an extraordinary general meeting of shareholders from the company decided, under Article 270, point 2, of the Kodeks sppłek handlowych, of 15 September 2000 ('the Companies Code'), to transfer the registered office of the company to Luxembourg. It is useful to know that such Article 270 Companies Code states that a company shall be wound up pursuant to a shareholders' resolution to wind up the company or to transfer the company's registered office abroad, that resolution being confirmed by minutes drawn up by a notary. Under Article 19(1) of the Ustawa – Prawo prywatne międzynarodowe (Law on Private International Law) of 4 February 2011, upon transfer of its head office to another State, a legal person shall be subject to the law of that State. The legal personality acquired in the State where it previously had its head office shall be retained, if the law of each of the States concerned so provides. Transfer of the head office within the European Economic Area shall not lead to the loss of legal personality. Despite this, Article 272 of the Companies Code requires that a company shall be wound up, after being liquidated, by being removed from the register.

On the basis of that resolution, on 19 October 2011, Polbud lodged a request that the opening of a liquidation procedure be recorded by the court responsible for keeping the commercial register ('the registry court'). On 26 October 2011, the opening of the liquidation procedure was recorded in that register and the liquidator was appointed.

On 28 May 2013, the meeting of shareholders of Consoil Geotechnik Sàrl, whose registered office is in Luxembourg, adopted a resolution which, *inter alia*, implemented the resolution of 30 September 2011 and transferred the registered office of Polbud to Luxembourg, with a view to the application of Luxembourg law to it, without loss of its legal personality. According to the resolution of 28 May 2013, the transfer was to take effect on that date. On 28 May 2013, therefore, Polbud's registered office was transferred to Luxembourg and that company was no longer named 'Polbud' but became 'Consoil Geotechnik'.

On 24 June 2013, Polbud lodged an application at the registry court for its removal from the Polish commercial register. The reason stated for that application was the transfer of the company's registered office to Luxembourg. For the purposes of the removal procedure, by decision of 21 August 2013, Polbud was asked to produce (i) the resolution of the general meeting of shareholders containing the indication of the name of the depositary of the books and documents of the undertaking being wound up, (ii) the financial accounts relating to the periods from 1 January to 29 September 2011, 30 September to 31 December 2011, 1 January to 31 December 2012, and 1 January to 28 May 2013, signed by the liquidator and by the person responsible for keeping the accounts, and (iii) the resolution of the general meeting of shareholders approving the report on the process of liquidation.

Polbud stated that it did not see any need to produce those documents since it was not being wound up, its assets had not been distributed to the shareholders, and the application for removal from the register had been lodged because of the transfer of the company's registered office to Luxembourg, where it was continuing its existence as a company incorporated under Luxembourg law. In those circumstances, by decision of 19 September 2013, the registry court refused the application for removal on the ground that the above-mentioned documents had not been submitted.

Polbud brought an action against that decision before the Sąd Rejonowy w Bydgoszczy (District Court of Bydgoszcz, Poland), which dismissed the action. The company brought an appeal against that dismissal before the Sąd Okręgowy w Bydgoszczy (Regional Court of Bydgoszcz, Poland), which dismissed the appeal by order of 4 June 2014. Polbud then brought an appeal on a point of law before the referring court.

Before that court, Polbud claims that, when its registered office was transferred to Luxembourg, it had lost its status as a company incorporated under Polish law and had become a company incorporated under Luxembourg law. Consequently, according to Polbud, the liquidation procedure should have been closed and its name should have been removed from the commercial register in Poland. In addition, Polbud states that compliance with the requirements of the liquidation procedure laid down under Polish law was neither necessary nor possible, since it had not lost its legal personality.

In those circumstances, the Sąd Najwyższy (Supreme Court, Poland) decided to stay the proceedings and to refer the following questions to the Court for a preliminary ruling:

C-106/16, *Polbud - Wykonawstwo sp. z o.o., in liquidation*, [ECLI:EU:C:2017:804], § 18

'(1) Do Articles 49 and 54 TFEU preclude the application, by the Member State in which a (private limited liability) company was initially incorporated, of provisions of national law which make removal from the commercial register conditional on that company being wound up after liquidation has been carried out, if that company has been reincorporated in another Member State pursuant to a shareholders' decision to continue the legal personality acquired in the State of initial incorporation?

If the answer to that question is in the negative:

(2) Can Articles 49 and 54 TFEU be interpreted as meaning that the requirement under national law that a process of liquidation of a company be carried out - including the conclusion of current business, recovery of debts, performance of obligations and sale of company assets, satisfaction or securing of creditors, submission of a financial statement on the conduct of that process, and indication of the person to whom the books and documents are to be entrusted - which precedes the winding-up of the company, that occurs on removal from the commercial register, is a measure which is appropriate, necessary and proportionate to a public interest deserving of protection that consists in the safeguarding of the interests of creditors, minority shareholders, and employees of the migrant company?

(3) Must Articles 49 and 54 TFEU be interpreted as meaning that restrictions on freedom of establishment cover a situation in which - for the purpose of its conversion to a company of another Member State - a company transfers its registered office to that other Member State without changing its main head office, which remains in the State of initial incorporation?'

The CJEU decided first to resolve the issues arising from the third question – i.e., as to whether the transfer of the registered office of a company to another Member State without changing the main head office, which remains in the State of initial incorporation, shall be considered an expression of freedom of establishment under Articles 49 and 54 TFEU. Whilst the Polish government, supported by the Austrian government and the Advocate General J. Kokott, maintained that Articles 49 and 54 TFEU are not applicable to such a company transfer, to the contrary, the Court holds the following:

C-106/16, *Polbud - Wykonawstwo sp. z o.o., in liquidation*, [ECLI:EU:C:2017:804], §§ 26, 35, 38, 41, Operative Part 1

The third question

26 At the outset, it must be observed that the questions referred for a preliminary ruling are based on the premise, which Polbud disputes, that Polbud did not intend to transfer its real head office to Luxembourg.

35 [Notwithstanding this point] freedom of establishment confers on Polbud, a company incorporated under Polish law, the right to convert itself into a company incorporated under Luxembourg law, provided that the conditions laid down by Luxembourg legislation are satisfied and, in particular, that the test adopted by Luxembourg to determine the connection of a company or firm to its national legal order is satisfied.

38 The Court has held that freedom of establishment extends to a situation in which a company formed in accordance with the legislation of one Member State, where it has its registered office, wants to set up a branch in another Member State, even where that company was formed, in the first Member State, solely for the purpose of establishing itself in the second, where its main, or indeed entire, business is to be conducted (see, to that effect, judgment of 9 March 1999, Centros, C-212/97, EU:C:1999:126, paragraph 17). Equally, a situation in which a company formed in accordance with the legislation of one Member State wants to convert itself into a company under the law of another Member State, with due regard to the test applied by the second Member State in order to determine the connection of a company to its national legal order, falls within the scope of freedom of establishment, even though that company conducts its main, if not entire, business in the first Member State.

41 It follows that, in the main proceedings, the fact that it was decided to transfer to Luxembourg the registered office alone of Polbud, that transfer not affecting the real head office of that company, cannot, in itself, mean that such a transfer does not fall within the scope of Articles 49 and 54 TFEU.

Operative Part 1. Articles 49 and 54 TFEU must be interpreted as meaning that freedom of establishment is applicable to the transfer of the registered office of a company formed in accordance with the law of one Member State to the territory of another Member State, for the purposes of its conversion, in accordance with the conditions imposed by the legislation of the other Member State, into a company incorporated under the law of the latter Member State, when there is no change in the location of the real head office of that company.

Having clarified the answer to the third question, the CJEU addressed the remaining questions as follows:

C 106/16, Polbud – *Wykonawstwo sp. z o.o., in liquidation*, [ECLI:EU:C:2017:804], §§ 63, 64, Operative Part 2

63 [...] the mere fact that a company transfers its registered office from one Member State to another cannot be the basis for a general presumption of fraud and cannot justify a measure that adversely affects the exercise of a fundamental freedom guaranteed by the Treaty (see, by analogy, judgment of 29 November 2011, National Grid Indus, C-371/10, EU:C:2011:785, paragraph 84).

64 Since a general obligation to implement a liquidation procedure amounts to establishing a general presumption of the existence of abuse, the Court must hold that legislation, such as that at issue in the main proceedings, which imposes such an obligation, is disproportionate.

Operative Part 2 Articles 49 and 54 TFEU must be interpreted as precluding legislation of a Member State which provides that the transfer of the registered office of a company incorporated under the law of one Member State to the territory of another Member State, for the purposes of its conversion into a company incorporated under the law of the latter Member State, in accordance with the conditions imposed by the legislation of that Member State, is subject to the liquidation of the first company.

Discussion on the effects of *Polbud* will be covered in Chapter 7.

FURTHER READING

Hana Horak and Kosjenka Dumancic, 'Cross-Border Transfer of the Company Seat: One Step Forward, Few Steps Backward', 14 *US-China L. Rev.* 711–728 (2017).

Nicola de Luca, Andrea Gentile and Fabio Schiavottiello, 'Transfer of the registered office and Delaware effect. The Polbud case', 45 *Giurisprudenza commerciale*, II, 454–462 (2018).

Gitte Soegaard and Erik Werlauff, 'Cross-border Transfer and Change of Lex Societatis After Polbud, C-106/16: Old Companies Do Not Die ... They Simply Fade Away to Another Country', 15 *ECL* 21–24 (2018).

Ariel Mucha and Krzysztof Oplustil, 'Redefining the Freedom of Establishment under EU Law as the Freedom to Choose the Applicable Company Law: A Discussion after the Judgment of the Court of Justice (Grand Chamber) of 25 October 2017 in Case C-106/16, Polbud', 15 *ECFR* 270–307 (2018).

Aleksandrs Fillers, 'Free Movement of Companies After the *Polbud* Case', 21 *EBOR* 571–590 (2020) https://doi.org/10.1007/s40804-020-00178-9.

5.10 Summary

The case review permits a summary of the EU *acquis* on the right of primary establishment, as follows:

Companies are creatures of the law, and more specifically (apart from the EEIG, the SE and the SCE) creatures of national law, existing only by virtue of the varying national legislation, which determines their incorporation and functioning (*see*, C-81/87, *Daily Mail*, § 19).

The Treaty places on the same footing, as connecting factors, the registered office, central administration and principal place of business of a company (*see*, C-81/87, *Daily Mail*, § 21). Therefore, EU Law confers no right on a company incorporated under the legislation of a Member State and having its registered office there to transfer its central management and control to another Member State (*see*, C-81/87, *Daily Mail*, Operative Part 1).

Despite a Member State permitting a company to move its registered office and/or the central management and control (the real seat) to another Member State, this is not sufficient grounds to claim that the company retains its status as a company governed by the law of the Member State of incorporation, hence without any change as to the national law applicable (*see*, C-210/06, *Cartesio*, Operative Part 4). However, freedom of establishment encompasses the transfer of the registered office of a company for the purpose of its conversion in accordance with the laws of the destination Member State, with the possibility that the originating State requires the dissolution and liquidation of the company based on the grounds that there is no change in the location of the real head office of the company (*see*, C-106/2016, *Polbud*, Operative Part 1).

Conversely, the Member State of destination may not refuse to register the company seeking to move the registered office and/or the central management and control (the real seat), if this is permitted by the law of the State of incorporation. Therefore:

(a) in cases where the Member State of origin does not permit the moving company to retain its status as a company governed by the law of the Member State of incorporation, the Member State of destination must allow a cross-border conversion (or a cross-border merger), provided that the moving company complies with all requirements set out by the applicable provisions of its national law on the conversion (or merger) of national companies (other than that of being already formed under a model provided by the national law of the Member State of destination) (*see*, C-378/10, *Vale*, operative part 2; *see also*, C-411/03, *Sevic*, operative part);

(b) in cases where the Member State of origin does permit a company to move the real seat and/or the registered office whilst retaining its status as a company governed by the law of the Member State of incorporation, the Member State of destination may not deny the company (rather, must recognise) legal capacity and, consequently, the capacity to bring legal proceedings before its national courts (*see*, C-208/00, *Überseering*, § 52, operative part 1).

6

Secondary Establishment in CJEU Case Law

6.1 General

As already mentioned (*see*, Chapter 1, § 1.2) the freedom of establishment shall also include the right for companies to set-up agencies, branches or subsidiaries as this is permitted by nationals of any Member State established in the territory of any other Member State (Article 49 TFEU). It is commonly understood that this provision grants a *right of secondary establishment*.

As for the primary establishment, interpretation of Article 49(1) TFEU has also involved the CJEU in several cases of secondary establishment, which we are about to discuss. After the case study, it will be possible to state the EU *acquis* on the matter.

FURTHER READING

Erik Werlauff, 'Common European Company Law Status 1998 Part II: The Background to Harmonisation, Disclosure, Capital, etc.', 9 *EBLR* 210–216 (1998).

Helen Xanthaki, 'The Secondary Establishment of Companies within the EU: Challenge or Missed Opportunity?', 10 *EBLR* 120–139 (1999).

Luca Enriques, 'EC Company Law and the Fears of a European Delaware', 15 *EBLR* 1259–1274 (2004).

Christian Kirchner, Richard W. Painter, and Wulf A. Kaal, 'Regulatory Competition in EU Corporate Law after Inspire Art: Unbundling Delaware's Product for Europe', 2 *ECFR* 159–206 (2005).

Ulrich Klinke, 'European Company Law and the ECJ: The Court's Judgements in the Years 2001 to 2004', 2 *ECFR* 270–321 (2005).

6.2 *Segers* Case

In *Segers* (C-79/85, *D. H. M. Segers* v. *Bestuur van de Bedrijfsvereniging voor Banken Verzekeringswezen, Groothandel en Vrije Beroepen*, [1986] ECR I-*02375*) the questions were raised in connection with an action brought by Mr Segers, a Dutch national and the director of a company incorporated under English law, against the refusal of the Dutch authorities, specifically the Bedrijfsvereniging voor banken verzekeringswezen, groothandel en vrije beroepen (banking, insurance, wholesale trade, and professions' association, hereafter referred to as 'the Association') to accord him sickness insurance benefits under the Ziektewet (Dutch law establishing a general sickness insurance scheme).

In April 1981, the private limited-liability company Slenderose Ltd, whose registered office is in London, was formed in accordance with English law. In June 1981, Mr Segers and his wife took over that company, each holding an equal number of shares. In July 1981, Mr Segers incorporated into Slenderose Ltd as a subsidiary of that company his one-man business, Free Promotion International, whose registered office was in the Netherlands. At the same time, he became a director of Slenderose. In practice all of Slenderose's business was then conducted by its subsidiary and solely in the Netherlands.

In July 1981, in order to obtain sickness insurance benefits, Mr Segers registered as sick with the Association. That body refused to grant him such benefits on the grounds that he had no employment contract with Slenderose and that consequently he was not subordinate to an employer. The Ziektewet provides, *inter alia*, that any person who is in a subordinate position in relation to another person, an employer, is insured.

Following the rejection by the Court of First Instance of his action against that decision, Mr Segers appealed to the Centrale Raad van Beroep. That court referred to its own decisions according to which the director of a company who himself holds 50 per cent or more of the shares of that company must be deemed to work for that company in a position subordinate to it. The Association, however, contended before the national court that that case law should apply only to directors of companies whose registered office was in the Netherlands and not to a company incorporated under foreign law.

The Centrale Raad van Beroep took the view that the Association's argument had some force and that an interpretation of Community law was required. It therefore stayed the proceedings and referred the following questions to the court of justice for a preliminary ruling.

C-79/85, D. H. M. Segers v. Bestuur van de Bedrijfsvereniging voor Banken Verzekeringswezen, Groothandel en Vrije Beroepen, [1986] ECR I-02375, §§ 3–6

(1) Do the principles of freedom of establishment within the EEC and freedom to provide services within the EEC – in particular the last sentence of article 52 read with article 58 of the EEC treaty [current Articles 49 and 54 TFEU] and the last sentence of article 60 read with article 66 of that treaty [current Articles 57 and 62 TFEU] – mean that, when deciding whether there is an insurance obligation under the Netherlands social security legislation, Netherlands courts may not make any distinction between the director/major shareholder of a private company incorporated under Netherlands law and a

director/major shareholder of a private company incorporated under the laws of another member state, even if the foreign company clearly does not carry out any actual business in the other member state concerned but carries on business only in the Netherlands?

(2) If that question must be answered in the negative, does community social security law (in particular, Article 3(1) of Regulation no 1408/71) or any other provision of community law prohibit such a distinction?

The CJEU resolved the above-mentioned questions as follows:

C-79/85, D. H. M. Segers v. Bestuur van de Bedrijfsvereniging voor Banken Verzekeringswezen, Groothandel en Vrije Beroepen, [1986] ECR I-02375, § 19

Where a company has exercised its right of freedom of establishment, articles 52 and 58 of the EEC treaty [current Articles 49 and 54 TFEU] must be interpreted as prohibiting the authorities of a member state from excluding the company's director from a national sickness insurance benefit scheme solely on the ground that the company was formed in accordance with the law of another member state, where it also has its registered office but does not conduct any business.

6.3 *Centros* Case

In *Centros* (C-212/97, *Centros Ltd* v. *Erhvervs- og Selskabsstyrelsen*, [1999] ECR I-01459), the question referred to the CJEU was raised in proceedings between Centros Ltd, a private limited company set up by Mr and Mrs Bryde (Danish nationals residing in Denmark) and registered on 18 May 1992 in England and Wales, and Erhvervs- og Selskabsstyrelsen (the Trade and Companies Board, '*the Board*') which comes under the Danish Department of Trade, concerning that authority's refusal to register a branch of Centros in Denmark.

Since the law of England and Wales imposes no requirement on limited-liability companies as to the provision for and the paying-up of a minimum share capital, Centros' share capital, which amounted to GBP 100, had been neither paid up nor made available to the company. The capital was divided into two shares held by Mr and Mrs Bryde. Mrs Bryde is the director of Centros, whose registered office is situated in the United Kingdom, at the home of a friend of Mr Bryde.

During the summer of 1992, Mrs Bryde requested the Board to register a branch of Centros in Denmark. The Board refused that registration on the grounds, *inter alia*, that Centros, which does not trade in the UK, was in fact seeking to establish in Denmark, not a branch, but a principal establishment, by circumventing the national rules concerning, in particular, the paying-up of minimum capital fixed at DKK 200,000 by Law No 886 of 21 December 1991.

Centros brought an action before the Østre Landsret against the refusal of the Board to effect that registration.

The Østre Landsret upheld the arguments of the Board in a judgment of 8 September 1995, whereupon Centros appealed to the Højesteret.

The Højesteret decided to stay proceedings and to refer a question to the Court for a preliminary ruling. As the CJEU puts it,

C-212/97, Centros Ltd v. Erhvervs- og Selskabsstyrelsen, [1999] ECR I-01459, § 14

by its question, the national court is in substance asking whether it is contrary to Articles 52 and 58 of the Treaty [current Articles 49 and 54 TFEU] for a Member State to refuse to register a branch of a company formed in accordance with the legislation of another Member State in which it has its registered office but where it does not carry on any business when the purpose of the branch is to enable the company concerned to carry on its entire business in the State in which that branch is to be set up, while avoiding the formation of a company in that State, thus evading application of the rules governing the formation of companies which are, in that State, more restrictive so far as minimum paid-up share capital is concerned.

The CJEU decided the referred question as follows:

C-212/97, Centros Ltd v. Erhvervs- og Selskabsstyrelsen, [1999] ECR I-01459, § 39, Operative Part

It is contrary to Articles 52 and 58 of the Treaty [current Articles 49 and 54 TFEU] for a Member State to refuse to register a branch of a company formed in accordance with the law of another Member State in which it has its registered office but in which it conducts no business where the branch is intended to enable the company in question to carry on its entire business in the State in which that branch is to be created, while avoiding the need to form a company there, thus evading application of the rules governing the formation of companies which, in that State, are more restrictive as regards the paying up of a minimum share capital. Given that the right to form a company in accordance with the law of a Member State and to set up branches in other Member States is inherent in the exercise, in a single market, of the freedom of establishment guaranteed by the Treaty, the fact that a national of a Member State who wishes to set up a company chooses to form it in the Member State whose rules of company law seem to him the least restrictive and to set up branches in other Member States cannot, in itself, constitute an abuse of the right of establishment.

That interpretation does not, however, prevent the authorities of the Member State concerned from adopting any appropriate measure for preventing or penalising fraud, either in relation to the company itself, if need be in cooperation with the Member State in which it was formed, or in relation to its members, where it has been established that they are in fact attempting, by means of the formation of a company, to evade their obligations towards private or public creditors established in the territory of the Member State concerned.

FURTHER READING

Erik Werlauff, 'Using a Foreign Company for Domestic Activities', 10 *EBLR* 306–313 (1999).

Janeen Carruthers and Charlotte Villiers, 'Company Law in Europe – Condoning the Continental Drift?', 11 *EBLR* 91–101 (2000).

Erik Werlauff, 'The Main Seat Criterion in a New Disguise', 12 *EBLR* 2–6 (2001).

Marc Lauterfeld, '"Centros" and the EC Regulation', 12 *EBLR* 79–88 (2001).

Catherin Holst, 'European Company Law after Centros: Is the EU on the Road to Delaware?', 8 *Colum. J. Eur. L.* 323–341 (2002).

Erik Werlauff, 'A "Copenhagen Effect"? Denmark's Answer to Centros: A Far-reaching Company Law Reform Aimed at Strengthening the "Free Movement of Companies"', 6 *ECL* 160–168 (2009).

Horst Eidenmüller, Luca Enriques, Geneviève Helleringer, and Kristin van Zwieten, 'Centros at 20: Regulatory Arbitrage and Beyond – An Introduction', 20 *EBOR* 399–405 (2019).

Anne-Lise Sibony, 'Centros and the Internal Market', 20 *EBOR* 407–424 (2019).

Carsten Gerner-Beuerle, Federico Mucciarelli, Edmund Schuster, and Mathias Siems, 'The Illusion of Motion: Corporate (Im)Mobility and the Failed Promise of Centros', 20 *EBOR* 425–465 (2019).

Martin Gelter, 'Centros and Defensive Regulatory Competition: Some Thoughts and a Glimpse at the Data', 20 *EBOR* 467–492 (2019).

See also:

Marco Ventoruzzo, Pierre-Henry Conac, Gen Goto, Sebastan Mock, Mario Notari, and Arad Reisberg, *Comparative Corporate Governance 65–74* (St Paul MN, West Academic Publishing, 2015).

6.4 *Inspire Art* Case

In *Inspire Art* (C-167/01, *Kamer van Koophandel en Fabrieken voor Amsterdam* v. *Inspire Art Ltd*, [2003] ECR I-10155), the questions referred to the CJEU were raised in proceedings between the Kamer van Koophandel en Fabrieken voor Amsterdam (Amsterdam Chamber of Commerce and Industry), Netherlands (the '*Chamber of Commerce*') and Inspire Art Ltd, a company governed by the law of England and Wales ('*Inspire Art*'), concerning the obligation imposed on Inspire Art's branch in the Netherlands to record, with its registration in the Dutch commercial register, its description as a formeel buitenlandse vennootschap (formally foreign company) and to use that description in its business dealings, such obligations being imposed by the

Wet op de Formeel Buitenlandse Vennootschappen (Law on Formally Foreign Companies, hereafter WFBV) of 17 December 1997.

Inspire Art was formed on 28 July 2000 in the legal form of a private company limited by shares under the law of England and Wales and it had its registered office at Folkestone (United Kingdom). Its sole director, whose domicile was in The Hague (Netherlands), was authorised to act alone and independently in the name of the company. The company, which carries on activity under the business name Inspire Art Ltd in the sphere of dealing in objets d'art, began trading on 17 August 2000 and had a branch in Amsterdam.

Inspire Art was registered in the commercial register of the Chamber of Commerce without any indication of the fact that it might be considered a formally foreign company within the meaning of Article 1 of the WFBV.

Taking the view that that indication was mandatory on the ground that Inspire Art traded exclusively in the Netherlands, the Chamber of Commerce applied to the Kantongerecht te Amsterdam on 30 October 2000 for an order that there should be added to that company's registration in the commercial register the statement that it is a formally foreign company, in accordance with Article 1 of the WFBV, which would entail other obligations laid down by law.

In its order of 5 February 2001, the Kantongerecht held that Inspire Art was a formally foreign company within the meaning of Article 1 of the WFBV. As regards the compatibility of the WFBV with Community law, it decided to stay proceedings and refer the following questions to the Court of Justice for a preliminary ruling:

C-167/01, Kamer van Koophandel en Fabrieken voor Amsterdam v. Inspire Art Ltd, [2003] ECR I-10155, §§ 34–36, 38–39

1. Are Articles 43 EC and 48 EC [current Articles 49 and 54 TFEU] to be interpreted as precluding the Netherlands, pursuant to the Wet op de formeel buitenlandse vennootschappen of 17 December 1997, from attaching additional conditions, such as those laid down in Articles 2 to 5 of that law, to the establishment in the Netherlands of a branch of a company which has been set up in the United Kingdom with the sole aim of securing the advantages which that offers compared to incorporation under Netherlands law, given that Netherlands law imposes stricter rules than those applying in the United Kingdom with regard to the setting-up of companies and payment for shares, and given that the Netherlands law infers that aim from the fact that the company carries on its activities entirely or almost entirely in the Netherlands and, furthermore, does not have any real connection with the State in which the law under which it was formed applies?
2. If, on a proper construction of those articles, it is held that the provisions of the Wet op de formeel buitenlandse vennootschappen are incompatible with them, must Article 46 EC [current Article 52 TFEU] be interpreted as meaning that the said Articles 43 EC and 48 EC [current Articles 49 and 54 TFEU] do not affect the applicability of the Netherlands rules laid down in that law, on the ground that the provisions in question are justified for the reasons stated by the Netherlands legislature?

The CJEU decided the referred questions as follows:

C-167/01, Kamer van Koophandel en Fabrieken voor Amsterdam v. Inspire Art Ltd, [2003] ECR I-10155, § 62, §§ 65, 69–70, 72, 143, Operative Part 1, §§ 105, 136–139, 143, Operative Part 2

Where a Community regulation does not specifically provide any penalty for an infringement or refers for that purpose to national laws, regulations and administrative provisions, Article 10 EC [current Article 4(3) TEU] requires the Member States to take all measures necessary to guarantee the application and effectiveness of Community law. For that purpose, while the choice of penalties remains within their discretion, the Member States must ensure in particular that infringements of Community law are penalised in conditions, both procedural and substantive, which are analogous to those applicable to infringements of national law of a similar nature and importance and which, in any event, make the penalty effective, proportionate and dissuasive.

It is contrary to Article 2 of the Eleventh Directive 89/666 concerning disclosure requirements in respect of branches opened in a Member State by certain types of company governed by the law of another State, which contains a list of the information which must be disclosed in the Member State in which the branch is established and a list of optional measures imposing disclosure requirements, for national legislation to impose on the branch of a company formed in accordance with the laws of another Member State disclosure obligations not provided for by that directive, such as recording in the commercial register the fact that the company is formally foreign, recording in the business register of the host Member State the date of first registration in the foreign business register and information relating to sole members, the compulsory filing of an auditor's certificate to the effect that the company satisfies the conditions as to minimum capital, subscribed capital and paid-up share capital or mention of the company's status of a formally foreign company on all documents it produces. Without affecting the information obligations imposed on branches under social or tax law, or in the field of statistics, harmonisation of the disclosure to be made by branches, as brought about by the Eleventh Directive, is exhausted.

It is contrary to Articles 43 EC and 48 EC [current Articles 49 and 54 TFEU] for national legislation to impose on the exercise of freedom of secondary establishment in that State by a company formed in accordance with the law of another Member State certain conditions provided for in domestic law in respect of company formation relating to minimum capital and directors' liability. The reasons for which the company was formed in that other Member State, and the fact that it carries on its activities exclusively or almost exclusively in the Member State of establishment, do not deprive it of the right to invoke the freedom of establishment guaranteed by the Treaty, save where the existence of an abuse is established on a case-by-case basis. A Member State is certainly entitled to take measures designed to prevent certain of its nationals from attempting, under cover of the rights created by the Treaty, improperly to circumvent their national legislation or to prevent individuals from improperly or fraudulently taking advantage of provisions of Community law. However, the provisions of the Treaty on freedom of establishment are intended specifically to enable companies formed in accordance with the law of a Member State and having their registered office, central administration or principal place of business within the Community to pursue activities in other Member States through an agency, branch or subsidiary. That being so, the fact that a national of a Member State who wishes to set up a company can choose to do so in the Member State the company-law rules of which seem to him the least restrictive and then set up branches in other Member States is inherent in the exercise, in a single market, of the freedom of establishment guaranteed by the Treaty. In addition, the fact that a company does not conduct any business in the Member State in which it has its registered office and pursues its activities only or principally in the Member State where its branch is established is not sufficient to prove the existence of abuse or fraudulent conduct which would entitle the latter Member State to deny that company the benefit of the provisions of Community law relating to the right of establishment.

FURTHER READING

Frank Wooldridge, 'The Advocate General's Submissions in Kamer van Koophandel: Further Emphasis on the Right of Establishment', 14 *EBLR* 497–505 (2003).

Harm-Jan de Kluiver, 'Inspiring a New European Company Law? – Observations on the ECJ's Decision in Inspire Art from a Dutch Perspective and the Imminent Competition for Corporate Charters between EC Member States', 1 *ECFR* 121–134 (2004).

Hans C. Hirt, 'Freedom of Establishment, International Company Law and the Comparison of European Company Law Systems after the ECJ's Decision in Inspire Art Ltd', 15 *EBLR* 1189–1222 (2004).

6.5 Summary

The case review permits a summary of the EU *acquis* on the right of secondary establishment, as follows:

The right of secondary establishment, consisting in that of setting-up agencies, branches or subsidiaries, includes the right to register a branch of a company formed in accordance with the law of another Member State in which it has its registered office but in which it conducts no business. In that regard, it is immaterial that the company was formed in the first Member State only for the purpose of establishing itself in the second, where its main, or indeed entire, business is to be conducted (*see*, C-79/85, *Segers*, § 16; C-212/97, *Centros*, §§ 17, 39 and operative part). Similarly, the right of secondary establishment prohibits the authorities of a Member State to treat disparately members or directors of a company incorporated under the laws of a different Member State, where it also has its registered office but does not conduct any business, solely on the ground that the company was formed in accordance with the law of another Member State (*see*, C-79/85, *Segers*, § 19).

Notwithstanding the above, Member States may adopt any appropriate measure for preventing or penalising fraud, either in relation to the company itself or in relation to its members, where it has been established that they are in fact attempting, by means of the formation of a company, to evade their obligations towards private or public creditors established in the territory of the Member State concerned (*see*, C-212/97, *Centros*, § 39, operative part).

According to a long established principle – the so-called Gebhard test – the national measures liable to hinder or make less attractive the exercise of fundamental freedoms guaranteed by the Treaty must fulfil four conditions:

(i) they must be applied in a non-discriminatory manner;
(ii) they must be justified by imperative requirements in the general interest;
(iii) they must be suitable for securing the attainment of the objective which they pursue; and
(iv) they must not go beyond what is necessary in order to attain it (*see* C-19/92 *Kraus* v. *Land Baden-Württemberg* [1993] ECR I-1663, § 32; C-55/94 *Gebhard* v. *Consiglio dell'Ordine degli Avvocati e Procuratori di Milano* [1995] ECR I-4165, § 37; C-212/97, *Centros*, § 34; C-167/01, *Inspire Art*, § 133).

However, this is not the case where EU nationals of a Member State decide to form a company in another Member State with the aim of evading application of more restrictive rules as regards the paying-up of a minimum share capital (*see*, C-212/97, *Centros*, § 39, operative part; C-167/01, *Inspire Art*, §§ 105, 136–139, 143, operative part 2).

Furthermore, it is contrary to Article 2 of the Eleventh Directive for national legislation to impose on the branch of a company formed in accordance with the laws of another Member State disclosure obligations not provided for by that directive, such as recording in the commercial register the fact that the company is formally foreign, recording in the business register of the host Member State the date of first registration in the foreign business register and information relating to sole members, the compulsory filing of an auditor's certificate to the effect that the company satisfies the conditions as to minimum capital, subscribed capital, and paid-up share capital or mention of the company's status of a formally foreign company on all documents it produces (*see*, C-167/01, *Inspire Art*, §§ 65, 69–70, 72, 143, operative part 1).

7

Cross-Border Mobility: From Case Law to Statutory Law

7.1 Cross-Border Transfer of Seat and Cross-Border Operations: An Overview

During the formation of the *acquis* on the freedom of establishment, the European Commission promoted discussion (*see*, § 7.3) of the adoption of legislative tools able to enhance cross-border mobility for companies and firms, in particular by permitting a company to transfer the seat with a view to changing the applicable company law (*lex societatis*), without going into liquidation.

This goal has been achieved, in the first instance, for EEIGs (in 1985), SEs (in 2001), and SCEs (in 2003): indeed, for all these legal entities formed under EU Regulations, the transfer of seat to a Member State other than that of incorporation entails the change of applicable (national) law, without requiring any winding-up or dissolution. However, the limited use of these legal forms required further efforts to foster cross-border mobility of companies and firms, especially for those which are incorporated under national law.

This process has taken a long time. In 2005, soon after the CJEU had already declared the validity of a cross-border merger in *Sevic*, based on the same provisions of the TFEU granting freedom of establishment for companies and firms, a Tenth Company Law Directive – Tenth Company Law Directive 2005/56/EC, *on cross-border mergers of limited liability companies*, now replaced by Directive 2017/1132/EU (Chapter 2, § 2.5) – entered into force. Similarly to the US system – where companies may reincorporate in another State by way of a (reverse) cross-border merger into an entirely owned NewCo (often, a Delaware company) – this directive provided for a useful workaround permitting a change of nationality, hence of *lex societatis*, for EU companies. Important cross-border operations, such as the Fiat–Chrysler merger in 2014, took advantage of this legal framework.

Notwithstanding that the EU Commission has, for some time, promoted the adoption of a Fourteenth Directive on the cross-border tranfer of the registered office – which resulted, *inter alia*, in consultations carried out in 2013 – all attempts to pass such a directive were unsuccessful. Conversely, soon after the CJEU had declared the validity of a cross-border conversion in *Polbud*, based on the same provisions of the TFEU granting freedom of establishment for companies and firms, an agreement was easily found not only for a modernisation of the Tenth Directive, on cross-border mergers, but also for other cross-border operations, which were not yet covered by EU directives, such as division and conversion.

On 27 November 2019, the European Parliament and the Council adopted Directive 2019/2121/EU amending Directive 2017/1132/EU as regards *cross-border conversions, mergers and divisions* (henceforth, the Cross-Border Operations Directive). Interesting thoughts on the reasons for a new directive are expressed in the first recitals.

Recitals 1–5 Directive 2019/2121/EU (Cross-Border Operations Directive)

(...) The rules on cross-border mergers represent a significant milestone in improving the functioning of the internal market for companies and firms and their exercise of the freedom of establishment. However, evaluation of those rules shows that they need to be changed. Furthermore, it is appropriate to provide for rules regulating cross-border conversions and divisions, since Directive (EU) 2017/1132 only provides for rules on domestic divisions of public limited liability companies.

Freedom of establishment is one of the fundamental principles of Union law. Under the second paragraph of Article 49 of the Treaty on the Functioning of the European Union ('TFEU'), when read in conjunction with Article 54 of the TFEU, the freedom of establishment for companies or firms includes, inter alia, the right to form and manage such companies or firms under the conditions laid down by the legislation of the Member State of establishment. This has been interpreted by the Court of Justice of the European Union as encompassing the right of a company or firm formed in accordance with the legislation of a Member State to convert itself into a company or firm governed by the law of another Member State, provided that the conditions laid down by the legislation of that other Member State are satisfied and, in particular, that the test adopted by the latter Member State to determine the connection of a company or firm with its national legal order is satisfied.

In the absence of harmonisation of Union law, defining the connecting factor that determines the national law applicable to a company or firm falls, in accordance with Article 54 of the TFEU, within the competence of each Member State. Article 54 of the TFEU places the connecting factors of the registered office, the central administration and the principal place of business of a company or firm on an equal footing. Therefore, as clarified in case-law, the fact that only the registered office, and not the central administration or principal place of business, is transferred does not as such exclude the applicability of the freedom of establishment under Article 49 of the TFEU.

Developments in the case-law have opened up new opportunities for companies in the internal market to foster economic growth, effective competition and productivity. At the same time, the objective of an internal market without internal borders for companies has also to be reconciled with other objectives of European integration, such as social protection as set out in Article 3 of the Treaty on European Union (TEU) and Article 9 of the TFEU, as well as the promotion of social dialogue as set out in Articles 151 and 152 of the TFEU. The rights of companies to convert, merge and divide across borders should go hand in hand, and be properly balanced, with the protection of employees, creditors and members.

The lack of a legal framework for cross-border conversions and divisions leads to legal fragmentation and legal uncertainty, and thus to barriers to the exercise of the freedom of establishment. It also leads to the suboptimal protection of employees, creditors and minority members within the internal market.

This chapter describes the process of transfer of the seat for EEIGs, SEs, and SCEs, before outlining the cross-border conversion, which is also discussed in Chapter 19 in relation to the rules on domestic mergers and divisions.

7.2 The Cross-Border Transfer of the Seat for EEIG, SE, and SCE

Council Regulation 2137/85 *on the European Economic Interest Grouping* (EEIG), Council Regulation 2157/2001 *on the Statute for a European Company* (SE), and Council Regulation 1435/2003 *on the Statute for a European Cooperative Society* (SCE) broach the subject of the cross-border transfer of the seat for, respectively, EEIG, SE, and SCE.

Given that these procedures are quite similar to one another, it is useful to begin with a description of the SE procedure to identify the differences between all three regulations. First of all, Council Regulation 2157/2001 on the Statute for a European Company (SE), while guaranteeing the transfer of the seat without the winding-up of the SE or the creation of a new legal entity, clarifies that both the SE's registered office and its head office ought to be in the same Member State.

This particular cross-border operation could not take place if proceedings for winding-up, liquidation, insolvency, or suspension of payments had begun against the company willing to move. In addition, Article 8 of Regulation 2001/2157/CE goes through all the steps, mentioned below, that ought to be made to transfer the seat. The management or administrative organ prepares both a draft transfer proposal and a report explaining the legal and economic aspects and implications. Noteworthy is the attention towards shareholders and creditors. As a matter of fact, not only could they examine and obtain copies of the mentioned documentation, but also the respect of their rights and interests is verified by the competent authority.

A further certificate attesting the compliance of the whole operation precedes the registration of the SE in the new registry, its contextual entry into force, and the subsequent subjection of the SE to the national laws of the host Member State. The deletion of the old registration closes the entire procedure.

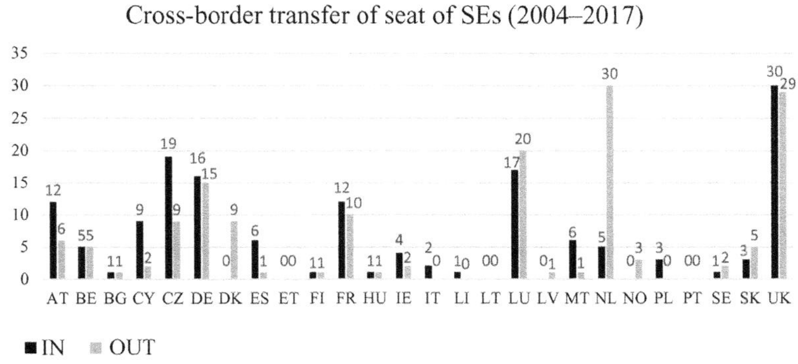

Figure 7.1. Cross-border transfer of seat of SEs (2004–2017)

The Regulation also pinpoints the role of the Member States, concerning, for example, their possibility of adopting particular provisions to protect minority shareholders or opposing the operation due to public interest.

It is worth noting that the European Commission has carried out a survey reporting that, as of 31 December 2017, 148 SEs (4.7 per cent of the overall number) have moved their seat throughout Europe (including transformed and deregistered SEs). Figure 7.1 shows that, whilst in many EEA countries, a similar number of SEs move in and out of the country each year, a significant net influx of SEs is recorded in Austria and the Czech Republic, whilst significantly more SEs left Denmark and the Netherlands than moved in (surprisingly, as the Netherlands is considered to be the European Delaware). Data post-Brexit are not available at the time of writing, although it is reasonable to expect that, as the UK has decided to withdraw from the EEA, it will probably account for a significant net loss of SEs (currently, the UK shows a significant overall number of SEs crossing the border in both directions).

Council Regulation 1435/2003 on the Statute for a European Cooperative Society (SCE) also describes the transfer procedure for SCEs, retracing the steps described above for SEs. However, worthy of attention are the provisions about resignation, not present in the SE Regulation.

Article 7 Regulation 2003/1435/CE

(5) Any member who opposed the transfer decision at the general meeting or at a sectorial or section meeting may tender his/her resignation within two months of the general meeting's decision. Membership shall terminate at the end of the financial year in which the resignation was tendered; the transfer shall not take effect in respect of that member. Resignation shall entitle the member to repayment of shares on the conditions laid down in Articles 4(4) and 16.

To conclude, Council Regulation 2137/85 on the European Economic Interest Grouping (EEIG) also allows the transfer of the seat without having to wind up the grouping and re-establish it in the host State. In particular, the transfer either may or may not result in the change of the applicable law.

In the first case, the provisions of Article 13 ought to be followed.

Article 13 Regulation 1985/2137/EEC

(1) The official address of a grouping may be transferred within the Community.

(2) When such a transfer does not result in a change in the law applicable pursuant to Article 2, the decision to transfer shall be taken in accordance with the conditions laid down in the contract for the formation of the grouping.

In the second case, Article 14 should be applied. After the preparation and the publication of the transfer proposal, unanimity of members' favourable votes ought to be achieved for any decision. These votes can not be cast for a period of two months following the publication of the transfer proposal, and the transfer then takes effect on the date of the new registry pursuant to the laws of the host Member State.

FURTHER READING

Manuel Garcia-Riestra, 'The Transfer of Seat of the European Company v. Free Establishment Case-Law', 15 *EBLR* 1295–1323 (2004).

Wino J.M. van Veen, 'The Law Governing SEs: An Interpretation Based on a Textual Analysis and the Referencing Methodology in the Regulation', 1 *ECL* 111–116 (2004).

Erik Werlauff, 'Cross-border Transfers of SE Companies', 1 *ECL* 121–125 (2004).

Enrico Vaccaro, 'Transfer of Seat and Freedom of Establishment in European Company Law', 16 *EBLR* 1348–1365 (2005).

Marios Bouloukos, 'The European Company (SE) as a Vehicle for Corporate Mobility within the EU: A Breakthrough in European Corporate Law?', 18 *EBLR* 535–557 (2007).

Federico M. Mucciarelli, 'E pluribus unum? Language diversity and the harmonization of company law in the European Union', 26 *Maastricht J. Eur. & Comp. L.* 669 (2019).

Article 7 Regulation 2003/1435/CE

(5) Any member who opposed the transfer decision at the general meeting or at a sectorial or section meeting may tender his/her resignation within two months of the general meeting's decision. Membership shall terminate at the end of the financial year in which the resignation was tendered; the transfer shall not take effect in respect of that member. Resignation shall entitle the member to repayment of shares on the conditions laid down in Articles 4(4) and 16.

Article 13 Regulation 1985/2137/EEC

(3) The official address of a grouping may be transferred within the Community.

(4) When such a transfer does not result in a change in the law applicable pursuant to Article 2, the decision to transfer shall be taken in accordance with the conditions laid down in the contract for the formation of the grouping.

7.3 Cross-Border Conversions

After a first draft proposal submitted in 1997, several consultations (i.e., in 1997, 2002, and 2005), a subsequent impact assessment in 2007 and the European Parliament's added value assessment in 2012, a public online consultation on the *Fourteenth Company Law Draft Directive on the cross-border transfer of registered office within the EU* was launched from 14 January 2013 to 17 April 2013. The results of the consultation made unclear whether, in the presence of many indirect tools (such as, in particular, the transfer of seat for SEs and the cross-border merger), permitting a company established in a Member State A to achieve the result of adopting the nationality and the applicable company law of Member State B, a directive regulating the cross-border transfer of the registered office was desirable. Some were of the opinion that the implementation of a directive would result not only in the strengthening of the basic principles of the freedom of movement and establishment of the Single Market, but also in significant savings for companies in terms of transaction costs. It was expected that the direct procedure provided by the Fourteenth Company Law Directive could avoid time-consuming procedures and subsequent prohibitive costs, considering that, in the absence of such provisions, moving through one of the above-mentioned indirect means could involve between thirteen and over thirty-five procedures, and could require sums which SMEs may be unable to afford.

The decision of the CJEU in *Polbud* has had a significant impact on this debate. It has been noted that, as in *Sevic*, so also in *Polbud*, through a smart interpretation of the TFEU, the CJEU has affirmed a right to a cross-border conversion, thereby requiring the Member States to take note of it. This has facilitated the task of other EU institutions in finding convergence on detailed rules.

Nicola de Luca, Andrea Gentile, and Fabio Schiavottiello, 'Transfer of the registered office and Delaware effect. The Polbud case', 45 *Giurisprudenza commerciale*, II, 454–462 (2018), at 460–462.

Indeed, in the light of the evolution of the case-law of the European Court of Justice, one may question whether a new directive in the matter of cross-border transfer of the seat is still necessary; or, else, whether the path followed by the European Court of Justice, through its rulings, from *Daily Mail* to *Polbud*, has conclusively outlined the principles, also granting the cross-border transfer of the seat, which directly derives from the provisions of the Treaty on freedom of establishment in the European Union.

To confirm the second alternative, it is appropriate to start from the possibility to transfer only the headquarters of a company, namely the central administration or the principal place of business, to a Member State other than that of establishment. There is no doubt that, in application of the freedom of establishment, for companies incorporated in Member States that adopt the principle of incorporation, the transfer of the headquarters to another Member State must be allowed (*Centros* and *Inspire Art*). In these cases, the *lex societatis* of the Member State of incorporation remains applicable to the company, if so is provided for or imposed by the Member State of incorporation (*Daily Mail*). This entails the consequence that the Member State of destination, even if it adopts the principle of the real seat, cannot deny the legal personality recognised by that of origin (*Überseering*) – nor impose significant regulatory measures (*Inspire Art*) – and cannot require the re-incorporation of the company, except in cases where the rules on private international law of the Member State of origin refer to those of the Member State of destination for determining whether the transferred company may keep the *lex societatis* of the State of origin (*Vale*). On the contrary, for companies incorporated in Member States adopting the principle of the real seat, it is possible to move the headquarters to another Member State only if this is accompanied by a change of the applicable *lex societatis* (*Cartesio*). This results in the consequence, arguable by some precedents (*Sevic* and *Vale*), that the Member State of destination will have to allow reincorporation (imposing its own internal rules if not in conflict with the freedom of establishment), acknowledging the continuation of the legal person going through the cross-border merger or conversion process.

As concerns the transfer of the registered office for the purpose of applying the *lex societatis* of the Member State of destination, it may be affirmed that, where expressly permitted by the Member State of origin, this is allowed both in cases where also the headquarters shall be transferred (*Vale*), and in cases where these are maintained in the Member State of origin (*Polbud*).

Conversely, the question of whether all the Member States shall allow the transfer of the registered office, for the purpose of a change of *lex societatis*, regardless of whether such Member States adopt the principle of incorporation or that of the real seat, and regardless of whether the involved companies maintain their effective headquarters in the Member State of origin, seems unanswered. Therefore, one should question whether in a case equivalent to that of *Polbud*, but occurred in another EU Member State, the Court would have affirmed a right to change the *lex societatis*, without prejudice of the location of the central administration and of the principal place of business, and regardless of the applicable rules of private international law.

To answer this question it shall be considered that the goal, the achievement of which is uncertain through a cross-border transfer of the registered office, can be certainly reached through the creation of a company in the Member State of destination and a reverse cross-border merger (or other turnarounds identified in the consultations relating to the Fourteenth

Directive proposal). Having this in mind, it would be hard to believe that what can be done in two (or more) steps cannot be done in one only, through an operation that directly pursues a purpose, which is *aliunde* deemed legal, in an easier and cheaper way.

Therefore, the answer to the question should be affirmative already in the present state of Community law.

Given that the right of establishment referred to in Articles 49 and 54 TFEU is to be read also in accordance with the principles that emerge from the Cross-border Merger Directive (and from the Regulations on SEs and SCEs, despite these require that the location of the registered office shall be the same of the real seat), Member States not allowing the transfer of the registered office abroad, for the purpose of a cross-border conversion, would end up violating the same principles granting the freedom of establishment. Under this perspective, some commentators have openly declared that some European legal systems are currently violating Community law, in that they prohibit or pose excessive obstacles to the right to change the legal system and *lex societatis* [Mucciarelli].

In sum, it shall be concluded that the right to a cross-border conversion is already granted by Community law, so that the Member States must take note of it, adapting their provisions of domestic law. In this regard, it should be underlined that a similar principle emerged in *Sevic*, when the Court of Justice affirmed the existence of the right to cross-border mergers, regardless of the fact that the directive on cross-border mergers had not yet entered in force on the date of publication (it would enter into force the following day).

Indeed, the Cross-Border Operations Directive acknowledges that the TFEU had been already interpreted by the Court of Justice of the European Union as encompassing the right of a company or firm formed in accordance with the legislation of a Member State to convert itself into a company or firm governed by the law of another Member State, provided that the conditions laid down by the legislation of that other Member State are satisfied and, in particular, that the test adopted by the latter Member State to determine the connection of a company or firm with its national legal order is satisfied. However, the lack of a legal framework for cross-border conversions would lead to legal fragmentation and legal uncertainty, and thus to barriers to the exercise of the freedom of establishment. It would also lead to the suboptimal protection of employees, creditors and minority members within the internal market.

On these grounds, the Cross-Border Operations Directive introduced Articles 86a-86t Directive 2017/1132/EU, laying down the rules on cross-border conversions. Cross-border conversion means an operation whereby a company, without being dissolved or wound up or going into liquidation, converts the legal form under which it is registered in a departure Member State into a legal form of the destination Member State and transfers at least its registered office to the destination Member State, while retaining its legal personality.

It is worth noting that the Cross-Border Operations Directive (extensively quoting *Daily Mail*) maintains the opinion that:

Recital 3 Directive 2019/2121/EU (Cross-Border Operations Directive)

In the absence of harmonisation of Union law, defining the connecting factor that determines the national law applicable to a company or firm falls, in accordance with Article 54 of the TFEU, within the competence of each Member State. Article 54 of the TFEU places the connecting factors of the registered office, the central administration and the principal place of business of a company or firm on an equal footing. Therefore, as clarified in case-law, the fact that only the registered office, and not the central administration or principal place of business, is transferred does not as such exclude the applicability of the freedom of establishment under Article 49 of the TFEU.

As commentators to *Polbud* have underlined, however, this principle expressed in *Daily Mail* – i.e., that the definition of the connecting factor that determines the national law applicable to a company or firm falls, in accordance with Article 54 of the TFEU, within the competence of each Member State – has become questionable. It has been argued that:

Nicola de Luca, Andrea Gentile, and Fabio Schiavottiello, 'Transfer of the registered office and Delaware effect. The Polbud case', 45 *Giurisprudenza commerciale*, II, 454–462 (2018), at 462

It is time for a substantial overruling of one of the cardinal principles that were affirmed with *Daily Mail*. Indeed, despite "companies are creatures of the law and, in the present state of Community law, creatures of national law", over time it has become true that incorporation in one particular Member State does not indissolubly link the company with the *lex societatis* of the Member State of origin. Any company created in the EU may move – through a cross-border merger or [sharing the Authors' opinion] through a cross-border conversion – to any other EU Member State, and therefore exists as creature of European Union law.

Indeed, Member States are free to define the connecting factor that determines the national law applicable to a company or firm only provided that – as has been pointed out in *Überseering* (*see,* Chapter 5, § 5.4) – the chosen connecting factor does not prevent a company incorporated under a certain national law adopting the incorporation theory from locating the real seat elsewere whilst retaining that legal personality granted by the Member State of incorporation. This principle somehow conflicts with the quoted principle affirmed in *Daily Mail*, as sometimes EU law solves conflicts between legislation of Member States concerning connecting factors, and declares that the validity of the real seat theory shall be reconsidered.

Moreover, the principle emerged in *Polbud* and strengthened in the Cross-Border Operations Directive, affirming that a simple transfer of the registered office of a company suffices in a view to changing the *lex societatis*, conflicts with the quoted principle affirmed in *Daily Mail*, that Article 54 of the TFEU places the connecting factors of the registered office, the central administration, and the principal place of business of a company or firm on an equal footing. Indeed, ECL requires that – in case of a cross-border operation – the nationality of a company established under the rules of any of the EU Member States is determined solely by its registered office, regardless of the location of the central management or the principal place of business.

This choice seems to resolve, for the avoidance of doubt, any question about whether a company, like natural persons, may have dual citizenship.

Gitte Soegaard and Erik Werlauff, 'Cross-border Transfer and Change of Lex Societatis After Polbud, C-106/16: Old Companies Do Not Die ... They Simply Fade Away to Another Country', 15 ECL 21–24 (2018), at 24

Figuratively speaking, although Polbud already has one foot in Luxembourg, it still has the other in Poland.

So, will Polbud now be a legal person with a 'double citizenship' meaning also two different company statutes?

In Vale it was stated that a conversion to a host Member State's law presupposes the consecutive application of two national laws.

It works for natural persons. Will it, in the long term, also work for companies? – Or will some common IP-based harmonization be more effective and preferable?

In conclusion, principles expressed in *Daily Mail* shall be amended, affirming that, despite the judgement that companies are creatures of the law, in the present state of EU law they are either a creature of national law, or of Union law (SEs and SCEs). Companies formed under the laws of any Member State (or a State member of the EEA), as well as companies formed under EU Regulations, are nationals of one Member State at once, based on the connecting factor chosen by the Member State of incorporation or by the EU Regulation concerned: i.e., the registered office, the central management, and/or the principal place of business. However, these companies are also EU-relevant subjects, as they enjoy the freedom of establishment and are subject to EU laws. In particular, companies formed under national law may adopt a different *lex societatis* by transferring, at least, their registered office in another Member State (cross-border conversion). In this case, the registered office, the central management, or the principal place of business are no longer on the same footing as connecting factors, as the one determining the new nationality is the registered office only, even in cases where the Member State of destination adopts another connecting factor for establishing nationality of legal persons.

FURTHER READING

Anneloes Baert, 'Crossing Borders: Exploring the Need for a Fourteenth EU Company Law Directive on the Transfer of the Registered Office', 26 *EBLR* 581–612 (2015).

Nicola de Luca, Andrea Gentile, and Fabio Schiavottiello, 'Transfer of the registered office and Delaware effect. The Polbud case', 45 *Giurisprudenza commerciale*, II, 454–462 (2018).

Gitte Soegaard and Erik Werlauff, 'Cross-border Transfer and Change of Lex Societatis After Polbud, C-106/16: Old Companies Do Not Die … They Simply Fade Away to Another Country', 15 *ECL*, no. 1, 21–24 (2018).

Jessica Schmidt, 'The Mobility Aspects of the EU Commission's Company Law Package: Or – the Good, the Bad and the Ugly', 16 *ECL* 13–17 (2019).

Jessica Schmidt, 'Cross-Border Mergers, Divisions and Conversions: Accomplishments and Deficits of the Company Law Package', 16 *ECFR* 222–272 (2019).

See also:

Mads Andenas and Frank Wooldridge, *European Comparative Company Law* 29–32 (Cambridge University Press, 2012).

Part III
Formation

8

The Setting Up of a New Company

8.1 Formation by a Single Member

One or more founders may decide to form a new company (NewCo) for carrying out a business activity.

Under ECL, the laws of Member States must permit single members to form a new private limited company, whilst Member States *may also* permit the formation of public limited companies by single members. In cases where the laws of Member States do not allow the formation of single-member public limited companies, a PLC formed by a single member shall be declared null and void (Article 11 Directive 2017/1132/EU).

As specified by the new Second Company Law Directive, private and public limited companies formed by more founders may subsequently become single-member companies when one person holds all the shares. This situation may lead to dissolution only in case, after an order of a Court, the company does not regularise its position within a given deadline.

Article 6 Directive 2017/1132/EU

1. Where the laws of a Member State require a company to be formed by more than one member, the fact that all the shares are held by one person or that the number of members has fallen below the legal minimum after incorporation of the company shall not lead to the automatic dissolution of the company.
2. If, in the cases referred to in paragraph 1, the laws of a Member State permit the company to be wound up by order of the court, the judge having jurisdiction must be able to give the company sufficient time to regularise its position.
3. Where a winding-up order as referred to in paragraph 2 is made the company shall enter into liquidation.

For the purpose of preventing the abuse of legal personality to the detriment of creditors, restrictions may be provided for in case a natural person is a single member of several companies or in case a legal person is the sole member of another company.

Article 2 Directive 2009/102/EC

1. A company may have a sole member when it is formed and also when all its shares come to be held by a single person (single-member company).
2. Member States may, pending coordination of national laws relating to groups, lay down special provisions or penalties for cases where:
   (a) a natural person is the sole member of several companies; or
   (b) a single-member company or any other legal person is the sole member of a company.

8.2 The Process of Setting Up a New Company: (A) The Instrument of Constitution and the Statutes

The formation of a NewCo must follow a process, including three steps: (i) the redaction of the instrument of constitution and of the statutes if they are contained in a separate instrument; (ii) the preventive control; (iii) the entry in the public register.

The first step of the process consists in the redaction of a contract (or a unilateral act) entered into and between natural or legal persons with the aim of creating a NewCo. Under Article 10 Directive 2017/1132/EU, the instrument of constitution, the company statutes, and any amendments to those documents shall be drawn up and certified in due legal form.

It must be noted that SEs (as well as EEIGs and SCEs) may not be formed *ex nihilo* by signing an instrument of constitution, rather only by merger of existing companies, by formation of a common subsidiary or parent company, or by conversion or division (so called 'incubation').

Article 2 Regulation 2001/2157/EC

1. Public limited-liability companies such as referred to in Annex I, formed under the law of a Member State, with registered offices and head offices within the Community may form an SE by means of a merger provided that at least two of them are governed by the law of different Member States.
2. Public and private limited-liability companies such as referred to in Annex II, formed under the law of a Member State, with registered offices and head offices within the Community may promote the formation of a holding SE provided that each of at least two of them:
   (a) is governed by the law of a different Member State, or
   (b) has for at least two years had a subsidiary company governed by the law of another Member State or a branch situated in another Member State.
3. Companies and firms within the meaning of the second paragraph of Article 48 of the Treaty and other legal bodies governed by public or private law, formed under the law of

a Member State, with registered offices and head offices within the Community may form a subsidiary SE by subscribing for its shares, provided that each of at least two of them:

(a) is governed by the law of a different Member State, or

(b) has for at least two years had a subsidiary company governed by the law of another Member State or a branch situated in another Member State.

4. A public limited-liability company, formed under the law of a Member State, which has its registered office and head office within the Community may be transformed into an SE if for at least two years it has had a subsidiary company governed by the law of another Member State.
5. A Member State may provide that a company the head office of which is not in the Community may participate in the formation of an SE provided that company is formed under the law of a Member State, has its registered office in that Member State and has a real and continuous link with a Member State's economy.

These methods for creating new SEs will be discussed in Chapter 9.

As already mentioned when describing the aims of the First Company Law Directive, national company law shall be harmonised so that the public register gives access to the basic information on the company, for the benefit of any third parties such as creditors. After the Second Company Law Directive has defined the details to be included in the instrument of constitution, the purpose of the First Company Law Directive is better achieved because this information will be published in the public register.

Recital 4 Directive 2017/1132/EU

(4) In the Union, the statutes or instrument of incorporation of a public limited liability company must make it possible for any interested person to acquaint himself with the basic particulars of the company, including the exact composition of its capital.

Consequently, Articles 3 and 4 of Directive 2017/1132/EU read as follows:

Article 3 Directive 2017/1132/EU

The statutes or the instrument of incorporation of the company shall always give at least the following information:

(a) the type and name of the company;

(b) the objects of the company;

(c) when the company has no authorised capital, the amount of the subscribed capital;
(d) when the company has an authorised capital, the amount thereof and also the amount of the capital subscribed at the time the company is incorporated or is authorised to commence business, and at the time of any change in the authorised capital, without prejudice to point (e) of Article 2 of Directive 2009/101/EC;
(e) in so far as they are not legally determined, the rules governing the number of and the procedure for appointing members of the bodies responsible for representing the company with regard to third parties, administration, management, supervision or control of the company and the allocation of powers among those bodies;
(f) the duration of the company, except where this is indefinite.

Article 4 Directive 2017/1132/EU

The following information at least must appear in either the statutes or the instrument of incorporation or a separate document published in accordance with the procedure laid down in the laws of each Member State in accordance with Article 3 of Directive 2009/101/EC:

(a) the registered office;
(b) the nominal value of the shares subscribed and, at least once a year, the number thereof;
(c) the number of shares subscribed without stating the nominal value, where such shares may be issued under national law;
(d) the special conditions, if any, limiting the transfer of shares;
(e) where there are several classes of shares, the information referred to in points (b), (c) and (d) for each class and the rights attaching to the shares of each class;
(f) whether the shares are registered or bearer, where national law provides for both types, and any provisions relating to the conversion of such shares unless the procedure is laid down by law;
(g) the amount of the subscribed capital paid up at the time the company is incorporated or is authorised to commence business;
(h) the nominal value of the shares or, where there is no nominal value, the number of shares issued for a consideration other than in cash, together with the nature of the consideration and the name of the person providing that consideration;
(i) the identity of the natural or legal persons or companies or firms by whom or in whose name the statutes or the instrument of incorporation, or where the company was not formed at the same time, the drafts of those documents, have been signed;
(j) the total amount, or at least an estimate, of all the costs payable by the company or chargeable to it by reason of its formation and, where appropriate, before the company is authorised to commence business; and
(k) any special advantage granted, at the time the company is formed or up to the time it receives authorisation to commence business, to anyone who has taken part in the formation of the company or in transactions leading to the grant of such authorisation.

FURTHER READING

Christine Hodt Dickens, 'Establishment of the SE Company: An Overview over the Provisions Governing the Formation of the European Company', 18 *EBLR* 1423–1464 (2007).

8.3 The Process of Setting Up a New Company: (B) The Preventive Control

As mentioned, ECL provides for preventive control of the instruments of constitution, this being a reminder of the old times when a legal person could only be created by act of the State (e.g., in England and Wales, by Royal Charter or Act of Parliament). Nowadays, preventive control is generally carried on by an administrative or judicial authority of the Member State. In case no administrative or judicial control is provided for (e.g., in Italy), the instrument of constitution shall be drawn up and certified in due legal form, to imply control by a notary or similar authority.

Article 10 Directive 2017/1132/EU

In all Member States whose laws do not provide for preventive, administrative or judicial control, at the time of formation of a company, the instrument of constitution, the company statutes and any amendments to those documents shall be drawn up and certified in due legal form.

EU law does not clarify the nature of any object for preventive control. As a matter of fact, it does not go beyond the conditions laid down for the validity of the instrument of constitution; indeed, in contrast with the old times, when the official grant was given based on the merits, no authority is now entrusted with the powers to challenge the business activity declared as object of the company, except when this is unlawful.

The *Job Centre I–II* cases are relevant for the discussion of this point.

8.4 *Job Centre I–II* Cases

In *Job Centre* (C-111/94, *Job Centre Coop. a r.l. (Job Centre I)*, [1995] ECR I-03361; C-55/96, *Job Centre Coop. a r.l. (Job Centre II)*, [1997] ECR I-07119), reference for a preliminary ruling under Article 177 of the EC Treaty [current Article 267 TFEU] was made by order of 31 March 1994 by the *Tribunale Civile e Penale di Milano* (Civil and Criminal District Court, Milan) concerning two questions on the interpretation of Articles 48, 55, 59, 60, 66, 86, and 90 of the EC Treaty [current Articles 54, 62, 66, 75, 74, 106, 110 TFEU]. Those questions were raised in the context of an application submitted by the representatives of Job Centre (*'JCC'*) to the *Tribunale Civile e Penale di Milano* for confirmation of its memorandum of association, in accordance with Article 2330(3) of the Italian Civil Code (formerly providing for judicial preventive control in Italy).

JCC was a cooperative society with limited liability that was in the course of being set up with its head office in Milan. Under its articles of association, its activities were to include, in particular, serving as an intermediary between supply and demand on the employment market and providing temporary staff for third parties. Its object was to enable workers and undertakings, whether they were members or not, to draw on such services on the employment market in Italy and the Union.

In Italy, the employment market is subject to a mandatory placement system administered by public employment agencies and regulated by Law No. 264 of 29 April 1949. Article 11(1) of that Law prohibits the pursuit of any activity, even unremunerated, as an intermediary between supply and demand for paid employment. The first paragraph of Article 1 of Law No. 1369 of 23 October 1960 lays down a prohibition on acting as an intermediary or subcontractor in employment relationships, failure to comply with which gives rise, *inter alia*, to penal sanctions.

In the proceedings before the *Tribunale Civile e Penale di Milano*, JCC submitted that the prohibition of private placement and provision of temporary workers were contrary to EU law. The national court therefore sought a preliminary ruling from the CJEU on the following questions:

C-111/94, Job Centre Coop. a r.l. (Job Centre I), [1995] ECR I-03361, § 5

1. May the national laws on employment procurement and temporary work, which relate to matters of public policy because their purpose is to protect the interests of workers and of the national economy, be considered as instances of the exercise of official authority within the meaning of the combined provisions of Articles 66 and 55 of the EEC Treaty?
2. May the Community rules relied upon by the applicants, in the absence of specific implementing provisions in that area, be considered directly applicable (calling into question the public policy aims of the Italian laws currently governing employment procurement and temporary work) and do they permit any person subject to public or private law to pursue, without specific supervision or authorization, any activity as an intermediary between supply and demand on the employment market and/or as provider of labour on a temporary basis for third persons, in the event that a Member State is not able through its own administrative apparatus fully to meet the demand for services on the labour market?

The CJEU maintained that it had no jurisdiction to rule on the questions raised by the *Tribunale Civile e Penale di Milano*:

C-111/94, Job Centre Coop. a r.l. (*Job Centre I*), [1995] ECR I-03361, § 11

When, in accordance with the applicable national legislation and under the 'giurisdizione volontaria' procedure, the national court rules on an application for confirmation of a company's articles of association with a view to its registration, it is performing a non-judicial function which, in other Member States, is entrusted to administrative authorities. It is exercising administrative authority without being at the same time called upon to settle any dispute. Only if the person empowered under national law to apply for such confirmation seeks judicial review of a decision rejecting that application – and thus of the application for registration – may the court seised be regarded as exercising a judicial function, for the purposes of Article 177, in respect of an application for the annulment of a measure adversely affecting the petitioner (see Case 32/74 Haaga [1974] ECR 1201).

Following this judgment, by decision of 18 December 1995 the *Tribunale Civile e Penale di Milano* dismissed the application for confirmation of the instrument establishing JCC submitted by its representative, on the ground that its business objects were incompatible with certain mandatory rules of Italian employment legislation.

JCC appealed against that refusal, under Article 2330(4) of the Italian Civil Code, to the *Corte d'Appello di Milano* (Court of Appeal), seeking to have the Tribunale's decision set aside and the instrument establishing it confirmed.

By order of 30 January 1996 the *Corte d'Appello di Milano* considered that JCC's appeal raised questions of interpretation of EU law and decided to stay the proceedings and refer to the CJEU for a preliminary ruling on the following questions:

C-55/96, Job Centre Coop. a r.l. (*Job Centre II*), [1997] ECR I-07119, § 10

1. May the provisions of Italian national law contained in Article 11(1) of Law No 264 of 29 April 1949 and the first paragraph of Article 1 of Law No 1369 of 23 October 1960, whereby the business of acting as an intermediary and negotiator between supply and demand on the employment market, whether as an employment agency or as an employment business, is prohibited unless carried on by the public offices specified in those provisions, be regarded as relating to the exercise of official authority within the meaning of the combined provisions of

Articles 66 and 55 of the EC Treaty in view of the fact that they are treated by Italian law as relating to matters of public policy because their purpose is to protect the interests of workers and the national economy?

2. Must those provisions, in view of their general scope, be regarded as conflicting with the principles of Community law laid down by Articles 48, 49, 59, 60, 62, 66, 86 and 90 of the said Treaty concerning the right to work, freedom of economic initiative, freedom of movement for workers and others, freedom of supply and demand for work and services, free and fair competition between economic agents and the prohibition of abuse of dominant positions?
3. In the event that the above-mentioned legislation of the Italian State concerning operation of an employment agency or an employment business is in breach of the principles of Community law mentioned in the foregoing question, must the judicial and administrative authorities of that Member State consider themselves bound to apply those principles directly, allowing public and private bodies and undertakings to act as intermediaries between those offering and those seeking employment and temporary work, provided that the provisions governing employment contracts and mandatory social security are complied with and subject to the controls provided for by law?

In those circumstances, the CJEU deemed it had jurisdiction to solve the referred question, and hence ruled as follows:

C-55/96, Job Centre Coop. a r.l. (*Job Centre II*), [1997] ECR I-07119, § 38 and Operative Part

Public placement offices are subject to the prohibition contained in Article 86 of the EC Treaty [current Article 106 TFEU], so long as application of that provision does not obstruct the performance of the particular task assigned to them. A Member State which prohibits any activity as an intermediary between supply and demand on the employment market, whether as an employment agency or as an employment business, unless carried on by those offices, is in breach of Article 90(1) of the Treaty [current Article 110 TFEU] where it creates a situation in which those offices cannot avoid infringing Article 86 of the Treaty. That is the case, in particular, in the following circumstances:

- the public placement offices are manifestly unable to satisfy demand on the market for all types of activity; and
- the actual placement of employees by private companies is rendered impossible by the maintenance in force of statutory provisions under which such activities are prohibited and non-observance of that prohibition gives rise to penal and administrative sanctions; and
- the placement activities in question could extend to the nationals or to the territory of other Member States.

Consequently, the *Corte d'Appello di Milano* set aside the decision of the *Tribunale Civile e Penale di Milano* and ordered registration of the Job Centre instrument of constitution in the public register.

FURTHER READING

C-41/90, *Höfner and Elser* v. *Macrotron*, [1991] ECR I-1979.

8.5 The Process of Setting Up a New Company: (C) The Registration

After preventive control, if this is necessary according to the laws of the Member States, the instrument of constitution is published in the public registry; therefore, the information included in it is made available to all interested parties.

After revision of the First Company Law Directive in 2009, following the suggestions of the SLIM Group, all information made available by the public registry is sent initially and received at its destination by means of electronic equipment for the processing (including digital compression) and storage of data, and entirely transmitted, conveyed, and received in a manner to be determined by Member States by wire, by radio, by optical means or by other electromagnetic means: i.e., by electronic means.

Article 3 Directive 2017/1132/EU

1. In each Member State, a file shall be opened in a central register, commercial register or companies register, for each of the companies registered therein.

...

3. All documents and particulars which must be disclosed pursuant to Article 2 shall be kept in the file, or entered in the register; the subject matter of the entries in the register must in every case appear in the file ...
4. A copy of the whole or any part of the documents or particulars referred to in Article 2 must be obtainable on application. Applications may be submitted to the register by paper means or by electronic means as the applicant chooses.

...

The price of obtaining a copy of the whole or any part of the documents or particulars referred to in Article 2, whether by paper means or by electronic means, shall not exceed the administrative cost thereof.

Paper copies supplied shall be certified as 'true copies', unless the applicant dispenses with such certification. Electronic copies supplied shall not be certified as 'true copies', unless the applicant explicitly requests such a certification.

Member States shall take the necessary measures to ensure that certification of electronic copies guarantees both the authenticity of their origin and the integrity of their contents, by means at least of an advanced electronic signature within the meaning of Article 2(2) of Directive 1999/93/EC.

5. Disclosure of the documents and particulars referred to in paragraph 3 shall be effected by publication in the national gazette designated for that purpose by the Member State, either of the full text or of a partial text, or by means of a reference to the document which has been deposited in the file or entered in the register. The national gazette designated for that purpose may be kept in electronic form.

Member States may decide to replace publication in the national gazette with equally effective means, which shall entail at least the use of a system whereby the information disclosed can be accessed in chronological order through a central electronic platform.

6. The documents and particulars may be relied on by the company as against third parties only after they have been disclosed in accordance with paragraph 5, unless the company proves that the third parties had knowledge thereof.

However, with regard to transactions taking place before the sixteenth day following the disclosure, the documents and particulars shall not be relied on as against third parties who prove that it was impossible for them to have had knowledge thereof. ...

Under Article 17 Directive 2017/1132/EU, documents and particulars shall be drawn up and filed in one of the languages permitted by the Member State, i.e., – generally – the official languages of the respective Member States.

Furthermore, reference to the public registry shall also be made in the correspondence of the company, so that third parties may detect and access the file. Websites have become important means of information too. EU law does not require that all companies have an official website; this becomes mandatory only for listed companies, as we will see in Chapter 15, § 15.5.

Article 26 Directive 2017/1132/EU

Member States shall prescribe that letters and order forms, whether they are in paper form or use any other medium, are to state the following particulars:

(a) the information necessary in order to identify the register in which the file mentioned in Article 3 is kept, together with the number of the company in that register;
(b) the legal form of the company, the location of its registered office and, where appropriate, the fact that the company is being wound up.

> Where, in those documents, mention is made of the capital of the company, the reference shall be to the capital subscribed and paid up.
>
> Member States shall prescribe that company websites are to contain at least the particulars mentioned in the first paragraph and, if applicable, a reference to the capital subscribed and paid up.

Each Member State shall determine through which persons the disclosure formalities are to be carried out. Generally, this task is entrusted to members of the board of directors. Failure to disclose mandatory information shall be sanctioned with penalties (Articles 28 Directive 2017/1132/EU).

8.6 Use of Digital Tools and Processes in the Setting up of Companies and the Registration of Branches: The CorpTech Directive

After promoting reports and studies on the digitalisation in company law – carried out by consultants such as ICLEG, Everis, E&Y, and Optimity – the European Commission decided to promote the use of digital tools and processes in company law, as part of the Company Law Package 2019.

In these circumstances, Directive 2019/1151/EU was passed amending Directive 2017/1132/EU, with regards to the online formation of companies, registration of branches, and consultation of commercial registers. The new Directive – which may be referred to as the CorpTech Directive – shall be implemented by 1 August 2021. The CorpTech Directive aims to initiate economic activity in an easier, quicker, and less costly manner, by permitting the setting up of a company or the opening of a branch of that company in another Member State. It also aims to provide more comprehensive and accessible information on companies, for the benefit of both national and cross-border users. However, as online procedures entail risks of fraud and company hijacking, the CorpTech Directive also aims to ensure that these risks are prevented.

In order to facilitate the formation of companies, the CorpTech Directive seeks to enable the online completion of all three of the ordinary steps for the formation of a new company – i.e., i) the drawing up of the instrument of constitution; ii) the preventive control; iii) the registration.

Member States are required to lay down detailed rules for online formation. In particular, these rules shall grant that it is possible to carry out online formation with the submission of documents or information in electronic form, without prejudice to material and procedural requirements, including those relating to legal procedures for drawing up instruments of constitution, and to the authenticity, accuracy, reliability, trustworthiness, and appropriate legal form of documents or information that are submitted.

In drafting these rules, Member States define, in conformity with their traditions, the role of notaries or lawyers in any part of such online procedures. As mentioned, one of the aims of the CorpTech Directive is to tackle fraud and company hijacking and to grant the reliability and trustworthiness of documents and information contained within national registers (Article 13c Directive 2017/1132/EU). These professionals play an important role, as they are generally entrusted by national law with the task of making controls on the identity and legal capacity (as well as the capacity to act) of persons seeking to form a company or register a branch or to file documents or information. Verification of identity shall be preferably carried out with the use of digital identity tools. In order to prevent frauds, however, the CorpTech Directive allows Member States to require – but does not itself require – the physical presence of the applicant before any authority or person or body mandated under national law to deal with any aspect of online procedures (Article 13b (4) and Article 13g (8) Directive 2017/1132/EU).

Member States are allowed to limit online formation to certain types of companies, such as private limited companies and simplified companies where such types are permitted (Article 13g Directive 2017/1132/EU). In any case, online formation may be excluded in cases where the share capital of the company is paid by way of contributions in kind (Article 13g (4)(d) Directive 2017/1132/EU). The payment of contributions in cash shall occur online: as such, not only all means of electronic payment are allowed (Article 13e Directive 2017/1132/EU), rather, also, the opening of a bank account online in the name of a pre-company shall be made possible (Article 13g (g) Directive 2017/1132/EU).

As already provided for in many Member States, the use of templates is very useful to facilitate the formation of companies (Article 13h Directive 2017/1132/EU): a template is a model for the instrument of constitution of a company which is drawn up by Member States in compliance with national law and is used for the online formation of a company. The use of templates is generally aimed at reducing costs, as these contain a predefined set of options in accordance with national law which applicants may select, in case they do not prefer to form a company with bespoke instruments of constitution. Furthermore, the CorpTech Directive requires that registration of companies formed exclusively by natural persons who use the templates occurs within five days, instead of the ordinary ten days (Article 13g (7) Directive 2017/1132/EU).

With regards to corporate information, the CorpTech Directive fosters the once-only principle (Recital 28 CorpTech Directive). Applying the once-only principle entails that companies are not asked to submit the same information to public authorities more than once. For example, companies should not have to submit the same information both to the national register and to the national gazette. Instead, the register should provide the information already submitted directly to the national gazette. Similarly, where a company is formed in one Member State and subsequently wishes to register a branch in another Member State, it should be possible for the company to make use of the documents or information previously submitted to a register. Furthermore, where a company is formed in one Member State but has a branch in another Member State, it should be possible for the company to submit certain changes to their company information only to the register where the company is registered, without the need to submit the same information to the register where the branch is registered. Instead, information such as a change of company name or change of registered office of the company should be exchanged electronically, between the register where the company is registered and the register where the branch is registered using the system of interconnection of registers.

FURTHER READING

Alessio Bartolacelli, 'A New (?) Framework (?) on Digitalization in European (?) Company (?) Law', 5 *InterEULawEast: J. Int'l & Eur. L., Econ. & Market Integrations* 1 (2018).

Sebastian Omlor, 'Digitalization and EU Company Law: Innovation and Tradition in Tandem', 16 *ECL* 6–12 (2019).

Christoph Teichmann, 'The Company Law Package. Content and State of Play', 16 *ECFR* 3–14 (2019).

8.7 Disclosure Requirements for Single-member Companies and for Branches

Additional disclosure is required in case a company has a sole member or opens a branch in another Member State.

Article 3 Directive 2009/102/EC

Where a company becomes a single-member company because all its shares come to be held by a single person, that fact, together with the identity of the sole member, must either be recorded in the file or entered in the register as referred to in Article 3(1) and (2) of Directive 68/151/EEC or be entered in a register kept by the company and accessible to the public.

In addition, decisions taken by the sole member in the field on which the general meeting has powers to decide shall be recorded in minutes or drawn up in writing, as well as contracts between the sole member and his company as represented by him (Articles 4–5 Directive 2009/102/EC).

As regards branches, ECL requires that information relating to the company is also disclosed in the public register of the State where the branch is opened.

Article 29 Directive 2017/1132/EU

1. Documents and particulars relating to a branch opened in a Member State by a company of a type listed in Annex II, which is governed by the law of another Member State, shall be disclosed pursuant to the law of the Member State of the branch, in accordance with Article 16.
2. Where disclosure requirements in respect of the branch differ from those in respect of the company, the branch's disclosure requirements shall take precedence with regard to transactions carried out with the branch.

Similarly to the (new) Second Company Law Directive requirements, in case of a branch the following information shall be disclosed:

Article 30 Directive 2017/1132/EU

1. The compulsory disclosure provided for in Article 1 shall cover the following documents and particulars only:
   (a) the address of the branch;
   (b) the activities of the branch;
   (c) the register in which the company file mentioned in Article 16 is kept, together with the registration number in that register;
   (d) the name and legal form of the company and the name of the branch if that is different from the name of the company;
   (e) the appointment, termination of office and particulars of the persons who are authorized to represent the company in dealings with third parties and in legal proceedings;
   - as a company organ constituted pursuant to law or as members of any such organ, in accordance with the disclosure by the company as provided for in Article 14(d),
   - as permanent representatives of the company for the activities of the branch, with an indication of the extent of their powers;

   (f) the winding-up of the company, the appointment of liquidators, particulars concerning them and their powers and the termination of the liquidation in accordance with disclosure by the company as provided for in Article 14 (h) and (k),
   - insolvency proceedings, arrangements, compositions, or any analogous proceedings to which the company is subject;

   (g) the accounting documents in accordance with Article 31;
   (h) the closure of the branch.
2. The Member State in which the branch has been opened may provide for the disclosure, as referred to in Article 29, of
   (a) the signature of the persons referred to in paragraph 1(e) and (f) of this Article;
   (b) the instruments of constitution and the memorandum and articles of association if they are contained in a separate instrument in accordance with points (a), (b) and (c) of Article 14, together with amendments to those documents;

(c) an attestation from the register referred to in point (c) of paragraph 1 of this Article relating to the existence of the company;
(d) an indication of the securities on the company's property situated in that Member State, provided such disclosure relates to the validity of those securities.

Of no trivial importance is the provision of Article 32 Directive 2017/1132/EU, providing that the Member State in which the branch has been opened may stipulate that the documents to be filed with the register must be published in another official language of the EU and that the translation of such documents must be certified.

8.8 Validity of Obligations Entered into by the Company

Although the three steps for creating a NewCo are generally very close to one another, time may elapse between the signing of the instrument of constitution and the moment in which this gets registered with the public registry. Some Member States' legislations (e.g., Germany, Poland, and Spain) address a company whose contract has been signed, but not yet registered with the public register, as a 'pre-company' (in German, *Vorgesellschaft*). This 'pre-company' is deemed to be an existing legal entity, although not yet enjoying legal personality, which only follows registration. As such, the pre-company acquires from shareholders contributions in cash and in kind, including real estate subject to formalities (e.g., the filing in the land registry in the name of the company), may dispose of such contributions or acquire new property rights, make and receive payments, and so on. It is, however, uncertain whether third parties that engage in transactions with the pre-company may claim rights vis-à-vis the pre-company itself and/or the persons who act in the name of the company.

ECL provides for rules preventing the company – once registered with the public register – to challenge the validity of certain obligations entered into before registration, on the grounds that the company was not in a condition to conclude binding contracts or, otherwise, to engage in obligations, for not enjoying of a legal personality yet. For these obligations, the (natural) persons who acted are jointly and severally liable, unless otherwise agreed.

Article 7 Directive 2017/1132/EU

If, before a company being formed has acquired legal personality, action has been carried out in its name and the company does not assume the obligations arising from such action, the persons who acted shall, without limit, be jointly and severally liable therefore, unless otherwise agreed.

Article 7 is somewhat ambiguous. Indeed, considering that not all Member States accept the pre-company doctrine, this rule grants that in cases where the company in course of formation does not acquire the legal personality, for any reason, creditors have an action vis-à-vis the natural persons acting in its name and on its behalf: hence, under common private law principles, a representative (i.e., someone acting in another's name and on their behalf) would bear no personal liability for the obligations arising from its actions. For Member States accepting the pre-company doctrine, however, since the pre-company exists regardless of whether it then acquires legal personality, joint and several liability of the natural persons shall be interpreted as an additional guarantee.

The same Article 7, however, refers also to cases where the company has acquired legal personality. In such cases, it is unclear why the legal person shall be permitted not to assume the obligations arising from previous actions and why shall natural persons continue to bear joint and several liability. As ECL aims at protecting the interest of creditors, Article 7 should be interpreted as precluding Member States from permitting companies to not assume obligations entered into by directors appointed as the instrument of constitution is signed. Also, as the joint and several liability of natural persons is a guarantee, which creditors may withdraw, Article 7 should also be interpreted as requiring that in all cases where natural persons pay a company's debt, the former shall have a right of recourse regardless of whether the company has assumed the obligation or not.

An interesting case on obligations entered into by a company before registration – *Ubbink Isolatie BV* – has been brought before the CJEU: we will discuss this case after the provisions on the nullity of a company have been discussed (§ 8.9).

It should also be added that the Second Company Law Directive considered that, despite the registration in the public register, some companies operating in certain business sectors, such as banking and insurance, may not commence business without authorisation of the relevant authority. For instance, one may question what happens if a company whose object is to carry on banking activity commences the business in the absence of the authorisation of the banking authority.

Article 5 Directive 2017/1132/EU

1. Where the laws of a Member State prescribe that a company may not commence business without authorisation, they shall also make provision for responsibility for liabilities incurred by or on behalf of the company during the period before such authorisation is granted or refused.
2. Paragraph 1 shall not apply to liabilities under contracts concluded by the company conditionally upon its being granted authorisation to commence business.

In general, once the company has registered with the public register, obligations entered into by the company, and on its behalf by the persons who, as an organ of the company, are authorised to represent it, shall be binding for the company. Registration, indeed, shall constitute a bar to any irregularity in appointment of these representatives being relied upon as against third parties unless the company proves that such third parties had knowledge thereof (Article 8 Directive 2017/1132/EU).

It must be noted that some Courts of the EU and outside the EU adopt the so-called *ultra vires doctrine*, by which acts attempted by a company that are beyond the scope of powers granted by the company's objects clause, included in the statutes or similar founding documents, are void or voidable. ECL, however, rejects the *ultra vires doctrine*.

Article 9 Directive 2017/1132/EU

1. Acts done by the organs of the company shall be binding upon it even if those acts are not within the objects of the company, unless such acts exceed the powers that the law confers or allows to be conferred on those organs.
2. However, Member States may provide that the company shall not be bound where such acts are outside the objects of the company, if it proves that the third party knew that the act was outside those objects or could not in view of the circumstances have been unaware of it; disclosure of the statutes shall not of itself be sufficient proof thereof.
3. The limits on the powers of the organs of the company, arising under the statutes or from a decision of the competent organs, may not be relied on as against third parties, even if they have been disclosed.
4. If the national law provides that authority to represent a company may, in derogation from the legal rules governing the subject, be conferred by the statutes on a single person or on several persons acting jointly, that law may provide that such a provision in the statutes may be relied on as against third parties on condition that it relates to the general power of representation; the question whether such a provision in the statutes can be relied on as against third parties shall be governed by Article 3.

8.9 Nullity of Companies

As companies are created based on a legal process starting from an act of private persons, generally a contract for the constitution of a company, it must be considered what consequences may arise in case these acts of private persons are deemed invalid for some reasons. One may question whether this leads to nullity of the company itself.

ECL provides for the affirmative answer to this question, whilst it (i) limits the cases in which a declaration of nullity may occur and (ii) determines which effects this declaration shall entail.

Article 11 Directive 2017/1132/EU

The laws of the Member States may not provide for the nullity of companies otherwise than in accordance with the following provisions:

(a) nullity must be ordered by decision of a court of law;
(b) nullity may be ordered only on the grounds: (i) that no instrument of constitution was executed or that the rules of preventive control or the requisite legal formalities were not complied with; (ii) that the objects of the company are unlawful or contrary to public policy; (iii) that the instrument of constitution or the statutes do not state the name of the company, the amount of the individual subscriptions of capital, the total amount of the capital subscribed or the objects of the company; (iv) of failure to comply with the provisions of the national law concerning the minimum amount of capital to be paid up; (v) of the incapacity of all the founder members; (vi) that, contrary to the national law governing the company, the number of founder members is less than two.

Apart from the foregoing grounds of nullity, a company shall not be subject to any cause of non-existence, absolute nullity, relative nullity or declaration of nullity.

Two interesting cases brought before the CJEU – *Ubbink Isolatie BV* and *Marleasing* – are useful to illustrate the point.

8.10 *Ubbink Isolatie BV* Case

In *Ubbink Isolatie BV* (C-136/87, *Ubbink Isolatie BV* v. *Daken Wandtechniek BV*, [1988] ECR I-04665), reference was made to the Court under Article 177 by the Hoge Raad der Nederlanden (Supreme Court of the Netherlands) for a preliminary ruling on the interpretation of the rules on nullity laid down by the First Directive.

The questions referred to the CJEU arose in proceedings concerning the performance of a contract between Daken Wandtechniek BV and the company calling itself Ubbink Isolatie BV.

At the time of the contested contract, a partnership was registered in the commercial register under the name Ubbink Isolatie BV i.o. (Ubbink Isolatie, a private limited company in the course of formation), listing as partners Ubbink Nederland BV and Isetco BV, both private limited companies, and as general representative, with the title of director, a certain Mr Juraske. However, there was no private limited company registered in the commercial register under the name Ubbink Isolatie BV. The national court found that as there had been no notarial instrument establishing a private limited company under the name Ubbink Isolatie BV, the company had not been duly formed.

This 'pre-company' concluded the contested contract with Daken Wandtechniek under the name Ubbink Isolatie BV without the addition of the expression 'in the course of formation' and proceedings were brought against it under that name by Daken Wandtechniek before the Arrondissementsrechtbank (District Court), Arnhem for the termination of that contract and to establish liability thereunder; the appellant also initially submitted its defence under that name.

During the proceedings before that court, the appellant contended that Daken Wandtechniek was wrong to bring its action against Ubbink Isolatie BV. The summons issued upon the application of Daken Wandtechniek was void and the application could not be granted because Ubbink Isolatie BV did not exist. In an interlocutory judgment, the Arrondissementsrechtbank, Arnhem held that even if Ubbink Isolatie BV had not been formed at all or if the instrument intended to form it was defective, the private limited-liability company could not be said not to exist merely on that ground. The company existed until such time as it was wound up or a declaration of nullity was made in accordance with the Netherlands Civil Code. Article 182(1) of Book 2 of that Code provides that where business has been carried on in the name of a private limited-liability company which has not been registered in the commercial register and before an instrument forming the company has been drawn up and certified by a notary or without a declaration that the minister has no objection to the formation of the company, a declaration of nullity may be obtained on the application of any interested party or of the public prosecutor.

The appellant appealed against that judgment to the Gerechtshof (Court of Appeal), Arnhem, which confirmed the judgment at first instance. The appellant then appealed to the Hoge Raad, claiming to be 'the party to the proceedings which, at earlier instances, was named as defendant and appeared as Ubbink Isolatie BV, a private limited liability company'. According to the statement of the grounds of appeal, Article 182 does not apply to a case such as this in which no private limited-liability company has been constituted and where actions have been wrongfully carried out on behalf or in the name of a fictitious private limited-liability company which does not have the structure required for the existence of such a company and in regard to which no instrument constituting the company has been executed.

Since it considered that Article 182 must be interpreted in the light of the provisions of Section III of the First Directive, in particular Articles 11 and 12 thereof, the Hoge Raad stayed the proceedings pending a preliminary ruling from the Court of Justice on the following questions:

C-136/87, Ubbink Isolatie BV v. Daken Wandtechniek BV, [1988] ECR I-04665, § 8

(1) Where business is carried on in the name of a company within the meaning of the First Directive which has not, however, been constituted under the applicable national law because no authentic instrument of constitution within the meaning of

Article 11(2)(a) of the directive was executed or the rules of preventive control, also within the meaning of Article 11(2)(a), were not complied with, do the rules laid down in Section III of the First Directive mean that in proceedings brought against it 'the company' must be treated as being in existence so long as its nullity has not been declared in separate proceedings for a declaration of nullity and for the winding-up of 'the company'?

(2) Does it make any difference to the answer to Question 1 whether (a) only the instrument of constitution was not executed or only the rules of preventive control were not complied with, or (b) the instrument was not executed and the aforesaid rules were not complied with either?

(3) Does it make any difference to the answer to Question 1 whether (a) business is carried on within the framework of an organization of persons and assets which – apart from the fact that business is done in the name of a company – gives the outward appearance of a company or (b) business is carried on where there is no question of the existence of such an organization?

(4) Is it relevant to the answer to Question 1 that business is carried on within the framework of an organization which, according to the applicable national law, has a different legal form from that of a company within the meaning of the First Directive, for example the legal form of a 'vennootschap onder firma' (partnership), and is registered as such in the commercial register under a name which, save as regards the indication of the legal form, is identical to the name of the unconstituted company under which business is carried on?

The CJEU answered the referred questions as follows:

C-136/87, Ubbink Isolatie BV v. Daken Wandtechniek BV, [1988] ECR I-04665, §§ 10–18 and Operative Part

Section I of the First Directive of the Council on coordination of safeguards which, for the protection of the interests of members and others, are required of companies (Directive 68/151) provides for formalities in regard to disclosure intended to provide third parties with prior information on the essential features of companies within the meaning of the said directive. Third parties may thus legitimately rely on the information available concerning such a company, but only if that information has been disclosed in the manner provided for. Consequently, the rules concerning the nullity of companies laid down in Section III of the First Directive apply only where third parties have been led to believe by the information published in accordance with Section I that a company within the meaning of the First Directive exists. They do not apply where the acts in question were performed in the name of a private limited liability company whose existence is not confirmed by the public register because the formalities for incorporation required by national law have not been completed. However, in so far as acts performed in the name of a limited liability company not yet incorporated are regarded by the applicable national law as having been performed in the name of a company being formed within the meaning of Article 7 of the directive, it is for the national law in question to provide, in accordance with that provision, that the persons who perform them are to be jointly and severally liable.

8.11 *Marleasing* Case

In *Marleasing* (C-106/89, *Marleasing SA* v. *La Comercial Internacional de Alimentación* SA, [1990] ECR I-04135), the Juzgado de Primera Instancia e Instrucción No 1, Oviedo, referred a question to the CJEU pursuant to Article 177 of the EEC Treaty for a preliminary ruling on the interpretation of Article 11 of Council Directive 68/151/EEC of 9 March 1968, on nullity of companies. The question arose in a dispute between Marleasing SA, the plaintiff in the main proceedings, and a number of defendants including La Comercial Internacional de Alimentación SA ('*La Comercial*'). The latter was established in the form of a public limited company by three persons, including Barviesa SA, which contributed its own assets.

Marleasing's primary claim, based on Articles 1261 and 1275 of the Spanish Civil Code (according to which contracts without cause or whose cause is unlawful have no legal effect) was for a declaration that the founders' contract establishing La Comercial was void on the ground that the establishment of the company lacked cause, was a sham transaction and was carried out in order to defraud the creditors of Barviesa SA, a co-founder of the defendant company. La Comercial contended that the action should be dismissed in its entirety on the grounds that Article 11 of Directive 68/151, which lists exhaustively the cases in which the nullity of a company may be ordered, does not include lack of cause amongst them.

The national court observed that in accordance with Article 395 of the Act concerning the Conditions of Accession of Spain and the Portuguese Republic to the European Communities (Official Journal 1985 L 302, p. 23) the Kingdom of Spain was under an obligation to bring the directive into effect as from the date of accession, but that that had still not been done at the date of the order for reference. Taking the view, therefore, that the dispute raised a problem concerning the interpretation of Community law, the national court referred the following question to the Court:

C-106/89, Marleasing SA v. La Comercial Internacional de Alimentacion SA, [1990] ECR I-04135, § 4

Is Article 11 of Council Directive 68/151/EEC of 9 March 1968, which has not been implemented in national law, directly applicable so as to preclude a declaration of nullity of a public limited company on a ground other than those set out in the said article?

The CJEU considered the referred question as follows:

C-106/89, Marleasing SA v. La Comercial Internacional de Alimentacion SA, [1990] ECR I-04135, §§ 5–8, §§ 9–12 and Operative Part

1. The Member States' obligation arising from a directive to achieve the result envisaged by the directive and their duty under Article 5 of the Treaty to take all appropriate measures, whether general or particular, to ensure the fulfilment of that obligation, is binding on all the authorities of Member States including, for matters within their jurisdiction, the courts. It follows that, in applying national law, whether the provisions in question were adopted before or after the directive, the national court called upon to interpret it is required to do so, as far as possible, in the light of the wording and the purpose of the directive in order to achieve the result pursued by it and thereby comply with the third paragraph of Article 189 of the Treaty.
2. A national court hearing a case which falls within the scope of Directive 68/151 on the coordination of safeguards which, for the protection of the interests of members and others, are required by Member States of companies within the meaning of the second paragraph of Article 58 of the Treaty, with a view to making such safeguards equivalent throughout the Community, is required to interpret its national law in the light of the purpose and the wording of that directive in order to preclude a declaration of nullity of a public limited company on a ground other than those listed in Article 11 of the directive. Those grounds must themselves be strictly interpreted, in the light of that purpose, so as to ensure that nullity on the ground that the objects of the company are unlawful or contrary to public policy must be understood as referring exclusively to the objects of the company as described in the instrument of incorporation or the articles of association.

Furthermore, the CJEU provided the interpretation of Article 11 (now included in Directive 2017/1132/EU), with reference to the expression 'objects of association of the company', as follows:

C-106/89, Marleasing SA v. La Comercial Internacional de Alimentacion SA, [1990] ECR I-04135, §§ 11–12

According to the Commission, the expression 'objects of the company' must be interpreted as referring exclusively to the objects of the company as described in the instrument of incorporation or the articles of association. It follows, in the Commission's view, that a declaration of nullity of a company cannot be made on the basis of the activity actually pursued by it, for instance defrauding the founders' creditors.

That argument must be upheld. As is clear from the preamble to Directive 68/151, its purpose was to limit the cases in which nullity can arise and the retroactive effect of a declaration of nullity in order to ensure 'certainty in the law as regards relations between the company and third parties, and also between members' (sixth recital). Furthermore, the protection of third parties 'must be ensured by provisions which restrict to the greatest possible extent the grounds on which obligations entered into in the name of the company are not valid'. It follows, therefore, that each ground of nullity provided for in Article 11 of the directive must be interpreted strictly. In those circumstances the words 'objects of the company' must be understood as referring to the objects of the company as described in the instrument of incorporation or the articles of association.

FURTHER READING

C-152/84 *Marshall* v. *Southampton and South-West Hampshire Area Health Authority* [1986] ECR 723; C-14/83 *Von Colson and Kamann* v. *Land Nordrhein-Westfalen* [1984] ECR 1891;

O.O.R. Saunders, 'Marleasing – A Fatal Blow to the Rule of Construction', 3 *EBLR* 339–341 (1992).

9

The Formation of a *Societas Europaea*

9.1 General

As mentioned earlier, SEs are not created following the procedure laid down in Directive 2017/1132/EU, but only:

(i) by merger of at least two companies originating in different EU countries;
(ii) by establishment of a holding company or subsidiary by at least two companies originating in different EU countries or having had a subsidiary or branch in another EU country for at least two years;
(iii) by conversion of a company having had a subsidiary in another EU country for at least two years;
(iv) by formation of a subsidiary by an SE or division of an existing SE (SE incubator).

Article 2 Regulation 2001/2157/EC

1. Public limited-liability companies such as referred to in Annex I, formed under the law of a Member State, with registered offices and head offices within the Community may form an SE by means of a merger provided that at least two of them are governed by the law of different Member States.
2. Public and private limited-liability companies such as referred to in Annex II, formed under the law of a Member State, with registered offices and head offices within the Community may promote the formation of a holding SE provided that each of at least two of them:
   (a) is governed by the law of a different Member State, or
   (b) has for at least two years had a subsidiary company governed by the law of another Member State or a branch situated in another Member State.
3. Companies and firms within the meaning of the second paragraph of Article 48 of the Treaty and other legal bodies governed by public or private law, formed under the law of a Member State, with registered offices and head offices within the

Community may form a subsidiary SE by subscribing for its shares, provided that each of at least two of them:

(a) is governed by the law of a different Member State, or

(b) has for at least two years had a subsidiary company governed by the law of another Member State or a branch situated in another Member State.

4. A public limited-liability company, formed under the law of a Member State, which has its registered office and head office within the Community may be transformed into an SE if for at least two years it has had a subsidiary company governed by the law of another Member State.
5. A Member State may provide that a company the head office of which is not in the Community may participate in the formation of an SE provided that company is formed under the law of a Member State, has its registered office in that Member State and has a real and continuous link with a Member State's economy.

The above-mentioned survey by the European Commission dated 31 December 2017 acknowledged that the Member States with the highest concentration of SEs are: the Czech Republic, Germany, Slovakia, the UK (although Brexit will also comprise leaving the EEA, thus requiring existing SEs to convert or move their registered office), the Netherlands, Luxembourg, Austria, and Belgium. Figure 9.1 shows in the vertical axis the total number of SEs (with separate indication of those employing more than five workers) and in the horizontal axis the ten EU countries with the largest number of SEs.

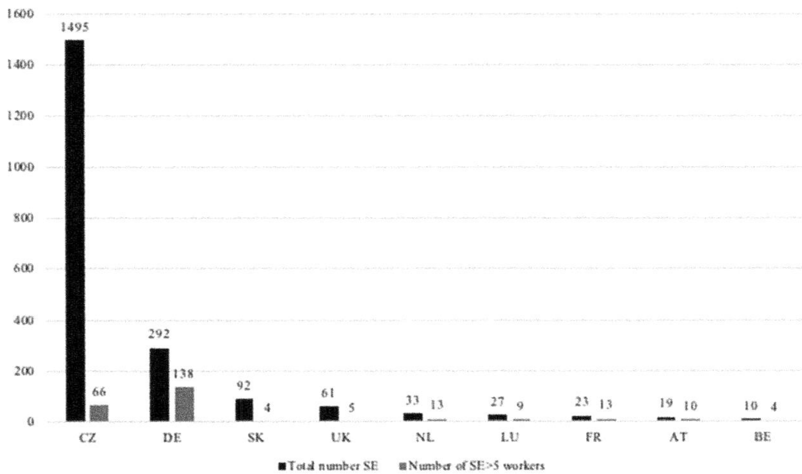

Figure 9.1 Ten EU countries with largest number of SEs

9.2 Formation by Merger

An SE may be formed by means of a merger following one of the two procedures laid down in Directive 2011/35/EU: i.e., merger by acquisition or by formation of a new company (*see*, Chapter 19). In the case of a merger by acquisition, the acquiring company shall take the form of an SE when the merger takes place. In the case of a merger by formation of a new company, the SE shall be the newly formed company (Article 17(2) Regulation 2001/2157/EC).

As we will see in Chapter 19, a merger involves three steps: (i) the drafting of the terms of merger; (ii) the decision by the general meetings of the companies to be merged; (iii) the deed of merger.

Article 20 Regulation 2001/2157/EC

1. The management or administrative organs of merging companies shall draw up draft terms of merger. The draft terms of merger shall include the following particulars:
   (a) the name and registered office of each of the merging companies together with those proposed for the SE;
   (b) the share-exchange ratio and the amount of any compensation;
   (c) the terms for the allotment of shares in the SE;
   (d) the date from which the holding of shares in the SE will entitle the holders to share in profits and any special conditions affecting that entitlement;
   (e) the date from which the transactions of the merging companies will be treated for accounting purposes as being those of the SE;
   (f) the rights conferred by the SE on the holders of shares to which special rights are attached and on the holders of securities other than shares, or the measures proposed concerning them;
   (g) any special advantage granted to the experts who examine the draft terms of merger or to members of the administrative, management, supervisory or controlling organs of the merging companies;
   (h) the statutes of the SE;
   (i) information on the procedures by which arrangements for employee involvement are determined pursuant to Directive 2001/86/EC.
2. The merging companies may include further items in the draft terms of merger.

After publication of the draft terms of merger in the national gazette, the general meeting of each of the merging companies shall approve the draft terms of merger (Article 23 Regulation 2001/2157/EC).

The legality of a merger shall be scrutinised, as regards the part of the procedure concerning each merging company, in accordance with the law on mergers of public limited-liability companies of the Member State to which the merging company is subject. In addition, as regards the part of the procedure concerning the completion of the merger and the formation of the SE, the same shall be scrutinised by the court, notary, or other authority competent in the Member State of the proposed registered office of the SE to scrutinise that aspect of the legality of mergers of public limited-liability companies.

Article 25 Regulation 2001/2157/EC

1. The legality of a merger shall be scrutinised, as regards the part of the procedure concerning each merging company, in accordance with the law on mergers of public limited-liability companies of the Member State to which the merging company is subject.
2. In each Member State concerned the court, notary or other competent authority shall issue a certificate conclusively attesting to the completion of the pre-merger acts and formalities.
3. If the law of a Member State to which a merging company is subject provides for a procedure to scrutinise and amend the share-exchange ratio, or a procedure to compensate minority shareholders, without preventing the registration of the merger, such procedures shall only apply if the other merging companies situated in Member States which do not provide for such procedure explicitly accept, when approving the draft terms of the merger in accordance with Article 23(1), the possibility for the shareholders of that merging company to have recourse to such procedure. In such cases, the court, notary or other competent authorities may issue the certificate referred to in paragraph 2 even if such a procedure has been commenced. The certificate must, however, indicate that the procedure is pending. The decision in the procedure shall be binding on the acquiring company and all its shareholders.

Article 26 Regulation 2001/2157/EC

1. The legality of a merger shall be scrutinised, as regards the part of the procedure concerning the completion of the merger and the formation of the SE, by the court, notary or other authority competent in the Member State of the proposed registered office of the SE to scrutinise that aspect of the legality of mergers of public limited-liability companies.
2. To that end each merging company shall submit to the competent authority the certificate referred to in Article 25(2) within six months of its issue together with a copy of the draft terms of merger approved by that company.
3. The authority referred to in paragraph 1 shall in particular ensure that the merging companies have approved draft terms of merger in the same terms and that arrangements for employee involvement have been determined pursuant to Directive 2001/86/EC.
4. That authority shall also satisfy itself that the SE has been formed in accordance with the requirements of the law of the Member State in which it has its registered office in accordance with Article 15.

The merger shall take effect, and the SE shall be deemed to be formed, on the date of registration of the deed of merger (Article 27 Regulation 2001/2157/EC).

Article 29 Regulation 2001/2157/EC

1. A merger carried out as laid down in Article 17(2)(a) shall have the following consequences ipso jure and simultaneously:
   (a) all the assets and liabilities of each company being acquired are transferred to the acquiring company;
   (b) the shareholders of the company being acquired become shareholders of the acquiring company;
   (c) the company being acquired ceases to exist;
   (d) the acquiring company adopts the form of an SE.
2. A merger carried out as laid down in Article 17(2)(b) shall have the following consequences ipso jure and simultaneously:
   (a) all the assets and liabilities of the merging companies are transferred to the SE;
   (b) the shareholders of the merging companies become shareholders of the SE;
   (c) the merging companies cease to exist.
3. Where, in the case of a merger of public limited-liability companies, the law of a Member State requires the completion of any special formalities before the transfer of certain assets, rights and obligations by the merging companies becomes effective against third parties, those formalities shall apply and shall be carried out either by the merging companies or by the SE following its registration.
4. The rights and obligations of the participating companies on [the] terms and conditions of employment arising from national law, practice and individual employment contracts or employment relationships and existing at the date of the registration shall, by reason of such registration be transferred to the SE upon its registration.

Similarly to the formation of a new company in accordance with Directive 2017/1132/EU, a merger aimed at the formation of an SE may not be declared null and void once the SE has been registered (Article 30 Regulation 2001/2157/EC).

9.3 Formation by Establishment of a Holding Company or Subsidiary

In contrast to the formation by merger, in case of formation of a holding or subsidiary SE, the promoting companies shall continue to exist.

Public and private companies (or firms), formed under the law of a Member State, with registered offices and head offices within the Union, may promote the formation of a holding or subsidiary SE provided that each of at least two of them:

(a) is governed by the law of a different Member State; or
(b) has had for at least two years a subsidiary company governed by the law of another Member State or a branch situated in another Member State.

Formation of the holding, or of the subsidiary, shall follow a similar procedure.

Article 32 Regulation 2001/2157/EC

...

2. The management or administrative organs of the companies which promote such an operation shall draw up, in the same terms, draft terms for the formation of the holding SE. The draft terms shall include a report explaining and justifying the legal and economic aspects of the formation and indicating the implications for the shareholders and for the employees of the adoption of the form of a holding SE. The draft terms shall also set out the particulars provided for in Article 20(1)(a), (b), (c), (f), (g), (h) and (i) and shall fix the minimum proportion of the shares in each of the companies promoting the operation which the shareholders must contribute to the formation of the holding SE. That proportion shall be shares conferring more than 50% of the permanent voting rights.
3. For each of the companies promoting the operation, the draft terms for the formation of the holding SE shall be publicised in the manner laid down in each Member State's national law in accordance with Article 3 of Directive 68/151/EEC at least one month before the date of the general meeting called to decide thereon.
4. One or more experts independent of the companies promoting the operation, appointed or approved by a judicial or administrative authority in the Member State to which each company is subject in accordance with national provisions adopted in implementation of Directive 78/855/EEC, shall examine the draft terms of formation drawn up in accordance with paragraph 2 and draw up a written report for the shareholders of each company. By agreement between the companies promoting the operation, a single written report may be drawn up for the shareholders of all the companies by one or more independent experts, appointed or approved by a judicial or administrative authority in the Member State to which one of the companies promoting the operation or the proposed SE is subject in accordance with national provisions adopted in implementation of Directive 78/855/EEC.
5. The report shall indicate any particular difficulties of valuation and state whether the proposed share-exchange ratio is fair and reasonable, indicating the methods used to arrive at it and whether such methods are adequate in the case in question.
6. The general meeting of each company promoting the operation shall approve the draft terms of formation of the holding SE.

   Employee involvement in the holding SE shall be decided pursuant to Directive 2001/86/EC. The general meetings of each company promoting the operation may reserve the right to make registration of the holding SE conditional upon its express ratification of the arrangements so decided.
7. These provisions shall apply mutatis mutandis to private limited-liability companies.

It is worth noting that in case of formation of a holding SE, the shareholders of the companies promoting such an operation shall have a period of three months in which to inform the promoting companies whether they intend to contribute their shares to the formation of the holding SE.

The holding SE shall be formed only if the shareholders of the companies promoting the operation have assigned the minimum proportion of shares in each company in accordance with the draft terms of formation and if all the other conditions are fulfilled.

Shareholders who have contributed their securities to the formation of the SE shall receive shares in the holding SE.

9.4 Conversion into a *Societas Europaea*

An SE may be formed by conversion of a public limited-liability company, formed under the law of a Member State, which has its registered office and head office within the Union; conversion into an SE may only occur when the company seeking conversion has had a subsidiary company governed by the law of another Member State for at least two years.

Article 37 Regulation 2001/2157/EC

1. An SE may be formed in accordance with Article 2(4).
2. Without prejudice to Article 12 the conversion of a public limited-liability company into an SE shall not result in the winding up of the company or in the creation of a new legal person.
3. The registered office may not be transferred from one Member State to another pursuant to Article 8 at the same time as the conversion is effected.
4. The management or administrative organ of the company in question shall draw up draft terms of conversion and a report explaining and justifying the legal and economic aspects of the conversion and indicating the implications for the shareholders and for the employees of the adoption of the form of an SE.
5. The draft terms of conversion shall be publicised in the manner laid down in each Member State's law in accordance with Article 3 of Directive 68/151/EEC at least one month before the general meeting called upon to decide thereon.
6. Before the general meeting referred to in paragraph 7 one or more independent experts appointed or approved, in accordance with the national provisions adopted in implementation of Article 10 of Directive 78/855/EEC, by a judicial or administrative authority in the Member State to which the company being converted into an SE is subject shall certify

in compliance with Directive 77/91/EEC(8) mutatis mutandis that the company has net assets at least equivalent to its capital plus those reserves which must not be distributed under the law or the Statutes.

7. The general meeting of the company in question shall approve the draft terms of conversion together with the statutes of the SE. The decision of the general meeting shall be passed as laid down in the provisions of national law adopted in implementation of Article 7 of Directive 78/855/EEC.
8. Member States may condition a conversion to a favourable vote of a qualified majority or unanimity in the organ of the company to be converted within which employee participation is organised.
9. The rights and obligations of the company to be converted on terms and conditions of employment arising from national law, practice and individual employment contracts or employment relationships and existing at the date of the registration shall, by reason of such registration be transferred to the SE.

9.5 The SE Incubator

'Incubation' is an additional way of forming an SE and, despite the fact that this method is not included in the list of Article 2 Regulation 2001/2157/EC, data reported by the European Commission (dated 31 March 2017) do show its crucial importance (*see*, Chapter 3, § 3.2).

Article 3(2) Regulation 2001/2157/EC

An SE may itself set up one or more subsidiaries in the form of SEs. The provisions of the law of the Member State in which a subsidiary SE has its registered office that require a public limited-liability company to have more than one shareholder shall not apply in the case of the subsidiary SE. The provisions of national law implementing the twelfth Council Company Law Directive (89/667/EEC) of 21 December 1989 on single-member private limited-liability companies shall apply to SEs mutatis mutandis.

As Figure 9.2 shows, 80 per cent of SEs are created by way of incubation (subsidiary), this meaning that the largest part of SEs are companies designed for carrying out new businesses. Existing companies seeking to become SEs take advantage of conversions and mergers, but they only represent 12 per cent of the overall number. Formation of a holding company is of trivial importance.

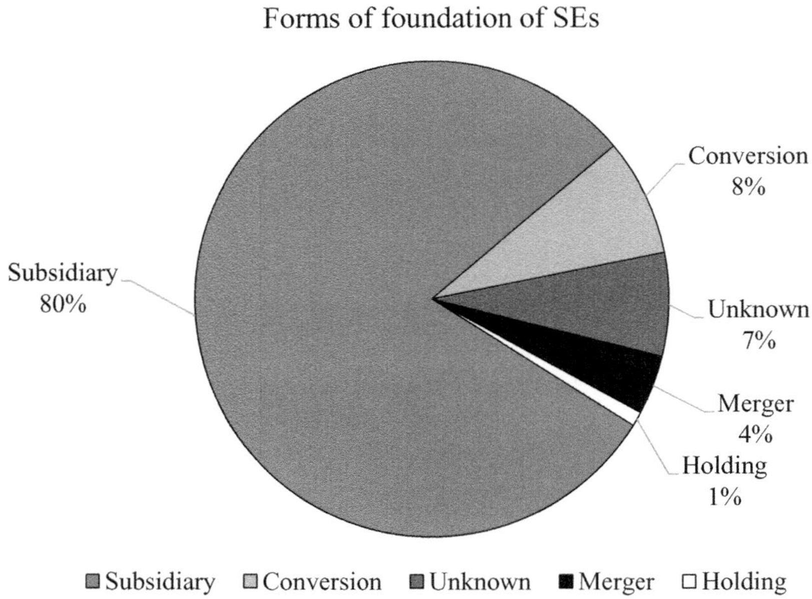

Figure 9.2 Forms of foundation of SEs

Part IV
Finance and Accounts

10

Legal Capital and Capital Formation

10.1 Legal Capital: General

Legal capital is the sum of assets contributed to a company by shareholders when they are issued shares. This sum is disclosed both in the public register (being part of the instrument of constitution or of the statutes) and in the annual financial statements. This information is important for both shareholders and creditors.

ECL requires that SEs and public limited companies have a legal capital greater than a certain sum: i.e., the minimum capital.

Article 4 Regulation 2001/2157/EC

1. The capital of an SE shall be expressed in euros.
2. The subscribed capital shall not be less than EUR 120,000.
3. The laws of a Member State requiring a greater subscribed capital for companies carrying on certain types of activity shall apply to SEs with registered offices in that Member State.

Article 4(1) Directive 2017/1132/EU

The laws of the Member States shall require that, in order that a company may be incorporated or obtain authorisation to commence business, a minimum capital shall be subscribed the amount of which shall be not less than EUR 25,000.

ECL provides rules assuring correct formation and maintenance of the legal capital. These rules also apply to SEs.

Article 5 Regulation 2001/2157/EC

Subject to Article 4(1) and (2), the capital of an SE, its maintenance and changes thereto, together with its shares, bonds and other similar securities shall be governed by the provisions which would apply to a public limited-liability company with a registered office in the Member State in which the SE is registered.

Capital formation rules mainly concern contribution of assets to the company and, in particular, the assessment of their value, in case these are other than contributions in cash: we will address capital formation rules in this chapter. Capital maintenance rules are more heterogeneous, as they include rules requiring that dividends are not paid when a company is not showing a profit above the level of historically recorded legal capital, rules requiring that an action is taken in cases where the net assets fall below the legal capital (serious losses), other rules on capital increases and reductions, on the acquisition of the companies' own shares, and so on: we will discuss capital maintenance rules in Chapter 11.

10.2 The Debate on Legal Capital

As mentioned, Recital 3 Directive 2017/1132/EU reads as follows:

Recital 3 Directive 2017/1132/EU

(3) In order to ensure minimum equivalent protection for both shareholders and creditors of public limited-liability companies, the coordination of national provisions relating to their formation and to the maintenance, increase or reduction of their capital is particularly important.

It has also been mentioned that the ability of EU capital formation and maintenance rules to effectively protect the interest of shareholders and creditors has been challenged by influential academics (Enriques and Macey; Lutter; Rickford; Schutte-Veenstra, Boschma and Lennarts), including those appointed by the Commission to make recommendations for the simplification and modernisation of ECL (the SLIM Group and the High Level Group).

Luca Enriques and Jonathan R. Macey, 'Creditors Versus Capital Formation: The Case Against Legal Capital Rules', 86 Cornell L. Rev. 1165–1204, at 1166 (2001)

This Article presents a critical economic analysis of the European Union's legal capital rules as codified by the Second Directive. Professors Enriques and Macey explore the fundamental differences between US and EU approaches to the conflict between fixed and equity claimants and argue that the EU should abandon its inefficient approach. The costs associated with the European legal capital rules – particularly costs to shareholders, creditors, and society as a whole significantly outweigh any benefits accrued by creditors. The authors suggest that a public-choice theory best explains the existence of the European legal capital rules, in that certain influential interest groups benefit from the rules despite their inefficiency. In conclusion, this Article advocates that the EU should abandon its current legal capital rules in favour of more flexible, contractarian rules in order to facilitate entrepreneurship and business in European markets.

The SLIM Group and the High Level Group also criticised the EU capital formation and maintenance rules and made proposals for their improvement. Whilst the SLIM Group only proposed the adoption of new rules with the view to simplifying existing capital formation and maintenance rules, the High Level Group Report – having usefully summarised the current debate – proposed several approaches to modernise ECL.

Final Report of the High Level Group of Company Law Experts on a Modern Regulatory Framework for Company Law in Europe 78–81

Chapter IV – Capital Formation and Maintenance

1 The Function of Legal Capital and the Competitive Effect of the Current Rules

The Consultation Document included a description of the traditional functions of legal capital in European Company Law, followed by three possible approaches for reform, and some special topics in the regulation of legal capital that deserved more detailed attention.

The concept of legal capital is generally seen as one of the cornerstones of European Company Law. In the Consultative Document, the functions of legal capital, as described by orthodox legal and financial theory, were listed. A large majority of the respondents highlighted the fundamental functions of protecting creditors' and existing shareholders' interests. Many respondents highlighted this function of legal capital as a 'retention figure' that prevents unlawful transfers of assets from the company to its members. Most respondents, and the Group itself, however do not believe that legal capital serves any function of indicating the adequacy of a company's assets for its entrepreneurial activity ('capital adequacy'), leaving aside the special regime of capital adequacy for certain regulated business activities. In short, a considerable majority of the respondents agree that the most important functions developed by legal capital are the protection of creditors' and shareholders' rights. It is important to note, however, that many respondents added that the functions performed by legal capital are more important in theory than in practice: there is wide agreement that the concept of legal capital is not effective in attaining the objectives that are assigned to it. The rules on capital formation and maintenance have an impact on the cost of capital and credit, although that impact may be extremely difficult to assess. Most of the respondents do not believe that the peculiarities of the European legal capital regime put European companies at a competitive disadvantage in comparison with their competitors in other legal systems. Evidently, this question deserves thorough empirical research, which is difficult because the competitive effect of the legal capital regime is obscured by the presence of many other variables. However, none of the respondents argue that European companies enjoy an advantage thanks to the legal capital regime existing in the EU.

2 Approaches to the Reform of Legal Capital in Europe

In the Consultative Document, we referred to criticisms levelled against the legal capital regime in the Second Company Law Directive. The legal capital regime, it is argued, fails to adequately protect creditors, who are not so much interested in the capital of the company (and certainly not in the minimum capital) but much more in its ability to pay its short term and long term debts. It can also be said that the amount of legal capital, as shown in the articles of association, is a very primitive and inaccurate indication of the company's ability to pay its debts. There is an argument against the inflexibility and costs of the current regime, that could hamper in some way the ability of companies to obtain equity funding.

Finally, it is argued that the annual accounts have become an inadequate yard-stick for deciding whether the company has sufficient distributable reserves for it to make distributions to shareholders. As a result of changes in accounting standards, like standards on goodwill impairment and accounting for pension fund performance and costs of share and share option schemes, the accounts – and the reserves they show – become more and more volatile and less and less an indicator of the ability of companies to pay their current and future debts. Capital protection based on such accounts is becoming a delusion.

Most of the respondents agree that there is room for improvement of the current regime, although there is controversy on which is the best possible course to reform the present system.

In the Consultative Document, three alternative approaches were considered:

- The first approach is based on the 'SLIM' (Simpler Legislation for the Internal Market) proposals. This approach consists of an evolution of the current regime to a more simplified and modern capital regime. The purpose of the SLIM exercise was to simplify the Second Company Law Directive; as a consequence of this, more fundamental changes to the rules could not be considered by the SLIM Group, which proposed a number of measures intended to simplify and modernise the current legal capital regime. In the Consultative Document, this was suggested as one of the possible approaches to reform, supplemented by other recommendations that could be included in a wider reform of the Second Company Law Directive ('SLIM-plus').
- The second approach is roughly based on the experience of US jurisdictions that have passed statutes based on the Model Business Corporations Act. This approach would mean a radical departure from many of the features of European Company Law: the concept of legal capital does not exist in such a regime, and most of the rules related to capital formation and maintenance are different from the European rules, or even totally opposed to them.

Apart from those basic features, in the US jurisdictions that follow this approach, the balance of powers between the general meeting of shareholders and the board of directors is usually tilted in favour of the latter, while the situation in Europe is different. In these US jurisdictions, the board of directors may issue new shares without any shareholders' involvement, but subject to the directors' fiduciary duties. Pre-emption rights are not recognised as basic shareholder rights, and they only exist where they are expressly recognised in the articles of association.

- The third approach contemplated in the Consultative Document is also based on the elimination of the concept of legal capital, but seeks to integrate that fundamental change with some of the basic features of European Company Law, specifically the need for shareholder approval for operations that affect shareholders' equity.

Very few respondents expressed support for the second approach. A substantial number of respondents preferred the first and third approach, with some of the respondents opting for one of them, but without excluding the other.

Taking into account the consultation results, the Group recommends a two-step approach:

1. The Commission should, as a matter of priority, present a proposal for reform of the Second Company Law Directive, along the lines suggested by the SLIM Group, with the modifications and supplementary measures that are suggested in the present Report ('SLIM-plus').
2. The Commission should, at a later stage, conduct a review into the feasibility of an alternative regime, based on the third approach. The alternative regime need not replace the capital formation and maintenance rules of the Directive as amended according to the 'SLIM-plus' proposals. Rather, the new regime could be offered as an alternative option for Member States, who should be able to freely decide to change to the new regime and impose it on companies subject to their jurisdiction or to retain the Second Directive rules as modified by the 'SLIM-plus' reform. Obviously, the creation of a new regime will demand further study and consultation, but there is a very substantial and relevant percentage of answers to the Consultative Document that shows a strong interest in pursuing this alternative to the present capital formation and maintenance rules. In addition, the Group believes that the criticism directed at the current regime is so fundamental and serious that indeed an alternative regime aimed at efficient shareholder and creditor protection needs to be developed.

The Commission's Action Plan of 2003 (*Modernising Company Law and Enhancing Corporate Governance in the European Union – A Plan to Move Forward*) welcomed both suggestions.

A proposal to amend the Second Directive along the lines drafted by the SLIM Group was regarded as a priority for the short term. As consequence, on 6 September 2006, the European Parliament and the Council approved Directive 2006/68/EC, carrying amendments to the Second Directive with regards to capital formation and maintenance rules, such as: (i) contributions in kind not requiring an expert's report; (ii) simplification of the rules on the acquisition of a company's own shares and on; (iii) the financial assistance for the acquisition of the company's own shares by a third party; (iv) rules related to the reduction of capital.

Recitals 3-6 Directive 2006/68/EC

(3) Member States should be able to permit public limited liability companies to allot shares for consideration other than in cash without requiring them to obtain a special expert valuation in cases in which there is a clear point of reference for the valuation of such consideration. Nonetheless, the right of minority shareholders to require such valuation should be guaranteed.

(4) Public limited liability companies should be allowed to acquire their own shares up to the limit of the company's distributable reserves and the period for which such an acquisition may be authorised by the general meeting should be increased so as to enhance flexibility and reduce the administrative burden for companies which have to react promptly to market developments affecting the price of their shares.

(5) Member States should be able to permit public limited liability companies to grant financial assistance with a view to the acquisition of their shares by a third party up to the limit of the company's distributable reserves so as to increase flexibility with regard to changes in the ownership structure of the share capital of companies. This possibility should be subject to safeguards, having regard to this Directive's objective of protecting both shareholders and third parties.

(6) In order to enhance standardised creditor protection in all Member States, creditors should be able to resort, under certain conditions, to judicial or administrative proceedings where their claims are at stake as a consequence of a reduction in the capital of a public limited liability company.

The Commission also considered the proposal of the High Level Group to introduce at a later stage an alternative regime that would not be based on the concept of legal capital. The Commission considered that, before deciding to introduce an alternative regime which would fundamentally depart from the capital maintenance regime organised by the Second Directive, further work was needed as to both the exact characteristics of a possible alternative regime and its ability to achieve an effective protection of shareholders and third parties. Consequently, a study into the feasibility of an alternative to the capital maintenance regime was to be launched by the Commission in the medium term. The study should have to identify in particular the precise benefits that an alternative regime would offer in comparison with the Second Directive rules amended in the short term.

The study was commissioned in October 2006 and led by KPMG, one of the world's largest auditing firms. The study provides a factual background on some of the main features of the legal capital regime established by the Second Company Law Directive, notably:

- the administrative costs of the rules on capital formation and maintenance;
- the costs and benefits of solvency tests or other alternative methods to determine distributable dividends;

- the shareholders' and creditors' protection in alternative regimes;
- the implementation costs of an alternative regime (e.g., the compliance costs required for companies to adjust to new requirements).

The study examines the situation in five Member States of the EU (namely France, Germany, Poland, Sweden, and the UK) and four foreign jurisdictions (Australia, Canada, US – California and Delaware – and New Zealand). It also reviews four academic proposals for alternative regimes to the capital maintenance rules: in addition to the High Level Group Report, these proposals are referred to by the feasibility study as the Rickford Group, the Lutter Group, and the Dutch Group Reports.

KPMG, Feasibility Study on an Alternative to the Capital Maintenance Regime Established by the Second Company Law Directive 77/91/EEC of 13 December 1976 and an Examination of the Impact on Profit Distribution of the New EU-accounting Regime 1–6, 314

1 Executive Summary

The guiding objective of this study is to evaluate the feasibility of an alternative to the current regime of legal capital established by the 2nd Company Law Directive (CLD) and to examine the impacts of International Financial Reporting Standards (IFRS) on profit distribution. The study is intended to help the European Commission to evaluate whether an alternative regime would better support the efficiency and competitiveness of EU businesses. A particular challenge for the capital regime as currently embedded in the 2nd CLD is the introduction of IFRS in the European Union. Under the IAS Regulation (1606/2002), EU Member States may permit or require companies to use IFRS for their individual financial statements. This instantly raises the question whether IFRS as an accounting framework is adequate to be used as the basis for profit distribution under the current capital regime of the 2nd CLD when IFRS are not primarily designed for this purpose.

The decision on the introduction of an alternative to the current regime is a highly complex task. Several disciplines on which alternative regimes may have an effect or influence, will need due consideration. This primarily concerns the areas of company law and accountancy. Furthermore, certain aspects of insolvency and securities' legislation or taxation may also come into play. For specific industries, such as the banking and insurance sector, certain regulations e.g. Basel II or Solvency II may also affect the capital regimes of the companies concerned. This study focuses on the core aspects of company law and accountancy as relevant for any company falling under the 2nd CLD, not making specific considerations for a particular industry. Taking into account the impact of IFRS on the current capital regime of the 2nd CLD, the study examines the feasibility of an alternative system by way of measuring the administrative burdens for EU businesses.

Overall, the cost analysis of the existing models adopted in the five EU Member States and five non-EU jurisdictions has shown that the compliance costs related to the capital regimes in all jurisdictions are generally not overly burdensome as [on] average they do not exceed €30,000 for a specific process. Comparative synthesis tables can be found in section 4.4 of this study report. A first conclusion of the study is that the reduction of compliance costs is unlikely to be a motivation for the transition to an alternative, solvency-based system.

Concerning the accounting aspects, EU Member States may require or permit the use of IFRS for individual accounts. As a consequence, IFRS individual accounts could also be used as a basis for profit distribution subject to Member States' legislation. This is currently the case in 17 of the 27 EU Member States. The practice on how IFRS are applied for distribution purposes shows a mixed picture throughout these 17 EU Member States. In 7 of these 17 Member States, the IFRS accounting profits are modified for distribution purposes. The basic modification consists in declaring certain 'unrealised' profits resulting from IFRS individual financial statements as non-distributable.

Comparative Cost Analysis of Capital Regimes in Selected EU/Non-EU Jurisdictions and in Literature

Based on a legal analysis, the study conducts an economic analysis of the capital regimes of five EU Member States (France, Germany, Poland, Sweden and the United Kingdom) and of four non-EU countries (the USA, Canada, Australia and New Zealand) [for the legal analysis see Annexes – part 1, section 3 of this study report]. Furthermore, four models which can be found in the literature (High Level Group, Rickford Group, Lutter Group and Dutch Group) are analysed. The aim of this economic analysis is the identification of the administrative costs, i.e. the incremental burdens linked to company law provisions concerning the capital regimes in existence and the proposed models in the literature. The comparison of the administrative costs of different regimes may allow assessing whether a certain capital regime is more advantageous than another for EU companies from a cost perspective. In order to obtain comparable data throughout the various jurisdictions with different economic levels, we have employed standardised cost rates of €100/€70 per hour for the main cost factor of the provisions, the internal man hours spent on compliance. The basis for the economic analysis formed in-depth interviews with high-ranking representatives of 35 companies of different sizes in the five EU and the four non-EU countries. The interviews were complemented by the results of a CFO questionnaire sent out to 3,578 companies in these countries; thereof 157 companies have responded to the questionnaire which represents

4.39 percent of the 3,578 companies [for the CFO questionnaire, see Annexes – part 1, section 2.1 of this study report].

Administrative Costs in Five EU Member States

A main building block of the current capital regime of the European Union is the concept of a subscribed capital which is protected from distributions. The concept of subscribed capital is extended to the 2nd CLD's approach to capital maintenance, which provides restrictions on share repurchases, capital reductions, the withdrawal of shares and financial assistance. Another building block is the use of balance sheet test to determine any distribution under the 2nd CLD. The balance sheet profit is the profit realised for the financial year after setting off losses and profits brought forward as well as sums in mandatory and optional reserves. The accounting framework from which the realised profits are derived is either national GAAP harmonised to a certain degree by the 4th CLD or IFRS. A third building block of the current regime of the 2nd CLD is the decision making authority of the general meeting concerning all matters relating to an amendment of the subscribed capital or fundamental decisions concerning transactions linked to capital maintenance issues.

The legal analysis of the company law regime adopted in five EU Member States showed that all of them closely follow the 2nd CLD. However, in some EU Member States there are a few significant additional protective measures in national legislation which partly concern profit distribution. This is the case, for instance, for national provisions concerning the protection of premiums and of certain reserves from distributions; the prohibition of transactions with shareholders that are not conducted at 'arm's length'; the necessity of resolutions by the general meeting to distribute profits; different quorums for general meetings and additional rules regarding sanctions.

In implementing the 2nd CLD, the five EU Member States have set minimum subscribed capital requirements which in all cases exceed the minimum of €25,000 required by the 2nd CLD and extend up to €225,000 for French listed companies [see section 4.1.6 of this study report]. In company practice, the subscribed capital regularly exceeds the minimum amounts by far. However, the interviews conducted with EU companies indicated that the practical relevance of the subscribed capital for the assessment of the viability of a company is seen as low. The companies as well as their peers like banks, rating agencies and analysts rather refer to other equity figures such as 'net equity' and 'market capitalisation'. A comparison of the ratio of subscribed capital to the total shareholders' equity for the companies on the main stock exchange indices of the five EU Member States showed that due to the low percentage of subscribed capital, equity financing is not largely dependent on it and that there should be [a] sufficient equity base for adequate distributions. In this context, it must be noted that the results of the CFO questionnaire underpin that the majority of the responding CFOs in all five EU Member States do currently not particularly question the distribution restrictions implied by the concept of legal capital. The majority of the responding CFOs considered the subscribed capital to be necessary for equity financing and, in their opinion the subscribed capital does not constitute a barrier to the distribution of excess capital.

The general dividend policies of the companies interviewed differentiate from company to company as they depend on their individual circumstances. The level of dividends as such is a 'political decision' of the parent company with a view to the share price. This includes aspects like dividend continuity or sending certain signals to the capital market. The starting point for the consideration of potential dividend levels is usually the consolidated financial statements and the cash flow situation of the group. The results of the interviews in this respect have been validated by the results of the CFO questionnaire. From an economic perspective, the reference to the group situation shows that the legal profit distribution concept which is based on the single legal entity, receives less consideration when discussing the actual level of dividends.

In general, all five EU Member States follow the requirements of the 2nd CLD in restricting profit distributions. The results of the CFO questionnaire showed that the responding CFOs considered legal requirements concerning distributions as well as possible violations of insolvency law as important deterrents regarding excessive levels of dividend payments, i.e. payments which endanger the viability of a company. Other market-led solutions such as bank covenants and rating agencies' requirements play a less significant role.

To bring the parent company's financial situation in line with the group perspective, a large part of the companies interviewed steer the profit and cash flow situation of the parent company. This is mostly done in a structured planning process over several years. This can entail significant costs for companies. However, as this process is mainly undertaken to achieve tax optimisation for intra-group distributions, we have disregarded the associated costs as incremental burdens stemming from company law.

Altogether, we have tried to assemble the administrative costs associated with key processes concerning compliance with the provisions of the implemented 2nd CLD. These processes included capital increases and profit distributions as well as certain aspects of capital maintenance such as the acquisition by the company of its own shares, capital reductions and redemption/withdrawal of shares. We have mainly been able to retrieve meaningful data for capital increases, profit distributions and acquisition by the company of its own shares as companies are regularly using these processes. The average costs for each process do not exceed €30,000. For capital reductions and the redemption/withdrawal of shares, there are no meaningful data as the sampled companies have not made use of these processes. For contractual self-protection such as covenants, we have found the use of such instruments but have not received associated cost data. Furthermore, we have not found that compliance costs vary according to the size of the company, in general.

In total, we conclude that the administrative costs concerning the 2nd CLD company law requirements are generally low for companies interviewed throughout the five EU Member States [for details please refer to section 4.1.6 of this study report]; more significant costs arise outside the area of the core company law requirements, specifically with regard to securities legislation (e.g. capital increases; acquisition by the company of its own shares). In view of the most recent changes to the 2nd CLD in 2006, we have not been in a position to verify the cost implications of these measures as they have not yet been applied by the EU companies interviewed.

In addition, we have analysed the situation of private companies in four of the five EU Member States (Sweden has no separate legal form). In essence, the legal requirements related to the capital regime of private companies are less restrictive than the regime for the companies falling under the 2nd CLD [For an overview and further details, please refer to Annexes – part 1, section 4 of this study report]. Private companies maintain the capital as contributions can usually not be distributed, although there is a trend at least to lower the amounts or de facto abolish the minimum capital. Capital increases and decreases require a resolution by the shareholder meeting. The basis for profit distributions are usually the net accounting profits as shown in the annual financial statements; the UK deviates by referring to 'realised profits', an approach also applied to UK companies falling under the 2nd CLD. The repurchase of own shares is generally not restricted, except for the UK where basically the same rules as for public companies apply.

Administrative Costs in Four Non-EU Countries The four non-EU countries show different alternatives to the capital regime used in the EU. We have examined two US state laws

(Delaware and California), the Canadian federal legislation as well as the company laws of Australia and New Zealand [for an overview see section 4.2.7]. Furthermore, we have outlined the provisions of the US Model Business Corporation Act (MBCA) which is a guideline for the company laws of a significant number of US states [see section 4.2.1].

With the exception of Delaware, none of the non-EU jurisdictions prescribe a subscribed capital or a minimum capital. In Delaware, the traditional capital system continues to be applied although it does not play an important role in practice. Because Delaware corporations usually issue shares with a very low par value (e.g. US$ 0.01 and less), capital is negligibly low. As with EU companies, the equity figures 'net equity' and 'market capitalisation' are much more important to the companies interviewed.

Instead, the emphasis has shifted to increased testing procedures for dividend payments and other kinds of distributions such as the repurchase of the company's own shares. This is achieved through various solvency and balance sheet tests. In some of the jurisdictions considered, the performance of the balance sheet test is based on audited consolidated accounts for legal or practical considerations (e.g. for the United States US GAAP). The results of the CFO questionnaire indicate that the responding CFOs of non-EU companies are satisfied with the concept of a balance sheet test and that they consider their audited accounts as a good starting point to determine the level of dividends. On the other hand, the majority of the responding CFOs, with the exception of Australia, believes that a solvency test taking into account future cash-flows better determines the ability to actually pay dividends than a balance sheet test.

In the non-EU countries, the distribution decision lies with the board of directors which has full discretion in this respect. The assessment by the company's management about the adequate level of dividend payments results, as in the EU Member States, in a 'political' decision driven by a share price objective. Aspects such as dividend continuity and other signalling effects to the capital market play a role. Again, these companies regularly refer to their consolidated accounts and cash-flow position as a starting point for such considerations. This is reconfirmed by the results of the CFO questionnaire. One interesting fact in this context, however, is that the responding CFOs in the considered non-EU countries rank the issue of the compliance with covenants much higher than their EU counterparts.

One common feature of the non-EU capital regimes is that the increased responsibility of the board in this regard translates into a fiduciary duty or personal liability. Particularly in the United States, directors may also be subject to fraudulent transfer legislation.

As for EU Member States, we have tried to track the administrative costs associated with key processes for the non-EU jurisdictions. These processes included capital increases and profit distributions as well as certain aspects of capital maintenance such as the repurchase of shares, capital reductions, redemption/withdrawal of shares. We have been able to retrieve meaningful data only for capital increases, profit distributions and repurchase of shares as companies regularly use such processes. The average cost for each operation does not exceed €25,000. For capital reductions and the redemption/withdrawal of shares, there is no meaningful data available as companies have not made use of these options. With respect to contractual self-protection such as covenants, we found significant compliance costs amounting on average up to €90,000. However, the costs relating to covenants mainly depend on individual circumstances, especially how covenants are negotiated. Furthermore, we have not found that compliance costs vary depending on the size of the company, in general. However, it should be noted that the non-EU companies interviewed were all in good financial health. The compliance effort may, in these models, significantly increase once a company enters into a more difficult financial situation because the management assessment to justify a dividend payment would become much more detailed.

In total, we conclude that the administrative costs are also generally low for companies interviewed throughout the five non-EU jurisdictions [for details please refer to section 4.2.7 of this study report]; as market-led solutions, namely covenants, play a more prominent role, additional costs may arise in this respect. More significant costs rather arise outside the area of the core company law requirements, specifically with regard to securities legislation (e.g. capital increases; repurchase of shares).

Administrative Costs of Four Models in the Literature

All four proposals in the literature (High Level Group, Rickford Group, Lutter Group, Dutch Group) consider possible changes to the current regime of profit distributions in the EU. These proposals vary from partial to full scale reform of the 2nd CLD capital regime. All systems differ as to how this affects the overall set-up of the capital regime.

The Lutter Group proposal [see section 4.3.3] to a large extent maintains the current system of the 2nd CLD and only changes provisions on the distribution of profits to accommodate the use of IFRS in the individual financial statements. To this end, the Lutter Group proposes a solvency test, in addition to the balance sheet test already foreseen by the 2nd CLD. The other three models (High Level Group, Rickford Group, Dutch Group) discuss a fundamental change to the current capital regime by abolishing the concept of legal capital in favour of distribution testing by means of additional solvency tests. The latter goes hand-in-hand with the transition from a par value concept of shares to a true no-par value share concept. The High Level Group [see section 4.3.1 of this study report] and the Dutch Group [see section 4.3.4 of this study report] require the companies to meet both the balance sheet test as well as the solvency test. The High Level Group additionally discusses the introduction of a solvency margin. The Rickford Group [see section 4.3.2 of this study report] ultimately only requires that a solvency test must be met to allow for distributions.

The solvency margin proposed by the High Level Group is an instrument which can only be used in the context of a balance sheet test and may replace the concept of a fixed legal capital. It ensures that the assets, after the distribution, exceed the liabilities by a certain margin. In this respect, it is decisive to determine an appropriate margin level to avoid excessive restrictions for companies to distribute dividends. In California, which is the only jurisdiction under consideration which embeds a solvency margin in law, the margin only needs to be met if a company does not have sufficient retained earnings for a distribution. We have not encountered any practical case of a California incorporated company where such a margin test has been actually performed.

The economic effects of these models are not fully clear, as they leave the most burdensome administrative aspects of the 2nd CLD intact. This specifically concerns the preparation of the general meeting in the case of capital increases, dividend distributions and the repurchase of shares. This is the reason why we have used the EU average administrative cost as a starting point for cost considerations. Presumably, this would also be true for capital reductions and redemptions/withdrawals. However, as specified above, we have not been able to gather reliable EU data in this regard.

All four models are, in differing degrees, incomplete in their suggestions on how to exactly conduct changes to the 2nd CLD. One important example is the impact of different designs of solvency tests. The existing gaps in these models partly allow for a wide interpretation and can immensely influence the associated burdens for the companies concerned. For the High Level Group, it seems relatively easy to comply as a reference to current balance sheet ratios is proposed (current assets/current liabilities). For the Rickford and Lutter Group, cash-flow projections are required. The Dutch Group leaves the design completely open. Except for the reference to current ratios, we have not encountered a formalised detailed application of any of these design approaches in the five non-EU jurisdictions. Therefore, we have not been in a position to build on this experience and, thus, have not attempted to estimate the costs associated with the different formats of the solvency tests [see section 4.3.5 of this study report].

Result of the Comparative Cost Analysis

Overall, the cost analysis of the existing models in the five EU Member States and four non-EU countries has shown that the administrative costs of company law in this regard for the companies in all jurisdictions are generally not overly burdensome as on average they do not exceed €30,000 in a specific process. The comparative synthesis tables can be found in section 4.4 of this study report. Thus, such considerations do not seem to play a decisive role in determining whether the transition to an alternative system would actually benefit EU businesses by lowering administrative burdens. However, administrative burdens can be of significant relevance when considering the implementation of certain measures in a jurisdiction. This is especially true for the design of solvency tests. Moreover, we have considered qualitative aspects of shareholder and creditor protection within each model. Both the EU and non-EU jurisdictions have certain shareholder and creditor protection instruments in place. In particular, the EU jurisdictions generally require the involvement of the general meeting concerning capital measures, whereas non-EU jurisdictions more often rely on the board of directors to take decisions in this respect.

...

Overall, the cost analysis of the existing models in five EU Member States and four non-EU countries has shown that the incremental burdens of company law in this regard for the companies in all jurisdictions are not overly burdensome and, thus, cannot play a decisive role in determining whether the transition to an alternative system would actually benefit EU business by lowering administrative burdens. However, incremental burdens can be of considerable relevance when considering the implementation of certain measures in a jurisdiction. This is especially true of the design of solvency tests. Moreover, aspects of shareholder and creditor protection have to be considered.

As a consequence of the KPMG Feasibility Study that assessed the substantial lack of benefits of an alternative regime to the legal capital, the Commission decided that the EU capital formation and maintenance rules expressed in the Second Company Law Directive should be kept. Therefore, a recast Second Directive was approved in 2012 (Directive 2012/30/EU); the new rules are now included in Directive 2017/1132/EU.

FURTHER READING

Luca Enriques and Jonathan R. Macey, 'Creditors Versus Capital Formation: The Case Against Legal Capital Rules', 86 *Cornell L. Rev.* 1165–1204 (2001).

Jonathan Rickford (ed.), 'Reforming Capital: Report of the Interdisciplinary Group on Capital Maintenance', 15 *EBLR* 919–1027 (2004).

Jonathan Rickford, 'Reforming Capital: An Introductory Note', 15 *EBLR* 1029–1030 (2004).

Friedrich Kübler, 'A Comparative Approach to Capital Maintenance: Germany', 15 *EBLR* 1031–1035 (2004).

Hanno Merkt, 'Creditor Protection and Capital Maintenance from a German Perspective', 15 *EBLR* 1045–1057 (2004).

Massimo Miola, 'Legal Capital and Limited Liability Companies: The European Perspective', 2 *ECFR* 413–486 (2005).

Hanny Schutte-Veenstra, Hylda Boschma, and Marie-Louise Lennarts, 'Alternative Systems for Capital Protection (Final Report dated 18 August 2005)', in Marcus Lutter (ed.), *Legal Capital in Europe, Special Volume 1 ECFR* (2006).

Jennifer Payne, 'Legal Capital and Creditor Protection in UK Private Companies', 5 *ECL* 220–228 (2008).

John Kong Shan Ho, 'Revisiting the Legal Capital Regime in Modern Company Law', 12 *J. Comp. L.* 1–22 (2017).

Eilìs Ferran, 'Revisiting Legal Capital', 20 *EBOR* 521–545 (2019).

See also:

Marco Ventoruzzo, Pierre-Henry Conac, Gen Goto, Sebastan Mock, Mario Notari, and Arad Reisberg, *Comparative Corporate Governance 144–151* (St Paul MN, West Academic Publishing, 2015).

10.3 The Capital Formation: General

To familiarise ourselves with the ECL rules on capital formation and maintenance, some legal concepts should be kept in mind.

First of all, the difference between (i) authorised capital, (ii) subscribed capital and (iii) issued and paid-up capital.

Authorised capital means the maximum amount of assets that the directors of the company are authorised to raise as contributions from shareholders or third parties by issuing the new shares. Authorisation to issue new shares is given by the shareholders either in the instrument of constitution or by resolution of the general meeting and lasts for a maximum of five years.

Article 68(2) Directive 2017/1132/EU

2. Nevertheless, the statutes or instrument of incorporation or the general meeting, the decision of which must be published in accordance with the rules referred to in paragraph 1, may authorise an increase in the subscribed capital up to a maximum amount which they shall fix with due regard for any maximum amount provided for by law. Where appropriate, the increase in the subscribed capital shall be decided on within the limits of the amount fixed by the company body empowered to do so. The power of such body in this respect shall be for a maximum period of five years and may be renewed one or more times by the general meeting, each time for a period not exceeding five years.

Subscribed capital means the amount of assets that existing shareholders are already engaged to contribute to the company (*see*, Item A.I. *Subscribed capital* in the Capital, reserves, and liability column, Table 10.1). Therefore, subscribed capital and legal capital are synonymous concepts. In addition, subscription of capital or of shares means the engagement to contribute to the company with new assets.

Issued and paid-up capital means the amount of assets that the company has already received from its shareholders in exchange for the issuance of shares, thus, as contribution to the capital formation (*see*, Item A. *Subscribed capital unpaid* of the Assets column, Table 10.1). Accordingly, shares may be paid-up in full or in part, depending on whether the shareholder has entirely fulfilled its obligation towards the company. Table 10.1 represents a simplified horizontal layout of the balance sheet, where the items A. *Subscribed capital unpaid* and A.I. *Subscribed capital* in the Assets and Capital, reserves, and liabilities columns have been embolded for comparative purposes.

Second, we shall consider the difference between *consideration in cash* and *consideration other than in cash*. Whilst there is no need to explain the

Table 10.1 Simplified horizontal layout of a balance sheet

Assets	Capital, reserves, and liabilities
A. Subscribed capital unpaid	A. Capital and reserves
	I. Subscribed capital
B. Formation expenses	II. Share premium account
	III. Revaluation reserve
C. Fixed assets	IV. Reserves
	V. Profit or loss brought forward
D. Current assets	VI. Profit or loss of the financial year
	B. Provisions
E. Prepayments and accrued incomes	C. Creditors
	D. Accruals and deferred income

meaning of 'cash', by 'contribution other than in cash', ECL refers to contributions of assets in kind (including credits) and to undertakings to perform work or supply. Not all assets other than cash may be contributed and form part of the capital of a public limited company.

Article 46 Directive 2017/1132/EU

The subscribed capital may be formed only of assets capable of economic assessment. However, an undertaking to perform work or supply services may not form part of those assets.

10.4 The Shares: Nominal Value and Accountable Par

There is a close linkage between shares and legal capital. Indeed, 'share' means 'part of something'. In legal systems like those of the EU Member States where legal capital is mandatory, shares represent parts of the legal capital and measure the shareholders' interest in a company. As legal capital is the sum of money that corresponds to the value of contributions, shares also represent a sum of money. In this respect, shares are deemed to have a nominal value, this being the part of the legal capital that each share represents.

The overall amount of all shares' nominal values corresponds to that of the legal capital. As consequence, provided that the nominal value of all shares is equal, division of the legal capital into the overall number of issued shares results in the nominal value of each share. However, ECL does not require that all shares have the same nominal value. Indeed, whilst the majority of EU legislations require that the nominal value is always equal, two Member States (Germany and Spain) permit shares of different classes to have different nominal values.

Moreover, ECL does not require that shares have an expressed nominal value. In case a nominal value is not expressed, the concept of 'accountable par' becomes relevant. Accountable par is the proportion between the price paid for the shares and the value accounted for in contributions made to the company and being part of the legal capital.

Article 47(1) Directive 2017/1132/EU

Shares may not be issued at a price lower than their nominal value, or, where there is no nominal value, their accountable par.

Nominal value and accountable par are therefore the lowest price at which shares are issued; as such, it is apparent that shares may be subscribed at a higher price. The difference between the nominal value or accountable par and the total consideration paid constitutes a share premium. This is accounted for in a reserve named the share premium account.

For example, assume that Harry purchases three shares out of ten in the X NewCo for €100 each, for an overall consideration of €300. Considering that the legal capital of the X NewCo is deemed to be €700, the price paid by Harry covers the part of legal capital represented by his three shares (€210) and the remaining part shall be accounted for in the share premium account.

Under certain conditions, and if the laws of the Member States provide accordingly, it is also possible to issue shares at a price lower than the nominal value or the accountable par.

Article 47(2) Directive 2017/1132/EU

However, Member States may allow those who undertake to place shares in the exercise of their profession to pay less than the total price of the shares for which they subscribe in the course of that transaction.

Reference is made to the possibility that an issuer entrusts a professional investor, such as a merchant bank, with the task of underwriting all of the shares to be issued after a capital increase in view of placing the shares by the final investors at its own risk (Article 72(7) Directive 2017/1132/EU). In this case, the overall price paid by the professional investor is less than the total nominal value or accountable par of the shares, as it includes the fees for the investment service provided to the issuer.

Furthermore, it is uncertain whether ECL permits one shareholder to pay a price less than the nominal value or accountable par for his shares, whilst another pays sufficient money to balance the total price paid with the total nominal value or accountable par of the shares. For example, considering that the legal capital of the X NewCo is deemed to be €700, Harry purchases three shares out of ten for €100 each, for an overall consideration of €300, whilst Ron purchases the remaining seven shares for an overall consideration of €400. Some EU legislations (e.g., the Italian one) permit such compensations.

10.5 Performance of the Contribution: Subscribed and Paid-up Capital

As mentioned, under ECL, *authorised, subscribed*, and *paid-up* capital are different concepts. In particular, subscription of new shares implies an engagement of the shareholders to pay a consideration to the company. When this engagement is then entirely performed, the subscribed shares and the corresponding capital are said to be paid-up.

ECL requires that at the time the company is incorporated or is authorised to commence business, or at the time of a subscription in case of a capital increase, at least 25 per cent of the total contributions are paid-up.

Article 48(1) Directive 2017/1132/EU

Shares issued for a consideration must be paid up at the time the company is incorporated or is authorised to commence business at not less than 25 per cent of their nominal value or, in the absence of a nominal value, their accountable par.

Article 69 Directive 2017/1132/EU

Shares issued for a consideration, in the course of an increase in subscribed capital, must be paid up to at least 25% of their nominal value or, in the absence of a nominal value, of their accountable par. Where provision is made for an issue premium, it must be paid in full.

The remaining part of the consideration is paid upon request of the company's directors. ECL does not require that the directors' call is made within a certain time limit, unless shareholders are engaged in making contributions in kind.

Article 48(2) Directive 2017/1132/EU

However, where shares are issued for a consideration other than in cash at the time the company is incorporated or is authorised to commence business, the consideration must be transferred in full within five years of that time.

Article 48(1) Directive 2017/1132/EU

1. Where shares are issued for a consideration other than in cash in the course of an increase in the subscribed capital the consideration must be transferred in full within a period of five years from the decision to increase the subscribed capital.

It must be noted that the major part of EU legislations require that contributions other than in cash are performed at once, when shares are issued. Other EU legislations (such as Germany's and Spain's) permit contributions in kind to be performed at a later stage (within five years). In these circumstances, it is not clear whether ECL also requires that 25 per cent is paid-up immediately (Article 48(1) Directive 2017/1132/EU). Assuming, for example, that one shareholder is engaged to transfer a business division to the company in five years, as contribution in kind, shall he or she be requested to pay up 25 per cent thereof immediately? The answer shall be negative, as the transfer of a business division may not be partially performed. Therefore, Article 48(1) Directive 2017/1132/EU shall be deemed applicable to only contributions in cash.

The right of the company to compel shareholders to pay up their unperformed contributions may not elapse. It may only be released in case of a capital reduction.

Article 53 Directive 2017/1132/EU

Subject to the provisions relating to the reduction of subscribed capital, the shareholders may not be released from the obligation to pay up their contributions.

10.6 Contributions Other Than in Cash

There is no need to assess the value of contributions in cash, provided that the contributed cash is the same currency in which the legal capital and, in general, all items of the balance sheet are expressed.

However, the value of contributions other than in cash, either credits or contributions in kind, must be assessed. In order to ensure the protection of creditors and other shareholders that contributions other than in cash are not overvalued, ECL mandates for a report by an expert appointed or approved by an administrative or judicial authority.

Article 49(1–3) Directive 2017/1132/EU (Similarly, Article 70(2) Directive 2017/1132/EU)

1. A report on any consideration other than in cash shall be drawn up before the company is incorporated or is authorised to commence business, by one or more independent experts appointed or approved by an administrative or judicial authority. Such experts may be natural persons as well as legal persons and companies or firms under the laws of each Member State.
2. The expert's report referred to in paragraph 1 shall contain at least a description of each of the assets comprising the consideration as well as of the methods of valuation used and shall state whether the values arrived at by the application of those methods correspond at least to the number and nominal value or, where there is no nominal value, to the accountable par and, where appropriate, to the premium on the shares to be issued for them.
3. The expert's report shall be published in the manner laid down by the laws of each Member State, in accordance with Article 16.

ECL does not require that the directors make a further assessment of the assets contributed in kind before these are accounted for in the balance sheet. Some legislations (e.g., Italy's), however, require such assessment. In cases of a relevant discrepancy between the assessment of the contributing shareholder, as confirmed by the expert's report, and that of the directors, it is uncertain whether the latter should prevail over the former, or whether an appraisal regime should apply. As we will see in § 10.7, such an appraisal regime has been provided for at Union level in cases of contributions in kind not requiring an expert's report.

10.7 Contributions in Kind Not Requiring an Expert's Report

As the SLIM Group pointed out in their report, in case of contributions in kind, protection of creditors and of shareholders does not always require the report of an appointed expert. In accordance with the SLIM Group proposal, the new Second Company Law Directive provides for cases in which an expert report is not necessary, unless the Member States' legislations so require. Notwithstanding that the Member States' legislation allows for such derogations, an expert report is always possible and, if requested, independent experts shall always be appointed or approved by the administrative or judicial authority designated by the national law.

Exemptions from the mandatory expert report rule are provided for in three cases: (i) where the consideration paid consists of transferable securities admitted to stock exchange listing (*see*, Chapter 17, § 17.2) or money-market instruments; (ii) assets contributed which have already been subject to a fair value opinion by a recognised independent expert; (iii) assets whose fair value is derived by individual asset from the statutory accounts of the previous financial year. In these cases, however, the decision not to have an expert report is taken by the administrative or management body of the company.

Article 50 Directive 2017/1132/EU

1. Member States may decide not to apply Article 49(1), (2) and (3) of this Directive where, upon a decision of the administrative or management body, transferable securities as defined in point 44 of Article 4(1) of Directive 2004/39/EC of the European Parliament and of the Council of 21 April 2004 on markets in financial instruments or money-market instruments as defined in point 17 of Article 4(1) of that Directive are contributed as consideration other than in cash, and those securities or money-market instruments are valued at the weighted average price at which they have been traded on one or more regulated markets as defined in point 21 of Article 4(1) of that Directive during a sufficient period, to be determined by national law, preceding the effective date of the contribution of the respective consideration other than in cash.

However, where that price has been affected by exceptional circumstances that would significantly change the value of the asset at the effective date of its contribution, including situations where the market for such transferable securities or money-market instruments has become illiquid, a revaluation shall be carried out on the initiative and under the responsibility of the administrative or management body.

For the purposes of such revaluation, Article 49(1), (2) and (3) shall apply.

2. Member States may decide not to apply Article 49(1), (2) and (3) where, upon a decision of the administrative or management body, assets other than the transferable securities and money-market instruments referred to in paragraph 1 of this Article are contributed as consideration other than in cash which have already been subject to a fair value opinion by a recognised independent expert and where the following conditions are fulfilled:
   (a) the fair value is determined for a date not more than six months before the effective date of the asset contribution; and
   (b) the valuation has been performed in accordance with generally accepted valuation standards and principles in the Member State which are applicable to the kind of assets to be contributed.

In the case of new qualifying circumstances that would significantly change the fair value of the asset at the effective date of its contribution, a revaluation shall be carried out on the initiative and under the responsibility of the administrative or management body.

For the purposes of such revaluation, Article 49(1), (2) and (3) shall apply.

In the absence of such a revaluation, one or more shareholders holding an aggregate percentage of at least 5% of the company's subscribed capital on the day the decision on the increase in the capital is taken may demand a valuation by an independent expert, in which case Article 49(1), (2) and (3) shall apply.

Such shareholder(s) may submit a demand up until the effective date of the asset contribution, provided that, at the date of the demand, the shareholder(s) in question still hold(s) an aggregate percentage of at least 5% of the company's subscribed capital as it was on the day the decision on the increase in the capital was taken.

3. Member States may decide not to apply Article 49(1), (2) and (3) where, upon a decision of the administrative or management body, assets other than the transferable securities and money-market instruments referred to in paragraph 1 of this Article are contributed as consideration other than in cash whose fair value is derived by individual asset from the statutory accounts of the previous financial year provided that the statutory accounts have been subject to an audit in accordance with Directive 2006/43/EC .

The second to fifth subparagraphs of paragraph 2 of this Article shall apply mutatis mutandis.

Additional exemptions are provided for in two more cases: (iv) where 90 per cent of the nominal value or the accountable par of all the shares is issued to one or more companies for a consideration other than in cash; (v) where, by the formation of a new company by way of merger or division, a report by one or more independent experts on the draft terms of merger or division is drawn up. In these cases, there is no need for a decision taken by the administrative or management body of the company.

Article 49(4–5) Directive 2017/1132/EU (Similarly, Article 70 (3–4) Directive 2017/1132/EU)

4. Member States may decide not to apply this Article where 90% of the nominal value, or where there is no nominal value, of the accountable par, of all the shares is issued to one or more companies for a consideration other than in cash, and where the following requirements are met:
   (a) with regard to the company in receipt of such consideration, the persons referred to in point (i) of Article 4 have agreed to dispense with the experts' report;
   (b) such agreement has been published as provided for in paragraph 3;
   (c) the companies furnishing such consideration have reserves which may not be distributed under the law or the statutes and which are at least equal to the nominal value or, where there is no nominal value, the accountable par of the shares issued for consideration other than in cash;
   (d) the companies furnishing such consideration guarantee, up to an amount equal to that indicated in point (c), the debts of the recipient company arising between the time the shares are issued for a consideration other than in cash and one year after the publication of that company's annual accounts for the financial year during which such consideration was furnished; any transfer of those shares is prohibited within this period;
   (e) the guarantee referred to in point (d) has been published as provided for in paragraph 3; and
   (f) the companies furnishing such consideration shall place a sum equal to that indicated in point (c) into a reserve which may not be distributed until three years after publication of the annual accounts of the recipient company for the financial year during which such consideration was furnished or, if necessary, until such later date as all claims relating to the guarantee referred to in point (d) which are submitted during that period have been settled.
5. Member States may decide not to apply this Article to the formation of a new company by way of merger or division where a report by one or more independent experts on the draft terms of merger or division is drawn up.

Where Member States decide to apply this Article in the cases referred to in the first subparagraph, they may provide that the report under this Article and the report by one or more independent experts on the draft terms of merger or division may be drawn up by the same expert or experts.

In these five cases, in which there is no expert report, the directors of the company must confirm that the value arrived at corresponds at least to the number, to the nominal value or the accountable par and to the premium on the shares to be issued for such consideration. The new Second Company Law Directive provides that, within one month after the effective date of the asset contribution, a declaration containing, *inter alia*, this confirmation shall be published.

Article 51 Directive 2017/1132/EU

1. Where consideration other than in cash as referred to in Article 11 occurs without an experts' report as referred to in Article 49(1), (2) and (3), in addition to the requirements set out in point (h) of Article 4 and within one month after the effective date of the asset contribution, a declaration containing the following shall be published:
   (a) a description of the consideration other than in cash at issue;
   (b) its value, the source of that valuation and, where appropriate, the method of valuation;
   (c) a statement whether the value arrived at corresponds at least to the number, to the nominal value or, where there is no nominal value, the accountable par and, where appropriate, to the premium on the shares to be issued for such consideration; and
   (d) a statement that no new qualifying circumstances with regard to the original valuation have occurred.

That publication shall be effected in the manner laid down by the laws of each Member State in accordance with Article 16.

2. Where consideration other than in cash is proposed to be made without an experts' report as referred to in Article 49(1), (2) and (3) in relation to an increase in the capital proposed to be made under Article 68(2), an announcement containing the date when the decision on the increase was taken and the information listed in paragraph 1 of this Article shall be published, in the manner laid down by the laws of each Member State in accordance with Article 16, before the contribution of the asset as consideration other than in cash is to become effective. In that event, the declaration pursuant to paragraph 1 of this Article shall be limited to the statement that no new qualifying circumstances have occurred since the aforementioned announcement was published.
3. Each Member State shall provide for adequate safeguards ensuring compliance with the procedure set out in Article 11 and in this Article where a contribution for a consideration other than in cash is made without an experts' report as referred to in Article 49(1), (2) and (3).

Despite general consent on the new approach relaxing requirements for contributions in kind, some criticism has been raised.

Mario Notari, 'The Appraisal Regime of Contributions in Kind in the Light of Amendments to the Second EEC Directive', 7 *ECFR* 63–80, at 63 (2010)

The new art. 10a of the Second EEC Directive regarding the incorporation of public companies and the maintenance and alteration of their capital provides for three cases where it is possible to contribute assets as a consideration in kind without requiring the report drawn up by an expert 'appointed or approved by an administrative or judicial authority' as required by the 'old' art. 10 of the Second Directive. The amendment of the Directive is not mandatory and has been adopted only by some of the Member States. This article examines the two 'general' derogations of art. 10 of the Second Directive, based on another appraisal already available or on values reported in statutory accounts. Doubts are raised on both the rules approved by EC lawmakers: the first because it ends up replacing, with fewer safeguards, the 'ordinary' system for the assessment of the value of contributions in kind, which is definitively left with a merely residual function; the second because it is not consistent with the options given to Member States on the adoption of international accounting standards, making any 'fair value' entered in the statutory accounts always and unconditionally attributable to share capital, even after an extensive period of time, the only safeguard being provided in this case by a subsequent control check by directors.

FURTHER READING

Mario Notari, 'The Appraisal Regime of Contributions in Kind in the Light of Amendments to the Second EEC Directive', 7 *ECFR* 63–80 (2010).

10.8 Acquisitions by Members or Directors

Circumvention of the rules on the mandatory expert report is not difficult, as members or directors of a NewCo could easily engage in contributions in cash, whilst selling to the company the assets they truly intend to contribute in kind at a price which is determined without any assessment by an expert. Both the contribution in kind and the sale of the asset could be later performed by compensation of mutual claims, thereby circumventing the requirement of an expert report.

Considering this weakness of the mandatory expert report rule, ECL provides an additional rule that aims at preventing the most blatant circumvention.

Article 52 Directive 2017/1132/EU

1. If, before the expiry of a time-limit laid down by national law of at least two years from the time the company is incorporated or is authorised to commence business, the company acquires any asset belonging to a person or company or firm referred to in point (i) of Article 4 for a consideration of not less than one-tenth of the subscribed capital, the acquisition shall be examined and details of it published in the manner provided for in Article 49(1), (2) and (3) and it shall be submitted for the approval of the general meeting.

   Articles 50 and 51 shall apply mutatis mutandis.

   Member States may also require those provisions to be applied when the assets belong to a shareholder or to any other person.

2. Paragraph 1 shall not apply to acquisitions effected in the normal course of the company's business, to acquisitions effected at the instance or under the supervision of an administrative or judicial authority, or to stock exchange acquisitions.

11

Capital Maintenance

11.1 Dividend Distribution

As already mentioned, ECL provides not only capital formation rules, i.e., rules ensuring correct assessment of assets contributed for the formation of the legal capital, but also capital maintenance rules. These include a rule requiring that dividends are only paid when a company is showing a profit above the level of historically recorded legal capital. More precisely, Article 56(1) Directive 2017/1132/EU makes reference to the value of the *net assets* shown in the company's annual accounts.

Neither the Annual and Consolidated Accounts Directive (Directive 2013/34/EU or new Fourth and Seventh Directive), nor the new Second Directive provide a definition of *net assets*. This concept corresponds to that of *equity*, which is also defined neither by the new Second nor the new Fourth and Seventh Directives. However, depending on the balance sheet layout adopted by Member States, net assets or equity are shown in Item A. *Capital and reserves* of the Capital, reserves, and liabilities column of Table 11.1, or in Item L. *Capital and reserves* of the vertical layout (*see*, Chapter 12, § 2). These items measure the resources contributed to the company or accumulated by it, which are not liabilities or debts towards third parties. Contrary to US law, under ECL not all these resources are available for distribution to shareholders. **Table 11.1** represents a simplified horizontal layout of the balance sheet, where all six items included in A. *Capital and reserves* of the Capital, reserves, and liabilities column have been highlighted in emboldened characters.

ECL requires that, prior to a distribution, the company performs a so-called *balance sheet test*, confirming that assets corresponding to the value of the legal capital and to reserves which may not be distributed under the law or the statutes are not reimbursed to shareholders as dividends. Reimbursement of these resources may only occur after dissolution of the company, or following a reduction of the subscribed capital, in case the general meeting provides accordingly and creditors do not object within a certain time limit. In any case, a reduction of capital below the minimum set out by the law is not permitted.

Table 11.1 Simplified horizontal layout of a balance sheet

Assets	Capital, reserves, and liabilities
A. Subscribed capital unpaid	**A. Capital and reserves**
B. Formation expenses	**I. Subscribed capital**
	II. Share premium account
	III. Revaluation reserve
C. Fixed assets	**IV. Reserves**
	V. Profit or loss brought forward
D. Current assets	**VI. Profit or loss of the financial year**
	B. Provisions
E. Prepayments and accrued incomes	C. Creditors
	D. Accruals and deferred income

Article 56(1-3) Directive 2017/1132/EU

1. Except for cases of reductions of subscribed capital, no distribution to shareholders may be made when on the closing date of the last financial year the net assets as set out in the company's annual accounts are, or following such a distribution would become, lower than the amount of the subscribed capital plus those reserves which may not be distributed under the law or the statutes.
2. Where the uncalled part of the subscribed capital is not included in the assets shown in the balance sheet, that amount shall be deducted from the amount of subscribed capital referred to in paragraph 1.
3. The amount of a distribution to shareholders may not exceed the amount of the profits at the end of the last financial year plus any profits brought forward and sums drawn from reserves available for this purpose, less any losses brought forward and sums placed to reserve in accordance with the law or the statutes.

Requiring that profits are distributed only in cases where the balance sheet test is positive, ECL does not permit the distribution of so-called *nimble dividends*. Nimble dividends are dividends paid out of the net profits of a company, in cases where there is a deficit in the account from which dividends may be paid (out of surplus). Nimble dividends are permitted under Delaware General Corporation Law.

Delaware General Corporation Law

§ 170 Dividends; Payment; Wasting Asset Corporations

(a) The directors of every corporation, subject to any restrictions contained in its certificate of incorporation, may declare and pay dividends upon the shares of its capital stock either:

(1) Out of its surplus, as defined in and computed in accordance with §§ 154 and 244 of this title; or
(2) In case there shall be no such surplus, out of its net profits for the fiscal year in which the dividend is declared and/or the preceding fiscal year.

ECL does not require a *solvency test* in order to make distributions. On the contrary, the US MBCA requires both balance sheet and solvency tests.

Model Business Corporation Act

§ 6.40(c) Distributions to Shareholders

(c) No distribution may be made if, after giving it effect:
(1) the corporation would not be able to pay its debts as they become due in the usual course of business; or
(2) the corporation's total assets would be less than the sum of its total liabilities plus (unless the articles of incorporation permit otherwise) the amount that would be needed, if the corporation were to be dissolved at the time of the distribution, to satisfy the preferential rights upon dissolution of shareholders whose preferential rights are superior to those receiving the distribution.

As mentioned earlier, the High Level Group Report recommended a mandatory solvency test (along with a mandatory balance sheet test). The Rickford and Dutch Groups have proposed similar approaches, while under the Lutter Group proposal, a solvency test should be mandatory only for companies subject to IAS/IFRS standards.

Furthermore, ECL allows that profits are distributed as dividends as well as interests relating to shares.

Article 56(4) Directive 2017/1132/EU

4. The expression 'distribution' used in paragraphs 1 and 3 includes in particular the payment of dividends and of interest relating to shares.

Distributions of dividends made contrary to the provisions of Directive 2017/1132/EU shall be deemed irregular. Hence, money paid to shareholders shall be returned to the company. However, for the protection of shareholders unaware that the distribution was irregular, ECL requires that the company proves the irregularity of the distribution made to them.

Article 57 Directive 2017/1132/EU

Any distribution made contrary to Article 17 must be returned by shareholders who have received it if the company proves that those shareholders knew of the irregularity of the distributions made to them, or could not in view of the circumstances have been unaware of it.

In addition, it should be noted that dividends are declared and paid after the general meeting or the supervisory board approve the annual accounts. ECL does not take a position as to whether directors or the general meeting should declare dividends. EU Member States' legislations, as the US MBCA, diverge in this respect.

Model Business Corporation Act

§ 6.40(a)(b) Distributions to Shareholders

(a) A board of directors may authorize and the corporation may make distributions to its shareholders subject to restriction by the articles of incorporation and the limitation in subsection (c).

(b) If the board of directors does not fix the record date for determining shareholders entitled to a distribution (other than one involving a purchase, redemption, or other acquisition of the corporation's shares), it is the date the board of directors authorizes the distribution.

FURTHER READING

John Armour, 'Share Capital and Creditor Protection: Efficient Rules for a Modern Company Law?', 63 *MLR* 355–378, at 373–375 (2000).

Luca Enriques and Jonathan R. Macey, 'Creditors Versus Capital Formation: The Case Against Legal Capital Rules', 86 *Cornell L. Rev.*, 1165–1204, at 1195–1198 (2001).

Eilìs Ferran, 'The Place for Creditor Protection on the Agenda for Modernisation of Company Law in the European Union', 3 *ECFR* 179–221, at 200–215 (2006).

Holger Fleischer, 'Disguised Distributions and Capital Maintenance in European Company Law,' in Marcus Lutter (ed.), *Legal Capital in Europe, Special Volume 1 ECFR* at 94 (2006).

See also:

John Armour, Gerhard Hertig, and Hideki Kanda, 'Transactions with Creditors', in John Armour, Luca Enriques et al., *The Anatomy of Corporate Law: A Comparative and Functional Approach* 110–145, at 124–127 (Oxford University Press, 3rd ed., 2017).

11.2 Interim Dividends

Under ECL, Member States' legislation may allow interim dividends, these being a dividend payment made before a company's general meeting to approve final financial statements. Interim dividends are generally paid at semesters, so that dividend payments, as bonds' interest, also occur semi-annually.

In order to have interim dividends paid, ECL requires that two conditions are met.

Article 56(5) Directive 2017/1132/EU

5. When the laws of a Member State allow the payment of interim dividends, the following conditions at least shall apply:

   (a) interim accounts shall be drawn up showing that the funds available for distribution are sufficient;

   (b) the amount to be distributed may not exceed the total profits made since the end of the last financial year for which the annual accounts have been drawn up, plus any profits brought forward and sums drawn from reserves available for that purpose, less losses brought forward and sums to be placed to reserve pursuant to the requirements of the law or the statutes.

6. Paragraphs 1 to 5 shall not affect the provisions of the Member States as regards increases in subscribed capital by capitalisation of reserves.

11.3 Other Means for Making Distributions and Creditors' Protection: (A) Capital Reduction

Nicola de Luca, 'Unequal Treatment and Shareholders' Welfare Growth: "Fairness" v. "Precise Equality"', 34 *Del. J. Corp. L.* 853–920, at 855 (2009)

Solvent corporations have two means for making distributions to shareholders: dividends and share repurchases. Corporations may also reduce their stated capital, and reimburse to the shareholders part of their contribution to the assets of the firm. European law does not permit 'spill-outs' of assets such as distributions of dividends or share repurchases, unless they are made out of surplus or upon a capital reduction; American corporate law generally does. Both solutions have advantages and correspond to the social and economic background to which they refer.

Although ECL acknowledges both acquisitions of companies' own shares and capital reductions as means for making distributions to shareholders, in these cases it mandates for the adoption of certain safeguards to protect the interests of creditors.

As regards capital reductions, ECL requires that existing creditors are allowed to object to the execution of the corporate transaction, in case the distribution of assets or release of shareholders from the obligation to pay up their shares in full could prejudice the company's ability to pay debts as they become due, i.e., the company's solvency. In these cases, creditors may obtain immediate payment or adequate safeguards for their claims.

Article 75 Directive 2017/1132/EU

1. In the event of a reduction in the subscribed capital, at least the creditors whose claims antedate the publication of the decision on the reduction shall at least have the right to obtain security for claims which have not fallen due by the date of that publication. Member States may not set aside such a right unless the creditor has adequate safeguards, or unless such safeguards are not necessary having regard to the assets of the company.

Member States shall lay down the conditions for the exercise of the right provided for in the first subparagraph. In any event, Member States shall ensure that the creditors are authorised to apply to the appropriate administrative or judicial authority for adequate safeguards provided that they can credibly demonstrate that due to the reduction in the subscribed capital the satisfaction of their claims is at stake, and that no adequate safeguards have been obtained from the company.

2. The laws of the Member States shall also stipulate at least that the reduction shall be void, or that no payment may be made for the benefit of the shareholders, until the creditors have obtained satisfaction or a court has decided that their application should not be acceded to.
3. This Article shall apply where the reduction in the subscribed capital is brought about by the total or partial waiving of the payment of the balance of the shareholders' contributions.

Capital reductions not aimed at making assets available for distribution, nor at releasing shareholders from their obligations to pay up their shares in full, do not fall within the scope of Article 75, Directive 2017/1132/EU.

Article 76 Directive 2017/1132/EU

1. Member States need not apply Article 75 to a reduction in the subscribed capital whose purpose is to offset losses incurred or to include sums of money in a reserve provided that, following that operation, the amount of such reserve is not more than 10% of the reduced subscribed capital. Except in the event of a reduction in the subscribed capital, that reserve may not be distributed to shareholders; it may be used only for offsetting losses incurred or for increasing the subscribed capital by the capitalisation of such reserve, in so far as the Member States permit such an operation.
2. In the cases referred to in paragraph 1 the laws of the Member States must at least provide for the measures necessary to ensure that the amounts deriving from the reduction of subscribed capital may not be used for making payments or distributions to shareholders or discharging shareholders from the obligation to make their contributions.

It must be added that under Article 80(2) Directive 2017/1132/EU, in case the capital reduction only affects shares acquired by the company itself and held as treasury shares, the company need not allow creditors to secure their credits, as long as treasury shares are fully paid up, have been acquired with funds available for distribution, and a reserve unavailable for distribution has been included in the liabilities. After the capital reduction, this reserve becomes available for distribution.

FURTHER READING

Nicola de Luca, 'Unequal Treatment and Shareholders' Welfare Growth: "Fairness" v. "Precise Equality"', 34 *Del. J. Corp. L.* 853–920 (2009).

11.4 Other Means for Making Distributions and Creditors' Protection: (B) Transactions on the Company's Own Shares, Share Redemption, and Compulsory Withdrawal

As regards transactions on the company's own shares, ECL prohibits a self-subscription of shares (Article 39 Directive 2017/1132/EU) as well as a subscription of shares of the parent company by its subsidiary (Article 67 Directive 2017/1132/EU).

Article 59(1) Directive 2017/1132/EU

1. The shares of a company may not be subscribed for by the company itself.

Member States may, however, permit other transactions, such as (i) the acquisition of the company's own shares (Article 60 Directive 2017/1132/EU); (ii) the financial assistance (i.e., advancing funds or making loans or providing security) for the acquisition of the company's own shares by a third party (Article 64 Directive 2017/1132/EU); (iii) the acceptance of the company's own shares as security (Article 66 Directive 2017/1132/EU); (iv) the acquisition or holding of shares of a parent company by its subsidiary (Article 67 Directive 2017/1132/EU). Where such transactions are permitted, conditions ensuring creditors' protection must be met.

The direct or indirect repurchase of the company's own shares (buy-back) is by far the most important among these transactions. Redemption and compulsory withdrawal of shares are similar transactions, and thus require similar safeguards in the interest of creditors: *redemption* generally refers to redeemable shares, these being shares which are issued on the basis that they are to be or may be repurchased at a later date by the company; *compulsory withdrawal* refers to the decision of the company to buy back shares from shareholders with or without their consent, in view of enacting a capital reduction.

Article 60(1) Directive 2017/1132/EU

Member States may permit a company to acquire its own shares, either itself or through a person acting in his own name but on the company's behalf. To the extent that the acquisitions are permitted, Member States shall make such acquisitions subject to the following conditions:

...

(b) the acquisitions, including shares previously acquired by the company and held by it, and shares acquired by a person acting in his own name but on the company's behalf, may not have the effect of reducing the net assets below the amount mentioned in Article 56 (1) and (2); and
(c) only fully paid-up shares may be included in the transaction.

Furthermore, Member States may subject acquisitions within the meaning of the first subparagraph to any of the following conditions:

...

(c) that the company complies with appropriate reporting and notification requirements;
(d) that certain companies, as determined by Member States, may be required to cancel the acquired shares provided that an amount equal to the nominal value of the shares cancelled must be included in a reserve which cannot be distributed to the shareholders, except in the event of a reduction in the subscribed capital; that reserve may be used only for the purposes of increasing the subscribed capital by the capitalisation of reserves; and
(e) that the acquisition shall not prejudice the satisfaction of creditors' claims.

In addition, in order to prevent the company from distributing the same funds twice, it is required that if treasury shares are accounted for in the assets, an equivalent reserve unavailable for distribution shall be included among the liabilities.

Article 63(1)(b) Directive 2017/1132/EU

(b) if the shares are included among the assets shown in the balance sheet, a reserve of the same amount, unavailable for distribution, shall be included among the liabilities.

As mentioned earlier, similar conditions are required for the redemption of shares without reduction of capital, as well as for the redemption of redeemable shares.

Article 78 Directive 2017/1132/EU (Similarly, Article 82 Directive 2017/1132/EU)

Where the laws of a Member State authorise total or partial redemption of the subscribed capital without reduction of the latter, they shall at least require that the following conditions are observed:

...

(b) only sums which are available for distribution within the meaning of Article 56(1) to (4) may be used for redemption purposes;

Article 82 Directive 2017/1132/EU

Where the laws of a Member State authorise companies to issue redeemable shares, they shall require that the following conditions, at least, are complied with for the redemption of such shares:

...

(b) the shares must be fully paid up;

...

(d) redemption can be only effected by using sums available for distribution in accordance with Article 56(1) to (4) or the proceeds of a new issue made with a view to effecting such redemption;
(e) an amount equal to the nominal value or, in the absence thereof, to the accountable par of all the redeemed shares must be included in a reserve which cannot be distributed to the shareholders, except in the event of a reduction in the subscribed capital; it may be used only for the purpose of increasing the subscribed capital by the capitalisation of reserves;
(f) point (e) shall not apply to redemption using the proceeds of a new issue made with a view to effecting such redemption;
(g) where provision is made for the payment of a premium to shareholders in consequence of a redemption, the premium may be paid only from sums available for distribution in accordance with Article 56(1) to (4), or from a reserve other than that referred to in point (e) of this Article which may not be distributed to shareholders except in the event of a reduction in the subscribed capital; that reserve may be used only for the purposes of increasing the subscribed capital by the capitalisation of reserves or for covering the costs referred to in point (j) of Article 4 or the cost of issuing shares or debentures or for the payment of a premium to holders of redeemable shares or debentures;
(h) notification of redemption shall be published in the manner laid down by the laws of each Member State in accordance with Article 16.

Partially different rules apply in case of a compulsory withdrawal of shares, as this aims at permitting the company to perform a reduction of the subscribed capital. As such, creditors may always secure their credits under Article 75 Directive 2017/1132/EU, except in cases of withdrawal of fully paid-up shares which are made available to the company free of charge or acquired using sums available for distribution.

Article 79 Directive 2017/1132/EU

1. Where the laws of a Member State may allow companies to reduce their subscribed capital by compulsory withdrawal of shares, they shall require that at least the following conditions are observed:

...

(d) Article 75 shall apply except in the case of fully paid-up shares which are made available to the company free of charge or are withdrawn using sums available for distribution in accordance with Article 56(1) to (4); in those cases, an amount equal to the nominal value or, in the absence thereof, to the accountable par of all the withdrawn shares must be included in a reserve; except in the event of a reduction in the subscribed capital that reserve may not be distributed to shareholders; it can be used only for offsetting losses incurred or for increasing the subscribed capital by the capitalisation of such reserve, in so far as Member States permit such an operation; and

...

Article 80 Directive 2017/1132/EU

1. In the case of a reduction in the subscribed capital by the withdrawal of shares acquired by the company itself or by a person acting in his own name but on behalf of the company, the withdrawal must always be decided on by the general meeting.
2. Article 75 shall apply unless the shares are fully paid up and are acquired free of charge or using sums available for distribution in accordance with Article 56(1) to (4); in those cases an amount equal to the nominal value or, in the absence thereof, to the accountable par of all the shares withdrawn must be included in a reserve. Except in the event of a reduction in the subscribed capital, that reserve may not be distributed to shareholders. It may be used only for offsetting losses incurred or for increasing the subscribed capital by the capitalisation of such reserve, in so far as the Member States permit such an operation.
3. Articles 74, 76 and 83 shall not apply to the cases to which paragraph 1 of this Article refers.

Both Articles 79(1)(d) and 80(2) Directive 2017/1132/EU can be critiqued for their incoherence. Indeed, provided that compulsory withdrawal of shares is regarded as a means to reduce the company's subscribed capital, no compulsory withdrawal occurs in a situation where fully paid-up shares are acquired by the company free of charge, or with sums available for distribution in view of holding such shares as treasury shares: these transactions are rather an acquisition of the company's own shares, regardless of the fact that the affected shareholders are forced to sell. In case of a share repurchase, as already mentioned, a reserve that is unavailable for distribution shall be included in the liabilities *only* if the shares are included among the assets shown in the balance sheet (Article 63(1)(b) Directive 2012/30/EU). Therefore, Member States that do not require the inclusion of repurchased shares in the assets, shall not require companies to include a reserve that is unavailable for distribution in the liabilities (the same remark shall be addressed to Article 82(1)(e) Directive 2017/1132/EU, regarding redeemable shares). In addition, acquisition of shares with sums available for distribution or free of charge are not similar cases: in the latter case, no 'distribution' of sums occurs, therefore there is no adequate reason for rendering a sum equivalent to the shares' total nominal value or accountable par unavailable for distribution; in the former case, as 'distribution' has already occurred, the reserve – if required by Member States' law – shall neither be used for further distribution, nor to offset losses (nor to increase the subscribed capital by the capitalisation of reserves, as provided for by Article 82(1)(e) Directive 2017/1132/EU, regarding redeemable shares): such a 'reserve' is not a reserve in the proper meaning of accumulated profits, and serves only to balance assets and liabilities when the treasury (or redeemed shares) are included in the assets. Redrafting of such provisions is therefore absolutely necessary.

As regards the conditions for the repurchase of the company's own shares, Member States may permit derogations to the two basic conditions required for the interest of creditors – i.e., that: (i) shares are fully paid up, and (ii) acquisition is made with sums available for distributions – in cases where creditors' interests are not at risk.

Article 61 Directive 2017/1132/EU

1. Member States may decide not to apply Article 60 to:

   (a) shares acquired in carrying out a decision to reduce capital, or in the circumstances referred to in Article 82;

   (b) shares acquired as a result of a universal transfer of assets;

   (c) fully paid-up shares acquired free of charge or by banks and other financial institutions as purchasing commission;

   (d) shares acquired by virtue of a legal obligation or resulting from a court ruling for the protection of minority shareholders in the event, particularly, of a merger, a change in the company's object or form, transfer abroad of the registered office, or the introduction of restrictions on the transfer of shares;

   (e) shares acquired from a shareholder in the event of failure to pay them up;

   (f) shares acquired in order to indemnify minority shareholders in associated companies;

(g) fully paid-up shares acquired under a sale enforced by a court order for the payment of a debt owed to the company by the owner of the shares; and

(h) fully paid-up shares issued by an investment company with fixed capital, as defined in the second subparagraph of Article 56(7), and acquired at the investor's request by that company or by an associate company. Point (a) of the third subparagraph of Article 56(7) shall apply. Those acquisitions may not have the effect of reducing the net assets below the amount of the subscribed capital plus any reserves the distribution of which is forbidden by law.

2. Shares acquired in the cases listed in points (b) to (g) of paragraph 1 must, however, be disposed of within not more than three years of their acquisition unless the nominal value or, in the absence of a nominal value, the accountable par of the shares acquired, including shares which the company may have acquired through a person acting in his own name but on the company's behalf, does not exceed 10% of the subscribed capital.
3. If the shares are not disposed of within the period laid down in paragraph 2, they must be cancelled. The laws of a Member State may make that cancellation subject to a corresponding reduction in the subscribed capital. Such a reduction must be prescribed where the acquisition of shares to be cancelled results in the net assets having fallen below the amount specified in Article 56(1) and (2).

In connection with all permitted transactions on a company's own shares, the redemption, and the compulsory withdrawal of shares, further conditions are required for the interest of minority shareholders: these will be discussed in Chapter 16.

For the time being, it is worth noting that contravention of the rules prohibiting self-subscription of shares (by the company itself or its subsidiary), or of the conditions set forth for the validity of a buyback, entails peculiar consequences. Indeed, notwithstanding that both contraventions would normally lead to common remedies to an invalid transaction, in the view of protecting the interest of creditors, ECL primarily cares that such transactions do not negatively affect the company's assets.

On the one hand, in case of a prohibited self-subscription of shares:

Article 59(2–3) Directive 2017/1132/EU

2. If the shares of a company have been subscribed for by a person acting in his own name, but on behalf of the company, the subscriber shall be deemed to have subscribed for them for his own account.
3. The persons or companies or firms referred to in point (i) of Article 3 or, in cases of an increase in subscribed capital, the members of the administrative or management body shall be liable to pay for shares subscribed in contravention of this Article.

However, the laws of a Member State may provide that any such person may be released from his obligation if he proves that no fault is attributable to him personally.

On the other hand, in case of a buyback contravening the conditions set forth by the national laws in accordance with ECL:

Article 62 Directive 2017/1132/EU

Shares acquired in contravention of Articles 60 and 61 shall be disposed of within one year of their acquisition. Should they not be disposed of within that period, Article 61(3) shall apply.

FURTHER READING

Nicola de Luca, 'The Corporation as Shareholder and the Market for its Own Securities', available at SSRN: http://ssrn.com/abstract=2025778.

11.5 Other Means for Making Distributions and Creditors' Protection: (C) Financial Assistance

Before the Second Directive was amended in 2006, ECL prohibited companies from advancing funds or making loans or providing security, with a view to the acquisition of its shares by a third party (so-called financial assistance). Under the suggestion of the SLIM Group, the financial assistance's prohibition has been relaxed. Member States' laws may now permit it, provided that safeguards similar to those required for buybacks are granted.

Article 61(1, 4–6) Directive 2017/1132/EU

1. Where Member States permit a company to, either directly or indirectly, advance funds or make loans or provide security, with a view to the acquisition of its shares by a third party, they shall make such transactions subject to the conditions set out in paragraphs 2 to 5.

...

4. The aggregate financial assistance granted to third parties shall at no time result in the reduction of the net assets below the amount specified in Article 17(1) and (2), taking into account also any reduction of the net assets that may have occurred through the acquisition, by the company or on behalf of the company, of its own shares in accordance with Article 60(1).

The company shall include, among the liabilities in the balance sheet, a reserve, unavailable for distribution, of the amount of the aggregate financial assistance.

5. Where a third party by means of financial assistance from a company acquires that company's own shares within the meaning of Article 60(1) or subscribes for shares issued in the course of an increase in the subscribed capital, such acquisition or subscription shall be made at a fair price.
6. Paragraphs 1 to 5 shall not apply to transactions concluded by banks and other financial institutions in the normal course of business, nor to transactions effected with a view to the acquisition of shares by or for the company's employees or the employees of an associate company.

However, those transactions may not have the effect of reducing the net assets below the amount specified in Article 56(1).

...

In addition to financial assistance, further conditions are required for the interest of minority shareholders: these will be discussed in Chapter 14, § 14.8.

It should be added that acceptance of the company's own shares as security for the loan – required for the subscription or the acquisition of the company's own shares for other reasons – may lead to a buyback, in case the debtor is not able to repay the debt he or she has secured from the company. Therefore, this transaction is also to be treated as a (possible) buyback, requiring that the same safeguards are provided for.

Article 66 Directive 2017/1132/EU

1. The acceptance of the company's own shares as security, either by the company itself or through a person acting in his own name but on the company's behalf, shall be treated as an acquisition for the purposes of Article 60, Article 61(1), and Articles 63 and 64.
2. The Member States may decide not to apply paragraph 1 to transactions concluded by banks and other financial institutions in the normal course of business.

FURTHER READING

Søren Friis Hansen and Karsten Engsig Sørensen, 'Reforming the Financial Assistance Provision in the Second Company Law Directive: A Danish Perspective', *EBLR* 3–23 (2003).

Eilis Ferran, 'Simplification of European Company Law on Financial Assistance', 6 *EBOR* 93–99 (2005).

Kees Hooft, 'The Financial Assistance Prohibition: Origins, Evolution, and Future', 8 *ECL* 157–160 (2011).

Giovanni Strampelli, 'Rendering (Once More) the Financial Assistance Regime More Flexible', 9 *ECFR* 530–570 (2012).

11.6 Serious Losses and Recapitalise or Liquidate Rule

Under ECL, legal capital and net assets are the reference for conducting a balance sheet test in order to make distributions. Net assets and legal capital also serve as benchmark for signalling a risk that the company may become insolvent due to the poor performance of its business activity.

In circumstances of serious loss of the subscribed capital (or, more precisely, in case the net assets fall below half of the subscribed capital), ECL requires that the board of directors calls a general meeting of shareholders to decide on appropriate measures, such as a change in the objects of the company, the pursuit of new financial resources, including a capital increase, or the dissolution of the company.

Article 58 Directive 2017/1132/EU

1. In the case of a serious loss of the subscribed capital, a general meeting of shareholders must be called within the period laid down by the laws of the Member States, to consider whether the company should be wound up or any other measures taken.
2. The amount of a loss deemed to be serious within the meaning of paragraph 1 may not be set by the laws of Member States at a figure higher than half the subscribed capital.

The general meeting may also consider that the remaining net assets are sufficient means to pursue the object of the company. Accordingly, shareholders might decide to reduce the legal capital to offset losses incurred, so that the legal capital matches the value of residual net assets. Such a reduction of capital enables the company to have future profits available for distribution as – in the absence of further losses – future balance sheet tests will be positive.

A capital reduction to offset losses incurred is permitted, unless the new subscribed capital would be less than the minimum required by the legislation of the Member States: as mentioned, this minimum shall be no less than €25,000 for public limited companies created under national law and €120,000 for SEs.

Article 77 Directive 2017/1132/EU

The subscribed capital may not be reduced to an amount less than the minimum capital laid down in accordance with Article 45.

However, Member States may permit such a reduction if they also provide that the decision to reduce the subscribed capital may take effect only when the subscribed capital is increased to an amount at least equal to the prescribed minimum.

In other words, ECL prohibits that a capital reduction is decided to offset losses bringing the net assets below the minimum legal capital; it does not require, however, that, in similar circumstances, a company is mandatorily liquidated or recapitalised.

Some EU Member States' legislations (such as Italy's, Spain's, Sweden's, and to a certain extent France's) strengthen the EU rules providing that, in case of losses bringing the net assets below the minimum capital, a recapitalise or liquidate (ROL) rule applies. Other EU Member States' legislations (such as Germany's) require that, in case the net assets fall below zero, the company files for bankruptcy.

Influential scholars have criticised the ROL rule.

Luca Enriques and Jonathan R. Macey, 'Creditors Versus Capital Formation: The Case Against Legal Capital Rules', 86 *Cornell L. Rev.* 1165–1204, at 1201–1202 (2001)

C. The 'Recapitalize or Liquidate' Rule: An Inefficient Alternative

The 'recapitalize or liquidate' rules of individual European Union Member States are undeniably much more effective at protecting creditors than the other legal capital rules, at least so long as such rules are easily enforceable. However, because these rules penalize risk-taking, they are highly inefficient and severely retard the growth of equity markets.

First of all, from a more formalistic point of view, such rules are inconsistent with the very concept of limited liability. In a hypothetical world in which every single company abided by these rules, no company would ever become insolvent because every company would either liquidate or reorganize before that. This, in turn, would mean that there would be no operational role for limited liability.

Second, rules requiring a company to liquidate or recapitalize when the value of the company's net assets fall[s] below some preordained behavior. Shareholders can, in fact, take advantage of such provisions in disputes with other shareholders.

Third, majority shareholders may use such rules in order to get rid of financially constrained minority shareholders. If the company's capital falls to zero, a shareholder who is unable or unwilling to contribute more money to the venture will lose her shareholder status. Another reason why these rules are inappropriate is because they are based on unreliable balance-sheet data. The relevant legal inquiry is whether the value of a firm's net assets as shown on its balance sheet has fallen below the requisite statutory minimum. A company with a real economic value significantly higher than the minimum legal capital amount will nonetheless have to undergo the radical restructuring that these rules require because its balance sheet does not reflect the true economic value of its assets. In order to avoid liquidation, such a company will either have to transform itself into a private limited-liability company (thereby losing the opportunity to access outside financing) or issue more equity. If the company in question really does face financial risk, then the cost of equity financing will be very high. Controlling shareholders may not have sufficient finds to contribute, and will face a Hobson's choice of either liquidating the company or diluting their control position by finding other investors willing to subscribe to the new issue. Ex ante, the prospect of having to choose between contributing more funds to a company in distress and diluting one's own control will be a disincentive for people to found new companies. Finally (needless to say), if liquidation is the only result of this rule, the creditors as well as shareholders will suffer. After all, the assets of the company will, ipso facto, devalue in liquidation.

Such criticism has raised an interesting debate, as some other scholars claim an informational value of the recapitalise or liquidate rule.

Lorenzo Stanghellini, 'Directors' Duties and the Optimal Timing of Insolvency: A Reassessment of the "Recapitalize or Liquidate" Rule', in Paolo Benazzo, Mario Cera, and Sergio Patriarca (eds.), *Il diritto delle società oggi: Innovazioni e persistenze* 733–768, at 766–768 (Turin, Utet, 2011)

13. Conclusion

Creditors are not perfectly informed on the conditions of the firm, and they are therefore not able to react immediately to a significant increase on the risk of losses. Contracting, it is arguable, is not sufficient. This is why a rule concerning the directors' duties with respect to the time that precedes a formal declaration of insolvency is advisable. An optimal rule should have the following features:

(a) it should trigger before cash flow insolvency, and also before balance sheet insolvency, if insolvency is foreseeable as a real and serious possibility (i.e., when there is still some equity but it is predictable that it will shortly vanish);
(b) it should leave directors freedom as to the appropriate steps to be taken to prevent or minimize losses to creditors. Those steps would include either out-of-court restructuring or filing for insolvency proceedings;
(c) it should be tied to a factual situation that the directors can readily ascertain without resorting to complex valuations, and that the court can assess ex post with reasonable accuracy.

In short, an optimal rule should be specific as to the moment at which it triggers, but flexible as to the consequences. In this light, the 'recapitalize or liquidate' [ROL] rule, the costs of which, in my opinion, have generally been overstated, displays some interesting attributes.

Such a rule can exist independently of rules mandating a minimum capital, and independently of capital maintenance rules altogether. Therefore, it is not [our] goal ... to recommend or defend the capital maintenance system. First, it is worth noting that, at least in Europe, following the 2006 reform of the Second Directive on Company law ..., this criticized system is little more than a limitation on profit distribution based on a positive net assets test. Moreover, to the extent that the EU Member States allow (or require) companies to use International Financial Reporting Standards (IFRS), the role of legal capital may be changing significantly, as companies start using valuation standards that could yield more volatile results. An increase in the importance of debt covenants, and legal reforms explicitly introducing a solvency test for profit distributions, may follow.

As we have seen, [o]n the basis of a negative assets test ROL does more than limit the distribution of profits: it calls [o]n insiders to reveal their estimation of the true value of the firm, under penalty of liquidation (solvent or insolvent liquidation, as the case may be). In so doing, the ROL shares the goal of the many legal techniques aimed at disciplining directors during the twilight period: the time during which shareholders have not yet been displaced but directors ought to consider creditors' interests.

FURTHER READING

Luca Enriques and Jonathan R. Macey, 'Creditors Versus Capital Formation: The Case Against Legal Capital Rules', 86 *Cornell L. Rev.* 1165–1204 (2001).

Lorenzo Stanghellini, 'Directors' Duties and the Optimal Timing of Insolvency: A Reassessment of the "Recapitalize or Liquidate" Rule', in Paolo Benazzo, Mario Cera, and Sergio Patriarca (eds.), *Il diritto delle società oggi: Innovazioni e persistenze* 733–768 (Turin, Utet, 2011).

Michelangelo Granato, 'The Myth of the Optimal Capital Structure and the Dogma of Creditor Protection', 18 *EBOR* 617–658 (2017).

See also:

John Armour, Gerhard Hertig, and Hideki Kanda, 'Transactions with Creditors', in John Armour, Luca Enriques et al., *The Anatomy of Corporate Law: A Comparative and Functional Approach* 110–145, at 126–127 (Oxford University Press, 3rd ed., 2017).

12

Annual and Consolidated Accounts

12.1 The Annual Accounts in General

An important chapter of EU company law includes annual and consolidated accounts. The following paragraphs will offer a brief overview of Directive 2013/34/EU, and in particular will focus on: (a) the annual accounts layouts, the management report and the duty of publication; (b) the accounting principles; (c) the consolidated accounts. Information will also be given on the IAS/IFRS accounting principles, as well as on statutory audits.

Under Directive 2013/34/EU, the annual financial statements are to comprise (at least) a balance sheet, a profit and loss account, and the notes to the accounts. These documents constitute a composite whole.

Article 4(1) General Provisions, Directive 2013/34/EU

1. The annual financial statements shall constitute a composite whole and shall for all undertakings comprise, as a minimum, the balance sheet, the profit and loss account and the notes to the financial statements.

Member States may require undertakings other than small undertakings to include other statements in the annual financial statements in addition to the documents referred to in the first subparagraph.

Essentially, Directive 2013/34/EU provides for two balance sheet alternative layouts (vertical and horizontal: *see*, Figure 12.1), leaving it to the Member States to choose, and lists the balance sheet items and comments on them. Also, Directive 2013/34/EU proposes two layouts for the profit and loss account from which Member States are free to choose, and provides a commentary on certain items. Notes must be drafted in accordance with some principles expressed in Directive 2013/34/EU. In addition to the three documents constituting the annual financial statements, Directive 2013/34/EU requires that the management board issues an annual report. The alternative

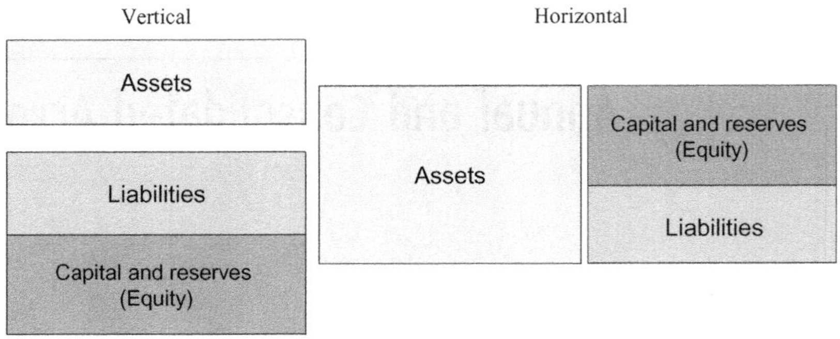

Figure 12.1 Vertical and horizontal layouts

layouts, the management report, the presentation, approval, and publication of these documents will be discussed in § 12.2.

Along with the layouts, Directive 2013/34/EU lays down the principles that govern the drawing up of these documents.

Annual financial statements pursue various objectives: above all, to provide information for investors in capital markets, as well as for creditors and other third parties, to give an account of past transactions and enhance corporate governance. Given their mainly informational role:

Recital 9 Directive 2013/34/EU

Annual financial statements should be prepared on a prudent basis and should give a true and fair view of an undertaking's assets and liabilities, financial position and profit or loss.

Prudence and true and fair view, along with the going concern and the accrual bases, are EU general accounting principles: these are also applicable to consolidated financial statements. Accounting principles will be discussed in § 12.3.

Whilst the Fourth Company Law Directive laid down less strict rules for SMEs, the Recast Fourth and Seventh Directives have consistently strengthened this multi-level approach.

Recitals 1–2 Directive 2013/34/EU

(1) This Directive takes into account the Commission's better regulation programme, and, in particular, the Commission Communication entitled 'Smart Regulation in the European Union', which aims at designing and delivering regulation of the highest quality whilst respecting the principles of subsidiarity and proportionality and ensuring that the administrative burdens are proportionate to the benefits they bring. The Commission

Communication entitled 'Think Small First – Small Business Act for Europe', adopted in June 2008 and revised in February 2011, recognises the central role played by small and medium-sized enterprises (SMEs) in the Union economy and aims to improve the overall approach to entrepreneurship and to anchor the 'think small first' principle in policy-making concerning regulation to public service. The European Council of 24 and 25 March 2011 welcomed the Commission's intention to present the 'Single Market Act' with measures creating growth and jobs, bringing tangible results to citizens and businesses.

The Commission Communication entitled 'Single Market Act', adopted in April 2011, proposes to simplify the Fourth Council Directive 78/660/EEC of 25 July 1978 based on Article 54(3)(g) of the Treaty on the annual accounts of certain types of companies and the Seventh Council Directive 83/349/EEC of 13 June 1983 based on Article 54(3)(g) of the Treaty on consolidated accounts (the Accounting Directives) as regards financial information obligations and to reduce administrative burdens, in particular for SMEs. 'The Europe 2020 Strategy' for smart, sustainable and inclusive growth aims to reduce administrative burdens and improve the business environment, in particular for SMEs, and to promote the internationalisation of SMEs. The European Council of 24 and 25 March 2011 also called for the overall regulatory burden, in particular for SMEs, to be reduced at both Union and national level and suggested measures to increase productivity, such as the removal of red tape and the improvement of the regulatory framework for SMEs.

(2) On 18 December 2008 the European Parliament adopted a non-legislative resolution on accounting requirements as regards small and medium-sized companies, particularly micro-entities, stating that the Accounting Directives are often very burdensome for small and medium-sized companies, and in particular for micro-entities, and asking the Commission to continue its efforts to review those Directives.

Having this goal to achieve, the Directive 2013/34/EU better defines large, medium, and small-sized companies, and introduces a definition of micro-undertaking in order to differentiate the burdens they shall be committed to. In addition, it provides a definition of the public-interest entity which corresponds to the one referred to in both Directive 2006/43/EC and Regulation 2014/537/EU (on statutory audits), and in Regulations 2002/1606/EC and 2008/1126/EC (on the application of IAS).

Recitals 12–15 Directive 2013/34/EU

(12) Small, medium-sized and large undertakings should be defined and distinguished by reference to balance sheet total, net turnover and the average number of employees during the financial year, as those criteria typically provide objective evidence as to the size of an undertaking. However, where a parent undertaking is not preparing consolidated financial statements for the group, Member States should be allowed to take steps they deem necessary to require that such an undertaking be classified as a larger

undertaking by determining its size and resulting category on a consolidated or aggregated basis. Where a Member State applies one or more of the optional exemptions for micro-undertakings, micro-undertakings should also be defined by reference to balance sheet total, net turnover and the average number of employees during the financial year. Member States should not be obliged to define separate categories for medium-sized and large undertakings in their national legislation if medium-sized undertakings are subject to the same requirements as large undertakings.

(13) Micro-undertakings have limited resources with which to comply with demanding regulatory requirements. Where no specific rules are in place for micro-undertakings, the rules applying to small undertakings apply to them. Those rules place on them administrative burdens which are disproportionate to their size and are, therefore, relatively more onerous for micro-undertakings as compared to other small undertakings. Therefore, it should be possible for Member States to exempt micro-undertakings from certain obligations applying to small undertakings that would impose excessive administrative burdens on them. However, micro-undertakings should still be subject to any national obligation to keep records showing their business transactions and financial position. Moreover, investment undertakings and financial holding undertakings should be excluded from the benefits of simplifications applicable to micro-undertakings.

(14) Member States should take into account the specific conditions and needs of their own markets when making a decision about whether or how to implement a distinct regime for micro-undertakings within the context of this Directive.

(15) Publication of financial statements can be burdensome for micro-undertakings. At the same time, Member States need to ensure compliance with this Directive. Accordingly, Member States making use of the exemptions for micro-undertakings provided for in this Directive should be allowed to exempt micro-undertakings from a general publication requirement, provided that balance sheet information is duly filed, in accordance with national law, with at least one designated competent authority and that the information is forwarded to the business register, so that a copy should be obtainable upon application. In such cases, the obligation laid down in this Directive to publish any accounting document in accordance with Article 3(5) of Directive 2009/101/EC of the European Parliament and of the Council of 16 September 2009 on coordination of safeguards which, for the protection of the interests of members and third parties, are required by Member States of companies within the meaning of the second paragraph of Article 48 of the Treaty, with a view to making such safeguards equivalent, should not apply.

Article 2(1) Definitions, Directive 2013/34/EU

(1) 'public-interest entities' means undertakings within the scope of Article 1 which are:

(a) governed by the law of a Member State and whose transferable securities are admitted to trading on a regulated market of any Member State within the meaning of point (14) of Article 4(1) of Directive 2004/39/EC of the European Parliament and of the Council of 21 April 2004 on markets in financial instruments;

(b) credit institutions as defined in point (1) of Article 4 of Directive 2006/48/EC of the European Parliament and of the Council of 14 June 2006 relating to the taking up and pursuit of the business of credit institutions, other than those referred to in Article 2 of that Directive;

(c) insurance undertakings within the meaning of Article 2(1) of Council Directive 91/674/EEC of 19 December 1991 on the annual accounts of insurance undertakings; or

(d) designated by Member States as public-interest entities, for instance undertakings that are of significant public relevance because of the nature of their business, their size or the number of their employees; ...

Article 3 Categories of Undertakings and Groups, Directive 2013/34/EU

1. In applying one or more of the options in Article 36, Member States shall define microundertakings as undertakings which on their balance sheet dates do not exceed the limits of at least two of the three following criteria:
   (a) balance sheet total: EUR 350 000;
   (b) net turnover: EUR 700 000;
   (c) average number of employees during the financial year: 10.
2. Small undertakings shall be undertakings which on their balance sheet dates do not exceed the limits of at least two of the three following criteria:
   (a) balance sheet total: EUR 4 000 000;
   (b) net turnover: EUR 8 000 000;
   (c) average number of employees during the financial year: 50.

Member States may define thresholds exceeding the thresholds in points (a) and (b) of the first subparagraph. However, the thresholds shall not exceed EUR 6 000 000 for the balance sheet total and EUR 12 000 000 for the net turnover.

3. Medium-sized undertakings shall be undertakings which are not micro-undertakings or small undertakings and which on their balance sheet dates do not exceed the limits of at least two of the three following criteria:
   (a) balance sheet total: EUR 20 000 000;
   (b) net turnover: EUR 40 000 000;
   (c) average number of employees during the financial year: 250.
4. Large undertakings shall be undertakings which on their balance sheet dates exceed at least two of the three following criteria:
   (a) balance sheet total: EUR 20 000 000;
   (b) net turnover: EUR 40 000 000;
   (c) average number of employees during the financial year: 250.

5. Small groups shall be groups consisting of parent and subsidiary undertakings to be included in a consolidation and which, on a consolidated basis, do not exceed the limits of at least two of the three following criteria on the balance sheet date of the parent undertaking:
   (a) balance sheet total: EUR 4 000 000;
   (b) net turnover: EUR 8 000 000;
   (c) average number of employees during the financial year: 50.

Member States may define thresholds exceeding the thresholds in points (a) and (b) of the first subparagraph. However, the thresholds shall not exceed EUR 6 000 000 for the balance sheet total and EUR 12 000 000 for the net turnover.

6. Medium-sized groups shall be groups which are not small groups, which consist of parent and subsidiary undertakings to be included in a consolidation and which, on a consolidated basis, do not exceed the limits of at least two of the three following criteria on the balance sheet date of the parent undertaking:
   (a) balance sheet total: EUR 20 000 000;
   (b) net turnover: EUR 40 000 000;
   (c) average number of employees during the financial year: 250.
7. Large groups shall be groups consisting of parent and subsidiary undertakings to be included in a consolidation and which, on a consolidated basis, exceed the limits of at least two of the three following criteria on the balance sheet date of the parent undertaking:
   (a) balance sheet total: EUR 20 000 000;
   (b) net turnover: EUR 40 000 000;
   (c) average number of employees during the financial year: 250.

12.2 Annual Accounts: Layouts, Management Report and Publication

As mentioned in § 12.1, Member States have an option on the balance sheet as well as on the profits and loss accounts layouts.

Article 10 Presentation of the Balance Sheet, Directive 2013/34/EU

For the presentation of the balance sheet, Member States shall prescribe one or both of the layouts set out in Annexes III and IV. If a Member State prescribes both layouts, it shall permit undertakings to choose which of the prescribed layouts to adopt.

Article 13, Presentation of the profit and loss account, Directive 2013/34/EU

1. For the presentation of the profit and loss account, Member States shall prescribe one or both of the layouts set out in Annexes V and VI. If a Member State prescribes both layouts, it may permit undertakings to choose which of the prescribed layouts to adopt.

2. By way of derogation from Article 4(1), Member States may permit or require all undertakings, or any classes of undertaking, to present a statement of their performance instead of the presentation of profit and loss items in accordance with Annexes V and VI, provided that the information given is at least equivalent to that otherwise required by Annexes V and VI.

Annex III Horizontal Layout of the Balance Sheet Provided for in Article 10

Assets

A. Subscribed capital unpaid of which there has been called (unless national law provides that called-up capital is to be shown under 'Capital and reserves', in which case the part of the capital called but not yet paid shall appear as an asset either under A or under D(II)(5)).

B. Formation expenses as defined by national law, and in so far as national law permits their being shown as an asset. National law may also provide for formation expenses to be shown as the first item under 'Intangible assets'.

C. Fixed assets
- I. Intangible assets
  1. Costs of development, in so far as national law permits their being shown as assets.
  2. Concessions, patents, licences, trade marks and similar rights and assets, if they were:
     (a) acquired for valuable consideration and need not be shown under C(I)(3); or
     (b) created by the undertaking itself, in so far as national law permits their being shown as assets.
  3. Goodwill, to the extent that it was acquired for valuable consideration.
  4. Payments on account.
- II. Tangible assets
  1. Land and buildings.
  2. Plant and machinery.
  3. Other fixtures and fittings, tools and equipment.
  4. Payments on account and tangible assets in the course of construction.
- III. Financial assets
  1. Shares in affiliated undertakings.
  2. Loans to affiliated undertakings.
  3. Participating interests.
  4. Loans to undertakings with which the undertaking is linked by virtue of participating interests.
  5. Investments held as fixed assets.
  6. Other loans.

D. Current assets
  I. Stocks
    1. Raw materials and consumables.
    2. Work in progress.
    3. Finished goods and goods for resale.
    4. Payments on account.
  II. Debtors (Amounts becoming due and payable after more than one year shall be shown separately for each item.)
    1. Trade debtors.
    2. Amounts owed by affiliated undertakings.
    3. Amounts owed by undertakings with which the undertaking is linked by virtue of participating interests.
    4. Other debtors.
    5. Subscribed capital called but not paid (unless national law provides that called-up capital is to be shown as an asset under A).
    6. Prepayments and accrued income (unless national law provides that such items are to be shown as assets under E).
  III. Investments
    1. Shares in affiliated undertakings.
    2. Own shares (with an indication of their nominal value or, in the absence of a nominal value, their accounting par value), to the extent that national law permits their being shown in the balance sheet.
    3. Other investments.
  IV. Cash at bank and in hand
E. Prepayments and accrued income (Unless national law provides that such items are to be shown as assets under D(II)(6).)

Capital, reserves and liabilities

A. Capital and reserves
  I. Subscribed capital (Unless national law provides that called-up capital is to be shown under this item, in which case the amounts of subscribed capital and paid-up capital shall be shown separately.)
  II. Share premium account
  III. Revaluation reserve
  IV. Reserves
    1. Legal reserve, in so far as national law requires such a reserve.
    2. Reserve for own shares, in so far as national law requires such a reserve, without prejudice to point (b) of Article 24(1) of Directive 2012/30/EU.
    3. Reserves provided for by the articles of association.
    4. Other reserves, including the fair value reserve.
  V. Profit or loss brought forward
  VI. Profit or loss for the financial year

B. Provisions
   1. Provisions for pensions and similar obligations.
   2. Provisions for taxation.
   3. Other provisions.

C. Creditors (Amounts becoming due and payable within one year and amounts becoming due and payable after more than one year shall be shown separately for each item and for the aggregate of those items.)
   1. Debenture loans, showing convertible loans separately.
   2. Amounts owed to credit institutions.
   3. Payments received on account of orders, in so far as they are not shown separately as deductions from stocks.
   4. Trade creditors.
   5. Bills of exchange payable.
   6. Amounts owed to affiliated undertakings.
   7. Amounts owed to undertakings with which the undertaking is linked by virtue of participating interests.
   8. Other creditors, including tax and social security authorities.
   9. Accruals and deferred income (unless national law provides that such items are to be shown under D).

D. Accruals and deferred income (Unless national law provides that such items are to be shown under C (9) under 'Creditors'.)

Annex IV Vertical Layout of the Balance Sheet Provided for in Article 10

A. Subscribed capital unpaid of which there has been called (unless national law provides that called-up capital is to be shown under L, in which case the part of the capital called but not yet paid must appear either under A or under D (II) (5).)

B. Formation expenses as defined by national law, and in so far as national law permits their being shown as an asset. National law may also provide for formation expenses to be shown as the first item under 'Intangible assets'.

C. Fixed assets
   I. Intangible assets
      1. Costs of development, in so far as national law permits their being shown as assets.
      2. Concessions, patents, licences, trade marks and similar rights and assets, if they were:
         (a) acquired for valuable consideration and need not be shown under C (I) (3); or
         (b) created by the undertaking itself, in so far as national law permits their being shown as assets.
      3. Goodwill, to the extent that it was acquired for valuable consideration.
      4. Payments on account.

II. Tangible assets
   1. Land and buildings.
   2. Plant and machinery.
   3. Other fixtures and fittings, tools and equipment.
   4. Payments on account and tangible assets in the course of construction.

III. Financial assets
   1. Shares in affiliated undertakings.
   2. Loans to affiliated undertakings.
   3. Participating interests.
   4. Loans to undertakings with which the undertaking is linked by virtue of participating interests.
   5. Investments held as fixed assets.
   6. Other loans.

D. Current assets

I. Stocks
   1. Raw materials and consumables.
   2. Work in progress.
   3. Finished goods and goods for resale.
   4. Payments on account.

II. Debtors (Amounts becoming due and payable after more than one year must be shown separately for each item.)
   1. Trade debtors.
   2. Amounts owed by affiliated undertakings.
   3. Amounts owed by undertakings with which the company is linked by virtue of participating interests.
   4. Other debtors.
   5. Subscribed capital called but not paid (unless national law provides that called-up capital is to be shown as an asset under A).
   6. Prepayments and accrued income (unless national law provides that such items are to be shown as assets under E).

III. Investments
   1. Shares in affiliated undertakings.
   2. Own shares (with an indication of their nominal value or, in the absence of a nominal value, their accounting par value), to the extent that national law permits their being shown in the balance sheet.
   3. Other investments.

IV. Cash at bank and in hand

E. Prepayments and accrued income (Unless national law provides that such items are to be shown under D(II)(6).)

F. Creditors: amounts becoming due and payable within one year
   1. Debenture loans, showing convertible loans separately.
   2. Amounts owed to credit institutions.

3. Payments received on account of orders, in so far as they are not shown separately as deductions from stocks.
4. Trade creditors.
5. Bills of exchange payable.
6. Amounts owed to affiliated undertakings.
7. Amounts owed to undertakings with which the company is linked by virtue of participating interests.
8. Other creditors, including tax and social security authorities.
9. Accruals and deferred income (unless national law provides that such items are to be shown under K).

G. Net current assets/liabilities (Taking into account prepayments and accrued income when shown under E and accruals and deferred income when shown under K.)

H. Total assets less current liabilities

I. Creditors: amounts becoming due and payable after more than one year
1. Debenture loans, showing convertible loans separately.
2. Amounts owed to credit institutions.
3. Payments received on account of orders, in so far as they are not shown separately as deductions from stocks.
4. Trade creditors.
5. Bills of exchange payable.
6. Amounts owed to affiliated undertakings.
7. Amounts owed to undertakings with which the company is linked by virtue of participating interests.
8. Other creditors, including tax and social security authorities.
9. Accruals and deferred income (unless national law provides that such items are to be shown under K).

J. Provisions
1. Provisions for pensions and similar obligations.
2. Provisions for taxation.
3. Other provisions.

K. Accruals and deferred income (Unless national law provides that such items are to be shown under F(9) or I(9) or both.)

L. Capital and reserves

I. Subscribed capital (Unless national law provides that called-up capital is to be shown under this item, in which case the amounts of subscribed capital and paid-up capital must be shown separately.)

II. Share premium account

III. Revaluation reserve

IV. Reserves
1. Legal reserve, in so far as national law requires such a reserve.
2. Reserve for own shares, in so far as national law requires such a reserve, without prejudice to point (b) of Article 24(1) of Directive 2012/30/EU.

3. Reserves provided for by the articles of association.
4. Other reserves, including the fair value reserve.

V. Profit or loss brought forward

VI. Profit or loss for the financial year

Annex V Layout of the Profit and Loss Account – By Nature of Expense, Provided for in Article 13

1. Net turnover.
2. Variation in stocks of finished goods and in work in progress.
3. Work performed by the undertaking for its own purposes and capitalised.
4. Other operating income. 5. ...
   (a) Raw materials and consumables.
   (b) Other external expenses.
6. Staff costs:
   (a) wages and salaries;
   (b) social security costs, with a separate indication of those relating to pensions.
7. ...
   (a) Value adjustments in respect of formation expenses and of tangible and intangible fixed assets.
   (b) Value adjustments in respect of current assets, to the extent that they exceed the amount of value adjustments which are normal in the undertaking concerned.
8. Other operating expenses.
9. Income from participating interests, with a separate indication of that derived from affiliated undertakings.
10. Income from other investments and loans forming part of the fixed assets, with a separate indication of that derived from affiliated undertakings.
11. Other interest receivable and similar income, with a separate indication of that derived from affiliated undertakings.
12. Value adjustments in respect of financial assets and of investments held as current assets.
13. Interest payable and similar expenses, with a separate indication of amounts payable to affiliated undertakings.
14. Tax on profit or loss.
15. Profit or loss after taxation.
16. Other taxes not shown under items 1 to 15.
17. Profit or loss for the financial year.

Annex VI Layout of the Profit and Loss Account – By Function of Expense, Provided for in Article 13

1. Net turnover.
2. Cost of sales (including value adjustments).
3. Gross profit or loss.
4. Distribution costs (including value adjustments).

5. Administrative expenses (including value adjustments).
6. Other operating income.
7. Income from participating interests, with a separate indication of that derived from affiliated undertakings.
8. Income from other investments and loans forming part of the fixed assets, with a separate indication of that derived from affiliated undertakings.
9. Other interest receivable and similar income, with a separate indication of that derived from affiliated undertakings.
10. Value adjustments in respect of financial assets and of investments held as current assets.
11. Interest payable and similar expenses, with a separate indication of amounts payable to affiliated undertakings.
12. Tax on profit or loss.
13. Profit or loss after taxation.
14. Other taxes not shown under items 1 to 13.
15. Profit or loss for the financial year.

Whatever the chosen layout, companies subject to Directive 2013/34/EU must comply with the general provisions concerning the balance sheet and the profit and loss account provided for under Article 9. Simplifications are provided for companies qualifying as either medium- or small-size, or for micro-undertakings (Article 14 Directive 2013/34/EU).

Article 9 General Provisions Concerning the Balance Sheet and the Profit and Loss Account, Directive 2013/34/EU

1. The layout of the balance sheet and of the profit and loss account shall not be changed from one financial year to the next. Departures from that principle shall, however, be permitted in exceptional cases in order to give a true and fair view of the undertaking's assets, liabilities, financial position and profit or loss. Any such departure and the reasons therefor shall be disclosed in the notes to the financial statements.
2. In the balance sheet and in the profit and loss account the items set out in Annexes III to VI shall be shown separately in the order indicated. Member States shall permit a more detailed subdivision of those items, subject to adherence to the prescribed layouts. Member States shall permit the addition of subtotals and of new items, provided that the contents of such new items are not covered by any of the items in the prescribed layouts. Member States may require such subdivision or subtotals or new items.
3. The layout, nomenclature and terminology of items in the balance sheet and profit and loss account that are preceded by arabic numerals shall be adapted where the special nature of an undertaking so requires. Member States may require such adaptations for undertakings which form part of a particular economic sector.

Member States may permit or require balance sheet and profit and loss account items that are preceded by arabic numerals to be combined where they are immaterial in amount for the purposes of giving a true and fair view of the undertaking's assets, liabilities, financial position and profit or loss or where such combination makes for greater clarity, provided that the items so combined are dealt with separately in the notes to the financial statements.

4. By way of derogation from paragraphs 2 and 3 of this Article, Member States may limit the undertaking's ability to depart from the layouts set out in Annexes III to VI to the extent that this is necessary in order for the financial statements to be filed electronically.
5. In respect of each balance sheet and profit and loss account item, the figure for the financial year to which the balance sheet and the profit and loss account relate and the figure relating to the corresponding item for the preceding financial year shall be shown. Where those figures are not comparable, Member States may require the figure for the preceding financial year to be adjusted. Any case of non-comparability or any adjustment of the figures shall be disclosed, with explanations, in the notes to the financial statements.
6. Member States may permit or require adaptation of the layout of the balance sheet and profit and loss account in order to include the appropriation of profit or the treatment of loss.
7. In respect of the treatment of participating interests in annual financial statements:
   (a) Member States may permit or require participating interests to be accounted for using the equity method as provided for in Article 27, taking account of the essential adjustments resulting from the particular characteristics of annual financial statements as compared to consolidated financial statements;
   (b) Member States may permit or require that the proportion of the profit or loss attributable to the participating interest be recognised in the profit and loss account only to the extent of the amount corresponding to dividends already received or the payment of which can be claimed; and
   (c) where the profit attributable to the participating interest and recognised in the profit and loss account exceeds the amount of dividends already received or the payment of which can be claimed, the amount of the difference shall be placed in a reserve which cannot be distributed to shareholders.

In addition to the balance sheet and the profit and loss accounts, the annual financial statements must include the notes.Whilst Article 16 Directive 2013/ 34/ EU refers to the content of the notes to the financial statements relating to all undertakings, Articles 17 and 18 Directive 2013/34/EU require additional disclosures for medium-sized and large undertakings, as well as for public-interest entities.

Also, a management report shall be added to the annual financial accounts. This shall include a fair review of the development and performance of the undertaking's business and of its position, together with a description of the principal risks and uncertainties that it faces (Article 19 Directive 2013/34/ EU). Companies qualifying as public-interest entities shall also include in the management report a corporate governance statement (further described in Chapter 13, § 13.2).

Annual financial accounts will comply with their informational function provided that they are accessible to the public, or at least to the addressees of the information. As a general rule, both annual and consolidated accounts of all companies shall be published in the ways prescribed by Directive 2009/101/EC. However, Member States may exempt small undertakings from the obligation to publish their profit and loss accounts and management reports and may permit medium-size ones to publish abridged balance sheets and notes (Article 31 Directive 2013/34/EU).

Article 30 General Publication Requirement, Directive 2013/34/EU

1. Member States shall ensure that undertakings publish within a reasonable period of time, which shall not exceed 12 months after the balance sheet date, the duly approved annual financial statements and the management report, together with the opinion submitted by the statutory auditor or audit firm referred to in Article 34 of this Directive, as laid down by the laws of each Member State in accordance with Chapter 2 of Directive 2009/101/EC.

Member States may, however, exempt undertakings from the obligation to publish the management report where a copy of all or part of any such report can be easily obtained upon request at a price not exceeding its administrative cost.

2. Member States may exempt an undertaking referred to in Annex II to which the coordination measures prescribed by this Directive apply by virtue of point (b) of Article 1(1) from publishing its financial statements in accordance with Article 3 of Directive 2009/101/EC, provided that those financial statements are available to the public at its head office, in the following cases:
   (a) all the members of the undertaking concerned that have unlimited liability are undertakings referred to in Annex I governed by the laws of Member States other than the Member State whose law governs that undertaking, and none of those undertakings publishes the financial statements of the undertaking concerned with its own financial statements;
   (b) all the members of the undertaking concerned that have unlimited liability are undertakings which are not governed by the laws of a Member State but which have a legal form comparable to those referred to in Directive 2009/101/EC.

Copies of the financial statements shall be obtainable upon request. The price of such a copy may not exceed its administrative cost.

3. Paragraph 1 shall apply with respect to consolidated financial statements and consolidated management reports.

Where the undertaking drawing up the consolidated financial statements is established as one of the types of undertaking listed in Annex II and is not required by the national law of its Member State to publish the documents referred to in paragraph 1 in the same manner as prescribed in Article 3 of Directive 2009/101/EC, it shall, as a minimum, make those documents available to the public at its head office and a copy shall be provided upon request, the price of which shall not exceed its administrative cost.

In *Texdata*, a case analysed in § 12.4, the CJEU has clarified that the time limit for the publication of the annual accounts to be decided by Member States is also applicable to branches of companies established in other Member States. The fact that time limits may be different in such circumstances does not result in a restriction to the freedom of establishment.

12.3 Accounting Principles

As already mentioned, the EU accounting principles include the true and fair view, the going concern, the prudence, and the accrual bases.

The first and most important accounting principle is that of requiring a true and fair view.

Recital 9 Directive 2013/34/EU

(9) Annual financial statements should be prepared on a prudent basis and should give a true and fair view of an undertaking's assets and liabilities, financial position and profit or loss. It is possible that, in exceptional cases, a financial statement does not give such a true and fair view where provisions of this Directive are applied. In such cases, the undertaking should depart from such provisions in order to give a true and fair view. The Member States should be allowed to define such exceptional cases and to lay down the relevant special rules which are to apply in those cases. Those exceptional cases should be understood to be only very unusual transactions and unusual situations and should, for instance, not be related to entire specific sectors.

Article 4(2–4) General Provisions, Directive 2013/34/EU

2. The annual financial statements shall be drawn up clearly and in accordance with the provisions of this Directive.
3. The annual financial statements shall give a true and fair view of the undertaking's assets, liabilities, financial position and profit or loss. Where the application of this Directive would not be sufficient to give a true and fair view of the undertaking's assets, liabilities, financial position and profit or loss, such additional information as is necessary to comply with that requirement shall be given in the notes to the financial statements.
4. Where in exceptional cases the application of a provision of this Directive is incompatible with the obligation laid down in paragraph 3, that provision shall be disapplied in order to give a true and fair view of the undertaking's assets, liabilities, financial position and profit or loss. The disapplication of any such provision shall be disclosed in the notes to the financial statements together with an explanation of the reasons for it and of its effect on the undertaking's assets, liabilities, financial position and profit or loss.

   The Member States may define the exceptional cases in question and lay down the relevant special rules which are to apply in those cases.

The expression 'true and fair view' is not strictly defined in the accounting literature. In a rough definition, this expression means that the annual financial statements are free from material misstatements and faithfully represent the economic and financial performance and position of the entity.

In particular: *true* suggests that the annual financial statements are factually correct and have been prepared according to applicable reporting standards (such as GAAP, IFRS, and others) and they do not contain any material misstatements that may mislead the users (misstatements may result from material errors or omissions of transactions and balances in the annual accounts); *fair* implies that the annual financial statements present the information faithfully without any element of bias and they reflect the economic substance of transactions rather than just their legal form.

A true and fair view is compromised by missing information, but also by an excess of information and detail. Therefore, the Directive 2013/34/EU expresses the principle that *immaterial information* may be omitted or aggregated in case this favours the true and fair view.

Recital 17 Directive 2013/34/EU

(17) The principle of materiality should govern recognition, measurement, presentation, disclosure and consolidation in financial statements. According to the principle of materiality, information that is considered immaterial may, for instance, be aggregated in the financial statements. However, while a single item might be considered to be immaterial, immaterial items of a similar nature might be considered material when taken as a whole. Member States should be allowed to limit the mandatory application of the principle of materiality to presentation and disclosure. The principle of materiality should not affect any national obligation to keep complete records showing business transactions and financial position.

The CJEU has further clarified the concept of true and fair view in *Tomberger*, a case examined in § 12.6 as its understanding implies some information on consolidated financial statements and the so-called equity method.

Correctness of the annual financial statements implies, *inter alia*, compliance with the going concern, the prudence and the accrual bases principles.

Recital 16 Directive 2013/34/EU

(16) To ensure the disclosure of comparable and equivalent information, recognition and measurement principles should include the going concern, the prudence, and the accrual bases. Set-offs between asset and liability items and income and expense items should not be allowed and components of assets and liabilities should be valued

separately. In specific cases, however, Member States should be allowed to permit or require undertakings to perform set-offs between asset and liability items and income and expense items. The presentation of items in financial statements should have regard to the economic reality or commercial substance of the underlying transaction or arrangement. Member States should, however, be allowed to exempt undertakings from applying that principle.

Article 6 General Financial Reporting Principles, Directive 2013/34/EU

1. Items presented in the annual and consolidated financial statements shall be recognised and measured in accordance with the following general principles:
   (a) the undertaking shall be presumed to be carrying on its business as a going concern;
   (b) accounting policies and measurement bases shall be applied consistently from one financial year to the next;
   (c) recognition and measurement shall be on a prudent basis, and in particular: (i) only profits made at the balance sheet date may be recognised, (ii) all liabilities arising in the course of the financial year concerned or in the course of a previous financial year shall be recognised, even if such liabilities become apparent only between the balance sheet date and the date on which the balance sheet is drawn up, and (iii) all negative value adjustments shall be recognised, whether the result of the financial year is a profit or a loss;
   (d) amounts recognised in the balance sheet and profit and loss account shall be computed on the accrual basis;
   (e) the opening balance sheet for each financial year shall correspond to the closing balance sheet for the preceding financial year;
   (f) the components of asset and liability items shall be valued separately;
   (g) any set-off between asset and liability items, or between income and expenditure items, shall be prohibited;
   (h) items in the profit and loss account and balance sheet shall be accounted for and presented having regard to the substance of the transaction or arrangement concerned;
   (i) items recognised in the financial statements shall be measured in accordance with the principle of purchase price or production cost; and
   (j) the requirements set out in this Directive regarding recognition, measurement, presentation, disclosure and consolidation need not be complied with when the effect of complying with them is immaterial.

In particular, prudence requires that items included in the annual financial statements show the purchase price or production cost incurred by the company. Devaluations and revaluations may be permitted only in cases and under conditions specified by Directive 2013/34/EU.

Recital 18 Directive 2013/34/EU

(18) Items recognised in annual financial statements should be measured on the basis of the principle of purchase price or production cost to ensure the reliability of information contained in financial statements. However, Member States should be allowed to permit or require undertakings to revalue fixed assets in order that more relevant information may be provided to the users of financial statements.

Article 2(6–7) Definitions, Directive 2013/34/EU

(6) 'purchase price' means the price payable and any incidental expenses minus any incidental reductions in the cost of acquisition;

(7) 'production cost' means the purchase price of raw materials, consumables and other costs directly attributable to the item in question. Member States shall permit or require the inclusion of a reasonable proportion of fixed or variable overhead costs indirectly attributable to the item in question, to the extent that they relate to the period of production. Distribution costs shall not be included.

Article 7 Alternative Measurement Basis of Fixed Assets at Revalued Amounts, Directive 2013/34/EU

1. By way of derogation from point (i) of Article 6(1), Member States may permit or require, in respect of all undertakings or any classes of undertaking, the measurement of fixed assets at revalued amounts. Where national law provides for the revaluation basis of measurement, it shall define its content and limits and the rules for its application.
2. Where paragraph 1 is applied, the amount of the difference between measurement on a purchase price or production cost basis and measurement on a revaluation basis shall be entered in the balance sheet in the revaluation reserve under 'Capital and reserves'.

The revaluation reserve may be capitalised in whole or in part at any time.

The revaluation reserve shall be reduced where the amounts transferred to that reserve are no longer necessary for the implementation of the revaluation basis of accounting. The Member States may lay down rules governing the application of the revaluation reserve, provided that transfers to the profit and loss account from the revaluation reserve may be made only where the amounts transferred have been entered as an expense in the profit and loss account or reflect increases in value which have actually been realised. No part of the revaluation reserve may be distributed, either directly or indirectly, unless it represents a gain actually realised.

Save as provided under the second and third subparagraphs of this paragraph, the revaluation reserve may not be reduced.

3. Value adjustments shall be calculated each year on the basis of the revalued amount. However, by way of derogation from Articles 9 and 13, Member States may permit or require that only the amount of the value adjustments arising as a result of the purchase price or production cost measurement basis be shown under the relevant items in the layouts set out in Annexes V and VI and that the difference arising as a result of the measurement on a revaluation basis under this Article be shown separately in the layouts.

Notwithstanding the purchase price principle, Directive 2013/34/EU provides that financial instruments are accounted for at fair value, as IAS/IFRS principles require (*see*, § 12.7).

Recital 19 Directive 2013/34/EU

(19) The need for comparability of financial information throughout the Union makes it necessary to require Member States to allow a system of fair value accounting for certain financial instruments. Furthermore, systems of fair value accounting provide information that can be of more relevance to the users of financial statements than purchase price or production cost-based information. Accordingly, Member States should permit the adoption of a fair value system of accounting by all undertakings or classes of undertaking, other than micro-undertakings making use of the exemptions provided for in this Directive, in respect of both annual and consolidated financial statements or, if a Member State so chooses, in respect of consolidated financial statements only. Furthermore, Member States should be allowed to permit or require fair value accounting for assets other than financial instruments.

FURTHER READING

Md Anowar Zahid, '"True and Fair View" Versus "Fair Presentation" Accountings: Are They Legally Similar or Different?', 19 *EBLR* 677–690 (2008).

12.4 *Texdata* Case

In *Texdata* (C-418/11, *Texdata Software GmbH*, [ECLI:EU:C:2013:588]) the request for a preliminary ruling concerned the interpretation of Article 6(1) and (3) TEU, Articles 49 TFEU and 54 TFEU, Articles 47 and 50 of the Charter of Fundamental Rights of the European Union ('*the Charter*'), Article 6(2) of the European Convention for the Protection of Human Rights and Fundamental Freedoms, signed in Rome on 4 November 1950 ('the *ECHR*'), Article 6 of First Council Directive 68/151/EEC, Article 60a of Fourth Council Directive 78/660/EEC and Article 38(6) of Seventh Council Directive 83/349/EEC. The request was made in proceedings initiated by Texdata Software GmbH ('*Texdata*'), contesting the periodic penalties imposed on it by the Landesgericht Innsbruck (Regional Court, Innsbruck) for its breach of the obligation to submit its annual accounts to that court, which is responsible for maintaining the commercial register.

Texdata is a limited company, established in Germany, which designs and markets software. It pursues its activities in Austria through a branch that has, since 4 March 2008, been registered in the Austrian commercial register as a branch of a company established in another Member State.

By two orders of 5 May 2011, the Landesgericht Innsbruck imposed two periodic penalties on Texdata under Paragraph 283(2) of the Unternehmensgesetzbuch (Austrian commercial code, UGB), as amended by the Undesbeschaffung GmbH (Austrian Federal Procurement Agency, BBG), in the amount of €700 each, on the ground that Texdata had failed to submit annual accounts for two fiscal years – ending on 31 December 2008 and 31 December 2009, respectively – within the prescribed period, that is to say, pursuant to the transitional measures, either before 28 February 2011 or the day before the delivery of those orders.

On 23 May 2011, Texdata lodged, within the prescribed period, two objections against those orders before the same court. In support of those objections, it claimed, first, that in the absence of prior notice, the imposition of a penalty for infringement of the disclosure obligation referred to in Paragraph 283 of the UGB, as amended by the BBG, was unlawful, and, secondly, that the annual accounts had been filed within the prescribed period at the Amtsgericht Karlsruhe (Local Court, Karlsruhe, Germany), which has territorial jurisdiction in view of the location of Texdata's registered office, and that those accounts had long been accessible there via electronic means.

On the same date, Texdata filed the annual accounts at issue before the Landesgericht Innsbruck, which entered them in the commercial register on 25 and 26 May 2011.

By two decisions of 25 May 2011, the Landesgericht Innsbruck rendered inoperative the orders adopted on 5 May 2011 on the ground that the objections had been raised in good time. However, in the light of the fact that the annual accounts at issue had not been filed within the prescribed period, that court again imposed, under the ordinary procedure pursuant to Paragraph 283 (3) and (7) of the UGB, as amended by the BBG, two periodic penalties in the same amount.

Seised of Texdata's appeal against those decisions, the Oberlandesgericht Innsbruck (Higher Regional Court, Innsbruck), the referring court, was uncertain as to whether the Austrian rules on penalties, as amended in 2011, which provide for a periodic penalty to be imposed immediately on a company that fails to file its annual accounts with the relevant court, were compatible with EU law. The referring court noted that, before the reform of 2011, it had become standard practice for the courts keeping the commercial register in Austria to first send a non-compliant company an informal notice granting an additional period of four weeks, after the nine-month period laid down in Paragraphs 277 and 283 of the UGB had expired. Upon the expiry of that period, if the failure to comply persisted, further notice would be given to the effect that, if the annual accounts were not forthcoming within a particular period or if it was not demonstrated that the obligation did not apply, a periodic penalty would be imposed. Only if the second notice also proved unfruitful and no obstacle to the disclosure had been invoked would the courts impose periodic penalties. The referring court noted the following elements, which it regarded as 'structural shortcomings' inherent in the national procedure: (i) the excessive formal requirements that require objections which are submitted out of time or which fail to state any reasons to be simply rejected, necessitating new pleas at the appeal stage, with the only caveat to these rejections being where the omission is excusable; (ii) the lack of any guarantee that a hearing will be held; (iii) the breach of the rights of the defence arising from the fact that there is no opportunity to submit observations prior to the imposition of the periodic penalty; (iv) the reliance on a statutory presumption of liability whereby the burden of proof is placed on the company; (v) the unreasonable rules on time-barring and the lack of prior notice, resulting in a lack of legal certainty for companies established in another Member State; and (vi) the fact that, in the event of continued failure to fulfil the disclosure obligation, further periodic penalties may be imposed when the initial decisions imposing a periodic penalty have not yet acquired the force of res judicata.

In those circumstances, the Oberlandesgericht Innsbruck decided to stay the proceedings and to refer the following question to the Court for a preliminary ruling:

C-418/11, Texdata Software GmbH, [ECLI:EU:C:2013:588], § 25

Does EU law, as it stands at present, and in particular:

(a) freedom of establishment, as laid down in Articles 49 TFEU and 54 TFEU;
(b) the general legal principle (Article 6(3) TEU) of effective judicial protection (principle of effectiveness);
(c) the principle of the right to a fair hearing laid down in the second paragraph of Article 47 of the Charter (Article 6(1) TEU) and in Article 6(2) of the ECHR (Article 6(1) TEU);
(d) the principle of non bis in idem laid down in Article 50 of the Charter; or
(e) the rules governing penalties in the disclosure procedure under Article 6 of the First Directive, Article 60a of the Fourth Directive and Article 38(6) of the Seventh Directive;

preclude national rules under which, in cases where the statutory nine-month period allowed for compiling and disclosing annual accounts to the relevant court maintaining the commercial register is exceeded, that court is required, first, to impose immediately a minimum periodic penalty of EUR 700 on the company and on each of the bodies authorised to represent it, on the ground that, in the absence of proof to the contrary, they are liable for that failure to effect timely disclosure and, secondly, to impose immediately a new minimum periodic penalty of EUR 700 on the company and on each of the bodies authorised to represent it, in respect of further failure for every two-month period thereafter, on the basis of the same presumption of liability, and in both cases

- without first allowing them an opportunity to state views on the existence of the obligation to disclose or to invoke any obstacles to doing so and, in particular, without

prior examination as to whether those annual accounts have in fact already been submitted to the court which maintains the register in the judicial district of which the principal place of business is situated; and
- without first giving the company or the bodies authorised to represent it notice to comply with the disclosure obligation?

The CJEU answered the referred questions as follows:

C-418/11, Texdata Software GmbH, [ECLI:EU:C:2013:588], § 89

89 In the light of all the foregoing considerations, the answer to the question referred is that, subject to the verifications to be carried out by the referring court, Articles 49 TFEU and 54 TFEU, the principles of effective judicial protection and respect for the rights of the defence, and Article 12 of the Eleventh Directive are to be interpreted as not precluding national legislation, such as that at issue in the main proceedings, which provides that, where the statutory nine-month period for disclosing accounting documents is exceeded, a minimum periodic penalty of EUR 700 is to be imposed immediately on the capital company whose branch is located in the Member State concerned, without prior notice and without the company first being given an opportunity to state its views on the alleged breach of the disclosure obligation.

12.5 Consolidated Accounts

As already mentioned, annual financial statements pursue various objectives, including, *inter alia*, to provide information for investors in capital markets, to give an account of past transactions, and to enhance corporate governance. Consolidated financial statements pursue the objective of providing information to members and third parties.

Recital 29 Directive 2013/34/EU

Many undertakings own other undertakings and the aim of coordinating the legislation governing consolidated financial statements is to protect the interests subsisting in companies with share capital. Consolidated financial statements should be drawn up so that financial information concerning such undertakings may be conveyed to members and third parties. National law governing consolidated financial statements should therefore be coordinated in order to achieve the objectives of comparability and equivalence in the information which undertakings should publish within the Union.

In brief, consolidated financial statements present the activities of a parent undertaking and its subsidiaries as a single economic entity (a group).

An undertaking is deemed to be subsidiary to a parent undertaking when the latter has control over the former. The concept of control is fundamentally based on holding a majority of voting rights in the general meeting; however, control may also exist where there are agreements with fellow shareholders or members and, in certain circumstances, control may be effectively exercised where the parent holds a minority or none of the shares in the subsidiary: the first situation occurs when the shares of the subsidiary are widespread, the second situation occurs in case of a contractual relationship between the parent and the subsidiary giving the parent company dominant influence without participation in the subscribed capital.

In this context, Directive 2013/34/EU provides many useful definitions.

Article 2 Definitions, Directive 2013/34/EU

(2) 'participating interest' means rights in the capital of other undertakings, whether or not represented by certificates, which, by creating a durable link with those undertakings, are intended to contribute to the activities of the undertaking which holds those rights. The holding of part of the capital of another undertaking is presumed to constitute a participating interest where it exceeds a percentage threshold fixed by the Member States which is lower than or equal to 20%;

(9) 'parent undertaking' means an undertaking which controls one or more subsidiary undertakings;

(10) 'subsidiary undertaking' means an undertaking controlled by a parent undertaking, including any subsidiary undertaking of an ultimate parent undertaking;

(11) 'group' means a parent undertaking and all its subsidiary undertakings;

(12) 'affiliated undertakings' means any two or more undertakings within a group;

(13) 'associated undertaking' means an undertaking in which another undertaking has a participating interest, and over whose operating and financial policies that other undertaking exercises significant influence. An undertaking is presumed to exercise a significant influence over another undertaking where it has 20% or more of the shareholders' or members' voting rights in that other undertaking;

Notwithstanding that the Directive provides no direct definition of control, the conditions under which a parent company shall be required to draw up the consolidated financial statements are clearly laid down.

Article 22 The Requirement to Prepare Consolidated Financial Statements, Directive 2013/34/EU

1. A Member State shall require any undertaking governed by its national law to draw up consolidated financial statements and a consolidated management report if that undertaking (a parent undertaking):

(a) has a majority of the shareholders' or members' voting rights in another undertaking (a subsidiary undertaking);
(b) has the right to appoint or remove a majority of the members of the administrative, management or supervisory body of another undertaking (a subsidiary undertaking) and is at the same time a shareholder in or member of that undertaking;
(c) has the right to exercise a dominant influence over an undertaking (a subsidiary undertaking) of which it is a shareholder or member, pursuant to a contract entered into with that undertaking or to a provision in its memorandum or articles of association, where the law governing that subsidiary undertaking permits its being subject to such contracts or provisions.

A Member State need not prescribe that a parent undertaking must be a shareholder in or member of its subsidiary undertaking. Those Member States the laws of which do not provide for such contracts or clauses shall not be required to apply this provision; or

(d) is a shareholder in or member of an undertaking, and: (i) a majority of the members of the administrative, management or supervisory bodies of that undertaking (a subsidiary undertaking) who have held office during the financial year, during the preceding financial year and up to the time when the consolidated financial statements are drawn up, have been appointed solely as a result of the exercise of its voting rights; or (ii) controls alone, pursuant to an agreement with other shareholders in or members of that undertaking (a subsidiary undertaking), a majority of shareholders' or members' voting rights in that undertaking. The Member States may introduce more detailed provisions concerning the form and contents of such agreements.

Member States shall prescribe at least the arrangements referred to in point (ii). They may subject the application of point (i) to the requirement that the voting rights represent at least 20% of the total.

However, point (i) shall not apply where a third party has the rights referred to in points (a), (b) or (c) with regard to that undertaking.

2. In addition to the cases mentioned in paragraph 1, Member States may require any undertaking governed by their national law to draw up consolidated financial statements and a consolidated management report if:
   (a) that undertaking (a parent undertaking) has the power to exercise, or actually exercises, dominant influence or control over another undertaking (the subsidiary undertaking); or
   (b) that undertaking (a parent undertaking) and another undertaking (the subsidiary undertaking) are managed on a unified basis by the parent undertaking.
3. For the purposes of points (a), (b) and (d) of paragraph 1, the voting rights and the rights of appointment and removal of any other subsidiary undertaking as well as those of any person acting in his own name but on behalf of the parent undertaking or of another subsidiary undertaking shall be added to those of the parent undertaking.

4. For the purposes of points (a), (b) and (d) of paragraph 1, the rights mentioned in paragraph 3 shall be reduced by the rights:
   (a) attaching to shares held on behalf of a person who is neither the parent undertaking nor a subsidiary of that parent undertaking; or
   (b) attaching to shares: (i) held by way of security, provided that the rights in question are exercised in accordance with the instructions received, or (ii) held in connection with the granting of loans as part of normal business activities, provided that the voting rights are exercised in the interests of the person providing the security.
5. For the purposes of points (a) and (d) of paragraph 1, the total of the shareholders' or members' voting rights in the subsidiary undertaking shall be reduced by the voting rights attaching to the shares held by that undertaking itself, by a subsidiary undertaking of that undertaking or by a person acting in his own name but on behalf of those undertakings.
6. Without prejudice to Article 23(9), a parent undertaking and all of its subsidiary undertakings shall be undertakings to be consolidated regardless of where the registered offices of such subsidiary undertakings are situated.
7. Without prejudice to this Article and Articles 21 and 23, a Member State may require any undertaking governed by its national law to draw up consolidated financial statements and a consolidated management report if:
   (a) that undertaking and one or more other undertakings to which it is not related as described in paragraphs 1 or 2, are managed on a unified basis in accordance with: (i) a contract concluded with that undertaking, or (ii) the memorandum or articles of association of those other undertakings; or
   (b) the administrative, management or supervisory bodies of that undertaking and of one or more other undertakings to which it is not related, as described in paragraphs 1 or 2, consist in the majority of the same persons in office during the financial year and until the consolidated financial statements are drawn up.
8. Where the Member State option referred to in paragraph 7 is exercised, the undertakings described in that paragraph and all of their subsidiary undertakings shall be consolidated, where one or more of those undertakings is established as one of the types of undertaking listed in Annex I or Annex II.
9. Paragraph 6 of this Article, Article 23(1), (2), (9) and (10) and Articles 24 to 29 shall apply to the consolidated financial statements and the consolidated management report referred to in paragraph 7 of this Article, subject to the following modifications:
   (a) references to parent undertakings shall be understood to refer to all of the undertakings specified in paragraph 7 of this Article; and
   (b) without prejudice to Article 24(3), the items 'capital', 'share premium account', 'revaluation reserve', 'reserves', 'profit or loss brought forward', and 'profit or loss for the financial year' to be included in the consolidated financial statements shall be the aggregate amounts attributable to each of the undertakings specified in paragraph 7 of this Article.

It should be added that a parent undertaking may be subsidiary to another undertaking. In this case, unless Member States provide otherwise, only the ultimate parent undertaking shall be required to draw up consolidated financial statements. Similarly, unless Member States provide otherwise, only undertakings of certain types (listed in the Annexes to the Directive) shall be considered the ultimate parent undertaking. Also, small groups are exempt from the obligation to prepare consolidated financial statements as the users of small undertakings' financial statements do not have sophisticated information needs and it can be costly to prepare consolidated financial statements in addition to the annual financial statements of the parent and subsidiary undertakings. Other exemptions from consolidation are listed in Article 23 Directive 2013/34/EU.

Consolidation requires the full incorporation of the assets and liabilities, of the income and expenditure of group undertakings, of the separate disclosure of non-controlling interests in the consolidated balance sheet within capital and reserves as well as the separate disclosure of non-controlling interests in the profit and loss of the group in the consolidated profit and loss accounts. Recognition and measurement principles applicable to the preparation of annual financial statements should also apply to the preparation of consolidated financial statements.

Article 24 The Preparation of Consolidated Financial Statements, Directive 2013/34/EU

...

2. The assets and liabilities of undertakings included in a consolidation shall be incorporated in full in the consolidated balance sheet.
3. The book values of shares in the capital of undertakings included in a consolidation shall be set off against the proportion which they represent of the capital and reserves of those undertakings in accordance with the following:

...

4. Where shares in subsidiary undertakings included in the consolidation are held by persons other than those undertakings, the amount attributable to those shares shall be shown separately in the consolidated balance sheet as non-controlling interests.
5. The income and expenditure of undertakings included in a consolidation shall be incorporated in full in the consolidated profit and loss account.
6. The amount of any profit or loss attributable to the shares referred to in paragraph 4 shall be shown separately in the consolidated profit and loss account as the profit or loss attributable to non-controlling interests.
7. Consolidated financial statements shall show the assets, liabilities, financial positions, profits or losses of the undertakings included in a consolidation as if they were a single

undertaking. In particular, the following shall be eliminated from the consolidated financial statements:

(a) debts and claims between the undertakings;

(b) income and expenditure relating to transactions between the undertakings; and

(c) profits and losses resulting from transactions between the undertakings, where they are included in the book values of assets.

8. Consolidated financial statements shall be drawn up as at the same date as the annual financial statements of the parent undertaking.

...

9. If the composition of the undertakings included in a consolidation has changed significantly in the course of a financial year, the consolidated financial statements shall include information which makes the comparison of successive sets of consolidated financial statements meaningful. This obligation may be fulfilled by the preparation of an adjusted comparative balance sheet and an adjusted comparative profit and loss account.

10. Assets and liabilities included in consolidated financial statements shall be measured on a uniform basis and in accordance with Chapter 2.

11. An undertaking which draws up consolidated financial statements shall apply the same measurement bases as are applied in its annual financial statements. However, Member States may permit or require that other measurement bases in accordance with Chapter 2 be used in consolidated financial statements. Where use is made of this derogation, that fact shall be disclosed in the notes to the consolidated financial statements and reasons given.

12. Where assets and liabilities included in consolidated financial statements have been measured by undertakings included in the consolidation using bases differing from those used for the purposes of the consolidation, those assets and liabilities shall be re-measured in accordance with the bases used for the consolidation. Departures from this requirement shall be permitted in exceptional cases. Any such departures shall be disclosed in the notes to the consolidated financial statements and reasons given.

13. Deferred tax balances shall be recognised on consolidation provided that it is probable that a charge to tax will arise within the foreseeable future for one of the undertakings included in the consolidation.

14. Where assets included in consolidated financial statements have been the subject of value adjustments solely for tax purposes, they shall be incorporated in the consolidated financial statements only after those adjustments have been eliminated.

Similarly to the annual financial statements, consolidated accounts shall also include notes (Article 28 Directive 2013/34/EU) and be complemented by a management report (Article 28 Directive 2013/34/EU). Also the annual financial statements shall be published in accordance with Directive 2017/1132/EU (Article 30 Directive 2013/34/EU).

Finally, it should be added that, unlike subsidiaries, associated undertakings are included in consolidated financial statements by means of the *equity method*. In accounting, the equity method is the process of treating equity investments in associated companies as an asset. The investor's proportional share of the associated company's net income increases the investment (and a net loss decreases the investment), and proportional payments of dividends decrease it. In the investor's income statement, the proportional share of the investee's net income or net loss is reported as a single-line item.

Article 27 Equity Accounting of Associated Undertakings, Directive 2013/34/EU

1. Where an undertaking included in a consolidation has an associated undertaking, that associated undertaking shall be shown in the consolidated balance sheet as a separate item with an appropriate heading.
2. When this Article is applied for the first time to an associated undertaking, that associated undertaking shall be shown in the consolidated balance sheet either:
   (a) at its book value calculated in accordance with the measurement rules laid down in Chapters 2 and 3. The difference between that value and the amount corresponding to the proportion of capital and reserves represented by the participating interest in that associated undertaking shall be disclosed separately in the consolidated balance sheet or in the notes to the consolidated financial statements. That difference shall be calculated as at the date on which that method is used for the first time; or
   (b) at an amount corresponding to the proportion of the associated undertaking's capital and reserves represented by the participating interest in that associated undertaking. The difference between that amount and the book value calculated in accordance with the measurement rules laid down in Chapters 2 and 3 shall be disclosed separately in the consolidated balance sheet or in the notes to the consolidated financial statements. That difference shall be calculated as at the date on which that method is used for the first time.

...

4. The book value referred to in point (a) of paragraph 2, or the amount corresponding to the proportion of the associated undertaking's capital and reserves referred to in point (b) of paragraph 2, shall be increased or reduced by the amount of any variation which has taken place during the financial year in the proportion of the associated undertaking's capital and reserves represented by that participating interest; it shall be reduced by the amount of the dividends relating to that participating interest.

...

6. The proportion of the profit or loss of the associated undertakings attributable to the participating interests in such associated undertakings shall be shown in the consolidated profit and loss account as a separate item under an appropriate heading.

...

9. This Article need not be applied where the participating interest in the capital of the associated undertaking is not material.

The use of the equity method is relevant for both the consolidated and the annual financial statements; as such it has an influence in the determination of the profits of the parent company available for distribution.

Article 2(7) General Provisions Concerning the Balance Sheet and the Profit and Loss Account, Directive 2013/34/EU

7. In respect of the treatment of participating interests in annual financial statements:
   (a) Member States may permit or require participating interests to be accounted for using the equity method as provided for in Article 27, taking account of the essential adjustments resulting from the particular characteristics of annual financial statements as compared to consolidated financial statements;
   (b) Member States may permit or require that the proportion of the profit or loss attributable to the participating interest be recognised in the profit and loss account only to the extent of the amount corresponding to dividends already received or the payment of which can be claimed; and
   (c) where the profit attributable to the participating interest and recognised in the profit and loss account exceeds the amount of dividends already received or the payment of which can be claimed, the amount of the difference shall be placed in a reserve which cannot be distributed to shareholders.

In *Tomberger*, the CJEU further clarified that dividends declared by a subsidiary company, although not yet paid by it, may be accounted for by means of the equity method in the balance sheet of a parent company, and can be distributed by the parent company, as this is not against the principle of the true and fair view. Next, in § 12.6, the facts of the case are examined more closely.

12.6 *Tomberger* Case

In *Tomberger* (C-234/94, *Waltraud Tomberger* v. *Gebrüder von der Wettern GmbH*, [1996] ECR I-03133), the Bundesgerichtshof (German Federal Court) referred to the Court for a preliminary ruling on a question on the interpretation of Articles 31(1) and 59 of the Fourth Council Directive 78/660/EEC of 25 July 1978 on the annual accounts of certain types of companies (hereafter '*the Fourth Directive*'). That question was raised in proceedings between Mrs Tomberger (hereafter '*the plaintiff*') and Gebrüder von der Wettern GmbH (hereafter '*the defendant*'), a company governed by German law and established in Germany.

The plaintiff, a shareholder in the defendant company, challenges that company's annual accounts for the financial year 1 January 1989 to 31 December 1989 as approved on 19 October 1990 by the general meeting of the company. The defendant, in particular, has a 100 per cent shareholding in the companies Technische Sicherheitssystem GmbH and Gesellschaft für Bauwerksabdich-tungen mbH (hereafter '*TSS and GfB*').

On 29 June 1990 the annual accounts of TSS and GfB, likewise for the financial year 1 January 1989 to 31 December 1989, were approved by resolutions of their respective general meetings. Those accounts showed that certain profits had been appropriated to the defendant for the financial year 1989 but had not yet been paid to it.

The defendant's annual accounts for 1989 showed the profits distributed to it by TSS and GfB for the financial year 1988 but not those appropriated to it for the financial year 1989.

The plaintiff considered that under the Fourth Directive the defendant's annual accounts for the financial year 1989 should have included the profits appropriated to it by TSS and GfB for that same year; she therefore brought an action before the Landgericht (Regional Court) for annulment of the resolution of the general meeting approving the defendant's annual accounts for 1989. The action was dismissed at first instance and on appeal, whereupon the plaintiff appealed to the Bundesgerichtshof on a point of law.

The Bundesgerichtshof considers that the entitlement of an undertaking (the parent company) which is the sole or majority shareholder of another company (the subsidiary) to the profits of the subsidiary is sufficiently certain at the balance sheet date for it to be regarded as forming part of the assets of the parent company. It follows, in its view, that the debt receivable by the parent company from its subsidiary company must be included in the annual accounts of the parent company as from the date when the corresponding liability of the subsidiary company came into being. However, the Bundesgerichtshof is in doubt as to the compatibility of that view with the requirements of the Fourth Directive. The Bundesgerichtshof therefore decided to stay proceedings pending a ruling from the Court of Justice on the following question:

C-234/94, Waltraud Tomberger v. Gebrüder von der Wettern GmbH, [1996] ECR I-03133, § 14

Is there an infringement of Article 31(1)(c)(aa) of the Fourth Directive 78/660/EEC of 25 July 1978, according to which only profits made at the balance-sheet date may be included, and of the principles laid down in Article 59 of that directive on the 'equity method', if the profit entitlement of an undertaking, as against a private limited company in which it is the sole or majority shareholder and in respect of which the presumptions of dependency within the meaning of Paragraph 17(2) of the Aktiengesetz (Law on Private Companies) and of belonging to a single group within the meaning of the third sentence of Paragraph 18(1) of that Law have not been rebutted, is regarded as forming part as from the balance-sheet date of the subsidiary company of the assets of the undertaking which is the sole or majority shareholder and must therefore be shown as an asset of the latter 'as from that date', on the assumption that the financial years of the two undertakings coincide and the meeting of shareholders in the private limited company controlled by the other resolves to adopt the annual accounts and appropriate the profits at a time when the auditing of the annual accounts of the undertaking which is the sole shareholder has not yet been completed?

The CJEU decided the proposed question as follows:

C-234/94, Waltraud Tomberger v. Gebrüder von der Wettern GmbH, [1996] ECR I-03133, § 15–25

15 It should be emphasized at the outset that, as appears from the terms of the question referred and the order for reference, the question arises in the context of a highly specific set of circumstances:

- the parent company is the sole shareholder in the subsidiary, and controls it,
- under national law, the parent company and the subsidiary form a group,
- the financial years of the two companies coincide,
- the subsidiary's annual accounts for the financial year in question were adopted by its general meeting before completion of the audit of the parent company's annual accounts for that year,
- the subsidiary's annual accounts for the financial year in question, as adopted by its general meeting, show that on the subsidiary's balance-sheet date – namely the last day of that financial year – the subsidiary appropriated profits to the parent company, and
- in the light of the presumptions of national law as to the relationship between the parent company and its subsidiary, the national court considers that the parent company's entitlement to the profits in question is sufficiently certain at the balance-sheet date of the two companies for it to be regarded as forming, at that date, part of the assets of the parent company.

16 As regards Article 59 of the Fourth Directive, as amended, to which the national court refers, it is sufficient to note, as the Advocate General has done at point 12 of his Opinion, that this provision can have no bearing on the resolution of the dispute in the main proceedings since the German legislature has not exercised the option made available to it under that article, so that the methods of valuation there provided for do not apply in Germany.

17 With regard to Article 31 of the Fourth Directive, it should be borne in mind that the Fourth Directive seeks to coordinate national provisions concerning the presentation and

content of annual accounts of certain types of companies (see the first recital of the preamble). In order to coordinate the content of annual accounts, the directive lays down the principle of the 'true and fair view', compliance with which is the primary objective of the directive. According to that principle, the annual accounts of the companies to which the Fourth Directive applies must give a true and fair view of their assets and liabilities, financial position and profit or loss (see the fourth recital in the preamble to the Fourth Directive and Article 2(3) and (5) thereof).

18 Application of that principle must, as far as possible, be guided by the general principles contained in Article 31 of the Fourth Directive. In this case, the principles set out in Article 31(1)(c)(aa) and (bb) and (d) are of particular importance.

19 First, Article 31(1)(c)(aa) provides that only profits made at the balance-sheet date may be included in the balance sheet.

20 Second, Article 31(1)(d) provides that account must be taken in the balance sheet for a financial year of all income and charges relating to that year, irrespective of the date of receipt or payment of such income or charges.

21 Third, in accordance with Article 31(1)(c)(bb), account must be taken of liabilities and losses arising in the course of a financial year even if they become apparent only between the end of the financial year and the date on which the balance sheet for that year is drawn up.

22 It is clear from those provisions that taking account of all elements 'profits made, charges, income, liabilities and losses' which actually relate to the financial year in question ensures observance of the requirement of a true and fair view.

23 In the present case, according to the subsidiary's annual accounts, the profits in question were made by that company during the financial year 1989 and were appropriated by it to the parent company as at 31 December 1989, that is to say before the end of that financial year. Before examining the parent company's accounts, the national court must be satisfied that there is no reason to question that that presentation of the subsidiary's financial position complies with the principle of the true and fair view.

24 It follows from all the foregoing that, if the subsidiary's accounts themselves comply with the principle of the true and fair view, it is not contrary to the rule laid down in Article 31(1)(c)(aa) of the Fourth Directive for the national court to consider that, in the circumstances described, the profits in question must be entered in the parent company's balance sheet for the financial year in respect of which the subsidiary appropriated them.

25 The answer to the question referred by the national court must therefore be that, where

- one company (the parent company) is the sole shareholder in another company (the subsidiary), and controls it,
- under national law, the parent company and the subsidiary form a group,
- the financial years of the two companies coincide,
- the subsidiary's annual accounts for the financial year in question were adopted by the general meeting before completion of the audit of the parent company's annual accounts for that year,

- the subsidiary's annual accounts for the financial year in question, as adopted by its general meeting, show that on the subsidiary's balance-sheet date - namely the last day of that financial year - the subsidiary appropriated profits to the parent company, and
- the national court is satisfied that the subsidiary's annual accounts for the financial year in question give a true and fair view of its assets and liabilities, financial position and profit or loss,

it is not contrary to the rule laid down in Article 31(1)(c)(aa) of the Fourth Directive for the national court to consider that the profits in question must be entered in the parent company's balance sheet for the financial year in respect of which they were appropriated by the subsidiary.

FURTHER READING

Wolfgang Schön, 'Case C-234/94, Waltraud Tomberger v. Gebrüder v.d. Wettern GmbH, 5th Chamber, Judgment of 27 June 1996, not yet reported', *Common Market Law Review* 34, no. 3, 681–693 (1997).

12.7 IAS/IFRS Principles

As mentioned earlier, in the field of consolidated accounts, the EU institutions have delivered additional regulations in order to have a uniform legislation for all publicly traded companies of the EU. This uniform legislation includes Regulation 2002/1606/EC of the European Parliament and of the Council of 19 July 2002 *on the application of international accounting standards* (hereafter IAS/IFRS) and Commission Regulation 2008/1126/EC of 3 November 2008 adopting certain international accounting standards (replacing Commission Regulation 2003/1725/EC of 29 September 2003).

Article 1 Aim, Regulation 2002/1606/EC

This Regulation has as its objective the adoption and use of international accounting standards in the Community with a view to harmonising the financial information presented by the companies referred to in Article 4 in order to ensure a high degree of transparency and comparability of financial statements and hence an efficient functioning of the Community capital market and of the Internal Market.

First of all, it is useful to become familiar with the acronyms IAS and IFRS.

Recital 7 Regulation 2002/1606/EC

International Accounting Standards (IASs) are developed by the International Accounting Standards Committee (IASC), whose purpose is to develop a single set of global accounting standards. Further to the restructuring of the IASC, the new Board on 1 April 2001, as one of its first decisions, renamed the IASC as the International Accounting Standards Board (IASB) and, as far as future international accounting standards are concerned, renamed IAS as International Financial Reporting Standards (IFRS). These standards should, wherever possible and provided that they ensure a high degree of transparency and comparability for financial reporting in the Community, be made obligatory for use by all publicly traded Community companies.

It is also useful to clarify that IAS/IFRS standards are not automatically adopted as they are issued or modified by the IASB. In order to ensure that such standards comply with the accounting principles set forth in the Directives, IAS/IFRS standards shall be 'endorsed' by the EU Commission.

Article 3 Adoption and Use of International Accounting Standards, Regulation 2002/1606/EC

1. In accordance with the procedure laid down in Article 6(2), the Commission shall decide on the applicability within the Community of international accounting standards.

...

4. Adopted international accounting standards shall be published in full in each of the official languages of the Community, as a Commission Regulation, in the Official Journal of the European Communities.

Article 6 Committee Procedure, Regulation 2002/1606/EC

1. The Commission shall be assisted by an accounting regulatory committee hereafter referred to as 'the Committee'.
2. Where reference is made to this paragraph, Articles 5 and 7 of Decision 1999/468/EC shall apply, having regard to the provisions of Article 8 thereof.

   The period laid down in Article 5(6) of Decision 1999/468/EC shall be set at three months.

3. The Committee shall adopt its rules of procedure.

Article 7 Reporting and Coordination, Regulation 2002/1606/EC

1. The Commission shall liaise on a regular basis with the Committee about the status of active IASB projects and any related documents issued by the IASB in order to coordinate positions and to facilitate discussions concerning the adoption of standards that might result from these projects and documents.
2. The Commission shall duly report to the Committee in a timely manner if it intends not to propose the adoption of a standard.

Compliance with the IAS/IFRS standards adopted by the EU Commission is mandatory for the preparation of the consolidated accounts of all companies – being ultimate parent companies – whose securities are admitted to trading on a regulated market of any Member State. However, Member States may permit or require these companies to prepare the annual financial statements in accordance with IASs. Member States may also permit or require that all other companies adopt the IASs.

Article 4 Consolidated Accounts of Publicly Traded Companies, Regulation 2002/1606/EC

For each financial year starting on or after 1 January 2005, companies governed by the law of a Member State shall prepare their consolidated accounts in conformity with the international accounting standards adopted in accordance with the procedure laid down in Article 6(2) if, at their balance sheet date, their securities are admitted to trading on a regulated market of any Member State within the meaning of Article 1(13) of Council Directive 93/22/ EEC of 10 May 1993 on investment services in the securities field.

Article 5 Options in Respect of Annual Accounts and of Non Publicly-traded Companies, Regulation 2002/1606/EC

Member States may permit or require:

(a) the companies referred to in Article 4 to prepare their annual accounts,
(b) companies other than those referred to in Article 4 to prepare their consolidated accounts and/or their annual accounts, in conformity with the international accounting standards adopted in accordance with the procedure laid down in Article 6(2).

Commission Regulation 2008/1126/EC of 3 November 2008 adopting certain IASs in accordance with Regulation 2002/1606/EC (replacing Commission Regulation 2003/1725/EC of 29 September 2003) sets out the IAS/IFRS and related interpretations. This regulation has been amended several times to include all the standards presented by the IASB since 2008, including certain amendments from 2012 on consolidated financial statements, partnerships and information to be provided on interests held in other entities.

Adopted IAS/IFRS, along with all interpretations presented by the International Financial Reporting Interpretations Committee (IFRIC) and by the Standards Interpretation Committee (SIC), the predecessor of IFRIC until 2002, are a complete set of accounting standards.

International Accounting Standards

IAS 1 Presentation of financial statements IAS 2 Inventories

IAS 7 Cash-flow statements

IAS 8 Accounting policies, changes in accounting estimates and errors IAS 10 Events after the balance sheet date

IAS 11 Construction contracts IAS 12 Income taxes

IAS 16 Property, plant and equipment IAS 17 Leases

IAS 18 Revenue

IAS 19 Employee benefits

IAS 20 Accounting for government grants and disclosure of government assistance IAS 21 The effects of changes in foreign exchange rates

IAS 23 Borrowing costs

IAS 24 Related party disclosures

IAS 26 Accounting and reporting by retirement benefit plans IAS 27 Consolidated and separate financial statements

IAS 28 Investments in associates

IAS 29 Financial reporting in hyperinflationary economies IAS 31 Interests in joint ventures

IAS 32 Financial instruments: presentation IAS 33 Earnings per share

IAS 34 Interim financial reporting IAS 36 Impairment of assets

IAS 37 Provisions, contingent liabilities and contingent assets IAS 38 Intangible assets

IAS 39 Financial instruments: recognition and measurement IAS 40 Investment property

IAS 41 Agriculture

IFRS 1 First-time Adoption of International Financial Reporting Standards IFRS 2 Share-based Payment

IFRS 3 Business Combinations IFRS 4 Insurance Contracts

IFRS 5 Non-current Assets Held for Sale and Discontinued Operations IFRS 6 Exploration for and Evaluation of Mineral Resources

IFRS 7 Financial Instruments: Disclosures IFRS 8 Operating Segments

IFRS 10 Consolidated Financial Statements IFRS 11 Joint Arrangements

IFRS 12 Disclosure of Interests in Other Entities IFRS 13 Fair Value Measurement

IFRIC 1 Changes in existing decommissioning, restoration and similar liabilities IFRIC 2 Members' shares in co-operative entities and similar instruments

IFRIC 4 Determining whether an arrangement contains a lease

IFRIC 5 Rights to interests arising from decommissioning, restoration and environmental rehabilitation funds

IFRIC 6 Liabilities arising from participating in a specific market – waste electrical and electronic equipment

IFRIC 7 Applying the Restatement Approach under IAS 29 Financial reporting in hyperinflationary economies

IFRIC 8 Scope of IFRS 2

IFRIC 9 Reassessment of embedded derivatives IFRIC 10 Interim financial reporting and impairment IFRIC 12 Service concessions arrangements

IFRIC 13 Customer loyalty programmes

IFRIC 14 IAS 19 The limit on a defined benefit asset, minimum funding requirements and their interaction

IFRIC 15 Agreements for the construction of real estate IFRIC Hedges of a net investment in a foreign operation IFRIC 17 Distributions of non-cash assets to owners IFRIC 18 Transfers of assets from customers

IFRIC 19 Extinguishing financial liabilities with equity instruments IFRIC 20 Stripping costs in the production phase of a surface mine IFRIC 21 Levies

SIC 7 Introduction of the euro

SIC 10 Government assistance – no specific relation to operating activities SIC 12 Consolidation – special purpose entities

SIC 13 Jointly controlled entities – non-monetary contributions by venturers SIC 15 Operating leases – incentives

SIC 21 Income taxes – recovery of revalued non-depreciable assets

SIC 25 Income taxes – changes in the tax status of an entity or its shareholders

SIC 27 Evaluating the substance of transactions involving the legal form of a lease SIC 29 Disclosure – service concession arrangements

SIC 31 Revenue – barter transactions involving advertising services SIC 32 Intangible assets – website costs

It is not possible to go into the details of all the IASs. It does, however, suffice to give some information on IAS 1 *Presentation of financial statements* and on IFRS 13 *Fair Value Measurement.*

IAS 1 Presentation of Financial Statements

Objective

1. The objective of this standard is to prescribe the basis for presentation of general purpose financial statements, to ensure comparability both with the entity's financial statements of previous periods and with the financial statements of other entities. To achieve this objective, this standard sets out overall requirements for the presentation of financial

statements, guidelines for their structure and minimum requirements for their content. The recognition, measurement and disclosure of specific transactions and other events are dealt with in other standards and in interpretations.

...

Purpose of Financial Statements

7. Financial statements are a structured representation of the financial position and financial performance of an entity. The objective of general purpose financial statements is to provide information about the financial position, financial performance and cash flows of an entity that is useful to a wide range of users in making economic decisions. Financial statements also show the results of management's stewardship of the resources entrusted to it. To meet this objective, financial statements provide information about an entity's:
   (a) assets;
   (b) liabilities;
   (c) equity;
   (d) income and expenses, including gains and losses;
   (e) other changes in equity; and
   (f) cash flows.

This information, along with other information in the notes, assists users of financial statements in predicting the entity's future cash flows and, in particular, their timing and certainty.

Components of Financial Statements

8. A complete set of financial statements comprises:
   (a) a balance sheet;
   (b) an income statement;
   (c) a statement of changes in equity showing either: (i) all changes in equity; or (ii) changes in equity other than those arising from transactions with equity holders acting in their capacity as equity holders;
   (d) a cash-flow statement; and
   (e) notes, comprising a summary of significant accounting policies and other explanatory notes.
9. Many entities present, outside the financial statements, a financial review by management that describes and explains the main features of the entity's financial performance and financial position and the principal uncertainties it faces. Such a report may include a review of:
   (a) the main factors and influences determining financial performance, including changes in the environment in which the entity operates, the entity's response to those changes and their effect, and the entity's policy for investment to maintain and enhance financial performance, including its dividend policy;

(b) the entity's sources of funding and its targeted ratio of liabilities to equity; and
(c) the entity's resources not recognised in the balance sheet in accordance with IFRSs.

10. Many entities also present, outside the financial statements, reports and statements such as environmental reports and value added statements, particularly in industries in which environmental factors are significant and when employees are regarded as an important user group. Reports and statements presented outside financial statements are outside the scope of IFRSs.

One of the most important amongst the IAS/IFRS principles is expressed in IFRS 13 *Fair Value Measurement*. Unlike the new Fourth and Seventh Directives, requiring that items included in the assets are accounted for at historical cost (purchase price or production cost), IAS/IFRS standards (e.g., IAS 2 Inventories, IAS 16 Property, plant and equipment, IAS 38 Intangible assets, IAS 39 Financial instruments: recognition and measurement and IAS 40 Investment property) require that items included in the assets are accounted for at *net realisable value* or *fair value*, these being the expected net selling price in the ordinary course of business or the amount for which an asset could be exchanged, or a liability settled, between knowledgeable, willing parties in an arm's length transaction.

IAS 2 Inventories

Definitions

...

Net realisable value is the estimated selling price in the ordinary course of business less the estimated costs of completion and the estimated costs necessary to make the sale.

Fair value is the amount for which an asset could be exchanged, or a liability settled, between knowledgeable, willing parties in an arm's length transaction.

On 12 May 2011, the IASB issued the IFRS 13 Fair Value Measurement, which has since been endorsed by the European Commission. This IFRS (a) defines fair value; (b) sets out in a single IFRS a framework for measuring fair value; and (c) requires disclosures about fair value measurements.

IFRS 13 Fair Value Measurement

Objective

...

2. Fair value is a market-based measurement, not an entity-specific measurement. For some assets and liabilities, observable market transactions or market information might be

available. For other assets and liabilities, observable market transactions and market information might not be available. However, the objective of a fair value measurement in both cases is the same – to estimate the price at which an orderly transaction to sell the asset or to transfer the liability would take place between market participants at the measurement date under current market conditions (i.e. an exit price at the measurement date from the perspective of a market participant that holds the asset or owes the liability).

3. When a price for an identical asset or liability is not observable, an entity measures fair value using another valuation technique that maximises the use of relevant observable inputs and minimises the use of unobservable inputs. Because fair value is a market-based measurement, it is measured using the assumptions that market participants would use when pricing the asset or liability, including assumptions about risk. As a result, an entity's intention to hold an asset or to settle or otherwise fulfil a liability is not relevant when measuring fair value.
4. The definition of fair value focuses on assets and liabilities because they are a primary subject of accounting measurement. In addition, this IFRS shall be applied to an entity's own equity instruments measured at fair value.

Although being estimates, rather than certain data, the fair value measurements reflect more closely the actual value of the company's assets and contribute to better showing the company's state of health in comparison with traditional accounting principles. This does however entail problems as regards the determination of losses and distributable profits, which are still governed by the principle of realisation.

Indeed, a widely discussed issue related to the adoption of IAS/IFRS standards concerns the role of capital and, in particular, that of capital maintenance rules, in particular for those countries, such as Italy, where IAS/IFRS standards are mandatory not only for the consolidated, but also for the annual financial statements of listed companies. A scholarly article thoroughly highlights the point, focusing in particular on the different goals pursued by the EU directive on annual and consolidated accounts and by the IAS/IFRS standards.

Giovanni E. Colombo, 'International Accounting Principles (IAS/IFRS), Share Capital and Net Worth', 4 ECFR 553–570, at 554–555, 570 (2007)

International accounting principles are not oriented towards the drawing up of a balance sheet aimed at capital maintenance. Whilst in the discipline of the Italian civil code – and in the civil code of other continental European countries – the balance sheet carries out (at the same time) the role both of indicating the composition and the value of the property of the company and of measuring the distributable profit (the basic criteria of historic costs, the principle of realization, the principle of dissymmetry, etc. are aimed at this goal), the International Accounting Principles assign the balance sheet with the sole role of informing the investors about the effective value of the company as a whole and on the performance of the annual management ('effective' result of the accounting period) and they show no interest in the problem of distributability of the profits which emerge from the accounting document. The annual accounts have to enable the forecast of the company's ability to generate cash flows in the future, i.e., the evaluation of its current and prospective profitability. Among the various users of the financial statement investors in risk capital are given premier position since they need to be able to receive information on whether to hold, buy or sell shares.

The rules of the IAS/IFRS are coherent with this approach. They allow the balance sheet to take into consideration not only the income created from the exchanges with third-parties but also from the positive value variations (which take place during the accounting period) of the company's property: such variations are measured on the basis of fair value criteria. Although according to IAS/IFRS principles too, the cost normally constitutes the initial criterion of evaluation of assets in the balance sheet, for many categories of assets the IAS/ IFRS allow for (more rarely-speaking, 'impose') the consequent application of fair value: the results being the application of capital gains, originating from estimates, on assets which remain within company property. The ban on the inclusion of non-realized capital gains – characteristic of traditional historic cost balance sheets – is not considered any more.

It is a consequence that the profits (both accountable in the profit and loss account or directly included to the net worth) resulting from an IAS/IFRS financial statement are not – differently from a traditional cost-based financial statement – realized profits but are, so to speak, 'realizable' profits.

It is also true that, in some way, the adoption of international principles may also cause a 'compression' of values which would result in a balance sheet drawn up according to the civil code. However, the overriding effect of the passage from traditional prudence principle-based accounting to IAS/IFRS is certainly connected to the increase in balance sheet values.

There is no need here for a deeper examination in order to justify the conclusion that the IAS/IFRS balance sheet is not best-suited to carry out – without adjustments – the organizational role attributable to such a document as laid down by the rules of the civil code. Above all it is not suited to determine any sort of distributable profit (Art. 2433) or limitations on various operations whose lawfulness is conditioned by the distributable profit limitations and available reserves (purchase of own shares or shares in the controlling company: Arts. 2357, 2359 bis, 2358 sub-section 3). It is also not suited to indicate loss of capital according to the terms of the provisions laid down by Arts. 2446, 2447. It is, finally, not suited to determine the sum of the reserves made available for the share capital increase (Art. 2442).

...

To sum up, the traditional accounting system is best suited to outline the dynamics of share capital protection offered by the other net worth rates limited to changes – whether increases or reductions over time – of only those reserves corresponding to the shareholders' contributions and realized profits. By contrast, the system originating from the IAS principles integrated with the rulings of decree 38/2005 also shows users the dynamics of that additional net worth share which corresponds to fair value capital gains.

In other words, the representation of the net worth dynamics originating from a traditional balance sheet has been somewhat fossilized, or at least slowed down, by the rigidity of the cost criterion. Indeed, until a positive net worth component is realized, creditors (and shareholders alike) ignore how much it is worth at its current value. In addition, creditors do not become aware of any change in value until the positive net worth value, greater than the cost, fails to occur, and the cost value has started to become tarnished. On the other hand, the use of fair value criteria, and the mandatory inclusion of their corresponding fair value-increases into unavailable reserves as well as the increase or deterioration of such reserves according to whether capital gains increase or decrease can provide users with a dynamic vision of that additional net worth share, which must be excluded from distribution as foreseen by Art. 6 of d. lgs. 38/2005. As a consequence, not only can knowledge of the net worth dynamics be garnered in advance, but it can also experience quantitative augmentation.

That is why I believe that the new net worth configuration originating from the integration of the International Accounting Principles with the enforcement of Art. 6 of d. lgs. 38/2005 is likely to improve, informatively speaking, the usefulness of the creditor protection scheme based on capital maintenance.

FURTHER READING

Giovanni E. Colombo, 'International Accounting Principles (IAS/IFRS): Share Capital and Net Worth', 4 *ECFR* 553–570 (2007).

Giovanni Strampelli, 'The IAS/IFRS after the Crisis: Limiting the Impact of Fair Value Accounting on Companies' Capital', 8 *ECFR* 1–29 (2011).

Steven Hijink, 'Towards European Accounting Law', 9 *ECL* 201–208 (2012).

Giovanni Strampelli, 'The EU Issuers' Accounting Disclosure Regime and Investors' Information Needs: The Essential Role of Narrative Reporting', 19 *EBOR* 541–579 (2018).

12.8 The Audit Report

As mentioned earlier, statutory audits are also related to the fields covered by Directive 2013/34/EU. Indeed, despite statutory audits having a much broader relevance in the corporate governance of companies (*see*, Chapter 14, § 14.11), 'statutory audit' means an audit of annual financial statements or consolidated financial statements.

Article 34 General Requirement, Directive 2013/34/EU

b. Member States shall ensure that the financial statements of public-interest entities, medium-sized and large undertakings are audited by one or more statutory auditors or audit firms approved by Member States to carry out statutory audits on the basis of Directive 2006/43/EC.

The statutory auditor(s) or audit firm(s) shall also:

(a) express an opinion on: (i) whether the management report is consistent with the financial statements for the same financial year, and (ii) whether the management report has been prepared in accordance with the applicable legal requirements;

(b) state whether, in the light of the knowledge and understanding of the undertaking and its environment obtained in the course of the audit, he, she or it has identified material misstatements in the management report, and shall give an indication of the nature of any such misstatements.

2. The first subparagraph of paragraph 1 shall apply mutatis mutandis with respect to consolidated financial statements. The second subparagraph of paragraph 1 shall apply mutatis mutandis with respect to consolidated financial statements and consolidated management reports.

Auditors express their opinion in the audit report, a document complementing the annual and consolidated financial statements.

Article 28 Audit Reporting, Directive 2006/43/EC

1. The audit report shall include:

(a) an introduction which shall, as a minimum, identify the financial statements that are the subject of the statutory audit, together with the financial reporting framework that has been applied in their preparation;

(b) a description of the scope of the statutory audit which shall, as a minimum, identify the auditing standards in accordance with which the statutory audit was conducted; an audit opinion; which shall be either unqualified, qualified or an adverse opinion and shall state clearly the opinion of the statutory auditor as to: (i) whether the annual financial statements give a true and fair view in accordance with the relevant financial reporting framework, and, (ii) where appropriate, whether the annual financial statements comply with statutory requirements.

If the statutory auditor is unable to express an audit opinion, the report shall contain a disclaimer of opinion;

(d) a reference to any matters to which the statutory auditor draws attention by way of emphasis without qualifying the audit opinion;

(e) the opinion and statement referred to in the second subparagraph of Article 34(1) of Directive 2013/34/EU of the European Parliament and of the Council of 26 June 2013 on the annual financial statements, consolidated financial statements and related reports of certain types of undertakings, amending Directive 2006/43/EC of the European Parliament and of the Council and repealing Council Directives 78/660/EEC and 83/349/EEC.

2. The audit report shall be signed and dated by the statutory auditor. Where an audit firm carries out the statutory audit, the audit report shall bear the signature of at least the statutory auditor(s) carrying out the statutory audit on behalf of the audit firm. In exceptional circumstances Member States may provide that such signature(s) need not be disclosed to the public if such disclosure could lead to an imminent and significant threat to the personal security of any person. In any case the name(s) of the person(s) involved shall be known to the relevant competent authorities.
3. The audit report on the consolidated financial statements shall comply with the requirements set out in paragraphs 1 and 2. In reporting on the consistency of the management report and the financial statements as required by point (e) of paragraph 1, the statutory auditor or audit firm shall consider the consolidated financial statements and the consolidated management report. Where the annual financial statements of the parent undertaking are attached to the consolidated financial statements, the audit reports required by this Article may be combined.

Part V
Corporate Governance

13

Corporate Governance

13.1 Corporate Governance: An Introduction

An important part of the modern company law debate focuses on corporate governance, in particular for listed companies. Although it would not be possible to go into the details of such a debate, it is useful to have at least an introduction to the topic. This will permit an understanding of existing EU provisions concerning corporate governance, as well as how the EU Commission's Action Plans of 2003 and of 2012 propose to foster good corporate governance and enhance its quality in Europe.

What does 'corporate governance' mean?

In December 1992 the UK Cadbury Committee, chaired by Sir Adrian Cadbury, released their final report, including a definition of corporate governance. Sir Adrian Cadbury later contributed to the OECD Principles of Corporate Governance, first issued in 1999 and now in their third edition (2015): the OECD Principles also provide a definition of corporate governance. Both the Cadbury Report and the OECD Principles are referred to in the Commission's Action Plans of 2003 and of 2012; the 2012 Action Plan includes a comprehensive definition of corporate governance.

Cadbury Committee Report, Financial Aspects of Corporate Governance (1992), § 2.5

Corporate governance is the system by which companies are directed and controlled. Boards of directors are responsible for the governance of their companies. The shareholders' role in governance is to appoint the directors and the auditors and to satisfy themselves that an appropriate governance structure is in place. The responsibilities of the board include setting the company's strategic aims, providing the leadership to put them into effect, supervising the management of the business and reporting to shareholders on their stewardship. The board's actions are subject to laws, regulations and the shareholders in general meeting.

OECD Principles of Corporate Governance (1999), Preamble

Corporate governance involves a set of relationships between a company's management, its board, its shareholders and other stakeholders. Corporate governance also provides the structure through which the objectives of the company are set, and the means of attaining those objectives and monitoring performance are determined.

Action Plan: European Company Law and Corporate Governance – A Modern Legal Framework for More Engaged Shareholders and Sustainable Companies (2012)

Corporate governance defines relationships between a company's management, its board, its shareholders and its other stakeholders. It determines the way companies are managed and controlled. An effective corporate governance framework is of crucial importance because well-run companies are likely to be more competitive and more sustainable in the long term. Good corporate governance is first and foremost the responsibility of the company concerned, and rules at European and national level are in place to ensure that certain standards are respected.

The corporate governance debate aims at answering the most challenging questions in the history of company law. Whose interests is a company, and hence its directors, committed to satisfy? Only those of the shareholders, or also those of other stakeholders, such as other investors, commercial and financial creditors, workers or suppliers, consumers, of the State or of the local community around the undertaking? In particular, what is the interest of the shareholders as a whole: to influence the company's governance, to receive dividends, to sell their shares at a higher price in the short or long term? Does the company as a whole have an interest of its own? May directors pursue personal interests while managing the company?

Company law and corporate governance practice deal with such fundamental questions and strive to provide answers. Although there are differences in the corporate structures of companies around the world (considering in particular Europe, the US, and Japan), there is substantial convergence on the conclusion that, in managing a company, directors are committed to maximising the so-called shareholders' value in the long term. In cases where the ownership of the firm is concentrated, protection of the interests of minorities is necessary and directors are burdened with the duty of ensuring such protection. Other interests circulating around a company are not matters of corporate law, rather of other laws (labour, consumers, environmental law and so on) influencing from the outside how the company is managed. There is also convergence that directors are not committed to pursuing the interests of creditors, although company law – and ECL in particular – focuses not only on the protection of shareholders, but also on creditors: as long as the company is solvent, however, the directors' focus shall be on maximising the shareholders' value as this is the best means for the pursuit of the aggregate social welfare.

Hansmann and Kraakman, two prominent American scholars, maintain that the history of corporate law has therefore come to an end as the shareholder-oriented or standard model (developed in the USA and in the UK) has prevailed over the managerialist model (developed in the USA until the 1960s), the State-oriented model (developed in France, Italy, and Japan) and the labour-oriented model (developed in Germany) after the Second World War. The reading of some excerpts from their piece is highly instructive.

Henry Hansmann and Reinier Kraakman, 'The End of History for Corporate Law', 89 *Geo. L.J.* 439–468 (2001)

Much recent scholarship has emphasized institutional differences in corporate governance, capital markets, and law among European, American, and Japanese companies. Despite very real differences in the corporate systems, the deeper tendency is toward convergence, as it has been since the nineteenth century. The basic law of corporate governance – indeed, most of corporate law – has achieved a high degree of uniformity across developed market jurisdictions, and continuing convergence toward a single, standard model is likely. The core legal features of the corporate form were already well established in advanced jurisdictions one hundred years ago, at the turn of the twentieth century. Although there remained considerable room for variation in governance practices and in the fine structure of corporate law throughout the twentieth century, the pressures for further convergence are now rapidly growing. Chief among these pressures is the recent dominance of a shareholder-centered ideology of corporate law among the business, government, and legal elites in key commercial jurisdictions. There is no longer any serious competitor to the view that corporate law should principally strive to increase long-term shareholder value. This emergent consensus has already profoundly affected corporate governance practices throughout the world. It is only a matter of time before its influence is felt in the reform of corporate law as well.

...

... [T]here is today a broad normative consensus that shareholders alone are the parties to whom corporate managers should be accountable, resulting from widespread disenchantment with a privileged role for managers, employees, or the state in corporate affairs. This is not to say that there is agreement that corporations should be run in the interests of shareholders alone – much less that the law should sanction that result. All thoughtful people believe that corporate enterprise should be organized and operated to serve the interests of society as a whole, and that the interests of shareholders deserve no greater weight in this social calculus than do the interests of any other members of society. The point is simply that now, as a consequence of both logic and experience, there is convergence on a consensus that the best means to this end (that is, the pursuit of aggregate social welfare) is to make corporate managers strongly accountable to shareholder interests and, at least in direct terms, only to those interests. It follows that even the extreme proponents of the so-called 'concession theory' of the corporation can embrace the primacy of shareholder interests in good conscience.

Of course, asserting the primacy of shareholder interests in corporate law does not imply that the interests of corporate stakeholders must or should go unprotected. It merely indicates that the most efficacious legal mechanisms for protecting the interests of non-shareholder constituencies – or at least all constituencies other than creditors – lie outside of corporate law. For workers, this includes the law of labor contracting, pension law, health and safety law, and antidiscrimination law. For consumers, it includes product safety regulation, warranty law, tort law governing product liability, antitrust law, and mandatory disclosure of product contents and characteristics. For the public at large, it includes environmental law and the law of nuisance and mass torts.

Creditors, to be sure, are to some degree an exception. There remains general agreement that corporate law should directly regulate some aspects of the relationship between a business corporation and its creditors. Conspicuous examples include rules governing veil-piercing and limits on the distribution of dividends in the presence of inadequate capital. The reason for these rules, however, is that there are unique problems of creditor contracting that are integral to the corporate form, owing principally to the presence of limited liability as a structural characteristic of that form. These types of rules, however, are modest in scope. Outside of bankruptcy, they do not involve creditors in corporate governance, but rather are confined to limiting shareholders' ability to use the characteristics of the corporate form opportunistically to exploit creditors.

...

The shareholder-oriented model does more than assert the primacy of shareholder interests, however. It asserts the interests of all shareholders, including minority shareholders. More particularly, it is a central tenet in the standard model that minority or noncontrolling shareholders should receive strong protection from exploitation at the hands of controlling shareholders. In publicly traded firms, this means that all shareholders should be assured an essentially equal claim on corporate earnings and assets.

There are two conspicuous reasons for this approach, both of which are rooted in efficiency concerns. One reason is that, absent credible protection for noncontrolling shareholders, business corporations will have difficulty raising capital from the equity markets. The second reason is that the devices by which controlling shareholders divert to themselves a disproportionate share of corporate benefits commonly involve inefficient investment choices and management policies.

...

It is sometimes said that the shareholder-oriented model of corporate law is well suited only to those jurisdictions in which one finds large numbers of firms with widely dispersed share ownership, such as the US and the UK. A different model is appropriate, it is said, for those jurisdictions in which ownership is more concentrated, such as the nations of continental Europe. This view, however, is unconvincing.

Closely held corporations, like publicly held corporations, operate most efficiently when the law helps assure that managers are primarily responsive to shareholder interests and that controlling shareholders do not opportunistically exploit noncontrolling shareholders. The shareholder primacy model does not logically privilege any particular ownership structure. Indeed, both concentrated and dispersed shareholdings have been celebrated, at different times and by different commentators, for their ability to advance shareholder interests in the face of serious agency problems.

Equally important, every jurisdiction includes a range of corporate ownership structures. While both the US and UK have many large firms with dispersed ownership, both countries also contain a far larger number of corporations that are closely held. Similarly, every major continental European jurisdiction has at least a handful of firms with dispersed ownership, and the number of such firms is evidently growing. It follows that every jurisdiction must have a system of corporate law that is adequate to handle the full range of ownership structures. Thus, just as there was rapid crystallization of the core features of the corporate form in the late nineteenth century, at the beginning of the twenty-first century we are witnessing rapid convergence on the standard shareholder-oriented model as a normative view of corporate structure and governance. We should also expect this normative convergence to produce substantial convergence in the practices of corporate governance and in corporate law.

...

Over the past decade, the literature on corporate governance and corporate law has sometimes advocated 'stakeholder' models as a normatively attractive alternative to a strongly shareholder-oriented view of the corporation. The stakeholders involved may be employees, creditors, customers, merchants in a firm's local community, or even broader interest groups such as beneficiaries of a well-preserved environment. The stakeholders, it is argued, will be subject to opportunistic exploitation by the firm and its shareholders if corporate managers are accountable only to the firm's shareholders; corporate law must therefore ensure that managers are responsive to stakeholder interests as well.

While stakeholder models start with a common problem, they posit two different kinds of solutions. One group of stakeholder models looks to what we term a 'fiduciary' model of the corporation, in which the board of directors functions as a neutral coordinator of the contributions and returns of all stakeholders in the firm. Under this model, only investors are given direct representation on the corporate board. Other stakeholders are protected by relaxing the board's duty or incentive to represent only the interests of shareholders, thus giving the board greater discretion to look after other stakeholders' interests.

The fiduciary model finds its most explicit recognition in US law in the form of constituency statutes that permit boards to consider the interests of constituencies other than shareholders in mounting takeover defenses. Margaret Blair and Lynn Stout, sophisticated American advocates of the fiduciary model, also claim to find support for this normative model in other, broader aspects of US corporate law. In the UK, the fiduciary model is a key element in the ongoing debate over the duties of corporate directors.

The second group of stakeholder models substitutes direct stakeholder representatives for fiduciary directors. In this 'representative' model of the corporation, two or more stakeholder constituencies appoint representatives to the board of directors, which then elaborates policies that maximize the joint welfare of all stakeholders, subject to the bargaining leverage that each group brings to the boardroom table. The board functions ideally then as a kind of collective fiduciary, even though its individual members remain partisan representatives. The board of directors (or supervisory board) then becomes an unmediated 'coalition of stakeholder groups' and functions as 'an arena for cooperation with respect to the function of monitoring the management,' as well as an arena for resolving 'conflicts with respect to the specific interests of different stakeholder groups.'

Neither the fiduciary nor the representative stakeholder models, however, constitute at bottom a new approach to the corporation. Rather, despite the new rhetoric with which the stakeholder models are presented, and the more explicit economic theorizing that sometimes accompanies them, they are at heart just variants on the older manager-oriented and labor-oriented models. Stakeholder models of the fiduciary type are in effect just reformulations of the manager-oriented model, and they suffer the same weaknesses. While untethered managers may better serve the interests of some classes of stakeholders, such as a firm's existing employees and creditors, the managers' own interests will often come to have disproportionate prominence in their decisionmaking, with costs to some interest groups – such as shareholders, customers, and potential new employees and creditors – that outweigh any gains to the stakeholders who benefit. Moreover, the courts are evidently incapable of formulating and enforcing fiduciary duties of sufficient refinement to ensure that managers behave more efficiently and fairly.

Stakeholder models of the representative type closely resemble yesterday's labor-oriented model, though generalized to extend to other stakeholders as well, and are again subject to the same weaknesses. The mandatory inclusion of any set of stakeholder representatives on the board is likely to impair corporate decisionmaking processes with costly consequences that outweigh any gains to the groups that obtain representation. Thus, the same forces that have been discrediting the older models are also undermining the stakeholder model as a viable alternative to the shareholder-oriented model.

…

The triumph of the shareholder-oriented model of the corporation over its principal competitors is now assured, even if it was problematic as recently as twenty-five years ago. Logic alone did not establish the superiority of this standard model or of the prescriptive rules that it implies, which establish a strong corporate management with duties to serve the interests of shareholders alone, as well as strong minority shareholder protections. Rather, the standard model earned its position as the dominant model of the large corporation the hard way, by out-competing during the post-World War II period the three alternative models of corporate governance: the managerialist model, the labor-oriented model, and the state-oriented model. If the failure of the principal alternatives has established the ideological hegemony of the standard model, though, perhaps this should not come as a complete surprise. The standard model has never been questioned for the vast majority of corporations. It dominates the law and governance of closely held corporations in every jurisdiction. Most German companies do not participate in the codetermination regime, and most Dutch companies are not regulated by the managerialist 'structure' regime. Similarly, the standard model of shareholder primacy has always been the dominant legal model in the two jurisdictions where the choice of models might be expected to matter most: the US and the UK. The choice of models matters in these jurisdictions because large companies often have highly fragmented ownership structures. In continental Europe, where most large companies are controlled by large shareholders, the interests of controlling shareholders traditionally dominate corporate policy no matter what the prevailing ideology of the corporate form.

We predict, therefore, that as equity markets evolve in Europe and throughout the developed world, the ideological and competitive attractions of the standard model will become indisputable, even among legal academics. And as the goal of shareholder primacy becomes second nature even to politicians, convergence in most aspects of the law and practice of corporate governance is sure to follow.

FURTHER READING

Mark J. Roe, 'Some Differences in Corporation Structure in Germany, Japan, and the United States', 102 *Yale L.J.* 1927 (1993).

Bernard S. Black and John C. Coffee, 'Hail Britannia? Institutional Investor Behavior Under Limited Regulation', 92 *Mich. L. Rev.* 1997 (1994).

Margaret M. Blair and Lynn A. Stout, 'A Team Production Theory of Corporate Law', 85 *Va L. Rev.* 247–319 (1999).

Henry Hansmann and Reinier Kraakman, 'The End of History for Corporate Law', 89 *Geo. L. J.* 439–468 (2001).

See also:

Reinier Kraakman, 'Disclosure and Corporate Governance: An Overview Essay', in Guido Ferrarini, Klaus J. Hopt, Jaap Winter, and Eddy Wymeersch (eds.), *Reforming Company and Takeover Law in Europe* 95–115 (Oxford University Press, 2004).

John Armour, Henry Hansmann, Reinier Kraakman, and Marianna Pargendler, 'What is Corporate Law?', in John Armour, Luca Enriques et al., *The Anatomy of Corporate Law: A Comparative and Functional Approach* 1–29 (Oxford University Press, 3rd ed., 2017).

John Armour, Luca Enriques, Henry Hansmann, and Reinier Kraakman, 'The Basic Governance Structure: The Interests of Shareholders as a Class'; Luca Enriques, Henry Hansmann, Reinier Kraakman, and Marianna Pargendler, 'The Basic Governance Structure: Minority Shareholders and Non-Shareholder Constituencies', in John Armour, Luca Enriques et al., *The Anatomy of Corporate Law: A Comparative and Functional Approach* 49–109 (Oxford University Press, 3rd ed., 2017).

13.2 ECL Approach to Corporate Governance

As already mentioned, the ECL approach to corporate governance has significantly changed over time. Whilst in the 1970s the Original Fifth Draft Directive considered the adoption of the two-tier system and workers' participation on an equal footing in the supervisory organ (co-determination) mandatory, the

Amended Proposal and the Third Draft, as well as the SE Statute expressed a substantial neutrality as to whether good corporate governance requires a two-tier structure and workers' co-determination within the supervisory organ.

In its 2003 Action Plan, the EU Commission made it clear that Member States have different systems of corporate governance, which reflect their different cultures and the various views about the roles of corporations and the way in which their industry should be financed. In its 2012 Action Plan, the EU Commission definitely declared that the EU has no intention of challenging or modifying this arrangement. This completely new approach does not mean that the EU does not recognise the importance of fostering good corporate governance in Europe by making convergent efforts to this end. To the contrary, both Action Plans aim at enhancing corporate governance in the EU by the adoption of several measures at various levels. These measures particularly focus on the governance of listed companies, as this consistently affects the smooth functioning of financial markets.

Considering the financial scandals of the early beginning of the millennium, in the 2003 Action Plan the EU Commission considered it necessary to enhance corporate governance by focusing on the reduction of the legal barriers to an effective shareholders' engagement. Therefore, the EU Commission proposed to undertake actions aiming at (i) enhancing disclosure, mainly through an annual corporate governance statement to be included in the consolidated financial statements and information on the institutional investors' involvement; (ii) strengthening shareholders' powers through various measures; (iii) modernising the board functioning, as regards, in particular, the board's composition, responsibility, and remuneration; and (iv) coordinating corporate governance efforts of Member States.

Modernising Company Law and Enhancing Corporate Governance in the European Union – A Plan to Move Forward (2003)

3.1 Corporate Governance

Corporate Governance, which can be defined in many ways, is usually understood as the system by which companies are directed and controlled. It is, in the light of the recent corporate scandals, now a major issue globally. Poor corporate governance performance, by some companies, has greatly undermined confidence in capital markets.

Within the EU, Member States have different systems of corporate governance, which reflect their different cultures and the various views about the roles of corporations and the way in which their industry should be financed. Over the last years, corporate governance has been the subject of an increasingly intense debate. Forty or so corporate governance codes relevant to the European Union have been adopted over the last decade, at national or international level, with the aim of better protecting the interests of shareholders and/or stakeholders.

Differences in national corporate governance arrangements may create uncertainty and costs for both issuers and investors, which need to be addressed to promote an efficient integration of EU capital markets. As announced in its 1999 Financial Services Action Plan, the Commission launched in 2001 a review of the main corporate governance codes relevant to the EU. The full comparative study, prepared for the Commission by Weil, Gotshal & Manges LLP, was finalised in March 2002 and concluded that the EU should not devote time and effort to the development of a European corporate governance code: the study identified as a more valuable area for the European Commission to focus its efforts on the reduction of legal and regulatory barriers to shareholder engagement in cross-border voting ('participation barriers') as well as the reduction of barriers to shareholders' ability to evaluate the governance of companies ('information barriers').

The need for a European code and for additional disclosure of corporate governance practices, as well as a series of additional issues raised by the Oviedo Council in April 2002 in the wake of the US scandals (the role of non-executive directors and of supervisory boards, management remuneration, management responsibility for financial statements, and auditing practices), were also considered by the High Level Group of Company Law Experts. In its Final Report, it confirmed that there is no need for an EU corporate governance code.

In this line of thinking, the Commission observes, firstly, that the main differences between Member States are found in differing company law and securities regulation, as opposed to the corporate governance codes which, according to the March 2002 study, show a remarkable degree of convergence, and, secondly, that the existence of many codes in the EU is not generally perceived as a difficulty by issuers (many issuers continue to be active primarily on their domestic market; when they are active on other markets, they are faced with codes that are pretty similar; and in the rare instances where codes provisions are divergent, the 'comply or explain' principle offers a satisfactory solution).

Moreover the Commission considers that:

(a) the adoption of a European code would not achieve full information for investors about the key corporate governance rules applicable to companies across Europe, as these rules would still be based on – and part of – national company laws that are in certain respects widely divergent;
(b) the adoption of such a code would not contribute significantly to the improvement of corporate governance in the EU, as this code would have either to allow for many different options or confine itself to abstract principles. Trying to harmonise all the elements of a European code would take years and would not be achievable in a reasonable timeframe.

There is nevertheless an active role for the EU to play in corporate governance, because some specific rules and principles need to be agreed at EU level in Directives or Recommendations and a certain co-ordination of corporate governance codes in the EU should be organised to encourage further convergence and the exchange of best practice.

Therefore at this stage the Commission considers that:

- There is little indication that the development of a European corporate governance code as an additional layer between principles developed at the international level and codes adopted at national level would offer significant added value. In that respect, the Commission notes that corporate governance is now at the forefront of the activities of the OECD, which recently decided to revise its corporate governance principles of 1999 with the aim of adopting a modernised version of these principles in 2004. The Commission is taking an active part in this exercise.

- A self-regulatory market approach, based solely on non-binding recommendations, is clearly not always sufficient to guarantee the adoption of sound corporate governance practices. Only in the presence of a certain number of made-to-measure rules, markets are able to play their disciplining role in an efficient way. In view of the growing integration of European capital markets, a common approach should be adopted at EU level with respect to a few essential rules and adequate co-ordination of corporate governance codes should be ensured.

More specifically, the Commission, largely in line with the High Level Group's suggestions, intends to proceed along the following lines.

3.1.1 Enhancing Corporate Governance Disclosure Annual Corporate Governance Statement

Listed companies should be required to include in their annual report and accounts a coherent and descriptive statement covering the key elements of their corporate governance structure and practices, which should at least include the following items:

(a) the operation of the shareholder meeting and its key powers, and the description of shareholder rights and how they can be exercised;
(b) the composition and operation of the board and its committees;
(c) the shareholders holding major holdings, and their voting and control rights as well as key agreements;
(d) the other direct and indirect relationships between these major shareholders and the company;
(e) any material transactions with other related parties;
(f) the existence and nature of a risk management system;
(g) and a reference to a code on corporate governance, designated for use at national level, with which the company complies or in relation to which it explains deviations.

A proposal for a Directive containing the principles applicable to such an annual corporate governance statement, which should appear prominently in the annual documents published by listed companies, is regarded by the Commission as a priority for the short term, so as to rapidly allow market pressures to be better exerted. The definition of these principles will properly take into account the related requirements present in existing (e.g. major holdings) or proposed (e.g. take-over bids) instruments.

Information about the Role Played by Institutional Investors

Institutional investors should be obliged:

(a) to disclose their investment policy and their policy with respect to the exercise of voting rights in companies in which they invest;
(b) to disclose to their beneficial holders at their request how these rights have been used in a particular case.

Such requirements would not only improve the internal governance of institutional investors themselves, but would also enhance participation by institutional investors in the affairs of the companies in which they invest. A requirement for institutional investors to systematically exercise their voting rights is not considered desirable, in view of its potential counterproductive effects (due to a lack of time or resources, institutional investors might simply vote in favour of any proposed resolution to fulfil the requirement).

Institutional investors have an important role to play in the governance of companies in which they invest. Fostering this role will require amendments to a series of existing legal texts (relating to insurance companies, pension funds, mutual and other investment funds, ...), and even more importantly the introduction of such a requirement would deliver its full effects only once the problems related to cross-border voting will have been solved. The Commission therefore intends to take the necessary steps in the medium term.

3.1.2 Strengthening Shareholders' Rights Access to Information

Shareholders of listed companies should be provided with electronic facilities to access the relevant information in advance of General Meetings. This issue is currently addressed by the Proposal for a Transparency Directive, which essentially enables listed companies to use electronic means to inform their shareholders and contains specific provisions guaranteeing a timely access to regulated information when securities are listed in another Member State than the home Member State. The Commission considers this solution as a significant and proportionate first step, which does not preclude the adoption of further measures (which would generally require listed companies to use electronic means to inform their shareholders) in the medium term, if this looks desirable in the light of the implementation of the Transparency Directive (which itself contains a revision clause).

Other Shareholders' Rights

There is a need for enhancing the exercise of a series of shareholders' rights in listed companies (right to ask questions, to table resolutions, to vote in absentia, to participate in general meetings via electronic means). These facilities should be offered to shareholders across the EU, and specific problems relating to cross-border voting should be solved urgently. The Commission considers that the necessary framework should be developed in a Directive, since an effective exercise of these rights requires a number of legal difficulties to be solved. In view of the important benefits expected from such a framework, the Commission regards the relevant proposal as a priority for the short term.

Shareholder Democracy

Strengthening shareholders' rights should be based essentially on (a) the provision of comprehensive information on what the various existing rights are and how they can be exercised and (b) the development of the facilities necessary to make sure that these existing rights can be effectively exercised. This approach is fully consistent with the OECD Principles of Corporate Governance.

The Commission considers that there is a strong medium to long term case for aiming to establish a real shareholder democracy in the EU. The Comparative Study of Corporate Governance Codes relevant to the EU evidenced that corporate governance codes tend to support the one share/one vote principle, although many codes favour some flexibility in this respect. The hardest line is taken by the codes issued by bodies affiliated with investors, which clearly do not support the issuance of shares with reduced or no voting rights. The Commission nevertheless observes that any initiative in this direction, which would give further effect to the principle of proportionality between capital and control advocated by the High Level Group in its First Report on issues related to take-over bids, requires prior study. The Commission therefore intends to undertake a study, in the short to medium term, on the consequences which such an approach would entail.

3.1.3 Modernising the Board of Directors Board Composition

In key areas where executive directors clearly have conflicts of interests (i.e. remuneration of directors, and supervision of the audit of the company's accounts), decisions in listed companies should be made exclusively by non-executive or supervisory directors who are in the majority independent. With respect to the nomination of directors for appointment by the body competent under national company law, the responsibility for identifying candidates to fill board vacancies should in principle be entrusted to a group composed mainly of executive directors, since executive directors can usefully bring their deep knowledge of the challenges facing the company and of the skills and experience of the human resources grown up within the company. Non-executive directors should, nonetheless, also be included and specific safeguards should be put in place to deal with conflicts of interests when they arise, for example when a decision has to be made on the reappointment of a director.

These requirements should be enforced by Member States at least on a 'comply or explain' basis. Certain minimum standards of what cannot be considered to be independent should be established at EU level. With a view to fostering a concrete and active role for non-executive or supervisory directors, particular attention will be paid to the issue of the number of mandates that may be held concurrently. Moreover, the impact of interlocking directorships on the independence of directors should be properly addressed in the minimum standards to be established. The Commission regards these measures as key to the restoration of confidence in the markets, and therefore intends to adopt a Commission Recommendation to this effect in the short term.

Such a Recommendation will define minimum standards applicable to the creation, composition and role of the nomination, remuneration and audit committees. In view of the recent accounting scandals, special emphasis will be placed on the audit committee (or equivalent body), with a view to fostering the key role it should play in supervising the audit function, both in its external aspects (selecting the external auditor for appointment by shareholders, monitoring the relationship with the external auditor including non-audit fees if any) and its internal aspects (reviewing the accounting policies, and monitoring the internal audit procedures and the company's risk management system).

The High Level Group further recommended that at least listed companies in the EU should generally have the option between a one-tier board structure (with executive and non-executive directors) and a two-tier board structure (with managing directors and supervisory directors). The Commission welcomes the idea to offer additional organisational freedom to listed companies, but recognises that the implications of such a proposal should be carefully studied. Much has to be learned in this respect from the adaptation of national law to the Regulation and the Directive on the European Company Statute. The Commission therefore proposes that this recommendation from the High Level Group should be followed up in the medium term.

Directors' Remuneration

Shareholders should be able to appreciate fully the relation between the performance of the company and the level of remuneration of directors, both ex ante and ex post, and they should be able to make decisions on the remuneration items linked to the share price.

Agreeing with the High Level Group, the Commission considers that an appropriate regulatory regime should be composed of four key items (disclosure of remuneration policy in the annual accounts, disclosure of details of remuneration of individual directors in the annual accounts, prior approval by the shareholder meeting of share and share option schemes in which directors participate, proper recognition in the annual accounts of the costs of such schemes for the company).

In order to promote a swift application of such a regime, a Commission Recommendation should be adopted to this effect. The Commission regards this action as key to the restoration of confidence, and intends to adopt such a Recommendation in the short term and to closely monitor its application with a view to identifying whether any further additional rulemaking may be desirable in the medium term.

Directors' Responsibilities

With a view to enhancing directors' responsibilities, the collective responsibility of all board members for financial and key non-financial statements (including the annual corporate governance statement mentioned above in Section 3.1.1) should be confirmed as a matter of EU law. The Commission considers that such a confirmation in framework provisions constitutes a first step which may be achieved rapidly, and intends to take the necessary initiatives in the short term.

The High Level Group made several other recommendations designed to enhance directors' responsibilities: (a) introduction of a special investigation right, whereby shareholders holding a certain percentage of the share capital should have the right to ask a court or administrative authority to authorise a special investigation into the affairs of the company; (b) development of a wrongful trading rule, whereby directors would be held personally accountable for the consequences of the company's failure, if it is foreseeable that the company cannot continue to pay its debts and they don't decide either to rescue the company and ensure payment or to put it into liquidation; (c) imposition of directors' disqualification across the EU as a sanction for misleading financial and non-financial statements and other forms of misconduct by directors. The Commission supports these ideas, whose implementation requires further analysis, and therefore intends to present the relevant proposal for a Directive in the medium term.

3.1.4 Co-ordinating Corporate Governance Efforts of Member States

The Commission shares the view of the High Level Group that the EU should actively coordinate the corporate governance efforts of Member States through their company laws, securities laws, listing rules, codes, or otherwise. In particular, each Member State should progress towards designating a code of corporate governance, designated for use at national level, as the code with which listed companies subject to their jurisdiction are to comply or in relation to which they are to explain deviations. Co-ordination should not only extend to the making of these national codes, but also to the procedures Member States have in place to monitor and enforce compliance and disclosure. Member States should participate in the co-ordination process set by the EU, but the process itself should be voluntary and non-binding with a strong involvement of market participants.

The comparative study of codes relevant to the EU concluded one year ago that these codes show a remarkable degree of convergence. The Commission nevertheless observes that such a situation may change rapidly: several Member States are currently engaged in important policy initiatives, and the EU will soon be enlarged by 10 new Member States. In addition, standards are increasingly set at the international level and they should be implemented in Member States in a consistent way.

For these reasons, the Commission regards it important to encourage the co-ordination and convergence of national codes through regular high level meetings of the European Corporate Governance Forum. Participants to such a Forum, which could meet once or twice a year, will comprise representatives from Member States, European regulators (including CESR), issuers and investors, other market participants and academics. Interested MEP's will also be invited to present their views. The Forum will be chaired by the Commission.

As we will see in this chapter and those that follow, many of the proposed actions have been undertaken: (i) the new Fourth and Seventh Company Law Directives (Directive 2013/34/EU) require that companies qualifying as public-interest entities form a corporate governance statement as part of the management report annexed to the annual and consolidated financial accounts; also the new Directive addresses the directors' responsibility and liability for drawing up and publishing the financial statements and the management report (*see further* in this chapter); (ii) the Shareholder Rights Directive (Directive 2007/36/EC, as amended by Directive 2014/59/EU and Directive 2017/828/EU) strengthens shareholder rights in listed companies (*see*, Chapter 15); (iii) in addition, efforts were also made to enhance the role of auditors in the governance of listed companies (Directive 2006/43/EC, replacing the Eighth Company Law Directive): indeed, in connection to the financial scandals of the early beginning of the millennium, rating agencies and auditing firms (such as Arthur Andersen and Deloitte) were considered to be as liable as unfaithful directors of companies such as Enron and WorldCom (in the US) and Parmalat (in the EU) for not having served the role of gatekeeper they were committed to.

It must also be pointed out that soft law of the EU – i.e., by means of recommendations – played an important role in this process: indeed, Recommendations 2004/913/EC, 2005/162/EC, and 2009/385/EC deal with the issue of board composition and members' remuneration (*see*, Chapter 14, §§ 14.5–14.7). The reason for issuing not only binding legislation, but also soft law by means of recommendations, is clarified in the Preamble of Recommendation 2005/162/EC on the role of non-executive or supervisory directors of listed companies, as follows:

Recital 4 Recommendation 2005/162/EC

(4) In view of the complexity of many of the issues at stake, the adoption of detailed binding rules is not necessarily the most desirable and efficient way of achieving the objectives pursued. Many corporate governance codes adopted in Member States tend to rely on disclosure to encourage compliance, based on the 'comply or explain' approach: companies are invited to disclose whether they comply with the code and to explain any material departures from it. This approach enables companies to reflect sector- and enterprise-specific requirements, and the markets to assess the explanations and justifications provided. With a view to fostering the role of non-executive or supervisory directors, it is therefore appropriate that all Member States be invited to take the steps necessary to introduce at national level a set of provisions based on the principles set out in this Recommendation, to be used by listed companies either on the basis of the 'comply or explain' approach or pursuant to legislation.

As underlined in the 2003 Action Plan, the Commission acknowledged the adoption in the preceding decade of forty or so corporate governance codes relevant to the EU, in particular for listed companies. These codes are drafted by national or international organisations with the aim of better protecting the interests of shareholders and/or stakeholders, on a 'comply or explain' basis. The EU Commission clarified that there is no need for a European corporate governance code.

As a consequence, as the EU Commission put it:

Action Plan: European Company Law and Corporate Governance – A Modern Legal Framework for More Engaged Shareholders and Sustainable Companies (2012)

The EU corporate governance framework is a combination of legislation and soft law, namely national corporate governance codes applied on a 'comply or explain' basis which gives companies and their shareholders an important degree of flexibility.

As mentioned, the accounting Directive requires that public-interest entities include a corporate governance statement in their management report, providing information on the adoption of a corporate governance code and on any departments from rules provided for in the code.

Article 20 Corporate Governance Statement, Directive 2013/34/EU

1. Undertakings referred to in point (1)(a) of Article 2 shall include a corporate governance statement in their management report. That statement shall be included as a specific section of the management report and shall contain at least the following information:
   (a) a reference to the following, where applicable: (i) the corporate governance code to which the undertaking is subject, (ii) the corporate governance code which the undertaking may have voluntarily decided to apply, (iii) all relevant information about the corporate governance practices applied over and above the requirements of national law.

   Where reference is made to a corporate governance code referred to in points (i) or (ii), the undertaking shall also indicate where the relevant texts are publicly available. Where reference is made to the information referred to in point (iii), the undertaking shall make details of its corporate governance practices publicly available;

   (b) where an undertaking, in accordance with national law, departs from a corporate governance code referred to in points (a)(i) or (ii), an explanation by the undertaking as to which parts of the corporate governance code it departs from and the reasons for doing so; where the undertaking has decided not to refer to any provisions of a corporate governance code referred to in points (a)(i) or (ii), it shall explain its reasons for not doing so;

   (c) a description of the main features of the undertaking's internal control and risk management systems in relation to the financial reporting process;

   (d) the information required by points (c), (d), (f), (h) and (i) of Article 10(1) of Directive 2004/25/EC of the European Parliament and of the Council of 21 April 2004 on takeover bids, where the undertaking is subject to that Directive;

   (e) unless the information is already fully provided for in national law, a description of the operation of the shareholder meeting and its key powers and a description of shareholders' rights and how they can be exercised; and

   (f) the composition and operation of the administrative, management and supervisory bodies and their committees.

...

FURTHER READING

John Armour, Luca Enriques, Henry Hansmann, and Reinier Kraakman, 'The Basic Governance Structure: The Interests of Shareholders as a Class', in John Armour, Luca Enriques et al., *The Anatomy of Corporate Law: A Comparative and Functional Approach* 49–79, at 62–66 (Oxford University Press, 3rd ed., 2017).

13.3 What are the Future Plans for EU Corporate Governance? More Transparency and More Engaged Shareholders

Whilst not all the goals of the 2003 Action Plan have been accomplished, further goals have been put forward in the 2012 Action Plan taking significant advantage of the debate raised by the Green Paper named *The EU corporate governance framework* of 5 April 2011. These new goals include: (i) enhancing transparency by (1) requiring disclosure of board diversity policy and management of non-financial risks; (2) improving corporate governance reporting; (3) permitting shareholder identification; (4) strengthening transparency rules for institutional investors; (ii) engaging shareholders by (1) better shareholder oversight of remuneration policy; (2) better shareholder oversight of related party transactions; (3) regulating proxy advisors; (4) clarification of the relationship between investor cooperation on corporate governance issues and the 'acting in concert' concept; (5) employee share ownership.

Action Plan: European Company Law and Corporate Governance – A Modern Legal Framework for More Engaged Shareholders and Sustainable Companies (2012)

2 Enhancing Transparency

2.1 Disclosure of Board Diversity Policy and Management of Non-financial Risks

In Europe, different board structures coexist. Depending on the country, listed companies may put in place either a 'single board' system (also called 'monistic' or 'unitary board' system), a two-tier (or 'dual board') system or some form of mixed system. The Commission acknowledges the coexistence of these board structures, which are often deeply rooted in the country's overall economic governance system, and has no intention of challenging or modifying this arrangement.

Regardless of the board structure, board composition plays a key role in a company's success. Effective oversight of the executive directors or the management board by the non-executive directors or supervisory boards leads to successful governance of the company. In this regard, diversity of competences and views among the board's members is very important. It facilitates understanding of the business organisation and affairs and thus enables the board to challenge the management's decisions objectively and constructively. In contrast, insufficient diversity could lead to a so-called group-think process, translating into less debate, fewer ideas and challenges in the boardroom and potentially less effective oversight of the management board or executive directors. The Commission, encouraged by the results of the 2011 Green Paper consultation, considers that increased transparency as regards board diversity policy could make companies reflect more on the issue and take better account of the need for greater diversity on their boards. This initiative will also be complementary to the specific proposal on improving the gender balance among non-executive directors of listed companies.

The Commission believes also that (supervisory) boards should give broader consideration to the entire range of risks faced by their company. Extending the reporting requirements with regard to non-financial parameters would help in establishing a more comprehensive risk profile of the company, enabling more effective design of strategies to address those risks. This additional focus on non-financial aspects would encourage companies to adopt a sustainable and long-term strategic approach to their business.

In order to encourage companies to enhance board diversity and give greater consideration to non-financial risks, the Commission will make in 2013 a proposal to strengthen disclosure requirements with regard to their board diversity policy and risk management through amendment of the accounting Directive.

2.2 Improving Corporate Governance Reporting

The quality of the corporate governance reports produced by listed companies has been subject to criticism. Corporate governance codes in the EU are applied on a 'comply or explain' basis. This approach allows companies to depart from particular recommendations of the applicable code, provided they explain the reasons for doing so. However, the explanations provided by companies are often insufficient. They either simply state that they had departed from a recommendation without any further explanation, or provide only a general or limited explanation. As these explanations are used by investors to make their investment decisions and assess the value of a company, such shortcomings limit the system's usefulness and viability. A large majority of respondents to the 2011 Green Paper were in favour of requiring companies to provide better explanations for departing from [the] codes' recommendations.

Following on from the 2011 Green Paper, some Member States have initiated discussions or issued guidelines on the quality of the explanations provided by companies. For example, in Finland, the Securities Markets Association issued on 20 January 2012 guidelines on explanations that companies should provide. The Belgian Corporate Governance Committee commissioned an independent study on the quality of explanation and, on the basis of the findings of this study, issued a number of practical recommendations in 2012. In the UK, the Financial Reporting Council launched in December 2011 a discussion between companies and investors on what constitutes appropriate explanation and, consequently, introduced guidelines on the 'comply or explain approach' in the Corporate Governance Code. The Commission welcomes these initiatives. It also intends to encourage further cooperation between the national bodies in charge of monitoring the application of the corporate governance codes, in particular through exchange of best practices developed in different Member States.

The Commission will take in 2013 an initiative, possibly in the form of a Recommendation, to improve the quality of corporate governance reports, and in particular the quality of explanations to be provided by companies that depart from the corporate governance codes.

2.3 Shareholder Identification

The 2011 Green Paper asked whether stakeholders saw a need for a European mechanism to help issuers identify their shareholders in order to facilitate dialogue on corporate governance issues. In addition, the Green Paper enquired whether this information should also be made available to other investors. A clear majority of respondents were in favour of such a mechanism. Particularly strong support came from both businesses and investors.

Opinions on what would be the best way forward were significantly divided though. Some respondents felt that requiring issuers to offer a forum to shareholders on their corporate websites was sufficient. Others, on the contrary, spoke out in favour of a fully-fledged EU shareholder identification mechanism. Quite a lot of respondents suggested lowering the thresholds for notification of major holdings in the Transparency Directive instead. Finally, a substantial group held that Member States should be required to provide mutual recognition for existing national identification mechanisms and, if necessary, should be obliged to introduce a national transparency tool respecting some minimum requirements.

The European Parliament supports the view that companies issuing name shares should be entitled to know the identity of their owners, but that owners of bearer shares should have the right not to see their identity disclosed. This echoes concerns expressed earlier as to the privacy of retail investors.

The Commission considers that additional information on who owns shares in a listed company can improve the corporate governance dialogue between the company and its shareholders. The existing tools are either not detailed enough or lack the necessary cross-border dimension.

The Commission will propose, in 2013, an initiative to improve the visibility of shareholdings in Europe as part of its legislative work programme in the field of securities law.

2.4 Strengthening Transparency Rules for Institutional Investors

Research conducted in preparation for the Commission Green Papers of 2010 and 2011 and the responses to them highlighted a need for improvement in the transparency of voting policies adopted by institutional investors, including asset management firms, and the exercise of these policies. Currently, the UK Stewardship Code and the Dutch Eumedion best practices for engaged share-ownership as well as the Code for external governance of the European Fund and Asset Management Association and the International Corporate Governance Network Global Corporate Governance Principles already recommend institutional investors to be transparent about the way they exercise their ownership/stewardship responsibilities, which includes in particular information about voting and engagement.

Disclosure of such information could have a positive impact on investor awareness, enable ultimate investors to optimise investment decisions, facilitate the dialogue between investors and companies, encourage shareholder engagement and could strengthen companies' accountability to civil society. Moreover, this information could be useful for investors before entering into a portfolio management contract or for beneficiaries of institutional investors acting on behalf of or for the benefit of others. In the light of its overall objective to engage shareholders, the Commission believes this to be the right step forward.

The Commission will in 2013 come with an initiative, possibly through modification of the shareholders' rights Directive, on the disclosure of voting and engagement policies as well as voting records by institutional investors.

3 Engaging Shareholders

Effective, sustainable shareholder engagement is one of the cornerstones of [a] listed companies' corporate governance model, which depends inter alia on checks and balances between the different organs and different stakeholders. If for instance the majority of shareholders remain passive, do not seek interaction with the company and do not vote, the functioning of the current corporate governance system is less effective. In such circumstances, no corrective action can be expected from the shareholders' side and supervision of management rests entirely on the shoulders of the (supervisory) board.

3.1 Better Shareholder Oversight of Remuneration Policy

Executive remuneration has been the topic of much discussion in recent years. The Commission believes that companies could benefit from remuneration policies which stimulate longer-term value creation and genuinely link pay to performance. Poor remuneration policies and/or incentive structures lead to unjustified transfers of value from companies, their shareholders and other stakeholders to executives. Therefore, and taking into account existing oversight possibilities, in particular as regards in companies with two-tier board structures, shareholders should be enabled to exercise better oversight of remuneration policies applying to directors of listed companies and the implementation of those policies. Accordingly, and as evidenced by the results of the 2011 Green Paper consultation, shareholders need clear, comprehensive and comparable information on remuneration policies and individual remuneration of directors. This can be achieved through basic harmonisation of disclosure requirements. Moreover, shareholders should be able to express their views on the matter, through a mandatory shareholder vote on the company's remuneration policy and the remuneration report, providing an overview of the manner in which the remuneration policy has been implemented. Currently, not all Member States give shareholders the right to vote on remuneration policy and/or the report, and information disclosed by companies in different Member States is not easily comparable.

The Commission will propose in 2013 an initiative, possibly through a modification of the shareholder rights Directive, to improve transparency on remuneration policies and individual remuneration of directors, as well as to grant shareholders the right to vote on remuneration policy and the remuneration report.

3.2 Better Shareholder Oversight of Related Party Transactions

Related party transactions, i.e. dealings where the company contracts with its directors or controlling shareholders, may cause prejudice to the company and its minority shareholders, as they give the related party the opportunity to appropriate value belonging to the company. Thus, adequate safeguards for the protection of shareholders' interests are of great importance.

Current EU rules require companies to include in their annual accounts a note on transactions entered into with related parties, stating the amount and the nature of the transaction and other necessary information. However, since this requirement tends to be regarded as insufficient, the European Corporate Governance Forum issued a statement on related party transactions recommending the introduction of common principles across Europe. The Forum proposed in particular that transactions above a certain threshold should be subject to evaluation by an independent advisor and that the most substantial transactions should be approved by shareholders. The 2011 Green Paper raised the question of providing more protection against related party transactions. A considerable proportion of respondents called for stronger safeguards. Having regard to this response and to the guidelines contained in the statement of the European Corporate Governance Forum, the Commission considers that shareholders' control over related party transactions should be strengthened.

The Commission will propose in 2013 an initiative aimed at improving shareholders' control over related party transactions, possibly through an amendment to the shareholder rights Directive.

3.3 Regulating Proxy Advisors

Institutional investors with highly diversified equity portfolios face practical difficulties in properly assessing how they should vote on items on the agenda of general meetings of investee companies. Therefore, they make frequent use of the services of proxy advisors, such as voting advice, proxy voting and corporate governance ratings. As a result, proxy advisors' influence on voting is substantial. Moreover, it has been argued that institutional investors rely more heavily on voting advice for their investments in foreign companies than for investments in their home markets. Thus, the influence of proxy advisors is likely to be greater in markets with a high percentage of international investors. Currently, proxy advisors are however not regulated at EU level.

The influence of proxy advisors raises some concerns. During the preparation of the 2011 Green Paper, investors and investee companies expressed concern about a lack of transparency in the methods used by proxy advisors for the preparation of their advice. More specifically, it is claimed that the analytical methodology used by proxy advisors fails to take into account company-specific characteristics and/or elements of national legislation and best corporate governance practices. Another concern is that proxy advisors are subject to conflicts of interest, such as when they also act as corporate governance consultants to investee companies. Conflicts of interest also arise when a proxy advisor advises investors on shareholder resolutions proposed by one of its clients. Finally, the lack of competition in the sector raises concerns, partly about the quality of the advice and whether it meets investors' needs.

In 2012 ESMA issued a discussion paper on proxy advisors requesting views on possible regulatory options for proxy advisors, ranging from no action and voluntary measures to quasi-binding or binding EU instruments. The Commission may draw on the results of the discussion to ensure a coherent and effective operational framework for proxy advisors.

The Commission will consider an initiative in 2013, possibly in the context of the revision of the shareholder rights Directive, with a view to improving the transparency and conflict of interest frameworks applicable to proxy advisors.

3.4 Clarification of the Relationship between Investor Cooperation on Corporate Governance Issues and the 'Acting in Concert' Concept

A large number of respondents to the 2011 Green Paper called for clarification of the concept of 'acting in concert'. Indeed, the lack of legal certainty provided by the current rules contained in the Takeover Bids Directive and the Transparency Directive and their transposition in national law is perceived as an obstacle to effective shareholder cooperation. Shareholders need to know when they can exchange information and cooperate with one another without running the risk that their actions may trigger unexpected legal consequences.

If such clarification is not provided, shareholders may avoid cooperation, which in turn could undermine the potential for long-term engaged share ownership under which shareholders effectively hold the board accountable for its actions. The Commission recognises the need for guidance to clarify the conceptual boundaries and to provide more legal certainty on this issue in order to make shareholder cooperation easier.

During 2013, the Commission will work closely with the competent national authorities and ESMA with a view to developing guidance to increase legal certainty on the relationship between investor cooperation on corporate governance issues and the rules on acting in concert.

3.5 Employee Share Ownership

The Commission believes that employees' interest in the sustainability of their company is an element that ought to be considered in the design of any well-functioning governance framework. Employees' involvement in the affairs of a company may take the form of information, consultation and participation in the board. But it can also relate to forms of financial involvement, particularly to employees becoming shareholders.

Employee share ownership schemes already have a successful tradition and track record in many Member States. Research conducted in preparation for the 2011 Green Paper and responses to it indicate that employee share ownership schemes could play an important role in increasing the proportion of long-term oriented shareholders. Since there are many angles to this issue (for instance taxation, social security and labour law) the Commission finds it important to analyse this subject in more detail, in particular as regards its internal market dimension. In the light of this analysis, it will identify which initiatives may be appropriate to encourage the development of trans-national employee share ownership schemes in Europe. The Commission will identify and investigate potential obstacles to trans-national employee share ownership schemes, and will subsequently take appropriate action to encourage employee share ownership throughout Europe.

The most important achievement is the approval of Directive 2017/828/EU of the European Parliament and of the Council of 17 May 2017 amending Directive 2007/36/EC (so-called Shareholder Rights Directive, *see* § 15.6 as regards the encouragement of long-term shareholder engagement).

14

Management and Control

14.1 Systems Options and Involvement of Employees

As mentioned, the concept of corporate governance includes the system by which companies are directed and controlled. In Europe different board structures coexist as, depending on the country, companies may put in place either a 'one-tier' or 'single board' system (also called 'monistic' or 'unitary board' system), a two-tier (or 'dual board' or 'dualistic') system, or some form of mixed system. The EU acknowledges the coexistence of these board structures, which are often deeply rooted in the country's overall economic governance system, and has no further intention of challenging or modifying this arrangement.

The SE governance structure is a clear example of this approach and this chapter therefore mainly refers to the SE Statute as expressing shared principles at Union level.

Article 38 Regulation 2001/2157/EC

Under the conditions laid down by this Regulation an SE shall comprise:

(a) a general meeting of shareholders; and
(b) either a supervisory organ and a management organ (two-tier system) or an administrative organ (one-tier system) depending on the form adopted in the statutes.

Notwithstanding that the Draft Fifth Company Law Directive has never been approved, it is not only the SE Statute that adopts the approach of permitting an option between systems. Rather, some EU Member States – such as France (1967) and Italy (2003) – also allow companies formed under their national law to freely opt for a one-tier or two-tier board structure.

Available data as of 31 December 2017 show that choices on board structure of SEs are largely path dependent: founders of an SE residing in a Member State adopting a monistic board structure will follow that path and choose a monistic structure for the newly established SE; conversely, founders residing

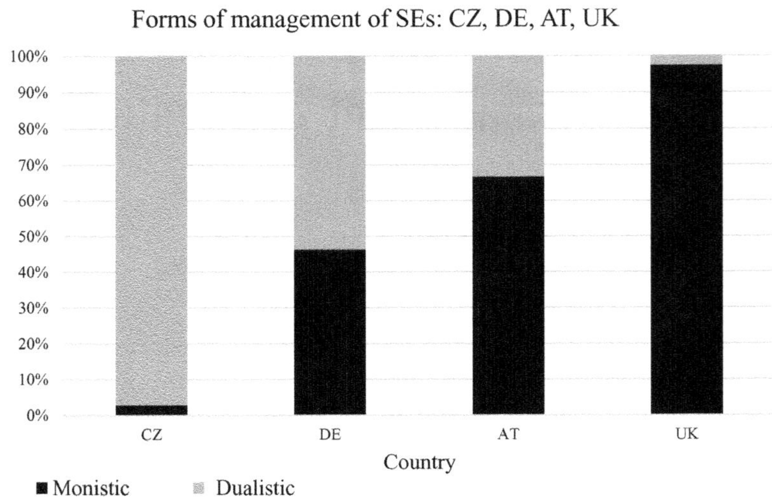

Figure 14.1 Forms of management of SEs

in a dualistic environment will maintain their tradition. A deeper investigation, however, shows a certain degree of contamination in countries, like Germany and Austria, where the formation of an SE is a tool permitting the adoption of a corporate governance structure which is otherwise not permitted by national company law. In particular, Figure 14.1 compares four States – the Czech Republic (CZ), Germany (DE), Austria (AT), and the UK (before Brexit) – three of which have a dualistic tradition (CZ, DE, AT). Data show that whilst CZ and the UK follow their respective paths, DE and AT diverge – and for good reason, i.e., in order to minimise the influence of workers on boards, as will be illustrated in due course.

Whilst the statutes decide whether the SE shall adopt a two-tier or a one-tier system, the shareholders' meeting shall decide on:

(a) the appointment and removal of members of the management organ in the one-tier system and, exceptionally, in the two-tier system (Articles 39 (2) and 43(3) Regulation 2001/2157/EC);
(b) the appointment and removal of members of the supervisory board in the two-tier system (Article 40(2) Regulation 2001/2157/EC).

Furthermore, the SE Statute expresses the principle that the shareholders' meeting appoints the organs upon majority vote. This implies that all members of the organs are chosen by the existing majority shareholder, if a majority shareholder exists.

The SE Statute does not preclude, however, that national law permits that some of the members of a company organ are appointed by constituencies other than shareholders, such as workers or public bodies, or by minority shareholders.

Article 47(4) Regulation 2001/2157/EC

4. This Regulation shall not affect national law permitting a minority of shareholders or other persons or authorities to appoint some of the members of a company organ.

With this in mind, it is an appropriate time to recall that the Directive 2001/86/EC, of 8 October 2001 *supplementing the Statute for a European company with regard to the involvement of employees* recognises the place and role of workers in the business of companies. However, as both the process of approving the Draft Fifth Company Law Directive and the SE Statute faced a significant deadlock as to whether workers shall be given the power to elect members of the board – be it in the supervisory organ in the two-tier system or in the administrative organ in the one-tier system – Directive 2001/86/EC leaves greater room for manoeuvre for the legislations of Member States as regards the involvement of employees.

The basic principle expressed by Directive 2001/86/EC is that no SE may be established without a model of employee involvement being selected by agreement between the management and the employees themselves. This agreement must of necessity include information and consultation procedures and, where appropriate, employee involvement in the management bodies of the SE. This involvement is nevertheless only mandatory if the employees already benefited from it before the creation of the SE. In other words, involvement of the employees is mandatory for those SEs originating from companies incorporated in EU Member States, such as Germany, where workers' corporate co-determination is mandatory.

In all other cases, for both companies adopting a one-tier or two-tier structure, workers' participation would be assured by direct appointment, co-optation, or collective agreement. Additionally, companies could assure employee participation by processes which do not entail membership on the supervisory organ: such processes shall provide access to both the managements' and the supervisory boards' decisions and extensive information.

Despite these being the principles expressed by the Directive, available data as of 31 December 2017 show that almost 95 per cent of all SEs provide workers with no involvement rights at all; 2.5 per cent provide workers with only information and consultation rights; only another 2.5 per cent (mainly registered in Germany and Austria, and some in France) provide workers with information, consultation, and participation rights. In other words, employee involvement seems to be the exception, not the rule in SEs: it may be also argued that in Germany and Austria, where the law provides workers with strong participation rights, the creation of an SE is often a way to circumvent workers' co-determination.

This being considered, as we will later discuss in detail, in the two-tier system the management organ is (generally) appointed by the supervisory

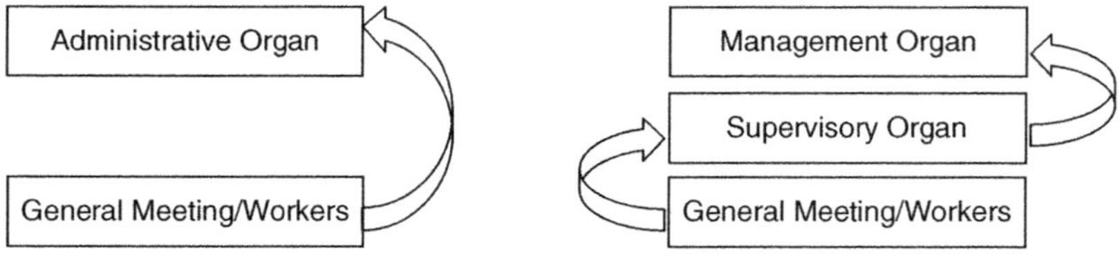

Figure 14.2 Monistic and dualistic systems

organ and the supervisory organ is appointed by the general meeting, whilst in the one-tier system the administrative organ is appointed by the general meeting. However, depending on the arrangement made with the employees, part of the members of the administrative or supervisory board – ranging from a third to a half, depending on the number of workers employed – may be elected by the workers. Figure 14.2 illustrates the two systems and the possible involvement of employees.

The SE Statute provides for rules applicable specifically to the two-tier system or the one-tier system, and for common rules applicable to both. In the next two paragraphs we will deal with the rules set forth by the SE Statute for the two-tier and the one-tier systems. In §§ 14.4–14.10 we will deal with the rules applicable to all directors – including members of the supervisory organ or the so-called non-executives or independent directors – regardless of the adopted systems: these rules are set forth by the SE Statute, as well as by other pieces of EU legislation of soft law.

FURTHER READING

On *system options*: Federico Ghezzi and Corrado Malberti, 'The Two-tier Model and the One-tier Model of Corporate Governance in the Italian Reform of Corporate Law', 5 *ECFR* 1–47 (2008).

Erik Werlauff, 'Board of Directors or Supervisory Board: Legal Aspects of the Choice Between One-tier and Two-tier Management in Danish Public Limited Companies after the 2009/2010 Company Reform', 6 *ECL* 257–263 (2009).

On *involvement of employees*: Paul L. Davies, 'Workers on the Board of the European Company', 32 *Indus. L.J.* 75–96 (2003).

Lone L. Hansen, 'Employee Involvement and the Formation of a European Company (SE)', 1 *ECL* 126–130 (2004).

Claire Leca, 'The Participation of Employees' Representatives in the Governance Structure of the Societas Europaea', 18 *EBLR* 403–441 (2007).

Claudia Schubert, 'The National Implementation of Employee Participation in the Administrative Board of the SE in the One-tier Model – A Legal Comparison on the Basis of Germany, Austria, Sweden, and France', 5 *ECFR* 422–452 (2008).

See also:

Luca Enriques, Henry Hansmann, Reinier Kraakman, and Marianna Pargendler, 'The Basic Governance Structure: Minority Shareholders and Non-shareholders' Constituencies', in John Armour, Luca Enriques et al., *The Anatomy of Corporate Law: A Comparative and Functional Approach* 79–109, at 89–92 (Oxford University Press, 3rd ed., 2017).

14.2 Two-Tier System

The two-tier system is characterized by the presence, alongside the general meeting, of a management organ responsible for managing the company and of a supervisory organ responsible for supervising the management.

Article 39(1) Regulation 2001/2157/EC

1. The management organ shall be responsible for managing the SE. A Member State may provide that a managing director or managing directors shall be responsible for the current management under the same conditions as for public limited-liability companies that have registered offices within that Member State's territory.

The management organ may be composed of a single member or of more members, appointed and removed by the supervisory organ: the statutes shall determine the number of members of the management organ, within the minimum and maximum amount eventually fixed by the Member States.

Article 39(2) Regulation 2001/2157/EC

2. The member or members of the management organ shall be appointed and removed by the supervisory organ.

   A Member State may, however, require or permit the statutes to provide that the member or members of the management organ shall be appointed and removed by the general meeting under the same conditions as for public limited-liability companies that have registered offices within its territory.
3. No person may at the same time be a member of both the management organ and the supervisory organ of the same SE. The supervisory organ may, however, nominate one of its members to act as a member of the management organ in the event of a vacancy. During such a period the functions of the person concerned as a member of the supervisory organ shall be suspended. A Member State may impose a time limit on such a period.
4. The number of members of the management organ or the rules for determining it shall be laid down in the SE's statutes. A Member State may, however, fix a minimum and/or a maximum number.
5. Where no provision is made for a two-tier system in relation to public limited-liability companies with registered offices within its territory, a Member State may adopt the appropriate measures in relation to SEs.

On the other hand, the supervisory organ shall supervise the work of the management organ; therefore it may not manage the company itself (Article 40(1) Regulation 2001/2157/EC), nor appoint its members as members of the management organ (Article 39(3) Regulation 2001/2157/EC).

Members of the supervisory organ are appointed and removed by the general meeting (or the statutes): the statutes shall determine the number of members of the supervisory organ, within the minimum and maximum amount eventually fixed by the Member States. The wording of the SE Statute seems to preclude that the supervisory organ is composed of a single member.

Article 40(2-3) Regulation 2001/2157/EC

2. The members of the supervisory organ shall be appointed by the general meeting. The members of the first supervisory organ may, however, be appointed by the statutes. This shall apply without prejudice to Article 47(4) or to any employee participation arrangements determined pursuant to Directive 2001/86/EC.
3. The number of members of the supervisory organ or the rules for determining it shall be laid down in the statutes. A Member State may, however, stipulate the number of members of the supervisory organ for SEs registered within its territory or a minimum and/or a maximum number.

The SE Statute grants the chairman of each organ a casting vote in case of a tie. The roots of this rule – and of its complementing rules – may be easily found in the German law on workers' co-determination of 1976, where a casting vote is granted to the chairman of the supervisory board of those companies employing more than 2,000 workers where half of the members are appointed by the employees. Since under the German stock-corporation law of 1965 the overall number of members shall be necessarily even, in the case of co-determination, the chairman is elected among the members of the organ appointed by the general meeting and, in the case of a tie, he or she may solve the deadlock by exercising a casting vote.

Similar rules are provided for in the SE Statute.

Article 42 Regulation 2001/2157/EC

The supervisory organ shall elect a chairman from among its members. If half of the members are appointed by employees, only a member appointed by the general meeting of shareholders may be elected chairman.

Article 50(3-4) Regulation 2001/2157/EC

2. Where there is no relevant provision in the statutes, the chairman of each organ shall have a casting vote in the event of a tie. There shall be no provision to the contrary in the statutes, however, where half of the supervisory organ consists of employees' representatives.

3. Where employee participation is provided for in accordance with Directive 2001/86/EC, a Member State may provide that the supervisory organ's quorum and decision-making shall, by way of derogation from the provisions referred to in paragraphs 1 and 2, be subject to the rules applicable, under the same conditions, to public limited-liability companies governed by the law of the Member State concerned.

The SE Statute does not specify how the supervisory organ shall supervise the management of the company, nor does it determine its duties and responsibilities. It only: (i) allows the Member States to grant the supervisory organ itself the power to make certain categories of transactions subject to authorisation; (ii) requires the management organ to provide the supervisory organ with information on the business and on events that may have an appreciable effect on the company; (iii) generically grants the supervisory organ powers of investigation.

Article 41 Regulation 2001/2157/EC

1. The management organ shall report to the supervisory organ at least once every three months on the progress and foreseeable development of the SE's business.
2. In addition to the regular information referred to in paragraph 1, the management organ shall promptly pass [to] the supervisory organ any information on events likely to have an appreciable effect on the SE.
3. The supervisory organ may require the management organ to provide information of any kind which it needs to exercise supervision in accordance with Article 40(1). A Member State may provide that each member of the supervisory organ also be entitled to this facility.
4. The supervisory organ may undertake or arrange for any investigations necessary for the performance of its duties.
5. Each member of the supervisory organ shall be entitled to examine all information submitted to it.

14.3 One-Tier System

The one-tier system is characterised by the presence, alongside the general meeting, of a single organ responsible for managing the company.

Similarly to the management organ in the two-tier system, when the option is made for the one-tier system the administrative organ shall manage the company.

Article 43(1) Regulation 2001/2157/EC

1. The administrative organ shall manage the SE. A Member State may provide that a managing director or managing directors shall be responsible for the day-to-day management under the same conditions as for public limited-liability companies that have registered offices within that Member State's territory.

However, similarly to the supervisory organ in the two-tier system, members of the administrative organ in the one-tier system are appointed and removed by the general meeting (or the statutes): the statutes shall determine the number of members of the supervisory organ, within the minimum and maximum amount eventually fixed by the Member States. Also in this case, the wording of the SE Statute seems to preclude that the administrative organ is composed of a single member.

In addition, the SE Statute requires that in case of corporate co-determination of employees, the number of members shall be at least three. Similarly to the supervisory organ in the two-tier system, in the case where the administrative organ is composed of an even number of members and half are appointed by the employees, the chairman shall be elected among the members appointed by the shareholders and, in the case of a tie, shall have a casting vote.

Article 43(2–4) Regulation 2001/2157/EC

2. The number of members of the administrative organ or the rules for determining it shall be laid down in the SE's statutes. A Member State may, however, set a minimum and, where necessary, a maximum number of members.

   The administrative organ shall, however, consist of at least three members where employee participation is regulated in accordance with Directive 2001/86/EC.
3. The member or members of the administrative organ shall be appointed by the general meeting. The members of the first administrative organ may, however, be appointed by the statutes. This shall apply without prejudice to Article 47(4) or to any employee participation arrangements determined pursuant to Directive 2001/86/EC.
4. Where no provision is made for a one-tier system in relation to public limited-liability companies with registered offices within its territory, a Member State may adopt the appropriate measures in relation to SEs.

Article 45 Regulation 2001/2157/EC

The administrative organ shall elect a chairman from among its members. If half of the members are appointed by employees, only a member appointed by the general meeting of shareholders may be elected chairman.

The SE Statute does not specify how the administrative organ in the one-tier system shall manage the company, nor does it determine its duties and responsibilities. It only: (i) requires the organ to meet at least once every three months to discuss the progress and foreseeable development of the business; and (ii) mandates for equal treatment of all members as regards information submitted to the organ.

Article 44 Regulation 2001/2157/EC

1. The administrative organ shall meet at least once every three months at intervals laid down by the statutes to discuss the progress and foreseeable development of the SE's business.
2. Each member of the administrative organ shall be entitled to examine all information submitted to it.

Last, it shall be emphasised that, in particular when the administrative organ includes more members, not all shall necessarily engage in the day-to-day management of the company. Members who do not engage in the day-to-day management of the company are referred to as *non-executive directors*: these are involved in policymaking and planning exercises, along with the function of supervising the activities of the executives. Therefore, these directors are often entrusted with functions similar to that of the supervisory organ in the two-tier system. As we will see later, the distinction between executive and non-executive directors is relevant in the field of listed companies.

14.4 Appointment of Members and Board Functioning

Members of the organs of an SE – as well as members of the organs of public companies established according to many domestic legislations – may not be appointed for a lifelong period; rather, notwithstanding members may be re-elected, appointment shall not exceed six years.

Article 46 Regulation 2001/2157/EC

1. Members of company organs shall be appointed for a period laid down in the statutes not exceeding six years.
2. Subject to any restrictions laid down in the statutes, members may be reappointed once or more than once for the period determined in accordance with paragraph 1.

Members of a company's organ shall be natural persons not being disqualified for such a function. However, the SE regulation allows – although this is a widely discussed issue under the domestic laws of the Member States – that, if the statutes so provide, members sitting in the boards of an SE are legal entities, provided that they designate a natural person to exercise their functions. It must be added that, under domestic legislations where this is permitted, an SE may be appointed as director of another company or partnership: a good example is that of Bertelsmann SE & Co. KGaA, where Bertelsmann SE is the management company of a German unlisted partnership limited by shares acting as holding company of a large group including RTL Group (television), Penguin Random

House (books), Gruner + Jahr (magazines), Arvato (services), and Be Printers (print); further details on Bertelsmann's acquisition of RTL will be given when examining the *Audiolux* case in Chapter 18, § 18.3.

Article 47(1–3) Regulation 2001/2157/EC

1. An SE's statutes may permit a company or other legal entity to be a member of one of its organs, provided that the law applicable to public limited-liability companies in the Member State in which the SE's registered office is situated does not provide otherwise.

That company or other legal entity shall designate a natural person to exercise its functions on the organ in question.

2. No person may be a member of any SE organ or a representative of a member within the meaning of paragraph 1 who:
   (a) is disqualified, under the law of the Member State in which the SE's registered office is situated, from serving on the corresponding organ of a public limited-liability company governed by the law of that Member State, or
   (b) is disqualified from serving on the corresponding organ of a public limited-liability company governed by the law of a Member State owing to a judicial or administrative decision delivered in a Member State.
3. An SE's statutes may, in accordance with the law applicable to public limited-liability companies in the Member State in which the SE's registered office is situated, lay down special conditions of eligibility for members representing the shareholders.

Although some organs of the SE may be composed of a single member, the SE Statute assumes that organs are generally composed of more than one member, this implying the need for internal rules relating to quorums and decision-taking.

Article 50(1) Regulation 2001/2157/EC

1. Unless otherwise provided by this Regulation or the statutes, the internal rules relating to quorums and decision-taking in SE organs shall be as follows:
   (a) quorum: at least half of the members must be present or represented;
   (b) decision-taking: a majority of the members [must be] present or represented.

Requiring that a quorum and a majority are determined based on the number of members being present or represented at the meeting, the SE Statute expresses the widely accepted principle that all members of a company's organ are equal, regardless of their appointment by the general meeting or by other constituencies, and express votes on a *per capita* basis.

However, the SE Statute grants the chairman of each organ a casting vote in the case of a tie. As mentioned, this rule has a particular meaning in companies adopting a two-tier system, in particular where half of the supervisory organ consists of employees' representatives.

The SE Statute does not require that companies follow mandatory rules on how the organs shall be convened and how meetings shall be held: in particular, as to who shall have the power to convene the organ, how and when the notice of meeting shall be given to members, whether items on the agenda shall be disclosed and related information shall be given beforehand, and so on. In contrast, such issues are very important for the shareholders' meeting and, as we will see later (Chapter 15, § 15.5), both the SE Statute and the Shareholder Rights Directive (for publicly traded companies) require a legal procedure that ensures an effective and informed participation of all shareholders.

Under the SE Statute, single members of the management organ (in the two-tier system) or of the administrative organ (in the one-tier system) may individually engage in transactions on behalf of the company. However, the Member States or the statutes may require that for certain categories of transactions – e.g., the sale of an important asset of the company, or other important transactions – there is an involvement of all members of the administrative or management organ and/or of the supervisory organ. Involvement of such organs may take the form of a decision of the organ as a whole or of an authorisation.

Article 48 Regulation 2001/2157/EC

1. An SE's statutes shall list the categories of transactions which require authorisation of the management organ by the supervisory organ in the two-tier system or an express decision by the administrative organ in the one-tier system.
   A Member State may, however, provide that in the two-tier system the supervisory organ may itself make certain categories of transactions subject to authorisation.
2. A Member State may determine the categories of transactions which must at least be indicated in the statutes of SEs registered within its territory.

In this respect, it is useful to recall that, under Directive 2009/101/EC, statutory limits on the powers of the organs of the company may not be relied on as against third parties. However, if general powers of representation are conferred to several persons acting jointly, the company may consider the transactions performed by single persons not binding.

Article 10(2) Directive 2009/101/EC

2. The limits on the powers of the organs of the company, arising under the statutes or from a decision of the competent organs, may not be relied on as against third parties, even if they have been disclosed.

3. If the national law provides that authority to represent a company may, in derogation from the legal rules governing the subject, be conferred by the statutes on a single person or on several persons acting jointly, that law may provide that such a provision in the statutes may be relied on as against third parties on condition that it relates to the general power of representation; the question whether such a provision in the statutes can be relied on as against third parties shall be governed by Article 3.

FURTHER READING

John Armour, Luca Enriques, Henry Hansmann, and Reinier Kraakman, 'The Basic Governance Structure: The Interests of Shareholders as a Class', in John Armour, Luca Enriques et al., *The Anatomy of Corporate Law: A Comparative and Functional Approach* 49–79, at 62–63 (Oxford University Press, 3rd ed., 2017).

14.5 Board Composition in Listed Companies

As mentioned, the distinction between executive and non-executive directors is relevant in the field of listed companies. In particular, Recommendation 2005/162/EC focuses on the role of non-executive or supervisory directors of listed companies and on the committees of the administrative and supervisory board.

As the Preamble to the Recommendation 2004/913/EC puts it,

Recital 3 Recommendation 2004/913/EC

(3) Non-executive or supervisory directors are recruited by companies for a variety of purposes. Of particular importance is their role in overseeing executive or managing directors and dealing with situations involving conflicts of interests. It is vital to foster that role in order to restore confidence in financial markets ...

However, non-executive or supervisory directors may still have personal interests related to the management of the company. These would hinder their ability to oversee executive directors and deal with situations involving conflicts of interests. Therefore, the Recommendation 2004/913/EC recognises and fosters the role of not only non-executive, but also independent directors, in that they are free of any material conflict of interest with the company itself, its management, the majority shareholder, or other interested parties.

Recitals 7–8 Recommendation 2004/913/EC

(7) The presence of independent representatives on the board, capable of challenging the decisions of management, is widely considered as a means of protecting the interests of

shareholders and other stakeholders. In companies with a dispersed ownership, the primary concern is how to make managers accountable to weak shareholders. In companies with controlling shareholders, the focus is more on how to make sure that the company will be run in a way that sufficiently takes into account the interests of minority shareholders. Ensuring adequate protection for third parties is relevant in both cases. Whatever the formal board structure of a company, the management function should therefore be subject to an effective and sufficiently independent supervisory function. Independence should be understood as the absence of any material conflict of interest; in this context, proper attention should be given in particular to any threats which might arise from the fact that a representative on the board has close ties with a competitor of the company.

(8) In order to ensure that the management function will be submitted to an effective and sufficiently independent supervisory function, the (supervisory) board should comprise a sufficient number of committed non-executive or supervisory directors, who play no role in the management of the company or its group and who are independent in that they are free of any material conflict of interest. In view of the different legal systems existing in Member States, the proportion of (supervisory) board members to be made up of independent directors should not be defined precisely at Community level.

Article 13 Independence, Recommendation 2004/913/EC

13.1. A director should be considered to be independent only if he is free of any business, family or other relationship, with the company, its controlling shareholder or the management of either, that creates a conflict of interest such as to impair his judgement.

13.2. A number of criteria for assessment of the independence of directors should be adopted at national level, taking into account the guidance set out in Annex II, which identifies a number of situations reflecting the relationships or circumstances usually recognised as likely to generate material conflict of interest. The determination of what constitutes independence is fundamentally an issue for the (supervisory) board itself to determine. The (supervisory) board may consider that, although a particular director meets all the criteria laid down at national level for assessment of the independence of directors, he cannot be considered independent owing to the specific circumstances of the person or the company, and the converse also applies.

13.3. Proper information should be disclosed on the conclusions reached by the (supervisory) board in its determination of whether a particular director should be regarded as independent.

13.3.1. When the appointment of a non-executive or supervisory director is proposed, the company should disclose whether it considers him to be independent; if one or more of the criteria laid down at national level for assessment of independence of directors is not met, the company should disclose its reasons for nevertheless considering that director to be independent. Companies should also disclose annually which directors they consider to be independent.

13.3.2. If one or more of the criteria laid down at national level for assessment of independence of directors has not been met throughout the year, the company should disclose its reasons for considering that director to be independent. To ensure the accuracy of the information provided on the independence of directors, the company should require the independent directors to have their independence periodically re-confirmed.

Given the role of non-executive or supervisory directors and that of independent directors, the presence of a sufficient number of both is strongly recommended in the boards of listed companies.

Article 3 Presence of Non-executive or Supervisory Directors, Recommendation 2004/913/EC

3.1. The administrative, managerial and supervisory bodies should include in total an appropriate balance of executive/managing and non-executive/supervisory directors such that no individual or small group of individuals can dominate decision-making on the part of these bodies.

3.2. The present or past executive responsibilities of the (supervisory) board's chairman should not stand in the way of his ability to exercise objective supervision. On a unitary board, one way to ensure this is that the roles of chairman and chief executive are separate; in the case of unitary and dual boards, one option may be that the chief executive does not immediately become the chairman of the (supervisory) board. In cases where a company chooses to combine the roles of chairman and chief executive or to immediately appoint as chairman of the (supervisory) board the former chief executive, this should be accompanied with information on any safeguards put in place.

Article 4 Number of Independent Directors, Recommendation 2004/913/EC

A sufficient number of independent non-executive or supervisory directors should be elected to the (supervisory) board of companies to ensure that any material conflict of interest involving directors will be properly dealt with.

The supervisory role of non-executive or supervisory directors is commonly perceived as crucial in three areas, where the potential for conflict of interest of management is particularly high, especially when such matters are not a direct responsibility for shareholders: (i) nomination of directors; (ii) remuneration of directors; and (iii) audit.

With particular regard to these three areas, Recommendation 2004/913/EC also emphasises the importance of committees within the administrative and supervisory organ. Committees are generally entrusted with the task of making recommendations aimed at preparing the decisions to be taken by the administrative or the supervisory board. Recommendation 2004/913/EC advances that these committees are entirely or in major part composed by non-executive or independent members.

Recital 10 Recommendation 2004/913/EC

(10) In principle, and without prejudice to the powers of the general meeting, only the (supervisory) board as a whole has statutory decision-making authority and, as a collegiate body, is collectively accountable for the performance of its duties. The (supervisory) board has the power to determine the number and structure of the committees which it deems to be appropriate to facilitate its own work, but these committees are in principle not to be a substitute for the (supervisory) board itself. As a general rule, therefore, the nomination, remuneration and audit committees should make recommendations aimed at preparing the decisions to be taken by the (supervisory) board. However, the (supervisory) board should not be precluded from delegating part of its decision-making powers to committees when it considers it appropriate and when this is permissible under national law, even though the (supervisory) board remains fully responsible for the decisions taken in its field of competence.

Article 5 Organisation in Board Committees, Recommendation 2004/913/EC

Boards should be organised in such a way that a sufficient number of independent nonexecutive or supervisory directors play an effective role in key areas where the potential for conflict of interest is particularly high. To this end, but subject to point 7, nomination, remuneration and audit committees should be created within the (supervisory) board, where that board plays a role in the areas of nomination, remuneration and audit under national law, taking into account Annex I.

Article 6 Role of the Committees vis-à-vis the (Supervisory) Board, Recommendation 2004/913/EC

6.1. The nomination, remuneration and audit committees should make recommendations aimed at preparing the decisions to be taken by the (supervisory) board itself. The primary purpose of the committees should be to increase the efficiency of the (supervisory) board by making sure that decisions are based on due consideration, and to help organise its work with a view to ensuring that the decisions it takes are free of material conflicts of interest. The creation of the committees is not intended, in principle, to remove the matters considered from the purview of the (supervisory) board itself, which remains fully responsible for the decisions taken in its field of competence.

6.2. The terms of reference of any committee created should be drawn up by the (supervisory) board. Where permissible under national law, any delegation of decision-making power should be explicitly declared, properly described and made public in a fully transparent way.

Article 7 Flexibility in Setting up the Committees, Recommendation 2004/913/EC

7.1. Companies should make sure that the functions assigned to the nomination, remuneration and audit committees are carried out. However, companies may group the functions as they see fit and create fewer than three committees. In such a situation, companies should give a clear explanation both of the reasons why they have chosen an alternative approach and how the approach chosen meets the objective set for the three separate committees.

7.2. In companies where the (supervisory) board is small, the functions assigned to the three committees may be performed by the (supervisory) board as a whole, provided that it meets the composition requirements advocated for the committees and that adequate information is provided in this respect. In such a situation, the national provisions relating to board committees (in particular with respect to their role, operation, and transparency) should apply, where relevant, to the (supervisory) board as a whole.

An annex to the Recommendation 2004/913/EC clarifies the role of non-executive and independent directors in these areas.

The *nomination committee* should at least: (i) identify and recommend, for the approval of the (supervisory) board, candidates to fill board vacancies as and when they arise. In doing so, the nomination committee should evaluate the balance of skills, knowledge, and experience on the board, prepare a description of the roles and capabilities required for a particular appointment, and assess the time commitment expected; (ii) periodically assess the structure, size, composition, and performance of the unitary or dual board, and make recommendations to the (supervisory) board with regard to any changes; (iii) periodically assess the skills, knowledge, and experience of individual directors, and report on this to the (supervisory) board; (iv) properly consider issues related to succession planning.

The *remuneration committee* should at least: (i) make proposals, for the approval of the (supervisory) board, on the remuneration policy for executive or managing directors. Such policy should address all forms of compensation, including in particular the fixed remuneration, performance-related remuneration schemes, pension arrangements, and termination payments. Proposals related to performance-related remuneration schemes should be accompanied with recommendations on the related objectives and evaluation criteria, with a view to properly aligning the pay of executive or managing directors with the long-term interests of the shareholders and the objectives set by the (supervisory) board for the company; (ii) make proposals to the (supervisory) board on the individual remuneration to be attributed to executive or managing directors, ensuring that they are consistent with the remuneration policy adopted by the company and the evaluation of the performance of the directors concerned. In doing so, the committee should be properly informed as to the total compensation obtained by the directors from other companies affiliated to the group; (iii) make proposals to the (supervisory) board on suitable forms of contract for executive or managing directors; (iv) assist the (supervisory) board in overseeing the process whereby the company complies with existing provisions regarding disclosure of remuneration-related items (in particular the remuneration policy applied and the individual remuneration attributed to directors).

The *audit committee* should assist the administrative or supervisory board to at least: (i) monitor the integrity of the financial information provided by the company, in particular by reviewing the relevance and consistency of the accounting methods used by the company and its group (including the criteria for the consolidation of the accounts of companies in the group); (ii) review at least annually the internal control and risk management systems, with a view to ensuring that the main risks (including those related to compliance with existing legislation and regulations) are properly identified, managed, and disclosed; (iii) ensure the effectiveness of the internal audit function, in particular by making recommendations on the selection, appointment, reappointment, and removal of the head of the internal audit department and on the department's budget, and by monitoring the responsiveness of management to its findings and recommendations. If the company does not have an internal audit function, the need for one should be reviewed at least annually.

The constitution of an audit committee is mandatory for public-interest entities.

Article 41 Audit Committee, Directive 2006/43/EC

1. Each public-interest entity shall have an audit committee. The Member State shall determine whether audit committees are to be composed of non-executive members of the administrative body and/or members of the supervisory body of the audited entity and/or members appointed by the general meeting of shareholders of the audited entity.

At least one member of the audit committee shall be independent and shall have competence in accounting and/or auditing.

In public-interest entities which meet the criteria of Article 2(1), point (f) of Directive 2003/71/EC, Member States may permit the functions assigned to the audit committee to be performed by the administrative or supervisory body as a whole, provided at least that when the chairman of such a body is an executive member, he or she is not the chairman of the audit committee.

2. Without prejudice to the responsibility of the members of the administrative, management or supervisory bodies, or of other members who are appointed by the general meeting of shareholders of the audited entity, the audit committee shall, inter alia:
   (a) monitor the financial reporting process;
   (b) monitor the effectiveness of the company's internal control, internal audit where applicable, and risk management systems;
   (c) monitor the statutory audit of the annual and consolidated accounts;
   (d) review and monitor the independence of the statutory auditor or audit firm, and in particular the provision of additional services to the audited entity.
3. In a public-interest entity, the proposal of the administrative or supervisory body for the appointment of a statutory auditor or audit firm shall be based on a recommendation made by the audit committee.
4. The statutory auditor or audit firm shall report to the audit committee on key matters arising from the statutory audit, and in particular on material weaknesses in internal control in relation to the financial reporting process.
5. Member States may allow or decide that the provisions laid down in paragraphs 1 to 4 shall not apply to any public-interest entity that has a body performing equivalent functions to an audit committee, established and functioning according to provisions in place in the Member State in which the entity to be audited is registered. In such a case the entity shall disclose which body carries out these functions and how it is composed.
6. Member States may exempt from the obligation to have an audit committee:
   (a) any public-interest entity which is a subsidiary undertaking within the meaning of Article 1 of Directive 83/349/EEC if the entity complies with the requirements in paragraphs 1 to 4 of this Article at group level;
   (b) any public-interest entity which is a collective investment undertaking as defined in Article 1(2) of Directive 85/611/EEC. Member States may also exempt public-interest entities the sole object of which is the collective investment of capital provided by the public, which operate on the principle of risk spreading and which do not seek to take legal or management control over any of the issuers of its underlying investments, provided that those collective investment undertakings are authorised and subject to supervision by competent authorities and that they have a depositary exercising functions equivalent to those under Directive 85/611/EEC;
   (c) any public-interest entity the sole business of which is to act as issuer of asset-backed securities as defined in Article 2(5) of Commission Regulation (EC) No 809/2004. In such instances, the Member State shall require the entity to explain to the public the reasons for which it considers it not appropriate to have either an audit committee or an

administrative or supervisory body entrusted to carry out the functions of an audit committee;

(d) any credit institution within the meaning of Article 1(1) of Directive 2000/12/EC whose shares are not admitted to trading on a regulated market of any Member State within the meaning of point 14 of Article 4(1) of Directive 2004/39/EC and which has, in a continuous or repeated manner, issued only debt securities, provided that the total nominal amount of all such debt securities remains below EUR 100 000 000 and that it has not published a prospectus under Directive 2003/71/EC.

FURTHER READING

John Armour, Luca Enriques, Henry Hansmann, and Reinier Kraakman, 'The Basic Governance Structure: The Interests of Shareholders as a Class', in John Armour, Luca Enriques et al., *The Anatomy of Corporate Law: A Comparative and Functional Approach* 49–79, at 62 (Oxford University Press, 3rd ed., 2017).

Christoph Van der Elst, 'The European Legislative Framework for Audit Committees', 12 *ECL* 26–33 (2015).

14.6 Towards Gender Balance in Boards

Another important issue for board composition is that of gender representation, as it is widely acknowledged that women are under-represented in key roles. Data collected by the EU Commission in 2016 show that in the largest publicly held companies in the EU, only 23 per cent of board members and only 7 per cent of board chairs were women.

While the need to improve the gender balance in corporate boards is broadly recognised, many Member States are against a hard, quota-based approach, preferring voluntary measures. Taking account of this divergence, on 14 November 2012, the Commission presented a proposal for a directive on improving the gender balance in the boardroom. Accordingly, instead of obligatory quota, the Commission's proposal would have set a quantitative objective of increasing the proportion of women among non-executive company board members in publicly listed companies to 40 per cent by 2020.

In order to reach this objective:

- neutral criteria for ensuring fair recruitment would need to be applied together with transparency measures;
- public enterprises would be expected to make progress more quickly than private ones;
- an exemption clause would be offered to Member States that have already introduced successful measures;
- SMEs would be exempted;
- Member States may provide that listed companies in which members of the under-represented sex also represent less than 10 per cent of the employees would be exempted.

Notwithstanding that the Commission's proposal has not been approved, the discussion has had an influence in the legislation of many Member States. Some of these, such as Spain, Finland, and France, have introduced legislation requiring 40 per cent female representation on boards. Spain requires this degree of representation only for publicly traded companies and Finland only for state owned enterprises; France has imposed the gender equality for all companies. Other Member States, such as the Netherlands, require public companies with more than 250 employees to have 30 per cent of the board seats available filled by women. Similarly, Italy requires public companies to have at least 33 per cent of both gender representatives, whilst Belgium expands this requirement for all companies. Beyond Europe, California also requires women on boards.

FURTHER READING

Carlos Gorriz, 'Women on Boards: A European Proposal', 14 *Global Jurist*, 31–66 (2014).

Hana Horak and Kristijan Poljanec, 'Recent Developments in European Company Law: A Way Forward to More Social Europe?', 5 *InterEULawEast: J. Int'l & Eur. L., Econ. & Market Integrations* 151 (2018).

Monika Leszczyńska, 'Mandatory Quotas for Women on Boards of Directors in the European Union: Harmful to or Good for Company Performance?', 19 *EBOR* 35–61 (2018).

Cristiana Carletti, 'Gender Diversity Management and Corporate Governance: International Hard and Soft Laws Within the Italian Perspective', 5 *Italian Law Journal*, 251–279 (2019).

Jill Fisch and Steven Davidoff Solomon, 'Centros, California's "Women on Boards" Statute and the Scope of Regulatory Competition', 20 *EBOR* 493–520 (2019).

14.7 Executive Remuneration

Notwithstanding that board members' remuneration and, in particular, executive remuneration is a very important matter in the governance of companies, unsurprisingly the SE Statute does not directly address this issue. The reasons for the absence of rules in this field may be understood from reading the Preamble of Recommendation 2004/913/EC fostering an appropriate regime for the remuneration of directors of listed companies and in the Preamble to the already mentioned Recommendation 2005/162/EC.

Recital 2 Recommendation 2004/913/EC

(2) The form, structure and level of directors' remuneration are matters falling within the competence of companies and their shareholders. This should facilitate the recruitment and retention of directors having the qualities required to run a company. However, remuneration is one of the key areas where executive directors may have a conflict of interest and where due account should be taken of the interests of shareholders. Remuneration systems

should therefore be subjected to appropriate governance controls, based on adequate information rights. In this respect, it is important to respect fully the diversity of corporate governance systems within the Community, which reflect different Member States' views about the roles of corporations and of bodies responsible for the determination of policy on the remuneration of directors, and the remuneration of individual directors.

Recital 13 Recommendation 2005/162/EC

(13) In the area of remuneration, [the] corporate governance codes adopted in Member States tend to focus primarily on the remuneration of executive or managing directors, since the potential for abuse and conflicts of interest is essentially located there. Many codes also recognise that some consideration should be given at board level to the remuneration policy for senior management. Finally, the issue of stock options is granted special attention. Given the different approaches in the Member States with respect to the bodies responsible for setting the remuneration of directors, the role of a remuneration committee created within the (supervisory) board should essentially be to make sure that, where the (supervisory) board plays a role in the remuneration setting process (either through a power to table proposals or to make decisions, as defined by national law), this role is performed in as objective and professional a way as possible. The remuneration committee should therefore essentially make recommendations to the (supervisory) board with respect to those remuneration issues for decision by the body competent under national company law.

Given the above, the main objectives of Recommendation 2004/913/EC are to ensure transparency of remuneration practices, shareholder control on remuneration policy and individual remuneration through disclosure, the introduction of a mandatory or advisory vote on the remuneration statement and shareholder approval for share-based remuneration schemes, effective and independent non-executive supervision and at least an advisory role of the remuneration committee with regard to remuneration practices.

The shareholders' meeting plays a key role in preventing the conflict of interest of directors in determining their remuneration. Therefore, the annual general meeting shall express an advisory vote on the remuneration policy and any significant change to it. In addition, the annual general meeting shall approve beforehand any remuneration in shares (so-called stock option plans).

Article 4 Shareholders' Vote, Recommendation 2004/913/EC

4.1. Without prejudice to the role and organisation of the relevant bodies responsible for setting directors' remunerations, the remuneration policy and any significant change to the remuneration policy should be an explicit item on the agenda of the annual general meeting.

4.2. Without prejudice to the role and organisation of the relevant bodies responsible for setting directors' remunerations, the remuneration statement should be submitted to the annual general meeting of shareholders for a vote. The vote may be either mandatory or advisory.

Member States may, however, provide that such a vote will be held only if shareholders representing at least 25% of the total number of votes held by shareholders present or represented at the annual general meeting request it. This should nevertheless be without prejudice to the right for shareholders to table a resolution in accordance with national provisions.

4.3. The listed company should inform shareholders entitled to receive notice of the meeting of the intention to table a resolution approving the remuneration statement at the annual general meeting.

...

Article 6 Shareholders' Approval, Recommendation 2004/913/EC

6.1. Schemes under which directors are remunerated in shares, share options or any other right to acquire shares or to be remunerated on the basis of share price movements should be subject to the prior approval of shareholders by way of a resolution at the annual general meeting prior to their adoption. The approval should relate to the scheme in itself and not to the grant of such share-based benefits under that scheme to individual directors.

6.2. Approval by the annual general meeting should be obtained for the following:
(a) grant of share-based schemes, including share options, to directors;
(b) the determination of their maximum number and the main conditions of the granting process;
(c) the term within which options can be exercised;
(d) the conditions for any subsequent change in the exercise price of the options, if this is appropriate and legally permissible;
(e) any other long term incentive schemes for which directors are eligible and which is not offered under similar terms to all other employees.

6.3. The annual general meeting should also set the deadline within which the body responsible for directors' remuneration may award these types of compensation to individual directors.

6.4. Any substantial change in the terms and conditions of the schemes should also be subject to the approval of shareholders by way of a resolution at the annual general meeting prior to their adoption. In those cases, shareholders should be informed of the full terms of the proposed changes and should be given an explanation of the effect of the proposed changes.

6.5. If such arrangement is permissible under national law or under the Articles of Association of the listed company, any discounted option arrangement under which any rights are granted to subscribe to shares at a price lower than the market value of the share on the date when the price is determined, or the average of the market values over a number of days preceding the date when the exercise price is determined, should also receive the approval of shareholders.

6.6. Points 6.1. to 6.4. should not apply to schemes in which participation is offered on similar terms to employees of the listed company or any of its subsidiary undertaking[s] whose employees are eligible to participate in the scheme and which has been approved by the annual general meeting.

In the wake of the 2008 financial crisis, the Commission issued Recommendation 2009/385/EC complementing both Recommendation 2004/913/EC and Recommendation 2005/162/EC. In brief, this Recommendation aims at:

(i) encouraging the long-term sustainability of the company and ensuring that remuneration is based on performance; (ii) ensuring that termination payments, so-called 'golden parachutes', are not a reward for failure and that the primary purpose of termination payments is as a safety net in case of early termination of the contract; (iii) ensuring that schemes under which directors are remunerated in shares, share options or any other right to acquire shares or be remunerated on the basis of share price movements are linked to performance and long-term value creation of the company.

An important achievement in the field of the executive remuneration policies has been made by Directive 2017/828/EU of the European Parliament and of the Council of 17 May 2017 amending Directive 2007/36/EC (so-called Shareholder Rights Directive, *see* § 15.5) as regards the encouragement of long-term shareholder engagement (henceforth, Shareholder Rights Directive II).

The Shareholder Rights Directive II aims, *inter alia*, at giving to shareholders of listed companies a '*say on directors' pay*'. Indeed, shareholders of listed companies shall have the right to vote on director remuneration policy at least every four years and the vote may be binding or advisory, at the choice of the EU Member State. The remuneration policy should support company strategy. It should describe the fixed and variable components of directors' pay, including the main characteristics of pension and payments linked to the termination of a contract. In the case of variable remuneration, director performance should be assessed on both financial and non-financial criteria, where applicable. The policy should state whether clawback or any deferral or holding period applies.

Shareholders will also have the right to vote on annual remuneration reports that provide information on individual directors' pay during the previous financial year. EU countries may allow small and medium-sized enterprises to have a discussion at the general meeting as an alternative to a vote. The remuneration policy and the reports will also have to be publicly disclosed.

A reading of the Preambles to the Shareholder Rights Directive II might be more useful than going into detail.

Recitals 28–41 Directive 2017/828/EU

(28) Directors contribute to the long-term success of the company. The form and structure of directors' remuneration are matters primarily falling within the competence of the company, its relevant boards, shareholders and, where applicable, employee representatives. It is therefore important to respect the diversity of corporate governance systems within the Union, which reflect different Member States' views about the roles of companies and of bodies responsible for the determination of the remuneration policy and of the remuneration of individual directors. Since remuneration is one of the key instruments for companies to align their interests and those of their directors and in view of the crucial role of directors in companies, it is important that the remuneration policy of companies is determined in an appropriate manner by competent bodies within the company and that shareholders have the possibility to express their views regarding the remuneration policy of the company.

(29) In order to ensure that shareholders have an effective say on remuneration policy, they should be granted the right to hold a binding or advisory vote on the remuneration policy, on the basis of a clear, understandable and comprehensive overview of the company's remuneration policy. The remuneration policy should contribute to the business strategy, long-term interests and sustainability of the company and should not be linked entirely or mainly to short-term objectives. Directors' performance should be assessed using both financial and non-financial performance criteria, including, where appropriate, environmental, social and governance factors. The remuneration policy should describe the different components of directors' pay and the range of their relative proportions. It can be designed as a frame within which the pay of directors is to be held. The remuneration policy should be publicly disclosed, without delay, after the vote by the shareholders at the general meeting.

(30) In exceptional circumstances, companies may need to derogate from certain rules in the remuneration policy such as criteria for fixed or variable remuneration. Therefore, Member States should be able to allow companies to apply such temporary derogation to the applicable remuneration policy if they specify in their remuneration policy how it would be applied in certain exceptional circumstances. Exceptional circumstances should only cover situations where the derogation from the remuneration policy is necessary to serve the long-term interests and sustainability of the company as a whole or assure its viability. The remuneration report should include information on remuneration awarded under such exceptional circumstances.

(31) To ensure that the implementation of the remuneration policy is in line with that policy, shareholders should be granted the right to vote on the company's

remuneration report. In order to ensure corporate transparency, and accountability of the directors, the remuneration report should be clear and understandable and should provide a comprehensive overview of the remuneration of individual directors during the most recent financial year. Where the shareholders vote against the remuneration report, the company should explain, in the following remuneration report, how the vote of the shareholders was taken into account. However, for small and medium-sized companies, Member States should be able to provide, as an alternative to the vote on the remuneration report, for the remuneration report to be submitted to shareholders only for discussion in the annual general meeting as a separate item of the agenda. If a Member State uses this possibility, the company should explain, in the following remuneration report, in what manner the discussion at the general meeting was taken into account.

(32) In order to provide shareholders with easy access to the remuneration report, and to enable potential investors and stakeholders to be informed of directors' remuneration, the remuneration report should be published on the company's website. This should be without prejudice to the possibility of Member States also to require the publication of the report by other means, for example as part of the corporate governance statement or management report.

(33) The disclosure of individual directors' remuneration and the publication of the remuneration report are intended to provide increased corporate transparency and increased accountability of directors, as well as better shareholder oversight over directors' remuneration. This creates a necessary prerequisite for the exercise of shareholder rights and shareholder engagement in relation to remuneration. In particular, the disclosure of such information to shareholders is necessary to enable them to assess directors' remuneration and to express their views on the modalities and level of directors' pay as well as on the link between pay and performance of each individual director, in order to remedy potential situations in which the amount of remuneration of a director is not justified on the basis of his or her individual performance and the performance of the company. Publication of the remuneration report is necessary in order to enable not only shareholders, but also potential investors and stakeholders to assess directors' remuneration, to what extent that remuneration is linked to the performance of the company and how the company implements its remuneration policy in practice. The disclosure and publication of anonymised remuneration reports would not allow the achievement of those objectives.

(34) In order to increase corporate transparency, and the accountability of directors, and to enable shareholders, potential investors and stakeholders to obtain a full and reliable picture of the remuneration of each director, it is of particular importance that every element and total amount of remuneration are disclosed.

(35) In particular, in order to prevent the circumvention of the requirements laid down by this Directive by the company, to avoid any conflicts of interests and to ensure loyalty of the directors to the company, it is necessary to provide for the disclosure and the publication of the remuneration awarded or due to individual directors not only from the company itself, but also from any undertaking belonging to the same group. If remuneration

awarded or due to individual directors by undertakings belonging to the same group as the company were excluded from the remuneration report, there would be a risk that companies try to circumvent the requirements laid down by this Directive by providing directors with hidden remuneration via a controlled undertaking. In such a case, shareholders would not have a full and reliable picture of the remuneration granted to the directors by the company and the objectives pursued by this Directive would not be achieved.

(36) In order to provide a complete overview of directors' remuneration, the remuneration report should also disclose, where applicable, the amount of remuneration granted on the basis of the family situation of individual directors. The remuneration report should therefore also cover, where applicable, remuneration components such as family or child allowance. However, because personal data which refer to the family situation of individual directors or special categories of personal data within the meaning of Regulation (EU) 2016/679 of the European Parliament and of the Council (4) are particularly sensitive and require specific protection, the report should disclose only the amount of the remuneration and not the ground on which it was granted.

(37) Under this Directive, personal data included in the remuneration report should be processed for the purposes of increasing corporate transparency as regards directors' remuneration with the view to enhancing directors' accountability and shareholder oversight of directors' remuneration. This is without prejudice to Member State law providing for the processing of the personal data of directors for other purposes.

(38) It is essential to assess the remuneration and the performance of directors not only annually but also over an appropriate time period to enable shareholders, potential investors and stakeholders to assess properly whether the remuneration rewards long-term performance and to measure the middle-to-long-term evolution in directors' performance and remuneration, in particular in relation to company performance. In many cases, it is possible only after several years to evaluate whether the remuneration granted was in line with the long-term interests of the company. In particular the granting of long-term incentives may cover periods of up to seven to ten years and may be combined with deferral periods of several years.

(39) It is also important to be able to assess the remuneration of a director over the entire period of his or her directorship on a particular company's board. In the Union, directors remain on a company board for a period of six years on average, although in some Member States that period exceeds eight years.

(40) In order to limit interference with the directors' rights to privacy and to the protection of their personal data, public disclosure by companies of directors' personal data included in the remuneration report should be limited to 10 years. That period is consistent with other periods laid down by Union law related to the public disclosure of corporate governance documents. For example, under Article 4 of Directive 2004/109/EC of the European Parliament and the Council (5), the management report and the corporate governance statements must remain publicly available as part of the annual financial report for at least 10 years. There is a clear interest in having various types of corporate governance reports, including the remuneration report, available for 10 years, so as to provide the overall state of a company to shareholders and stakeholders.

(41) At the end of the 10-year period, the company should remove any personal data from the remuneration report or cease to disclose the remuneration report publicly as a whole. Following that period access to such personal data could be necessary for other purposes, such as in order to exercise legal actions. The provisions on remuneration should be without prejudice to the full exercise of fundamental rights guaranteed by the Treaties, in particular Article 153(5) of the Treaty on the Functioning of the European Union, general principles of national contract and labour law, Union and national law regarding involvement and the general responsibilities of the administrative, management and supervisory bodies of the company concerned, and the rights, where applicable, of the social partners to conclude and enforce collective agreements, in accordance with national law and customs. The provisions on remuneration should also, where applicable, be without prejudice to national law on the representation of employees in the administrative, management or supervisory body.

FURTHER READING

Guido Ferrarini and Niamh Moloney, 'Executive Remuneration and Corporate Governance in the EU: Convergence, Divergence, and Reform Perspectives', 1 *ECFR* 251–339 (2004), also in Guido Ferrarini, Klaus J. Hopt, Jaap Winter, and Eddy Wymeersch (eds.), *Reforming Company and Takeover Law in Europe* 267–347 (Oxford University Press, 2004).

Kimberly Crook, 'Accounting for Share-based Remuneration', in Guido Ferrarini, Klaus J. Hopt, Jaap Winter, and Eddy Wymeersch (eds.), *Reforming Company and Takeover Law in Europe* 347–373 (Oxford University Press, 2004).

Cornelis de Groot, 'The Level and Composition of Executive Remuneration: A View from the Netherlands', 3 *ECL* 11–17 (2006).

Cornelis de Groot, 'Executive Directors' Remuneration', 3 *ECL* 62–63 (2006).

Jennifer G. Hill, 'Regulating Executive Remuneration: International Developments in the Post-scandal Era', 3 *ECL* 64–74 (2006).

Sanjai Bhagat and Roberta Romano, 'Reforming Executive Compensation: Simplicity, Transparency and Committing to the Long-term', 7 *ECFR* 273–296 (2010).

Eilís Ferran, 'New Regulation of Remuneration in the Financial Sector in the EU', 9 *ECFR* 1–34 (2012).

Tom Dijkhuizen, 'On the Remuneration of Directors of Listed Companies (Again)', 11 *ECL* 199–200 (2014).

Christoph Van der Elst, 'Shareholders Holding the Reins on Remuneration: The European Say on Pay', 14 *ECL* 114–120 (2017).

Christoph Van der Elst and Anne Lafarre, 'Shareholder Voice on Executive Pay: A Decade of Dutch Say on Pay', 18 *EBOR* 51–83 (2017).

Tobias H. Tröger and Uwe Walz, 'Does Say on Pay Matter? Evidence from Germany', 16 *ECFR* 381–414 (2019).

14.8 Conflict of Interests: Financial Assistance as Example

As already mentioned, the potential for conflict of interest of management is particularly high as regards the nomination and remuneration of directors.

Therefore, the presence of independent non-executive or supervisory directors in committees advising on such matters is strongly recommended as a means of preventing conflict of interests.

As with remuneration policies, in other similar situations directors may tend to pursue their own interest to the detriment or in disregard of the interest of the company they manage: all these situations are addressed as conflicts of interests.

Notwithstanding that one of the main goals of good corporate governance is to prevent conflict of interests, as the CJEU pointed out in *Rabobank* – a case examined in § 14.9 – the general issue of conflict of interests with the company falls outside the normative framework of ECL. Nevertheless, it is possible to point to at least one set of provisions – other than those included in the recommendations examined in the foregoing paragraphs – that aims at preventing conflicts of interests in case the directors, on behalf of the company, advance funds or make loans or provide security with a view to the acquisition of the company's own shares by a third party, or in particular by individual members of the administrative or management body of the company.

Article 64(2–5) Directive 2017/1132/EU

2. The transactions shall take place under the responsibility of the administrative or management body at fair market conditions, especially with regard to interest received by the company and with regard to security provided to the company for the loans and advances referred to in paragraph 1.

   The credit standing of the third party or, in the case of multiparty transactions, of each counterparty thereto shall have been duly investigated.
3. The transactions shall be submitted by the administrative or management body to the general meeting for prior approval, whereby the general meeting shall act in accordance with the rules for a quorum and a majority laid down in Article 83.

   The administrative or management body shall present a written report to the general meeting, indicating:

   (a) the reasons for the transaction;
   (b) the interest of the company in entering into such a transaction;
   (c) the conditions on which the transaction is entered into;
   (d) the risks involved in the transaction for the liquidity and solvency of the company; and
   (e) the price at which the third party is to acquire the shares.

   That report shall be submitted to the register for publication in accordance with Article 16.
4. The aggregate financial assistance granted to third parties shall at no time result in the reduction of the net assets below the amount specified in Article 56(1) and (2), taking into account also any reduction of the net assets that may have occurred through the

acquisition, by the company or on behalf of the company, of its own shares in accordance with Article 60(1).

The company shall include, among the liabilities in the balance sheet, a reserve, unavailable for distribution, of the amount of the aggregate financial assistance.

5. Where a third party by means of financial assistance from a company acquires that company's own shares within the meaning of Article 60(1) or subscribes for shares issued in the course of an increase in the subscribed capital, such acquisition or subscription shall be made at a fair price.

Article 65 Directive 2017/1132/EU

In cases where individual members of the administrative or management body of the company being party to a transaction referred to in Article 64(1), or of the administrative or management body of a parent undertaking within the meaning of Article 22 Directive 2013/34/EU or such parent undertaking itself, or individuals acting in their own name but on behalf of the members of such bodies or on behalf of such undertaking, are counterparties to such a transaction, Member States shall ensure through adequate safeguards that such [a] transaction does not conflict with the company's best interests.

The reading of such provisions is useful to point out the general ideas of ECL for preventing conflicts of interests.

First of all, transactions in which directors could have a conflict of interest shall not be undertaken by single members, rather by the board in its entirety, and especially when independent non-executive directors are also part of the board.

Second, in the field of financial assistance, as well as for other transactions with related parties, a so-called 'whitewash procedure', whereby the shareholders authorise transactions that would otherwise be void, shall be followed. In view of obtaining an authorisation from the shareholders' meeting, the board is forced to disclose in writing: (a) the reasons for the transaction; (b) the interest of the company in entering into such a transaction; (c) the conditions on which the transaction is entered into; (d) the risks involved in the transaction for the liquidity and solvency of the company; and (e) the price at which the third party is to acquire the shares. On the one hand, the written report permits the shareholders' meeting to fully understand the reasons and conditions of the proposed transactions and to vote accordingly. On the other hand, in case the majority shareholder is also in a conflict of interest and authorises a transaction conflicting with the interests of the company as a whole, minority shareholders may challenge the validity of such a transaction.

In addition, in case the shares are sold from the corporate treasury or issued as new shares, directors are required to show that such acquisition or subscription is made at a *fair price*. In this case the company is a counterparty twice to the transaction because it sells or issues the shares, as well as advances funds or makes loans or provides security for the acquisition or subscription. Therefore, it is not sufficient that directors show the price at which the third party is to acquire the shares, rather they must assess that this price is fair.

Moreover, when the directors themselves are counterparties to the transaction, not only shall they show that the company has a *positive interest* in entering into such a transaction, but they are required to show that this does not conflict with the company's *best interests*. Although assessing what the company's best interests are may be difficult, this requirement seems a useful tool in case minority shareholders wish to challenge the validity of the transaction.

More recently, the same Shareholder Rights Directive II mentioned earlier (§ 14.7) has tackled the issue of transactions with related parties in listed companies. According to the definition made by IAS/IFRS Principles (referred to by the same Shareholder Rights Directive II), a related party is a person or an entity that is related to the reporting entity: a person or a close member of that person's family is related to a reporting entity if that person has control, joint control, or significant influence over the entity or is a member of its key management personnel.

The Shareholder Rights Directive II requires that in any material transaction (to be defined by each EU Member State) between a listed company and a related party: (a) the transaction must be publicly announced; (b) an independent report may have to be published assessing whether the transaction is fair and reasonable from the company's perspective and for the other shareholders; (c) the transaction must be approved by shareholders or the board (a 'whitewash procedure').

Recitals 42–44 Directive 2017/828/EU

(42) Transactions with related parties may cause prejudice to companies and their shareholders, as they may give the related party the opportunity to appropriate value belonging to the company. Thus, adequate safeguards for the protection of companies' and shareholders' interests are of importance. For this reason Member States should ensure that material related party transactions are submitted to approval by the shareholders or by the administrative or supervisory body according to procedures that prevent the related party from taking advantage of its position and provide adequate protection for the interests of the company and of the shareholders who are not a related party, including minority shareholders.

(43) Where the related party transaction involves a director or a shareholder, that director or shareholder should not take part in the approval or vote. However, Member States should have the possibility to allow the shareholder who is a related party to take part in the vote provided that national law foresees appropriate safeguards in relation to

the voting process to protect the interests of companies and of the shareholders who are not a related party, including minority shareholders, such as for example a higher majority threshold for the approval of transactions.

(44) Companies should publicly announce material transactions no later than at the time of the conclusion of the transaction, identifying the related party, the date and the value of the transaction and any other information that is necessary to assess the fairness of the transaction. Public disclosure of such transaction, for example on a company's website or by other easily available means, is needed in order to allow shareholders, creditors, employees and other interested parties to be informed of potential impacts that such transactions may have on the value of the company. The precise identification of the related party is necessary to better assess the risks implied by the transaction and to enable challenges to the transaction, including by means of legal action.

FURTHER READING

Klaus J. Hopt, 'Trusteeship and Conflicts of Interest in Corporate, Banking and Agency Law: Toward Common Legal Principles for Intermediaries in the Modern Service-oriented Society', in Guido Ferrarini, Klaus J. Hopt, Jaap Winter, and Eddy Wymeersch (eds.), *Reforming Company and Takeover Law in Europe* 51–89 (Oxford University Press, 2004).

Luca Enriques, Gerard Hertig, Hideki Kanda, and Marianna Pargendler, 'Related-party Transactions', in John Armour, Luca Enriques et al., *The Anatomy of Corporate Law: A Comparative and Functional Approach* 145–171 (Oxford University Press, 3rd ed., 2017).

John Armour, Luca Enriques, Marianna Pargendler, and Wolf-Georg Ringe, 'Beyond the Anatomy', in John Armour, Luca Enriques et al., *The Anatomy of Corporate Law: A Comparative and Functional Approach* 305–312 (Oxford University Press, 3rd ed., 2017).

Irene C.P. Groenland, 'Related Party Transactions in the Revised Shareholders' Rights Directive: The EU Perspective and Implementation in National Law', 16 *ECL*, 44–49 (2019).

14.9 *Rabobank* Case

In *Rabobank* (Case C-104/96, *Coöperatieve Rabobank 'Vecht en Plassengebied' BA* v. *Erik Aarnoud Minderhoud*, [1997] ECR I-07211) the Hoge Raad der Nederlanden (Supreme Court of the Netherlands) referred three questions to the Court raised in proceedings brought by the Coöperatieve Rabobank 'Vecht en Plassengebied' BA ('*Rabobank*') financier of the holding company Holland Data Groep BV ('*HDG*'), of five of its operating companies and of Mediasafe BV ('*Mediasafe*'), against the receiver of Mediasafe on the subject of his challenge to the validity of an agreement to offset debit balances against credit balances, entered into between HDG, the five companies, and Mediasafe on the one hand, and Rabobank on the other.

On 23 October 1989 Rabobank concluded an agreement with HDG and the five operating companies concerning the calculation of interest on joint accounts and the offsetting of debit balances against credit balances under which the companies were to be jointly and severally liable to Rabobank.

On 21 November 1989, HDG and Stichting Nieuwegein (Nieuwegein Foundation) set up Mediasafe, in which HDG held 99 shares and Stichting Nieuwegein 1 share. HDG was appointed sole director and two commissioners were appointed, on a proposal from Stichting Nieuwegein, to oversee the management and the general course of business of Mediasafe on behalf of Stichting Nieuwegein.

On 11 December 1989, Rabobank concluded another agreement concerning the offsetting of debit balances against credit balances, the substance and scope of which was the same as that of 23 October 1989. Mediasafe was represented by HDG, its sole director. Under that agreement all the companies in the HDG group, including Mediasafe, declared themselves jointly and severally liable for their debts to Rabobank.

On 22 May 1990, Mediasafe was declared bankrupt. Mr Minderhoud was appointed receiver of the company. At the time Mediasafe's account with Rabobank showed a credit balance of HFL 447,117.60.

By letter of 5 June 1990, Rabobank informed the receiver that, in accordance with the agreement of 11 December 1989 and Article 53 of the Faillessementswet (Bankruptcy Law), it proposed to offset credit balances against debit balances of the current accounts of the other companies in HDG in respect of which Mediasafe was joint and several co-debtor. Rabobank stated that, once the balances had been offset in this way, Mediasafe's credit balance with Rabobank at the date of the bankruptcy stood at HFL 67,337.36.

By the judgment of 31 July 1990, HDG and its five other operating companies were declared bankrupt.

The receiver sought payment from Rabobank of the difference between Mediasafe's credit balance before and after this offsetting operation, which amounted to HFL 379,780.24. He argued that the agreement to offset balances of 11 December 1989 could not be given effect because there was a conflict of interests within the meaning of Articles 12(3) and (4) of Mediasafe's statutes and Article 2:256 of the Netherlands Civil Code between Mediasafe and HDG – which concluded the agreements, *inter alia*, on behalf of Mediasafe in its capacity as sole director. Consequently, HDG had no authority to represent Mediasafe when the agreement was concluded.

Article 2:146 of the Netherlands Civil Code, which applies to 'naamloze vennootschappen' (public limited-liability companies), and Article 2:256, which applies to 'besloten vennootschappen met beperkte aansprakelijkheid' (private limited-liability companies), provides that where there is a conflict of interests between a company and the directors authorised to represent it when a legal instrument is being concluded, that instrument can only be concluded by the commissioners of that company. That statutory provision was also incorporated in Article 12(3) and (4) of Mediasafe's statutes.

By the judgment of 4 August 1993, the Arrondissementsrechtbank (District Court), Utrecht, held that, by reason of a conflict of interests within the meaning of Article 2:256 of the Civil Code, HDG had no authority to conclude, on behalf of Mediasafe, the agreement to offset balances with Rabobank and took the view that the latter, as a professional organisation, had constructive notice of that conflict of interest. The Arrondissementsrechtbank accordingly upheld the receiver's claim.

That judgment was upheld by the Gerechtshof (Regional Court of Appeal), Amsterdam, on the same grounds.

Before the Hoge Raad der Nederlanden, Rabobank argued that a conflict of interests within the meaning of Article 2:256 of the Civil Code could only exist in the case of an instrument concluded between a company and its director. The Hoge Raad rejected that argument, thus recognising the applicability of that provision to situations in which there was an indirect conflict of interests. However, it questions whether for a company to rely on Article 2:256 of the Civil Code as against a third party might not be incompatible with Article 9 of the First Directive (now Article 10 Directive 2009/101/EC), under which,

Article 9 Directive 2017/1132/EU

1. Acts done by the organs of the company shall be binding upon it even if those acts are not within the objects of the company, unless such acts exceed the powers that the law confers or allows to be conferred on those organs.

   However, Member States may provide that the company shall not be bound where such acts are outside the objects of the company, if it proves that the third party knew that the act was outside those objects or could not in view of the circumstances have been unaware of it; disclosure of the statutes shall not of itself be sufficient proof thereof.
2. The limits on the powers of the organs of the company, arising under the statutes or from a decision of the competent organs, may not be relied on as against third parties, even if they have been disclosed.
3. If the national law provides that authority to represent a company may, in derogation from the legal rules governing the subject, be conferred by the statutes on a single person or on several persons acting jointly, that law may provide that such a provision in the statutes may be relied on as against third parties on condition that it relates to the general power of representation; the question whether such a provision in the statutes can be relied on as against third parties shall be governed by Article 16.

Taking the view that Article 2:256 of the Civil Code should be interpreted in the light of the provisions of the First Directive, the Hoge Raad der Nederlanden referred the following questions to the Court for a preliminary ruling:

Case C-104/96, Coöperatieve Rabobank 'Vecht en Plassengebied' BA v. Erik Aarnoud Minderhoud, [1997] ECR I-07211, § 15

(1) Is it consistent with the First Directive for a company to be allowed to rely, as against a third party with whom a director generally authorized to represent the company has entered into a transaction on its behalf, on the fact that the director lacked authority on the ground that the transaction involved a conflict of interests between him and the company?
(2) Is Question 1 to be answered in the affirmative only if the third party had knowledge of the conflict of interests at the time when the transaction took place, or could reasonably have been expected to have knowledge of that conflict of interests on the basis of the information available to him at the time?
(3) Is Question 1 to be answered in the affirmative only if the conflict of interests at the time when the transaction took place was so plain that no reasonable third party could have believed that no such conflict existed?

The CJEU concluded that the rules governing the enforceability as against third parties of acts done by members of company organs in circumstances where there is a conflict of interests with the company fall outside the normative framework of the First Company Law Directive (now Directive 2017/1132/EU) and are matters for the national legislature. Furthermore the CJEU adds the following:

Case C-104/96, Coöperatieve Rabobank 'Vecht en Plassengebied' BA v. Erik Aarnoud Minderhoud, [1997] ECR I-07211, §§ 25–28

25 This conclusion is, moreover, confirmed by the proposal for a Fifth Directive to coordinate the safeguards which, for the protection of the interests of members and others, are required by Member States of companies within the meaning of the second paragraph of Article 58 of the EEC Treaty, as regards the structure of sociétés anonymes and the powers and obligations of their organs (Journal Officiel 1972 C 131, p. 49; OJ 1983 C 240, p. 2).
26 Article 10(1) of that proposal for a Fifth Directive provided that every agreement to which the company was party and in which a member of the management organ or of the supervisory organ, was to have an interest, even if only indirect, must be authorised by the supervisory organ at least.
27 Article 10(4) of the proposal for a Fifth Directive provided, further:

'Want of authorization by the supervisory organ or irregularity in the decision giving authorization shall not be adduced as against third parties save where the company proves that the third party was aware of the want of authorization or of the irregularity in the decision, or that in view of the circumstances he could not have been unaware thereof.'

28 Accordingly the answer to the question referred to the Court must be that the rules governing the enforceability as against third parties of acts done by members of company organs in circumstances where there is a conflict of interests with the company fall outside the normative framework of the First Directive and are matters for the national legislature.

14.10 Directors' Liability

The SE Statute stipulates that all members of the organs of an SE shall be liable for loss or damage sustained by the SE following any breach of the legal, statutory or other obligations inherent in their duties. However, except for the case where liability arises as consequence of members of an organ divulging confidential information during their office or after this is ceased (Article 49 Regulation 2001/2157/EC), the SE Statute does not cover the field of civil liability; therefore, civil liability of members shall be regulated in accordance with the provisions applicable to public limited-liability companies in the Member State in which the SE's registered office is situated (Article 51 Regulation 2001/2157/EC).

ECL only requires the Member States to cover the civil liability of members of the administrative, management and supervisory organs for drawing up and publishing the financial statements and the management report.

Article 33 Responsibility and Liability for Drawing Up and Publishing the Financial Statements and the Management Report, Directive 2013/34/EU

1. Member States shall ensure that the members of the administrative, management and supervisory bodies of an undertaking, acting within the competences assigned to them by national law, have collective responsibility for ensuring that:
   (a) the annual financial statements, the management report and, when provided separately, the corporate governance statement; and
   (b) the consolidated financial statements, consolidated management reports and, when provided separately, the consolidated corporate governance statement, are drawn up and published in accordance with the requirements of this Directive and, where applicable, with the international accounting standards adopted in accordance with Regulation (EC) No 1606/2002.
2. Member States shall ensure that their laws, regulations and administrative provisions on liability, at least towards the undertaking, apply to the members of the administrative, management and supervisory bodies of the undertakings for breach of the duties referred to in paragraph 1.

FURTHER READING

Holger Fleischer, 'The Responsibility of the Management and of the Board and its Enforcement', in Guido Ferrarini, Klaus J. Hopt, Jaap Winter, and Eddy Wymeersch (eds.), *Reforming Company and Takeover Law in Europe* 373–417 (Oxford University Press, 2004).

14.11 The Statutory Audit

As mentioned earlier, statutory audits are not only related to annual and consolidated financial statements, but rather have a much broader relevance in the corporate governance of companies. In addition to the audit report, a document where auditors express their opinion on the annual and consolidated financial statements, auditors are entrusted with other functions contributing to better corporate governance.

After the financial scandals of the early millennium, where one of the so-called big five auditing firms had to dismiss the licence (Arthur Andersen) and in response to the US Sarbanes–Oxley Act of 2002, the EU institutions adopted a new, more comprehensive Directive on statutory audits of annual accounts and consolidated accounts. As already mentioned, Directive 2006/43/EC or the so-called new Eighth Directive – last amended by Directive 2014/56/EU of 16 April 2014 – also lays down (in addition to the conditions for the approval and registration of persons that carry out statutory audits) the rules on independence, objectivity and professional ethics applying to those persons, and the framework for their public oversight.

Under the new Eighth Directive, only qualified auditors, having an adequate knowledge of matters such as company law, fiscal law, and social law, shall carry on statutory audits (Recital 7 Directive 2006/43/EC). Auditors shall be independent professionals, subject to professional ethics, and keeping strict confidentiality on the information acquired by their clients (Recitals 9–11 Directive 2006/43/EC). The statutory auditor or audit firm should be appointed by the general meeting of shareholders or members of the audited entity; however, in order to protect the independence of the auditor, a dismissal should be possible only where there are proper grounds (Recital 22 Directive 2006/43/EC).

In addition, the new Eighth Directive provides stricter rules applicable to the statutory audit of public-interest entities, such as listed companies, banks, insurance companies, undertakings for the collective investment in transferable securities (UCIT), and so on: auditors for these entities shall meet higher standards and, to reinforce their independence, the key audit partner auditing such entities shall rotate over time (Recitals 23–27 Directive 2006/43/EC). As for the consolidated accounts of listed companies, also with regards to auditing, the

EC Commission shall adopt international standards and issue recommendations on the auditors' civil liability (Recitals 13–15, 19 Directive 2006/43/EC). In 2014, the EU institutions approved a broad amendment to the new Eighth Directive. The grounds for such amendments are expressed as follows:

Recitals 1–2 Directive 2014/56/EU

(1) ... it is necessary to further harmonise those rules at Union level in order to allow for greater transparency and predictability of the requirements applying to such persons and to enhance their independence and objectivity in the performance of their tasks. It is also important to increase the minimum level of convergence with respect to the auditing standards on the basis of which the statutory audits are carried out. Moreover, in order to reinforce investor protection, it is important to strengthen public oversight of statutory auditors and audit firms by enhancing the independence of Union public oversight authorities and conferring on them adequate powers, including investigative powers and the power to impose sanctions, with a view to detecting, deterring and preventing infringements of the applicable rules in the context of the provision by statutory auditors and audit firms of auditing services.

(2) Because of the significant public relevance of public-interest entities, which arises from the scale and complexity of their business or from the nature of their business, the credibility of the audited financial statements of public-interest entities needs to be reinforced. Consequently, the special provisions for the statutory audits of public-interest entities set out in Directive 2006/43/EC have been further developed in Regulation (EU) No 537/2014 of the European Parliament and of the Council. The provisions on statutory audits of public-interest entities laid down in this Directive should be applicable to statutory auditors and audit firms only in so far as they carry out statutory audits of such entities.

On the one hand, Regulation 2014/537/EU of the European Parliament and of the Council of 16 April 2014, *on specific requirements regarding statutory audit of public-interest entities* and repealing Commission Decision 2005/909/EC, provided uniform legislation on statutory audits of public-interest entities. The grounds for delivering such a Regulation are further clarified as follows:

Recital 5 Regulation 2014/537/EU

(5) It is important to lay down detailed rules with a view to ensuring that the statutory audits of public-interest entities are of adequate quality and are carried out by statutory auditors and audit firms subject to stringent requirements. A common regulatory approach should enhance the integrity, independence, objectivity, responsibility, transparency and reliability of statutory auditors and audit firms carrying out statutory audits

of public-interest entities, contributing to the quality of statutory audits in the Union, thus to the smooth functioning of the internal market, while achieving a high level of consumer and investor protection. The development of a separate act for public-interest entities should also ensure consistent harmonisation and uniform application of the rules and thus contribute to a more effective functioning of the internal market. These strict requirements should be applicable to statutory auditors and audit firms only insofar as they carry out statutory audits of public-interest entities

On the other hand, Directive 2014/56/EU, amending the new Eighth Directive aimed at enhancing the credibility and transparency of the quality assurance reviews, thereby enhancing the powers of public oversight authorities over auditors and audit firms. The grounds for such enhancement of powers is clarified as follows:

Recitals 14 and 18 Directive 2014/56/EU

(14) In order to enhance the credibility and transparency of the quality assurance reviews performed in the Union, Member States' quality assurance systems should be governed by the competent authorities designated by the Member States to ensure public oversight of statutory auditors and audit firms. Quality assurance reviews are designed to prevent or address potential deficiencies in the manner in which statutory audits are carried out. In order to ensure that the quality assurance reviews are sufficiently comprehensive, the competent authorities, when carrying out such reviews, should take into account the scale and complexity of the activity of the statutory auditors and the audit firms ...

(18) The public oversight of statutory auditors and audit firms encompasses the approval and registration of statutory auditors and audit firms, the adoption of standards in respect of professional ethics and internal quality control of audit firms, continuing education, and the systems of quality assurance, investigation and sanctions for statutory auditors and audit firms. In order to enhance the transparency of auditor oversight and to allow for greater accountability, each Member State should designate a single authority to be in charge of public oversight of statutory auditors and audit firms. The independence of such public oversight authorities from the audit profession is a core prerequisite for the integrity, efficiency and orderly functioning of public oversight of statutory auditors and audit firms. Consequently, the public oversight authorities should be governed by non-practitioners and Member States should establish independent and transparent procedures for the selection of such non-practitioners.

In brief, public oversight authorities should be vested with sufficient powers to fulfil their tasks in an effective manner, including the power to bring a claim before a national court for the dismissal of the statutory auditor (Recitals 21–23 Directive 2014/56/EU). Furthermore, public authorities shall be empowered to issue administrative pecuniary sanctions, both on statutory auditors, audit firms, and public-interest entities in case of identified infringements of the rules (Recitals 15–16 Directive 2014/56/EU). To this end, national legislation shall encourage whistleblowers to alert the public authorities to possible infringements of provisions of both Regulation 2014/537/EU and Directive 2014/56/ EU (Recital 17 Directive 2014/56/EU).

As already mentioned, the new Eighth Directive expresses the opportunity for the EU Commission to issue recommendations on auditors' civil liability (Recitals 13–15, 19 Directive 2006/43/EC). In its Recommendation of 5 June 2008, the EU Commission has proposed the *limitation* of the civil liability of statutory auditors and audit firms, the Commission, based on the following grounds:

Recitals 3–6 Commission Recommendation of 5 June 2008

(3) Since unlimited joint and several liability may deter audit firms and networks from entering the international audit market for listed companies in the Community, there is little prospect of new audit networks emerging which are in a position to conduct statutory audits of such companies.

(4) As a consequence, the liability of auditors and audit firms, including group auditors, carrying out statutory audits of listed companies should be limited. However, any limitation on liability is not justified in cases of intentional breach of professional duties on the part of an auditor and should not apply in such cases. Nor should such a limitation prejudice the right of any injured party to be fairly compensated.

(5) In view of the considerable variations between civil liability systems in the Member States, it is appropriate at this stage that each Member State be able to choose the method of limitation which it considers to be the most suitable for its civil liability system.

(6) Member States should accordingly be able to determine under national law a cap in respect of auditors' liability. Alternatively Member States should be able to establish under national law a system of proportionate liability according to which statutory auditors and audit firms are liable only to the extent of their contribution to the damage caused, without being jointly and severally liable with other parties. In the Member States where any claims against statutory auditors might be brought only by the audited company and not by individual shareholders or any other third parties, Member States should also be able to allow the company, its shareholders and the auditor to determine the limitation of the auditor's liability, subject to appropriate safeguards for investors in the company audited.

The EU Commission proposes various methods as a means to limit the civil liability of auditors, among which Member States may choose.

Articles 5–6 Commission Recommendation of 5 June 2008

5. Member States should take measures to limit liability. For that purpose, it is recommended that any one or more of the following methods in particular be used:
   (a) establishment of a maximum financial amount or of a formula allowing for the calculation of such an amount;
   (b) establishment of a set of principles by virtue of which a statutory auditor or an audit firm is not liable beyond its actual contribution to the loss suffered by a claimant and is accordingly not jointly and severally liable with other wrongdoers;
   (c) provision allowing any company to be audited and the statutory auditor or audit firm to determine a limitation of liability in an agreement.
6. Where liability is limited by agreement as referred to in point 5(c), Member States should ensure that all the following conditions are met:
   (a) the agreement is subject to judicial review;
   (b) with regard to the company to be audited, the limitation is decided collectively by the members of the administrative, management and supervisory bodies referred to in Article 50b of Council Directive 78/660/EEC (2), or, in the case of a group audit, in Article 36a of Council Directive 83/349/EEC (3), and such a decision is approved by the shareholders of the company to be audited;
   (c) the limitation and any modification thereof are published in the notes to the accounts of the audited company.

The limitation of auditors' liability has raised an intense debate among legal scholars, some of whom do not support the idea that auditing firms should benefit from a limitation of liability.

FURTHER READING

John C. Coffee, Jr, 'Gatekeeper Failure and Reform: The Challenge of Fashioning Relevant Reforms', in Guido Ferrarini, Klaus J. Hopt, Jaap Winter, and Eddy Wymeersch (eds.), *Reforming Company and Takeover Law in Europe* 455–507 (Oxford University Press, 2004).

Werner F. Ebke, 'Corporate Governance and Auditor Independence: The Battle of the Private Versus Public Interest', in Guido Ferrarini, Klaus J. Hopt, Jaap Winter, and Eddy Wymeersch (eds.), *Reforming Company and Takeover Law in Europe* 507–539 (Oxford University Press, 2004).

Hans Beckman and Eva C.A. Nass, 'Auditors' Liability in the European Union', 4 *ECL* 103–108 (2007).

Cláudio Flores, 'New Trends in Auditor Liability', 12 *EBOR* 415–436 (2011).

Paolo Giudici, 'Auditors' Multi-layered Liability Regime', 13 *EBOR* 501–555 (2012).

Lise Kolding Foged-Ladefoged and Erik Werlauff, 'Limitation of Auditors' Liability', 11 *ECL* 271–275 (2014).

15

General Meeting

15.1 The Case for Increasing Shareholder Powers?

In its 2003 Action Plan, the EU Commission proposed various actions to increase shareholders' rights, as a means of enhancing corporate governance in Europe.

The relevant part of the Action Plan reads as follows:

Modernising Company Law and Enhancing Corporate Governance in the European Union – A Plan to Move Forward (2003)

3.1.2 Strengthening Shareholders' Rights

Access to Information

Shareholders of listed companies should be provided with electronic facilities to access the relevant information in advance of General Meetings. This issue is currently addressed by the Proposal for a Transparency Directive, which essentially enables listed companies to use electronic means to inform their shareholders and contains specific provisions guaranteeing a timely access to regulated information when securities are listed in another Member State than the home Member State. The Commission considers this solution as a significant and proportionate first step, which does not preclude the adoption of further measures (which would generally require listed companies to use electronic means to inform their shareholders) in the medium term, if this looks desirable in the light of the implementation of the Transparency Directive (which itself contains a revision clause).

Other Shareholders' Rights

There is a need for enhancing the exercise of a series of shareholders' rights in listed companies (right to ask questions, to table resolutions, to vote in absentia, to participate in general meetings via electronic means). These facilities should be offered to shareholders across the EU, and specific problems relating to cross-border voting should be solved urgently. The Commission considers that the necessary framework should be developed in a Directive, since an effective exercise of these rights requires a number of legal difficulties to be solved. In view of the important benefits expected from such a framework, the Commission regards the relevant proposal as a priority for the short term.

Shareholder Democracy

Strengthening shareholders' rights should be based essentially on (a) the provision of comprehensive information on what the various existing rights are and how they can be exercised and (b) the development of the facilities necessary to make sure that these existing rights can be effectively exercised. This approach is fully consistent with the OECD Principles of Corporate Governance.

The Commission considers that there is a strong medium to long term case for aiming to establish a real shareholder democracy in the EU. The Comparative Study of Corporate Governance Codes relevant to the EU evidenced that corporate governance codes tend to support the one share/one vote principle, although many codes favour some flexibility in this respect. The hardest line is taken by the codes issued by bodies affiliated with investors, which clearly do not support the issuance of shares with reduced or no voting rights. The Commission nevertheless observes that any initiative in this direction, which would give further effect to the principle of proportionality between capital and control advocated by the High Level Group in its First Report on issues related to take-over bids, requires prior study. The Commission therefore intends to undertake a study, in the short to medium term, on the consequences which such an approach would entail.

It should be noted that, notwithstanding that the US corporate governance model is traditionally management-oriented, in contrast to the EU model which is more shareholder-oriented, influential American scholars, after Enron, have also claimed that, in the US, sound corporate governance requires increasing shareholder powers.

Lucian Arye Bebchuk, 'The Case for Increasing Shareholder Power', 118 *Harv. L. Rev.* 833–914, at 833–834 (2005)

This paper reconsiders the basic allocation of power between management and shareholders in publicly traded companies. US corporate law has long precluded shareholders in such companies from directly intervening in any major corporate decisions. I argue that the case for such insulation is weak, and I put forward a regime in which shareholders have the power to initiate, and approve by vote, major corporate decisions.

Providing shareholders with the power to intervene can significantly address important governance problems that have long occupied the attention of corporate law scholars and financial economists. In particular, shareholder power to make 'rules-of-the-game' decisions – to amend the corporate charter or change the state of incorporation – would ensure that corporate governance arrangements change over time in ways that serve shareholder interests. Shareholder power to make 'game-ending' decisions – to merge, sell all assets, or dissolve – would address managers' excessive tendency to retain their independence. Finally, shareholder power to make 'scaling-down' decisions – to contract the company's size by ordering a cash or in-kind distribution – would address problems of empire building and free cash flow. A regime with shareholder power to intervene could greatly improve corporate governance.

Bebchuk's paper has stimulated a wide debate – especially among American scholars – largely oriented towards a law and economics approach on company law matters.

Iman Anabtawi, 'Some Skepticism About Increasing Shareholder Power', 53 *UCLA L. Rev.* 561–579, at 561–562 (2007)

In the shareholder power debate over how best to apportion corporate decision-making among directors and officers, on the one hand, and shareholders, on the other hand, shareholder primacists are gaining ground. According to shareholder primacy theory, shareholders of the modern publicly held corporation are principals, and managers are their agents in running the firm. Because of the separation of ownership and control in large corporations, however, managers' interests are not fully aligned with those of shareholders. In particular, shareholder primacists contend that shareholders would like managers to maximize shareholder value, but managers are unlikely to do so because they generally own only a small percentage of their companies' stock and therefore do not bear the full costs of their actions. Increasing shareholder power would, according to shareholder primacists, go a long way toward solving the agency problem between shareholders and managers.

On the other side of the debate are director primacists – those who argue in favor of vesting primary decision-making authority in a firm's board of directors.

In Stephen Bainbridge's director primacy theory, for example, the board of directors is a mechanism for solving the organizational design problem that arises when one views the firm as a nexus of contracts among various factors of production, each with different interests and asymmetrical information. The board of directors provides an efficient central decision-maker within this scheme. Centralizing corporate decision-making in a board of directors, however, necessitates conferring upon it considerable discretion, which, in turn, implies limiting shareholder power.

... This Article disputes the characterization of shareholders as having interests that are fundamentally in harmony with one another. While the conception of shareholders may once have been an accurate generalization, it no longer reflects the pattern of share ownership in US public companies. Pitted against shareholders' common interest in enhancing share value are significant private interests. Take, for example, a hedge fund shareholder that is about to raise capital for a new fund. As part of its marketing efforts, it wants to show impressive returns on its prior funds. To generate such returns, the hedge fund is likely to favor policies by the firms in which it invests that produce short-term gains, even if a more patient investment orientation would generate higher long-term returns. In contrast, a pension fund or life insurance company shareholder is more likely to be concerned about the long-term value of its investments, which will allow it to meet its future obligations. Shareholders have numerous other private interests, some of which have emerged relatively recently, and these are described in Part III of this Article. On close analysis, shareholder interests look highly fragmented.

When we recognize that shareholders have significant private interests, it becomes apparent that shareholders may use [the] incremental power conferred upon them to pursue those interests to the detriment of shareholders as a class. As a result, transferring power from boards to shareholders may create new costs. In other words, more shareholder power could reduce overall shareholder welfare. This, of course, is a result directly opposite that predicted by proponents of increasing shareholder power.

Some scholars have been more harsh with Bebchuk's proposal, mostly basing their critiques on the deemed flawlessness of the US company law system which, in their view, would make any amendment not only unnecessary but also potentially detrimental.

Stephen M. Bainbridge, 'Director Primacy and Shareholder Disempowerment', 119 Harv. L. Rev. 5–25, at 5–19 (2006)

Lucian Bebchuk has emerged as a – perhaps the – leading academic proponent of these efforts [i.e. the efforts to extend the shareholder franchise].

... In this journal [118 Harv. L. Rev. 883–914 (2005)], Bebchuk recently put forward a related set of proposals designed to allow 'shareholders to initiate and vote to adopt changes in the company's basic corporate governance arrangements'. As Bebchuk explains, the housekeeping rules of corporation law effectively preclude shareholders from initiating corporate action. Indeed, the extent to which corporate law is stacked against what Bebchuk calls 'intervention power' goes beyond just the housekeeping rules; much of both corporate and securities law serves to sharply limit shareholder involvement in corporate decision-making, a point which becomes quite significant later in our analysis. Taken together, these myriad rules form a regime I have called 'director primacy', although in retrospect the phrase 'board primacy' might have been a more felicitous choice.

Hence, I do not quibble with Bebchuk's extensive empirical demonstration of shareholder weakness; to the contrary, I celebrate it as further evidence that my director primacy model accurately describes how corporation[s] work. Nor would I quibble very much with Bebchuk's proposal were it to be framed as an alternative into which corporations could opt. As a good contractarian, I believe that corporate law is generally comprised of default rules, from which shareholders are free to depart, rather than mandatory rules. As a normative matter ... this is just as it should be. As I understand Bebchuk's proposal, however, he wishes to replace the existing mostly mandatory rules disempowering shareholders with a new set of mostly mandatory rules empowering them. In contrast, I argue herein that the existing system of director primacy should be preserved as the default rule.

... Bebchuk's rhetoric arguably is more temperate, but the basic account remains unchanged. Indeed, his basic argument for empowering shareholders is that without the constraints provided by shareholder-initiated governance terms, management 'might divert resources through excessive pay, self dealing, or other means; reject beneficial acquisition offers to maintain its independence and private benefits of control; over-invest and engage in empire-building; and so forth'. In the absence of granting shareholders such powers, management will continue to use its agenda-setting control to adopt corporate governance terms it favors and induce 'states to provide rules favored by management'.

... Finally, the issues as to which Bebchuk proposes empowering shareholders are assigned by corporation law to the board of directors rather than managers, yet Bebchuk routinely refers to directors and officers as a single 'team'. As I have observed of other work by Bebchuk, conflating the roles of directors and managers is a critical error. Once we disentangle their roles, Bebchuk's managerial power model loses much of its traction. In the last couple of decades, several trends have provided boards of directors with important incentives to exercise more active and effective oversight of management. Increasingly, for example, director compensation is paid in stock, which helps align director and shareholder interests. The market for corporate control and the risk of shareholder litigation also provide such incentives. Courts have insisted upon proof of effective board decision-making processes and oversight before granting board decisions the deference traditionally accorded them under the business judgment rule, especially insofar as the category of decisions Bebchuk refers to as 'game-ending' are concerned. The stock markets have adopted tough new director independence and corporate governance rules. Given that these rules are still quite new, with as yet uncertain effects, it is desirable to hold off on additional reforms of the sort Bebchuk proposes here. Again, the claim is not that the principal–agent problem has not been solved. Obviously, the principal–agent problem is intractable. The claim here is only that the corporate governance system mostly functions well, despite the principal–agent problem, in large part because boards of directors have awoken and found that they are strong. Accordingly, the theory of the second best comes into play. It holds that, in a complex and interdependent system, inefficiencies in one part of the system should be tolerated if 'fixing' them would create even greater inefficiencies elsewhere in the system as a whole.

Even stronger criticism has been evinced by others.

Theodore N. Mirvis, Paul K. Rowe and William Savitt, 'Bebchuk's "Case for Increasing Shareholder Power": An Opposition', 121 *Harv. L. Rev.* 43–53, at 43–50 (2007)

In our view, the 'case for increasing shareholder power' is exceedingly weak, and in this space we summarize several of our core objections.

First, Bebchuk's proposal involves the abrupt overthrow of core Delaware corporate law principles and therefore risks extraordinarily costly disruption without any assurance of corresponding benefit. Second, Bebchuk's proposal – which rests on the (virtually explicit) hypothesis that corporate boards cannot be trusted to respect their fiduciary duty – finds no resonance in the observed experience of boardroom practitioners. And third, Bebchuk's proposal exalts shareholder power in a manner that is not only inconsistent with statute and decades of Delaware case law, but also is particularly suspect in light of the palpable practical problems of any shareholder-centric approach.

...

Thorny new practical and legal problems would also ensue [i.e. should Bebchuk's approach be enacted]. For example, would shareholders setting corporate policy owe fiduciary duties to one another? What legal recourse (if any) would be available when a majority shareholder (or group) changes 'the rules of the road' to the detriment of the minority? Would shareholders (like directors under the current regime) owe fiduciary duties to non-shareholder corporate constituencies in non-Revlon circumstances [Revlon, Inc. v. MacAndrews & Forbes Holdings, Inc., 506 A.2d 176 (1985)]? If so, how and by whom might be they enforced? And if not, what other redress, if any, would be available for these dispossessed constituencies? And what result when the shareholders vote for divergent 'rules of the road' – which are to be binding and which ignored, and who decides? What if these rules are constantly changed?

The Bebchuk proposal likewise raises complex issues relating to the allocation of risk and reward between shareholders and corporations. As a general rule, those entrusted with corporate management – officers and directors – bear legal risk for the actions of their corporations. Shareholders do not: the law deems investments in corporate enterprises sufficiently socially desirable that it allows shareholders to reap the benefits of corporate performance through share ownership without risk of liability for harm that the corporation may cause to others. In exchange for the privilege of investing without exposure to personal liability, shareholders must cede control and responsibility over corporate conduct to others, namely directors and officers. But would this trade-off continue to make sense under the Bebchuk regime of shareholder empowerment?

... Now, we are not quite ready to declare that blood will run red in the streets of Wilmington if Bebchuk has his way. But it is critical to appreciate just how radical a break with all history Bebchuk proposes. This would be an abrupt and fundamental reordering of power within the corporate form. In view of the enormous long-term success of the Delaware approach and the apparent satisfaction of the marketplace, and given the absence of any persuasive empirical basis for Bebchuk's proposal, we believe that such a break is plainly unwarranted.

... Bebchuk's proposal is not only fundamentally ahistorical, but it also rests on an inaccurate account of boardroom behavior. To read The Case for Increasing Shareholder Power is to enter an alternative universe in which directors do not seek to advance shareholder interest but are to the contrary engaged in a constant struggle to extract private benefits at shareholders' expense. We are thus treated to arguments built on the hypothesis that 'for self-serving reasons, management does not wish to initiate ... value-increasing change[s]', and asked to entertain fanciful models of the 'bargaining' that takes place between directors on the one hand and shareholders on the other, in which directors' 'monopoly' over corporate policy allows them to avoid value-enhancing policies and line their own pockets instead.

The trouble with this line of argument is that it bears no relationship to reality. Advisors who actually work with public company directors know that directors are keenly aware of their fiduciary duties to shareholders and others, extensively advised as to how to satisfy those duties, and vigilant to identify and cure potential conflicts. No one who has actually been in the board room of a major US corporation in recent times could plausibly argue that directors are not focused on shareholder interests. To be sure, some directors, and some boards, are more effective than others, and there will always be an occasional outlier or miscreant. But the assumption that undergirds much of Bebchuk's analysis – that directors are generally engaged in a constant struggle to maximize their private benefits at shareholders' expense – cannot be even remotely squared with the experience of those of us who actually work with directors as they strive to meet their fiduciary obligations.

... It is an irony that Bebchuk has chosen to make his 'case for increasing shareholder power' at a time when the conceptual underpinnings of the shareholder primacy theory are under increasing and well-deserved scrutiny. The shareholder-centric thesis rests on the premise that shareholders are animated by the common objective of maximizing share value – put simply, the reason Bebchuk wishes to empower shareholders is that he believes they will use their power to achieve the common goal of higher share value. By the same token, however, if a shareholder has private interests distinct from shareholders generally, that shareholder should be expected to use its vote to advance its distinct agenda, possibly to the detriment of fellow shareholders or the corporation generally.

Comparisons with the American company law system are imposed by the importance of the US corporate and financial market being the largest worldwide: whoever wishes to approach the study of company law has a duty to take into due consideration the American experience. Of course, the same holds true for American scholars looking at the European system as the foregoing debate clearly shows.

When it comes to corporate governance-related issues – as in any other field of company law (and, perhaps, of law in general) – one must reckon that there is no perfect model. There are just functional models. The US managerialist model of corporate governance works as it is because it is enshrined in a whole complex of complementary provisions (what, in constitutional law, would be referred to as 'checks and balances') that shape it as functional for the needs and features of that economic reality. Likewise, although being very different, the EU model also proves to be self-sufficient and well-functioning, rooting its rationale in a tradition of recognition of a major role for shareholders, long established in all European Member States.

Cherry-picking and dragging single pieces of legislation out of their context can be costly, inefficient, or even harmful. Transplantations often result in rejections. However, problems posed by company law practice are the same in every jurisdiction; solutions differ. Studying similarities and differences amongst systems helps understand how to solve problems in harmony with the whole environment where such applicative shortcomings have emerged.

FURTHER READING

Eilìs Ferran, 'The Role of the Shareholder in the Internal Corporate Governance: Shareholder Information, Communication and Decision-making', in Guido Ferrarini, Klaus J. Hopt, Jaap Winter, and Eddy Wymeersch (eds.), *Reforming Company and Takeover Law in Europe* 417–455 (Oxford University Press, 2004).

Lucian Arye Bebchuk, 'The Case for Increasing Shareholder Power', 118 *Harv. L. Rev.* 833–914 (2005).

Stephen M. Bainbridge, 'Director Primacy and Shareholder Disempowerment', 119 *Harv. L. Rev.* 5–25 (2006).

Theodore N. Mirvis, Paul K. Rowe, and William Savitt, 'Bebchuk's "Case for Increasing Shareholder Power": An Opposition', 121 *Harv. L. Rev.* 43–53 (2007).

Iman Anabtawi, 'Some Skepticism About Increasing Shareholder Power', 53 *UCLA L. Rev.* 561–579 (2007).

Edward Rock, Paul Davies, Hideki Kanda, Reinier Kraakman, and Wolf-Georg Ringe, 'Fundamental Changes', in John Armour, Luca Enriques et al., *The Anatomy of Corporate Law: A Comparative and Functional Approach* 171–205 (Oxford University Press, 3rd ed., 2017).

15.2 Matters on which the General Meeting Decides

Shareholders' engagement in corporate governance first of all depends on the matters on which the general meeting decides. To define such matters it is useful to refer to the SE Statute.

Article 52 Regulation 2001/2157/EC

The general meeting shall decide on matters for which it is given sole responsibility by:

(a) this Regulation or
(b) the legislation of the Member State in which the SE's registered office is situated adopted in implementation of Directive 2001/86/EC.

Furthermore, the general meeting shall decide on matters for which responsibility is given to the general meeting of a public limited-liability company governed by the law of the Member State in which the SE's registered office is situated, either by the law of that Member State or by the SE's statutes in accordance with that law.

The SE Statute requires the shareholders' meeting to decide on:

(a) the appointment and removal of members of the management organ in the one-tier system and, exceptionally, in the two-tier system (Articles 39 (2) and 43(3) Regulation 2001/2157/EC);
(b) the appointment and removal of members of the supervisory board (Article 40(2) Regulation 2001/2157/EC);
(c) any amendment of the SE Statute (Article 59 Regulation 2001/2157/EC);
(d) the winding-up (Article 63 Regulation 2001/2157/EC);
(e) the conversion of the SE (Article 66 Regulation 2001/2157/EC).

As regards the matters on which the general meeting decides under national law, it is useful mentioning that Directive 2012/30/EU mandates that some fundamental decisions, such as an increase or reduction of capital, a redemption of shares not implying a reduction of capital or a compulsory withdrawal of shares (in case the statutes merely allow such withdrawal) are decided upon by the general meeting.

Article 68(1) Directive 2017/1132/EU

1. Any increase in capital must be decided upon by the general meeting. Both that decision and the increase in the subscribed capital shall be published in the manner laid down by the laws of each Member State, in accordance with Article 16.

Article 73 Directive 2017/1132/EU

Any reduction in the subscribed capital, except under a court order, must be subject at least to a decision of the general meeting acting in accordance with the rules for a quorum and a majority laid down in Article 85 without prejudice to Articles 79 and 80. Such decision shall be published in the manner laid down by the laws of each Member State in accordance with Article 16.

The notice convening the meeting must specify at least the purpose of the reduction and the way in which it is to be carried out.

Article 78(1) Directive 2017/1132/EU

Where the laws of a Member State authorise total or partial redemption of the subscribed capital without reduction of the latter, they shall at least require that the following conditions are observed:

(a) where the statutes or instrument of incorporation provide for redemption, the latter shall be decided on by the general meeting voting at least under the usual conditions of quorum and majority; where the statutes or instrument of incorporation do not provide for redemption, the latter shall be decided upon by the general meeting acting at least under the conditions of quorum and majority laid down in Article 83; the decision must be published in the manner prescribed by the laws of each Member State, in accordance with Article 16;

Article 79(1) Directive 2017/1132/EU

1. Where the laws of a Member State may allow companies to reduce their subscribed capital by compulsory withdrawal of shares, they shall require that at least the following conditions are observed:

...

(b) where the compulsory withdrawal is authorised merely by the statutes or instrument of incorporation, it shall be decided upon by the general meeting unless it has been unanimously approved by the shareholders concerned;

Article 80(1) Directive 2017/1132/EU

1. In the case of a reduction in the subscribed capital by the withdrawal of shares acquired by the company itself or by a person acting in his own name but on behalf of the company, the withdrawal must always be decided on by the general meeting.

As we will later examine, in a group of cases, which include *Karella and Karellas* as the leading case, the CJEU was asked to assess the validity of legal provisions granting in case of a crisis of the undertaking an administrative authority to decide, outside any decision by the general meeting of shareholders, to effect an increase in the company's capital which would have the effect either of obliging the original shareholders to increase their contributions to the capital or of imposing on them the addition of new shareholders, thus reducing their involvement in the decision-taking power of the company. Later cases, such as *Kotnik* and *Dowling*, have distinguished (or maybe overruled) the *Karella and Karellas* doctrine, in cases of financial crises of companies of such economic relevance that a reorganisation is necessary to avoid a failure in the context of a serious disturbance of the national economy and the financial system of a Member State.

The same Directive 2017/1132/EU requires that other important decisions, such as the acquisition of the company's own shares (Article 60(1), Directive 2017/1132/EU) or to provide financial assistance for the acquisition of the company's own shares by a third party (Article 64(2), Directive 2017/1132/EU), are taken by directors upon an authorisation of the general meeting. As already mentioned with regards to conflict of interests of directors (*see*, Chapter 14, § 14.8), these authorisations are part of the so-called 'whitewash procedure'.

In addition, some EU Member States (such as Italy and France) require that the general meeting decides on the annual and consolidated financial statements, unless the company adopts a two-tier board system: in this case, as provided for in other member States (e.g., Germany and Austria), the supervisory board is entrusted with the task of approving the annual and consolidated financial statements.

As mentioned earlier, ECL does not take a position as to whether directors or the general meeting shall declare dividends. Most EU laws entrust this task to the general meeting; in the UK, however, dividend policy is left to the statutes (generally the board recommends the policy and the general meeting decides, as in other EU countries).

Lastly, it should be added that the law of some Member States (such as Spain) – or, in absence of statutory law, case law (such as in Germany: so-called *Holzmüller* doctrine) – requires that decisions involving basic or primordial interests of members (from French: *intérêt primordiale*), such as the sale of the entire business of the company or of a historical trademark, shall only be taken upon shareholders' meeting resolution, in absence of a specific clause, either provided by the law or the statutes of the company, which includes such decision amongst the matters for the general meeting to decide.

15.3 *Karella and Karellas* and Related Cases

In *Karella and Karellas* (Joined Cases C-19/90 and C-20/90, *Karella and Karellas* v. *Minister of Industry, Energy and Technology and Another,* [1991] ECR I-2691), the Symvoulio Epikrateias (Greek Council of State) referred to the Court pursuant to Article 177 of the EEC Treaty three questions for a preliminary ruling on the interpretation of Articles 25, 41, and 42 of the Second Company Law Directive. Those questions were raised in two sets of proceedings between two shareholders in the company Klostiria Velka AE, on the one hand, and the Minister of Industry, Energy and Technology and Organismos Anasygkrotiseos Epicheiriseon AE (Business Reconstruction Organization, hereafter referred to as '*the OAE*'), on the other. Those proceedings are concerned with an increase in that company's capital that was decided upon by the OAE and approved by the State Secretary for Industry, Energy and Technology.

The OAE is a public sector body having the form of a public limited-liability company that acts in the public interest under the control of the State. It was set up by Greek Law No 1386/1983 of 5 August 1983. Under Article 2(2) of that law, the purpose of the OAE is to contribute to the economic and social development of the country through the financial rejuvenation of undertakings, the importation and application of foreign know-how and the development of Greek know-how and through the establishment and operation of nationalised or mixed economy undertakings.

Article 2(3) of Law No 1386/1983 lists the powers conferred on the OAE in order to achieve those objects. It may take over the administration and day-to-day operation of undertakings undergoing rejuvenation or nationalised undertakings; participate in the capital of undertakings; grant loans and issue or agree certain loans; acquire bonds; and make over shares, in particular to employees or their representative bodies, local government bodies, or other legal entities governed by public law, charitable institutions, social organisations, or private individuals.

In particular, Article 8(8) of Law No 1386/1983 provides that, during its provisional administration of the company subject to the system established by the Law, the OAE may decide, by way of derogation from the provisions in force relating to public limited-liability companies, to increase the capital of the company concerned. The increase, which has to be approved by the minister, may take the form of contributions in cash or in kind. The undertaking's capital may also be increased by set-off. However, the original shareholders retain their pre-emptive rights, which they may exercise within a time-limit laid down in the ministerial decision granting approval.

By a decision of 14 December 1983 the State Secretary for the Economy subjected Klostiria Velka AE to the provisions of Law No 1386/1983. The OAE took over the administration of that company in accordance with Article 8 of the Law.

During its provisional administration the OAE decided, under Article 8(8) of Law No 1386/1983, to increase the capital of the company subjected to the system established by the Law by DR 400 million. The State Secretary for Industry, Energy and Technology approved that decision. The decree provided that the original shareholders would have an unlimited pre-emptive right that they had to exercise within one month of the publication of the decision.

Marina Karella and Nikolaos Karellas, who were shareholders in Klostiria Velka AE, brought actions for the annulment of that decree in the Greek Council of State on the ground that it was contrary to the Greek Constitution and the Second Directive.

In its judgments of 25 May 1989, the Council of State held that the applicants' pleas in law seeking the annulment of the decree on the ground of its unconstitutionality were unfounded. However, it decided that it should refer to the Court for a preliminary ruling the following questions – identically worded in the two cases – on the interpretation of the Second Directive:

Joined Cases C-19/90 and C-20/90, Karella and Karellas v. Minister of Industry, Energy and Technology and Another, [1991] ECR I-2691, § 12

(1) Are the provisions of Article 25 in conjunction with Article 41(1) and Article 42 of Council Directive 77/91/EEC of 13 December 1976 free of conditions which lie within the discretion of the Member States and sufficiently precise that they can be relied upon against the State before a national court by an individual claiming that a provision of a law is incompatible with those provisions of the directive?

(2) Does a legal provision come within the scope of Article 25 of Directive 77/91/EEC where it does not permanently govern matters relating to increases in the capital of a limited liability company but is intended to deal with the exceptional circumstances of over-indebted companies which are of particular economic and social importance for society as a whole and provides, in order to ensure the survival and continued operation of those companies for the adoption by administrative act of a decision to increase the company capital, without prejudice, however, to the pre-emptive right of the existing shareholders when the new shares are distributed, and if so to what extent is it compatible with that provision in conjunction with Article 41(1) of the directive?

(3) Is such a law compatible with the provisions of Article 42 of Directive 77/91/EEC in view of the fact that it does not prescribe that the price of the shares is to be fixed by the State on the basis of the objectively established net worth of the undertaking and the resultant inherent value of the old shares but leaves it to the discretion of the administration to fix the price so as to make possible the necessary immediate inflow of capital into companies which, because of their difficulties, have had confidence in them shaken, although it does safeguard the pre-emptive right of existing shareholders when the new shares are distributed?

The CJEU solved the first question in the affirmative:

Joined Cases C-19/90 and C-20/90, Karella and Karellas v. Minister of Industry, Energy and Technology and Another, [1991] ECR I-2691, § 23

23 It is appropriate therefore to answer the national court by stating that Article 25(1) of the Second Directive may be relied upon by individuals against the public authorities before national courts.

Therefore, the CJEU focused on the scope of Article 25(1) of the Second Directive, now Article 29(1) Directive 2012/30/EU, requiring that the general meeting decides on a capital increase.

Joined Cases C-19/90 and C-20/90, Karella and Karellas v. Minister of Industry, Energy and Technology and Another, [1991] ECR I-2691, §§ 24–26

24 As for the scope of Article 25(1) of the Second Directive with respect to a law, such as Law No 1386/1983, it should be examined in the first place whether such a law falls within the field of application of the directive, since that legislation does not set out the basic rules on increases of capital and merely seeks to deal with exceptional situations. If that legislation falls within the field of application of the Second Directive, it should then be considered whether it can qualify for the benefit of the derogation provided for in Article 41(1) of that directive.

25 As far as the field of application of the Second Directive is concerned, it should be stated first of all that, in accordance with Article 54(3)(g) of the Treaty, it seeks to coordinate the safeguards which, for the protection of the interests of members and others, are required by Member States of companies and firms within the meaning of the second paragraph of Article 58 of the Treaty with a view to making such safeguards equivalent. Consequently, the aim of the Second Directive is to provide a minimum level of protection for shareholders in all the Member States.

26 That objective would be seriously frustrated if the Member States were entitled to derogate from the provisions of the directive by maintaining in force rules – even rules categorized as special or exceptional – under which it is possible to decide by administrative measure, outside any decision by the general meeting of shareholders, to effect an increase in the company's capital which would have the effect either of obliging the original shareholders to increase their contributions to the capital or of imposing on them the addition of new shareholders, thus reducing their involvement in the decision-taking power of the company.

The CJEU considers that derogations are permitted in certain circumstances, but maintains that no derogations are permitted in case of a crisis.

Joined Cases C-19/90 and C-20/90, Karella and Karellas v. Minister of Industry, Energy and Technology and Another, [1991] ECR I-2691, § 28

28 In this connection, it must be held that no derogating provision which would allow the Member States to derogate from Article 25(1) of the directive in crisis situations is provided for either in the EEC Treaty or in the Second Directive itself. On the contrary, Article 17(1) of the directive provides expressly that, in the case of a serious loss of the subscribed capital, a general meeting of shareholders must be called within the period laid down by the laws of the Member States to consider whether the company should be wound up or any other measures taken. Consequently, that provision confirms the principle laid down by Article 25(1) and applies even where the company concerned is undergoing serious financial difficulties.

The CJEU further added that, whilst the directive does not preclude the taking of execution measures and, in particular, liquidation measures placing the company under compulsory administration in the interests of safeguarding creditors' rights, it nevertheless continues to apply as long as the company's shareholders and normal bodies have not been divested of their powers. Certainly, this is true where there is a straightforward rejuvenation measure involving public bodies or companies governed by private law where the members' right to the capital and to decision-making power in the company is in question.

Joined Cases C-19/90 and C-20/90, Karella and Karellas v. Minister of Industry, Energy and Technology and Another, [1991] ECR I-2691, § 31

31 It follows that, in the absence of a derogation provided for by Community law, Article 25(1) of the Second Directive must be interpreted as precluding the Member States from maintaining in force rules incompatible with the principle set forth in that article, even if those rules cover only exceptional situations. To recognize the existence of a general reservation covering exceptional situations, outside the specific conditions laid down in the provisions of the Treaty and the Second Directive, would, moreover, be liable to impair the binding nature and uniform application of Community law (see, to this effect, the judgment in Case 222/84 Johnston v. Chief Constable of the Royal Ulster Constabulary, [1986] ECR 1651, paragraph 26).

In conclusion, the CJEU solved the second and third questions as follows:

Joined Cases C-19/90 and C-20/90, Karella and Karellas v. Minister of Industry, Energy and Technology and Another, [1991] ECR I-2691, Operative Part

(2) Article 25 in conjunction with Article 41(1) of the Second Directive must be interpreted as meaning that they preclude national rules which, in order to ensure the survival and

continued operation of undertakings which are of particular economic and social importance for society as a whole and are in exceptional circumstances by reason of their excessive debt burden, provide for the adoption by administrative act of a decision to increase the company capital, without prejudice to the right of pre-emption of the original shareholders when the new shares are issued.

As mentioned, other cases were raised before the CJEU concerning the application of Article 29(1) Directive 2012/30/EU (formerly Article 25(1) Second Company Law Directive); all of these cases originated from the application of Greek law. Whilst details on the facts may be omitted, it is useful to list the cases and to point out how these contribute to shape the EU *acquis* on the point.

In *Syndesmos Melon* (C-381/89, *Syndesmos Melon tis Eleftheras Evangelikis Ekklisias and Others*, [1992] ECR I-2111) and in *Pafitis* (C-441/93, *Panagis Pafitis and Others* v. *Trapeza Kentrikis Ellados A.E. and Others*, [1996] ECR I-1347), the Court reaffirmed the principles expressed in *Karella and Karellas*, as follows:

C-381/89, Syndesmos Melon tis Eleftheras Evangelikis Ekklisias and Others, [1992] ECR I-2111, Operative Part

1. [ECL] precludes the application of rules which, being designed to ensure the rationalization and continued trading of undertakings that are of particular importance to the economy of a Member State and are in an exceptional situation because of their debts, allow an increase of capital to be decided upon by administrative measure, without any resolution being passed by the general meeting, and enable a decision to be taken, by administrative measure, that new shares are to be allotted without being offered on a pre-emptive basis to the shareholders in proportion to the capital represented by their shares;
2. [ECL rules] may be relied upon by individuals as against the public authorities before the national courts.

C-441/93, Panagis Pafitis and Others v. Trapeza Kentrikis Ellados A.E. and Others, [1996] ECR I-1347, §§ 67–70 and Operative Part

1. [ECL] precludes national legislation under which the capital of a bank constituted in the form of a public limited liability company which, as a result of its debt burden, is in exceptional circumstances may be increased by an administrative measure, without a resolution of the general meeting.
2. Publication of an offer of subscription in daily newspapers does not constitute information given in writing to the holders of registered shares within the meaning of the third sentence of Article 29(3) of Directive 77/91.

In *Kefalas* (C-367/96, *Alexandros Kefalas and Others* v. *Greek State and Others*, [1998] ECR I-2843) and, similarly, in *Diamantis* (C-373/97, *Dionysios Diamantis* v. *Elliniko Dimosio (Greek State) and Organismos Ikonomikis Anasygkrotisis Epicheiriseon AE (OAE)*, [2000] ECR I-01705) an additional question was referred to the Court, as to whether:

C-367/96, Alexandros Kefalas and Others v. Greek State and Others, [1998] ECR I-2843, § 18

1. Can the national court apply a provision of national law (in this case Article 281 of the Greek Civil Code) in order to assess whether a right granted by the Community provisions at issue is being exercised abusively by the party possessing it, or are there other Community law principles, and if so which, to be found in legislation or settled case-law, on which the national court may, if need be, base itself?
2. If the reply to Question 1 is in the negative, if, that is, the Court of Justice reserves such competence for itself, for reasons relating, for instance, to the uniform application of Community provisions, may the specific circumstances as formulated by the defendant respondent State as an objection, which constituted the issue of proof in judgment No 5943/1994 of this court, and which were set out succinctly in the previous paragraph of this judgment, or certain of them and if so which, prevent an action founded on infringement of Article 25(1) of the Second Council Directive 77/91/EEC from succeeding?

In *Kefalas*, the CJEU solved the main question as follows:

C-367/96, Alexandros Kefalas and Others v. Greek State and Others, [1998] ECR I-2843, Operative Part

Community law does not preclude national courts from applying a provision of national law in order to assess whether a right arising from a provision of Community law is being exercised abusively. However, where such an assessment is made, a shareholder relying on Article 25(1) of the Second Council Directive 77/91/EEC of 13 December 1976 on coordination of safeguards which, for the protection of the interests of members and others, are required by Member States of companies within the meaning of the second paragraph of Article 58 of the Treaty, in respect of the formation of public limited liability companies and the maintenance and alteration of their capital, with a view to making such safeguards equivalent, cannot be deemed to be abusing the right arising from that provision merely because the increase in capital contested by him has resolved the financial difficulties threatening the existence of the company concerned and has clearly ensured to his economic benefit, or because he has not exercised his preferential right under Article 29(1) of that directive to acquire new shares issued on the increase in capital at issue.

In *Diamantis*, the Court added that:

C-373/97, Dionysios Diamantis v. Elliniko Dimosio (Greek State) and Organismos Ikonomikis Anasygkrotisis Epicheiriseon AE (OAE), [2000] ECR I-01705, Operative Part

... In contrast, Community law does not preclude national courts from applying the provision of national law concerned if, of the remedies available for a situation that has arisen in breach of that provision, a shareholder has chosen a remedy that will cause such serious damage to the legitimate interests of others that it appears manifestly disproportionate.

15.4 *Kotnik* and *Dowling* Cases

As the global financial crisis of 2007 unfolded, some EU member States were confronted with situations in which their banking system would collapse in the absence of a bail-out. In these circumstances, between 2008 and 2013, the EU Commission published a series of communications on State aid to banks, named the *Crisis Communications*: the last Communication from the Commission on the application, from 1 August 2013, of *State aid rules to support measures in favour of banks in the context of the financial crisis ('Banking Communication')* was published in 2013. Thereafter, a Directive 2014/59/EU of the European Parliament and of the Council of 15 May 2014 establishing a framework for the recovery and resolution of credit institutions and investment firms was passed (the BRRD Directive).

Both the Banking Communication and the BRRD Directive express the principle of *burden sharing*. Under this principle, before granting any kind of restructuring aid, be it a recapitalisation or impaired asset measure, shareholders and creditors of the distressed bank must share some of the burden by having a portion of their position written off. The burden sharing principle is also referred to as 'bail-in', a new word originally coined by *The Economist*, then officially included in pieces of legislation of the EU.

According to Recital 66 of the BRRD Directive, the bail-in tool ensures that shareholders and creditors of the failing institution suffer appropriate losses and bear an appropriate part of the costs arising from the failure of the institution. The bail-in tool will therefore give shareholders and creditors of institutions a stronger incentive to monitor the health of an institution during normal circumstances.

In the light of the principles emerging from the Crisis Communications, the Banking Communication, and the BRRD Directive, some member States or public agencies have begun to inject financial resources into distressed banks. Some programmes included the possibility to have capital increases and withdrawal of pre-emptive rights of existing shareholders without resolution of the general meeting, along with issues of new shares at a price lower than nominal value or accountable par. Therefore, questions of compatibility with ECL principles were raised. In particular, two cases regarding Slovenia (*Kotnik*) and Ireland (*Dowling*) were brought before the CJEU. As mentioned earlier, solutions given to these new cases are quite divergent from those which emerged in *Karella and Karellas* and related cases.

In *Kotnik* (Case C-526/14, *Tadej Kotnik and Others* v. *Državni zbor Republike Slovenije*, [2016] *Digital reports* ECLI:EU:C:2016:570) the request for a preliminary ruling concerns the validity and interpretation of points 40 to 46 of the Banking Communication, and the interpretation of Articles 29, 34, 35, and 40 to 42 of Directive 2012/30/EU [now Articles 68, 73, 74, and 79 to 81 of Directive 2017/1132/EU], as well as of the seventh indent of Article 2 of Directive 2001/24/EC of the European Parliament and of the Council of 4 April 2001 on the reorganisation and winding-up of credit institutions.

The Banka Slovenije (the Bank of Slovenia) determined, in September 2013, that five Slovenian banks, namely Nova Ljubljanska banka d.d., Nova Kreditna banka Maribor d.d., Abanka Vipa d.d., Probanka d.d., and Factor banka d.d., were showing capital shortfalls. Given the scale of those shortfalls, those banks did not have sufficient assets to satisfy their creditors and to cover the value of deposits. On 17 December 2013, the Bank of Slovenia adopted decisions which put in place exceptional measures to effect the recapitalisation of the first two banks, the rescue of the third, and the winding-up of the last two banks ('the contested measures'). On 18 December 2013 the Commission authorised the granting of State aid to the five banks concerned, prior notice of that aid having been given by the Slovenian authorities. The contested measures, which were adopted on the basis of the law on the banking sector, in particular Articles 261a to 261c and Article 261e of that law, included writing off equity capital, as well as hybrid capital and subordinated debt (together: 'subordinated rights').

Subordinated rights are constituted by financial instruments which share certain characteristics with debt products and certain characteristics with shares in equity capital. In the event of the insolvency or winding-up of the issuing entity, the holders of subordinated rights ('subordinated creditors') are paid after the holders of ordinary debentures, but before shareholders. In exchange for the financial risk thus assumed by their holders, those financial instruments offer a higher rate of return.

A number of applications for review of constitutionality were brought before the Ustavno sodišče (Constitutional Court, Slovenia) by, on the one hand, private individuals and, on the other, by the Državni svet Republike Slovenije (the Council of State, Slovenia) and the Varuh človekovih pravic Republike Slovenije (the Slovenian Ombudsman). Those applications related to whether provisions of the law on the banking sector, on the basis of which the contested measures were adopted, were compatible with the Slovenian Constitution, and in particular with the principle of non-retroactivity, the principles of protection of legitimate expectations and proportionality, and the right to property. It is stated in the order for reference that the objective of the provisions of the law on the banking sector was to transpose the Banking Communication into national law, in order to enable the national authorities to grant State aid in that sector which was compatible with the internal market. Consequently, according to the referring court, while the objections of the applicants in the main proceedings are directed against those provisions, their actual target is the Banking Communication. Those applicants consider that that communication is contrary not only to the Slovenian Constitution, but also to Article 17 of the Charter of Fundamental Rights of the European Union ('the Charter') and to Directives 2012/30 and 2001/24.

In those circumstances, the Ustavno sodišče (Constitutional Court) decided to stay the proceedings and to refer the following questions to the CJEU for a preliminary ruling:

Case C-526/14, *Tadej Kotnik and Others v Državni zbor Republike Slovenije*, [2016] *Digital reports* ECLI:EU:C:2016:570, § 30

(1) Having regard to the legal effects actually produced by the Banking Communication, and given that the European Union has exclusive competence in relation to State aid, in accordance with Article 3(1)(b) [TFEU], and the Commission has competence to give decisions relating to State aid, pursuant to Article 108 [TFEU], must the Banking Communication be regarded as binding on Member States seeking to remedy a serious disturbance in the economy by granting State aid to credit institutions, where such aid is intended to be permanent and cannot be easily revoked ?

(2) Are points 40 to 46 of the Banking Communication – which make the possibility of granting State aid intended to remedy a serious disturbance in the national economy conditional upon compliance with the requirement to write off equity capital, [and subordinated rights] and/or to convert [subordinated rights] into equity, in order to limit the amount of aid to the minimum necessary in the light of the need to take account of moral hazard – incompatible with Articles 107 to 109 [TFEU], in so far as they exceed the Commission's competence, as defined in the provisions of the Treaty relating to State aid?

(3) If Question 2 is answered in the negative, are points 40 to 46 of the Banking Communication – which make the possibility of granting State aid conditional on the requirement of writing off and/or converting into equity capital, in so far as that requirement relates to shares (equity capital), and [subordinated rights] issued before the publication of the Banking Communication and which, at the time of issue, could have been written off or written down without full compensation only in the event of the bank's insolvency – compatible with the principle of the protection of legitimate expectations enshrined in EU law?

(4) If Question 2 is answered in the negative and Question 3 in the affirmative, are points 40 to 46 of the Banking Communication – which make the possibility of granting State aid conditional on the requirement to write off equity capital, [and subordinated rights] and/or to convert [subordinated rights] into equity, without the initiation and conclusion of an

insolvency procedure by which the debtor's assets may be liquidated by means of judicial proceedings in which the holders of subordinated financial instruments would have the opportunity to participate as parties to the proceedings – compatible with the right to property enshrined in Article 17(1) of the Charter ?

(5) If Question 2 is answered in the negative and Questions 3 and 4 in the affirmative, are points 40 to 46 of the Banking Communication – which make the possibility of granting State aid conditional on the requirement to write off equity capital, and/or to convert [subordinated rights] into equity, in so far as the implementation of those measures calls for a reduction and/or increase in the share capital of a public limited liability company on the basis of the decision of a competent administrative body, not that of the general meeting of shareholders of that company – contrary to Articles 29, 34, 35 and 40 to 42 of Directive 2012/30 [now Articles 68, 73, 74, and 79 to 81 of Directive 2017/1132/EU]...?

(6) With regard to point 19 of the Banking Communication, in particular the requirement laid down in that provision to respect fundamental rights, to point 20, and to the affirmation of the requirement, as a matter of principle, laid down in points 43 and 44 of the communication, to convert or write down [subordinated rights] before granting State aid, may the Banking Communication be interpreted as meaning that those measures do not compel Member States that seek to remedy a serious disturbance in their economy by granting State aid to credit institutions to impose an obligation to adopt such conversion and writing down measures as a condition for the grant of State aid on the basis of Article 107(3)(b) [TFEU], or as meaning that, in order to be able to grant State aid, it is sufficient that the conversion or writing down measure should merely operate in a manner that is proportionate?

(7) May the seventh indent of Article 2 of [Directive 2001/24] be interpreted as meaning that the measures requiring burden-sharing by shareholders and subordinated creditors provided for in points 40 to 46 of the Banking Communication (write-down of equity capital [and subordinated rights] and the conversion into equity of [subordinated rights] may also be classified as reorganisation measures?

For the matters concerned in this book, question number 5 is of greater relevance. The CJEU has addressed it as follows:

Case C-526/14, *Tadej Kotnik and Others v Državni zbor Republike Slovenije*, [2016] *Digital reports* ECLI:EU:C:2016:570, §§ 81–94

The fifth question

81 By its fifth question, the referring court seeks, in essence, to ascertain whether Articles 29, 34, 35 and 40 to 42 of Directive 2012/30 [now Articles 68, 73, 74, and 79 to 81 of Directive 2017/1132/EU] must be interpreted as precluding points 40 to 46 of the Banking Communication in so far as those points lay down a condition of

burden-sharing by shareholders and subordinated creditors as a prerequisite to the authorisation of State aid.

82 Articles 29, 34, 35 and 40 to 42 of Directive 2012/30 [now Articles 68, 73, 74, and 79 to 81 of Directive 2017/1132/EU] provide, in essence, that any increase or reduction in the capital of a public limited liability company must be subject to a decision by the general meeting of the company.

83 According to the referring court, to the extent that the Banking Communication provides that certain alterations to the share capital of banks do not have to be decided upon or approved by the general meeting, that communication is incompatible with that directive.

84 However [...] the Banking Communication contains no specific provision on the legal procedures whereby the burden-sharing measures set out in points 40 to 46 of that communication are to be implemented.

85 Consequently, while the Member States may possibly find it necessary, in a particular situation, to adopt such burden-sharing measures without the agreement of the general meeting of the company, that circumstance cannot however call into question the validity of the Banking Communication in the light of the provisions of Directive 2012/30 [now Directive 2017/1132].

86 Further, it must be observed that, according to recital 3 in the preamble of Directive 2012/30 [now Directive 2017/1132], the aim of that directive is to ensure minimum equivalent protection for both shareholders and creditors of public limited liability companies. To that end, that directive coordinates the national provisions relating to the formation of such companies, and to the maintenance, increase and reduction of their capital.

87 The background to Directive 2012/30 [now Directive 2017/1132] is the attainment of freedom of establishment in the internal market, and its principal objective is the protection of the interests of shareholders and others. The directive is intended to reassure investors that their rights will be respected throughout the internal market by the governing bodies of the companies in which they have invested, particularly when a company is formed and when its share capital is increased and reduced. Consequently, the measures provided for by Directive 2012/30 [now Directive 2017/1132] in order to guarantee that protection relate to the normal operation of public limited liability companies.

88 By contrast, the burden-sharing measures involving both shareholders and subordinated creditors constitute, when they are imposed by the national authorities, exceptional measures. They can be adopted only in the context of there being a serious disturbance of the economy of a Member State and with the objective of preventing a systemic risk and ensuring the stability of the financial system.

89 Contrary to what is claimed by the applicants in the main proceedings, Directive 2012/30 [now Directive 2017/1132] does not preclude measures relating to share capital being adopted, in certain specific circumstances, such as those mentioned in the Banking Communication, without the approval of the company general meeting. That interpretation cannot, moreover, be called into question by the judgment of 12 March 1993, *Pafitis and Others* (C-441/93, EU:C:1996:92).

90 In that judgment, the Court interpreted Council Directive 77/91/EEC of 13 December 1976 [...], in the context of a dispute characterised by the insolvency of a single bank, whereas, in the main proceedings, the burden-sharing measures that are the subject of points 40 to 46 of the Banking Communication are envisaged as a prerequisite for the grant, to banks faced with a capital shortfall, of State aid intended, in an exceptional context of a national economy being affected by a serious disturbance, to overcome a systemic financial crisis capable of adversely affecting the national financial system as a whole and the financial stability of the European Union.

91 It must be emphasised, in that regard, that, as the Advocate General stated in points 105 and 107 of his Opinion, the national measures that were challenged in *Pafitis and Others* (C-441/93, EU:C:1996:92) had been adopted in the 1986-1990 period and the Court delivered its judgment in 1996, thus well before the start of the third stage for the implementation of the Economic and Monetary Union, with the introduction of the euro, the establishment of the Eurosystem and the related amendments to the EU Treaties. Although there is a clear public interest in ensuring throughout the European Union a strong and consistent protection of investors, that interest cannot be held to prevail in all circumstances over the public interest in ensuring the stability of the financial system.

92 The referring court considers, however, that the provisions of Directive 2014/59 may lead to a finding that the Banking Communication is incompatible with Directive 2012/30 [now Directive 2017/1132].

93 However, in addition to what was stated in paragraphs 72 and 84 of this judgment, the fact that, under Article 123 of Directive 2014/59, from 1 January 2016, Articles 29, 34 and 35, and 40 to 42 of Directive 2012/30 [now Articles 68, 73, 74, and 79 to 81 of Directive 2017/1132/EU] do not apply in the case of use of the resolution mechanisms provided for by Directive 2014/59, does not permit the conclusion that, before that date, derogations of that kind were prohibited.

94 In the light of the foregoing, the answer to the fifth question is that Articles 29, 34, 35 and 40 to 42 of Directive 2012/30 [now Articles 68, 73, 74, and 79 to 81 of Directive 2017/1132/EU] must be interpreted as not precluding points 40 to 46 of the Banking Communication in so far as those points lay down a condition of burden-sharing by shareholders and subordinated creditors as a prerequisite to the authorisation of State aid.

Case C-526/14, Tadej Kotnik and Others v Državni zbor Republike Slovenije, [2016] Digital reports ECLI:EU:C:2016:570, Operative part

On those grounds, the Court (Grand Chamber) hereby rules:

[...]

4. Articles 29, 34, 35 and 40 to 42 of Directive 2012/30/EU of the European Parliament and of the Council of 25 October 2012 on coordination of safeguards which, for the protection

of the interests of members and others, are required by Member States of companies within the meaning of the second paragraph of Article 54 of the Treaty on the Functioning of the European Union [now Articles 68, 73, 74, and 79 to 81 of Directive 2017/1132/EU], in respect of the formation of public limited liability companies and the maintenance and alteration of their capital, with a view to making such safeguards equivalent, must be interpreted as not precluding points 40 to 46 of the Banking Communication in so far as those points lay down a condition of burden-sharing by shareholders and holders of subordinated rights as a prerequisite to the authorisation of State aid.

5. The Banking Communication must be interpreted as meaning that the measures for converting hybrid capital and subordinate debt or writing down their principal, as provided for in point 44 of that communication, must not exceed what is necessary to overcome the capital short-fall of the bank concerned.
6. The seventh indent of Article 2 of Directive 2001/24/EC of the European Parliament and of the Council of 4 April 2001 on the reorganisation and winding up of credit institutions must be interpreted as meaning that burden-sharing measures such as those provided for in points 40 to 46 of the Banking Communication fall within the scope of the concept of 'reorganisation measures', within the meaning of that provision of that directive.

In *Dowling* (Case C-41/15, *Gerard Dowling, Padraig McManus, Piotr Skoczylas and Scotchstone Capital Fund Limited* v. *Irish Minister for Finance*, [2016] *Digital reports* ECLI:EU:C:2016:836), the High Court of Ireland made a request for a preliminary ruling concerning the interpretation of Articles 8, 25, and 29 of the Second Council Directive 77/91/EEC of 13 December 1976 [now Articles 47, 68, and 72 of Directive 2017/1132/EU]. The request had been made in the course of proceedings between, on the one hand, Mr Gerard Dowling, Mr Padraig McManus, Mr Piotr Skoczylas, and Scotchstone Capital Fund Limited and, on the other, the Irish Minister for Finance, where the former sought the setting aside of the direction order made by the High Court on 26 July 2011, directing a company, of which the applicants in the main proceedings are members and shareholders, to increase its share capital and to issue, in favour of the Minister for Finance, new shares at a price lower than their nominal value.

The dispute concerns Permanent TSB plc, formerly Irish Life and Permanent plc, ('ILP'), a credit institution operating in Ireland. Permanent TSB Group Holdings plc, formerly Irish Life and Permanent Group Holdings plc, ('ILPGH') is a company incorporated with limited liability in Ireland. ILPGH is not a credit institution. During the period at issue in the main proceedings, ILPGH owned the entire share capital of ILP. The applicants in the main proceedings are members and shareholders of ILPGH.

The economic and financial crisis, faced by Ireland in 2008, had serious effects on the financial stability both of the Irish banks and of Ireland, the two being particularly strongly linked because of the relative size of the banking sector compared to the size of the national economy and the significant guarantees of bank liabilities that Ireland had granted to those national banks in 2008. Notwithstanding the measures taken by Ireland to support the banking sector, the markets continued to lose faith in the Irish banks and the financial situation of Ireland continued to deteriorate. In those circumstances, the Irish authorities produced an economic and financial adjustment programme, for which, on 21 November 2010, they sought, *inter alia*, European Union financial assistance. In that programme, Ireland undertook to reorganise and recapitalise the banking sector.

By Implementing Decision 2011/77, the Council approved that programme and made available to Ireland European Union financial assistance under the European financial stabilisation mechanism, established by Regulation No 407/2010. On 16 December 2010 Ireland and the Commission entered into a Memorandum of Understanding on the basis of Article 1(4) of that decision ('the Memorandum of Understanding'). In accordance with the commitments made in that Memorandum of Understanding and with Articles 3(4), (5), and 7(g) of that decision, Ireland was to ensure the recapitalisation of the national banks by the end of July 2011, on the basis of the results of a Prudential Capital Assessment Review and a Prudential Liquidity Assessment Review published by the Central Bank of Ireland.

The Central Bank of Ireland published the results of its reviews on 31 March 2011. On the basis of those results, the Governor of the Central Bank of Ireland ordered ILP, by a decision adopted on that date, to raise additional capital of €4 billion. In July 2011 the Minister submitted to the shareholders of ILPGH a proposal designed to facilitate the recapitalisation of ILP by means of, *inter alia*, a capital injection of €2.7 billion. That proposal was rejected by the extraordinary general meeting of ILPGH held on 20 July 2011, which mandated the directors of that company to examine other recapitalisation options and to request, for that purpose, an extension of the recapitalisation deadline laid down in Implementing Decision 2011/77.

Pursuant to Sections 7 and 9 of the 2010 Act, in order to recapitalise ILP the Minister prepared a Proposed Direction Order, which he submitted to the High Court. The Direction Order was adopted by the High Court on the terms sought, directing ILPGH to issue, in return for the capital injection of €2.7 billion, new shares to the Minister at a share price dictated by him, that is at a price 10 per cent below the quoted share price of 23 June 2011. Consequently, the Minister obtained, without any decision having been made by the general meeting of shareholders of ILPGH, 99.2 per cent of the shares of that company. In addition, the delisting of the company on the Irish and London Stock Exchanges was ordered.

The applicants in the main proceedings brought before the High Court, on the basis of Section 11 of the 2010 Act, an application for the setting aside of the Direction Order. Before that court, they claimed that the increase in share capital resulting from that order is incompatible with Articles 8, 25, and 29 of the Second Directive, since it was effected without the approval of the general meeting of ILPGH. The Minister and both ILPGH and ILP rejected that argument, relying on Directive 2001/24, Regulation No 407/2010, Implementing Decision 2011/77, Articles 49, 65, 107, 119, 120, and 126 TFEU and on the provisions in Title VIII of Part III of the FEU Treaty. In their opinion, those provisions of EU law authorised Ireland to take measures necessary to defend the integrity of its own financial system notwithstanding the provisions of the Second Directive. Pursuant to its obligations under Title VIII of Part III of the FEU Treaty and, in particular, Articles 119 and 120 thereof, Ireland was required to take those measures in order to secure the safety of an institution of systemic importance for Ireland and the European Union.

The referring court concluded, on the balance of probabilities, that ILP could not have raised the required amount of capital of €4 billion either from private investors or from existing shareholders, after the extraordinary general meeting of ILPGH had rejected, on 20 July 2011, the Minister's recapitalisation proposal. In the opinion of that court, if ILP had not been recapitalised by the deadline laid down in Implementing Decision 2011/77, that would have led to the failure of ILP, due to a number of possible developments, such as a run on deposits held with ILP, a call for repayment of various notes or a cessation of funding under the emergency liquidity assistance scheme, or a combination of some or all of those possibilities. Further, the High Court considered that ILP's failure would not only have led to the complete loss of value of the shares to the shareholders, but would also have had adverse consequences for Ireland. The court referred to, *inter alia*, the possibility of a run on deposits held with the national banks, the subsequent call on the guarantee granted to ILP by the Irish State and the possibility of full or partial withdrawal of funding to Ireland under the economic and financial adjustment programme for non-compliance with the terms of that programme. In the opinion of the referring court, those adverse consequences for Ireland would probably have worsened the threat to the financial stability of other Member States and of the European Union.

In those circumstances, the High Court decided to stay the proceedings and to refer the following questions to the Court for a preliminary ruling:

Case C-41/15, *Gerard Dowling, Padraig McManus, Piotr Skoczylas and Scotchstone Capital Fund Limited v. Irish Minister for Finance,* [2016] *Digital reports* ECLI:EU:C:2016:836, § 32

(1) Does the Second Directive [now Directive 2017/1132/EU] preclude in all circumstances, including the circumstances of this case, the making of a Direction Order pursuant to Section 9 of the 2010 Act, on foot of the opinion of the Minister that it is necessary, where such an order has the effect of increasing a company's capital without the consent of the general meeting; allotting new shares without offering them on a pre-emptive basis

to existing shareholders, without the consent of the general meeting; lowering the nominal value of the company's shares without the consent of the general meeting and, to that end, altering the company's memorandum and articles of association without the consent of the general meeting?

(2) Was the Direction Order made by the High Court pursuant to Section 9 of the 2010 Act in relation to ILPGH and ILP in breach of European Union Law?

In order to solve the case, the Court clearly stated that the Direction Order unequivocally infringed Article 8(1) and Articles 25 and 29 of the Second Directive [now Articles 47(1), 68, and 72 of Directive 2017/1132/EU]. Indeed, the effect of that order was that shares in ILPGH were issued at a price lower than their nominal value and that the share capital of that company was increased, while the pre-emptive right to subscribe was denied, without the agreement of the general meeting of that company.

That being the case, the CJEU observed that the two questions referred must be understood as meaning that the referring court is seeking, in essence, to ascertain whether these rules also preclude a measure adopted where there is a serious disturbance of the economy and financial system of a Member State that threatens the financial stability of the European Union, the effect of that measure being to increase the share capital of a public limited-liability company, without the approval of the general meeting of that company, new shares being issued at a price lower than their nominal value and the existing shareholders being denied any pre-emptive right to subscribe.

Case C-41/15, *Gerard Dowling, Padraig McManus, Piotr Skoczylas and Scotchstone Capital Fund Limited v. Irish Minister for Finance*, [2016] *Digital reports* ECLI:EU:C:2016:836, §§ 44–55

44 In that regard, it is clear from the information provided by the referring court that the Direction Order was adopted in the context of the financial and economic crisis which led Ireland, in 2008, to grant significant guarantees to the national banks affected by that crisis and, in late 2010, when the financial situation of those banks was continuing to deteriorate and was also threatening the financial stability of that Member State, to request financial assistance from the European Union and to undertake to restructure and recapitalise the national banking sector.

45 According to the referring court, that situation of serious disturbance of the national economy made it essential, because of the fact that it was impossible for ILP itself to achieve the recapitalisation by the end of July 2011, as required in particular by the Memorandum of Understanding, that the Irish State take action in order to avoid a failure of ILP that would threaten both the financial stability of Ireland and that of other Member States and of the European Union.

46 The recapitalisation of national banks, including ILP, by 31 July 2011 was also laid down by Article 1(4) and Article 3(2), (4), (5) and (7)(g) of Implementing Decision 2011/77, as a condition for the payment of European Union financial assistance to Ireland. That financial assistance constituted, in accordance with recitals 4 and 5 and Article 1 of Regulation No 407/2010 – itself adopted on the basis of Article 122(2) TFEU which is designed to allow action to be taken to deal with 'exceptional occurrences' – a measure taken as a matter of urgency with a view to maintaining the financial stability of the European Union.

47 Admittedly, in order to recapitalise ILP, the Direction Order required an increase in the share capital of ILPGH. However, Article 3(7)(g) of Implementing Decision 2011/77 provides for the recapitalisation of national banks, one such being ILP, but does not specify how that was to be achieved. Consequently, the Irish authorities were not obliged to make a direct injection of capital into the share capital of ILP, but could carry out that recapitalisation by means of increasing the share capital of ILPGH.

48 Further, as stated in paragraphs 30 and 31 of this judgment, the referring court, after weighing the competing interests, came to the conclusion that, once the decision of ILPGH's extraordinary general meeting of 20 July 2011 was made to reject the Minister's proposed recapitalisation, the Direction Order was the only means of ensuring, within the time limit laid down by Implementing Decision 2011/77, the recapitalisation of ILP that was necessary to prevent the failure of that financial institution and thereby to forestall a serious threat to the financial stability of the European Union.

49 The aim of the Second Directive [now Directive 2017/1132/EU] is to achieve, as stated in its second recital, minimum equivalent protection for both shareholders and creditors of public limited liability companies. Accordingly, as ILPGH and ILP and also Ireland have stated in their observations submitted to the Court, the measures provided for by that directive relating to the formation of public limited liability companies and to the maintenance, increase or reduction of their capital guarantee such protection against acts taken by the governing bodies of those companies and relate, therefore, to their normal operation (see, by analogy, judgment of 19 July 2016, *Kotnik and Others*, C-526/14, EU:C:2016:570, paragraphs 86 and 87).

50 However, as is clear from paragraphs 44 to 48 of this judgment, the Direction Order is not a measure taken by a governing body of a public limited liability company as part of its normal operation, but is an exceptional measure taken by the national authorities intended to prevent, by means of an increase in share capital, the failure of such a company, which failure, in the opinion of the referring court, would threaten the financial stability of the European Union. The protection conferred by the Second Directive [now Directive 2017/1132/EU] on the shareholders and creditors of a public limited liability company, with respect to its share capital, does not extend to a national measure of that kind that is adopted in a situation where there is a serious disturbance of the economy and financial system of a Member State and that is designed to overcome a systemic threat to the financial stability of the European Union, due to a capital shortfall in the company concerned.

51 The provisions of the Second Directive [now Directive 2017/1132/EU] do not therefore preclude an exceptional measure affecting the share capital of a public limited liability company, such as the Direction Order, taken by the national authorities where there is a serious disturbance of the economy and financial system of a Member State, without the approval of the general meeting of that company, with the objective of preventing a systemic risk and ensuring the financial stability of the European Union (see, by analogy, judgment of 19 July 2016, *Kotnik and Others*, C-526/14, EU:C:2016:570, paragraphs 88 to 90).

52 That conclusion cannot be called into question by the fact that the Direction Order could be classified, as claimed by the applicants in the main proceedings, not as a 'judicial measure', but a 'provisional administrative act'. It follows from the two preceding paragraphs that the Second Directive [now Directive 2017/1132/EU] does not preclude, in circumstances such as those at issue in the main proceedings, the adoption of a measure such as the Direction Order, the nature of the national authority which issued that order being of no relevance in that regard.

53 The above interpretation is in no way irreconcilable with the interpretation adopted by the Court in the judgment of 12 March 1996, *Pafitis and Others* (C-441/93, EU:C:1996:92), contrary to what is claimed by the applicants in the main proceedings. The factors set out in paragraphs 44 to 48 of this judgment distinguish the situation at issue in the main proceedings from the case that gave rise to the judgment of 12 March 1996, *Pafitis and Others* (C-441/93, EU:C:1996:92), the feature of that case being that it concerned the insolvency of a single bank. While the Court held that the Second Directive [now Directive 2017/1132/EU] continues to apply in the case of 'ordinary reorganisation measures' (judgment of 12 March 1996, *Pafitis and Others*, C-441/93, EU:C:1996:92, paragraph 57), the Court did not, however, give a ruling, as the Advocate General observed in point 45 of his Opinion, on extraordinary reorganisation measures, such as a direction order designed to avoid, in a situation where there is a serious disturbance of the national economy and of the financial system of a Member State, the failure of a bank and thereby to maintain the financial stability of the European Union.

54 Further, as ILPGH and ILP and also Ireland have stated in their observations submitted to the Court, the national measures contested in the *Pafitis and Others* case (C-441/93, EU:C:1996:92) had been adopted in the 1986-1990 period and the Court delivered its judgment on 12 March 1996, thus well before the start of the third stage for the implementation of the Economic and Monetary Union, with the introduction of the euro, the establishment of the Eurosystem and the related amendments to the EU Treaties. Although there is a clear public interest in ensuring, throughout the European Union, a strong and consistent protection of shareholders and creditors, that interest cannot be held to prevail in all circumstances over the public interest in ensuring the stability of the financial system established by those amendments (see, to that effect, judgment of 19 July 2016, *Kotnik and Others*, C-526/14, EU:C:2016:570, paragraph 91).

55 In the light of the foregoing, the answer to the questions referred is that Article 8(1) and Articles 25 and 29 of the Second Directive [now Articles 47(1), 68 and 72 of Directive

2017/1132/EU] must be interpreted as not precluding a measure, such as the Direction Order at issue in the main proceedings, adopted in a situation where there is a serious disturbance of the economy and the financial system of a Member State threatening the financial stability of the European Union, the effect of that measure being to increase the share capital of a public limited liability company, without the agreement of the general meeting of that company, new shares being issued at a price lower than their nominal value and the existing shareholders being denied a pre-emptive right to subscribe.

Case C-41/15, *Gerard Dowling, Padraig McManus, Piotr Skoczylas and Scotchstone Capital Fund Limited v. Irish Minister for Finance*, [2016] *Digital reports* ECLI:EU:C:2016:836, Operative part

On those grounds, the Court (Grand Chamber) hereby rules:

Article 8(1) and Articles 25 and 29 of the Second Council Directive 77/91/EEC of 13 December 1976 on coordination of safeguards which, for the protection of the interests of members and others, are required by Member States of companies within the meaning of [the second paragraph of Article 54 TFEU], in respect of the formation of public limited liability companies and the maintenance and alteration of their capital, with a view to making such safeguards equivalent [now Articles 47(1), 68 and 72 of Directive 2017/1132/EU], must be interpreted as not precluding a measure, such as the Direction Order at issue in the main proceedings, adopted in a situation where there is a serious disturbance of the economy and the financial system of a Member State threatening the financial stability of the European Union, the effect of that measure being to increase the share capital of a public limited liability company, without the agreement of the general meeting of that company, new shares being issued at a price lower than their nominal value and the existing shareholders being denied any pre-emptive subscription right.

After having analysed the two cases, it is necessary to address the question as to whether the new trend distinguishes or rather overrules the old principles. The Court holds that the interpretation given in *Kotnik* or in *Dowling* is in no way irreconcilable with the interpretation adopted in *Pafitis* (and in other similar cases), where the insolvency of a single bank was concerned. As consequence, whilst ECL principles continue to apply in the case of 'ordinary reorganisation measures', these might be derogated by 'extraordinary reorganisation measures', such as measures designed to avoid, in a situation where there is a serious disturbance of the national economy and of the financial system of a Member State, the failure of a bank and thereby to maintain the financial stability of the European Union.

The reasoning of the CJEU is not totally convincing. Indeed, it may be true that measures taken by the Slovenian and Irish authorities were intended to avoid a serious disturbance of the economy, and therefore qualified as an extraordinary reorganisation. Nonetheless, there is no doubt that the measures also taken by the Greek authorities in all other cases were intended as tools to avoid a serious disturbance of the national economy, and not as ordinary reorganisation measures for individual companies. In light of the above, it may be observed that the distinguishing of the CJEU made in *Kotnik* and *Dowling* should have led the Court to apply similar principles to the Greek cases also. This does not interfere with the general principle, that in cases of ordinary reorganisation measures of a company, ECL principles concerning the matters on which the general meeting decides cannot be derogated.

FURTHER READING

Gianni Lo Schiavo, 'Burden Sharing Arrangements vs. Shareholders and Creditors: Kotnik, Dowling and the Current State Aid Policy in the Banking Sector', 19 *EBOR* 581–613 (2018).

15.5 The Shareholders' Meetings Procedure: (A) The Convocation

Shareholders' meetings are held at any time when their decision is required or appropriate, upon convocation of the administrative, management or supervisory organ. In any case, the shareholders' meeting shall be held at least once a year (annual meeting). Such a rule is provided for in the SE Statute as well as many legislations of the Member States: the annual meeting is generally called for the approval of the annual financial statements and, where provided for by the Member States' legislation, or by the statutes, for the distribution of dividends.

Article 54 Regulation 2001/2157/EC

1. An SE shall hold a general meeting at least once each calendar year, within six months of the end of its financial year, unless the law of the Member State in which the SE's registered office is situated applicable to public limited-liability companies carrying on the same type of activity as the SE provides for more frequent meetings. A Member State may, however, provide that the first general meeting may be held at any time in the 18 months following an SE's incorporation.
2. General meetings may be convened at any time by the management organ, the administrative organ, the supervisory organ or any other organ or competent authority in accordance with the national law applicable to public limited-liability companies in the Member State in which the SE's registered office is situated.

Shareholders holding a certain number of shares (thus, representing a certain percentage of the subscribed capital) may request the administrative or management organ to convene a meeting on certain items to be put on the agenda. In case of non-compliance by the administrative or management organ, the competent judicial or administrative authority shall call the meeting.

Article 55 Regulation 2001/2157/EC

1. One or more shareholders who together hold at least 10% of an SE's subscribed capital may request the SE to convene a general meeting and draw up the agenda therefor; the SE's statutes or national legislation may provide for a smaller proportion under the same conditions as those applicable to public limited-liability companies.
2. The request that a general meeting be convened shall state the items to be put on the agenda.
3. If, following a request made under paragraph 1, a general meeting is not held in due time and, in any event, within two months, the competent judicial or administrative authority within the jurisdiction of which the SE's registered office is situated may order that a general meeting be convened within a given period or authorise either the shareholders who have requested it or their representatives to convene a general meeting. This shall be without prejudice to any national provisions which allow the shareholders themselves to convene general meetings.

In all legislations of the EU Member States, shareholders' meetings shall follow a legal procedure granting that shareholders are put in a condition to take part in the meeting on a certain date, with all the necessary information on the items put on the agenda so that they may express a conscious vote. Frequently, shareholders' meetings are convened on a second convocation, in case in the first convocation the necessary quorum is not reached: the notice of convocation may contain both dates.

Whilst the SE Statute does not refer to the content of the notice of meeting, nor stipulate how it is published or sent to the recipients, the SCE Statute does.

Article 56 Regulation 2003/1435/EC

1. A general meeting shall be convened by a notice in writing sent by any available means to every person entitled to attend the SCE's general meeting in accordance with Article 58 (1) and (2) and the provisions of the statutes. That notice may be given by publication in the official internal publication of the SCE.
2. The notice calling a general meeting shall give at least the following particulars:
   - the name and registered office of the SCE,
   - the venue, date and time of the meeting,
   - where appropriate, the type of general meeting,
   - the agenda, indicating the subjects to be discussed and the proposals for decisions.

3. The period between the date of dispatch of the notice referred to in paragraph 1 and the date of the opening of the general meeting shall be at least 30 days. It may, however, be reduced to 15 days in urgent cases. Where Article 61(4) is applied, relating to quorum requirements, the time between a first and second meeting convened to consider the same agenda may be reduced according to the law of the Member State in which the SCE has its registered office.

For listed companies, the Shareholder Rights Directive requires that shareholders are given comprehensive information prior to the general meeting regarding in particular the place and date of the meeting, the items on the agenda and the procedures to take part in it and how to vote their shares (either in presence or by proxy). Such information is given through a notice of meeting issued no later than 21 days before the day of the annual meeting (or no later than 14 days before the day of other meetings) and either sent to all shareholders personally, or disseminated through media ensuring fast access to it on a non-discriminatory basis; in any case, the information included in the notice shall be published on the Internet site of the company.

Article 5 Directive 2007/36/EC reads as follows:

Article 5 Information Prior to the General Meeting, Directive 2007/36/EC

1. Without prejudice to Articles 9(4) and 11(4) of Directive 2004/25/EC of the European Parliament and of the Council of 21 April 2004 on takeover bids, Member States shall ensure that the company issues the convocation of the general meeting in one of the manners specified in paragraph 2 of this Article not later than on the 21st day before the day of the meeting.

   Member States may provide that, where the company offers the facility for shareholders to vote by electronic means accessible to all shareholders, the general meeting of shareholders may decide that it shall issue the convocation of a general meeting which is not an annual general meeting in one of the manners specified in paragraph 2 of this Article not later than on the 14th day before the day of the meeting. This decision is to be taken by a majority of not less than two thirds of the votes attaching to the shares or the subscribed capital represented and for a duration not later than the next annual general meeting.

   Member States need not apply the minimum periods referred to in the first and second subparagraphs for the second or subsequent convocation of a general meeting issued for lack of a quorum required for the meeting convened by the first convocation, provided that this Article has been complied with for the first convocation and no new item is put on the agenda, and that at least 10 days elapse between the final convocation and the date of the general meeting.

2. Without prejudice to further requirements for notification or publication laid down by the competent Member State as defined in Article 1(2), the company shall be required to issue the convocation referred to in paragraph 1 of this Article in a manner ensuring fast access to it on a non-discriminatory basis. The Member State shall require the company to use such media as may reasonably be relied upon for the effective dissemination of information to the public throughout the Community. The Member State may not impose an obligation to use only media whose operators are established on its territory.

   The Member State need not apply the first subparagraph to companies that are able to identify the names and addresses of their shareholders from a current register of shareholders, provided that the company is under an obligation to send the convocation to each of its registered shareholders.

   In either case the company may not charge any specific cost for issuing the convocation in the prescribed manner.
3. The convocation referred to in paragraph 1 shall at least:
   (a) indicate precisely when and where the general meeting is to take place, and the proposed agenda for the general meeting;
   (b) contain a clear and precise description of the procedures that shareholders must comply with in order to be able to participate and to cast their vote in the general meeting. This includes information concerning: (i) the rights available to shareholders under Article 6, to the extent that those rights can be exercised after the issuing of the convocation, and under Article 9, and the deadlines by which those rights may be exercised; the convocation may confine itself to stating only the deadlines by which those rights may be exercised, provided it contains a reference to more detailed information concerning those rights being made available on the Internet site of the company; (ii) the procedure for voting by proxy, notably the forms to be used to vote by proxy and the means by which the company is prepared to accept electronic notifications of the appointment of proxy holders; and (iii) where applicable, the procedures for casting votes by correspondence or by electronic means;
   (c) where applicable, state the record date as defined in Article 7(2) and explain that only those who are shareholders on that date shall have the right to participate and vote in the general meeting;
   (d) indicate where and how the full, unabridged text of the documents and draft resolutions referred to in points (c) and (d) of paragraph 4 may be obtained;
   (e) indicate the address of the Internet site on which the information referred to in paragraph 4 will be made available.
4. Member States shall ensure that, for a continuous period beginning not later than on the 21st day before the day of the general meeting and including the day of the meeting, the company shall make available to its shareholders on its Internet site at least the following information:
   (a) the convocation referred to in paragraph 1;
   (b) the total number of shares and voting rights at the date of the convocation (including separate totals for each class of shares where the company's capital is divided into two or more classes of shares);

(c) the documents to be submitted to the general meeting;
(d) a draft resolution or, where no resolution is proposed to be adopted, a comment from a competent body within the company, to be designated by the applicable law, for each item on the proposed agenda of the general meeting; moreover, draft resolutions tabled by shareholders shall be added to the Internet site as soon as practicable after the company has received them;
(e) where applicable, the forms to be used to vote by proxy and to vote by correspondence, unless those forms are sent directly to each shareholder.

Where the forms referred to in point (e) cannot be made available on the Internet for technical reasons, the company shall indicate on its Internet site how the forms can be obtained on paper. In this case the company shall be required to send the forms by postal services and free of charge to every shareholder who so requests.

Where, pursuant to Articles 9(4) or 11(4) of Directive 2004/25/EC, or to the second subparagraph of paragraph 1 of this Article, the convocation of the general meeting is issued later than on the 21st day before the meeting, the period specified in this paragraph shall be shortened accordingly.

5. Member States shall ensure that for the purposes of Directive 2014/59/EU the general meeting may, by a majority of two-thirds of the votes validly cast, issue a convocation to a general meeting, or modify the statutes to prescribe that a convocation to a general meeting is issued, at shorter notice than as laid down in paragraph 1 of this Article, to decide on a capital increase, provided that that meeting does not take place within ten calendar days of the convocation, that the conditions of Article 27 or 29 of Directive 2014/59/EU are met, and that the capital increase is necessary to avoid the conditions for resolution laid down in Articles 32 and 33 of that Directive.
6. For the purposes of paragraph 5, the obligation on each Member State to set a single deadline in Article 6(3), the obligation to ensure timely availability of a revised agenda in Article 6(4) and the obligation on each Member State to set a single record date in Article 7(3) shall not apply.

Both the SE Statute and the Shareholders' Rights Directive permit that minority shareholders, before the day of the meeting, request that one or more additional items be put on the agenda of any general meeting.

Article 56 Regulation 2001/2157/EC

One or more shareholders who together hold at least 10% of an SE's subscribed capital may request that one or more additional items be put on the agenda of any general meeting. The procedures and time limits applicable to such requests shall be laid down by the national law of the Member State in which the SE's registered office is situated or, failing that, by the SE's statutes. The above proportion may be reduced by the statutes or by the law of the Member

State in which the SE's registered office is situated under the same conditions as are applicable to public limited-liability companies.

Recital 7 Directive 2007/36/EC

(7) Shareholders should, in principle, have the possibility to put items on the agenda of the general meeting and to table draft resolutions for items on the agenda. Without prejudice to different time-frames and modalities which are currently in use across the Community, the exercise of those rights should be made subject to two basic rules, namely that any threshold required for the exercise of those rights should not exceed 5% of the company's share capital and that all shareholders should in every case receive the final version of the agenda in sufficient time to prepare for the discussion and voting on each item on the agenda.

Article 6 Right to Put Items on the Agenda of the General Meeting and to Table Draft Resolutions, Directive 2007/36/EC

1. Member States shall ensure that shareholders, acting individually or collectively:
   (a) have the right to put items on the agenda of the general meeting, provided that each such item is accompanied by a justification or a draft resolution to be adopted in the general meeting; and
   (b) have the right to table draft resolutions for items included or to be included on the agenda of a general meeting.

   Member States may provide that the right referred to in point (a) may be exercised only in relation to the annual general meeting, provided that shareholders, acting individually or collectively, have the right to call, or to require the company to call, a general meeting which is not an annual general meeting with an agenda including at least all the items requested by those shareholders.

   Member States may provide that those rights shall be exercised in writing (submitted by postal services or electronic means).
2. Where any of the rights specified in paragraph 1 is subject to the condition that the relevant shareholder or shareholders hold a minimum stake in the company, such minimum stake shall not exceed 5% of the share capital.
3. Each Member State shall set a single deadline, with reference to a specified number of days prior to the general meeting or the convocation, by which shareholders may exercise the right referred to in paragraph 1, point (a). In the same manner each Member State may set a deadline for the exercise of the right referred to in paragraph 1, point (b).
4. Member States shall ensure that, where the exercise of the right referred to in paragraph 1, point (a) entails a modification of the agenda for the general meeting already communicated to shareholders, the company shall make available a revised agenda in the same manner as the previous agenda in advance of the applicable record date as defined in Article 7(2) or, if no record date applies, sufficiently in advance of the date of the general meeting so as to enable other shareholders to appoint a proxy or, where applicable, to vote by correspondence.

In addition, the Shareholder Rights Directive requires that shareholders are permitted to ask questions on the items put on the agenda: questions may be asked before or during the meeting.

Recital 8 Directive 2007/36/EC

(8) Every shareholder should, in principle, have the possibility to ask questions related to items on the agenda of the general meeting and to have them answered, while the rules on how and when questions are to be asked and answered should be left to be determined by Member States.

Article 9 Right to Ask Questions, Directive 2007/36/EC

1. Every shareholder shall have the right to ask questions related to items on the agenda of the general meeting. The company shall answer the questions put to it by shareholders.
2. The right to ask questions and the obligation to answer are subject to the measures which Member States may take, or allow companies to take, to ensure the identification of shareholders, the good order of general meetings and their preparation and the protection of confidentiality and business interests of companies. Member States may allow companies to provide one overall answer to questions having the same content.

Member States may provide that an answer shall be deemed to be given if the relevant information is available on the company's Internet site in a question and answer format.

15.6 The Shareholders' Meetings Procedure: (B) Participation in the General Meeting in Listed Companies

When shareholdings are split amongst a multitude of small and very small investors, participation in the shareholders' meeting is significantly reduced and the meeting's role in the governance of the company remains unexpressed. To enhance the degree of participation of equity investors to shareholders' meetings, Member States may adopt two different strategies, both favouring their involvement. First, final investors' participation may be encouraged by easing direct voting from shareholders: this result is achieved by allowing remote attendance at the meeting and voting with electronic means, or, as an alternative, by allowing voting by correspondence upon draft resolutions. We may refer to this option as a direct shareholders' democracy model.

Also, final investors' participation may be strengthened by widely permitting proxy voting: this option is particularly effective if final investors give proxies to banks and investing firms. Indeed, being entrusted with the task of taking care of their clients' interests in the shareholders' meeting, banks and investing firms could play a critical role for the corporate governance of issuers. This result may be achieved both by the use of proxies, or by directly attributing to the intermediary financial institutions the task of voting the shares in their clients' interests. We may refer to this option as an indirect shareholders' democracy model.

Both models have advantages and disadvantages. The main disadvantages of a direct shareholders' democracy model consist in the difficulties of disclosure of relevant information before voting, an unawareness of investors as how to vote, and a high potential of influencing their decisions. On the other hand, the indirect shareholders' democracy model may give rise to significant conflicts of interests, thus requiring both strong deterrence rules preventing abuses and independent gatekeeping. Indirect shareholders' democracy also increases the level of risk for institutional investors being responsible towards final investors: this may lead them to avoid this risk in some ways.

Having focused on this picture, Directive 2007/36/CE allows both strategies. However, it requires in any case that Member States' legislations provide for a direct shareholders' democracy model, in case shareholders prefer to cast votes directly.

The goal of enhancing shareholders' direct or indirect participation in meetings may be only achieved if existing obstacles, deterring shareholders from voting, such as the so-called *blocking of shares*, are removed. The blocking of shares consists in the burden of depositing the shares with the company or banks (or other burdens having similar effects) before the general meeting: the function of the deposit constraint, especially in the past where also shares of listed companies were issued in the form of paper certificates, is that of permitting the company to organise a list of shareholders legitimated to participate in the meeting. The deposit, however, does not permit the shareholders to sell or dispose of their shares until after the meeting (hence the expression: 'share blocking'). As this practice would deter shareholders (and in particular institutional investors) from participating in meetings, the same is prohibited by the Shareholder Rights Directive; at the same time, however, the Directive proposes the adoption of more efficient and less burdensome systems permitting the company to timely organise the participation of shareholders in the meeting.

Recital 3 Directive 2007/36/EC

(3) Holders of shares carrying voting rights should be able to exercise those rights given that they are reflected in the price that has to be paid at the acquisition of the shares. Furthermore, effective shareholder control is a pre-requisite to sound corporate governance and should, therefore, be facilitated and encouraged. It is therefore necessary to adopt measures to approximate the laws of the Member States to this end. Obstacles which deter shareholders from voting, such as making the exercise of voting rights

subject to the blocking of shares during a certain period before the general meeting, should be removed. However, this Directive does not affect existing Community legislation on units issued by collective investment undertakings or on units acquired or disposed of in such undertakings.

Article 7 Requirements for Participation and Voting in the General Meeting, Directive 2007/36/EC

1. Member States shall ensure:
   (a) that the rights of a shareholder to participate in a general meeting and to vote in respect of any of his shares are not subject to any requirement that his shares be deposited with, or transferred to, or registered in the name of, another natural or legal person before the general meeting; and
   (b) that the rights of a shareholder to sell or otherwise transfer his shares during the period between the record date, as defined in paragraph 2, and the general meeting to which it applies are not subject to any restriction to which they are not subject at other times.

As mentioned, whilst the blocking of shares shall not be permitted, the Shareholder Rights Directive is aware that organising a shareholders' meeting in listed companies is not as easy, as it requires the management to previously identify which shareholders (maybe hundreds or thousands of people) are entitled to take part in the meeting. Unless companies are able to identify their shareholders on the very same day of the meeting, such identification shall be performed by implementing a so-called *record date system*. A record date is the date within which shareholders are made eligible to exercise a given social right, usually the right to vote. The Directive requires that the record date shall not lie more than thirty days before the date of the general meeting to which it applies.

Article 7(2–4) Requirements for Participation and Voting in the General Meeting, Directive 2007/36/EC

2. Member States shall provide that the rights of a shareholder to participate in a general meeting and to vote in respect of his shares shall be determined with respect to the shares held by that shareholder on a specified date prior to the general meeting (the record date).

   Member States need not apply the first subparagraph to companies that are able to identify the names and addresses of their shareholders from a current register of shareholders on the day of the general meeting.
3. Each Member State shall ensure that a single record date applies to all companies. However, a Member State may set one record date for companies which have issued bearer shares and another record date for companies which have issued registered

shares, provided that a single record date applies to each company which has issued both types of shares. The record date shall not lie more than 30 days before the date of the general meeting to which it applies. In implementing this provision and Article 5(1), each Member State shall ensure that at least eight days elapse between the latest permissible date for the convocation of the general meeting and the record date. In calculating that number of days those two dates shall not be included. In the circumstances described in Article 5(1), third subparagraph, however, a Member State may require that at least six days elapse between the latest permissible date for the second or subsequent convocation of the general meeting and the record date. In calculating that number of days those two dates shall not be included.

4. Proof of qualification as a shareholder may be made subject only to such requirements as are necessary to ensure the identification of shareholders and only to the extent that they are proportionate to achieving that objective.

It is important to stress that implementing a record date system is not a goal in itself, rather it constitutes a compromise that permits a listed company to efficiently organise the meeting, whilst not having the shares blocked in the meantime. Therefore, under EU law, the adoption of a record date system is not mandatory where companies are able to identify the names and addresses of their shareholders from a current register of shareholders on the day of the general meeting.

Indeed, as is well known in the American debate, the record date system entails potential conflict of interest or an empty voting issue (i.e., people expressing more votes than economic ownership allows), in that it precludes the acquirers of shares after the record date from exercising their shareholders' rights whilst permitting people who are no longer shareholders to take part in meetings and vote.

Carl Clottens, 'Empty Voting: A European Perspective', 9 ECFR 446–483, at 450–451 (2012)

The problem of empty voting is further aggravated by the record date system, in which the number of shares with voting rights held on a specified date some time before the general meeting of shareholders determines the amount of votes that can be validly cast at the general meeting. This creates additional scope for empty voting, by allowing for the possibility of buying shares before the record date (record date capture) and selling them between the record date and the general meeting (post record date trade). Shares can also be borrowed before the record date and sold short before the general meeting; this creates perverse incentives to vote against the company interest, because the shareholder as of [the] record date can profit from a (provoked) sudden drop of the share price to buy shares in the market at a discount in order to return them to the lender. This constitutes a major disadvantage of the record date system, as compared to the traditional rule where the entitlement to attend the general meeting and to vote was determined at the (day of the) general meeting. A shareholder could still buy shares just before the meeting and sell them afterwards, but he would normally suffer the negative impact on the share price of a suboptimal voting outcome, unless he had otherwise hedged the risk of his shares or unless the market had not fully absorbed the information and reflected it in the stock price before he sold his shares. Obviously, this is not the case with a sale before the general meeting. A post record date sale is suspect since a shareholder who expects (to contribute to) an increase in value would normally prefer to hold his shares, unless the sale can be explained by other motives such as a sudden need for liquidity. In theory, the problem of post record date trade can easily be solved by a voting proxy from the seller to the buyer, but in practice this is impossible when shares are traded anonymously on the stock exchange.

In order to avoid empty voting, since 2009, Delaware legislation permits the board of directors to determine two different record dates: a first one is referred to for determining who are the addressees of the notice of meeting, potentially allowed to take part in the meeting and vote; a second one, very close to or on the date of the meeting, is referred to for determining who amongst the shareholders recorded at the first record date is in fact to be granted the right to vote.

In so doing, those registered as shareholders on the first record date but who have sold the shares in the interim are not allowed to vote.

Delaware General Corporation Law

§ 213 (a) Fixing Date for Determination of Stockholders of Record

(a) In order that the corporation may determine the stockholders entitled to notice of any meeting of stockholders or any adjournment thereof, the board of directors may fix a record date, which record date shall not precede the date upon which the resolution fixing the record date is adopted by the board of directors, and which record date shall not be more than 60 nor less than 10 days before the date of such meeting. If the board of directors so fixes a date, such date shall also be the record date for determining the stockholders entitled to vote at such meeting unless the board of directors determines, at the time it fixes such record date, that a later date on or before the date of the meeting shall be the date for making such determination. If no record date is fixed by the board of directors, the record date for determining stockholders entitled to notice of and to vote at a meeting of stockholders shall be at the close of business on the day next preceding the day on which notice is given, or, if notice is waived, at the close of business on the day next preceding the day on which the meeting is held. A determination of stockholders of record entitled to notice of or to vote at a meeting of stockholders shall apply to any adjournment of the meeting; provided, however, that the board of directors may fix a new record date for determination of stockholders entitled to vote at the adjourned meeting, and in such case shall also fix as the record date for stockholders entitled to notice of such adjourned meeting the same or an earlier date as that fixed for determination of stockholders entitled to vote in accordance with the foregoing provisions of this subsection (a) at the adjourned meeting.

As the issue of empty voting is related not only to the record date system but also, and mainly, to the so-called hidden ownership phenomenon (which may be described as undisclosed economic ownership accompanied by informal voting rights), we will therefore return to this issue later.

This being said, the core of the Shareholder Rights Directive lies within the part encouraging direct or indirect participation in the meeting. The grounds for such provisions are expressed in the Preamble, as follows:

Recitals 5–6, 9–13 Directive 2007/36/EC

(5) Significant proportions of shares in listed companies are held by shareholders who do not reside in the Member State in which the company has its registered office. Non-resident shareholders should be able to exercise their rights in relation to the general meeting as easily as shareholders who reside in the Member State in which the company has its registered office. This requires that existing obstacles which hinder the access of non-resident shareholders to the information relevant to the general meeting and the exercise of voting rights without physically attending the general meeting be removed. The removal of these obstacles should also benefit resident shareholders who do not or cannot attend the general meeting.

(6) Shareholders should be able to cast informed votes at, or in advance of, the general meeting, no matter where they reside. All shareholders should have sufficient time to consider the documents intended to be submitted to the general meeting and determine how they will vote their shares. To this end, timely notice should be given of the general meeting, and shareholders should be provided with the complete information intended to be submitted to the general meeting. The possibilities which modern technologies offer to make information instantly accessible should be exploited. This Directive presupposes that all listed companies already have an Internet site.

…

(9) Companies should face no legal obstacles in offering to their shareholders any means of electronic participation in the general meeting. Voting without attending the general meeting in person, whether by correspondence or by electronic means, should not be subject to constraints other than those necessary for the verification of identity and the security of electronic communications. However, this should not prevent Member States from adopting rules aimed at ensuring that the results of the voting reflect the intentions of the shareholders in all circumstances, including rules aimed at addressing

situations where new circumstances occur or are revealed after a shareholder has cast his vote by correspondence or by electronic means.

(10) Good corporate governance requires a smooth and effective process of proxy voting. Existing limitations and constraints which make proxy voting cumbersome and costly should therefore be removed. But good corporate governance also requires adequate safeguards against a possible abuse of proxy voting. The proxy holder should therefore be bound to observe any instructions he may have received from the shareholder and Member States should be able to introduce appropriate measures ensuring that the proxy holder does not pursue any interest other than that of the shareholder, irrespective of the reason that has given rise to the conflict of interests. Measures against possible abuse may, in particular, consist of regimes which Member States may adopt in order to regulate the activity of persons who actively engage in the collection of proxies or who have in fact collected more than a certain significant number of proxies, notably to ensure an adequate degree of reliability and transparency. Shareholders have an unfettered right under this Directive to appoint such persons as proxy holders to attend and vote at general meetings in their name. This Directive does not, however, affect any rules or sanctions that Member States may impose on such persons where votes have been cast by making fraudulent use of proxies collected. Moreover, this Directive does not impose any obligation on companies to verify that proxy holders cast votes in accordance with the voting instructions of the appointing shareholders.

(11) Where financial intermediaries are involved, the effectiveness of voting upon instructions relies, to a great extent, on the efficiency of the chain of intermediaries, given that investors are frequently unable to exercise the voting rights attached to their shares without the cooperation of every intermediary in the chain, who may not have an economic stake in the shares. In order to enable the investor to exercise his voting rights in cross-border situations, it is therefore important that intermediaries facilitate the exercise of voting rights. Further consideration should be given to this issue by the Commission in the context of a Recommendation, with a view to ensuring that investors have access to effective voting services and that voting rights are exercised in accordance with the instructions given by those investors.

(12) While the timing of disclosure to the administrative, management or supervisory body as well as to the public of votes cast in advance of the general meeting electronically or by correspondence is an important matter of corporate governance, it can be determined by Member States.

(13) Voting results should be established through methods that reflect the voting intentions expressed by shareholders, and they should be made transparent after the general meeting at least through the company's Internet site.

As mentioned, direct shareholders' participation is achieved by allowing remote attendance at the meeting and voting with electronic means, or, as an alternative, by allowing a vote by correspondence upon draft resolutions. The Shareholder Rights Directive allows both.

Article 8 Participation in the General Meeting by Electronic Means, Directive 2007/36/EC

1. Member States shall permit companies to offer to their shareholders any form of participation in the general meeting by electronic means, notably any or all of the following forms of participation:
   (a) real-time transmission of the general meeting;
   (b) real-time two-way communication enabling shareholders to address the general meeting from a remote location;
   (c) a mechanism for casting votes, whether before or during the general meeting, without the need to appoint a proxy holder who is physically present at the meeting.
2. The use of electronic means for the purpose of enabling shareholders to participate in the general meeting may be made subject only to such requirements and constraints as are necessary to ensure the identification of shareholders and the security of the electronic communication, and only to the extent that they are proportionate to achieving those objectives.

This is without prejudice to any legal rules which Member States have adopted or may adopt concerning the decision-making process within the company for the introduction or implementation of any form of participation by electronic means.

Article 12 Voting by Correspondence, Directive 2007/36/EC

Member States shall permit companies to offer their shareholders the possibility to vote by correspondence in advance of the general meeting. Voting by correspondence may be made subject only to such requirements and constraints as are necessary to ensure the identification of shareholders and only to the extent that they are proportionate to achieving that objective.

As also mentioned, indirect shareholders' participation may be achieved both by the use of proxies, or by directly attributing to the intermediary financial institutions the task of voting the shares in their clients' interests. The Shareholder Rights Directive opts for the first solution.

Article 10 Proxy Voting, Directive 2007/36/EC

1. Every shareholder shall have the right to appoint any other natural or legal person as a proxy holder to attend and vote at a general meeting in his name. The proxy holder shall enjoy the same rights to speak and ask questions in the general meeting as those to which the shareholder thus represented would be entitled.

   Apart from the requirement that the proxy holder possess legal capacity, Member States shall abolish any legal rule which restricts, or allows companies to restrict, the eligibility of persons to be appointed as proxy holders.
2. Member States may limit the appointment of a proxy holder to a single meeting, or to such meetings as may be held during a specified period.

Without prejudice to Article 13(5), Member States may limit the number of persons whom a shareholder may appoint as proxy holders in relation to any one general meeting. However, if a shareholder has shares of a company held in more than one securities account, such limitation shall not prevent the shareholder from appointing a separate proxy holder as regards shares held in each securities account in relation to any one general meeting. This does not affect rules prescribed by the applicable law that prohibit the casting of votes differently in respect of shares held by one and the same shareholder.

3. Apart from the limitations expressly permitted in paragraphs 1 and 2, Member States shall not restrict or allow companies to restrict the exercise of shareholder rights through proxy holders for any purpose other than to address potential conflicts of interest between the proxy holder and the shareholder, in whose interest the proxy holder is bound to act, and in doing so Member States shall not impose any requirements other than the following:
   (a) Member States may prescribe that the proxy holder disclose certain specified facts which may be relevant for the shareholders in assessing any risk that the proxy holder might pursue any interest other than the interest of the shareholder;
   (b) Member States may restrict or exclude the exercise of shareholder rights through proxy holders without specific voting instructions for each resolution in respect of which the proxy holder is to vote on behalf of the shareholder;
   (c) Member States may restrict or exclude the transfer of the proxy to another person, but this shall not prevent a proxy holder who is a legal person from exercising the powers conferred upon it through any member of its administrative or management body or any of its employees.

   A conflict of interest within the meaning of this paragraph may in particular arise where the proxy holder:
   (i) is a controlling shareholder of the company, or is another entity controlled by such shareholder;
   (ii) is a member of the administrative, management or supervisory body of the company, or of a controlling shareholder or controlled entity referred to in point (i);
   (iii) is an employee or an auditor of the company, or of a controlling shareholder or controlled entity referred to in (i);
   (iv) has a family relationship with a natural person referred to in points (i) to (iii).
4. The proxy holder shall cast votes in accordance with the instructions issued by the appointing shareholder.

Member States may require proxy holders to keep a record of the voting instructions for a defined minimum period and to confirm on request that the voting instructions have been carried out.

5. A person acting as a proxy holder may hold a proxy from more than one shareholder without limitation as to the number of shareholders so represented. Where a proxy holder holds proxies from several shareholders, the applicable law shall enable him to cast votes for a certain shareholder differently from votes cast for another shareholder.

In addition to the above, it shall be considered that final investors may also choose to entrust a professional investor, being either a natural or legal person, to act as trustee. In such circumstances the professional investor is recognised as shareholder, whilst it acts in the course of a business on behalf of another natural or legal person (beneficial owner or client). In order to act on behalf of the client, the trustee need not receive a proxy. However, Member States may impose disclosure requirements as a prerequisite for the exercise of voting rights by such shareholders (trustees).

As these may result in an impediment to the effective exercise of voting rights, such requirements shall not go beyond a list disclosing to the company the identity of each client and the number of shares voted on his behalf.

Article 13 Removal of Certain Impediments to the Effective Exercise of Voting Rights, Directive 2007/36/EC

1. This Article applies where a natural or legal person who is recognised as a shareholder by the applicable law acts in the course of a business on behalf of another natural or legal person (the client).
2. Where the applicable law imposes disclosure requirements as a prerequisite for the exercise of voting rights by a shareholder referred to in paragraph 1, such requirements shall not go beyond a list disclosing to the company the identity of each client and the number of shares voted on his behalf.
3. Where the applicable law imposes formal requirements on the authorisation of a shareholder referred to in paragraph 1 to exercise voting rights, or on voting instructions, such formal requirements shall not go beyond what is necessary to ensure the identification of the client, or the possibility of verifying the content of voting instructions, respectively, and is proportionate to achieving those objectives.
4. A shareholder referred to in paragraph 1 shall be permitted to cast votes attaching to some of the shares differently from votes attaching to the other shares.
5. Where the applicable law limits the number of persons whom a shareholder may appoint as proxy holders in accordance with Article 10(2), such limitation shall not prevent a shareholder referred to in paragraph 1 of this Article from granting a proxy to each of his clients or to any third party designated by a client.

Identification of the beneficial owners behind institutional investors acting on their behalf ('shareholders' identification') is an issue strictly related to that of *hidden ownership*, that is a possible decoupling between *legal* or *formal ownership* over shares, giving access to the right to vote, and *economic ownership*. Indeed, hidden ownership may hinder the ability of the company to detect conflicts of interest and, as voting rights are given to shareholders on the assumption that they pursue a similar economic interest to maximisation of the shareholders' value, it may also give rise to empty voting. An excerpt from a scholarly article will help to clarify the point.

Henry T.C. Hu and Bernard Black, 'The New Vote Buying: Empty Voting and Hidden (Morphable) Ownership', 79 *So. Cal. L. Rev.* 811–908, at 906–908 (2006)

Shareholder voting is a core aspect of corporate governance. The central role of voting depends on a link between votes and economic interest. Financial innovation, however, is undermining that link. In this Article, we explain how both investors and insiders can engage in large-scale, low-cost, often hidden decoupling of voting rights from economic ownership. This decoupling – the new vote buying – comes in two main flavors, which we term empty voting (more votes than economic ownership) and hidden (morphable) ownership (undisclosed economic ownership accompanied by informal voting rights).

Hedge funds have been pioneers in both forms of new vote buying. Insiders have used decoupling strategies to retain votes while shedding economic exposure. New OTC [over-the-counter] derivatives developed to transfer risk turn out to be well adapted for transferring votes. A now-massive share lending market serves both the traditional needs of short-sellers and the needs of empty voters.

In the past several years, decoupling has played a central role in the boardrooms of public corporations worldwide. We have found more than twenty publicly known or rumored examples, almost all since 2002. Several involve empty voting by investors with negative economic interests, who would profit if the companies' share prices go down. How many more have remained hidden is unknown.

Not all vote buying is bad. Some could move votes from less informed to better informed investors and thus strengthen shareholders' oversight. Still, unless there are ways to separate good vote buying from bad, and allow only the former, the new vote buying, as we call it, threatens to unravel the longstanding connection between voting and economic ownership of shares. Voting outcomes might be decided by hidden welfare among company insiders and major investors, each employing financial technology to acquire votes. Adroitness in such financial technology may increasingly supplant the role of merit in determining the control of corporations.

Moreover, any regulatory response to decoupling must also consider its impact on derivatives and short-selling. Derivatives serve good purposes, as well [as] ill. Short sellers play a valuable role in securities markets, and depend on the same share lending market that facilitates the new vote buying. The right regulatory response to the new vote buying is not obvious.

The first step is to better understand the new vote buying. For that, disclosure is the near term answer. This Article therefore develops an 'integrated ownership disclosure' proposal that would both address new vote buying, and partially integrate and greatly simplify the five existing share ownership disclosure regimes. The core of the proposal is to require more consistent, symmetric disclosure of both voting and economic ownership. Our proposal is sensitive to compliance cost; its simplicity, compared to the current regulatory patchwork quilt, may actually reduce the overall costs of regulatory compliance. Indeed, our integrate[d] ownership disclosure proposal is worth considering for its simplicity and internal consistency alone, even apart from its value in relation to the new vote buying.

Disclosure may be sufficient to address hidden (morphable) ownership. For empty voting, it will likely prove to be only a first step. Eventually, perhaps soon, other responses to empty voting may be needed. We outline a menu of possible approaches, which fall into three broad families. One family focuses on voting rights themselves. A second addresses the aging architecture of our voting system. The third involves the supply and demand forces in the OTC derivatives and share lending market on which the new vote buying relies.

Which additional regulatory approaches should be adopted we cannot yet say. That will depend on information as yet unknown, which our disclosure rules are designed to collect. We do not know existing legal and economic theories of the public corporation presume a link between voting rights and economic ownership that can no longer be relied on.

As already mentioned, the Shareholder Rights Directive was amended in 2017 by the Shareholder Rights Directive II (Directive 2017/828/EU of the European Parliament and of the Council of 17 May 2017 amending Directive 2007/36/EC *as regards the encouragement of long-term shareholder engagement*). The Shareholder Rights Directive II addresses this issue according to the 2012 Action Plan (§ 2.3.).

The Shareholder Rights Directive II recognises that shares of listed companies are often held through complex chains of intermediaries which render the exercise of shareholder rights more difficult and may act as an obstacle to shareholder engagement. Companies are often unable to identify their shareholders, whilst the identification of shareholders is a prerequisite to direct communication between the shareholders and the company and therefore essential to facilitating the exercise of shareholder rights and shareholder engagement. This is particularly relevant in cross-border situations and when using electronic means. Listed companies should therefore have the right to identify their shareholders in order to be able to communicate with them directly. Intermediaries should be required, upon the request of the company, to communicate to the company the information regarding shareholder identity. However, Member States should be allowed to exclude from the identification requirement shareholders holding only a small number of shares (Recital 4 Shareholder Rights Directive II).

As a result, a new chapter of the Shareholder Rights Directive on identification of shareholders, transmission of information and facilitation of exercise of shareholder rights has been introduced.

Article 3a Identification of shareholders Directive 2007/36/EC

1. Member States shall ensure that companies have the right to identify their shareholders. Member States may provide for companies having a registered office on their territory to be only allowed to request the identification of shareholders holding more than a certain percentage of shares or voting rights. Such a percentage shall not exceed 0.5 %.

2. Member States shall ensure that, on the request of the company or of a third party nominated by the company, the intermediaries communicate without delay to the company the information regarding shareholder identity.
3. Where there is more than one intermediary in a chain of intermediaries, Member States shall ensure that the request of the company, or of a third party nominated by the company, is transmitted between intermediaries without delay and that the information regarding shareholder identity is transmitted directly to the company or to a third party nominated by the company without delay by the intermediary who holds the requested information. Member States shall ensure that the company is able to obtain information regarding shareholder identity from any intermediary in the chain that holds the information.

Member States may provide for the company to be allowed to request the central securities depository or another intermediary or service provider to collect the information regarding shareholder identity, including from the intermediaries in the chain of intermediaries and to transmit the information to the company.

Member States may additionally provide that, at the request of the company, or of a third party nominated by the company, the intermediary is to communicate to the company without delay the details of the next intermediary in the chain of intermediaries.

4. The personal data of shareholders shall be processed pursuant to this Article in order to enable the company to identify its existing shareholders in order to communicate with them directly with the view to facilitating the exercise of shareholder rights and shareholder engagement with the company.

Without prejudice to any longer storage period laid down by any sector-specific Union legislative act, Member States shall ensure that companies and intermediaries do not store the personal data of shareholders transmitted to them in accordance with this Article for the purpose specified in this Article for longer than 12 months after they have become aware that the person concerned has ceased to be a shareholder.

Member States may provide by law for processing of the personal data of shareholders for other purposes.

5. Member States shall ensure that legal persons have the right of rectification of incomplete or inaccurate information regarding their shareholder identity.
6. Member States shall ensure that an intermediary that discloses information regarding shareholder identity in accordance with the rules laid down in this Article is not considered to be in breach of any restriction on disclosure of information imposed by contract or by any legislative, regulatory or administrative provision.
7. By 10 June 2019, Member States shall provide the European Supervisory Authority (European Securities and Markets Authority) (ESMA), established by Regulation (EU) No 1095/2010 of the European Parliament and of the Council (10) with information on whether they have limited shareholder identification to shareholders holding more than a certain percentage of the shares or voting rights in accordance with paragraph 1 and, if so, the applicable percentage. ESMA shall publish that information on its website.

8. The Commission shall be empowered to adopt implementing acts to specify the minimum requirements to transmit the information laid down in paragraph 2 as regards the format of information to be transmitted, the format of the request, including their security and interoperability, and the deadlines to be complied with. Those implementing acts shall be adopted by 10 September 2018 in accordance with the examination procedure referred to in Article 14a(2).

Article 3b Transmission of information Directive 2007/36/EC

1. Member States shall ensure that the intermediaries are required to transmit the following information, without delay, from the company to the shareholder or to a third party nominated by the shareholder:
   (a) the information which the company is required to provide to the shareholder, to enable the shareholder to exercise rights flowing from its shares, and which is directed to all shareholders in shares of that class; or
   (b) where the information referred to in point (a) is available to shareholders on the website of the company, a notice indicating where on the website that information can be found.
2. Member States shall require companies to provide intermediaries in a standardised and timely manner with the information referred to in point (a) of paragraph 1 or the notice referred to in point (b) of that paragraph.
3. However, Member States shall not require that the information referred to in point (a) of paragraph 1 or the notice referred to in point (b) of that paragraph be transmitted or provided in accordance with paragraphs 1 and 2 where companies send that information or that notice directly to all their shareholders or to a third party nominated by the shareholder.
4. Member States shall oblige intermediaries to transmit, without delay, to the company, in accordance with the instructions received from the shareholders, the information received from the shareholders related to the exercise of the rights flowing from their shares.
5. Where there is more than one intermediary in a chain of intermediaries, information referred to in paragraphs 1 and 4 shall be transmitted between intermediaries without delay, unless the information can be directly transmitted by the intermediary to the company or to the shareholder or to a third party nominated by the shareholder.
6. The Commission shall be empowered to adopt implementing acts to specify the minimum requirements to transmit information laid down in paragraphs 1 to 5 of this Article as regards the types and format of information to be transmitted, including their security and interoperability, and the deadlines to be complied with. Those implementing acts shall be adopted by 10 September 2018 in accordance with the examination procedure referred to in Article 14a(2).

Article 3c Facilitation of the exercise of shareholder rights Directive 2007/36/EC

1. Member States shall ensure that the intermediaries facilitate the exercise of the rights by the shareholder, including the right to participate and vote in general meetings, which shall comprise at least one of the following:
   (a) the intermediary makes the necessary arrangements for the shareholder or a third party nominated by the shareholder to be able to exercise themselves the rights;
   (b) the intermediary exercises the rights flowing from the shares upon the explicit authorisation and instruction of the shareholder and for the shareholder's benefit.
2. Member States shall ensure that when votes are cast electronically an electronic confirmation of receipt of the votes is sent to the person that casts the vote.

Member States shall ensure that after the general meeting the shareholder or a third party nominated by the shareholder can obtain, at least upon request, confirmation that their votes have been validly recorded and counted by the company, unless that information is already available to them. Member States may establish a deadline for requesting such confirmation. Such a deadline shall not be longer than three months from the date of the vote.

Where the intermediary receives confirmation as referred to in the first or second subparagraph, it shall transmit it without delay to the shareholder or a third party nominated by the shareholder. Where there is more than one intermediary in the chain of intermediaries the confirmation shall be transmitted between intermediaries without delay, unless the confirmation can be directly transmitted to the shareholder or a third party nominated by the shareholder.

3. The Commission shall be empowered to adopt implementing acts to specify the minimum requirements to facilitate the exercise of shareholder rights laid down in paragraphs 1 and 2 of this Article as regards the types of the facilitation, the format of the electronic confirmation of receipt of the votes, the format for the transmission of the confirmation that the votes have been validly recorded and counted through the chain of intermediaries, including their security and interoperability, and the deadlines to be complied with. Those implementing acts shall be adopted by 10 September 2018 in accordance with the examination procedure referred to in Article 14a(2).

Likewise, a new chapter of the Shareholder Rights Directive has been introduced on transparency of institutional investors, asset managers, and proxy advisors (Articles 3g–3k Directive 2007/36/EC). The principles supporting the provision of this new chapter are synthesised in the Preambles of Shareholder Rights Directive II as follows.

Recitals 15–23 Directive 2017/828/EU

(15) Institutional investors and asset managers are often important shareholders of listed companies in the Union and can therefore play an important role in the corporate

governance of those companies, but also more generally with regard to their strategy and long-term performance. However, the experience of the last years has shown that institutional investors and asset managers often do not engage with companies in which they hold shares and evidence shows that capital markets often exert pressure on companies to perform in the short term, which may jeopardise the long-term financial and non-financial performance of companies and may, among other negative consequences, lead to a suboptimal level of investments, for example in research and development, to the detriment of the long-term performance of both the companies and the investors.

(16) Institutional investors and asset managers are often not transparent about their investment strategies, their engagement policy and the implementation thereof. Public disclosure of such information could have a positive impact on investor awareness, enable ultimate beneficiaries such as future pensioners optimise investment decisions, facilitate the dialogue between companies and their shareholders, encourage shareholder engagement and strengthen their accountability to stakeholders and to civil society.

(17) Institutional investors and asset managers should therefore be more transparent as regards their approach to shareholder engagement. They should either develop and publicly disclose a policy on shareholder engagement or explain why they have chosen not to do so. The policy on shareholder engagement should describe how institutional investors and asset managers integrate shareholder engagement in their investment strategy, which different engagement activities they choose to carry out and how they do so. The engagement policy should also include policies to manage actual or potential conflicts of interests, in particular situations in which the institutional investors or asset managers or their affiliated undertakings have significant business relationships with the investee company. The engagement policy or the explanation should be publicly available online.

(18) Institutional investors and asset managers should publicly disclose information about the implementation of their engagement policy and in particular how they have exercised their voting rights. However, with a view to reducing the possible administrative burden, investors should be able to decide not to publish every vote cast if the vote is considered to be insignificant due to the subject matter of the vote or to the size of the holding in the company. Such insignificant votes may include votes cast on purely procedural matters or votes cast in companies where the investor has a very minor stake compared to the investor's holdings in other investee companies. Investors should set their own criteria regarding which votes are insignificant on the basis of the subject matter of the vote or the size of the holding in the company, and apply them consistently.

(19) A medium to long-term approach is a key enabler of responsible stewardship of assets. The institutional investors should therefore disclose to the public, annually, information explaining how the main elements of their equity investment strategy are consistent with the profile and duration of their liabilities and how those elements contribute to the medium to long-term performance of their assets. Where they make use of an asset manager, either through discretionary mandates involving the management of assets on an individual basis or through pooled funds,

institutional investors should disclose to the public certain key elements of the arrangement with the asset manager, in particular how it incentivises the asset manager to align its investment strategy and decisions with the profile and duration of the liabilities of the institutional investor, in particular long-term liabilities, how it evaluates the asset manager's performance, including its remuneration, how it monitors portfolio turnover costs incurred by the asset manager and how it incentivises the asset manager to engage in the best medium to long-term interest of the institutional investor. This would contribute to a proper alignment of interests between the final beneficiaries of institutional investors, the asset managers and the investee companies and potentially to the development of longer-term investment strategies and longer-term relationships with investee companies involving shareholder engagement.

(20) Asset managers should give information to the institutional investor that is sufficient to allow the latter to assess whether and how the manager acts in the best long-term interests of the investor and whether the asset manager pursues a strategy that provides for efficient shareholder engagement. In principle, the relationship between the asset manager and the institutional investor is a matter for bilateral contractual arrangements. However, although big institutional investors may be able to request detailed reporting from the asset manager, especially if the assets are managed on the basis of a discretionary mandate, for smaller and less sophisticated institutional investors it is crucial to set a minimum set of legal requirements, so that they can properly assess, and hold to account, the asset manager. Therefore, asset managers should be required to disclose to institutional investors how their investment strategy and the implementation thereof contribute to the medium to long-term performance of the assets of the institutional investor or of the fund. That disclosure should cover reporting on the key material medium to long-term risks associated with the portfolio investments, including corporate governance matters and other medium to long-term risks. That information is key to allowing the institutional investor to assess whether the asset manager carries out a medium to long-term analysis of the equity and the portfolio which is a key enabler of efficient shareholder engagement. As those medium to long-term risks will impact the returns of the investors, more effective integration of those matters into investment processes may be crucial for institutional investors.

(21) Moreover, asset managers should disclose to institutional investors the composition, turnover and turnover costs of their portfolio as well as their policy on securities lending. The level of portfolio turnover is a significant indicator of whether an asset manager's processes are fully aligned with the identified strategy and interests of the institutional investor and indicates whether the asset manager holds equities for a period of time that enables it to engage with the company in an effective way. High portfolio turnover may be an indicator of a lack of conviction in investment decisions and momentum-following behaviour, neither of which is likely to be in the institutional investor's best interests in

the long term, especially as an increase in turnover raises the costs faced by the investor and can influence systemic risk. On the other hand, unexpectedly low turnover may signal inattention to risk management or a drift towards a more passive investment approach. Securities lending can cause controversy in the area of shareholder engagement under which the investors' shares are in effect sold, subject to a buyback right. Sold shares have to be recalled for engagement purposes, including voting at the general meeting. It is therefore important that the asset manager reports on its policy on securities lending and how it is applied to fulfil its engagement activities, particularly at the time of the general meeting of the investee company.

(22) The asset manager should also inform the institutional investor whether and, if so, how the asset manager makes investment decisions on the basis of an evaluation of the medium to long-term performance of the investee company, including its non-financial performance. Such information is particularly useful to indicate whether the asset manager adopts a long-term oriented and active approach to asset management and takes social, environmental and governance matters into account.

(23) The asset manager should provide proper information to the institutional investor on whether and, if so, which conflicts of interests have arisen in connection with engagement activities and how the asset manager has dealt with them. For example, conflicts of interests may prevent the asset manager from voting or from engaging at all. All such situations should be disclosed to the institutional investor.

FURTHER READING

Henry T.C. Hu and Bernard Black, 'The New Vote Buying: Empty Voting and Hidden (Morphable) Ownership', 79 *So. Cal. L. Rev.* 811–908 (2006).

Henry T.C. Hu and Bernard Black, 'Empty Voting and Hidden (Morphable) Ownership: Taxonomy, Implications, and Reforms', 61 *Bus. Law* 1011 (2006).

Henry T.C. Hu and Bernard Black, 'Hedge Funds, Insiders, and the Decoupling of Economic and Voting Ownership: Empty Voting and Hidden (Morphable) Ownership', 13 *J. Corp. Fin.* 343 (2007).

Eddy Wymeersch, 'Shareholders in Action: Towards a New Company Paradigm?', 4 *ECL* 50–57 (2007).

Henry T.C. Hu and Bernard Black, 'Equity and Debt, Decoupling and Empty Voting II: Importance and Extensions', 156 *U. Pa L. Rev.* 625 (2008).

Marcel Kahan and Eduard Rock, 'The Hanging Chads of Corporate Voting', 96 *Geo. L.J.* 1227 (2008).

Carl Clottens, 'Empty Voting: A European Perspective', 9 *ECFR* 446–483 (2012).

Sascha Stiegler, 'Shareholder Identification and Transmission of Information – Imbalance between Shareholders' Anonymity and Engagement?', 30 *EBLR* 763–784 (2019).

See also:

Nicola de Luca, 'On Record Date, Empty Voting and Hidden Ownership: Some Remarks on EU Directive 2007/36/EC from a European Perspective', available at SSRN: https://papers.ssrn.com/sol3/papers.cfm?abstract_id=1633749.

15.7 The Shareholders' Meetings Procedure: (C) The General Meetings' Resolutions

Neither the SE Statute nor the Shareholders' Rights Directive express the rules for the organisation and conduct of general meetings.

Article 53 Regulation 2001/2157/EC

Without prejudice to the rules laid down in this section, the organisation and conduct of general meetings together with voting procedures shall be governed by the law applicable to public limited-liability companies in the Member State in which the SE's registered office is situated.

The goal of shareholders' meetings is to facilitate discussion of the agenda items and permit the voting on proposed resolutions. As the majority principle characterises the shareholders' democracy, adoption of proposed resolutions requires that a majority of votes are cast in favour of the resolution.

Other than in partnerships and cooperatives, where voting rights are allocated on a *per capita* basis, in limited companies – either public or private – voting rights generally attach to shares under the one share, one vote principle; hence, shareholders holding more shares dispose of more voting rights, and eventually of the majority enabling decisions to be taken in the general meeting.

It is disputed whether one share, one vote is a European principle and, in case the answer is positive, how broad derogations from it shall be permitted. This issue will be examined twice: first with respect to so-called 'golden shares', shares issued in a company undergoing the process of privatisation often granting to Member States or other public bodies the right to elect additional board members, or to compulsorily repurchase the majority stake at will, or to express a majority in meeting regardless of the stake; as we will later discuss by examining the leading cases, including *ENI/Telecom Italia, EDF, Volkswagen*, and *AEM/ Edison* (*see*, Chapter 16, §§ 16.7–16.10), the CJEU has been asked to assess the validity of the golden shares system several times; second, with respect to the 'Breakthrough Rule', i.e., a rule neutralising multiple-voting shares in case of a takeover bid (*see*, Chapter 18, § 18.4).

This being said, regardless of whether the shares of the company confer single or multiple voting rights to their holders, the SE Statute adopts the simple majority of votes validly cast as a general principle. Sometimes, however, it requires that a majority is only reached in a given quorum, i.e., when a sufficient number of shareholders are present or represented in the general meeting.

Article 57 Regulation 2001/2157/EC

Save where this Regulation or, failing that, the law applicable to public limited-liability companies in the Member State in which an SE's registered office is situated requires a larger majority, the general meeting's decisions shall be taken by a majority of the votes validly cast.

Article 59 Regulation 2001/2157/EC

1. Amendment of an SE's statutes shall require a decision by the general meeting taken by a majority which may not be less than two thirds of the votes cast, unless the law applicable to public limited-liability companies in the Member State in which an SE's registered office is situated requires or permits a larger majority.
2. A Member State may, however, provide that where at least half of an SE's subscribed capital is represented, a simple majority of the votes referred to in paragraph 1 shall suffice.
3. Amendments to an SE's statutes shall be publicised in accordance with Article 13.

Save when the shareholders' meeting elects the members of the supervisory or the administrative organ, shareholders generally express their votes in a kind of binary code, as they are required to say 'yes' or 'no' to a proposed resolution. In addition to 'yes' or 'no' shareholders may, however, abstain from voting.

In case of shareholders abstaining from the vote, the SE Statute expresses the principle by which only 'yes' or 'no' votes shall be considered cast. Therefore, a majority of votes validly cast is reached when the 'yes' overreach the 'no'.

Article 58 Regulation 2001/2157/EC

The votes cast shall not include votes attaching to shares in respect of which the shareholder has not taken part in the vote or has abstained or has returned a blank or spoilt ballot paper.

It should be added, as we will later examine in more detail, that where companies have two or more classes of shares, decisions of the general meeting are sometimes only a part of a more articulated procedure, involving also the separate vote of the holders of each class of shares.

Article 60(1) Regulation 2001/2157/EC

1. Where an SE has two or more classes of shares, every decision by the general meeting shall be subject to a separate vote by each class of shareholders whose class rights are affected thereby.

As a final point, the Shareholder Rights Directive requires that the voting results are disclosed for all interested shareholders through publication on the Internet site.

Article 14 Voting Results, Directive 2007/36/EC

1. The company shall establish for each resolution at least the number of shares for which votes have been validly cast, the proportion of the share capital represented by those votes, the total number of votes validly cast as well as the number of votes cast in favour of and against each resolution and, where applicable, the number of abstentions.

However, Member States may provide or allow companies to provide that if no shareholder requests a full account of the voting, it shall be sufficient to establish the voting results only to the extent needed to ensure that the required majority is reached for each resolution.

2. Within a period of time to be determined by the applicable law, which shall not exceed 15 days after the general meeting, the company shall publish on its Internet site the voting results established in accordance with paragraph 1.
3. This Article is without prejudice to any legal rules that Member States have adopted or may adopt concerning the formalities required in order for a resolution to become valid or the possibility of a subsequent legal challenge to the voting result.

FURTHER READING

Guido Ferrarini, 'One Share – One Vote: A European Rule?', 3 *ECFR* 147–177 (2006).

George Psarakis, 'One Share – One Vote and the Case for a Harmonised Capital Structure', 19 *EBLR* 709–733 (2008).

See also:

Alberto Santamaria, *European Economic Law* 102–108 (Alphen aan den Rijn, Kluwer Law International, 3rd ed., 2014).

16

Protection of Minorities and Equal Treatment of Shareholders (I)

16.1 Reinforced Majorities and Double Voting

Nicola de Luca, 'Unequal Treatment and Shareholders' Welfare Growth: "Fairness" v. "Precise Equality"', 34 *Del. J. Corp. L.* 853–920, at 895 (2009)

Corporations are not only governed by a majority principle, but they are also governed by a majoritarian principle related to shares of interest. Indeed, the necessity to put all members of a community on the same playing field belongs to a very different economic and social model. This model is typically seen in mutual companies or by some non-profit organizations, where the majority principle is related to people and not to shares of interests, and votes are counted on a per capita basis. The majority principle related to shares of interest, however, is in itself an expression of inequality, because shareholders that are outside the majority group do not run the business either directly, or indirectly, through the appointment of directors. So they count less. This may lead some to question the justification for the shares of interests' majority principle or the morality of capitalism in general, that may invoke (or misinterpret) the Aristotelian concept of distributive justice. But this seems to be a sterile and fundamentally wrong debate. The majority rule is a fundamental device to solve the deadlock which absolutely equal parties would unavoidably face.

Adoption of the majority principle as a general rule requires adequate consideration of minority shareholders' interest. In this respect, ECL provides many rules aiming at protecting minority shareholders, such as: reinforced majorities for some fundamental matters, anti-dilution tools in case of a capital increase, double majorities for decisions affecting special classes of shares (or special consent of the affected shareholders), sterilisation of voting rights attached to treasury shares, and so on.

The SE Statute requires that all decisions of the general meeting that amend the articles of the company are decided upon a reinforced majority.

Article 59 Regulation 2001/2157/EC

1. Amendment of an SE's statutes shall require a decision by the general meeting taken by a majority which may not be less than two thirds of the votes cast, unless the law applicable to public limited-liability companies in the Member State in which an SE's registered office is situated requires or permits a larger majority.
2. A Member State may, however, provide that where at least half of an SE's subscribed capital is represented, a simple majority of the votes referred to in paragraph 1 shall suffice.
3. Amendments to an SE's statutes shall be publicised in accordance with Article 13.

Similarly, Article 83 Directive 2017/1132/EU requires that decisions of the general meeting concerning a capital increase (and restricting or withdrawing pre-emptive rights) or concerning a reduction of capital are taken upon a reinforced majority of not less than two thirds of the votes attaching to the securities or the subscribed capital represented. However, a simple majority is sufficient when at least half the subscribed capital is represented.

As regards the redemption of shares, ECL differentiates: (i) redemption of shares *provided for* in advance by the company's statute or instrument of incorporation; (ii) redemption of shares *not provided for* in advance by the company's statute or instrument of incorporation; (iii) redemption of redeemable shares.

Article 78 Directive 2017/1132/EU

Where the laws of a Member State authorise total or partial redemption of the subscribed capital without reduction of the latter, they shall at least require that the following conditions are observed:

(a) where the statutes or instrument of incorporation provide for redemption, the latter shall be decided on by the general meeting voting at least under the usual conditions of quorum and majority; where the statutes or instrument of incorporation do not provide for redemption, the latter shall be decided upon by the general meeting acting at least under the conditions of quorum and majority laid down in Article 83 [i.e. upon a reinforced majority of not less than two-thirds of the votes attaching to the securities or the subscribed capital represented]; the decision must be published in the manner prescribed by the laws of each Member State, in accordance with Article 16;

...

(c) shareholders whose shares are redeemed shall retain their rights in the company, with the exception of their rights to the repayment of their investment and participation in the distribution of an initial dividend on unredeemed shares.

Article 82 Directive 2017/1132/EU

Where the laws of a Member State authorise companies to issue redeemable shares, they shall require that the following conditions, at least, are complied with for the redemption of such shares:

(a) redemption must be authorised by the company's statutes or instrument of incorporation before the redeemable shares are subscribed for;

...

(c) the terms and the manner of redemption must be laid down in the company's statutes or instrument of incorporation;

...

In other words, when redemption of the shares is probable (because all shares may be redeemed, or because there is one or more class of redeemable shares), then the decision of the general meeting does not require a reinforced majority; conversely, a reinforced majority is required when redemption is possible, but not probable. In addition, as shareholders whose shares are redeemed shall retain their rights in the company (except for the right to reimbursement and to a certain quota of dividends) these are deemed not to be 'affected' by the decision.

Indeed, when decisions of the general meeting affect only certain classes of shares, the resolution of the general meeting shall be effective only upon consent – expressed by majority vote – of the holders of the class of shares whose rights are affected by the general meeting's decision. As the SE Statute puts it:

Article 60 Regulation 2001/2157/EC

1. Where an SE has two or more classes of shares, every decision by the general meeting shall be subject to a separate vote by each class of shareholders whose class rights are affected thereby.
2. Where a decision by the general meeting requires the majority of votes specified in Article 59(1) or (2) [i.e. a reinforced majority], that majority shall also be required for the separate vote by each class of shareholders whose class rights are affected by the decision.

In addition, Directive 2017/1132/EU mandates the same double voting system in cases of capital increase or reduction disparately affecting the various classes of shares.

Article 68(3) Directive 2017/1132/EU

3. Where there are several classes of shares, the decision by the general meeting concerning the increase in capital referred to in paragraph 1 or the authorisation to increase the capital referred to in paragraph 2 shall be subject to a separate vote at least for each class of shareholder whose rights are affected by the transaction.

Article 74 Directive 2017/1132/EU

Where there are several classes of shares, the decision by the general meeting concerning a reduction in the subscribed capital shall be subject to a separate vote, at least for each class of shareholders whose rights are affected by the transaction.

On the contrary, notwithstanding that only some shares or classes of shares are affected by the general meeting's decision, a double vote is not required for recovery of redeemable shares and compulsory withdrawal of shares. Both these two transactions require that the company's statutes provide accordingly before the shares are subscribed for by shareholders. In so doing, the shareholders accept that shares are later redeemed or compulsorily withdrawn and further consent at the time of the redemption or withdrawal is not necessary.

Article 79(1) Directive 2017/1132/EU

...

(a) compulsory withdrawal must be prescribed or authorised by the statutes or instrument of incorporation before the shares which are to be withdrawn are subscribed for;

Article 82(1) Directive 2017/1132/EU

...

(a) redemption [of redeemable shares] must be authorised by the company's statutes or instrument of incorporation before the redeemable shares are subscribed for;

Only in cases where the compulsory withdrawal is authorised merely by the statutes or instrument of incorporation is approval by the shareholders concerned necessary, unless withdrawal is decided upon by the general meeting

(Article 82(1)(b), Directive 2017/1132/EU). In this case, as withdrawal need not affect a certain class of shares, rather, all holders of the shares to be withdrawn, ECL requires either individual consent or a decision taken by the general meeting upon a reinforced majority.

Discussion on the redemption or withdrawal of shares, or on repurchase of the company's own shares shall be resumed later (Chapter 16, § 16.5) as we will introduce the principle of equal treatment of shareholders, carried by Articles 60(1) and 85 Directive 2017/1132/EU.

FURTHER READING

Luca Enriques, Henry Hansmann, Reinier Kraakman, and Marianna Pargendler, 'The Basic Governance Structure: Minority Shareholders and Non-shareholder Constituencies', in John Armour, Luca Enriques et al., *The Anatomy of Corporate Law: A Comparative and Functional Approach* 79–109, at 79–89 (Oxford University Press, 3rd ed., 2017).

16.2 Capital Increase and Pre-emptive Rights

As regards protection of minorities, pre-emptive rights on new issued shares is one of the major features distinguishing EU and US company law.

Marco Ventoruzzo, 'Issuing New Shares and Preemptive Rights: A Comparative Analysis', 12 *Richmond J. Global L. & B.* 517–542, at 519–521 (2013)

In the US, the power to issue new shares is primarily entrusted to the board of directors. Directors enjoy a great degree of freedom in issuing new shares; however one important limitation is that they can only issue the number of shares authorized by the articles of incorporation. Generally, corporations have outstanding shares, which are shares already sold to shareholders that form the capital of the corporation; but the articles of incorporation provide for additional authorized shares that director[s] can issue and sell ...

This rule gives shareholders some control over the financial structure of the corporation. Sales of shares that might dilute shareholders' ownership of the corporation above the threshold set by the authorized shares must be voted by shareholders as an amendment to the articles of incorporation. The practice, however, is to provide for a number of authorized shares significantly larger than the number of outstanding shares, so that if the new financial resources are needed, directors can easily issue new shares. In contrast to European law, issuing new shares in the US is substantially and practically in the hands of directors. In addition, minority shareholders in corporations with controlling shareholders derive little protection from this rule because majority shareholders can consent to increase the number of authorized shares.

One exception to this allocation of powers is established by MBCA § 6.21(f), which requires shareholders' approval if (i) the shares are issued for consideration other than in cash, and (ii) the voting power of shares that are issued comprises more than 20 percent of the voting power of the outstanding shares. Also in listed corporations, shareholders' approval is necessary when the issuing of new shares might determine a shift in control.

Preemptive rights.

Another way to protect shareholders in the event of new shares [being] issued is to grant them a preemptive right to purchase these shares. In this case, shareholders who want to avoid the dilution of their participation can acquire pro-rata the new shares paying the required consideration. Of course, this protection is effective only to the extent that shareholders have the financial means to buy the new shares but if they do, no dilution occurs.

... [In modern corporate statutes] the default rule is that shareholders do not have a preemptive right in case of issuance of new shares, unless the articles of incorporation (and sometimes the bylaws) expressly provide so. In Massachusetts this rule was adopted in 1964, under chapter 156B, section 20 of the general corporation statute. The MBCA and Delaware law also provide for similar rules.

In contrast to US law, ECL requires that pre-emptive rights are granted where the capital is increased by consideration in cash (for consideration other than in cash, the *Siemens* case discussed in § 16.3 is relevant); however, it also considers cases in which pre-emptive rights may be restricted or withdrawn, in the interest of the company as a whole.

Article 72 Directive 2017/1132/EU

1. Whenever the capital is increased by consideration in cash, the shares must be offered on a pre-emptive basis to shareholders in proportion to the capital represented by their shares.

...

3. Any offer of subscription on a pre-emptive basis and the period within which that right must be exercised shall be published in the national gazette appointed in accordance with Article 16. However, the laws of a Member State need not provide for such publication where all of a company's shares are registered. In such case, all the company's shareholders must be informed in writing. The right of pre-emption must be exercised within a period which shall not be less than 14 days from the date of publication of the offer or from the date of dispatch of the letters to the shareholders.

Since it involves a commitment for new contributions to the company, the exercise of pre-emptive rights is a single shareholder's choice that may not be compelled by the company and its directors.

Pre-emptive rights not exercised by shareholders within the period established by national law will expire. ECL does not take any position as to whether, after the expiry of such period, shares offered for subscription to shareholders may be sold to other shareholders or third parties for the same or a higher price.

ECL only requires that, unless the decision of the general meeting so provides, the capital increase shall be subscribed in full, or otherwise is aborted.

Article 72(1) Directive 2017/1132/EU

Where an increase in capital is not fully subscribed, the capital will be increased by the amount of the subscriptions received only if the conditions of the issue so provide.

To facilitate subscription of all new shares, issuers may offer to banks or other financial institutions to subscribe the whole capital increase, at a discounted price which might also be lower than the shares' aggregate nominal value or accounted par (*see above*, Chapter 10, § 10.4). Such professional investors undertake the obligation to offer the subscribed shares to existing shareholders at the price set by the company, thus indirectly granting the right of pre-emption.

Article 72(7) Directive 2017/1132/EU

7. The right of pre-emption is not excluded for the purposes of paragraphs 4 and 5 where, in accordance with the decision to increase the subscribed capital, shares are issued to banks or other financial institutions with a view to their being offered to shareholders of the company in accordance with paragraphs 1 and 3.

As mentioned earlier, a company may not compel shareholders to subscribe the new issued shares. However, the interests of the company as a whole may sometimes require that shareholders waive their individual pre-emptive rights, through a decision taken by the shareholders' meeting upon a reinforced majority. In this respect, ECL prohibits that pre-emptive rights are restricted or withdrawn by the statutes or instrument of incorporation. Pre-emptive rights may only be restricted or withdrawn on a case-by-case basis upon resolution of the general meeting.

Article 72(4–5) Directive 2017/1132/EU

4. The right of pre-emption may not be restricted or withdrawn by the statutes or instrument of incorporation. This may, however, be done by decision of the general meeting. The administrative or management body shall be required to present to such a

meeting a written report indicating the reasons for restriction or withdrawal of the right of pre-emption, and justifying the proposed issue price. The general meeting shall act in accordance with the rules for a quorum and a majority laid down in Article 44. Its decision shall be published in the manner laid down by the laws of each Member State, in accordance with Article 16.

5. The laws of a Member State may provide that the statutes, the instrument of incorporation or the general meeting, acting in accordance with the rules for a quorum, a majority and publication set out in paragraph 4, may give the power to restrict or withdraw the right of pre-emption to the company body which is empowered to decide on an increase in subscribed capital within the limit of the authorised capital. That power may not be granted for a longer period than the power for which provision is made in Article 68(2).

In addition, Member States may decide that pre-emptive rights are not allocated to holders of shares or classes of shares carrying limited right to participate in distributions.

Article 72(2) Directive 2017/1132/EU

2. The laws of a Member State:
   (a) need not apply paragraph 1 to shares which carry a limited right to participate in distributions within the meaning of Article 56 and/or in the company's assets in the event of liquidation; or
   (b) may permit, where the subscribed capital of a company having several classes of shares carrying different rights with regard to voting, or participation in distributions within the meaning of Article 56 or in assets in the event of liquidation, is increased by issuing new shares in only one of these classes, the right of pre-emption of shareholders of the other classes to be exercised only after the exercise of that right by the shareholders of the class in which the new shares are being issued.

It should be added that companies frequently issue convertible bonds, i.e., bonds whose consideration may be (or must be – depending on whether conversion is decided by the bondholder, or is mandatory) used as contribution for the issuance of new shares in exchange for the bonds: in this case, the bondholder becomes a shareholder. Also, companies may issue bonds carrying the right to subscribe for new shares ('cum-warrant'): in case the warrant is exercised, the bondholder *also* becomes a shareholder. In both cases, all existing shareholders at the time of the issuance shall enjoy a pre-emptive right to subscribe the convertible bonds or the cum-warrant bonds, so that they are not later diluted.

Article 72(6) Directive 2017/1132/EU

6. Paragraphs 1 to 5 shall apply to the issue of all securities which are convertible into shares or which carry the right to subscribe for shares, but not to the conversion of such securities, nor to the exercise of the right to subscribe.

Article 72(6) Directive 2017/1132/EU does not expressly refer to the possibility that the right of pre-emption is granted to also convertible – but not yet converted – bondholders. Some Member States' legislations (such as Spain's and Italy's) also grant a pre-emptive right to convertible bondholders: the question as to whether this provision complies with ECL has been raised by the EU Commission and the CJEU has solved it in *Commission* v. *Spain*, which will be discussed in § 16.4.

16.3 *Siemens* Case

In *Siemens* (C-42/95, *Siemens AG* v. *Henry Nold*, [1996] ECR I-06017), the German Bundesgerichtshof (Federal Court of Justice) referred to the Court for a preliminary ruling on a question on the interpretation of Article 29(1) and (4) of the Second Company Law Directive, now Article 72(1) and (4) Directive 2017/1132/EU.

The question was raised in proceedings between Siemens AG ('*Siemens*'), a company incorporated under the laws of Germany, and one of its shareholders, Mr Nold, who sought to have set aside a resolution of Siemens' general meeting authorising the management board to carry out an increase in capital by issuing ordinary shares up to a specified ceiling in return for consideration in cash or in kind. The increase in capital was purportedly intended, *inter alia*, to enable shares to be offered to employees and holdings to be acquired in other companies. By its resolution giving authority to the management board, the general meeting withdrew the shareholders' right of pre-emption.

Under German company law any shareholder who so requests is entitled to be allocated some of the new shares in proportion to the capital represented by his shares in the event of an increase in capital for consideration either in cash or in kind. That right of pre-emption may not be withdrawn by the general meeting unless 'among a number of other conditions' the management board has presented a written report setting out the reasons for withdrawing the right of pre-emption and justifying the proposed issue price.

In addition, the Bundesgerichtshof has formulated case law which, through the imposition of supplementary conditions, subjects resolutions of the general meeting providing for the withdrawal of the shareholders' right of pre-emption to substantive review.

Accordingly, in a judgment of 13 March 1978 (BGHZ 71, 40), the Bundesgerichtshof held that the shareholders' right of pre-emption could be withdrawn only if, having regard to the resulting consequences for shareholders from whom it is withdrawn, such a measure is justified on objective grounds in the company's interest. Reviewing that objective condition of validity entails considering the respective interests of the company and the shareholders and whether the means are proportionate to the intended aim.

Furthermore, in a judgment of 19 April 1982 (BGHZ 83, 319), which was concerned with an increase in capital within the limits of the authorised capital, the Bundesgerichtshof held that, if the general meeting resolves to withdraw the right of pre-emption in the actual resolution authorising the increase, the aforementioned conditions must be publicised at the time of the resolution and be sufficiently certain as to enable them to be assessed by the general meeting. In *Siemens*, the Bundesgerichtshof held that the resolution of the Siemens' general meeting did not satisfy the conditions set out in its case law in so far as it withdrew the shareholders' right of pre-emption in the event of the issue of ordinary shares in return for acquisitions of holdings in other companies, and therefore had to be regarded as unlawful.

The national court has, however, expressed doubts as to the compatibility of its case law with Article 29(1) of the Second Directive (now Article 72(1) Directive 2017/1132/EU), which provides for a right of pre-emption *only* where the capital is increased by consideration in cash, with the result that the rule set out in paragraph 4 may not apply to increases in capital by consideration in kind.

The Bundesgerichtshof took the view that if that provision had to be interpreted as meaning that an increase in capital for consideration in kind is not subject to any condition designed to protect shareholders against depreciation of their shares, but is subject only to review to establish possible abuse, it would preclude the substantive review laid down in its case law in so far as that review would subject resolutions of the general meeting providing for an increase in capital by consideration in kind and involving concurrent withdrawal of the shareholders' right of pre-emption to considerably stricter requirements than those necessitated by a mere review to establish possible abuse.

In those circumstances, the national court stayed proceedings and referred the following question to the Court for a preliminary ruling:

C-42/95, Siemens AG v. Henry Nold, [1996] ECR I-06017, § 11

Is it compatible with the Second Council Directive of 13 December 1976 (77/91/EEC; OJ 1977 L 26, p. 1), in particular Article 29(1) and (4) thereof, for the legality of a resolution of a general meeting of shareholders relating to an increase in capital in return for contributions in kind while at the same time withdrawing the shareholders' right of pre-emption to be determined on the basis of a substantive review in accordance with the principles laid down in the Bundesgerichtshof's judgments of 13 March 1978 (BGHZ 71, 40) and 19 April 1982 (BGHZ 83, 319)?

The CJEU answered the proposed question as follows:

C-42/95, Siemens AG v. Henry Nold, [1996] ECR I-06017, §§ 16, 22 and Operative Part

The Second Council Directive (77/91/EEC) on coordination of safeguards which, for the protection of the interests of members and others, are required by Member States of companies within the meaning of the second paragraph of Article 58 of the Treaty, in respect of the formation of public limited liability companies and the maintenance and alteration of their capital, with a view to making such safeguards equivalent, in particular Article 29(1) and (4), does not preclude a Member State's domestic law from granting a right of pre-emption to shareholders in the event of an increase in capital by consideration in kind and from subjecting the legality of a decision withdrawing that right of pre-emption to a substantive review which secures a higher level of protection for shareholders than that required by Article 29(4) of the directive in the case of contributions in cash.

The fact that that provision does not refer to increases in capital by consideration in kind does not mean that the conclusion can be drawn that the Community legislator elected to restrict the shareholders' right of pre-emption to increases in capital by consideration in cash, thereby precluding Member States from extending it also to increases in capital by consideration in kind. On the contrary, since the Second Directive merely prescribes a right of pre-emption in the event of increases in capital by consideration in cash, whilst refraining from laying down rules on the complex situation – unknown in most Member States – where the right of pre-emption is exercised in the event of increases in capital by consideration in kind, it left Member States at liberty to provide or not to provide for a right of pre-emption in the latter case. In addition, a national rule extending the principle that shareholders should have a right of pre-emption to increases in capital by consideration in kind, while providing for the possibility of restricting or withdrawing that right in certain circumstances, is consistent with one of the aims of the Second Directive, namely that of ensuring more effective protection for shareholders.

16.4 *Commission* v. *Spain* Case

In *Commission* v. *Spain* (C-338/06, *Commission of the European Communities* v. *Kingdom of Spain*, [2008] ECR I-10139), the EU Commission made an application requesting that the Court declare that:

C-338/06, Commission of the European Communities v. Kingdom of Spain, [2008] ECR I-10139, § 1

- by allowing the general meeting of shareholders to approve the issue of new shares without pre-emptive subscription rights, at a price below their fair value;

- by granting the right to pre-emptive subscription of shares in the event of a capital increase by consideration in cash, not only to shareholders, but also to holders of bonds convertible into shares;
- by granting the right to pre-emptive subscription rights for bonds convertible into shares not only to shareholders, but also to holders of bonds convertible into shares pertaining to earlier issues, and
- by failing to provide that the shareholders' meeting may decide to withdraw pre-emptive subscription rights for bonds convertible into shares, the Kingdom of Spain has failed to fulfil its obligations under Articles 29 and 42 of Second Council Directive 77/91/EEC of 13 December 1976 on coordination of safeguards which, for the protection of the interests of members and others, are required by Member States of companies within the meaning of the second paragraph of Article [48] of the Treaty, in respect of the formation of public limited liability companies and the maintenance and alteration of their capital, with a view to making such safeguards equivalent (OJ 1977 L 26, p. 1; 'the Second Directive').

The CJEU solved the proposed questions as follows (from the official summary):

C-338/06, Commission of the European Communities v. Kingdom of Spain, [2008] ECR I-10139, §§ 26, 30–31, 33–34

A Member State which maintains in force rules whereby the general meeting of shareholders of a listed company may freely determine the issue price of the new shares, when deciding on an increase in capital that entails the total or partial withdrawal of a right of pre-emption, does not fail to fulfil its obligations under Article 42 of Second Directive 77/91 on company law, read in conjunction with Article 29(1) and (4) thereof, provided that the meeting has available to it a report for the director of the company and a report from an auditor appointed for that purpose, and provided that the issue price of the shares is higher than their net asset value as apparent from the auditor's report.

Although the right of pre-emption granted to shareholders does not admit of any exception other than that expressly laid down in Article 29(4) of the Second Directive, the fact remains that the Second Directive lays down minimum requirements for the protection of shareholders and creditors of public limited companies, by leaving the Member States free to adopt provisions that are more favourable to them, which provide, inter alia, for more restrictive conditions on withdrawing the right of pre-emption.

In addition, the fact that the issue price of the new shares may be set below their market value, in accordance with those rules, cannot be regarded as liable to lead to unequal treatment, for the purposes of Article 42 of the Second Directive, between existing and new shareholders, in the absence of evidence to show, as required under Article 42 of the directive, that both those categories of shareholders are in the same position, and must therefore be treated equally. Furthermore, to require that the issue price of new shares must not be below their market value would have the effect that, even if that price were justified by the directors' report, the general meeting of shareholders could not apply it without infringing the principle of equal treatment referred to in Article 42 of the Second Directive.

C-338/06, Commission of the European Communities v. Kingdom of Spain, [2008] ECR I-10139, §§ 39–40, 46, Operative Part 1

A Member State which grants a pre-emption right in respect of shares, in the event of an increase in capital by contributions in cash, not only to shareholders, but also to holders of bonds convertible into shares, and which grants a pre-emption right in respect of bonds convertible into shares, not only to shareholders, but also to the holders of bonds convertible into shares pertaining to earlier issues, fails to fulfil its obligations under Article 29(1) and (6) of Second Directive 77/91 on company law.

As is apparent from the wording of Article 29(1) and (6), the new shares and the bonds convertible into shares are not to be offered to the shareholders and the bondholders simultaneously, but 'on a pre-emptive basis' to the shareholders. Thus, only in so far as the shareholders have not exercised their right of pre-emption can those shares and bonds be offered to other purchasers, including, in particular, the holders of convertible bonds.

C-338/06, Commission of the European Communities v. Kingdom of Spain, [2008] ECR I-10139, §§ 50–51, 55, 57, Operative Part 1

A Member State which fails to provide that the general meeting of shareholders may decide to withdraw pre-emption rights in respect of bonds convertible into shares on an issue of such bonds fails to fulfil its obligations under Article 29(6) of Second Directive 77/91 on company law, read in conjunction with Article 29(4) thereof.

Even though the Member States are free to adopt more restrictive conditions on withdrawal of the right of pre-emption at issue, the fact remains that Article 29(6) of the Second Directive, read in conjunction with Article 29(4) thereof, requires that, in certain circumstances, the general meeting of shareholders be able to decide to withdraw the right of pre-emption for all securities which are convertible into shares. National rules which make no express provision for the possibility of such withdrawal, even if they could be interpreted contrary to their wording, would not be likely to create a situation which is sufficiently precise, clear and transparent in order to allow individuals to know the full extent of their rights and rely on them before the national courts.

As emerges from the summary, *Commission* v. *Spain* is an important decision not only for clarifying the relationship between the shareholders and bondholders of a company, but also for considering a possible unequal treatment between existing and new shareholders, in case pre-emptive rights are withdrawn and the law requests that the price of the new shares be above the net asset value of the shares but may be less than the current market value. We will discuss this issue in greater depth in § 16.5, after introducing the relevant ECL rules concerning equal treatment of shareholders.

FURTHER READING

Kristoffel Grechenig, 'Discriminating Shareholders through the Exclusion of Preemption Rights?: The European Infringement Proceeding against Spain (C-338/06)', 4 *ECFR* 571–592 (2007).

See also:
Marco Ventoruzzo, Pierre-Henry Conac, Gen Goto, Sebastan Mock, Mario Notari, and Arad Reisberg, *Comparative Corporate Governance* 238–243 (St Paul, MN, West Academic Publishing, 2015).

16.5 Equal Treatment of Shareholders (I)

Article 85 Directive 2017/1132/EU reads as follows:

Article 85 Directive 2017/1132/EU

For the purposes of the implementation of this Directive, the laws of the Member States shall ensure equal treatment to all shareholders who are in the same position.

As of 2006, the principle of equal treatment has been reiterated as regards the acquisition of the company's own shares.

Article 60(1) Directive 2017/1132/EU

1. Without prejudice to the principle of equal treatment of all shareholders who are in the same position, and to Regulation (EU) No 596/2014, Member States may permit a company to acquire its own shares ...

In addition, Article 65 of Directive 2001/34/EC on admission of securities to the stock exchange listing, requires that the company ensures equal treatment of all shareholders who are in the same position, in particular with regards to the obligation of directors to provide information to all holders of securities.

Article 65 Directive 2001/34/EU

1. The company shall ensure equal treatment for all shareholders who are in the same position.

2. The company must ensure, at least in each Member State in which its shares are listed, that all the necessary facilities and information are available to enable shareholders to exercise their rights. In particular, it must:

(a) inform shareholders of the holding of meetings and enable them to exercise their right to vote,
(b) publish notices or distribute circulars concerning the allocation and payment of dividends, the issue of new shares including allotment, subscription, renunciation and conversion arrangements,
(c) designate as its agent a financial institution through which shareholders may exercise their financial rights, unless the company itself provides financial services.

Similarly to the Admission to Listing, the Shareholder Rights Directive has also included an equal treatment rule as regards participation and the exercise of voting rights in the general meeting.

Article 4 Equal Treatment of Shareholders, Directive 2007/36/EC

The company shall ensure equal treatment for all shareholders who are in the same position with regard to participation and the exercise of voting rights in the general meeting.

Lastly, the principle of equal treatment of all holders of securities, thus including those with minority holdings, when control of their companies has been acquired, is expressed in Article 3(1)(a) Directive 2004/25/EC, reading as follows:

Article 3(1) Directive 2004/25/EC

(a) all holders of the securities of an offeree company of the same class must be afforded equivalent treatment; moreover, if a person acquires control of a company, the other holders of securities must be protected;

An excerpt from a scholarly paper might be useful to clarify the debate behind these rules and their meaning. Also, as this paper shows, the equal treatment rule provided for in the Company Law Directive, in the Admission to Listing as well as the Shareholder Rights Directives, on the one hand, and the one included in the Takeover Bids Directive, on the other, are very different rules, as the former refers to the relationship between the company and the shareholders and the latter refers to the relationship amongst shareholders, in particular majority and minority shareholders: hence, the latter will be discussed in Chapter 18, § 18.2.

Nicola de Luca, 'Unequal Treatment and Shareholders' Welfare Growth: "Fairness" v. "Precise Equality"', 34 *Del. J. Corp. L.* 853–920, at 887–896 (2009)

V The Law & Economics of Equal Treatment in Corporate Distributions

... this part of the paper will shed light on the doctrinal background, causing broadly opposing approaches to emerge especially in the American case law.

Here, as also among legal scholars, the existence of an equal opportunity rule for all shareholders is highly controversial. Generally, those who stand for an equal opportunity rule claim that it is applicable to sales of control blocks. Yet Berle and Means argued that control is a corporate asset; therefore, if a premium should go anywhere, it 'must go into the corporate treasury,' indirectly benefiting all shareholders. A similar result is reached by those who affirm the right to equal opportunity; therefore, they counsel that in the sale of control blocks, the premium should be proportionally shared directly among all shareholders. Over time the equal opportunities approach has been suggested to several operations that normally precede or follow the acquisition or consolidation of corporate control (especially freeze-outs, squeeze-outs, going private transactions, leveraged and management buyouts); these operations involve fiduciary duties of directors or shareholders. Actually, it is the debate relating to these further problems that gave the arguments which led to the Donahue and Nixon decisions: these arguments were proposed by scholars based at Harvard and Chicago, whom I will further address as the Harvard School or the Chicago School Approach.

V.A Equal Opportunities in Sales of Control Blocks

The problem of equal opportunities in the sale of control blocks, in my point of view, must be set aside from the problems we are discussing in this paper. The equal sharing–Harvard School approach claims that, in case of sale of control blocks, all shareholders have an equal opportunity to sell the same portion as the controlling shareholder (proportional to the total amount offered). This idea relates to the principle that all shares (of the same class) are to be treated equally, because this is fair. Arguments in favor and against have been brought, and ultimately economic analyses have shown that both the equal treatment rule and the market rule may be efficient: in particular, the equal treatment rule stops some efficient transactions, but also stops some inefficient transactions. In fact, while the American case law follows the market rule, Article 5 Thirteenth Directive on takeovers bids adopts a general equal opportunity rule (where the target is a listed company). In my opinion, close corporations should be left to the market rule: drag-along, or other similar clauses may grant minorities the right to share the premium, or to take over the company; also, such clauses are effective devices for majorities to squeeze-out minorities through white knights at fair price. As the comparative overview has clearly shown, however, an equal opportunity rule should be relevant to drive the conduct of corporate bodies, such as the board of directors and the shareholders' meeting, when managing the corporation and its assets, but seems not relevant for the disposal of shareholders' personal rights, such as ultimately the sale of shares or control blocks. In my view, this is the deciding argument counseling not to overlap the principle of equal treatment of shareholders with the opportunity to share the premium among all shareholders in sales of control blocks. For the latter, indeed, European scholars focus on market egalitarianism, rather than on a principle of equal treatment of shareholders.

V.B The Harvard School Approach

That being said, the Harvard School approach also suggests that the board of directors (or the majority) follow an equal opportunity rule in case of purchases of a corporation's own shares, distributions in kind, cash-out mergers, forward and reverse stock splits. The Harvard School notes that most corporate laws, including the US, provide shareholders' (pro rata) equality rule in dividend distributions. In their point of view, dividends must be shared among shareholders on a pro rata basis, because this strengthens the expectations of minority shareholders. Were it possible for directors or majorities to share dividends upon a non pro rata basis, the costs for raising capital among investors would considerably increase. Indeed, if the capital suppliers were to bear the risk of sharing the profits of an activity less than proportionally to their investment (at directors' or majority's will), they would set a much higher price for capital supply, significantly restricting the total offer. Issuers should rely much more consistently if not exclusively on their own equity; all this would result in an inefficient allocation of resources which a system of free collective bargaining would surely avoid. 'Accordingly, corporation law and fiduciary principles provide a standardized contract which removes the element of uncertainty by presuming homogenized treatment of investors of the same class in distributions of dividends and on liquidations.'

What are the corollaries of this approach? Unequal treatment can be justified only if agreed in the charter and not at [the] majority's or directors' discretion. A distribution in kind is not permissible unless the same asset can be distributed to all shareholders or all shareholders consent to a distribution partly in kind and partly in cash. Minorities' freezeouts should be forbidden. The purchase of a company's own shares should not be permitted, except for buybacks of fractional shares and for close corporations, not having an available share market. Going private transactions should be allowed under an equal treatment rule, the effectiveness of which should be granted by judicial or administrative appointment of negotiators to act for the minority or by requiring prior approval of the transaction by an administrative agency or the courts.

V.C The Chicago School Approach

Since the Harvard School proposal results in very severe consequences, some have attempted to mitigate the effects. Relying on shareholders' welfare growth, some others – such as the Chicago School – have strongly criticized this approach.

As Easterbrook and Fischel clearly put it, many scholars, though few courts, conclude that one aspect of fiduciary duty is the equal treatment of investors. Their argument takes the following form: fiduciary principles require fair conduct; equal treatment is fair conduct; hence, fiduciary principles require equal treatment. The conclusion does not follow. The argument depends upon an equivalence between equal and fair treatment. To say that fiduciary principles require equal treatment is to beg the central question whether investors would contract for equal or even roughly equal treatment.

Their argument is that, if the terms under which the directors obtain control of the firm call for them to maximize the wealth of the investors, their duty is to select the highest-paying venture and, following that, to abide by the rules of distribution. If unequal distribution is necessary to make the stakes higher, then duty requires inequality ... The ex post inequality ... is no more 'unfair' than the ex post inequality of a lottery, in which all players invest a certain amount but only a few collect. The equal treatment of the investors ..., and the gains they receive from taking chances, make the ex post inequality both fair and desirable.

The ultimate conclusion of the Chicago School Approach is that whoever produces a gain should be allowed to keep it, 'subject to the constraint that other parties to the transaction be at least as well off as before the transaction. Any attempt to require sharing simply reduces the likelihood that there will be gains to share.'

Although mainly referring to corporate control transactions, I believe that the Chicago Approach is useful to solve also the issues here, but needs further development. Indeed, the Chicago School emphasizes that directors do not breach their fiduciary duties toward all shareholders by performing unequal treatments that benefit some but do not prejudice others. Unequal treatment can be a device to increase shareholders' welfare; and if shareholders' welfare increases, the added value may be shared unequally.

V.D Towards an Improvement of the Chicago School Approach

The Chicago School agrees that dividends must be shared on a pro rata basis because dividend policy transfers and does not increase welfare. Indeed, a rule allowing non pro rata distribution of dividends would not increase the value of the company, but impose a cost on shareholders by forcing them to [monitor] the outflow of capital from the company and ultimately reduce the aggregate welfare. These commentators – as the majority of American legal scholars – fail, however, to differentiate among the various techniques that achieve a distribution for shareholders. In particular they do not adequately consider the effects of distributions in kind and repurchases of shares. Not surprisingly, they strongly criticize the Donahue doctrine, by emphasizing the severe consequences of a strict equal opportunity rule upon the contractual equilibrium of close corporations.

The Chicago School Approach needs, therefore, some further improvement to combine more ideas: (i) unequal treatment of shareholders can be implemented if it determines a shareholder's welfare growth; (ii) also distributions may increase shareholders' welfare, not being only transfer of wealth, but also being suitable to create additional welfare; (iii) if the additional welfare derives from a disparate treatment of shareholders, such treatment is to be allowed as far as no shareholder can claim damage or is specifically compensated; (iv) unequal treatment of shareholders may not be allowed if it does not meet the requirement of fairness; (v) fairness means to consider others' interests in good faith, not to pursue others' interests to the detriment of one's own.

VI Unequal Treatment and Shareholders' Welfare Growth

In this Part, I show that neither equal treatment of shareholders under a different position, nor equal treatment of shareholders under the same position are necessarily efficient from an economic point of view. I show that equal, but not 'precise' equal treatment in corporate distributions may increase shareholders' welfare, and not prejudice anyone.

VI.A Equality of Shareholders v. Equality of Shares

Unlike European legislators and scholars, both the Harvard and the Chicago School approaches overlap 'equal treatment of shareholders' and 'equality among shares.' This leads to some misinterpretation. The rule of sharing dividends pro rata or the 'one-share, one-vote' rule belong to the principle of equality among shares, which is a fundamental device for building secondary markets, and which has nothing to do with 'justice' or 'fairness.' Indeed, secondary markets may only work if standardized and fungible goods may be traded: also capital secondary markets require standardized goods, as shares. Standardization does not necessarily mean uniformity. The practice of all capital markets acknowledges classes of shares characterized by preferential dividend rights or differentiated voting rights. The privileges that characterize the classes of shares are set up in advance, within the corporate charter, because the consent of investors relies basically on these characteristics. However, most jurisdictions allow alterations of these characteristics thereafter, subject to strict procedures that ensure the involvement of the stakeholders. The more common rule for such alterations is the double majority system provided for under the European Directives: the general meeting passes an amendment to the charter by majority vote, then special class meetings give their consent to these amendments. Purchasers of already issued shares always know what kind of investment they are about to make and, although the characteristics of a certain class of shares may change over time, a procedural framework is devoted to ensure that the alterations are not up to the majority's or directors' discretion.

These rules granting equality among shares prevent the pernicious effects that in particular the Harvard School thinks would result [from] not following the rule of equal treatment of shareholders. Indeed, a very different concern is a principle of equal treatment of shareholders. From an economic perspective of the corporate phenomenon, absolute equality among shareholders would require one to consider equal all shareholders, notwithstanding the different quality and quantity of shares each shareholder possesses. This approach would unavoidably strike against one of the fundamental principles of the western economy, employing corporations as the dominant entrepreneurial framework. Corporations not only are governed by a majority principle; they are governed by a majoritarian principle related to shares of interest. Indeed, the necessity to put all members of a community on the same level playing field belongs to a very different economic and social model, typically represented by mutual companies or by some not-for-profit organizations, where the majority principle is related to people and not to shares of interests, and votes are counted on a per capita basis. The majority principle related to shares of interest, however, is in itself an expression of inequality, for the obvious reason that shareholders outside the majority group do not run the business either directly, or appointing the directors. Some may perhaps want to question the justification of the shares of interests' majority principle or the morality of capitalism in general, invoking (or misinterpreting) the Aristotelian concept of distributive justice. This would seem to me, however, a sterile and fundamentally wrong debate. The majority rule, indeed, is a fundamental device to solve the deadlock which absolute equal parties would unavoidably face.

Given that the law cannot provide a principle of equal treatment of shareholders ignoring how many shares the shareholders own, it could be significant (first of all, from an economic point of view) to question whether a rule that requires equal treatment for those who are in a same position would make sense. Not by chance [does] the EU Second Directive [use] this language in its Articles 19 and 42 [now Articles 58 and 85 Directive 2017/1132/EU]. My belief is that both same position and equal treatment are vague concepts. An economic analysis shows, however, that shareholders in the same position need not always be treated equally; that shareholders in a different position should in some cases be treated similarly; that equal treatment cannot mean identical. Ultimately, if an equal treatment rule aims to prevent oppression of minority shareholders, it is not economically efficient.

Only on rare occasions has the CJEU been asked to assess the validity of provisions of national law with regard to Article 85 Directive 2017/1132/EU, or to interpret the meaning of this rule: one of these cases is the already mentioned *Commission* v. *Spain*; another is *Audiolux*, further discussed at Chapter 18, § 18.3. It must be added that, in fields other than company law, the CJEU has been asked to assess the existence (and to define the meaning) of an EU general principle of equal treatment. In so doing, the CJEU exactly refers to the Aristotelian ethic principle (referred to in de Luca (2009) above).

Case C-127/07, Arcelor Atlantique and Lorraine and Others, [2008] ECR I-09895, § 23

23. The general principle of equal treatment, as a general principle of Community law, requires that comparable situations must not be treated differently and different situations must not be treated in the same way unless such treatment is objectively justified (see, inter alia, Case 106/83 Sermide [1984] ECR 4209, paragraph 28; Joined Cases C-133/93, C-300/93 and C-362/93 Crispoltoni and Others [1994] ECR I-4863, paragraphs 50 and 51; and Case C-313/04 Franz Egenberger [2006] ECR I-6331, paragraph 33).

In *Commission* v. *Spain*, the CJEU was asked to declare whether a national rule allowing the general meeting of shareholders (of a listed company) to approve the issue of new shares without pre-emptive subscription rights, at a price below their fair value (current market price), should be regarded as liable to lead to unequal treatment, for the purposes of Article 85 Directive 2017/1132/EU (former Article 42 of the Second Directive), between existing and new shareholders.

C-338/06, Commission of the European Communities v. Kingdom of Spain, [2008] ECR I-10139, §§ 29–34

29 Whereas Article 29(4) of the Second Directive is limited to requiring that the issue price of the new shares be justified in the report of the company's administrative or management body, and does not set any minimum threshold for this, the second subparagraph of Article 159(1)(c) of the Ley de Sociedades Anónimas (LSA, now replaced by the Ley de Sociedades Comerciales, LSC) lays down, as regards quoted companies, a minimum issue price for the new shares, by requiring that that price be above the net asset value of the shares in question irrespective of the conclusions of the report.

30 This assessment of the national rules cannot, moreover, be undermined by the Commission's arguments to the effect that setting the issue price of the new shares at below their market value, as permitted by Article 159 of the LSA, is liable to lead to unequal treatment, for the purposes of Article 42 of the Second Directive, between existing and new shareholders.

31 First, it must be pointed out that the Commission has not provided any evidence to show, as is required under Article 42 of the directive, that those two categories of shareholders are in the same position, thus requiring the LSA to ensure them equal treatment.

32 Secondly, the effect of the Commission's interpretation would be to render Article 29(4) of the Second Directive redundant, since under that provision the issue price has to be justified by the directors' report, although it does not have to be set in accordance with the market value of the shares in question.

33 To require that the issue price of new shares must not be below their market value would have the effect that, even if that price were justified by the directors' report, the general meeting could not apply it without infringing the principle of equal treatment referred to in Article 42 of the Second Directive.

34 In the light of all the foregoing, the first complaint relied on by the Commission in support of its action must be rejected as unfounded.

In other words, the CJEU holds that the fact that the issue price of the new shares may be set below their market value, in accordance with those rules, cannot be regarded as liable to lead to unequal treatment between existing and new shareholders, in the absence of evidence to show, as required under Article 85 Directive 2017/1132/EU, that both those categories of shareholders are in the same position, and must therefore be treated equally. The CJEU, however, does not clarify whether the Commission (in its role of applicant) only failed to show that existing and new shareholders are in the same position, or rather these are by definition in a different position, thus always allowing unequal or disparate treatment. Indeed, the CJEU does not give clues on what could be relevant in the assessment as to whether different shareholders are in the same position or not: e.g., new and old shareholders, majority and minority shareholders, shareholders qualified for being also workers, or having more or less personal needs for a distribution, and so on.

Furthermore, in *Commission* v. *Spain*, the CJEU rejects a broad interpretation of the equal treatment rule. Indeed, to require that the issue price of new shares must not be below their market value would have the effect that, even if that price were justified by the directors' report, the general meeting of shareholders could not apply it without infringing the principle of equal treatment referred to in Article 85 Directive 2017/1132/EU. In so doing, the CJEU clearly rejects that the equal treatment rule prevents decisions, implying disparate treatments but based on reasonable grounds disclosed by the board of directors and approved by the general meeting upon a reinforced majority.

Further, thoughts on the general principle of equal treatment of shareholders are expressed in *Audiolux* – which is discussed in detail in Chapter 18, § 18.3. This case raised the question of whether there is a general principle under EU law of shareholder equality, under which minority shareholders are protected by an obligation on the dominant shareholder, when acquiring or exercising control of a company, to offer to buy the minority shareholders' shares under the same conditions as those agreed when a shareholding in that company conferring or strengthening the control of the dominant shareholder was acquired and, if so, the effects in time of such a principle. As already mentioned, this is a completely different issue, as it refers to the relationship amongst shareholders: the CJEU shares this opinion.

C-101/08, Audiolux SA et al. v. Groupe Bruxelles Lambert SA (GBL) et al. and Bertelsmann AG et al., [2009] ECR I-09823, §§ 37–40

37 Similarly, the obligation, laid down in Article 42 of Directive 77/91, to ensure equal treatment to all shareholders who are in the same position applies, as is clear from the phrase 'for the purposes of the implementation of this Directive', only within the framework of that directive, that is to say, as set out in the fifth recital of its preamble, in relation to the increase or reduction of capital. Thus, that article applies to situations which are completely different from those covered by the obligation which, in the case in the main proceedings, is said to bind the dominant shareholder pursuant to the putative general principle of Community law relied on by Audiolux.

38 The finding that the Community legislature did not intend the rule of equal treatment of shareholders provided for in Article 42 of Directive 77/91 to be applied outside the framework of that directive is confirmed by the latter's purpose.

39 That directive seeks only to ensure a minimum level of protection for shareholders in all the Member States (see, Case C-441/93 Pafitis and Others [1996] ECR I-1347, paragraph 38; Case C-42/95 Siemens [1996] ECR I-6017, paragraph 13; and Case C-338/06 Commission v. Spain [2008] ECR I-0000, paragraph 23).

40 Furthermore, it must be pointed out that, even in the context of Directive 77/91, Article 42 thereof cannot be considered to reflect a general principle of Community law. The Court has rejected a broad interpretation of Article 42 on the ground that it would render Article 29(4) of that directive, which relates to the conditions governing the restriction of the right of pre-emption, redundant (see, Commission v. Spain, paragraphs 32 and 33).

In conclusion, both *Commission* v. *Spain* and *Audiolux* confirm that the general principle of equal treatment of shareholders, despite its broad wording, has very limited room for application. This might also confirm the conclusion of some scholars, maintaining that the EU equal treatment rule only aims to prevent oppression of minority shareholders; therefore, its wording in the positive, requiring that EU Member States law grant equal treatment to all shareholders who are in the same position, has trivial importance in comparison with the principle that it expresses in the negative, which is particularly stressed by the CJEU itself in assessing the general meaning of equal treatment (*see*, Case C-127/07, *Arcelor Atlantique and Lorraine and Others*, [2008] ECR I-09895, § 23). Hence, unequal treatment of shareholders is permitted so long as this is not unfair to those who are treated unevenly: sometimes unequal treatments better achieve the interest of the company as a whole, i.e., the shareholders' overall welfare.

Nicola de Luca, 'Unequal Treatment and Shareholders' Welfare Growth: "Fairness" v. "Precise Equality"', 34 *Del. J. Corp. L.* 853–920, at 919–920 (2009)

This paper's main conclusion is that some decisions imply disparate treatments, but are not implausible. A strong equal treatment rule does not avoid all oppressions of the minorities, but also restricts the room to maneuver of boards and majorities in situations where no oppression occurs. The softer EU equal treatment rule requiring an equal treatment of shareholders who are in the same position is unclear and vague. If the goal of an equal treatment rule is to avoid oppression of minorities, the law should intervene only when a disparate treatment is unfair.

Inequalities should be permitted as far as they achieve economic results in terms of shareholders' welfare growth. The majority or the directors take their decisions, but must meet the requirement of fairness. The duty of fairness does not require best effort to satisfy the interests of minorities, but to consider others' interest in good faith. An oppression of the minority occurs when the directors or the majority act in bad faith; hence, when they disregard interests of minorities which could be taken into consideration at no cost. Consistent with this approach, the directors or the majorities shall not bear the burden to prove the validity, legitimacy or properness of the business purpose on which they rely. Nor may the courts question these issues. Still, directors and majorities must disclose the purpose upon which they make their decisions, and decisions must be reasonable. Minorities may challenge that an action or, in some cases, inaction is unreasonable.

Therefore, under Articles 60(1) and 85 Directive 2012/30/EU, some unequal treatments of shareholders are permitted, whilst others are prohibited. Some practical examples may explain the point.

First, imagine that Harry and Ron are shareholders of WWW Co.; Harry holds 60 per cent, Ron 40 per cent of the shares. WWW Co. shows in its balance sheet net assets worth €200,000.00, including €100,000.00 as subscribed and fully paid-up capital and €100,000.00 as reserves available for distribution. Assume that the general meeting decides a capital increase aimed at permitting the company to acquire a building as contribution in kind. Harry owns such a building, worth €100,000.00 (as assessed by an expert report). According to *Siemens*, in case the capital is increased by consideration other than in cash, the shares need not be offered to shareholders on a pre-emptive basis; as a consequence, the general meeting may decide the capital increase upon ordinary quorum and majority, and all shares may be offered to Harry, thus diluting Ron's stake. Notwithstanding his interest in the transaction, Harry has a deciding vote. According to *Commission* v. *Spain*, the principle of equal treatment of shareholders does not require that the new shares are issued at fair market price; rather, under Article 49(2) Directive 2017/1132/EU, the value of the building shall correspond at least to the number and nominal value or to the accountable par and, where appropriate, to the premium on the shares to be issued for it. However, it must be noted that also the decision as to whether a part of the consideration shall go into the share premium account is taken by the general meeting, thus by Harry having a deciding vote. In this respect, the company as a whole is indifferent, as it always acquires the building at the same price (€100,000.00). In turn, the two shareholders are not indifferent: in case all of the consideration goes to legal capital, as a mere consequence of the capital increase not only Ron is diluted (his 40 per cent becomes a 20 per cent stake), but also his share on the reserves available for distribution is reduced to 20 per cent; in case the consideration paid for the new shares is equally divided between capital and share premium account, notwithstanding dilution (Harry now holds ca. 73 per cent and Ron ca. 27 per cent), Ron maintains his share in the reserves available for distribution (Ron may claim ca. 27 per cent of ca. €50,000.00, which equals 40 per cent of €100,000.00).

In case the general meeting, i.e., the majority shareholder Harry, decides that none of the consideration shall go into the share premium account, one may question whether Ron could challenge the decision for breach of the equal treatment rule. The answer shall be affirmative, as the equal treatment rule permits an uneven treatment in cases where this is not unfair to the affected shareholder, which might not be where a fair alternative exists.

Second, imagine that the same WWW Co. has sums available for distribution and its directors decide – upon authorisation of the general meeting – to repurchase some of the company's own shares up to 5 per cent of the subscribed capital. Or, imagine that in the absence of sums available for distribution, the general meeting decides to reduce its subscribed capital to allow the reimbursement of shares corresponding up to 5 per cent of the subscribed capital. Does the equal treatment rule require that shares are proportionally purchased or withdrawn by Harry and Ron, or could the directors buyout or withdraw only Harry's or Ron's shares?

In these cases, one must consider that there is no interest of the company as a whole at issue, as distributions (either out of surplus, or out of capital) only concern the interests of shareholders as individuals. Notwithstanding that various opinions have been expressed on this matter, the correct answer is that directors need not buyout nor withdraw shares proportionally. Indeed, assuming that repurchase or withdrawal is made at a fair price, none of the shareholders is better or worse off after the transaction is performed. Assume, for example, that the company repurchases 5 per cent of only Harry's shares at a fair price, i.e., at net asset value equal to €10,000.00. After performance of the transaction, whilst Harry's share of interest will drop to 55 per cent, Ron maintains his 40 per cent and the remaining 5 per cent is represented by treasury shares. Similarly, whilst reserves available for distribution drop to €90,000.00, the subscribed capital remains €100,000.00. In these circumstances, Harry is not better off: in case of future distributions, both dividends and the treasury shares would go to Harry and Ron on a new 57, 89 per cent–42, 11 per cent ratio. In other words, the equal treatment rule only requires that directors and majority shareholders – owing fiduciary duties to all shareholders – act in good faith and make their choices reasonable.

FURTHER READING

Frank H. Easterbrook and Daniel R. Fischel, 'Corporate Control Transactions', 91 *Yale L.J.* 698 (1982).

Victor Brudney, 'Equal Treatment of Shareholders in Corporate Distributions and Reorganizations', 71 *Cal. L. Rev.* 1072 (1983).

Lucian Arye Bebchuk, 'Toward Undistorted Choice and Equal Treatment in Corporate Takeovers', 98 *Harv. L. Rev.* 1700 (1985).

M.L Lennarts and M.S. Koppert-van Beek, 'Loyalty Dividend and the EC Principle of Equal Treatment of Shareholders', 5 *ECL* 173–180 (2008).

Nicola de Luca, 'Unequal Treatment and Shareholders' Welfare Growth: "Fairness" v. "Precise Equality"', 34 *Del. J. Corp. L.* 853–920 (2009).

Rein Philips, 'The Inter Access Case Revisited: Corporate Interest = Public Interest?', 8 *ECL* 233–239 (2011).

16.6 The Golden Shares Case Law: An Overview

Also related to the issue of equal treatment of shareholders is that of the so-called 'golden shares', shares that are issued in a company undergoing the process of privatisation, often granting to Member States or other public bodies the right to elect additional board members, or to compulsorily repurchase the majority stake at will, or to express a majority in a meeting regardless of the stake.

As already mentioned, the legitimacy of the golden shares' system has been investigated in light of the principle of free movement of capital, as it may strike against the rule of the TFEU requiring that all citizens of the EU, including Member States and public bodies, are treated the same as regards participation in the capital of companies or firms.

Article 55 TFEU

Member States shall accord nationals of the other Member States the same treatment as their own nationals as regards participation in the capital of companies or firms.

Article 63(1) TFEU

All restrictions on the movement of capital between Member States and between Member States and third countries shall be prohibited.

As the breakthrough rule provided for in the Takeover Bids Directive points out, the concept of golden share is multifaceted. An excerpt from a scholarly piece will help illustrate this point.

Guido Ferrarini, 'One Share – One Vote: A European Rule?', 3 *ECFR* 147–177, at 168–169 (2006)

The breakthrough rule does not apply to golden shares and similar rights. Article 11(7) specifies it, firstly, with regard to 'securities in the offeree company which confer special rights on the Member States ...'; secondly, with respect to 'special rights provided for in national law ...'. The first concept refers to golden shares as originally adopted in the UK, where the articles of association of privatised companies used to provide for the issuance of special shares to the State. The second concept refers to the practice of privatisations in countries like France and Italy, where the law foresees that special rights (similar to those deriving from golden shares) may be attributed to the State with respect to privatised companies. In both cases, a problem arises of compatibility of the Member State's special rights with the EC Treaty. To the extent that a Member State is entitled, for instance, to authorise either transfers of control in the relevant company or mergers of the same with another company, the fundamental freedoms of the Treaty may be restricted as a result.

There is a useful summary of jurisprudence provided for by the EU institution that gives an overview on the issue. In the following paragraphs, selected cases will therefore be examined in detail.

http://ec.europa.eu/internal_market/capital/framework/court/index_en.htm

In strategically sensitive sectors or in the case of important/large national companies ('national champions'), some Member States' governments have felt the need to retain control of privatised companies and resorted to holding on to special rights in them. These rights are special in the sense that they go beyond the rights associated with normal shareholding. One means to install such special rights is a 'golden share', i.e. a preferred stockholding in a company that a public authority retains after privatisation. But over time, the term 'golden share' has become a generic term for special rights in general, whether those rights are associated with State shareholding or not.

The first judgment concerning golden shares was delivered on 23 May 2000 in a case against Italy (case C-58/99). The case concerned a framework privatisation law and related decrees ensuring government control in companies of the energy and telecommunications sector.

On 4 June 2002, the Court ruled on the cases brought against Portugal, France and Belgium. In the case of Portugal (case C-367/98), the provisions at issue were the framework laws and regulations concerning the privatisation of undertakings in the banking, insurance, energy and transport sectors. The case of France (case C-483/99) concerned a decree vesting in the state a special share in Société Nationale Elf-Aquitaine, which supplies France with petroleum products. The case against Belgium (case C-503/99) concerned two Royal Decrees which vested in the state golden shares in Distrigaz and Société Général de Transport par Canalisations. It provides valuable guidance on proportionality considerations regarding special rights.

On 23 May 2003 the Court ruled on cases brought against Spain and the United Kingdom. The case of Spain (case C-463/00) concerned provisions of a privatisation law and Royal Decrees, which gave government control in Repsol and Endesa (energy), Telefónica (telecommunications), Argentaria (banking) and Tabacalera (tobacco). In the case of the United Kingdom, (case C-98/01) the provision at issue pertained to the Articles of Association of Britain's biggest airport operator, British Airport Authorities (BAA), which owns e.g. Heathrow and Stansted.

In 2005, the Court ruled on a case brought against Italy (case C-174/04) for the suspension of voting rights attached to shareholdings exceeding 2% to public undertakings investing in gas and electricity companies.

In a case brought against Germany (C-112/05), the Court ruled in 2007 on a tailor-made state measure (the VW-law) designed to give public authorities special rights in Volkswagen AG, which they would not normally have under German company law.

In 2008, the Court ruled on cases brought against Italy and Spain. In Case C-326/07, the Court ruled against derogation from ordinary company law that ensured public authorities' participation beyond what their status as shareholders would normally allow. In the two cases brought against Spain (C-274/06 and C-207/07), which concerned the highly topical issue of screening investment in the energy sector, the Court established that a system of prior authorisation cannot in all cases guarantee secure energy supplies and imposing specific obligations on energy companies can represent a more proportionate means safeguarding the energy supply than a straightforward restriction of voting rights.

In 2010, the CJEU [Court of Justice of the European Union] ruled that Portugal's holding of special rights in Portugal Telecom (C-171/08) and in EDP – Energias de Portugal (C-543/08) was contrary to the free movement of capital. In the first of these cases, the Court outlawed special rights including the right to veto management decisions in Portugal Telecom (PT) conferred on the Portuguese State and other public sector entities as shareholders of a privilege class of shares following the privatisation of PT. In the second, the Court found that the Portuguese State's right of veto over a large number of company decisions, the right to oppose the election of directors and the right to appoint a director, a voting limit of 5% in the general assembly for all shareholders except for the State or public bodies were not justified. In both cases the Court found that such special rights discourage operators of other Member States from making direct investments and may have a deterrent effect on portfolio investors.

In 2011, the CJEU found that by maintaining special rights in favour of the State and other public bodies in GALP, Portugal had failed to fulfil its Treaty obligations (C-2012/069). The special rights involved include the right to veto over a large number of company decisions. Of interest to note that the Court not only confirmed that Articles of Association reflecting legal provisions on special rights are a State measure, but it also considered shareholders' agreements through which the State exercises special rights to be a State measure.

FURTHER READING

Guido Ferrarini, 'One Share – One Vote: A European Rule?', 3 *ECFR* 147–177 (2006).

Thomas Papadopoulos, 'Greek Legislation on Strategic Investments: The Next Golden Share Case before the European Court of Justice?', 6 *ECL* 264–270 (2009).

Thomas Papadopoulos, 'Privatized Companies, Golden Shares and Property Ownership in the Euro Crisis Era: A Discussion After Commission v. Greece', 12 *ECFR* 1–18 (2015).

See also:

Mads Andenas and Frank Wooldridge, *European Comparative Company Law* 14–21 (Cambridge University Press, 2012).

16.7 *ENI/Telecom Italia* Case

In *ENI/Telecom Italia* (C-58/99, *Commission of the European Communities* v. *Italian Republic (ENI/Telecom Italia),* [2000] ECR I-03811) the Commission of the European Communities brought an action under Article 169 of the EC Treaty (now Article 258 TFEU) for a declaration that, by adopting Articles 1 (5) and 2 of the consolidated text of Decree Law No 332 of 31 May 1994, converted, after amendment, into Law No 474 of 30 July 1994, providing for acceleration of the procedures for the sale of shareholdings held by the State and public bodies in joint stock companies, and the decrees concerning the special powers laid down in the case of the privatisation of ENI S.p.A. and Telecom Italia S.p.A., the Italian Republic had failed to fulfil its obligations under Articles 52 and 59 of the EC Treaty (now Articles 49 and 56 TFEU) and Article 73b of the EC Treaty (now Article 63 TFEU).

Article 2 of the consolidated legislation is concerned with the special powers reserved for the State and public bodies. Article 2(1) provides that the President of the Council of Ministers is to determine by decree which companies controlled directly or indirectly by the State and operating in the defence, transport, telecommunications, energy resources and other public service sectors in whose statutes, before the adoption of any measure resulting in the loss of control, a provision must be inserted, by decision taken at an extraordinary general meeting, conferring on the Minister for the Treasury one or more special powers. Those powers, which are set out in Article 2(1), include a power to grant express approvals, a power to appoint a minimum of one or several directors and an auditor, and a right to veto certain decisions. The special powers must be exercised having regard to national economic and industrial policy objectives.

On 5 October 1995, by decree of the President of the Council of Ministers, the Italian Government inserted in the statutes of ENI S.p.A. (which operates in the energy and petrochemical sectors) the special powers provided for in Article 2 of the consolidated legislation.

On 21 March 1997 a decree of the President of the Council of Ministers established that S.p.A. and Telecom Italia S.p.A. (respectively, holding and operating company in the telecommunications sector) should have included the special powers in their statutes before they were privatised. S.p.A. and Telecom Italia S.p.A. subsequently merged. On 24 March 1997 two decrees of the Minister for the Treasury were published; one laid down the content of the special powers, while the other set the relevant percentage for the purposes of the exercise of the special power of approval conferred on the Minister for the Treasury at 3 per cent of the voting rights.

By letter of formal notice of 3 February 1998, the Commission informed the Italian Government pursuant to Article 169 of the Treaty that the national provisions referred to above were incompatible with Articles 52, 59, and 73b of the Treaty.

Notwithstanding the Italian Government observations, the Commission decided, in accordance with the procedure set out in the second paragraph of Article 169 of the Treaty (now Article 258 TFEU), to bring an application before the Court.

C-58/99, Commission of the European Communities v. Italian Republic (ENI/Telecom Italia), [2000] ECR I-03811, § 13

13 With regard to the special powers conferred on the Treasury Ministry under Article 2 of the consolidated legislation, the Commission essentially argues that powers of that kind,

which are liable to hinder or render less attractive the exercise of the fundamental freedoms guaranteed by the Treaty, must satisfy four conditions: they must apply in a non-discriminatory manner, be justified by overriding considerations in the general interest, be appropriate for ensuring that the objective which they pursue is achieved and not go beyond what is necessary in order to achieve that objective. Since there is no indication whatever that those conditions are satisfied in the present case and the special powers thus confer on the Italian authorities a potential to discriminate which may be used in an arbitrary manner, the Commission considers that those special powers are incompatible with Articles 52 and 73b of the Treaty.

In such circumstances, the CJEU:

C-58/99, Commission of the European Communities v. Italian Republic (ENI/Telecom Italia), [2000] ECR I-03811, § 20 and Operative Part

Declare[d] that, by adopting Articles 1(5) and 2 of the consolidated text of Decree Law No 332 of 31 May 1994, converted, after amendment, into Law No 474 of 30 July 1994, providing for acceleration of the procedures for the sale of shareholdings held by the State and public bodies in joint stock companies, and the decrees concerning the special powers laid down in the case of the privatisation of ENI SpA and Telecom Italia SpA, the Italian Republic has failed to fulfil its obligations under Articles 52 and 59 of the EC Treaty (now, after amendment, Articles 43 EC and 49 EC) and Article 73b of the EC Treaty (now Article 56 EC);

16.8 *ELF* Case

In *ELF* (C-483/99, *Commission of the European Communities* v. *French Republic (Société Nationale Elf-Aquitaine*), [2002] ECR I-04781) the Commission of the European Communities brought an action under Article 226 EC for a declaration that,

C-483/99, Commission of the European Communities v. French Republic (Société Nationale Elf-Aquitaine), [2002] ECR I-04781, § 1

... by maintaining in force Article 2(1) and (3) of Decree No 93-1298 of 13 December 1993 vesting in the State a golden share in Société Nationale Elf-Aquitaine, according to which the following rights attach to the golden share held by the French Republic in that company:

(a) any direct or indirect shareholding by a natural or legal person, acting alone or in conjunction with others, which exceeds the ceiling of one tenth, one fifth or one third of the capital of, or voting rights in, the company must first be approved by the Minister for Economic Affairs (Article 2(1) of the Decree);

(b) the right to oppose any decision to transfer or use as security the assets listed in the annex to the Decree – the assets in question being the majority of the capital of four subsidiaries of the parent company, namely Elf-Aquitaine Production, Elf-Antar France, Elf-Gabon SA and Elf-Congo SA (Article 2(3) of the Decree),

and by failing to lay down sufficiently precise and objective criteria for approval of, or opposition to, the abovementioned operations, the French Republic has failed to comply with its obligations under Articles 52 (now, after amendment, Article 43 EC) to 58 of the EC Treaty (now Article 48 EC) and Article 73b of the EC Treaty (now Article 56 EC).

The Court observed that depending on the circumstances, certain concerns may justify the retention by Member States of a degree of influence within undertakings that were initially public and subsequently privatised where those undertakings are active in fields involving the provision of services in the public interest or strategic services. However, those concerns cannot entitle Member States to plead their own systems of property ownership by way of justification for obstacles, resulting from privileges attaching to their position as shareholder in a privatised undertaking, to the exercise of the freedoms provided for by the Treaty, such as the free movement of capital between Member States. That provision does not have the effect of exempting the Member States' systems of property ownership from the fundamental rules of the Treaty.

C-483/99, Commission of the European Communities v. French Republic (Société Nationale Elf-Aquitaine), [2002] ECR I-04781, §§ 42, 47, 53, Operative Part 1

A Member State which maintains in force national rules vesting in that State a golden share in an oil company, according to which the following rights attach to that golden share:

- a right of prior authorisation by the State where certain ceilings in respect of shareholdings or voting rights are exceeded;
- a right to oppose any decision to transfer or use as security the majority of the capital of various subsidiaries of the company, fails to comply with its obligations under Article 56 EC.

Such rules constitute a restriction on the movement of capital within the meaning of that article which cannot be justified. Although, in that regard, the objective of safeguarding supplies of petroleum products in the event of a crisis falls within the ambit of public security considerations which may justify an obstacle to the free movement of capital, in accordance with Article 58(1)(b) EC, such rules go beyond what is necessary in order to attain that objective, since the structure of the system established does not include any precise, objective criteria.

16.9 *Volkswagen* Case

In *Volkswagen* (C-112/05, *Commission of the European Communities v. Federal Republic of Germany – (Volkswagen)*, [2007] ECR I-08995), the Commission asked the CJEU to declare that Paragraphs 2(1) and 4(1) and (3) of the Law of 21 July 1960 on the privatisation of equity in the Volkswagenwerk limited company (Gesetz über die Überführung der Anteilsrechte an der Volkswagenwerk Gesellschaft mit beschränkter Haftung in private Hand, as further amended, 'the VW Law') infringed Article 43 TEC (now Article 49 TFEU), on the right of establishment, and Article 56 TEC (now Article 63 TFEU), on the free movement of capital.

Paragraph 2(1) of the VW Law, concerning the exercise of voting rights and the limitations on that right, provides: 'The voting rights of a shareholder whose par value shares represent more than one fifth of the share capital shall be limited to the number of votes granted by the par value of shares equivalent to one fifth of the share capital.'

Paragraph 4 of the VW Law, headed 'The company's articles of association', is worded as follows:

1. The Federal Republic of Germany and the Land of Lower Saxony may each appoint two members to the supervisory board on condition that they hold shares in the company ... 3. Resolutions of the general meeting which, under the Law on public limited companies, require the favourable vote of at least three quarters of the share capital represented at the time of their adoption, shall require the favourable vote of more than four fifths of the share capital represented at the time of that adoption.

On 1 April 2004, the Commission delivered a reasoned opinion stating that those provisions of national law constituted restrictions on the free movement of capital and on the freedom of establishment guaranteed by Articles 56 TEC and 43 TEC, respectively. Since that Member State did not adopt the measures necessary to comply with that opinion within the prescribed period, the Commission brought an action before the CJEU.

C-112/05, Commission of the European Communities v. Federal Republic of Germany – (Volkswagen), [2007] ECR I-08995, § 9

The Commission asserted, in essence, that, first, by limiting, in derogation from the general law, the voting rights of every shareholder to 20% of Volkswagen's share capital, secondly, by requiring a majority of over 80% of the shares represented for resolutions of the general assembly, which, according to the general law, require only a majority of 75%, and thirdly, by allowing, in derogation from the general law, the Federal State and the Land of Lower Saxony each to appoint two representatives to the company's supervisory board, the disputed provisions of the VW Law are liable to deter direct investment and for that reason constitute restrictions on the free movement of capital within the meaning of Article 56 TEC.

The CJEU ruled as follows:

C-112/05, Commission of the European Communities v. Federal Republic of Germany – (Volkswagen), [2007] ECR I-08995, §§ 43–46, 50–52, 54, 56, 59, 61–62, 64, 66, 68, 82, Operative Part

A Member State which maintains in force legislation which, in derogation from ordinary company law, combines a limitation of the voting rights of every shareholder in a given company to 20% of that company's share capital with the requirement of a majority of over 80% of the company's capital for the adoption of certain decisions by the general assembly, and which, in derogation from the general law, allows a Member State and a territorial entity of that State each to appoint two representatives to the company's supervisory board, fails to fulfil its obligations under Article 56(1) TEC.

The fixing of the threshold of the required majority at more than 80% of the capital, being a requirement derogating from general law and imposed by way of specific legislation, affords any shareholder holding 20% of the share capital a blocking minority and in this case creates an instrument enabling the public authorities to procure for themselves a blocking minority allowing them to oppose important resolutions, on the basis of a lower level of investment than would be required under general company law. By capping voting rights at the same level of 20%, the specific legislation supplements a legal framework which enables the said public authorities to exercise considerable influence on the basis of such a reduced investment. By limiting the possibility for other shareholders to participate in the company with a view to establishing or maintaining lasting and direct economic links with it which would make possible effective participation in the management of that company or in its control, such a situation is liable to deter direct investors from other Member States, thereby diminishing the interest in acquiring a stake in the capital of that company and thus constituting a restriction on the movement of capital.

The same applies to the right to appoint two representatives to the company's supervisory board, being a specific right, in derogation from general company law, laid down by a national legislative measure for the sole benefit of the public authorities. By enabling those authorities to participate in a more significant manner in the activity of the supervisory board than their status as shareholders would normally allow, that measure thus establishes an instrument which gives the public authorities the possibility of exercising influence which exceeds their levels of investment.

FURTHER READING

Jaron van Bekkum, Joost Kloosterman, and Jaap Winter, 'Golden Shares and European Company Law: The Implications of Volkswagen', 5 *ECL* 6–12 (2008).

Gert-Jan Vossestein, 'Volkswagen: The State of Affairs of Golden Shares, General Company Law and European Free Movement of Capital – A Discussion of Case C-112/05 Commission v. Germany of 23.10.2007', 5 *ECFR* 115–133 (2008).

Jaron van Bekkum, 'Golden Shares: A New Approach', 7 *ECL* 13–19 (2010).

16.10 *AEM/Edison* Case

In *AEM/Edison* (Joined Cases C-463/04 and C-464/04, *Federconsumatori and Others and Associazione Azionariato Diffuso dell'AEM S.p.A. and Others* v. *Comune di Milano*, [2007] ECR I-10419) references were made in proceedings between various associations for the protection of consumers, small shareholders, and private shareholders, namely *Federconsumatori, Adiconsum, ADOC and Mr Zucca* (Case C-463/04) and *Associazione Azionariato Diffuso dell'AEM S.p.A., Ms Sanchirico, Messrs Cuccia, Fragapane, Puggioni and Sartorio* (Case C-464/04), respectively, and Comune di Milano concerning a national provision under which the articles of association of a company limited by shares may confer on the State or a public body holding shares in that company the power to appoint directly one or more directors to the board of the latter.

AEM S.p.A. (Azienda Elettrica Milanese S.p.A., '*AEM*'), which was a company set up by the Comune di Milano in 1996, operated in the public service sector as a distributor of gas and electricity, the management of which it was granted by that Comune. In 1998 its shares were listed on the stock exchange and a first tranche of shares were sold, after which the Comune di Milano held 51 per cent of the company's capital.

Continuing the company's privatisation, by Decision No 4/04 of 17 February 2004 the municipal council of the Comune di Milano decided to reduce its shareholding in AEM to 33.4 per cent. However, it made that transfer of shares conditional on the prior amendment of AEM's articles of association.

By Decision No 5/04 of 8 March 2004, the municipal council decided 'to designate, as provided for in Article 2(3) of Law No 474/1994, AEM … as a company subject to privatisation of which the articles of association should be amended in accordance with the requirements of Law No 474/1994'. By the same decision it also decided to amend the articles of association of AEM, in particular the provisions regarding procedures for the appointment of directors to the board of that company.

On 29 April 2004, at an extraordinary general meeting AEM's shareholders adopted the measures necessary to amend the articles of association of that company in accordance with Decision No 5/04 of the municipal council by inserting, in particular, the exclusive right for the Comune di Milano to appoint directly, in proportion to its shareholding, directors pursuant to Article 2449 of the Civil Code, not exceeding one quarter of the members of the board of directors of that company. In addition, the articles of association of AEM conferred on the Comune di Milano, in accordance with Article 4 of Law No 474/1994, the right to participate in the election on the basis of lists of directors not directly appointed by it.

The combined effect of the right of direct appointment of directors and the right to participate in the election of the other members of the board of directors of AEM by voting on the basis of lists enabled the Comune di Milano, according to the facts as stated by the national court, to retain an absolute majority of appointments to the board of directors, even though it may hold, subsequent to the transfer of shares, only a relative majority in the capital of that company.

The appellants in the two main proceedings challenged Decisions Nos 4/04 and 5/04 before the Tribunale amministrativo regionale per la Lombardia (Regional Administrative Court, Lombardy) (Italy) seeking their annulment and suspension of their implementation. They complained in particular that the described machinery discouraged investors from purchasing shares in AEM or indeed from controlling it, such deterrent effect having inevitable negative repercussions on their own holdings in that company, which necessarily depreciated as a result.

By interim judgment of 10 June 2004, the Tribunale amministrativo regionale per la Lombardia ordered the suspension of the implementation of Decision No 5/04 on the ground that the provisions relating to the machinery for appointing the directors of AEM appeared, as they stood, to be contrary to the case law of the Court of Justice concerning special powers.

By interim judgment of 10 August 2004, the Consiglio di Stato (Council of State) (Italy) reversed that judgment, thereby rejecting the application for suspension of implementation on the ground, *inter alia*, that the Community caselaw on which that decision was based concerns cases relating to 'golden shares', a concept vastly different from that at issue in the cases brought before that court, which concern the special powers which one of the shareholders may have under civil law.

Nonetheless, the national court is unsure whether Article 2449 of the Civil Code complies with Article 56 TEC, as interpreted by the Court, in so far as its application, combined with the list system referred to in Article 4 of Law No 474/1994, introduces a severe restriction on the ability to participate effectively in the management and actual control of a company limited by shares outside the scope of lawful exercise of special powers.

In those circumstances, the Tribunale amministrativo regionale per la Lombardia decided to stay the proceedings and to refer the following questions, the wording of which is identical in Cases C-463/04 and C-464/04, to the Court of Justice for a preliminary ruling:

Joined Cases C-463/04 and C-464/04, Federconsumatori and Others and Associazione Azionariato Diffuso dell'AEM S.p.A. and Others v. Comune di Milano, [2007] ECR I-10419

1. Can Article 2449 of the Civil Code, as applied in the circumstances at issue in this case, be held to be compatible with Article 56 EC as interpreted in the judgments in Case C-58/99 [Commission v. Italy], Case C-503/99 and Case C-483/99 [Commission v. Belgium and

Commission v. France], Case C-98/01 and Case C-463/00 [Commission v. United Kingdom and Commission v. Spain], when it is invoked by a public entity which, although it has lost control by operation of law over a company limited by shares, retains a substantial shareholding (33.4%) as a shareholder holding a relative majority of the shares, thereby obtaining a disproportionate power of control?

2. Can Article 2449 of the Civil Code, applied in conjunction with Article 4 of Decree Law No 332 of 31 May 1994, which became Law No 474 of 30 July 1994, be held to be compatible with Article 56 EC as interpreted in the judgments of the Court of Justice in Case C-58/99 [Commission v. Italy], Case C-503/99 and Case C-483/99 [Commission v. Belgium and Commission v. France], Case C-98/01 and Case C-463/00 [Commission v. United Kingdom and Commission v. Spain], when it is invoked by a public entity which, although it has lost control by operation of law over a company limited by shares, retains a substantial shareholding (33.4%) as a shareholder holding a relative majority of the shares, and thereby obtaining a disproportionate power of control?
3. Can Article 2449 of the Civil Code be held to be compatible with Article 56 EC, as interpreted in the judgments of the Court of Justice in Case C-58/99 [Commission v. Italy], Case C-503/99 and Case C-483/99 [Commission v. Belgium and Commission v. France], Case C-98/01 and Case C-463/00 [Commission v. United Kingdom and Commission v. Spain], inasmuch as, when applied in specific cases, it brings about a result that is contrary to another provision of national law (in particular Article 2(1)(d) of Decree Law No 332 of 31 May 1994, which became Law No 474 of 30 July 1994) which itself complies with Article 56 EC and consequently reflects, in respect of the conditions on which special powers are exercised and the requirements to which they are subject, the principles established in that connection by the judgments of the Court of Justice cited above?

After joining the two cases, the CJEU ruled as follows:

Joined Cases C-463/04 and C-464/04, Federconsumatori and Others and Associazione Azionariato Diffuso dell'AEM SpA and Others v. Comune di Milano, [2007] ECR I-10419, §§ 22–24, 29, 33–34, 41–43, Operative Part

Article 56 EC must be interpreted as precluding a national provision under which the articles of association of a company limited by shares may confer on the State or a public body with a shareholding in that company the power to appoint directly one or more directors which, on its own or in conjunction with a provision which grants that State or public body the right to participate in the election on the basis of lists of the directors it has not appointed directly, is such as to enable that State or public body to obtain a power of control which is disproportionate to its shareholding in that company.

That provision enables public shareholders to participate in a more significant manner in the activity of the board of directors of a company limited by shares than their status as shareholders would normally allow, and thereby places at the disposal of those public shareholders an instrument which gives them the possibility of exercising influence which exceeds their levels of investment. By giving public shareholders an instrument enabling them to restrict the possibility of the other shareholders participating in the company with a view to establishing or maintaining lasting and direct economic links with it such as to enable them to participate effectively in the management of that company or in its control, such a national provision is liable to deter direct investors from other Member States from investing in the capital of that company, and thus constitutes a restriction on the free movement of capital.

Whilst it is true that the national legislation at issue does not confer that right of appointment directly upon the State or a public body, but requires a decision of the general meeting of the shareholders of the company concerned, the fact remains that that does not take away the restrictive character of the legislation in question. Irrespective of whether the public shareholder itself has the majority required to have its right of direct appointment of the company's directors included in the company's articles of association or whether it can have it included only with the consent of the other shareholders, it must be noted that it is only by virtue of the legislation at issue, which derogates from ordinary company law, that a public shareholder may, unlike a private shareholder, obtain the right to participate in the activities of the board of directors in a more significant manner than its status as shareholder would normally allow.

Concerns which may, depending on the circumstances, justify the retention by Member States of a degree of influence within undertakings that were initially public and subsequently privatised, where those undertakings are active in fields involving the provision of services in the public interest or strategic services, cannot justify such a provision, since it does not make inclusion in the articles of association of a company limited by shares of a right for the State or a public body holding shares in that company to appoint directly one or more directors subject to any condition.

FURTHER READING

Guido Ferrarini, 'One Share – One Vote: A European Rule?', 3 *ECFR* 147–177 (2006).

Part VI

Capital Markets and Takeover Regulation

17

Capital Markets

17.1 Official Stock Exchange Listing and Regulated Markets

Companies may also be regarded as issuers of shares, bonds, and other securities, these being the 'goods' traded in capital markets. EU law extensively regulates capital markets with the purpose of ensuring the free movement of capital. Therefore, in this chapter and Chapter 18 we will deal with some of the EU capital market regulations that have special relevance for ECL, such as the Admission to Listing Directive, the Prospectus Regulation, the Market Abuse Regulation, the Transparency Directive, and the Takeover Bids Directive.

Brief introductory notes on capital markets may be useful to understand the wider picture.

As with used cars, securities may also be sold to third parties at arm's length. However, whilst a used car is generally sold to buy a new one, securities are sold in case the holders need money for their personal needs, or because it is the appropriate time to liquidate the investment. In finance, the practice of selling securities when these have risen in price is called *profit taking*.

The more the securities are widespread, the more likely it is that their holders will find someone willing to purchase them; moreover, the more the securities are widespread, the more likely it is that there is a current 'market' price for units of a certain security reflecting that of previous transactions on similar securities. The existence of a market price facilitates determining when it is time for taking profits.

Unlike used cars, widespread securities such as shares and bonds issued by public companies are traded in specialised markets, known as stock exchanges: e.g., the London Stock Exchange, the New York Stock Exchange (NYSE), the NASDAQ, the Deutsche Börse, and so on. These markets ensure continuous trading and an official market price for all listed securities.

A *stock exchange* is a place where investors can buy and sell shares, bonds, and other securities or financial instruments. Such a place can be either physical or virtual: usually, there is a central location at least for record keeping, but trade is increasingly less linked to such a physical place, as modern markets use electronic networks, which gives them advantages of increased speed and reduced cost of transactions. Stock exchanges often function as 'continuous auction' markets, with buyers and sellers consummating transactions at a central location, such as the floor of the exchange. To be able to trade a security on a certain stock exchange, it must be listed there. Also, trade on an exchange is restricted to the intermediaries admitted to the market.

Stock exchange and listed (or publicly traded) companies are strictly related concepts: indeed, a *listed (or publicly traded) company* is a company issuing shares and/or bonds admitted to official listing and effectively traded in one or more stock exchanges.

In the EU, the creation and the operation of a stock exchange is regulated by Directive 2014/65/EU of the European Parliament and of the Council of 15 May 2014 *on markets in financial instruments* (amending Directive 2002/92/ EC and Directive 2011/61/EU and repealing Directive 2004/39/EC, generally known as the Markets in Financial Instruments Directive, or MiFID). Under the Directive 2014/65/EU (MiFID 2), stock exchanges are multilateral systems, among which regulated markets are to be distinguished from multilateral trading facilities (MTF) and organised trading facilities (OTF).

Article 4(1) Numbers 18–19, 21–23, Directive 2014/65/EU (MiFID 2)

(18) 'market operator' means a person or persons who manages and/or operates the business of a regulated market and may be the regulated market itself;

(19) 'multilateral system' means any system or facility in which multiple third-party buying and selling trading interests in financial instruments are able to interact in the system;

...

(21) 'regulated market' means a multilateral system operated and/or managed by a market operator, which brings together or facilitates the bringing together of multiple third-party buying and selling interests in financial instruments – in the system and in accordance with its non-discretionary rules – in a way that results in a contract, in respect of the financial instruments admitted to trading under its rules and/or systems, and which is authorised and functions regularly and in accordance with Title III of this Directive;

(22) 'multilateral trading facility' or 'MTF' means a multilateral system, operated by an investment firm or a market operator, which brings together multiple third-party buying and selling interests in financial instruments – in the system and in accordance with non-discretionary rules – in a way that results in a contract in accordance with Title II of this Directive;

(23) 'organised trading facility' or 'OTF' means a multilateral system which is not a regulated market or an MTF and in which multiple third-party buying and selling interests in bonds, structured finance products, emission allowances or derivatives are able to interact in the system in a way that results in a contract in accordance with Title II of this Directive;

Unlike an MTF or an OTF, a regulated market is operated or managed by an authorised market operator, functions regularly and enjoys the ability to admit financial instruments to trading under specified rules and/or systems. Therefore, a company qualifies as listed or publicly traded only provided that its securities are admitted to trading on a regulated market; to this end, as we will see in § 17.2, securities shall be admitted to official stock exchange listing under the rules provided for by the Member State where the regulated market is located or operates. It is useful to add that 'regulated' means that the stock exchange market has clear and transparent rules regarding the admission of financial instruments to trading (Article 51 Directive 2014/65/EU (MiFID 2)), as well as transparent and non-discriminatory rules, based on objective criteria governing access of investors to or membership of the regulated market (Article 53 Directive 2014/65/EU (MiFID 2)). These rules – the 'Market Regulation' – and any amendment to them shall be approved beforehand by the designated authority of the Member State.

Also, one must differentiate admission of securities to *official stock exchange listing* and admission of securities to *trading* in a regulated market or in an MTF. As we will see in § 17.2, securities of a company are admitted to official stock exchange listings only based on a request by the issuer; through this request, the issuer commits itself to comply with the legislative rules of the Member States where official listing of the securities is sought and with the trading rules set forth in the Market Regulation of the chosen regulated market. Furthermore, an issuer may decide to have securities admitted to official stock exchange listing in various Member States or admitted to trading in more regulated markets; in these cases, it shall comply with all the relevant legislative rules and with the various trading rules set forth by the Market Regulations.

Notwithstanding the above, once the securities of a company are admitted to official stock exchange listing and are consequently admitted to trading in a regulated market, these may be traded in other regulated markets of the same or of other Member States even without the consent of the issuer (Article 51(5) Directive 2014/65/EU (MiFID 2)). Therefore, it must be noted that under EU law, securities may be admitted to single, dual, or multiple *listing* and/or to single, dual, or multiple *trading*.

Article 51 Admission of Financial Instruments to Trading, Directive 2014/65/EU (MiFID 2)

1. Member States shall require that regulated markets have clear and transparent rules regarding the admission of financial instruments to trading.

Those rules shall ensure that any financial instruments admitted to trading on a regulated market are capable of being traded in a fair, orderly and efficient manner and, in the case of transferable securities, are freely negotiable.

2. In the case of derivatives, the rules referred to in paragraph 1 shall ensure in particular that the design of the derivative contract allows for its orderly pricing as well as for the existence of effective settlement conditions.
3. In addition to the obligations set out in paragraphs 1 and 2, Member States shall require the regulated market to establish and maintain effective arrangements to verify that

issuers of transferable securities that are admitted to trading on the regulated market comply with their obligations under Union law in respect of initial, ongoing or ad hoc disclosure obligations.

Member States shall ensure that the regulated market establishes arrangements which facilitate its members or participants in obtaining access to information which has been made public under Union law.

4. Member States shall ensure that regulated markets have established the necessary arrangements to review regularly the compliance with the admission requirements of the financial instruments which they admit to trading.
5. A transferable security that has been admitted to trading on a regulated market can subsequently be admitted to trading on other regulated markets, even without the consent of the issuer and in compliance with the relevant provisions of Directive 2003/71/EC. The issuer shall be informed by the regulated market of the fact that its securities are traded on that regulated market. The issuer shall not be subject to any obligation to provide information required under paragraph 3 directly to any regulated market which has admitted the issuer's securities to trading without its consent.
6. ESMA shall develop draft regulatory technical standards which:
   (a) specify the characteristics of different classes of financial instruments to be taken into account by the regulated market when assessing whether a financial instrument is issued in a manner consistent with the conditions laid down in the second subparagraph of paragraph 1 for admission to trading on the different market segments which it operates;
   (b) clarify the arrangements that the regulated market is required to implement so as to be considered to have fulfilled its obligation to verify that the issuer of a transferable security complies with its obligations under Union law in respect of initial, ongoing or ad hoc disclosure obligations;
   (c) clarify the arrangements that the regulated market has to establish pursuant to paragraph 3 in order to facilitate its members or participants in obtaining access to information which has been made public under the conditions established by Union law.

ESMA shall submit those draft regulatory technical standards to the Commission by 3 July 2015. Power is delegated to the Commission to adopt the regulatory technical standards referred to in the first subparagraph in accordance with Articles 10 to 14 of Regulation (EU) No 1095/2010.

As regards access of investors to a regulated market, Article 53 Directive 2014/65/EU (MiFID 2) reads as follows:

Article 53 Access to a Regulated Market, Directive 2014/65/EU (MiFID 2)

1. Member States shall require a regulated market to establish, implement and maintain transparent and non-discriminatory rules, based on objective criteria, governing access to or membership of the regulated market.

2. The rules referred to in paragraph 1 shall specify any obligations for the members or participants arising from:
   (a) the constitution and administration of the regulated market;
   (b) the rules relating to transactions on the market;
   (c) the professional standards imposed on the staff of the investment firms or credit institutions that are operating on the market;
   (d) the conditions established, for members or participants other than investment firms and credit institutions, under paragraph 3;
   (e) the rules and procedures for the clearing and settlement of transactions concluded on the regulated market.
3. Regulated markets may admit as members or participants investment firms, credit institutions authorised under Directive 2013/36/EU and other persons who:
   (a) are of sufficient good repute;
   (b) have a sufficient level of trading ability, competence and experience;
   (c) have, where applicable, adequate organisational arrangements;
   (d) have sufficient resources for the role they are to perform, taking into account the different financial arrangements that the regulated market may have established in order to guarantee the adequate settlement of transactions.
4. Member States shall ensure that, for the transactions concluded on a regulated market, members and participants are not obliged to apply to each other the obligations laid down in Articles 24, 25, 27 and 28. However, the members or participants of the regulated market shall apply the obligations provided for in Articles 24, 25, 27 and 28 with respect to their clients when they, acting on behalf of their clients, execute their orders on a regulated market.
5. Member States shall ensure that the rules on access to or membership of or participation in the regulated market provide for the direct or remote participation of investment firms and credit institutions.
6. Member States shall, without further legal or administrative requirements, allow regulated markets from other Member States to provide appropriate arrangements on their territory so as to facilitate access to and trading on those markets by remote members or participants established in their territory.

The regulated market shall communicate to the competent authority of its home Member State the Member State in which it intends to provide such arrangements. The competent authority of the home Member State shall communicate that information to the Member State in which the regulated market intends to provide such arrangements within 1 month. ESMA may request access to that information in accordance with the procedure and under the conditions set out in Article 35 of Regulation (EU) No 1095/2010.

The competent authority of the home Member State of the regulated market shall, on the request of the competent authority of the host Member State and, without undue delay, communicate the identity of the members or participants of the regulated market established in that Member State.

7. Member States shall require the market operator to communicate, on a regular basis, the list of the members or participants of the regulated market to the competent authority of the regulated market.

17.2 Admission of Securities to the Official Stock Exchange Listing

With a view to ensuring integrated, open, competitive, and efficient European financial markets and services, harmonisation was necessary to ensure similar conditions for the admission of securities to official stock exchange listing and information to be published on those securities.

Today, this field is regulated by Directive 2001/34/EC, of the European Parliament and Council from 28 May 2001, *on the admission of securities to official stock exchange listings and on information to be published on those securities.* The aim of this Directive is to provide equivalent protection for investors at Union level.

Furthermore, Directive 2001/34/EC aims to consolidate the existing measures concerning the conditions for admission of securities to official stock exchange listing and the financial information that listed companies must make available to investors. The existing measures were:

- Council Directive 79/279/EEC coordinating the conditions for the admission of securities to official stock exchange listing;
- Council Directive 80/390/EEC coordinating the requirements for the drawing up, scrutiny and distribution of the listing particulars to be published for the admission of securities to official stock exchange listing;
- Council Directive 82/121/EEC on the information to be published on a regular basis by companies the shares of which have been admitted to official stock exchange listing;
- Council Directive 88/627/EEC on the information to be published when a major holding in a listed company is acquired or disposed of.

The coordination introduced by the Directive 2001/34/EC concerns all securities for which admission to official listing is requested and those admitted, irrespective of the legal nature of their issuer. In order to protect investors, information on the financial circumstances of the issuer and details of the securities must be disclosed. More specifically, in the case of securities for which admission to official listing is requested, the information required is published in a prospectus.

In order to have their securities admitted to official stock exchange listing, issuers must file a request and comply with certain obligations and conditions.

Article 5 Directive 2001/34/EC

Member States shall ensure:

(a) that securities may not be admitted to official listing on any stock exchange situated or operating within their territory unless the conditions laid down by this Directive are satisfied, and

(b) that issuers of securities admitted to such official listing, regardless of the date on which this admission takes place, are subject to the obligations provided for by this Directive.

Directive 2001/34/EC lists these conditions and obligations in Articles 42 to 82.

Regarding the conditions relating to companies for the shares of which admission to official listing is sought, these shall ensure that the *market capitalisation* (which is the total market value of the shares of the company, equal to the share price times the number of shares outstanding), or, if this cannot be assessed, that the *net assets* of the company are at least one million euro; in addition, applicant companies shall have their annual accounts published (or filed for publication) for the three financial years preceding the application for official listing.

Article 43(1–2) Directive 2001/34/EC

1. The foreseeable market capitalisation of the shares for which admission to official listing is sought or, if this cannot be assessed, the company's capital and reserves, including profit or loss, from the last financial year, must be at least one million euro.
2. Member States may provide for admission to official listing, even when this condition is not fulfilled, provided that the competent authorities are satisfied that there will be an adequate market for the shares concerned.

Article 44 Directive 2001/34/EC

A company must have published or filed its annual accounts in accordance with national law for the three financial years preceding the application for official listing. By way of exception, the competent authorities may derogate from this condition where such derogation is desirable in the interests of the company or of investors and where the competent authorities are satisfied that investors have the necessary information available to be able to arrive at an informed judgement on the company and the shares for which admission to official listing is sought.

As regards the conditions relating to the shares for which admission is sought, among others, these shall be *freely negotiable* and there shall be a sufficient *free float*. The free float is the portion of shares of the company that are in the hands of public investors as opposed to locked-in shares held by the controlling or other relevant shareholders not available for sale in the market. In addition, the application for admission to official listing must cover all the shares of the same class already issued.

Article 46 Directive 2001/34/EC

1. The shares must be freely negotiable.
2. The competent authorities may treat shares which are not fully paid up as freely negotiable, if arrangements have been made to ensure that the negotiability of such

shares is not restricted and that dealing is made open and proper by providing the public with all appropriate information.

3. The competent authorities may, in the case of the admission to official listing of shares which may be acquired only subject to approval, derogate from paragraph 1 only if the use of the approval clause does not disturb the market.

Article 48(1-5) Directive 2001/34/EC

1. A sufficient number of shares must be distributed to the public in one or more Member States not later than the time of admission.

...

5. A sufficient number of shares shall be deemed to have been distributed either when the shares in respect of which application for admission has been made are in the hands of the public to the extent of at least 25% of the subscribed capital represented by the class of shares concerned or when, in view of the large number of shares of the same class and the extent of their distribution to the public, the market will operate properly with a lower percentage.

Article 49(1) Directive 2001/34/EC

1. The application for admission to official listing must cover all the shares of the same class already issued.

Specific rules are provided for in case of securities issued in physical form (paper certificates of shares) or issued by companies of a Member State other than that of the stock exchange where admission to listing is sought.

Furthermore, Directive 2001/34/EC requires that companies whose shares are admitted to official listing comply with some additional requirements. These include: (i) an obligation to ensure the equal treatment for all shareholders who are in the same position (Article 65 Directive 2001/34/EC), (ii) an obligation to provide information to the public (on amendments to the instrument of incorporation, on annual accounts, and on any major new developments in their sphere of activity) (Articles 66–69 Directive 2001/34/EC), (iii) an obligation to publish periodical information (Articles 70–71 Directive 2001/34/EC), (iv) an obligation to publish a half-yearly report (Articles 72–77 Directive 2001/34/EC).

As regards the equal treatment of shareholders and information to be given to investors, Article 65 Directive 2001/34/EC reads as follows:

Article 65 Directive 2001/34/EC

1. The company shall ensure equal treatment for all shareholders who are in the same position.
2. The company must ensure, at least in each Member State in which its shares are listed, that all the necessary facilities and information are available to enable shareholders to exercise their rights. In particular, it must:
   (a) inform shareholders of the holding of meetings and enable them to exercise their right to vote,
   (b) publish notices or distribute circulars concerning the allocation and payment of dividends, the issue of new shares including allotment, subscription, renunciation and conversion arrangements,
   (c) designate as its agent a financial institution through which shareholders may exercise their financial rights, unless the company itself provides financial services.

This rule – originally included in Article 17 Directive 2001/34/EC – has been discussed in *Audiolux* (*see*, Chapter 18, § 18.3) as follows:

C-101/08, Audiolux SA et al. v. Groupe Bruxelles Lambert SA (GBL) et al. and Bertelsmann AG et al., [2009] ECR I-09823, §§ 41–42

41 As regards point 2(A) of Schedule C in the Annex to Directive 79/279, according to which the company is to ensure equal treatment for all shareholders who are in the same position, it is sufficient to observe that that provision has subsequently been repealed and replaced by Article 17 of Directive 2001/34 which applies, according to its heading, only to the obligation to provide information to the holders of securities.

42 Thus the provisions of Directive 77/91 and of Directive 79/279 referred to by the referring court apply to well-defined situations that are clearly different from those at issue in the main proceedings. Furthermore, as the Advocate General notes, in point 84 of her Opinion, those provisions are essentially limited to regulating very specific company-law situations by imposing on companies certain obligations for the protection of all shareholders. They do not therefore possess the general, comprehensive character which is otherwise naturally inherent in general principles of law.

As regards the half-yearly report, Directive 2001/34/EC requires that this consists of figures and of an explanatory statement relating to the company's activities and profits and losses during the relevant six-month period, and that it is published within the time limit of four months of the end of the relevant six-month period. The half-yearly report is particularly relevant for companies intending to distribute interim dividends.

Article 72 Directive 2001/34/EC

1. The half-yearly report shall be published within four months of the end of the relevant six-month period.
2. In exceptional, duly substantiated cases, the competent authorities shall be permitted to extend the time limit for publication.

Article 73 Directive 2001/34/EC

1. The half-yearly report shall consist of figures and an explanatory statement relating to the company's activities and profits and losses during the relevant six-month period.
2. The figures, presented in table form, shall indicate at least:
   (a) the net turnover, and
   (b) the profit or loss before or after deduction of tax.

These terms shall have the same meanings as in the Directives on company accounts.

3. The Member States may allow the competent authorities to authorise companies, exceptionally and on a case-by-case basis, to supply estimated figures for profits and losses, provided that the shares of each such company are listed officially in only one Member State. The use of this procedure must be indicated by the company in its report and must not mislead investors.
4. Where the company has paid or proposes to pay an interim dividend, the figures must indicate the profit or loss after tax for the six-month period and the interim dividend paid or proposed.
5. Against each figure there must be shown the figure for the corresponding period in the preceding financial year.
6. The explanatory statement must include any significant information enabling investors to make an informed assessment of the trend of the company's activities and profits or losses together with an indication of any special factor which has influenced those activities and those profits or losses during the period in question, and enable a comparison to be made with the corresponding period of the preceding financial year.

It must also, as far as possible, refer to the company's likely future development in the current financial year.

7. Where the figures provided for in paragraph 2 are unsuited to the company's activities, the competent authorities shall ensure that appropriate adjustments are made.

Securities are admitted to official listing upon request of the issuing company.

A designated competent authority of the territory where the stock exchange is situated or operates, vested with all necessary powers, shall examine the request of the company. Member States may entrust a public body (e.g., as in the UK) or the market operator of a regulated market itself (e.g., as in Italy) with the authority to decide on the admission of securities to official listing. Such an authority shall verify that the conditions and obligations prescribed by Directive 2001/34/EC are met, and they may reject the application in cases where an admission would be detrimental to the interest of investors. The authority may also make the admission of a security subject to conditions deemed appropriate.

Article 11 Directive 2001/34/EC

1. The competent authorities referred to in Article 105 shall decide on the admission of securities to official listing on a stock exchange situated or operating within their territories.
2. Without prejudice to the other powers conferred upon them, the competent authorities may reject an application for the admission of a security to official listing if, in their opinion, the issuer's situation is such that admission would be detrimental to investors' interests.

Article 12 Directive 2001/34/EC

By way of derogation from Article 8, Member States may, solely in the interests of protecting the investors, give the competent authorities power to make the admission of a security to official listing subject to any special condition which the competent authorities consider appropriate and of which they have explicitly informed the applicant.

After admission to listing, where protection of investors or the smooth operation of the market so requires, the designated authority may compel the issuers to provide and publish further information.

Article 16 Directive 2001/34/EC

1. An issuer whose securities are admitted to official listing shall provide the competent authorities with all the information which the latter consider appropriate in order to protect investors or ensure the smooth operation of the market.
2. Where protection of investors or the smooth operation of the market so requires, an issuer may be required by the competent authorities to publish such information in such a form and within such time limits as they consider appropriate. Should the issuer fail to comply with such requirement, the competent authorities may themselves publish such information after having heard the issuer.

In case of subsequent non-compliance with the obligations laid down in the Directive or with requests of the authority, the latter may suspend the listing or decide that listing shall be discontinued.

Article 18 Directive 2001/34/EC

1. The competent authorities may decide to suspend the listing of a security where the smooth operation of the market is, or may be, temporarily jeopardised or where protection of investors so requires.
2. The competent authorities may decide that the listing of the security be discontinued where they are satisfied that, owing to special circumstances, normal regular dealings in a security are no longer possible.

It should be added that companies seeking for admission of their securities to official listing shall publish an information sheet, drafted in as easily analysable and comprehensible a form as possible (Article 22 Directive 2001/34/EC), referred to as *listing particulars*.

Article 20 Directive 2001/34/EC

Member States shall ensure that the admission of securities to official listing on a stock exchange situated or operating within their territories is conditional upon the publication of an information sheet, hereinafter referred to as 'listing particulars', in accordance with Chapter I of Title V.

Article 21 Directive 2001/34/EC

1. The listing particulars shall contain the information which, according to the particular nature of the issuer and of the securities for the admission of which application is being made, is necessary to enable investors and their investment advisers to make an informed assessment of the assets and liabilities, financial position, profits and losses, and prospects of the issuer and of the rights attaching to such securities.
2. Member States shall ensure that the obligation referred to in paragraph 1 is incumbent upon the persons responsible for the listing particulars as provided for in heading 1.1 of Schedules A and B of Annex I hereto.

As we will see later, in *Ntionik* the CJEU clarified that the wording of Article 21(2) Directive 2001/34/EC does not preclude a national legislature from laying down, for cases where the information recorded in listing particulars published with a view to admitting securities to official stock exchange listing proves to be inaccurate or misleading, administrative penalties imposable not only upon the persons expressly mentioned in those particulars as responsible but also upon the issuer of the securities and, indiscriminately, upon the members of the issuer's board of directors, regardless of whether the board members have been identified as responsible in the listing particulars.

The information sheet where the listing particulars are disclosed shall comply with the rules laid down in the Prospectus Directive, which we are about to discuss.

FURTHER READING

Jan Wouters, 'EC Harmonisation of National Rules Concerning Offerings, Stock Exchange Listing and Investment Services: An Overview', 4 *EBLR* 199–203 (1993).

Mathias M. Siems, 'The Foundations of Securities Law', 20 *EBLR* 141–171 (2009).

17.3 Prospectus

The Prospectus Regulation – Regulation 2017/1129/EU of the European Parliament and of the Council of 14 June 2017 *on the prospectus to be published when securities are offered to the public or admitted to trading* and repealing Directive 2003/71/EC – aims to establish a set of common standards on information, disclosure, and transparency for the enterprises issuing securities onto a regulated market *vis-à-vis* their potential security holders.

Article 1 Regulation 2017/1129/EU

This Regulation lays down requirements for the drawing up, approval and distribution of the prospectus to be published when securities are offered to the public or admitted to trading on a regulated market situated or operating within a Member State.

The Prospectus Regulation is part of the European Commission's proposal to introduce a regulation, establishing the criteria for the formation of a single prospectus valid across the EU.

The Regulation (originally a Directive) is also part of the so-called *Lamfalussy process* approach, a system that brought to light four Directives, also including the Market Abuse Directive (later replaced by the Market Abuse Regulation), the Transparency Directive and the MiFID 2, belonging to the Action Plan on Building a Capital Market Union.

Recital 6 Directive 2003/71/EC

(6) In its final report of 15 February 2001 the Committee of Wise Men proposed the introduction of new legislative techniques based on a four-level approach, namely framework principles, implementing measures, cooperation and enforcement. Level 1, the directive, should confine itself to broad, general 'framework' principles, while Level 2 should contain technical implementing measures to be adopted by the Commission with the assistance of a committee.

Coined from the name of Alexandre Lamfalussy, chair of the EU Advisory Committee who created it, this process consists of four different levels of lawmaking:

- at the first level, the Council of the European Union and the European Parliament adopt a piece of legislation, setting out framework principles and building guidelines on its implementation;
- at the second level, committees and regulators advise on technical details and set out the implementing measures that allow the above-mentioned principles to be put into practice;
- at the third level, new regulations are voted by the Member State representatives, which will delegate national regulators to work on coordinating the rules with other nations;
- the fourth level involves compliance and enforcement of the new laws.

The Prospectus Regulation is the result of the joint work of the European institutions, which gave a start to the first level of the legislative process, and the Committee of European Securities Regulators (CESR, now ESMA) that advised and gave feedback to the European Commission on the second-level ground, helping with the necessary updates and amendments.

The coordination of requirements for the drawing-up, approval and distribution of this prospectus, a sort of 'single passport' for issuers, is ensured by its mutual recognition. However, such mutual recognition does not in itself confer the right to admission to official listing.

The information provided to investors must be minimal, sufficient, regular, adequate and international:

- *minimal* since Member States may find it useful to establish nondiscriminatory minimum quantitative criteria which issuers must meet in order to benefit from the possibilities for exemption provided for in the Directive; this does not rule out the right of Member States to impose stricter rules should they so wish;
- *sufficient* to ensure that investors possess the relevant information;
- *regular* so that investors are supplied with appropriate information throughout the entire period during which the securities are listed; irrespective of whether the information is provided in the form of an annual financial report, a half-yearly report or interim management statements, it must accurately reflect the current situation and prospects of the issuer;
- *adequate* in that investors must be informed by shareholders of 'major' holdings of changes in those holdings;
- *international* since the principle of equivalence in respect of the disclosure requirement also applies to issuers located in non-member countries.

In order to simplify access to the prospectus and the information and, in the process, increase harmonisation of securities markets, the home Member State, i.e., the country where the issuer has its registered office, is the sole base for provision of the documents.

Moreover, the need for consistency and efficiency in relation to publication and disclosure of the information militates in favour of the use of a common language, be it a language accepted by the competent authorities of the home and/or host Member State(s) or a language that is customary in the international sphere.

As regards the listing particulars for the admission to official stock exchange listing, a prospectus is a disclosure document that provides prospective investors with material information about the issuer and the security itself.

Article 6(1) Regulation 2017/1129/EU

1. Without prejudice to Article 14(2) and Article 18(1), a prospectus shall contain the necessary information which is material to an investor for making an informed assessment of:
   (a) the assets and liabilities, profits and losses, financial position, and prospects of the issuer and of any guarantor;
   (b) the rights attaching to the securities; and
   (c) the reasons for the issuance and its impact on the issuer.

That information may vary depending on any of the following:

(a) the nature of the issuer;
(b) the type of securities;
(c) the circumstances of the issuer;
(d) where relevant, whether or not the non-equity securities have a denomination per unit of at least EUR 100 000 or are to be traded only on a regulated market, or a specific segment thereof, to which only qualified investors can have access for the purposes of trading in the securities.

The prospectus is therefore the 'visiting card' that presents the company and the securities to the market, a portfolio that contains and discloses all the relevant information that is useful to make an informed and trustworthy assessment at the time of the investment. This assessment is based on several different factors that, combined, display the issuer's profile. The disclosed information shall include notions regarding the assets and the liabilities of the company, its financial position, the profits and losses accounts of the current and of the recent fiscal years, along with all the necessary data about the rights attached to the securities.

All the information disclosed in the prospectus must be true, complete and up to date. Any discovered omissions have to be dealt with by the national competent authority. However, the authority may eventually authorise the omission from the prospectus of certain information in three cases: (i) where reasons of public interest so suggest; (ii) in the case where disclosure of such information would be seriously detrimental to the issuer, provided that the omission would not be likely to mislead the public with regard to facts and circumstances essential for an informed assessment of the issuer, offeror or guarantor, if any, and of the rights attached to the securities to which the prospectus relates; (iii) in the case where such information is of minor importance (*see*, Article 18(1) Regulation 2017/1129/EU).

Before the prospectus may be publicised by insertion in newspapers, distribution in public offices or by broadcasting via electronic means, this must be approved by the national competent authority: in contrast to the admission to listing, market operators operating regulated markets may not be entrusted with the function of approving the prospectus (listing particulars).

Article 31(1) Regulation 2017/1129/EU

1. Each Member State shall designate a single competent administrative authority responsible for carrying out the duties resulting from this Regulation and for ensuring that the provisions of this Regulation are applied. Member States shall inform the Commission, ESMA and the competent authorities of other Member States accordingly.

The competent authority shall be independent from market participants.

Article 20(1–2) Regulation 2017/1129/EU

1. A prospectus shall not be published unless the relevant competent authority has approved it, or all of its constituent parts in accordance with Article 10.
2. The competent authority shall notify the issuer, the offeror or the person asking for admission to trading on a regulated market of its decision regarding the approval of the prospectus within 10 working days of the submission of the draft prospectus.

Where the competent authority fails to take a decision on the prospectus within the time limits laid down in the first subparagraph of this paragraph and paragraphs 3 and 6, such failure shall not be deemed to constitute approval of the application.

The competent authority shall notify ESMA of the approval of the prospectus and any supplement thereto as soon as possible and in any event by no later than the end of the first working day after that approval is notified to the issuer, the offeror or the person asking for admission to trading on a regulated market.

...

Article 21 Regulation 2017/1129/EU

1. Once approved, the prospectus shall be made available to the public by the issuer, the offeror or the person asking for admission to trading on a regulated market at a reasonable time in advance of, and at the latest at the beginning of, the offer to the public or the admission to trading of the securities involved.

In the case of an initial offer to the public of a class of shares that is admitted to trading on a regulated market for the first time, the prospectus shall be made available to the public at least six working days before the end of the offer.

2. The prospectus, whether a single document or consisting of separate documents, shall be deemed available to the public when published in electronic form on any of the following websites:
   (a) the website of the issuer, the offeror or the person asking for admission to trading on a regulated market;
   (b) the website of the financial intermediaries placing or selling the securities, including paying agents;
   (c) the website of the regulated market where the admission to trading is sought, or where no admission to trading on a regulated market is sought, the website of the operator of the MTF.
3. The prospectus shall be published on a dedicated section of the website which is easily accessible when entering the website. It shall be downloadable, printable and in searchable electronic format that cannot be modified.

The documents containing information incorporated by reference in the prospectus, the supplements and/or final terms related to the prospectus and a separate copy of the summary shall be accessible under the same section alongside the prospectus, including by way of hyperlinks where necessary.

The separate copy of the summary shall clearly indicate the prospectus to which it relates.

4. Access to the prospectus shall not be subject to the completion of a registration process, the acceptance of a disclaimer limiting legal liability or the payment of a fee. Warnings specifying the jurisdiction(s) in which an offer or an admission to trading is being made shall not be considered to be disclaimers limiting legal liability.
5. The competent authority of the home Member State shall publish on its website all the prospectuses approved or at least the list of prospectuses approved, including a hyperlink to the dedicated website sections referred to in paragraph 3 of this Article as well as an identification of the host Member State or States where prospectuses are notified in accordance with Article 25. The published list, including the hyperlinks, shall be kept up-to-date and each item shall remain on the website at least for the period referred to in paragraph 7 of this Article.

At the same time as it notifies ESMA of the approval of a prospectus or of any supplement thereto, the competent authority shall provide ESMA with an electronic copy of the prospectus and any supplement thereto, as well as the data necessary for its classification by ESMA in the storage mechanism referred to in paragraph 6 and for the report referred to in Article 47.

The competent authority of the host Member State shall publish information on all notifications received in accordance with Article 25 on its website.

6. ESMA shall, without undue delay, publish all prospectuses received from the competent authorities on its website, including any supplements thereto, final terms and related translations where applicable, as well as information on the host Member State(s) where prospectuses are notified in accordance with Article 25. Publication

shall be ensured through a storage mechanism providing the public with free of charge access and search functions.

7. All prospectuses approved shall remain publicly available in electronic form for at least 10 years after their publication on the websites referred to in paragraphs 2 and 6.

Where hyperlinks are used for information incorporated by reference in the prospectus, and the supplements and/or final terms related to the prospectus, such hyperlinks shall be functional for the period referred to in the first subparagraph.

8. An approved prospectus shall contain a prominent warning stating when the validity of the prospectus will expire. The warning shall also state that the obligation to supplement a prospectus in the event of significant new factors, material mistakes or material inaccuracies does not apply when a prospectus is no longer valid.
9. In the case of a prospectus comprising several documents and/or incorporating information by reference, the documents and information that constitute the prospectus may be published and distributed separately provided that those documents are made available to the public in accordance with paragraph 2. Where a prospectus consists of separate documents in accordance with Article 10, each of those constituent documents, except for documents incorporated by reference, shall indicate that it is only one part of the prospectus and where the other constituent documents may be obtained.
10. The text and the format of the prospectus, and any supplement to the prospectus made available to the public, shall at all times be identical to the original version approved by the competent authority of the home Member State.
11. A copy of the prospectus on a durable medium shall be delivered to any potential investor, upon request and free of charge, by the issuer, the offeror, the person asking for admission to trading on a regulated market or the financial intermediaries placing or selling the securities. In the event that a potential investor makes a specific demand for a paper copy, the issuer, the offeror, the person asking for admission to trading on a regulated market or a financial intermediary placing or selling the securities shall deliver a printed version of the prospectus. Delivery shall be limited to jurisdictions in which the offer of securities to the public is made or where the admission to trading on a regulated market is taking place under this Regulation.
12. ESMA may, or where the Commission so requests shall, develop draft regulatory technical standards to specify further the requirements relating to the publication of the prospectus.

Power is delegated to the Commission to adopt the regulatory technical standards referred to in the first subparagraph in accordance with Articles 10 to 14 of Regulation (EU) No 1095/2010.

13. ESMA shall develop draft regulatory technical standards to specify the data necessary for the classification of prospectuses referred to in paragraph 5 and the practical arrangements to ensure that such data, including the ISINs of the securities and the LEIs of the issuers, offerors and guarantors, is machine readable.

ESMA shall submit those draft regulatory technical standards to the Commission by 21 July 2018.

Power is delegated to the Commission to adopt the regulatory technical standards referred to in the first subparagraph in accordance with Articles 10 to 14 of Regulation (EU) No 1095/2010.

Every significant new factor (occurring after the publication), material mistake or inaccuracy relating to the information included in the prospectus which is capable of affecting the assessment of the securities, shall be mentioned in a supplement to the prospectus to be published following the same procedure (Article 10(1) Regulation 2017/1129/EU).

Also after granting their approval, the national competent authority shall have the powers to: (i) require offerors, issuers (or their auditors/managers) to provide documents or supplementary information; (ii) in cases where there is reasonable suspicion of any infringement to the applicable rules, prohibit or suspend a public offer for ten days; (iii) make public an issuer's failure to comply with its obligation.

Infringements of rules set forth by the Prospectus Regulation are to be punished with administrative sanctions enforced by the Member States via their national competent authorities. The Directive specifies that these administrative sanctions do not act in prejudice to applicable criminal or civil liability regime (so-called prospectus liability).

Article 38(1) Regulation 2017/1129/EU

1. Without prejudice to the supervisory and investigatory powers of competent authorities under Article 32, and the right of Member States to provide for and impose criminal sanctions, Member States shall, in accordance with national law, provide for competent authorities to have the power to impose administrative sanctions and take appropriate other administrative measures which shall be effective, proportionate and dissuasive

Finally, it is worth mentioning that the prospectus operates as a European passport for securities admitted to official listing, under the home country control standard.

Article 24 Regulation 2017/1129/EU

1. Without prejudice to Article 37, where an offer of securities to the public or admission to trading on a regulated market occurs in one or more Member States, or in a Member State other than the home Member State, the prospectus approved by the home Member State and any supplements thereto shall be valid for the offer to the public or the admission to trading in any number of host Member States, provided that ESMA and the competent authority of each host Member State are notified in accordance with Article 25. Competent authorities of host Member States shall not undertake any approval

or administrative procedures relating to prospectuses and supplements approved by the competent authorities of other Member States, and relating to final terms.

2. Where a significant new factor, material mistake or material inaccuracy arises or is noted within the timeframe specified in Article 23(1), the competent authority of the home Member State shall require that the publication of a supplement be approved in accordance with Article 20(1). ESMA and the competent authority of the host Member State may inform the competent authority of the home Member State of the need for new information.

It is worth noting that another way of raising money from the public is equity or lending crowdfunding. Crowdfunding is an emerging alternative form of financing that connects those who can give, lend or invest money directly with those who need financing for a specific project. It usually refers to public online calls to contribute finance to specific projects.

The EU market for crowdfunding is underdeveloped as compared to other major world economies. One of the biggest hurdles faced by crowdfunding platforms seeking to offer their services across borders is the lack of common rules across the EU. This raises compliance and operational costs and prevents crowdfunding platforms from expanding.

In March 2018, as part of its Fintech action plan, the European Commission presented a proposal for a regulation on crowdfunding service providers. Once adopted at EU level, the new regulation will allow platforms to apply for an EU passport based on a single set of rules. This will make it easier for them to offer their services across the EU.

The new rules will improve access to this innovative form of finance for small investors and businesses in need of funding, particularly start-ups. Investors on crowdfunding platforms will benefit from a better protection regime and a higher level of guarantees, based on:

(a) clear rules on information disclosures for project owners and crowdfunding platforms;
(b) rules on governance and risk management;
(c) a coherent approach to supervision.

The Commission proposal only applies to those crowdfunding services entailing a financial return for investors, such as investment and lending-based crowdfunding.

FURTHER READING

Colin Mercer, 'EC Prospectus and Mutual Recognition Directives: UK Implementation', 2 *EBLR* 227–228 (1991).

Guido Alpa, 'The Harmonisation of the EC Law of Financial Markets in the Perspective of Consumer Protection', 13 *EBLR* 523–540 (2002).

Elizabeth Howell, 'An Analysis of the Prospectus Regime: The EU Reforms and the "Brexit" Factor', 15 *ECFR* 69–100 (2018).

See also:

Danny Bush and Guido Ferrarini (eds.), *Regulation of the EU Financial Markets* (Oxford University Press, 2017).

Hse-Yu Chiu, 'Plus Size Fits All? – Why Unitary Standards of Disclosure for Prospectuses under the Draft Prospectus Proposal by the European Commission Should be Reconsidered', 14 *EBLR* 727–741 (2003).

Christel Grundmann-van de Krol, 'New EC Prospectus Directive and the Lamfalussy Process', 1 *ECL* 32–35 (2004).

Guido Alpa, 'The Harmonisation of EC Law of Financial Markets in the Perspective of Consumer Protection', 15 *EBLR* 347–365 (2004).

Mirella Pellegrini, 'Critical Analysis of the Prospectus Directive', 17 *EBLR* 1679–1692 (2006).

See also:

Gerard Hertig, Reinier Kraakman, and Edward Rock, 'Corporate Law and Securities Markets', in John Armour, Luca Enriques et al., *The Anatomy of Corporate Law: A Comparative and Functional Approach* 243–267 (Oxford University Press, 3rd ed., 2017).

17.4 *Ntionik* Case

In *Ntionik* (C-430/05, *Ntionik Anonimi Etairia Emporias H/Y, Logismikou kai Paroxis Ypiresion Michanografisis and Ioannis Michail Pikoulas* v. *Epitropi Kefalaiagoras*, [2007] ECR I-05835), the question referred to the CJEU was raised in proceedings between Ntionik Anonimi Etairia Emporias I/I, Logismikou kai Parokhis Ipiresion Mikhanografisis ('*Ntionik*'), Ioannis Mikhail Pikoulas and Epitropi Kefalaiagoras.

In 2002 Ntionik, the applicant in the main proceedings, was sanctioned by the Greek authority 'CMC', which was instituted with the purpose of enforcing and policing the requirements imposed on companies by the Directive 2001/34/EC. The applicant had allegedly infringed the national (and European) provisions, according to which a company, who is willing to put onto a regulated market its securities, must provide the investors with a clear prospectus containing all the relevant and necessary information to permit an honest and true assessment of the economic and social current situation of the said company. The aim of this directive is deliberately to safeguard potential investors from the risk of undertaking an uninformed investment.

Ntionik provided a regular prospectus in the year 2001 for the admission to listing of its securities in order to issue a capital rise between February and March, althought it was not coherent in the assessments concerning the development of the sales and profits and losses of the company which were published at the end of the financial year 2000.

'CMC' imposed a fine, according to Greek law, on Ntionik and on Mr Pikoulas, a member of the board of directors of Ntionik, who was not, however, identified in the listing particulars at issue as responsible for the accuracy of the information contained therein.

Ntionik and Mr Pikoulas reacted by bringing the matter before the '*Simvoulio tis Epikratias*' (national court) saying that it was not lawful to sanction an undisclosed member of the board of directors.

The *Simvoulio tis Epikratias* stayed the proceedings and referred the following questions to the Court of Justice:

C-430/05, Ntionik Anonimi Etairia Emporias H/Y, Logismikou kai Paroxis Ypiresion Michanografisis and Ioannis Michail Pikoulas v. Epitropi Kefalaiagoras, [2007] ECR I-05835, § 36

In the light of Article 21 of Directive 2001/34 ..., can a national legislature lay down, for cases where the information recorded in listing particulars proves to be inaccurate or misleading, administrative penalties imposable not only upon the persons expressly mentioned in those particulars as responsible but also upon the issuer of the securities being admitted to listing on a stock exchange and, indiscriminately, upon the members of its board of directors, regardless of whether the board members have been identified as responsible in the abovementioned sense?

The CJEU decided the referred questions as follows:

C-430/05, Ntionik Anonimi Etairia Emporias H/Y, Logismikou kai Paroxis Ypiresion Michanografisis and Ioannis Michail Pikoulas v. Epitropi Kefalaiagoras, [2007] ECR I-05835, §§ 50, 52–53, 55–56, Operative Part

Article 21 of Directive 2001/34 on the admission of securities to official stock exchange listing and on information to be published on those securities is to be interpreted as not precluding a national legislature from laying down, for cases where the information recorded in listing particulars published with a view to admitting securities to official stock exchange listing proves to be inaccurate or misleading, administrative penalties imposable not only upon the persons expressly mentioned in those particulars as responsible but also upon the issuer of the securities and, indiscriminately, upon the members of the issuer's board of directors, regardless of whether the board members have been identified as responsible in the listing particulars.

Since the directive does not expressly provide for a system of penalties applicable to the persons on whom responsibility for the listing particulars is incumbent, the Member States are empowered to choose the penalties which seem appropriate to them. They must, however, exercise that power in accordance with Community law and its general principles, and consequently with the principle of proportionality.

In that regard, a system of civil, criminal or administrative penalties established at national level in respect of the abovementioned persons does not run counter to the objective of that directive, which is to ensure, inter alia, adequate information of investors, where the system is proportionate to the gravity of the infringement consisting in the giving of inaccurate or misleading information in the listing particulars.

17.5 The Market Abuse Regulation

Regulation (EU) No. 596/2014 of the European Parliament and of the Council of 16 April 2014, better known as the Market Abuse Regulation or MAD, has replaced Directive 2003/6/EC of the European Parliament and of the Council of 28 January 2003 *on insider dealing and market manipulation (market abuse)* (the Market Abuse Directive).

The 2003 Directive focused on preventing abuses through financial instruments admitted to trading on a regulated market, or for which a request for admission to trading on such a market had been made.

3.1.1 Commission Staff Working Paper Impact Assessment

If an instrument is admitted to trading on a regulated market then any trading in that instrument is covered by the MAD, whether the trading of that instrument occurs on a MTF, 'crossing network' or over-the-counter (OTC). Further, for insider dealing (although not for market manipulation), the prohibition extends also to financial instruments not admitted to trading on a regulated market, but whose value depends on such a financial instrument.

The Commission Impact Assessment, published in 2011, found that the 2003 Directive could no longer achieve its aim of creating a level playing field for economic actors. Three main issues were raised. First, the 2003 Directive failed to prevent market abuse in certain financial markets due to the legislative, market and technological developments that had emerged since it came into force. Secondly, the 2003 Directive failed to provide regulators with sufficient investigative powers, and sanctions were too meagre to provide a deterrent effect. Finally, any reform needed more legal certainty and less regulatory complexity, as excessive administration had acted as a barrier for small and medium size issuers to access the financial market.

Regulation 596/2014 was drafted in response to these issues. To achieve its aims, the Regulation targets certain market abuses.

Article 1 Regulation 596/2014

This Regulation establishes a common regulatory framework on insider dealing, the unlawful disclosure of inside information and market manipulation (market abuse) as well as measures to prevent market abuse to ensure the integrity of financial markets in the Union and to enhance investor protection and confidence in those markets.

These types of market abuse are defined in their respective provisions, however they can be broadly summarised as:

(a) *Insider dealing* (Article 8): trading a financial product on the market to one's own advantage through the use of inside information (i.e., information that is known only to those working inside or close to the company in question).
(b) *Unlawful disclosure of 'inside information'* (Article 10): the leaking of inside information to other market participants unless disclosure is in the normal exercise of the profession.
(c) *Market manipulation* (Article 12): artificially manipulating the price of a financial product by spreading false supply, demand or price information.

These abuses have potentially been made easier by the aforementioned legislative, market and technological developments. An increasingly global market has given rise to new technologies and trading platforms, such as MTFs and OTCs.

3.2.1 Commission Staff Working Paper Impact Assessment

If an instrument is not admitted to trading on a regulated market but is only traded on a MTF, another type of facility or OTC it will not be covered by MAD.

...

Of the 41 MTFs that trade shares in Europe, 25 admit to trading shares which are not admitted to trading on a regulated market. Trading in these instruments falls outside the scope of the MAD, and only three Member States have extended the MAD regime in full at national level to all MTFs. Eight other Member States have extended the MAD regime in part to all MTFs. Of the remainder, two have extended the MAD fully only to some MTFs, 6 have extended the MAD in part to some MTFs (including 4 of the six largest), and 8 Member States have not extended the MAD to any MTFs at all. Overall, the majority of Member States have only extended the MAD at national level to some MTFs, or to none at all. Therefore in most Member States there are at least some MTFs which are partially or fully outside the scope of market abuse legislation.

Therefore, the Market Abuse Regulation extends the prohibition of market abuse to financial instruments that are only traded on new platforms and to OTC transactions. Moreover, it clarifies that such market abuse is also prohibited across commodity and related derivative markets. It is hoped that the Market Abuse Regulation's increased scope will improve investor protection, preserve the integrity of markets and ensure that market abuse of such instruments is clearly prohibited.

These changes will prevent the Market Abuse Regulation becoming outdated, as the 2003 Directive did.

Recital 38 Regulation 596/2014

This Regulation should provide measures regarding market manipulation that are capable of being adapted to new forms of trading or new strategies that may be abusive. To reflect the fact that trading in financial instruments is increasingly automated, it is desirable that the definition of market manipulation provide examples of specific abusive strategies that may be carried out by any available means of trading including algorithmic and high-frequency trading. The examples provided are neither intended to be exhaustive nor intended to suggest that the same strategies carried out by other means would not also be abusive.

This idea of updating legislation against modern and future forms of abuse is further evidenced in Article 48 Regulation 596/2014 with the explicit mentioning of websites, blogs, and social media. It can be seen, therefore, that the Regulation achieves much of its principal aim to update and strengthen the existing legal framework set out in the MAD.

The 2003 Directive also granted limited investigative and sanction powers, which were insufficient for regulators to effectively enforce rules against market abuse.

The Commission Impact Assessment on the Market Abuse Directive, dated 20 October 2011, found inconsistencies in regulators' powers. For example, in some Member States regulators could not receive reports of suspicious transactions in OTC derivatives, and some regulators were unable to obtain existing telephone data despite this being necessary to providing evidence. Furthermore, there were also no tools to address 'attempts at market manipulation' for those who had tried and failed at market abuse.

The Regulation, being directly applicable, now deals with the inconsistency in the Directive's legal framework. It also grants a minimum set of supervisory and investigative powers, including to carry out on-site inspections and investigations, and to request the freezing or sequestration of assets. In addition, the Regulation includes a prohibition on 'attempts at market manipulation'.

The level of sanctions was also an issue highlighted by the Impact Assessment.

3.2.3 Commission Staff Working Paper Impact Assessment: Regulation of the European Parliament and of the Council on Insider Dealing Market Manipulation (Market Abuse)

The level of administrative pecuniary sanctions varies widely among Member States and in some cases the maximum fine can be considered low and insufficiently dissuasive. When the gains of a market abuse offence are higher than the expected sanctions, the deterrent effect of the sanctions is undermined. This is reinforced by the fact that the offender might consider that his offence could remain undetected. As shown in table 2, respectively 4 and 9 Member States have sanctions lower or equal to EUR 200,000 while respectively 10 and 14 Member States have sanctions of more than EUR 1 million for the same offences. These sanctions can be considered weak as insider dealing and market manipulation offences covered by Directive 2003/6/EC can lead to gains of several million euros, in excess of the maximum levels of fines provided for in some Member States.

Indeed, when the gains of a market abuse offence are higher than the expected sanctions, the deterrent effect of the sanctions is undermined. In addition, some Member States did not publish the sanctions that had been imposed, and great disparity was seen in relation to criminal sanctions.

3.2.3 Commission Staff Working Paper Impact Assessment: Regulation of the European Parliament and of the Council on Insider Dealing Market Manipulation (Market Abuse)

Analysis ... shows that none of the offences of insider dealing or market manipulation is subject to criminal sanctions in all EU Member States. For example, for the offence of improper disclosure of inside information by secondary insiders, 8 Member States lack criminal sanctions, while for the offence of 'tipping' by secondary insiders, 6 Member States lack criminal sanctions. Since market abuse can be carried out across borders, this divergence can be expected to have negative effects on the single market and could encourage potential offenders to carry out market abuse in Member States which have the least strict sanctions. It also complicates cross-border cooperation by law enforcement authorities.

The result of these shortcomings was that in some areas the legal framework lacked the 'bite' it needed for deterrence.

To remedy such faults, the Regulation requires EU countries to specify administrative pecuniary sanctions of at least €1 million to €15 million or 15 per cent of the total annual turnover for legal persons (such as companies) and between €500,000 and €5 million for individuals. Moreover, the affiliated Directive 2014/57/EU on criminal sanctions for market abuse (MAD) provides for criminal sanctions for such abuse. It is hoped that harmonisation of the regime will prevent the rules being undermined by inconsistent application. Finally, the Commission Communication of 25 June 2008 on 'A Small Business Act for Europe' found certain requirements, such as the need to keep and constantly update insider lists, was particularly burdensome for issuers in SME growth markets.

III – A Regulatory Environment in Support of SMEs' Needs, Council of the European Union: Conclusions on 'Think Small First – A Small Business Act for Europe'

The Council of the European Union:

(27) UNDERLINES the imperative need to continue cutting red tape and better adapting administrative rules to the needs of SMEs, in order to enable them to save time and money and devote the resulting resources to their development and improving their competitiveness;

(28) RECALLS therefore the importance of cutting administrative costs imposed on business arising from EU legislation by 25% by 2012 and of national measures of comparable ambition by Member States.

The Regulation gives an exemption for issuers in SMEs to continually keep and update these lists, merely requiring that one can be provided should it be needed. Furthermore, ESMA should be able to issue guidelines that assist issuers in SME growth markets, without compromising investor protection. It is hoped that these changes will reduce costly administrative burdens and facilitate access to finance for issuers in SME markets.

It will always be difficult to know the impact of the Market Abuse Regulation. The Impact Assessment surmises:

3.1.3 Commission Staff Working Paper Impact Assessment: Regulation of the European Parliament and of the Council on Insider Dealing Market Manipulation (Market Abuse)

It is difficult to estimate the extent to which market abuse takes place within Europe. One way to estimate the prevalence of market abuse is to consider the number of cases sanctioned by competent authorities in Member States, although inevitably this is likely to underestimate the true extent of abuse as some cases will go undetected due to the sophistication of the abuses or the limited resources available to investigate cases.

Nonetheless, the drafters of the Regulation have been sensitive to the difficulties faced by its predecessor, as raised in the Impact Assessment. Its provisions are well placed to create a more cohesive legal framework for a secure financial market, whilst balancing the costs for SMEs.

17.6 The Transparency Directive

Directive 2013/50/EU amended Directive 2004/109/EC of the European Parliament and of the Council. The former Directive 2004/109/EC sought to make a safer market for investors by requiring information disclosure.

Recital 2 Directive 2004/109/EC

The disclosure of accurate, comprehensive and timely information about security issuers builds sustained investor confidence and allows an informed assessment of their business performance and assets. This enhances both investor protection and market efficiency.

In the context of the 2008 financial crisis, it was considered necessary to review the Transparency Directive, in order to rebuild investor confidence. An External Study was commissioned.

1.1.6 Commission Staff Working Document

The Review of the Operation of Directive 2004/109/EC: Emerging Issues

Two points have been frequently made regarding the general architecture of the Directive in the survey conducted by the External Study. Firstly, the minimum harmonisation character of the Transparency Directive allows Member States to adopt more stringent requirements. Thus the transposition of the Directive is relatively uneven as a result of different national requirements. More stringent national requirements, in particular regarding the notification of major holdings of voting rights, are perceived as problematic by stakeholders. This results in real and costly implementation problems. This raises the question as to whether the current regime (i.e. a minimum harmonisation directive) is the appropriate tool to achieve an effective level harmonisation of transparency requirements in the EU.

Secondly, the absence of more flexible rules for smaller listed companies makes requirements too demanding and costly according to such companies, thus creating market inefficiency.

Additionally, it appears that the Directive's obligations need to be adapted to innovation in financial markets. In particular, insufficient disclosure of stock lending practices seemed to have increased the risk of empty voting and lack of disclosure regarding cash-settled derivatives has led to problems with 'hidden ownership'. Finally, the progress towards the establishment of a pan-European system of storage of regulated information, with a view to facilitate investors' access to information, is slow and the impact of the Directive in this area has been insufficient.

In response to the findings of the Commission Staff Working Document dated 27 May 2010 ('the Commission Report'), reform was therefore necessary for better harmonisation, more flexibility for smaller listed companies, improved measures to adapt to innovation in financial markets, and a Europewide system of storage for the information gathered.

First, the Directive has harmonised the regime for notification of major holdings of voting rights. Specific provision is made for situations where a holder of financial instruments exercises their rights such that the total holding of voting rights exceeds the notification threshold without affecting the overall percentage of the previously notified holdings, a new notification should be required. ESMA has been tasked with drafting technical standards for notification of major holdings especially those obtained through financial instruments.

Recital 12 Directive 2013/50/EU

A harmonised regime for notification of major holdings of voting rights, especially regarding the aggregation of holdings of shares with holdings of financial instruments, should improve legal certainty, enhance transparency and reduce the administrative burden for cross-border investors.

Greater notification requirements better achieve the aims of the Directive in providing transparency in financial markets. However, the cost of such transparency created a significant financial burden for smaller enterprises, thereby forcing them to raise capital through other means (e.g., private equity, banking loans, accessing alternative, non-regulated markets, or by issuing debt).

Secondly, therefore, the Commission Report acknowledged this financial burden and sought to devise solutions for how to make regulated markets more appealing for SMEs.

S.2.1 Commission Staff Working Document

The Review of the Operation of Directive 2004/109/EC: Emerging Issues

An important recurrent issue is how to make access to regulated market more attractive for small and medium-sized enterprises (SMEs). The argument is regularly advanced to the Commission staffs that the rules appear to be designed primarily for the 'blue-chip' companies in the first place and that, for SMEs or smaller listed companies, the costs of being listed are proportionally higher. In the External Study, stakeholders' views are in favour of a distinct transparency regime for SMEs (understood as smaller listed companies), in particular those of financial analysts, retail investors and issuers of shares (especially mid and small caps). Stock exchanges and institutional investors are however more reluctant to this.

...

there are specific simplification measures which could be envisaged, without undermining investor protection, such as for instance: (i) providing for more flexible deadlines to the disclosure of financial reports; (ii) alleviating the obligation to publish quarterly financial information; (iii) harmonising the maximum content of reports; or (iv) facilitating cross border visibility of smaller listed companies.

As such, Directive 2013/50/EU acknowledges the problems faced by SMEs.

Recital 2 Directive 2013/50/EU

[T]he report demonstrates the need to provide for the simplification of certain issuers' obligations with a view to making regulated markets more attractive to small and medium-sized issuers raising capital in the Union.

Steps have therefore been taken in Directive 2013/50/EU to reduce the administration and financial burdens of its predecessor, such that regulated markets are made more accessible for small and medium-size issuers.

To reduce the administrative burdens Directive 2013/50/EU has simplified reporting requirements. Article 1(2) abolished the requirement to publish interim management statements or quarterly reports and Member States may no longer require periodic financial information on more than an annual or six-month basis. However, with regard to the content of these reports, Member States retain powers to require additional financial information, should this not constitute a significant financial burden.

Further efforts are made in the Directive to reduce the burden, and simplify the process, for any other reports. For example, to reduce the burden of reporting, the period for issuers to publish their half-yearly reports has been extended from two to three months at the end of each period and, to simplify the process, uniform regulatory standards were to be introduced by 31 December 2016. The Directive also contains provisions for annual financial reports being prepared in a single electronic format.

Article 1(3)(b) Directive 2013/50/EU

With effect from 1 January 2020 all annual financial reports shall be prepared in a single electronic reporting format provided that a cost-benefit analysis has been undertaken by the European Supervisory Authority (European Securities and Markets Authority) (ESMA) established by Regulation (EU) No 1095/2010 of the European Parliament and of the Council.

ESMA shall develop draft regulatory technical standards to specify the electronic reporting format, with due reference to current and future technological options. Before the adoption of the draft regulatory technical standards, ESMA shall carry out an adequate assessment of possible electronic reporting formats and conduct appropriate field tests. ESMA shall submit those draft regulatory technical standards to the Commission at the latest by 31 December 2016.

It is hoped that these changes will have a meaningful impact in making regulated markets a legitimate option for SMEs seeking to raise capital.

Thirdly, Directive 2013 seeks greater transparency. This transparency regime has been used widely, as well as broadened to encompass new financial innovations. An example of greater transparency in the Directive is the amendment made by Article 1(5), which requires greater disclosure of payments made from extractive industries (e.g., logging, oil, and gas) to governments.

Article 1(5) Directive 2013/50/EU

Member States shall require issuers active in the extractive or logging of primary forest industries ... to prepare on an annual basis, in accordance with Chapter 10 of that Directive, a report on payments made to governments. The report shall be made public at the latest six months after the end of each financial year and shall remain publicly available for at least 10 years. Payments to governments shall be reported at consolidated level.

Disclosure of financial ties to government, such as this, promotes a system of transparency that, in turn, promotes investor confidence. Indeed, the Commission Report acknowledges the importance of disclosure in building investor confidence.

C1.20 Annex 1 Commission Staff Working Document

The Review of the Operation of Directive 2004/109/EC: Emerging Issues

Transparency of information about securities issuers enhances both investor protection and market efficiency and thus contributes to growth and job creation by better allocation of capital and by reducing costs. On the other hand, lack of transparency with regard to such information could hinder investor confidence and affect market resilience, reducing investment and slowing economic growth.

New financial instruments have developed since Directive 2004/109/EC came in to force, for which disclosure was not previously required. A lack of transparency in new financial instruments, particularly with regards to vote lending, increased the potential and effectiveness for empty voting. For example, cash-settled derivatives could be used to conceal economic ownership and acquire voting rights (also known as 'hidden ownership'). Therefore, Directive 2013/50/EU expanded the notification of major holdings of voting rights such that it now includes direct and indirect holdings of financial instruments that have the same economic effect as holding the shares themselves, regardless of them holding the right of physical settlement.

The harmonised regime for disclosing major holdings, along with the aforementioned new developments in financial instruments, has made cross-border investment more secure because investors are better informed of the markets into which they are entering.

Finally, for this transparency regime to benefit investors in a practical sense, the information gathered needed to be accessible. The Directive therefore also tasked the ESMA with creating a web portal for the dissemination of this information.

Article 1(14) Directive 2013/50/EU

European electronic access point

1. A web portal serving as a European electronic access point ('the access point') shall be established by 1 January 2018. ESMA shall develop and operate the access point.

Ultimately, the steps taken in the Transparency Directive positively build upon the legal framework set out in Directive 2004/109/EC to ensure better access to information for investors, and facilitate a more open financial market in the EU.

18

Takeover Regulation

18.1 General Principles

Within the series of directives specifically addressing listed companies and financial markets, the Takeover Bids Directive – Directive 2004/25/EC of the European Parliament and of the Council of 21 April 2004 *on Takeover Bids* – pursues the ambitious goal of achieving a full harmonisation of the rules of Member States in the field of takeover bids.

A 'takeover bid' or 'bid' means a public offer made to the holders of the securities of a company to acquire all or some of those securities, whether mandatory or voluntary, which follows or has as its objective the acquisition of control of the offeree company in accordance with national law (Article 2 Directive 2004/25/EC).

Directive 2004/25/EC was adopted after a long and constructive debate among the European institutions. Both the first and the second proposal for a Directive containing regulations on takeover bids presented by the Commission to the Council and the European Parliament were rejected for the lack of sufficient agreement among the Member States. Whilst the first proposal, submitted on 19 January 1989, contained detailed and mandatory rules, in light of the preference expressed by the Member States, the second proposal, submitted on 8 February 1996, expressed more general principles. Notwithstanding the new approach, the second proposal was also rejected. Therefore, the Commission entrusted the High Level Group (*see*, Chapter 4, § 4.3) with the task of drafting another proposal in an attempt to solve the most critical issues raised by the European Parliament during the discussion of the second proposal. Directive 2004/25/EC adopted on 21 April 2004 substantially benefits from the contribution of the High Level Group Report.

The grounds for adopting such a Directive are expressed in the Preamble as follows:

Recitals 1–3 Directive 2004/25/EC

(1) In accordance with Article 44(2)(g) of the Treaty, it is necessary to coordinate certain safeguards which, for the protection of the interests of members and others, Member

States require of companies governed by the law of a Member State the securities of which are admitted to trading on a regulated market in a Member State, with a view to making such safeguards equivalent throughout the Community.

(2) It is necessary to protect the interests of holders of the securities of companies governed by the law of a Member State when those companies are the subject of takeover bids or of changes of control and at least some of their securities are admitted to trading on a regulated market in a Member State.

(3) It is necessary to create Community-wide clarity and transparency in respect of legal issues to be settled in the event of takeover bids and to prevent patterns of corporate restructuring within the Community from being distorted by arbitrary differences in governance and management cultures.

As the Takeover Bids Directive Assessment Report ('External Study') puts it, the Directive aims at establishing the following conditions:

Takeover Bid Directive Assessment Report ('External Study')

(1) legal certainty on the takeover bid process and Community-wide clarity and transparency with respect to takeover bids, (2) protection of the interests of shareholders, in particular minority shareholders, employees and other stakeholders, when a company is subject to a takeover bid for control, and (3) reinforcement of the freedom for shareholders to deal in and vote on securities of companies and prevention of management action that could frustrate a bid.

In more detail, the Takeover Bids Directive aimed at harmonising takeover law by introducing, *inter alia*, the mandatory bid rule (Article 5), rules on information, disclosure and procedures to be followed during the bid (Articles 6–8), the passivity rule (Article 9), the breakthrough rule (Article 11) and the reciprocity exemption (Article 12), and the squeeze-out and sell-out rights (Articles 15–16).

The grounds for the introduction of such principles are expressed in the Preamble as follows:

Recitals 9, 12-21, 24 Directive 2004/25/EC

(9) Member States should take the necessary steps to protect the holders of securities, in particular those with minority holdings, when control of their companies has been acquired. The Member States should ensure such protection by obliging the person who has acquired control of a company to make an offer to all the holders of that company's securities for all of their holdings at an equitable price in accordance with a common

definition. Member States should be free to establish further instruments for the protection of the interests of the holders of securities, such as the obligation to make a partial bid where the offeror does not acquire control of the company or the obligation to announce a bid at the same time as control of the company is acquired ...

(12) To reduce the scope for insider dealing, an offeror should be required to announce his/her decision to launch a bid as soon as possible and to inform the supervisory authority of the bid.

(13) The holders of securities should be properly informed of the terms of a bid by means of an offer document. Appropriate information should also be given to the representatives of the company's employees or, failing that, to the employees directly.

(14) The time allowed for the acceptance of a bid should be regulated.

(15) To be able to perform their functions satisfactorily, supervisory authorities should at all times be able to require the parties to a bid to provide information concerning themselves and should cooperate and supply information in an efficient and effective manner, without delay, to other authorities supervising capital markets.

(16) In order to prevent operations which could frustrate a bid, the powers of the board of an offeree company to engage in operations of an exceptional nature should be limited, without unduly hindering the offeree company in carrying on its normal business activities.

(17) The board of an offeree company should be required to make public a document setting out its opinion of the bid and the reasons on which that opinion is based, including its views on the effects of implementation on all the company's interests, and specifically on employment.

(18) In order to reinforce the effectiveness of existing provisions concerning the freedom to deal in the securities of companies covered by this Directive and the freedom to exercise voting rights, it is essential that the defensive structures and mechanisms envisaged by such companies be transparent and that they be regularly presented in reports to general meetings of shareholders.

(19) Member States should take the necessary measures to afford any offeror the possibility of acquiring majority interests in other companies and of fully exercising control of them. To that end, restrictions on the transfer of securities, restrictions on voting rights, extraordinary appointment rights and multiple voting rights should be removed or suspended during the time allowed for the acceptance of a bid and when the general meeting of shareholders decides on defensive measures, on amendments to the articles of association or on the removal or appointment of board members at the first general meeting of shareholders following closure of the bid. Where the holders of securities have suffered losses as a result of the removal of rights, equitable compensation should be provided for in accordance with the technical arrangements laid down by Member States.

(20) All special rights held by Member States in companies should be viewed in the framework of the free movement of capital and the relevant provisions of the Treaty. Special rights held by Member States in companies which are provided for in private or

public national law should be exempted from the 'breakthrough' rule if they are compatible with the Treaty.

(21) Taking into account existing differences in Member States' company law mechanisms and structures, Member States should be allowed not to require companies established within their territories to apply the provisions of this Directive limiting the powers of the board of an offeree company during the time allowed for the acceptance of a bid and those rendering ineffective barriers, provided for in the articles of association or in specific agreements. In that event Member States should at least allow companies established within their territories to make the choice, which must be reversible, to apply those provisions. Without prejudice to international agreements to which the European Community is a party, Member States should be allowed not to require companies which apply those provisions in accordance with the optional arrangements to apply them when they become the subject of offers launched by companies which do not apply the same provisions, as a consequence of the use of those optional arrangements ...

(24) Member States should take the necessary measures to enable an offeror who, following a takeover bid, has acquired a certain percentage of a company's capital carrying voting rights to require the holders of the remaining securities to sell him/her their securities. Likewise, where, following a takeover bid, an offeror has acquired a certain percentage of a company's capital carrying voting rights, the holders of the remaining securities should be able to require him/her to buy their securities. These squeeze-out and sell-out procedures should apply only under specific conditions linked to takeover bids. Member States may continue to apply national rules to squeeze-out and sell-out procedures in other circumstances.

Before going into details, it is useful to illustrate some basic concepts relating to takeovers.

Article 1(1) Directive 2004/25/EC

(a) 'takeover bid' or 'bid' shall mean a public offer (other than by the offeree company itself) made to the holders of the securities of a company to acquire all or some of those securities, whether mandatory or voluntary, which follows or has as its objective the acquisition of control of the offeree company in accordance with national law;

A takeover bid may be voluntary or, where provided for by the applicable law, mandatory.

Voluntary bids may be tender offers or hostile takeovers. A tender offer is a public offer by a prospective acquirer to the shareholders of a listed company (the 'target') to tender their shares for sale at a specified price during a specified time. The target company may have an incumbent majority shareholder or a dispersed ownership without a majority shareholder. A friendly takeover occurs when the incumbent majority shareholder or, in the absence of a majority shareholder, the management of the company, agree on the takeover bid. In contrast, a hostile takeover occurs when a bidder attempts to take over a target company whose management is unwilling to agree to it.

In the alternative, the majority stake in a listed company may be acquired by means of private transactions from the incumbent majority shareholder, or of several acquisitions of shares from the market. Some legislations, including ECL, provide for a mandatory bid rule in case control over a listed company is acquired other than as a consequence of a voluntary bid (Article 5(2) Directive 2004/25/EC). The mandatory bid must address all shareholders at the same, equitable price.

It is useful to mention that Directive 2004/25/EC does not clarify the meaning of control. Nor – as already mentioned – is control defined by Directive 2013/34/EU on annual and consolidated accounts.

In view of a takeover, the participating interest deemed to confer control over a company shall be defined by the legislation of Member States in which the target company has its registered office.

Article 5(3) Directive 2004/25/EC

3. The percentage of voting rights which confers control for the purposes of paragraph 1 and the method of its calculation shall be determined by the rules of the Member State in which the company has its registered office.

Indeed, the Takeover Bids Directive takes into account that, notwithstanding a participating interest superior to 50 per cent grants *de facto* control, lesser stakes may also give a majority in the general meeting – in particular, the general meeting called to elect the management organ – considering that not all shareholders take part in the general meeting, thus lowering the necessary quorum and majority. Also, control may be exercised by virtue of shareholders' agreements.

In turn, the Takeover Bids Directive directly defines the concept of equitable price, as the highest price paid for the same securities by the offeror in the semester or year before the bid.

Article 5(4) Directive 2004/25/EC

4. The highest price paid for the same securities by the offeror, or by persons acting in concert with him/her, over a period, to be determined by Member States, of not less than

six months and not more than 12 before the bid referred to in paragraph 1 shall be regarded as the equitable price. If, after the bid has been made public and before the offer closes for acceptance, the offeror or any person acting in concert with him/her purchases securities at a price higher than the offer price, the offeror shall increase his/her offer so that it is not less than the highest price paid for the securities so acquired.

Provided that the general principles laid down in Article 3(1) are respected, Member States may authorise their supervisory authorities to adjust the price referred to in the first subparagraph in circumstances and in accordance with criteria that are clearly determined. To that end, they may draw up a list of circumstances in which the highest price may be adjusted either upwards or downwards, for example where the highest price was set by agreement between the purchaser and a seller, where the market prices of the securities in question have been manipulated, where market prices in general or certain market prices in particular have been affected by exceptional occurrences, or in order to enable a firm in difficulty to be rescued. They may also determine the criteria to be applied in such cases, for example the average market value over a particular period, the break-up value of the company or other objective valuation criteria generally used in financial analysis.

Any decision by a supervisory authority to adjust the equitable price shall be substantiated and made public.

Figure 18.1 should help explain why an offeror may prefer to gain control over the target before launching a takeover bid to the public, despite knowing that this shall occur at the highest price paid for the same securities over a six or twelve month period. Figure 18.1 shows that prices for shares up to 30 per cent (which is the custom threshold fixed by Member States, as such a block generally confers control over a listed company) are lower than the highest price paid (25). Notwithstanding that after the threshold is passed, the price for the outstanding

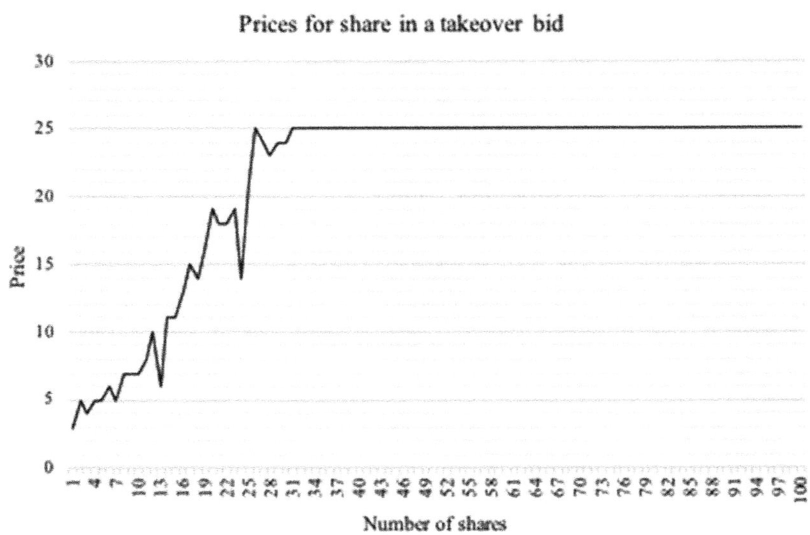

Figure 18.1 Prices for share in a takeover bid

shares shall be at least the highest price paid (25), the offeror is aware to have saved all the money represented in the area in between the line and 25. Should the bidder launch the takeover bid before gaining control over the target, then he or she would face more risks as: a) the price offered could be excessive, and the takeover would cost more money; b) the price could be too low, and the takeover attempt could fail, thereby wasting money.

The price offered as a consideration shall consist of cash. The offeror may also offer securities in exchange, or a combination of cash and securities: in this case, however, if the securities offered in exchange are not admitted to trading in a regulated market, offerees may compel a cash consideration. Member States may provide that a cash consideration must be offered, at least as an alternative, in all cases.

Article 5(5) Directive 2004/25/EC

5. By way of consideration the offeror may offer securities, cash or a combination of both. However, where the consideration offered by the offeror does not consist of liquid securities admitted to trading on a regulated market, it shall include a cash alternative.

In any event, the offeror shall offer a cash consideration at least as an alternative where he/she or persons acting in concert with him/her, over a period beginning at the same time as the period determined by the Member State in accordance with paragraph 4 and ending when the offer closes for acceptance, has purchased for cash securities carrying 5% or more of the voting rights in the offeree company.

Member States may provide that a cash consideration must be offered, at least as an alternative, in all cases.

The Takeover Bids Directive requires that shareholders are allowed to have a clear proposal on which they might take their decision as to whether to sell or not within a specified time allowed for acceptance. The supervisory authority designated by the Member States must be informed beforehand of the intention of the bidder and shall be required to endorse a detailed document – having the characteristics of a prospectus – which is later made public (Articles 6–8 Directive 2004/25/EC).

Furthermore, Directive 2004/25/EC expresses general principles that all Member States' legislation shall comply with.

Article 3 General Principles, Directive 2004/25/EC

1. For the purpose of implementing this Directive, Member States shall ensure that the following principles are complied with:
   (a) all holders of the securities of an offeree company of the same class must be afforded equivalent treatment; moreover, if a person acquires control of a company, the other holders of securities must be protected;

(b) the holders of the securities of an offeree company must have sufficient time and information to enable them to reach a properly informed decision on the bid; where it advises the holders of securities, the board of the offeree company must give its views on the effects of implementation of the bid on employment, conditions of employment and the locations of the company's places of business;

(c) the board of an offeree company must act in the interests of the company as a whole and must not deny the holders of securities the opportunity to decide on the merits of the bid;

(d) false markets must not be created in the securities of the offeree company, of the offeror company or of any other company concerned by the bid in such a way that the rise or fall of the prices of the securities becomes artificial and the normal functioning of the markets is distorted;

(e) an offeror must announce a bid only after ensuring that he/she can fulfil in full any cash consideration, if such is offered, and after taking all reasonable measures to secure the implementation of any other type of consideration;

(f) an offeree company must not be hindered in the conduct of its affairs for longer than is reasonable by a bid for its securities.

2. With a view to ensuring compliance with the principles laid down in paragraph 1, Member States:

(a) shall ensure that the minimum requirements set out in this Directive are observed;

(b) may lay down additional conditions and provisions more stringent than those of this Directive for the regulation of bids.

In the following paragraphs we will focus on the main issues raised by the EU legislation on takeovers, namely on the mandatory bid rule and its implied equal treatment rule, on the rules concerning the behaviour of the target company and its organs during the offer (passivity and breakthrough rules), and on the rights of squeeze-out and sell-out after a successful takeover bid.

FURTHER READING

Blanaid Clarke, 'European Takeover Regulation – The Latest Draft of the 13th Company Law Directive', 10 *EBLR* 482–491 (1999).

Patrick C. Leyens, 'European Take-overs', 12 *EBLR* 42–66 (2001).

Rolf Skog, 'The Takeover Directive – An Endless Saga?', 13 *EBLR* 301–312 (2002).

Steef Bartman, 'Analysis and Consequences of the EC Directive on Takeover Bids', 1 *ECL* 5–8 (2004).

Theodor Baums, 'The Regulation of Takeovers under German Law', 15 *EBLR* 1453–1460 (2004).

Andrea Guaccero, 'Recent Developments in European Takeover and Corporate Law', 12 *Cardozo J. Int'l & Comp. L.* 91–108 (2004).

Joseph A. McCahery, Luc Renneboog, Peer Ritter, and Sascha Haller, 'The Economics of the Proposed European Takeover Directive', in Guido Ferrarini, Klaus J. Hopt, Jaap Winter, and Eddy Wymeersch (eds.), *Reforming Company and Takeover Law in Europe* 575–647 (Oxford University Press, 2004).

Jonathan Rickford, 'The Emerging European Takeover Law from a British Perspective', 15 *EBLR* 1379–1421 (2004).
Frank Wooldridge, 'The Recent Directive on Takeover-Bids', 15 *EBLR* 147–158 (2004).
Michel Menjucq, 'The European Regime on Takeover', 3 *ECFR* 222–236 (2006).
Joseph A. McCahery and Erik P.M. Vermeulen, 'The Case Against Reform of the Takeover Bids Directive', 22 *EBLR* 541–557 (2011).
Klaus J. Hopt, 'European Takeover Reform of 2012/2013 – Time to Re-examine the Mandatory Bid', 15 *EBOR* 143–190 (2014).
Jonathan Mukwiri, 'Reforming EU Takeover Law Remains on Hold', 12 *ECL* 186–187 (2015).
Mathias Habersack, 'Non-Frustration Rule and Mandatory Bid Rule-Cornerstones of European Takeover Law', 15 *ECFR* 1–40 (2018).

See also:
Erik Werlauff, *EU Company Law* 93 (Copenhagen, DJØF Publishing, 2nd ed., 2003).
Vanessa Edwards, 'The Directive on Takeover Bids – Not Worth the Paper It's Written On?', 1 *ECFR* 416–439 (2004).
Heribert Hirte, 'The Takeover Directive – A Mini-Directive on the Structure of the Corporation: Is it a Trojan Horse?', 2 *ECFR* 1–19 (2005).
See further: Paul Davies, Klaus Hopt, and Wolf-Georg Ringe, 'Control Transactions', in John Armour, Luca Enriques et al., *The Anatomy of Corporate Law: A Comparative and Functional Approach* 205–243 (Oxford University Press, 3rd ed., 2017).
Mads Andenas and Frank Wooldridge, *European Comparative Company Law* 26–28 (Cambridge University Press, 2012).

18.2 Mandatory Bid Rule and Equal Treatment of Shareholders (II)

In order to protect the interests of minority shareholders, Directive 2004/25/EC provides for a mandatory bid rule to all holders of transferable securities carrying voting rights in the target company. Under this rule, an offeror having acquired control over a listed company, unless such control has been acquired following a voluntary bid, is forced to make a bid to all the remaining holders of securities carrying voting rights at an equitable price.

Article 5(1–2) Directive 2004/25/EC

1. Where a natural or legal person, as a result of his/her own acquisition or the acquisition by persons acting in concert with him/her, holds securities of a company as referred to in Article 1(1) which, added to any existing holdings of those securities of his/hers and the holdings of those securities of persons acting in concert with him/her, directly or indirectly give him/her a specified percentage of voting rights in that company, giving him/her control of that company, Member States shall ensure that such a person is required to make a bid as a means of protecting the minority shareholders of that company. Such a bid shall be addressed at the earliest opportunity to all the holders of those securities for all their holdings at the equitable price as defined in paragraph 4.
2. Where control has been acquired following a voluntary bid made in accordance with this Directive to all the holders of securities for all their holdings, the obligation laid down in paragraph 1 to launch a bid shall no longer apply.

The mandatory bid rule allows the minority shareholders to sell their shares to the new majority shareholder after a change of control over the company, thereby obtaining the same control premium paid by the offeror to the incumbent majority shareholder or to those shareholders holding the marginal shares. This rule, also known as the 'equal opportunity rule', opposes the so-called 'market rule', followed in the US, where the bidder is left free to make a public tender offer or to carry on private transactions: after the famous *Unocal* case (*Unocal Corp.* v. *Mesa Petroleum Co.*, 493 A.2nd 946 (Del. 1985)), however, also the US Securities and Exchange Commission (SEC) requires that, in case a public tender offer is launched, then an all-holders' rule (at the same price) applies.

17 CFR 240.14d-10 – Equal Treatment of Security Holders

No bidder shall make a tender offer unless: (1) the tender offer is open to all security holders of the class of securities subject to the tender offer; and (2) the consideration paid to any security holder for securities tendered in the tender offer is the highest consideration paid to any other security holder for securities tendered in the tender offer.

Two convergent economic analyses acknowledge that both the equal opportunity and the market rules have advantages and disadvantages.

Marcel Kahan, 'Sale of Corporate Control', 9 JLEO 368–379, at 379 (1993)

The tender offer rule overdeters desirable control sales, and the private negotiation rule underdeters undesirable control sales and also overdeters desirable control sales (though to a lesser extent than the tender offer rule). Both rules operate more efficiently the higher the fraction of shares sold in the sale of control transaction. Thus, a higher fraction of shares sold is not an inherent reason to move from tender offer rule to the private negotiation rule.

The present law, which incorporates such a move, may instead be justified by the effect of the fraction of shares held by the controlling person on [an] alternative mechanism for transferring control. These alternative mechanisms may induce desirable control transfers when the fraction of shares is low, thus making sales of control less necessary. Therefore, for low fractions, the primary objective may be to deter undesirable control sales, which would make the tender offer rule efficient. But when the fraction of shares sold is high, these alternative mechanisms fail to induce desirable control transfers. Thus, for high fractions, encouraging desirable control sales becomes a more important objective, justifying the application of the private negotiation rule.

Lucian Arye Bebchuk, 'Efficient and Inefficient Sales of Corporate Control', 109 QJE 957–993 (1994)

This paper develops a framework for analyzing transactions that transfer a company's controlling block from an existing controller to a new controller. This framework is used to compare the market rule, which is followed in the United States, with the equal opportunity rule, which prevails in some other countries. The market rule is superior to the equal opportunity rule in facilitating efficient transfers of control but inferior to it in discouraging inefficient transfers. Conditions under which one of the two rules is overall superior are identified; for example, the market rule is superior if existing and new controllers draw their characteristics from the same distributions. Finally, the rules' effects on surplus division are analyzed and this examination reveals a rationale for mandatory rules.

Considering companies not having a controlling shareholder prior to the takeover, the same Professor Bebchuk – in a seminal work of 1985 – criticised the US market rule, making the case for an equal treatment of shareholders: this is thoroughly motivated comparing merger and takeover law.

Lucian Arye Bebchuk, 'Towards Undistorted Choice and Equal Treatment in Corporate Takeovers', 98 *Harv. L. Rev.* 1693–1808, at 1696 and 1706 (1985)

... In takeovers accomplished under current law, the total acquisition price is disproportionately distributed among the target's shareholders. Some shareholders have all or most of their shares purchased for the bid price, while [other] shareholders have all their shares become minority shares with a value lower than the bid price. Consequently some shareholders, largely unsophisticated investors, end up with considerably less than their pro rata share of the acquisition price. This disproportionate division, I shall suggest, is both inefficient and unfair.

...

When an independent target is acquired through a merger, the acquisition price is generally divided among the target's shareholders in proportion to their holdings. The process that determines whether a merger proposal will be accepted has no bearing on how the acquisition price will be distributed if the proposal is accepted. Once a merger proposal is approved by shareholder vote and the merger goes through, each shareholder receives his pro rata share of the total acquisition price, regardless of whether or how he voted.

In contrast, when an independent target is currently acquired through a takeover, the target's shareholders might well be subject to unequal treatment. Under current rules, the process that determines whether a takeover bid will succeed also has a substantial bearing on the distribution of the acquisition price in the event that the bid does succeed; and the resulting distribution might be quite disproportionate. Moreover, a target's shareholders do not all have the same ex ante chance of being a victim of the current inequality of treatment; unsophisticated investors are much more likely than are sophisticated investors to end up in the event of a takeover with less than their pro rata share of the acquisition price. The existing inequality of treatment, it should [be] emphasized, is a product of current takeover rules; the regulations proposed in this Article would produce a proportionate division of acquisition prices.

On the other side of the Atlantic Ocean, however, the EU mandatory bid rule has been criticised, too.

Takeover Bids Directive Assessment Report ('External Study')

From this perspective, it can be argued that the mandatory bid rule impedes takeovers by forcing a potential offeror who may only wish to purchase, say, 35% of the shares, to be prepared to purchase 100%. This substantially increases the prospective cost of a takeover for the offeror and may deter it from launching a bid at all. If one follows the logic that shareholder control equates to economic value, this value may be diminished by a mandatory bid requirement because it increases the cost of a change of control for offerors who must now account for the possibility of having to purchase 100% of the shares even if they only want to hold significantly less shares.

Luca Enriques, 'The Mandatory Bid Rule in the Takeover Directive: Harmonization Without Foundation?', 1 *ECFR* 440–457, at 456–457 (2004)

The directive provides for a very generic, vague rule that control transfers must be followed by a mandatory bid, but entrusts national policymakers and national supervisory agencies with wide powers to grant partial and total exemptions.

As section 3 has shown, it is hard to demonstrate that the EC mandatory bid rule is justified on efficiency grounds. What is certain is that some interest groups will gain from it. Corporate managers (and blockholders retaining working control) of widely-held European companies are the usual suspects, as they stand to gain from rules that make hostile takeovers more costly. Less frequently mentioned, but even more suspect are the policymakers and securities agency officials to whom so much power and discretion are granted in deciding whether the rule applies and what the mandatory bid price should be. Finally, those providing advisory services in the market for corporate control, and above all lawyers specializing in mergers and acquisitions, stand to gain from having in place a mandatory bid rule such as that designed in the directive: their services will in fact be available to buyers and sellers who want to evade the mandatory bid or at least to obtain a discount.

One may object that mandatory bid regimes very similar to the directive are already in place in most Member States, so that there should be no increase in the rents securities agency officials and lawyers can extract, leaving them indifferent to its approval. The point, of course, is not that government officials and lawyers in countries with no mandatory bid rule yet in place will also be able to extract such rents following its transposition. Much more significantly, the directive would increase rents for government officials and lawyers across the EU in at least three ways. First, the proposed EC mandatory bid rule is more flexible in terms of price discounts (left to national supervisory authorities) than at least some of the Member State mandatory bid regimes now in place. To put it bluntly, this greater flexibility would allow supervisory authority officials to make decisions that may be of great value to the powerful people involved in acquisitions (whether as sellers or buyers), while at the same time providing lawyers with a wider range of weapons to earn fees and hopefully please their clients. Second, the petrification effect typical of all directives would keep Member States from scrapping their own mandatory bid rules, unless they agree to scrap the EC one. Finally, like any directive, the takeover directive would add another layer of complexity to a regulatory picture that is already highly technical and complex in all jurisdictions. Questions of consistency between national provisions or decisions and the directive can be raised, a highly pleasing prospect from the point of view of at least one of the interest groups mentioned.

As mentioned earlier, Article 3(1)(a) Directive 2004/25/EC provides – amongst the Directive's 'general principles' – for an equal treatment rule of all holders of securities when control of their companies has been acquired.

Article 3(1) Directive 2004/25/EC

(a) all holders of the securities of an offeree company of the same class must be afforded equivalent treatment; moreover, if a person acquires control of a company, the other holders of securities must be protected;

This rule and the equal treatment rule provided for under Article 46 Directive 2012/30/EU (or under Article 65 Directive 2001/34/EC) should not be overlapped. The latter refers to the relationship between the company and its shareholders; the former refers to the relationship between the offeror in a takeover bid and the existing shareholders of the target company. Not by chance, the Takeover Bids Directive is not applicable in case the offeror is the 'target company' itself, repurchasing its own shares. A scholarly note on *Audiolux* clarifies the point.

Federico M. Mucciarelli, 'Equal Treatment of Shareholders and European Union Law: Case Note on the Decision "Audiolux" of the European Court of Justice', 7 *ECFR* 158–167, at 163–164 (2010)

2 Equal Treatment of Shareholders Upon a Change of Control

Differently from equal treatment of shareholders vis-à-vis the company, the 'mandatory bid rule' provided for by the Takeover Directive aims at attaining equal treatment of shareholders upon a change of control and vis-à-vis the majority shareholders.

According to the mandatory bid rule, any change of control triggers the duty to launch a tender offer for all outstanding shares. The rationale behind this rule is debated: one important reason is to mitigate the pressure to tender on [the] target's shareholders, but also [the] equal treatment of minority shareholders can be one of its goals. Indeed, if the bidder purchases the target's control through a private transaction, the mandatory bid rule allows minority shareholders, who have been previously neglected, to sell their shares and to gain a portion of the control premium. In other words, if a mandatory bid rule is in place, all shareholders are treated equally regarding the opportunity to share the control premium. This is particularly true in the EU, as pursuant to the Takeover Directive the new control shareholder should offer the highest price paid for [the] target's shares during a period of 6 to 12 months prior to the bid, unless the competent authority allows an exception in specific circumstances to be established on a case by case basis according to domestic law.

However, according to Audiolux the mandatory bid rule is not simply a specific rule provided for by the Takeover Directive, but is the manifestation of a general principle, which applies also to non listed companies and beyond the scope of application of the Takeover Directive.

This theory is not completely new. In Germany, for instance, before a mandatory bid rule was in place, some scholars argued that, after having purchased the control of a company, the new majority shareholder owes to their fellow-shareholders a duty to share with them a portion of the control premium. According to these theories, such duty should be inferred from general fiduciary duties that shareholders owe one another, which should be extended to market decisions that might affect the interests of other shareholders. However, this ingenious theory can not be accepted, as minority shareholders are not in the same position as control shareholder and, hence, [the] control premium does not 'belong' to them and they should not have the right to share it. In addition, we should bear in mind that the mandatory bid rule reveals a significant drawback as it reduces the overall amount of control transactions and the disciplinary power of the market for corporate control upon directors' behaviours. The law-maker can obviously introduce such [a] rule, but this choice requires an explicit political decision that weights the interests of minority shareholders against the interest of potential acquirers and of the market.

The EU equal opportunity rule provided for in the Takeover Bids Directive has been further clarified by the CJEU in *Audiolux*, which we are about to discuss. As mentioned earlier, *Audiolux* raises the question as to whether there is a general principle of EU law of equality of shareholders under which minority shareholders are protected by an obligation on the dominant shareholder, when acquiring or exercising control of a company, to offer to buy the minority shareholders' shares under the same conditions as those agreed when a shareholding in that company conferring or strengthening the control of the dominant shareholder was acquired and, if so, the effects over time of such a principle.

FURTHER READING

Lucian Arye Bebchuk, 'Towards Undistorted Choice and Equal Treatment in Corporate Takeovers', 98 *Harv. L. Rev.* 1693–1808 (1985).

Paul L. Davies, 'The Notion of Equality in European Take-over Regulation' (2002), available at SSRN: http://ssrn.com/abstract=305979 or http://dx.doi.org/10.2139/ssrn.305979.

Mike Burkart and Fausto Panunzi, 'Mandatory Bids, Squeeze-out, Sell-out and the Dynamics of the Tender Offer Process', in Guido Ferrarini, Klaus J. Hopt, Jaap Winter, and Eddy Wymeersch (eds.), *Reforming Company and Takeover Law in Europe* 737–767 (Oxford University Press, 2004).

Luca Enriques, 'The Mandatory Bid Rule in the Takeover Directive: Harmonization Without Foundation?', 1 *ECFR* 440–457 (2004), also in Guido Ferrarini, Klaus J. Hopt, Jaap Winter, and Eddy Wymeersch (eds.), *Reforming Company and Takeover Law in Europe* 767–797 (Oxford University Press, 2004).

Joseph Lee, 'Four Models of Minority Shareholder Protection in Takeovers', 16 *EBLR* 803–830 (2005).

Federico M. Mucciarelli, 'Equal Treatment of Shareholders and European Union Law: Case Note on the Decision "Audiolux" of the European Court of Justice', 7 *ECFR* 158–167 (2010).

18.3 *Audiolux* Case

In *Audiolux* (C-101/08, *Audiolux SA et al.* v. *Groupe Bruxelles Lambert SA (GBL) et al. and Bertelsmann AG et al.*, [2009] ECR I-09823), the reference was made in the course of proceedings between, on the one hand, the minority shareholders in the RTL Group ('*RTL*') and, on the other, Groupe Bruxelles Lambert SA (GBL) ('*GBL*'), Bertelsmann AG ('*Bertelsmann*') and RTL concerning agreements concluded between GBL and Bertelsmann.

Audiolux SA and the other applicants in the dispute in the main proceedings (referred to collectively as '*Audiolux*') were minority shareholders in RTL, the shares of which were listed on regulated stock exchanges in Luxembourg, Brussels, and London.

Before the events that gave rise to the dispute in the main proceedings, GBL held 30 per cent of the shares in RTL. Bertelsmann held 80 per cent of the shares in Bertelsmann Westdeutsche TV GmbH, the other 20 per cent being held by Westdeutsche Allgemeine Zeitungsverlagsgesellschaft E. Brost & J Funke GmbH & Co. Bertelsmann Westdeutsche TV GmbH held 37 per cent of the shares in RTL, the UK group Pearson Television held 22 per cent and the remaining 11 per cent of the shares were held by the public, including Audiolux.

By several transactions which took place in the first half of 2001, GBL transferred its 30 per cent shareholding in RTL to Bertelsmann in exchange for 25 per cent of the latter's capital.

Subsequently, in December 2001, Bertelsmann acquired Pearson Television's holding and RTL 'delisted' its securities from the London Stock Exchange with effect from 31 December 2002.

The transfer of GBL's holding to Bertelsmann was the subject of a judgment of the Tribunal d'arrondissement (District Court) (Luxembourg) of 8 July 2003, which dismissed the claims brought by Audiolux on the ground that they were not based on any legal rule or principle recognised by Luxembourg law. Those claims concerned, *inter alia*, the validity of the transactions resulting in the transfer of that holding and compensation for loss caused by failure to comply with the obligation to offer the claimants the opportunity to exchange their shares in RTL for shares in Bertelsmann under the same conditions as those agreed with GBL.

According to that judgment, Luxembourg company law as it stands makes no provision, where one major shareholder transfers its shares to another, for any right of minority shareholders to dispose of their shares under the same conditions. Likewise, Luxembourg Stock Exchange rules cannot serve as a legal basis for the claims at issue. The judgment states, in particular, that no provision of Luxembourg law has been enacted to implement Recommendation 77/534. The delisting of RTL securities from the London Stock Exchange was the subject of a judgment of the Tribunal d'arrondissement de Luxembourg of 30 March 2004, which dismissed the claims brought by Audiolux concerning, in particular, the obligation to increase the availability of RTL's securities to the public and not to delist those securities from the London Stock Exchange.

The Cour d'appel (Court of Appeal) (Luxembourg), after joining the two cases, upheld those judgments stating, as regards the judgment of 8 July 2003, that the case concerned the existence of a general principle according to which minority shareholders of a Luxembourg listed company may claim the right to equal treatment by the majority shareholders when a major shareholding in that company is transferred. In that connection, the Court of Appeal considered that there was no general principle of equality of shareholders in the law as it stood, nor could such a principle serve as a legal basis for the appellants' claims.

The appeal in cassation lodged by Audiolux was directed solely against the parts of that judgment that upheld the judgment of 8 July 2003. In its appeal, Audiolux claimed a breach of the general principle of equality of shareholders, and argued that it should be treated in the same way as GBL was when the latter's shareholding in RTL was transferred to Bertelsmann in return for a control premium.

In those circumstances, the Cour de cassation decided to stay the proceedings and to refer the following questions to the Court for a preliminary ruling:

C-101/08, Audiolux SA et al. v. Groupe Bruxelles Lambert SA (GBL) et al. and Bertelsmann AG et al., [2009] ECR I-09823, § 29

1. Are the references to the equality of shareholders and, more specifically, to the protection of minority shareholders,
   (a) in Articles 20 and 42 of the Second Company Directive 77/91 ...;
   (b) in the third general principle and Supplementary principle 17 of ... Recommendation [77/534];
   (c) in Schedule C, point 2(A) annexed to ... Directive 79/279 carried over in [D]irective [2001/34];
   (d) in Article 3(1)(a) of Directive 2004/25 ... in the light of recital 8 in the preamble thereto, manifestations of a general principle of Community law?
2. If so, is that general principle of Community law to be applied only to the relations between a company and its shareholders or, to the contrary, does it also apply to the relations between majority shareholders exercising or acquiring control of a company and the minority shareholders of that company?
3. If the answer to the foregoing two questions is in the affirmative, must that general principle of Community law be regarded, having regard to the development in time of the references referred to in Question 1, as having existed and being binding on the relations between majority and minority shareholders within the meaning of Question 2 before the entry into force of the abovementioned Directive 2004/25/EC and before the facts at issue, which occurred in the first half of 2001?

The judgment of the CJEU is a very important one, as it clarifies certain criteria to define general principles of EU law.

First, the Court examines secondary EU law for 'conclusive indications' of the existence of such a general principle of EU law. It observes that the mere fact that EU legislation lays down provisions relating to the equality of shareholders in respect of some of their well-defined rights is not sufficient in itself for the principle in question to qualify as a general principle of ECL. According to the Court, such a classification presupposes that the principle in question possesses a truly general character, which in this case excludes taking into account provisions that are limited to regulating very specific company law situations, introducing rules protecting all shareholders. Moreover, the Court stresses that, when seeking 'conclusive indications' of the existence of a general principle of EU law, only measures of a binding nature can be taken into account.

Second, the Court examines whether the treatment to which the minority shareholders lay claim may be understood in this case as a specific expression, in company law, of the general principle of equal treatment. It observes in this respect that this principle cannot in itself either give rise to a particular obligation on the part of the dominant shareholder in favour of the other shareholders or determine the specific situation to which such an obligation relates, as this would be contrary to the principle of legal certainty. Such a principle presupposes legislative choices, based on a weighing of the interests at issue and the fixing in advance of precise and detailed rules.

Finally, according to the Court, the principle in question could not be regarded as a general principle as it is characterised by a degree of detail requiring a secondary law at Union level. It therefore concludes that no general principle of EU law of equality of shareholders exists, as defined by the referring court.

As regards the equal opportunity rule provided for in the Takeover Bids Directive, the CJEU expressed the following thoughts:

C-101/08, Audiolux SA et al. v. Groupe Bruxelles Lambert SA (GBL) et al. and Bertelsmann AG et al., [2009] ECR I-09823, §§ 44–52, 64 and Operative Part

47 As far as Directive 2004/25 is concerned, this introduces, in Article 5, a requirement that a shareholder who has acquired control of a company must launch a mandatory bid. In Article 16 it provides for the right of sell-out.

48 First, Recitals 2, 9, 10, 11 and 24 in the preamble to Directive 2004/25 relating to the mandatory bid and right of sell-out do not state either expressly or by implication that the rules introduced by that directive derive from a general principle of Community law. Furthermore, those recitals make no reference to the Code of Conduct or to Directives 77/91 and 79/279, and therefore do not enable the conclusion to be drawn that Directive 2004/25 is the culmination of a project begun by the Code of Conduct or the abovementioned directives.

49 Second, in accordance with Article 1 of Directive 2004/25, the mandatory bid and right of sell-out apply only to companies listed on the stock exchange. Moreover, the mandatory bid applies, according to Article 5(1) of that directive, only where a person holds, as a result of an acquisition, a holding which gives him control of that company and, according to Articles 15 and 16 of that directive, the right of sell-out applies only to situations in which a shareholder acquires, in a takeover, more than 90% of the capital carrying voting rights.

50 Thus, the provisions of Directive 2004/25 apply to specific situations, so that no general principle with a specific content can be inferred from them. In addition, they do not, as was already stated with respect to the provisions of Directives 77/91 and 79/279, in paragraph 42 of this judgment, possess the general, comprehensive character which is naturally inherent in general principles of law.

51 As regards, in particular, the provisions of Directive 2004/25 to which the national court refers, it must be observed that, although Recital 8 in the preamble to that directive alludes to general principles of Community law, the fact remains that that recital refers only to procedural safeguards and does not involve any principle of equal treatment of shareholders. Similarly, it cannot be inferred from the use of the term 'general principles' in Article 3 of that directive that the Community legislature thereby intends the principles mentioned in that article to be treated in the same way as general principles of Community law. As is clear from the words 'for the purposes of implementing this Directive', they are only guiding principles for the implementation of that directive by the Member States.

52 Having regard to the foregoing, it must be held that the provisions of secondary Community law to which the national court refers do not provide conclusive evidence of the existence of a general principle of equal treatment of minority shareholders.

...

64 Having regard to all the foregoing, the answer to the first and second questions must be that Community law does not include any general principle of law under which minority shareholders are protected by an obligation on the dominant shareholder, when acquiring or exercising control of a company, to offer to buy their shares under the same conditions as those agreed when a shareholding conferring or strengthening the control of the dominant shareholder was acquired.

FURTHER READING

Federico M. Mucciarelli, 'Equal Treatment of Shareholders and European Union Law: Case Note on the Decision "Audiolux" of the European Court of Justice', 7 *ECFR* 158–167 (2010).

Jaron van Bekkum, 'Commentary on the EU Court's Decision in Audiolux', 7 *ECL* 161–164 (2010).

Georgios Psaroudakis, 'The Mandatory Bid and Company Law in Europe', 7 *ECFR* 550–584 (2010).

18.4 Breakthrough Rule and Poison Pills

The rules concerning the defensive measures that the target company may adopt in order to counteract hostile takeovers are one of the key aspects of the Takeover Bids Directive. Indeed, such defences may prevent change of control over companies, making the acquisition too costly and protecting, as a consequence, the incumbent management and controlling shareholders from unfriendly raiders, even in cases where change of control is useful for the shareholders and the company itself.

Defensive measures are fundamentally of two kinds: *ex ante* defences, already in place before the takeover bid is launched, and *ex post* defences, enacted after the bid is launched.

Ex ante anti-takeover devices are clauses embedded in the company's instrument of incorporation or statutes deterring potential interested parties from making their bids.

In this regard, ECL requires that all relevant information on the target company that might constitute *ex ante* anti-takeover devices be disclosed to potential bidders.

Article 10 Information on Companies as Referred to in Article 1(1), Directive 2004/25/EC

1. Member States shall ensure that companies as referred to in Article 1(1) publish detailed information on the following:
   (a) the structure of their capital, including securities which are not admitted to trading on a regulated market in a Member State, where appropriate with an indication of the different classes of shares and, for each class of shares, the rights and obligations attaching to it and the percentage of total share capital that it represents;
   (b) any restrictions on the transfer of securities, such as limitations on the holding of securities or the need to obtain the approval of the company or other holders of securities, without prejudice to Article 46 of Directive 2001/34/EC;
   (c) significant direct and indirect shareholdings (including indirect shareholdings through pyramid structures and cross-shareholdings) within the meaning of Article 85 of Directive 2001/34/EC;
   (d) the holders of any securities with special control rights and a description of those rights;
   (e) the system of control of any employee share scheme where the control rights are not exercised directly by the employees;
   (f) any restrictions on voting rights, such as limitations of the voting rights of holders of a given percentage or number of votes, deadlines for exercising voting rights, or systems whereby, with the company's cooperation, the financial rights attaching to securities are separated from the holding of securities;
   (g) any agreements between shareholders which are known to the company and may result in restrictions on the transfer of securities and/or voting rights within the meaning of Directive 2001/34/EC;
   (h) the rules governing the appointment and replacement of board members and the amendment of the articles of association;
   (i) the powers of board members, and in particular the power to issue or buy back shares;
   (j) any significant agreements to which the company is a party and which take effect, alter or terminate upon a change of control of the company following a takeover bid, and the effects thereof, except where their nature is such that their disclosure would be seriously prejudicial to the company; this exception shall not apply where the company is specifically obliged to disclose such information on the basis of other legal requirements;

(k) any agreements between the company and its board members or employees providing for compensation if they resign or are made redundant without valid reason or if their employment ceases because of a takeover bid.

2. The information referred to in paragraph 1 shall be published in the company's annual report as provided for in Article 46 of Directive 78/660/EEC and Article 36 of Directive 83/349/EEC.
3. Member States shall ensure, in the case of companies the securities of which are admitted to trading on a regulated market in a Member State, that the board presents an explanatory report to the annual general meeting of shareholders on the matters referred to in paragraph 1.

Similar clauses – provided for either in the statutes or in shareholders' agreements – are not prohibited, notwithstanding that these are able to discourage unfriendly bidders from acquiring the control of the target company. Rather, ECL requires that Member States take the necessary measures to ensure that the market for corporate control is effective, at least by assuring that these clauses or contractual limitations are suspended during a takeover bid, whilst concerned shareholders are adequately compensated.

Recital 19 Directive 2004/25/EC

Member States should take the necessary measures to afford any offeror the possibility of acquiring majority interests in other companies and of fully exercising control of them. To that end, restrictions on the transfer of securities, restrictions on voting rights, extraordinary appointment rights and multiple voting rights should be removed or suspended during the time allowed for the acceptance of a bid and when the general meeting of shareholders decides on defensive measures, on amendments to the articles of association or on the removal or appointment of board members at the first general meeting of shareholders following closure of the bid. Where the holders of securities have suffered losses as a result of the removal of rights, equitable compensation should be provided for in accordance with the technical arrangements laid down by Member States.

Suspension of such clauses or agreements constituting *ex ante* anti-takeover measures is provided for by the so-called 'breakthrough rule'.

Article 11(2–6) Directive 2004/25/EC

2. Any restrictions on the transfer of securities provided for in the articles of association of the offeree company shall not apply vis-à-vis the offeror during the time allowed for acceptance of the bid laid down in Article 7(1).

   Any restrictions on the transfer of securities provided for in contractual agreements between the offeree company and holders of its securities, or in contractual agreements between holders of the offeree company's securities entered into after the adoption of this Directive, shall not apply vis-à-vis the offeror during the time allowed for acceptance of the bid laid down in Article 7(1).

3. Restrictions on voting rights provided for in the articles of association of the offeree company shall not have effect at the general meeting of shareholders which decides on any defensive measures in accordance with Article 9.

   Restrictions on voting rights provided for in contractual agreements between the offeree company and holders of its securities, or in contractual agreements between holders of the offeree company's securities entered into after the adoption of this Directive, shall not have effect at the general meeting of shareholders which decides on any defensive measures in accordance with Article 9.

   Multiple-vote securities shall carry only one vote each at the general meeting of shareholders which decides on any defensive measures in accordance with Article 9.

4. Where, following a bid, the offeror holds 75% or more of the capital carrying voting rights, no restrictions on the transfer of securities or on voting rights referred to in paragraphs 2 and 3 nor any extraordinary rights of shareholders concerning the appointment or removal of board members provided for in the articles of association of the offeree company shall apply; multiple-vote securities shall carry only one vote each at the first general meeting of shareholders following closure of the bid, called by the offeror in order to amend the articles of association or to remove or appoint board members.

   To that end, the offeror shall have the right to convene a general meeting of shareholders at short notice, provided that the meeting does not take place within two weeks of notification.

5. Where rights are removed on the basis of paragraphs 2, 3, or 4 and/or Article 12, equitable compensation shall be provided for any loss suffered by the holders of those rights. The terms for determining such compensation and the arrangements for its payment shall be set by Member States.
6. Paragraphs 3 and 4 shall not apply to securities where the restrictions on voting rights are compensated for by specific pecuniary advantages.

   An exception to the breakthrough rule is provided for with golden shares (see, Chapter 16, § 16.6) conferring special rights in the target company, so far as such special rights are compatible with the TFEU.

Article 11(7) Directive 2004/25/EC

7. This Article shall not apply either where Member States hold securities in the offeree company which confer special rights on the Member States which are compatible with the Treaty, or to special rights provided for in national law which are compatible with the Treaty or to cooperatives.

This exception in particular has led to questions about whether one share, one vote is a European rule. Influential legal scholars conclude that one share, one vote is not justified by economic efficiency and also that the breakthrough rule, which ultimately strikes down all deviations from one share, one vote, does not appear to be well grounded.

Guido Ferrarini, 'One Share – One Vote: A European Rule?', 3 *ECFR* 147–177, at 173–177 (2006)

IV Enhancing Harmonisation in the EU?

In order to answer the main question of this paper, it is necessary to establish, first of all, whether the issue of one share-one vote should be regulated at national level. Only if a positive answer were offered in this respect, would the issue of regulatory harmonisation have to be considered. In this section, I summarize this paper's outcomes and argue that harmonization at EU level is not needed (except for the transparency of ownership structures which is already regulated by the Takeover Directive).

1 Lessons from Economic Analysis

The study by Grossman [and] Hart examined above concludes that one share-one vote is frequently, but not always optimal. The two economists consider a company at the IPO [initial public offering] stage and ask what voting structure should be chosen in order to maximize the total value of the company. They assume that the company has a diffuse ownership structure after the offer and that two management teams (the incumbent managers and a rival team) consider taking over the company. They argue that the optimal voting structure depends on the likely distribution of private benefits between the two competing teams: if only one team has private benefits with respect to the target company, one share-one vote is optimal; if both teams have private benefits, a dual-class structure is preferable. In countries where private benefits of control are high, one might expect frequent deviations from one share-one vote. Grossman [and] Hart conclude that one share-one vote should not be mandated as a legal standard at least with respect to the IPO stage. Their conclusions are different with reference to deviations taking place at a later stage when the company's shareholders are dispersed, if these deviations are effected by the managers to entrench themselves and the relative costs are borne by the public shareholders. However, if the managers are already in the company's control, a change in the voting structure should not be interfered with.

The policy recommendations made by law and economics scholars are similar. The case of IPOs is always non-problematic, as the initial shareholders bear the cost of limited voting structures. Dual-class recapitalizations, on the contrary, create problems if they are used to entrench the managers at the expense of public shareholders who see their shares' value reduced. The consent given by public shareholders to similar transactions could be the result of coercion by the managers. On the contrary, if a new class of non-voting shares is issued to allow new capital to be raised without diluting the dominant group, the transaction should not be interfered with.

However, dual-class structures generate agency costs which increase with the size of the wedge between control rights and cash-flow rights, as shown by both theoretical and empirical studies. These agency costs are higher in countries where investor protection is weaker. Moreover, dual-class structures are more common in these countries for the controllers can obtain higher benefits of control. Not infrequently, in similar countries, the initial owners of a company adopt a dual-class structure before offering the company's securities to the public, as they do not want to leave control up for grabs in situations where the amount of private benefits could attract unfriendly takeover-bids. On a policy level, the relevant agency costs could be dealt with either by forbidding dual-class structures or by increasing investor protection. However, if separating control rights from cash-flow rights were not possible, the initial owners could rather choose not to go public, possibly generating social costs higher than those caused by dual-class structures. Also increasing investor protection could have a chilling effect if the costs of going public became relatively high.

2 Lessons from Comparative Analysis

The US approach to one share–one vote is consistent with the comments just made from an economic perspective. While the traditional NYSE rule forbidding all deviations from one share–one vote overshot the target, the rule subsequently adopted by the US exchanges and NASDAQ discriminates between types of transactions along lines similar to those suggested by scholars in the discussions leading to self-regulatory reform. Initial public offerings of securities with disparate voting rights and subsequent public offerings of lesser voting stock are permitted, while other types of transactions 'disenfranchising' existing shareholders, like the adoption of voting caps by listed companies, are forbidden.

The European approach is diversified. Rules forbidding deviations from one share–one vote were only recently adopted in some Member States, but offer partial solutions to the problems at issue. For instance, in Italy multiple voting shares were forbidden a long time ago and voting caps were excluded for listed companies by the recent company law reform, while a breakthrough rule applies to voting pacts under the 'Draghi law' in the case of a takeover; yet, pyramidal groups are still present in Italy and non-voting shares can be issued by joint-stock companies. The situation is similar in other Member States, where deviations from one share–one vote are relatively common. This may depend on weak investor protection, even though departures from one share–one vote do not always correlate to private benefits of control, as shown by the use of multiple voting shares in Sweden which is generally considered as a 'good law' country. The situation is no doubt evolving as a reflection of corporate governance practices and legal reforms introducing Anglo-American standards; however, path dependence and the rigidity of corporate ownership structures slow down the transition to one share–one vote as a general standard.

The European approach is partially consistent with the policy recommendations formulated by economists (and received by American law). Deviations from one share–one vote are permitted even in countries that forbid some of them. However, no distinction is made in

Europe concerning the ways in which similar deviations occur. Voting caps, where permitted, can be introduced either at the IPO stage or afterwards. Otherwise, they are generally forbidden to listed companies (as is the case in Germany and Italy). Similarly, non-voting shares can be issued either through a capital increase or by way of conversion of voting stock. Yet, dual-class recapitalizations do not seem to be an issue in Europe, possibly as a result of higher corporate ownership concentration.

On the contrary, the breakthrough rule suggested by the High Level Group and included in the Takeover Directive does not conform to the policy recommendations considered above. To be sure, this rule does not mandate one share–one vote, so that deviations are still possible. Moreover, Member States can opt-out of this rule. However, where applicable, the breakthrough rule will have an impact similar to an outright prohibition on voting structures. In fact, controlling shareholders will rather choose those structures, such as pyramidal groups and cross-shareholdings, which are not at risk of a breakthrough in the case of a takeover.

3 A European Rule?

In light of the comments made in the preceding two paragraphs, the need for European harmonization is in principle excluded. Mandating one share–one vote is not justified by economic efficiency, as also confirmed by comparative law. If there is no need for regulation at the national level, also the European breakthrough rule, which ultimately strikes down all deviations from one share–one vote, does not appear to be well grounded. Only transparency rules appear to be justified also at EU level as disclosure of ownership and voting structures serves a pricing and governance function, while harmonization of the relevant rules reduces transaction costs in integrated markets.

Some scholars have tried to find a rationale for the breakthrough rule in the European commitment to economic and political integration. According to J. Gordon ['An International Relations Perspective on the Convergence of Corporate Governance: German Shareholder Capitalism and the European Union, 1990–2000', ECGI Law Working Paper No. 06 (February 2003)], this rule is aimed to foster the development of diffusely-held public firms on the assumption that these companies better serve the EU integration project. In fact, cross-border takeovers would become easier if corporate ownership evolved towards Anglo-American standards, while economic nationalisms would be curbed if companies were more easily contestable.

Similarly, J. Coates ['Ownership, Takeovers and EU Law: How Contestable Should EU Corporations Be?', in G. Ferrarini, K. Hopt, J. Winter and E. Wymeersch (eds.), Reforming Company and Takeover Law in Europe 682 et seq. (Oxford University Press, 2004)] suggested that the best rationale for the breakthrough rule is that many companies with dual-class structures were established long ago when they had already achieved a self-sufficient scale. Now that the EU has liberalised markets, 'scale economies are not being achieved in the most efficient manner (through M&A transactions) because controllers are unwilling or in some cases legally unable to sell or share control'. Coates concludes, however, that the breakthrough rule is not necessarily the best remedy for such companies and that a better balance could be achieved with a periodic 'reopening' of control, as recommended by American scholars suggesting that takeover defences be revisited every ten or twenty years at a general meeting of shareholders.

These two scholars try to justify the breakthrough rule on grounds different from those usually referred to for legal harmonization. Indeed, if the Member States did not consider anything like this rule for their own laws, the reasons traditionally given for harmonization, such as reduction of transaction costs caused by divergent national rules and protectionism inherent in national regulations, cannot be invoked for the breakthrough rule. Nonetheless, the Treaty's freedoms do not seem to support such a drastic regulatory move. As argued above with respect to 'golden shares', the conclusions reached by the ECJ in the relevant cases could not be extended to all sorts of deviations from one share–one vote, as they concern deviations specifically provided for by the law. Similarly, the Treaty freedoms could not be invoked to strike down all deviations from one share–one vote under the breakthrough rule, as this would unduly restrict private autonomy, while it is not at all clear whether structures like dual-class shares are substantial impediments to economic integration in Europe.

The breakthrough rule is not able to neutralise all possible varieties of *ex ante* anti-takeover devices. In particular, whilst the breakthrough rule neutralises shares conferring multiple voting rights, this may not prevent all the so-called 'poison pills'. A poison pill is a clause often included in the instrument of constitution or statutes permitting the issue of new shares or the conversion of existing shares (not carrying voting rights, into shares carrying voting rights) upon occurrence of a triggering event: the triggering event is generally represented by a takeover bid or, in the absence thereof, by a significant change in the company's ownership. As a consequence of the issue of new shares or of the conversion, the offeror may gain control over the target company only buying many more shares, this resulting in an increased burden that may lead to withdrawal of the offer.

Given the EU rules on capital increases, requiring a shareholders' meeting decision and generally requiring to grant pre-emptive rights to shareholders, poison pills have no easy access in EU listed companies' statutes.

FURTHER READING

John A. Coates IV, 'Ownership, Takeovers and EU Law: How Contestable Should EU Corporations Be?', in Guido Ferrarini, Klaus J. Hopt, Jaap Winter, and Eddy Wymeersch (eds.), *Reforming Company and Takeover Law in Europe* 677–711 (Oxford University Press, 2004).

Peter O. Mülbert, 'Make It or Break It: The Breakthrough Rule as a Break-through for the European Takeover Directive?', in Guido Ferrarini, Klaus J. Hopt, Jaap Winter, and Eddy Wymeersch (eds.), *Reforming Company and Takeover Law in Europe* 711–737 (Oxford University Press, 2004).

Ulf Bernitz, 'The Attack on the Nordic Multiple Voting Rights Model: The Legal Limits under EU Law', 15 *EBLR* 1423–1437 (2004).

Rolf Skog, 'The Takeover Directive, the "Breakthrough" Rule and the Swedish System of Dual Class Common Stock', 15 *EBLR* 1439–1451 (2004).

Paul Krüger Andersen, 'The Takeover Directive and Corporate Governance: The Danish Experience', 15 *EBLR* 1461–1475 (2004).

18.5 Passivity Rule

The Takeover Bids Directive addresses *ex post* defences, by expressing a so-called passivity or board neutrality rule.

Recital 16 Directive 2004/25/EC

In order to prevent operations which could frustrate a bid, the powers of the board of an offeree company to engage in operations of an exceptional nature should be limited, without unduly hindering the offeree company in carrying on its normal business activities.

Article 9(2) Directive 2004/25/EC

2. During the period referred to in the second subparagraph, the board of the offeree company shall obtain the prior authorization of the general meeting of shareholders given for this purpose before taking any action, other than seeking alternative bids, which may result in the frustration of the bid and in particular before issuing any shares which may result in a lasting impediment to the offeror's acquiring control of the offeree company.

Such authorisation shall be mandatory at least from the time the board of the offeree company receives the information referred to in the first sentence of Article 6(1) concerning the bid and until the result of the bid is made public or the bid lapses. Member States may require that such authorisation be obtained at an earlier stage, for example as soon as the board of the offeree company becomes aware that the bid is imminent.

In other words, the passivity rule essentially requires the target company's board of directors to 'stay passive' or to 'be neutral' once a takeover bid has been launched, whilst it confers on the general meeting of shareholders the authority to decide the adoption of frustrating actions. Its aim would be to safeguard shareholders against any opportunistic behaviour of the incumbent management, thus ensuring the future of the company in the hands of the prospective new owner. In this view, the shareholders' meeting is also required to grant *ex post* authorisation of measures enacted by the board before the neutrality period begins (Article 9(3) Directive 2004/25/EC).

Ex post devices to counteract a hostile takeover are often shares' repurchases restricting the number of the free floating shares available; mergers increasing the value and number of shares granting control over the company or capital increases; the sale of the company's best assets ('crown jewels'), and so on. A relevant exception to the passivity rule is the search for a so-called 'white knight': in such a case, an authorisation from the general meeting is not required for the directors to seek alternative bids. This exception, however, has been criticised.

Federico M. Mucciarelli, 'White Knights and Black Knights – Does the Search for Competitive Bids always Benefit the Shareholders of "Target" Companies?', 3 *ECFR* 408–425, at 408 (2006)

According to the EC Directive on Takeover Bids, defensive measures should be authorised by the general meeting of the target company. The incumbent board can, nonetheless, search for a competing bid, a so-called 'white knight'.

The rationale underpinning this exception is that competing bids always benefit [the] target's shareholders. In this paper I will tackle this rationale, arguing that even competing bids could generate a pressure to tender on [the] target's shareholders and, therefore, in this case should not be considered as a benefit for them.

The board neutrality rule does not imply that the board may not express a negative opinion on the bid. On the contrary, ECL requires that the board officially express their opinion on the bid, thus qualifying the tender offer as friendly or hostile.

Recital 17 Directive 2004/25/EC

(17) The board of an offeree company should be required to make public a document setting out its opinion of the bid and the reasons on which that opinion is based, including its views on the effects of implementation on all the company's interests, and specifically on employment.

In assessing the proper role of a target's management in responding to a tender offer, some authors suggest that these should consider not only the target's shareholders' welfare but that of shareholders as a whole.

Frank H. Easterbrook and Daniel R. Fischel, 'The Proper Role of a Target's Management in Responding to a Tender Offer', *Harv. L. Rev.* 1161–1204, at 1176–1178 (1981)

Even resistance that ultimately elicits a higher bid is socially wasteful. Although the target's shareholders may receive a higher price, these gains are exactly offset by the bidder's payment and thus by a loss to the bidder's shareholders. Shareholders as a group gain nothing; the increase in the price is simply a transfer payment from the bidder's shareholders to the target's shareholders. Indeed, because the process of resistance consumes real resources, shareholders as a whole lose by the amount [the] targets spend in resistance plus the amount bidders and any rivals spend in overcoming resistance. These additional costs can be substantial. This argument may appear to be inconsistent with fiduciary principles. If resistance touches off an auction, it may drive up the price paid for the target's

> shares. Ordinarily managers are charged with the duty of maximizing the returns to the firm's shareholders without regard to adverse consequences to other firms' shareholders or to society at large. The standard economic assumption since Adam Smith introduced the invisible hand has been that the firm's rational pursuit of its self-interest yields more gains for it than losses for its rivals. The result is efficient because the winners gain more than enough to compensate the losers. But this is not invariably true, and the recent experience with pollution provides an example. When a firm treats the air as a free good, society as a whole may lose more than the firm gains. As long as the firm is entitled to disregard the effects on third parties of the pollution it emits, it will consume too much clean air in producing its products. A related 'externality' arises when a target's management resists a tender offer. The resulting increase in the prices paid for target firms will generally discourage prospective bidders for other targets; when the price of anything goes up, the quantity demanded falls. Changes in the incentives of bidders affect the utility of monitoring by outsiders, and that affects the size of agency costs and in turn the pre-offer price of potential targets' stock. In order to explore the nature of these effects, it would be useful to ask what rational shareholders would do if, before a tender offer was in prospect, they could bind the management to resist or to acquiesce in any offer. Consider the effects of two polar rules. Under the first rule, management is passive in the face of tender offers. If there are no competing bidders, the first tender offeror will prevail at the lowest premium that will induce the shareholders to surrender their shares. Under the second rule, management uses all available means to resist the offer. This resistance creates an auction, so that no bidder can acquire the target without paying a price almost as high as the shares would be worth under the best practicable management. For example, shares of firm X are trading for $40. Outsiders could manage the firm better so that the shares would be valued at $90 each. A bid of $50 would induce a substantial majority of X's shareholders to tender their shares. Under the first paradigm rule – managerial acquiescence – the bid of $50 would ensure success. Under the second paradigm – resistance – a tender offeror could not acquire X for much less than $90 per share. Which of these rules maximizes the welfare of X's shareholders? If the question is asked ex post, after a tender offer has been made, then plainly the shareholders would prefer the second rule and the bidding war. But if the shareholders were asked which strategy the managers should pursue ex ante, prior to the offer, they would have substantial reasons to choose acquiescence. It is easy to see why. If the target's shareholders obtain all the gains from the transaction, no one has an incentive to make a tender offer, and thus no one will offer a premium for the shares. The shareholders will be stuck with their $40 shares. Under the strategy of acquiescence, however, the shareholders obtain $50 and are better off.

Considering this economic background, unsurprisingly, the EU passivity rule is a widely discussed principle. Some hold its importance, some others its triviality. An excerpt from a scholarly paper highlights the strengths and weaknesses of the rule, in particular discussing the possibility granted to Member States to decide to opt-out from the regime (*see also*, § 18.5).

Carsten Gerner-Beuerle, David Kershaw and Matteo Solinas, 'Is the Board Neutrality Rule Trivial? Amnesia about Corporate Law in European Takeover Regulation', 22 *EBLR* 559–622, at 619–622 (2011)

The analysis set forth in this article suggests that there are two axes upon which we can assess the significance or triviality of the adoption of a board neutrality rule in European Union Member States. The first axis is the extent to which a Member State's adoption of an unqualified board neutrality rule makes a consequential difference to the ability of boards to fashion and deploy defences without requesting shareholder approval to do so: without a board neutrality rule does corporate law provide the tools to boards to construct defences and does it allow them to be used without restraint? If one emerges with a positive response from the analysis of these questions, the second axis comes into play, namely, the potency of such available defences. There are two elements that structure defence potency: the first depends upon the nature of the defence itself – an asset sale, for example, is significantly less potent than a poison pill; the second element is the background corporate governance rules such as rules on director removal and the calling of shareholder meetings that enable or restrain the defences' deployment for non-corporate/non-shareholder value purposes.

In all three of our selected jurisdictions we have seen that there are multiple and overlapping fields of regulation. And in each of these jurisdictions there is variation in the importance and effectiveness of these different fields of regulation: variation in what does the work of restricting board defensive power. The rules restricting formal availability are, for example, more important in Germany and Italy – where there are serious doubts about the formal availability of a poison pill or similar mechanism even with ex-ante shareholder approval – than in the UK. General rules requiring explicit shareholder authorization to use board power for defensive purposes are more important in the UK (the improper purpose doctrine) and Germany (the Holzmüller doctrine) than in Italy. In the UK and Italy, the background corporate governance rule set is a stronger constraint on the potency of available defences than it is in Germany where supervisory board and management board removal is more difficult. However, whilst there is variation in the role played by these different fields of regulation in each of the three jurisdictions, the conclusions we have reached for the UK, Germany and Italy are very similar. Although we acknowledge variation in the strength of the argument, the case for the triviality of the board neutrality rule can be made in each country.

In the UK the non-frustration rule is trivial. Only asset sale defences are available without shareholder involvement and even their use requires specific ex-ante or ex-post defensive authorization from the shareholders. Where explicit authorization is granted ex-ante to construct and deploy defences the background rule set, and the role of UK institutional investors would prevent their use for any purpose that was not compellingly justified in terms of corporate and shareholder betterment. In Germany, poison pills are unavailable, although their functional substitutes may be with explicit shareholder approval and considerable practical difficulty; share issues of greater than 10 per cent of the outstanding shares require, in effect, explicit shareholder authorization to be used defensively. This leaves less than 10 per cent share issues and share buy-backs with a general ex-ante shareholder authorization (that may always be subject to shareholder imposed conditionality) and only asset sales requiring no authorization (subject to Holzmüller). But asset sales are not potent defences – they are difficult to put in place in the tight time constraints of a bid and may be unavailable if the sold assets are closely interconnected with the remaining assets.

Of our three jurisdictions, Italy arguably presents the weakest case for the triviality thesis. Whilst we think that a strong case can be made that poison pills are not formally available at all in Italy, there is some doubt about this. But even if available they would require ex-ante authorization in order to issue a large grant of warrants. Furthermore, asset sale defences are available without shareholder involvement, and there is scope to issue a sizeable block of shares non pre-emptively to friendly third parties, but again with ex-ante shareholder authorization. Importantly, shareholders unhappy about managerial abuse of defensive capability could put a stop to this by imposing conditions on rolling grants of the authorization to allot shares. Furthermore, there is under Italian law a soft requirement to obtain the shareholders' view of defensive actions, but this is more of a market practice supported by academic commentary than a legal rule. As in the UK, the background Italian corporate governance rule set is strongly pro-shareholder and would constrain board use of these defences for entrenchment purposes.

What does this mean for the Takeover Directive's approach to its anticipated review of the implementation and effect of the board neutrality rule in the European Union? We cannot, of course, extrapolate from these three Member States to the remaining 24. However, what is clear from this article's findings is that there is a distinct possibility that the board neutrality rule is not merely trivial for the Member States analysed in this paper but trivial for the European Union as a whole. Accordingly, looking only at the adoption or rejection of the board neutrality rule by the Member States does not enable us to draw any conclusions about the extent to which boards of European companies can use defences to entrench themselves or throw sand in the wheels of European economic integration.

What is also clear from this analysis is that corporate law in European Member States provides regulation of takeover defences just as it provides for the regulation of any exercise of corporate power. Such regulation represents a balance of board and shareholder power that has evolved since the nineteenth century. Such a balance of power readily addresses surprises that may arise from how boards deploy corporate power. A mandatory board neutrality rule cuts through this crafted balance of power and in so doing, as any bright line does, overreaches itself. This is seen most clearly where it prevents informed shareholders from ex-ante electing to allow boards to use and control board power for defensive purposes when a hostile bid is made. Approaching 140 years ago in a different context where board loyalty was questioned, a famous English Lord Chancellor, Lord Hatherley, when asked to overrule the election that shareholders had made in the articles, observed that it was not 'for the Court to lay down rules for the guidance of men who are adult, and can manage and deal with their own interests'. It would, he observed, have been be 'a violent assumption if any thing of that kind were attempted'. We see in Germany, the UK and also in Italy that it is difficult for boards to manoeuvre defensively without explicit shareholder approval, and that the balance of power allows shareholders to respond if managers overstep the mark.

And we see from the United States that widely-held shareholders, often led by the bidder as shareholder but also pre-emptively prior to a bid, are not in this context cowered by rational apathy. In European Member States where the situation is similar to Germany, the UK and Italy it would indeed, therefore, be a 'violent assumption' to assume that a board neutrality rule would be beneficial for companies and shareholders and that it should be imposed through European legislation.

A practical conclusion follows from our analysis. In order to determine whether or not the board neutrality rule is an important regulatory tool that would justify revision of the Directive to make it a mandatory rule within the European Union, the Commission should carry out the type of analysis set forth in this article for all Member States. If the analysis of the corporate law of these Member States suggests that the corporate legal restrictions on defensive action are as significant as they are in the UK, Germany or Italy, then in our view it would be time for the European Commission to hang up its neutrality boots. There are more important matters that require its attention.

It should be added that according to some other commentators the passivity rule reflects the general freedom of establishment provided for by Article 49 TFEU, and is therefore applicable not only to the board of directors, but also to some activist shareholders.

Thomas Papadopoulos, 'Infringements of Fundamental Freedoms within the EU Market for Corporate Control', 9 *ECFR* 221–260, at 260 (2012)

Discriminatory conduct on the part of market operators, or action which restricts access to the market of other market operators, would seem capable of amounting to a restriction on a fundamental freedom. Hence, the hostile behaviour of the board (especially its expression through defensive measures) or the stance of certain activist shareholders of the target company towards the takeover bid, could both be characterized as a restriction of the freedom of establishment, because they inhibit the bidder from exercising this fundamental freedom through the acquisition of shares (and potentially the control of the company).

FURTHER READING

Jaap Winter, 'We All Want to Go to Heaven but Nobody Wants to Die', 1 *ECL* 4 (2004).

Peter Callens, Erik Werlauff, Yann Christin, Peter Veranneman, Kerstin Grupp, Diana Allegretti, Giovanna Adinolfi, Peter Dortmond, Javier Ybáñez, Alan Paul, and Jaya Gupta, 'Country Status Reports on Defensive Measures against Hostile Takeovers and the Impact of the 13th EC Directive', 1 *ECL* 9–31 (2004).

Ferna Ipekel, 'Defensive Measures under the Directive on Takeover Bids and their Effect on the UK and French Takeover Regimes', 16 *EBLR* 341–351 (2005).

Federico M. Mucciarelli, 'White Knights and Black Knights – Does the Search for Competitive Bids

always Benefit the Shareholders of "Target" Companies?', 3 *ECFR* 408–425 (2006).
Andrin Schnydrig, 'Should Defensive Measures in Takeover Settings be Permitted or Prohibited by Law? An Analysis of the Approach Adopted by US Law, UK Law, and Swiss Law in Light of the Economic Rationale of Takeovers', 20 *EBLR* 909–929 (2009).
Carsten Gerner-Beuerle, David Kershaw, and Matteo Solinas, 'Is the Board Neutrality Rule Trivial? Amnesia about Corporate Law in European Takeover Regulation', 22 *EBLR* 559–622 (2011).
Thomas Papadopoulos, 'Infringements of Fundamental Freedoms within the EU Market for Corporate Control', 9 *ECFR* 221–260 (2012).

18.6 Optional Arrangements and Reciprocity Exemption

Both rules restricting the target's ability to counteract a hostile takeover – passivity and breakthrough rules – are intended to promote the market for corporate control. However, Member States may consider that promotion of the market for corporate control in certain circumstances – i.e., in the case of a severe contraction of the national economy, such as for instance the COVID-19 of 2020 – shall not prevail over other interests. In such circumstances, they may 'opt-out' from both rules, whilst permitting listed companies to voluntarily 'opt-in'.

Recital 21 Directive 2004/25/EC

Taking into account existing differences in Member States' company law mechanisms and structures, Member States should be allowed not to require companies established within their territories to apply the provisions of this Directive limiting the powers of the board of an offeree company during the time allowed for the acceptance of a bid and those rendering ineffective barriers, provided for in the articles of association or in specific agreements. In that event Member States should at least allow companies established within their territories to make the choice, which must be reversible, to apply those provisions. Without prejudice to international agreements to which the European Community is a party, Member States should be allowed not to require companies which apply those provisions in accordance with the optional arrangements to apply them when they become the subject of offers launched by companies which do not apply the same provisions, as a consequence of the use of those optional arrangements.

Article 12(1–2) Directive 2004/25/EC

1. Member States may reserve the right not to require companies as referred to in Article 1 (1) which have their registered offices within their territories to apply Article 9(2) and (3) and/or Article 11.
2. Where Member States make use of the option provided for in paragraph 1, they shall nevertheless grant companies which have their registered offices within their territories

the option, which shall be reversible, of applying Article 9(2) and (3) and/or Article 11, without prejudice to Article 11(7).

The decision of the company shall be taken by the general meeting of shareholders, in accordance with the law of the Member State in which the company has its registered office in accordance with the rules applicable to amendment of the articles of association. The decision shall be communicated to the supervisory authority of the Member State in which the company has its registered office and to all the supervisory authorities of Member States in which its securities are admitted to trading on regulated markets or where such admission has been requested.

The possibility for Member States to opt-out from both passivity and breakthrough rules may result in an unequal treatment for companies of various Member States. This occurs in case a listed company having its registered office in Member State A, where both passivity and breakthrough rules apply, is the target of a hostile takeover bid by a company having its registered office in Member State B, where passivity and breakthrough rules are not provided for. In this case, ECL permits that Member States allow the target company not to comply with the passivity and breakthrough rules, opposing a so-called reciprocity exemption upon authorisation by the general meeting.

Article 12(3) Directive 2004/25/EC

3. Member States may, under the conditions determined by national law, exempt companies which apply Article 9(2) and (3) and/or Article 11 from applying Article 9(2) and (3) and/or Article 11 if they become the subject of an offer launched by a company which does not apply the same Articles as they do, or by a company controlled, directly or indirectly, by the latter, pursuant to Article 1 of Directive 83/349/EEC.
4. Member States shall ensure that the provisions applicable to the respective companies are disclosed without delay.
5. Any measure applied in accordance with paragraph 3 shall be subject to the authorisation of the general meeting of shareholders of the offeree company, which must be granted no earlier than 18 months before the bid was made public in accordance with Article 6(1).

FURTHER READING

Marco Brecht, 'Reciprocity in Takeovers', in Guido Ferrarini, Klaus J. Hopt, Jaap Winter, and Eddy Wymeersch (eds.), *Reforming Company and Takeover Law in Europe* 647–677 (Oxford University Press, 2004).

Mathias M. Siems, 'The Rules on Conflict of Laws in the European Takeover Directive', 1 *ECFR* 458–476 (2004).

Marco Lamandini, 'Takeover Bids and "Italian" Reciprocity', 5 *ECL* 56–57 (2008).

18.7 Squeeze-Out and Sell-Out Rights

The Takeover Bids Directive considers the situation of a target company after a successful bid, in particular when more than 90 per cent of the shares (or of securities carrying more than 90 per cent of the voting rights) are sold to the bidder. In such circumstances, ECL provides the bidder with a right to squeeze-out the residual shareholders at a fair price, whilst, in turn, the residual shareholders benefit from a right to sell-out the shares left in their holdings on the same conditions. Either the squeeze- or sell-out rights must be exercised within three months after the end of the time allowed for acceptance of the (mandatory or voluntary) bid.

Article 15 Directive 2004/25/EC providing for a squeeze-out right reads as follows:

Article 15 Directive 2004/25/EC

1. Member States shall ensure that, following a bid made to all the holders of the offeree company's securities for all of their securities, paragraphs 2 to 5 apply.
2. Member States shall ensure that an offeror is able to require all the holders of the remaining securities to sell him/her those securities at a fair price. Member States shall introduce that right in one of the following situations:
   (a) where the offeror holds securities representing not less than 90% of the capital carrying voting rights and 90% of the voting rights in the offeree company,

   or

   (b) where, following acceptance of the bid, he/she has acquired or has firmly contracted to acquire securities representing not less than 90% of the offeree company's capital carrying voting rights and 90% of the voting rights comprised in the bid.

In the case referred to in (a), Member States may set a higher threshold that may not, however, be higher than 95% of the capital carrying voting rights and 95% of the voting rights.

3. Member States shall ensure that rules are in force that make it possible to calculate when the threshold is reached.

Where the offeree company has issued more than one class of securities, Member States may provide that the right of squeeze-out can be exercised only in the class in which the threshold laid down in paragraph 2 has been reached.

4. If the offeror wishes to exercise the right of squeeze-out he/she shall do so within three months of the end of the time allowed for acceptance of the bid referred to in Article 7.
5. Member States shall ensure that a fair price is guaranteed. That price shall take the same form as the consideration offered in the bid or shall be in cash. Member States may provide that cash shall be offered at least as an alternative.

Following a voluntary bid, in both of the cases referred to in paragraph 2(a) and (b), the consideration offered in the bid shall be presumed to be fair where, through acceptance of the bid, the offeror has acquired securities representing not less than 90% of the capital carrying voting rights comprised in the bid.

Following a mandatory bid, the consideration offered in the bid shall be presumed to be fair.

The squeeze-out right is intended to protect the majority shareholder to become a sole shareholder and reorganise the target company as he or she prefers. A justification for granting a squeeze-out right has been highlighted by the High Level Group.

Report of the High Level Group of Company Law Experts on Issues Related to Takeover Bids 61

- without a squeeze-out right, takeover bids are less attractive to potential bidders because of the costs and risks related to the existence of minority shareholders after the bid. This will reduce the likelihood of voluntary bids and the prices offered in them and the range of circumstances in which such bids are economic. In the same way, the squeeze-out right may be viewed as a counterpart to the mandatory bid rule.

Still, squeeze-out rights are controversial under many Member States' jurisdictions as they might impact on the constitutional right to private property.

Conversely, ECL also provides the residual shareholders with a sell-out right, which they might exercise regardless of whether the majority shareholder plans to exercise his or her squeeze-out right. Article 16 Directive 2004/25/EC reads as follows:

Article 16 Directive 2004/25/EC

1. Member States shall ensure that, following a bid made to all the holders of the offeree company's securities for all of their securities, paragraphs 2 and 3 apply.
2. Member States shall ensure that a holder of remaining securities is able to require the offeror to buy his/her securities from him/her at a fair price under the same circumstances as provided for in Article 15(2).
3. Article 15(3) to (5) shall apply mutatis mutandis.

In other words, the sell-out right grants a second chance to residual minority shareholders who may require the successful bidder, notwithstanding the time allowed for acceptance of the bid has expired, to compulsorily purchase their remaining securities at a fair price.

Also in this respect, a justification for granting a sell-out right has been highlighted by the High Level Group in its Report.

Report of the High Level Group of Company Law Experts on Issues Related to Takeover Bids 62

- the sell-out right is an appropriate mechanism to counter the pressure on shareholders to tender in the takeover bid. In the consultations organised by the Group, the view has been expressed that there is no justification for a sell-out right in situations where a takeover bid has taken place, because the minority shareholders have the opportunity to sell in that bid. The Group does not share this view and considers instead that minority shareholders may have good reasons (unattractive price, promising perspectives for the company) for not selling in the course of the bid, but should be entitled to modify their decision in view of the outcome of the bid. A rule whereby the consideration required in the sell-out procedure should normally not be higher than the consideration offered in the bid would help to prevent purely speculative behaviours.

It should be added that, after a successful takeover, permitting the bidder to acquire more than 90 per cent of the shares, the target company shall be delisted, unless the same bidder sells sufficient shares to re-establish the free float: as already mentioned, this represents all the shares outstanding that can be publicly traded, necessary under the rules of the chosen regulated market to maintain admission to trading. In case the free float is not re-established, and the company is delisted, the remaining shareholders will not have the possibility to sell their shares in the market. Therefore, a sell-out right forcing the bidder to buyout all of the remaining shares shall be seen as the necessary burden upon the successful bidder for having caused the company to be delisted.

FURTHER READING

Sanford J. Grossman and Oliver D. Hart, 'Takeover Bids, the Free-rider Problem, and the Theory of the Corporation', 11 *Bell Journal of Economics* 42–64 (1980).

Lucian Arye Bebchuk, 'The Pressure to Tender: An Analysis and a Proposed Remedy', 12 *Del. J. Corp. L.* 911–949 (1987).

Mike Burkart and Fausto Panunzi, 'Mandatory Bids, Squeeze-out, Sell-out and the Dynamics of the Tender Offer Process', in Guido Ferrarini, Klaus J. Hopt, Jaap Winter, and Eddy Wymeersch (eds.), *Reforming Company and Takeover Law in Europe* 737–767 (Oxford University Press, 2004).

Mads Krohn, 'Minority Squeeze-outs and the European Convention on Human Rights', 15 *EBLR* 159–182 (2004).

Christoph van der Elst and Lientje van den Steen, 'Squeezing and Selling-out: A Patchwork of Rules in Five European Member States', 4 *ECL* 19–25 (2007).

Christoph van der Elst and Lientje van den Steen, 'Balancing the Interests of Minority and Majority Shareholders: A Comparative Analysis of Squeeze-out and Sell-out Rights', 6 *ECFR* 391–439 (2009).

Part VII

Merger, Division, Conversion, Dissolution, and Insolvency

19

Merger, Division, and Conversion

19.1 Extraordinary Transactions: Merger, Division, and Conversion

As a company is formed, it might be dissolved after winding-up and liquidation. However, a company may also be wound up *without* going into liquidation, such as in merger, division, or conversion transactions. In these cases, the company is not dissolved, but continues its operation through the new company or companies into which it has converted, into which it has been merged, or into which it has been divided. ECL addresses mergers and division of domestic companies: the rules of such transactions were formerly carried by the Third and Sixth Directives, now both included in the Directive 2017/1132/EU (Articles 87–117; 135–160 Directive 2017/1132/EU). Since 2005 ECL also regulates cross-border mergers: the rules of such a transaction were formerly carried by the Tenth Directive, and they too are now also included in the Directive 2017/1132/EU (Articles 118–134 Directive 2017/1132/EU). Since 2019, Directive 2019/2121/EU has introduced within Directive 2017/1132/EU two new chapters, respectively concerning cross-border divisions (Articles 160a–160u Directive 2017/1132/EU) and cross-border conversions (Articles 86a–86t Directive 2017/1132/EU).

In the following paragraphs, a brief picture of the EU law of extraordinary transactions will be outlined.

19.2 Types of Merger and Division

Both mergers and divisions may be performed by acquisition or by formation of a new company. If the legislation of the Member States provides accordingly, a merger or division may be also effected where one or more of the companies being acquired is in liquidation.

Article 89 Directive 2017/1132/EU

1. For the purposes of this Chapter, 'merger by acquisition' shall mean the operation whereby one or more companies are wound up without going into liquidation and

transfer to another all their assets and liabilities in exchange for the issue to the shareholders of the company or companies being acquired of shares in the acquiring company and a cash payment, if any, not exceeding 10% of the nominal value of the shares so issued or, where they have no nominal value, of their accounting par value.

2. A Member State's laws may provide that merger by acquisition may also be effected where one or more of the companies being acquired is in liquidation, provided that this option is restricted to companies which have not yet begun to distribute their assets to their shareholders.

Article 90 Directive 2017/1132/EU

1. For the purposes of this Chapter, 'merger by the formation of a new company' shall mean the operation whereby several companies are wound up without going into liquidation and transfer to a company that they set up all their assets and liabilities in exchange for the issue to their shareholders of shares in the new company and a cash payment, if any, not exceeding 10% of the nominal value of the shares so issued or, where they have no nominal value, of their accounting par value.
2. A Member State's laws may provide that merger by the formation of a new company may also be effected where one or more of the companies which are ceasing to exist is in liquidation, provided that this option is restricted to companies which have not yet begun to distribute their assets to their shareholders.

Article 106 Directive 2017/1132/EU

1. For the purposes of this Chapter, 'division by acquisition' shall mean the operation whereby, after being wound up without going into liquidation, a company transfers to more than one company all its assets and liabilities in exchange for the allocation to the shareholders of the company being divided of shares in the companies receiving contributions as a result of the division (hereafter referred to as 'recipient companies') and possibly a cash payment not exceeding 10% of the nominal value of the shares allocated or, where they have no nominal value, of their accounting par value.
2. Article 89(2) shall apply.
3. In so far as this Chapter refers to provisions of Chapter I of Title II, the term 'merging companies' shall mean 'the companies involved in a division', the term 'company being acquired' shall mean 'the company being divided', the term 'acquiring company' shall mean 'each of the recipient companies' and the term 'draft terms of merger' shall mean 'draft terms of division'.

Article 155 Directive 2017/1132/EU

1. For the purposes of this Chapter, 'division by the formation of new companies' means the operation whereby, after being wound up without going into liquidation, a company transfers to more than one newly-formed company all its assets and liabilities in exchange for the allocation to the shareholders of the company being divided of shares in the recipient companies, and possibly a cash payment not exceeding 10% of the nominal value of the shares allocated or, where they have no nominal value, of their accounting par value.
2. Article 90(2) shall apply.

Article 160b Directive 2017/1132/EU, giving the relevant definitions for a cross-border division, specifies that a 'division' means an operation whereby:

(a) a company being divided, on being dissolved without going into liquidation, transfers all its assets and liabilities to two or more recipient companies, in exchange for the issue to the members of the company being divided of securities or shares in the recipient companies and, if applicable, a cash payment not exceeding 10 % of the nominal value, or, in the absence of a nominal value, a cash payment not exceeding 10 % of the accounting par value of those securities or shares ('full division');
(b) a company being divided transfers part of its assets and liabilities to one or more recipient companies, in exchange for the issue to the members of the company being divided of securities or shares in the recipient companies, in the company being divided or in both the recipient companies and the company being divided, and, if applicable, a cash payment not exceeding 10 % of the nominal value, or, in the absence of a nominal value, a cash payment not exceeding 10 % of the accounting par value of those securities or shares ('partial division'); or
(c) a company being divided transfers part of its assets and liabilities to one or more recipient companies, in exchange for the issue to the company being divided of securities or shares in the recipient companies ('division by separation').

It is worth noting that a *division by separation* (commonly referred to as *spin-off*) is not recognised as division for domestic divisions, as it constitutes the setting-up of a NewCo by a single member. However, in the context of a cross-border operation, member States shall recognise it as a division.

As a result of the merger or the division, shareholders of the company to be merged or divided (except in cases of cross-border division by separation) become shareholders of the resulting company or companies under a specified share exchange ratio. Indeed, in all considered transactions, the cash payment may not exceed 10 per cent of the nominal value of the shares allocated or, where they have no nominal value, of their accounting par value.

In other words, ECL does not permit the so-called cash-out or freeze-out merger or division that are allowed – although with some reluctance – under Delaware law. Reference to articles, from both European and American scholars, will help to clarify the terms of the debate.

Victor Brudney and Marvin A. Chirelstein, 'A Restatement of Corporate Freezeouts', 87 *Yale L.J.* 1354–1376, at 1357–1358 (1978)

The essence of a freezeout is the displacement of public investors by those who own a controlling block of stock of a corporation, whether individuals or a parent company, for cash or senior securities. The public investors are thus required to give up their equity in the enterprise, while the controllers retain theirs. Freezeouts most commonly take the form of a merger of a corporation into its existing parent or into a shell corporation newly formed for the purpose by those who control the merged entity.

Freezeouts, by definition, are coercive: minority stockholders are bound by majority rule to accept cash or debt in exchange for their common shares, even though the price they receive may be less than the value they assign to those shares. But in this alone does not render freezeouts objectionable. Majority rule always entails coercion. It is, nonetheless, an acceptable rule of governance if all will be identically affected by the outcome of the vote. In the ordinary arm's length stockholders of the merged entity are properly viewed as having a common interest in maximizing the returns on their stock, whether through periodic dividends or through sale or liquidation of the firm. Once approved by a statutory majority, the terms of such a merger will apply equally to each of the merging company's stockholders, and the common decision will satisfy the principle that all members of the class be treated alike ...

Freezeouts obviously differ from arm's-length mergers in that all the members of the same class of stockholders do not receive identical treatment: the controlling stockholders retain their equity but force the minority, the public investors, to accept cash or debt.

Delaware's merger statutes were amended in 1967 expressly to permit cash mergers. Until 1983, however, there was some question about whether fiduciary principles would permit a merger to be undertaken solely or primarily to increase a majority shareholder's interest in a company or to eliminate minority shareholders. Overruling *Singer* v. *Magnavox Co.* (380 A.2d 969 (Del. 1977)), in a famous decision of 1983 – *Weinberger* v. *UOP, Inc.* (457 A.2d 701, 715 (Del. 1983)) – the Delaware Supreme Court affirmed that 'Delaware law allows the majority shareholder to cash-out with the minority shareholders solely for the purpose of increasing [the majority's] control provided, of course, that the majority shareholder treats the minority shareholder with entire fairness.' The entire fairness standard, drafted in *Weinberger*, is a stronger test as a business judgment rule, requiring directors to show a reasonable purpose for their action. Indeed, freeze-out mergers involve problems of equal treatment of shareholders. In this regard, it may be of interest to refer to another scholarly article that, although mainly discussing corporate takeovers, also focuses on the involvement of equal treatment in the several methods of corporate acquisition.

Lucian Arye Bebchuk, 'Toward Undistorted Choice and Equal Treatment in Corporate Takeovers', 98 *Harv. L. Rev.* 1695–1795, at 1696–1707 (1985)

Shareholders' decisions whether to tender in the face of a takeover bid are at present subject to substantial pressures and distortions. A target's shareholder might well tender his shares to a bidder even if he views the offered acquisition price as lower than the value of the independent target. For one thing, the shareholder might tender out of fear that, if he does not tender, the bidder might still gain control, in which case the shareholder would be left with low-value minority shares in the acquired target.

Because of the existing distortions of shareholder choice, a bidder might currently succeed in taking over a target even if the value-maximizing course of action for the target's shareholders would be to reject the bid. Consequently, a target might be acquired even if the most efficient use of its assets would require that it remain independent or that it be acquired by another buyer. The current distortions thus reduce social welfare by leading to an inefficient allocation of corporate assets. Moreover, these distortions provide the only possible justification for allowing target managements to use obstructive defensive tactics; eliminating these distortions would therefore remove the only defensible obstacle to prohibiting such tactics, which are very costly both to target shareholders and to society.

... In takeovers accomplished under current law, the total acquisition price is disproportionately distributed among the target's shareholders. Some shareholders have all or most of their shares purchased for the bid price, while other shareholders have all their shares become minority shares with a value lower than the bid price. Consequently, some shareholders, largely unsophisticated investors, end up with considerably less than their pro rata share of the acquisition price. This disproportionate division, I shall suggest, is both inefficient and unfair.

... equal treatment is a desirable objective not only for mergers but also for takeovers. One reason for this desirability is that equal treatment is instrumental to attaining undistorted choice. As the analysis will show, the current inequality of treatment distorts shareholders' tender decisions; consequently, attaining undistorted choice would require ensuring a proportionate distribution of acquisition prices.

Equal treatment is desirable, however, not only for its instrumental value but also as an independent objective, an end in itself. This independent value of equal treatment is based on what I view as widely held notions of fairness. These notion[s] of fairness suggest some presumption in favor of pro rata division. The presumption is that, absent some reason to the contrary, fairness require[s] that two shareholders holding the same number of shares in a company receive the same fraction of the acquisition price in the event of a takeover (or at least that they have ex ante the same prospects of sharing in such an acquisition price).

As already mentioned, under ECL, a cash merger may not occur, as only 10 per cent of the overall nominal value may be paid in cash, nor are freeze-outs permitted, as all shareholders must be treated exactly the same. It is, however, interesting to read another more recent scholarly article, comparing freeze-outs from an American and a European perspective.

Marco Ventoruzzo, 'Freeze-outs: Transcontinental Analysis and Reform Proposals', 50 *Va J. of Int'l L.* 841–916, at 842–847 (2010)

One of the most crucial, but systematically neglected, comparative differences between corporate law systems in Europe and the United States concerns regulation governing freezeout transactions in listed corporations. For the purposes of this Article, freeze-outs can be defined as transactions in which the controlling shareholders exercise a legal right to buy out the shares of the minority, consequently delisting the corporation and bringing it private. Beyond this essential definition, systems diverge profoundly.

... Much can be gained from a study of minority freeze-outs, from both a theoretical and practical perspective. From a theoretical point of view, freeze-outs of minorities lie on the contested frontier separating the powers (and duties) of controlling shareholders and directors from the rights of minority shareholders. It is a boundary drawn along the elusive and politically charged line of efficiency and fairness. Comparative scrutiny of the American and European attitudes towards freeze-outs allows for identification of some of the most defining features of different corporate law regimes, such as the kind of property interest that minorities are deemed to maintain in the corporation, the role of litigation in shaping corporate rules, and the propensity toward monetary damages versus other types of relief for the protection of minorities. From a more practical perspective, the opportunity to go private, its costs, and its timing affect not only the prosperity of single corporations at the micro level, but also the health of the financial system in which they operate at the macro level. One may question whether going-private transactions are value-maximizing and how efficiency gains, if any, are split among different stakeholders. As is often the case, the empirical evidence is not conclusive. It is, however, unquestionable that under specific circumstances, powerful financial, strategic, legal, and tax considerations incentivize the majority shareholders to buy out the minority's equity interests and delist the corporation. In many instances, going private is in the best interest of all parties involved: majority and minority shareholders, investors, creditors, employees, and other stakeholders.

... This Article proceeds on the general assumption that European regulation is more restrictive of freeze-outs than its US counterpart. This disparity reflects different philosophies concerning shareholders' rights and minority protection. The European model is based on the idea that every shareholder enjoys a substantially untouchable property right in her shares. Conversely, the American model allows greater flexibility as a consequence of regulatory competition among states and the common law case-based approach. At the same time, this model lacks certainty and leads to partially contradictory outcomes. This Article, after a critical discussion of freeze-out rules in the United States and Europe, builds a comparative analysis to propose reforms that would increase shareholder protection in the United States and foster more uniform rules in Europe that would facilitate, under certain conditions, going-private transactions.

As regards the possibility of substantial squeeze-outs or freeze-outs through divisions, it should be added that the Sixth Directive states the following:

Article 139 Directive 2017/1132/EU

1. A division shall require at least the approval of a general meeting of each company involved in the division. Article 93 shall apply with regard to the majority required for such decisions, their scope and the need for separate votes.
2. Where the shares in the recipient companies are allocated to the shareholders of the company being divided otherwise than in proportion to their rights in the capital of that company, Member States may provide that the minority shareholders of that company may exercise the right to have their shares purchased. In such [a] case, they shall be entitled to receive consideration corresponding to the value of their shares. In the event of a dispute concerning such consideration, it must be possible for the consideration to be determined by a court.

Article 139 Directive 2017/1132/EU therefore allows a so-called *disproportional* or *asymmetric division*, whereby shareholders of the divided company become shareholders of the recipient company in a proportion other than their share of interest in the capital of the company being divided or, rather, become sole shareholders of two or more new companies. Under ECL, also these kind of divisions are decided upon a majority vote (however, in some Member States it is argued that an asymmetric division should require unanimous consent of all shareholders). Unless Member States so provide, minority shareholders may not force the company to be cashed out, nor may they object that the division does not grant all shareholders the right to be allocated shares of all the recipient companies in proportion to the share of interest in the capital of the company being divided. For example, assume that Harry and Ron jointly own WWW Co., a company engaging in two businesses of uneven relevance: Harry owns 75 per cent of the share capital, therefore he has a majority in the general meeting of WWW Co. Harry may therefore decide that WWW Co. is divided into NewCo A, engaging in business A (worth three times business B), and into NewCo B, engaging in business B; instead of having both Harry and Ron shareholders in NewCo A and NewCo B, the general meeting might decide that Harry becomes the sole shareholder of NewCo A and Ron the sole shareholder of NewCo B. Unless a right to be cashed out is provided for, Ron must accept Harry's decision.

It is worth noting that a disproportional or an asymmetric division may be substantially performed through other transactions such as a repurchase of the company's own shares or a capital reduction to be paid in kind. To this regard, two important cases have occurred in the past. One of these dates back to 1894 (*BA Trustee*), whilst the other is much more recent, as it occurred in 1999 (*Novoprint*).

In *BA Trustee* (*British & American Trustee & Finance Corp.* v. *Couper* [1894], A.C. 399) a company incorporated under English law operated in Britain and the US. The shares were divided between two groups of shareholders, as was the board; the majority was British, and the minority was American. Because of the US part of the business, the company faced a deadlock and the shareholders agreed to a substantial split or spin-off. Since no such reorganisation was provided for under English law at the time, they agreed to reduce the legal capital to the extent that it was 'in excess of the wants of the company'. The company implemented the reduction by allocating the US assets to the American shareholders. Both the general meeting and the special-class meetings (ordinary's and founders') approved the proposal. As English law still requires, the proposal was subsequently subjected to the court's approval. One shareholder appealed, claiming that a capital reduction cannot affect only part of the shares of a single class. He argued that it was forbidden to allot parts of the company's assets to some shareholders only: the reimbursement should be the same for all. The House of Lords did not follow this view and confirmed the reduction plan. In doing so, the House of Lords recognised the legitimacy of a reduction or a selective purchase of the company's own shares affecting all shareholders unequally, as an asymmetric division decided upon majority vote.

In *Novoprint* (Spanish RDGN, 1 March 1999, n. 1372, *Novoprint*, [1999] La Ley, 6697), 99.85 per cent of the shareholders of the company attended the general meeting and unanimously adopted a resolution to reduce the share capital in order to repay in full all the shares held by three shareholders (holding around 40 per cent of the shares). The shares would be reimbursed in kind, through the award of a building. Since the reduction would affect the shareholders differently, a separate vote from the special meetings (both the special meeting of all shareholders whose shares were cancelled and refunded, and the special meeting of all the remaining shareholders) would be necessary. However, the Spanish General Direction of Register considered that the transaction was fair, no one objected, and even if 0.15 per cent had voted against the resolution, their vote would not have been equivalent to a right to veto.

It is now interesting to recall Article 85 Directive 2017/1132/EU on equal treatment and read it in the light of the solutions rendered by the national Courts in the foregoing two cases.

As seen previously (Chapter 16, § 16.5), such provision calls for the laws of the Member States to ensure equal treatment to all shareholders who are in the same position. A strict interpretation of such a rule would lead to *either* a ruling of illegitimacy for transactions such as the ones carried out in *BA Trustee* and *Novoprint*, where shareholders were treated disparately, *or* to require that such transactions are valid only provided that all shareholders grant their individual consent. Such an interpretation, however, would blatantly strike against the principles that may be carved out of Article 139 Directive 2017/1132/EU, whereby it allows an asymmetric division decided upon majority vote.

The foregoing confirms that, as it has been clarified, Article 85 Directive 2017/1132/EU – being an ambiguous provision, on which, not by chance, there is no CJEU case law – shall be interpreted as not preventing all disparate treatments of shareholders, rather requiring that all shareholders are treated fairly (*see* Chapter 16, § 16.5). Therefore, notwithstanding all such transactions involving disparate treatment are validly decided upon majority vote, the majority must still behave fairly to the minority. The minority may challenge the validity of decisions they deem unfair and seek pecuniary compensation.

FURTHER READING

Victor Brudney and Marvin A. Chirelstein, 'A Restatement of Corporate Freezeouts', 87 *Yale L.J.* 1354–1376 (1978).

Lucian Arye Bebchuk, 'Toward Undistorted Choice and Equal Treatment in Corporate Takeovers', 98 *Harv. L. Rev.* 1695–1795 (1985).

Marco Ventoruzzo, 'Freeze-outs: Transcontinental Analysis and Reform Proposals', 50 *Va J. of Int'l L.* 841–916 (2010).

Tom Vos, '"Baby, it's cold outside ..." – A Comparative and Economic Analysis of Freeze-outs of Minority Shareholders', 15 *ECFR* 148–196 (2018).

19.3 The Merger or Division Process

The merger or division process is articulated in three steps: (i) the preparation of the draft terms of merger or division; (ii) the shareholders' meeting or meetings' decision; (iii) the deed of merger or division.

The draft terms of merger or division are prepared by the administrative or management bodies of the merging companies or of the companies involved in a division.

Article 91 Directive 2017/1132/EU

1. The administrative or management bodies of the merging companies shall draw up draft terms of merger in writing.
2. Draft terms of merger shall specify at least:
   (a) the type, name and registered office of each of the merging companies;
   (b) the share exchange ratio and the amount of any cash payment;
   (c) the terms relating to the allotment of shares in the acquiring company;
   (d) the date from which the holding of such shares entitles the holders to participate in profits and any special conditions affecting that entitlement;

(e) the date from which the transactions of the company being acquired shall be treated for accounting purposes as being those of the acquiring company;
(f) the rights conferred by the acquiring company on the holders of shares to which special rights are attached and the holders of securities other than shares, or the measures proposed concerning them;
(g) any special advantage granted to the experts referred to in Article 96(1) and members of the merging companies' administrative, management, supervisory or controlling bodies.

Similarly, these are provided for in the Directive 2017/1132/EU as regards divisions. However, the draft terms of division must include additional disclosure as regards:

Article 140(2)(h–i), (3) Directive 2017/1132/EU

(h) the precise description and allocation of the assets and liabilities to be transferred to each of the recipient companies;
(i) the allocation to the shareholders of the company being divided of shares in the recipient companies and the criterion upon which such allocation is based.
3. (a) Where an asset is not allocated by the draft terms of division and where the interpretation of these terms does not make a decision on its allocation possible, the asset or the consideration therefore shall be allocated to all the recipient companies in proportion to the share of the net assets allocated to each of those companies under the draft terms of division.
(b) Where a liability is not allocated by the draft terms of division and where the interpretation of these terms does not make a decision on its allocation possible, each of the recipient companies shall be jointly and severally liable for it. Member States may provide that such joint and several liability be limited to the net assets allocated to each company.

After preparation of the draft term of a merger or division, publication shall occur.

Article 140 Directive 2017/1132/EU (Similarly, Article 138 Directive 2017/1132/EU)

Draft terms of merger must be published in the manner prescribed by the laws of each Member State in accordance with Article 16, for each of the merging companies, at least 1 month before the date fixed for the general meeting which is to decide thereon.

Any of the merging companies shall be exempt from the publication requirement laid down in Article 16 if, for a continuous period beginning at least 1 month before the day fixed for the general meeting which is to decide on the draft terms of merger and ending not earlier than the conclusion of that meeting, it makes the draft terms of such merger available on its website free of charge for the public. Member States shall not subject that exemption to any requirements or constraints other than those which are necessary in order to ensure the security of the website and the authenticity of the documents, and may impose such requirements or constraints only to the extent that they are proportionate in order to achieve those objectives.

By way of derogation from the second paragraph of this Article, Member States may require that publication be effected via the central electronic platform referred to in Article 16(5). Member States may alternatively require that such publication be made on any other website designated by them for that purpose. Where Member States avail themselves of one of those possibilities, they shall ensure that companies are not charged a specific fee for such publication.

Where a website other than the central electronic platform is used, a reference giving access to that website shall be published on the central electronic platform at least 1 month before the day fixed for the general meeting. That reference shall include the date of publication of the draft terms of merger on the website and shall be accessible to the public free of charge. Companies shall not be charged a specific fee for such publication.

The prohibition precluding the charging to companies of a specific fee for publication, laid down in the third and fourth paragraphs, shall not affect the ability of Member States to pass on to companies the costs in respect of the central electronic platform.

Member States may require companies to maintain the information for a specific period after the general meeting on their website or, where applicable, on the central electronic platform or the other website designated by the Member State concerned. Member States may determine the consequences of temporary disruption of access to the website or to the central electronic platform, caused by technical or other factors.

The draft terms of merger or division shall be examined by one or more experts, acting on behalf of the dividing company or of each of the merging companies but independent of them, appointed or approved by a judicial or administrative authority. These experts shall draw up a written report to the shareholders that will be submitted to the shareholders' meeting along with the management report (Articles 95 and 141 Directive 2017/1132/EU).

Article 96 Directive 2017/1132/EU (Similarly, Article 142 Directive 2017/1132/EU)

1. One or more experts, acting on behalf of each of the merging companies but independent of them, appointed or approved by a judicial or administrative authority, shall examine

the draft terms of merger and draw up a written report to the shareholders. However, the laws of a Member State may provide for the appointment of one or more independent experts for all the merging companies, if such appointment is made by a judicial or administrative authority at the joint request of those companies. Such experts may, depending on the laws of each Member State, be natural or legal persons or companies or firms.

2. In the report mentioned in paragraph 1 the experts must in any case state whether in their opinion the share exchange ratio is fair and reasonable. Their statement must at least:
   (a) indicate the method or methods used to arrive at the share exchange ratio proposed;
   (b) state whether such method or methods are adequate in the case in question, indicate the values arrived at using each such method and give an opinion on the relative importance attributed to such methods in arriving at the value decided on.

   The report shall also describe any special valuation difficulties which have arisen.

3. Each expert shall be entitled to obtain from the merging companies all relevant information and documents and to carry out all necessary investigations.
4. Neither an examination of the draft terms of merger nor an expert report shall be required if all the shareholders and the holders of other securities conferring the right to vote of each of the companies involved in the merger have so agreed.

Being amendments to the statutes of the company or companies involved, both merger and division are transactions for the general meeting to decide.

Article 93 Directive 2017/1132/EU (Similarly, Article 138 Directive 2017/1132/EU)

1. A merger shall require at least the approval of the general meeting of each of the merging companies. The laws of the Member States shall provide that this approval decision shall require a majority of not less than two thirds of the votes attached either to the shares or to the subscribed capital represented.

The laws of a Member State may, however, provide that a simple majority of the votes specified in the first subparagraph shall be sufficient when at least half of the subscribed capital is represented. Moreover, where appropriate, the rules governing alterations to the memorandum and articles of association shall apply.

2. Where there is more than one class of shares, the decision concerning a merger shall be subject to a separate vote by at least each class of shareholders whose rights are affected by the transaction.
3. The decision shall cover both the approval of the draft terms of merger and any alterations to the memorandum and articles of association necessitated by the merger.

However, Member States' legislation may waive the necessity of a shareholder meeting's decision provided that certain conditions are met.

Article 94 Directive 2017/1132/EU (Similarly, Articles 140 and 154 Directive 2017/1132/EU)

The laws of a Member State need not require approval of the merger by the general meeting of the acquiring company if the following conditions are fulfilled:

(a) the publication provided for in Article 92 must be effected, for the acquiring company, at least 1 month before the date fixed for the general meeting of the company or companies being acquired which is to decide on the draft terms of merger;
(b) at least 1 month before the date specified in point (a), all shareholders of the acquiring company must be entitled to inspect the documents specified in Article 97(1) at the registered office of the acquiring company;
(c) one or more shareholders of the acquiring company holding a minimum percentage of the subscribed capital must be entitled to require that a general meeting of the acquiring company be called to decide whether to approve the merger; this minimum percentage may not be fixed at more than 5%. Member States may, however, provide for the exclusion of non-voting shares from this calculation.

For the purposes of point (b) of the first paragraph, Article 97(2), (3), and (4) shall apply.

After a resolution of the general meeting or meetings, where the laws of a Member State do not provide for judicial or administrative preventive supervision of the legality of mergers or division, the management or administrative organs of the company or companies to be merged or divided may proceed to the deed of merger or division. In such a case, the deed of merger or division subsequent to such general meetings shall be drawn up and certified in due legal form.

Article 102 Directive 2017/1132/EU (Similarly, Article 148 Directive 2017/1132/EU)

1. Where the laws of a Member State do not provide for judicial or administrative preventive supervision of the legality of mergers, or where such supervision does not extend to all the legal acts required for a merger, the minutes of the general meetings which decide on the merger and, where appropriate, the merger contract subsequent to such general meetings shall be drawn up and certified in due legal form. In cases where the merger need not be approved by the general meetings of all the merging companies, the draft terms of merger must be drawn up and certified in due legal form.
2. The notary or the authority competent to draw up and certify the document in due legal form must check and certify the existence and validity of the legal acts and formalities required of the company for which that notary or authority is acting and of the draft terms of merger.

In addition, the laws of the Member States must provide for an adequate system of protection of the interests of creditors of the merging companies or the company to be divided (including holders of debentures and other securities) whose claims antedate the publication of the draft terms of merger or division and have not fallen due at the time of such publication. Protection of creditors may require that the deed of merger or division does not occur before a certain date after publication of the draft terms of merger or division.

Article 99(2) Directive 2017/1132/EU (Similarly, Article 146 Directive 2017/1132/EU)

2. To that end, the laws of the Member States shall at least provide that such creditors shall be entitled to obtain adequate safeguards where the financial situation of the merging companies makes such protection necessary and where those creditors do not already have such safeguards.

Member States shall lay down the conditions for the protection provided for in paragraph 1 and in the first subparagraph of this paragraph. In any event, Member States shall ensure that the creditors are authorised to apply to the appropriate administrative or judicial authority for adequate safeguards provided that they can credibly demonstrate that due to the merger the satisfaction of their claims is at stake and that no adequate safeguards have been obtained from the company.

19.4 The Effects of a Merger or Division

The date on which a merger or a division takes effect is determined by the laws of the Member States (Articles 103 and 149 Directive 2017/1132/EU). In any case, a merger or a division shall entail *ipso jure* and simultaneously the effects provided for by the relevant Directives.

Article 105 Directive 2017/1132/EU (Similarly, Article 151 Directive 2017/1132/EU)

1. A merger shall have the following consequences ipso jure and simultaneously:
   (a) the transfer, both as between the company being acquired and the acquiring company and as regards third parties, to the acquiring company of all the assets and liabilities of the company being acquired;
   (b) the shareholders of the company being acquired become shareholders of the acquiring company;
   (c) the company being acquired ceases to exist.
2. No shares in the acquiring company shall be exchanged for shares in the company being acquired held either:
   (a) by the acquiring company itself or through a person acting in his own name but on its behalf; or

(b) by the company being acquired itself or through a person acting in his own name but on its behalf.

3. The foregoing shall not affect the laws of Member States which require the completion of special formalities for the transfer of certain assets, rights and obligations by the acquired company to be effective as against third parties. The acquiring company may carry out these formalities itself; however, the laws of the Member States may permit the company being acquired to continue to carry out these formalities for a limited period which cannot, save in exceptional cases, be fixed at more than 6 months from the date on which the merger takes effect.

The laws of the Member States shall lay down rules governing the civil liability of the administrative or management bodies in preparing and implementing the merger or the division (Articles 106 and 152 Directive 2017/1132/EU), as well as that of the experts in the performance of their duties (Articles 147 and 152 Directive 2017/1132/EU).

Lastly, similarly to the nullity of a newly formed company, the nullity of a merger or division may also be declared only in a limited set of cases.

Article 108 Directive 2017/1132/EU (Similarly, Article 153 Directive 2017/1132/EU)

1. The laws of the Member States may lay down nullity rules for mergers in accordance with the following conditions only:
   (a) nullity must be ordered in a court judgment;
   (b) mergers which have taken effect pursuant to Article 103 may be declared void only if there has been no judicial or administrative preventive supervision of their legality, or if they have not been drawn up and certified in due legal form, or if it is shown that the decision of the general meeting is void or voidable under national law;
   (c) nullification proceedings may not be initiated more than 6 months after the date on which the merger becomes effective as against the person alleging nullity or if the situation has been rectified;
   (d) where it is possible to remedy a defect liable to render a merger void, the competent court shall grant the companies involved a period of time within which to rectify the situation;
   (e) a judgment declaring a merger void shall be published in the manner prescribed by the laws of each Member State in accordance with Article 16;
   (f) where the laws of a Member State permit a third party to challenge such a judgment, that party may do so only within 6 months of publication of the judgment in the manner prescribed by Section 1 of Chapter II of Title I;
   (g) a judgment declaring a merger void shall not of itself affect the validity of obligations owed by or in relation to the acquiring company which arose before the judgment was published and after the date on which the merger takes effect;

(h) companies which have been parties to a merger shall be jointly and severally liable in respect of the obligations of the acquiring company referred to in point (g).

2. By way of derogation from point (a) of paragraph 1, the laws of a Member State may also provide for the nullity of a merger to be ordered by an administrative authority if an appeal against such a decision lies to a court. Point (b) and points (d) to (h) of paragraph 1 shall apply by analogy to the administrative authority. Such nullification proceedings may not be initiated more than 6 months after the date on which the merger takes effect.
3. The laws of the Member States on the nullity of a merger pronounced following any supervision other than judicial or administrative preventive supervision of legality shall not be affected.

19.5 *IGI* v. *Cicenia* Case

In *IGI* v. *Cicenia* (C-394/18, *IGI* v. *Cicenia et al.*, ECLI:EU:C:2020:56) the request has been made in proceedings between I.G.I. Srl, on the one hand, and Maria Grazia Cicenia, Mario Di Pierro, Salvatore de Vito and Antonio Raffaele, on the other hand, concerning the possibility for the latter, as creditors of a company being divided which had a part of its assets transferred to I.G.I., to bring an *actio pauliana* so as to have the instrument of division declared without effect vis-à-vis them, and to bring enforcement or protective actions in relation to the assets transferred to I.G.I.

An Italian building company (Costruzioni Ing. G. Iandolo Srl, or the 'company being divided') transferred, within the context of a division by formation of a new company, a part of its assets to a newly established recipient company (I.G.I. Srl, or the 'recipient company'). Taking the view that the division had caused the company being divided to lose a large part of its assets and that the company now owned only land plots of low value, some creditors brought an action against both companies before the District Court of Avellino (Italy). Principally, they brought an action to set aside the transaction (a so-called *actio pauliana*), requesting that the transfer of assets being the consequence of the division be declared without effect vis-à-vis the plaintiff creditors. As an alternative, they requested that both companies be declared jointly and severally liable for the debts of the company being divided .

The District Court of Avellino allowed the principal claim of the creditors and declared the asset transfer instrument contained in the instrument of division without effect vis-à-vis the creditors. The two companies appealed against that judgment before the Court of Appeals of Naples (Italy), arguing that – both under Italian and EU law – creditors of companies involved in a division may enjoy a sole judicial remedy, i.e., to object to the division before it is registered in the commercial register. In addition, the appellant companies also stated that Italian insolvency law – which is more severe on this point than European Union law – precludes the possibility to declare invalid an instrument of division after its publication formalities have been completed.

Therefore, even an action to set aside a division transaction should be deemed inadmissible.

Considering wide discussion on these points in the Italian case law and law reviews, the Court of Appeals of Naples stayed the proceedings and referred two questions to the Court of Justice EU for a preliminary ruling with regards to Articles 12 and 19 of Sixth Council Directive 82/891/EEC of 17 December 1982 based on Article 54(3)(g) of the Treaty, concerning the division of public limited-liability companies ('the Sixth Directive').

As mentioned, it is highly disputed among Italian Courts whether an action to set aside a division is permissible, in other words, whether it conflicts with the law of divisions implementing the Sixth Directive (now Articles 135–160 Directive 2017/1132/EU). It is worth mentioning that the Italian law of divisions (as well as mergers and conversions) is applicable to all companies and firms, regardless of whether the interested company is a 'società per azioni' (the type of company referred to in the annex to the Directive for Italy) or another type of company.

Some court decisions, along with some commentators, believe that both Italian and EU law adopt a broad concept of 'nullity' of a division, also including actions to set aside, the purpose of which is to declare the division ineffective vis-à-vis the interested creditors. As a consequence, an *actio pauliana* would not be admissible in case of divisions. On the one hand, EU law does not list actions to set aside amongst the cases where 'nullity' of a division may be declared. On the other hand, Italian law – being more restrictive than EU law – does not permit a declaration of 'nullity' of a division in any case.

Moreover, the same line of reasoning holds that, since creditors are granted a right to object to the division before it is implemented, allowing an action to set aside would conflict with the rationale behind this remedy, which is to grant to interested creditors immediate payment or an adequate guarantee.

Lastly, it is argued that granting an action to set aside would be useless because the effects of the action are equivalent to the possibility, granted by both EU and Italian law, to claim payment of debts of the divided companies from all recipients of the division. These companies are jointly and severally liable – pro rata – for obligations entered by the divided company before the instrument of division has been implemented.

Other decisions, however, do not share the following assumptions: (1) that an action to set aside affects the validity of the division; (2) that the objection procedure prevents creditors from exercising other remedies (in cases where there are grounds for the exercise of such remedies); and (3) that the joint and several liability of the recipient companies is equivalent to an action to set aside a division operation. Therefore, these court decisions – amongst which that of the court of first instance in the case of *IGI* v. *Cicenia* – allow actions to set aside a division of companies.

Being aware of these diverging opinions, the Court of Appeals of Naples stayed the proceedings and referred the two aforementioned questions to the

CJEU for a preliminary ruling. With its first question, the referring court asked whether Article 12 of the Sixth Directive must be interpreted as precluding the creditors of the company being divided (whose credit interests antedate that division and who did not take advantage of the protection tools provided in the legislation implementing that article) from bringing an *actio pauliana* after the division has been implemented, in order to have the division declared ineffective and to bring enforcement or protective action in relation to the assets transferred to the recipient company.

By its second question, the referring court asked whether Article 19 of the Sixth Directive, which lays down nullity rules for divisions, must be interpreted as precluding the creditors of the company being divided from bringing, after the division has been implemented, an *actio pauliana* which does not affect the validity of that division but merely allows for that division to be rendered unenforceable against those creditors.

The CJEU has negatively solved both questions, affirming that:

C-394/18, *IGI v Cicenia et al.*, ECLI:EU:C:2020:56, Operative Parts

1. Article 12 of Sixth Council Directive 82/891/EEC of 17 December 1982 based on Article 54 (3)(g) of the Treaty, concerning the division of public limited liability companies, as amended by Directive 2007/63/EC of the European Parliament and of the Council of 13 November 2007, read in conjunction with Articles 21 and 22 of Directive 82/891, must be interpreted as not precluding the creditors of the company being divided whose credit interests antedate that division, who did not take advantage of the creditor protection tools provided for in the national legislation implementing that article, from bringing an actio pauliana after the division has been implemented, in order to obtain a declaration that the division in question has no effect against them and to bring enforcement or protective action in relation to the assets transferred to the newly formed company.
2. Article 19 of Directive 82/891, as amended by Directive 2007/63, read in conjunction with Articles 21 and 22 of Directive 82/891, which lays down nullity rules for divisions, must be interpreted as not precluding the creditors of the company being divided from bringing, after the division has been implemented, an actio pauliana which does not affect the validity of that division but merely allows for that division to be rendered unenforceable against those creditors.

The reasoning behind the CJEU judgment is crystal clear.

As regards the first question, the Court observes that under Article 12(1) of the Sixth Directive, the Member States must provide for an adequate system of protection for the interests of the creditors of the companies involved in a division whose claims antedate publication of the draft terms of division and have not yet fallen due at the time of such publication. The same Article 12 of the Sixth Directive, in its second paragraph, establishes that the Member States must at least provide that such creditors are to be entitled to obtain adequate safeguards where the financial situations of the company being divided and of the company to which the obligation will be transferred, make such protection necessary and where those creditors do not already have such safeguards. Furthermore, the Member States may provide that the newly formed companies are to be jointly and severally liable for the obligations of the company being divided (Article 12(3) of the Sixth Directive).

Given this picture of EU law of divisions, the Court observes that the *actio pauliana* is not listed amongst the tools for protecting the creditors of a company being divided. Despite this, the court marks that the use of the expression 'at least' in Article 12(2) of the Sixth Directive indicates that the article provides for a minimum system of protection for the interests of the creditors of the companies involved in a division whose claims antedate publication of the draft terms of division and have not yet fallen due at the time of such publication. Therefore, that paragraph does not prevent the Member States from providing tools for protecting the interests of those additional creditors in relation to those claims (IGI v Cicenia C-394/18, § 67).

As a consequence, Article 12 of the Sixth Directive does not exclude the possibility, for the creditors of a company being divided, to bring an *actio pauliana*, where the financial situation of the company being divided and that of the company to which the obligation will be transferred in accordance with the draft terms of division make such protection necessary.

In addition, it is noted that Article 12 of the Sixth Directive does not require the protection for the creditors of newly formed companies provided for by the Member States to be equivalent to that provided for the creditors of a company being divided. It therefore follows from all those provisions that under the Sixth Directive, the minimum harmonisation of the protection of the interests of the creditors of companies involved in a division does not preclude, within the context of a division by the formation of a new company, as is the case in the main proceedings, priority being given to the protection of the interests of the creditors of the company being divided (IGI v Cicenia C-394/18, §§ 73–74).

As regards the second question, the Court observes that Article 19 of the Sixth Directive (which outlines nullity rules for divisions) limits the cases in which nullity can arise, restricts the period within which nullification proceedings may be commenced, and provides that, where it is possible to remedy a defect liable to render a division void, a period of time is to be granted to the companies involved to rectify the situation.

Notwithstanding that the concept of 'nullity' is not defined in the Sixth Directive, it is arguable that 'the concept of "nullity", in its usual meaning, refers to actions seeking the annulment of an act, that result in its elimination and that have an effect erga omnes' (IGI v Cicenia C-394/18, § 80). Article 19 (1)(b) of the Sixth Directive states that divisions which have taken effect may be declared void in three cases only: (1) if there has been no judicial or administrative preventive supervision of their legality; (2) if they have not been drawn up and certified in due legal form; or (3) if it is shown that the decision of the general meeting which approved the draft terms of division is void or voidable under national law. 'Those three cases in which nullity can arise concern the coming into being of the division and affect its very existence. Therefore, these are cases which result in the elimination of the division' (IGI v Cicenia C-394/18, § 83).

The Court expresses the opinion that an *actio pauliana* 'has the sole aim of protecting creditors to whose rights the division has caused harm', not to penalise failure to comply with the requirements for the coming into being of the instrument of division. It follows that: the *actio pauliana* brought by the respondents in the main proceedings under Article 2901 of the Civil Code only allows for the division in question, in particular the transfer of certain assets referred to in the instrument of division, to be declared unenforceable against those respondents. That action does not affect the validity of that division, does not result in its elimination and does not have an effect erga omnes (*IGI* v Cicenia C-394/18, §§ 85–86).

In light of all of these considerations, as already reported, the Court concludes that the answer to both questions shall be negative.

The decision of the CJEU has been fully endorsed and it is useful to read the reasoning.

Nicola de Luca, '*Actio Pauliana* and Divisions (IGI v Cicenia, C-394/18): Not Everything That Is Done, Is Well Done', 17 *ECL* 97–101, at 100–101 (2020)

[I]n the Luxembourg judges' decision, it was somewhat obvious that to questions posed by the referring court 'the Court of Justice [would have given] a solution in the sense that the admissibility of the action to set aside, affecting the effectiveness of the transfer of assets and not the validity of the instrument of division, is not precluded by the European provisions'. The predictability of the CJEU's solution, however, does not diminish the relevance of the issue that arises in Italian law.

To analyse the impact of the CJEU's decision, it is useful to consider first the question raising the doubt that an action to set aside may conflict with the rule restricting the cases in which 'nullity' of a division operation may be declared. As the Court puts it, 'nullity' refers to actions seeking the annulment of an act, that result in its elimination and that have an effect erga omnes. The Court takes the view that an actio pauliana does not affect the validity of the division but merely allows for that division to be rendered unenforceable against those creditors; hence, it is admissible.

EU law defines a division by the formation of new companies as follows: an operation whereby a company transfers to one or more newly-formed companies (all or part of) its assets and liabilities in exchange for the allocation to the shareholders of the company being divided of shares in the recipient companies. Contrary to some decisions of Italian courts and the opinion of some authoritative legal scholars, an actio pauliana does not aim at declaring the newly-formed (recipient) company null and void, rather at making the transfer to that recipient company ineffective vis-à-vis the creditors. The consequence of a successful *actio pauliana* is that only some effects of the division operation are set aside: reference is made 'to the asset transfer instrument contained in the instrument of division'. So, even if the newly-formed company survives, its directors must re-transfer the assets (and liabilities) to the company being divided, in case it has not ceased to exist, for the benefit of the latter's creditors.

The idea that the transfer of assets may be ineffective, although the instrument of division is valid, perfectly fits with the doctrine that recognises the viability of an action to set aside a contribution in kind, whilst maintaining the validity of the instrument of constitution of a company. Indeed, Article 11 of Directive 2017/1132/EU defines the grounds for declaring the nullity of a company: as clarified in Marleasing, nullity of a company may not be declared for grounds not listed in the directive, e.g. a sham transaction, but in no case does such a restriction limit the possibility to set aside a contribution in kind found to be a fraud to creditors. As nullity of a company and that of a division are similar cases, solutions must be harmonious.

This being clarified, the solution to the other question referred to the CJEU – as to whether other means provided for in the interest of creditors preclude the admissibility of an action to set aside – may be better understood and approved. Some domestic decisions maintain that the objection granted to creditors before the division is the only tool of protection of which creditors may avail themselves. The decision of the CJEU easily proves this assumption to be wrong, as EU law requires that creditors are granted at least the right to object to the proposed division. The CJEU's decision, however, does not directly tackle another argument which is generally underlined by those who hold that the actio pauliana is not permissible in case of divisions. Indeed, some legal scholars are of the opinion that the joint and several liability of the recipient companies is equivalent to the effects of an action to set aside, as all assets transferred to the recipient companies are still available for the satisfaction of creditors of the company being divided.

There are at least two reasons to reject the above argument. First, the possibility to claim joint and several liability of the recipient companies does not give creditors of the company being divided a right to bring enforcement or protective actions in relation to the assets transferred, in case these are no longer in the availability of the recipient company; an action to set aside would indeed grant this opportunity. Second, if it were true that joint and several liability of the recipient companies grants the same effects as an action to set aside, it would be impossible to understand why EU law worries about creditors' protection and grants them at least the right to make an objection and request adequate guarantees. Instead, as creditors may be negatively affected by a division operation regardless of whether the recipient companies are jointly and severally liable with the company being divided, an action to set aside shall be deemed admissible, as it proves to be useful.

FURTHER READING

Nicola de Luca, '*Actio Pauliana* and Divisions (IGI v Cicenia, C-394/18): Not Everything That Is Done, Is Well Done', 17 *ECL* 97–101 (2020).

David Ramos Muñoz, 'Analysis of "I.G.I. v Maria Grazia Cicenia"', available at https://eulawlive.com/.

David Ramos Muñoz, Monserrat Rodriguez Riu, 'Reconciling legal certainty in corporate divisions with respect for Civil law remedies: Case C 394/18 IGI v. Maria Grazia Cicenia', 27 *Maastricht J. Eur. & Comp. L.* 358–378 (2020).

19.6 Cross-Border Mergers

Articles 118–133 Directive 2017/1132/EU – and formerly the Tenth Company Law Directive – set out the rules to facilitate mergers of limited-liability companies involving more than one country. More precisely: mergers of limited-liability companies formed in accordance with the law of a Member State and having their registered office, central administration, or principal place of business within the Union, provided that at least two of them are governed by the laws of different Member States (cross-border mergers). Given that the validity of the transaction in itself was already declared by the CJEU in *Sevic*, the tool of the Directive aims to provide a common legal framework according to which the merger procedure involving companies formed in accordance with laws of different Member States ought to be realised. Besides clarifying that, as a general rule, each merging company is governed by the provisions of its national law applicable also to domestic mergers, the Directive specifies all the steps that must be followed in order to complete the merger process.

First of all, the management or administrative organ of each of the merging companies draws up the common draft terms of the cross-border merger, which must include the mandatory basic content required by Article 122 Directive 2017/1132/EU (i.e., firms' main data, ratio applicable to shares and securities, timetable, rights or special advantages acquired) and be published in the manner prescribed by the norms of the respective State (Article 123 Directive 2017/1132/EU). Before the approval of the common draft terms by the general meeting of each merging company (Article 126 Directive 2017/1132/EU), two different reports are prepared. The first report explains and justifies the legal and economic aspects of the merger and presents its implications for shareholders, arranged by the management or administrative organ of each company (Article 124 Directive 2017/1132/EU). The second report, addressed to members and available at least one month before the date of the general meeting, is prepared by an independent expert (Article 125 Directive 2017/1132/EU). In 2019 it was clarified that Member States shall ensure that at least the members of the merging companies who voted against the approval of the common draft-terms of the cross-border merger have the right to dispose of their shares for adequate cash compensation (Article 126a Directive 2017/1132/EU). Also, additional safeguards shall be granted to creditors and workers (Articles 126b and 126c Directive 2017/1132/EU). A certificate of the designated competent authority is then issued in order to attest the proper completion of the pre-merger acts and formalities (Article 127 Directive 2017/1132/EU). The legal scrutiny of the whole procedure precedes the effective entry into force of the cross-border merger pursuant to the laws of the jurisdiction of the resulting company. Ultimately, the formalities concerning registration are completed in accordance with the norms of the respective merging companies' Member States.

The Directive, therefore, manages to provide the legal landmark to which companies could refer while giving, in addition, the opportunity to define the terms of some thorny issues such as the employee participation (Article 133 Directive 2017/1132/EU). Moreover, simplified formalities in the cases of mergers involving totally owned companies or companies which have 90 per cent of their shares held are also specified. Thus, the legal tool of the Directive, taking the path from *Sevic*, has clarified, simplified, and developed a framework fundamental for the enforcement of the freedom of establishment within the EU and effectively made the cross-border merger procedure more certain and less time- and cost-consuming.

FURTHER READING

Jonathan Rickford, 'The Proposed Tenth Company Law Directive on Cross Border Mergers and its Impact in the UK', 16 *EBLR* 1393–1414 (2005).

Matthias Pannier, 'The EU Cross Border Merger Directive – A New Dimension for Employee Participation and Company Restructuring', 16 *EBLR* 1424–1442 (2005).

Christian E. Decher, 'Cross Border Mergers: Traditional Structures and SE-Merger Structures', 4 *ECFR* 5–16 (2007).

Maria Doralt, 'Cross-border Mergers – A Glimpse into the Future', 4 *ECFR* 17–42 (2007).

Thomas Papadopoulos, *Cross-border Mergers. EU Perspectives and National Experiences* (Springer, 2019).

Marco Ventoruzzo, 'Cross-border Mergers, Change of Applicable Corporate Laws and Protection of Dissenting Shareholders: Withdrawal Rights under Italian Law', 4 *ECFR* 47–75 (2007).

Arianna Ugliano, 'The New Cross-border Merger Directive: Harmonisation of European Company Law and Free Movement', 18 *EBLR* 585–617 (2007).

19.7 Cross-Border Divisions and Conversions

As anticipated (§ 7.1), the Cross-Border Operations Directive has added provisions to Directive 2017/1132/EU regarding two more cross-border operations, namely divisions and conversions.

Articles 160a–160u Directive 2017/1132/EU lay down the rules on cross-border divisions. A cross-border division occurs where at least two of the limited-liability companies involved in the division are governed by the laws of different Member States. As already mentioned, in the case of a division transaction, a company transfers all of its assets and liabilities to two or more companies in the case of a *full division*, or transfers part of its assets and liabilities to one or more companies in the case of a *partial division* or *division by separation*: divisions by separation are recognised as such only in the context of a cross-border operation. Unlike the chapter on domestic divisions, that concerning cross-border divisions does not provide a harmonised framework for cross-border divisions in which a company transfers assets and liabilities to one or more existing companies (*division by acquisition*), rather than only by the *formation of new companies.*

Recital 8 Directive 2019/2121/EU (Cross-Border Operations Directive)

(...) as such cases have been viewed as being very complex, requiring the involvement of competent authorities from several Member States and entailing additional risks in terms of the circumvention of Union and national rules. The possibility of forming a company through a division by separation offers companies a new harmonised procedure in the internal market. However, companies should be free to directly set up subsidiaries in other Member States.

Similarly to cross-border mergers, the management or administrative organ of the dividing company draws up the draft terms of the cross-border division, which must include the particulars required by Article 160d Directive 2017/1132/EU. Before the approval of the draft terms by the general meeting of the dividing company (Article 160h Directive 2017/1132/EU), the report of the administrative or management body for members and employees (Article 160e Directive 2017/1132/EU) and that of an independent expert are prepared (Article 160f Directive 2017/1132/EU). Draft terms and reports (if such are required by the concerned Member State) are disclosed 30 days before the general meeting. Similarly to the new provisions on cross-border mergers, Article 160i Directive 2017/1132/EU also requires that Member States ensure that at least the members of a company being divided who voted against the approval of the draft terms of the cross-border division have the right to dispose of their shares for adequate cash compensation, provided that, as a result of the cross-border division, they would acquire shares in the recipient companies which would be governed by the law of a Member State other than the Member State of the company being divided. In case cash compensation offered to shareholders is considered inadequate, shareholders are entitled to claim additional cash compensation before the competent authority or body mandated under national law. Also, whilst Article 160j Directive 2017/1132/

UE draws up the requirements for creditors' protection, Articles 160k and 160l Directive 2017/1132/EU provide for information and consultation rights for employees, as well as for their participation in the recipient companies.

A certificate of the designated competent authority is then issued in order to attest the proper completion of the pre-division acts and formalities (Article 160m Directive 2017/1132/EU). The legal scrutiny of the whole procedure precedes the effective entry into force of the cross-border division pursuant to the laws of the jurisdiction of the recipient company or companies (Article 160o Directive 2017/1132/EU). The cross-border division is completed after registration (Article 160p Directive 2017/1132/EU), and entails the consequences provided for in Article 160r Directive 2017/1132/EU.

As regards cross-border conversions, the reasons for such an operation have already been discussed (§ 7.3). It is useful to give here some details on the operation itself and its process. Firstly, a cross-border conversion is defined as follows,

Article 86b(2) Directive 2017/1132/EU

'cross-border conversion' means an operation whereby a company, without being dissolved or wound up or going into liquidation, converts the legal form under which it is registered in a departure Member State into a legal form of the destination Member State, as listed in Annex II, and transfers at least its registered office to the destination Member State, while retaining its legal personality;

Considering that cross-border conversions affect only one company, incorporated under the rules of a certain Member State (the departure Member State), the law of the departure Member State shall govern those parts of the procedures and formalities to be complied with in connection with the cross-border conversion in order to obtain the pre-conversion certificate, and the law of the destination Member State shall govern those parts of the procedures and formalities to be complied with following receipt of the pre-conversion certificate (Article 86c Directive 2017/1132/EU). As with a cross-border merger, the management or administrative body of the company shall draw up the draft terms of a cross-border conversion, which must include the particulars listed by Article 86d Directive 2017/1132/EU and be published in the manner prescribed by the norms of the departure Member State (Article 86g Directive 2017/1132/EU). Before the approval of the draft terms by the general meeting of the company (Article 86h Directive 2017/1132/EU), similar reports as for cross-border mergers are prepared. The first report explains and justifies the legal and economic aspects of the conversion and presents its implications for shareholders, arranged by the management or administrative body of the company (Article 86e Directive 2017/1132/EU). The second report, addressed to members and available at least one month before the date of the general meeting, is prepared by an independent expert (Article 86f Directive 2017/1132/EU). The conversion shall be approved by the general meeting and requires a majority of not less than two thirds but not more than 90 per cent of the votes attached to the shares. Member States shall ensure that at least the members of the company who voted against the approval of the draft-terms of the cross-border conversion have the right to dispose of their shares for adequate cash compensation (Article 86i Directive 2017/1132/EU). Also, additional safeguards shall be granted to creditors and workers (Articles 86j–86l Directive 2017/1132/EU). A certificate of the designated competent authority is then issued in order to attest the proper completion of the pre-conversion acts and formalities (Article 86m Directive 2017/1132/EU). The pre-conversion certificate is then transferred to the competent authority of the destination Member State (Article 86n Directive 2017/1132/EU). The designed authority of the destination Member State scrutinises the legality of the cross-border conversion as regards that part of the procedure which is governed by the law of the destination Member State and approves the cross-border conversion (Article 86o Directive 2017/1132/EU). Then the cross-border conversion is registered and takes effect (Articles 86p–86q Directive 2017/1132/EU). Consequences of a cross-border conversion are described as follows,

Article 86r Directive 2017/1132/EU

A cross-border conversion shall, from the date referred to in Article 86q, have the following consequences:

(a) all the assets and liabilities of the company, including all contracts, credits, rights and obligations, shall be those of the converted company;
(b) the members of the company shall continue to be members of the converted company, unless they have disposed of their shares as referred to in Article 86i(1);
(c) the rights and obligations of the company arising from contracts of employment or from employment relationships and existing at the date on which the cross-border conversion takes effect shall be those of the converted company.

Article 86t Directive 2017/1132/EU

A cross-border conversion which has taken effect in compliance with the procedures transposing this Directive may not be declared null and void.

The first paragraph does not affect Member States' powers, inter alia, in relation to criminal law, the prevention and combatting of terrorist financing, social law, taxation and law enforcement, to impose measures and penalties, under national law, after the date on which the cross-border conversion took effect.

FURTHER READING

Jessica Schmidt, 'The Mobility Aspects of the EU Commission's Company Law Package: Or – the Good, the Bad and the Ugly', 16 *ECL* 13–17 (2019).

Jessica Schmidt, 'Cross-Border Mergers, Divisions and Conversions: Accomplishments and Deficits of the Company Law Package', 16 *ECFR* 222–272 (2019).

20

Dissolution and Insolvency

20.1 The Dissolution of Companies

As mentioned previously, merger, division, and conversion do not entail liquidation, nor dissolution of the company. Winding-up and liquidation aimed at the dissolution of the company may be voluntary or compulsory. Insolvency proceedings, where the assets of insolvent companies or firms are liquidated so that creditors may be paid at least in part, is the most important example of compulsory winding-up and liquidation.

ECL does not directly address winding-up, liquidation and dissolution of companies. Neither does a substantive European insolvency law – exception made for Directive 2019/1023/EU, examined later (§ 20.12) – exist. As the SE Statute plainly states it:

Article 63 Regulation 2001/2157/EC

As regards winding up, liquidation, insolvency, cessation of payments and similar procedures, an SE shall be governed by the legal provisions which would apply to a public limited-liability company formed in accordance with the law of the Member State in which its registered office is situated, including provisions relating to decision-making by the general meeting.

However, EU law partially covers cross-border insolvency, as regards the jurisdiction over the insolvent debtor and its assets. This issue will be addressed in §§ 20.2–20.10 in respect, in particular, of debtors being insolvent companies.

20.2 Cross-Border Insolvency in General

A situation of cross-border insolvency occurs when a debtor goes bankrupt – be it an individual or a company – and who has conducted his or her business in more than one Member State, and so has creditors and/or assets scattered across the Union.

This situation entails complicated consequences as, other than company law, insolvency law – and especially insolvency procedures – is not harmonised at Union level. The various Member States have their own regulations on insolvency proceedings that may be divergent from one another. Furthermore, such laws may be applicable either to undertakings (companies or firms) being nationals of the Member State itself, regardless of where the petition for bankruptcy is filed or the assets or the undertaking are located, or to any undertaking conducting businesses within the territory of the interested Member State, regardless of the nationality, or even a combination of the two criteria.

This situation may raise conflicts of jurisdiction between authorities of the Member States. These conflicts are to be settled by the applicable rules of international private law, thereby depending on bilateral or multilateral agreements in which Member States might take part.

With the aim of preventing such conflicts, the EU institutions – acting under the authority of Article 81 TFEU which allows them to achieve the scope of judicial cooperation in civil matters – have delivered Regulation 2000/1346/EC of the Council, of 29 May 2000, on insolvency proceedings (hereafter, the 'Regulation'), which has more recently been replaced by a recast (and deeply amended) Regulation 2015/848/EU of the European Parliament and of the Council, of 20 May 2015, (hereafter, the 'Recast Regulation'). The latter entered into force as of 17 June 2017.

Recital 6 Regulation 2015/848/EU

This Regulation should include provisions governing jurisdiction for opening insolvency proceedings and actions which are directly derived from insolvency proceedings and are closely linked with them. This Regulation should also contain provisions regarding the recognition and enforcement of judgments issued in such proceedings, and provisions regarding the law applicable to insolvency proceedings. In addition, this Regulation should lay down rules on the coordination of insolvency proceedings which relate to the same debtor or to several members of the same group of companies.

Insolvency of undertakings and, in particular, cross-border insolvency, has become a critical matter in the last two decades, where significant financial crises have led many EU and non-EU multinational firms to bankruptcy or at least to undergo reorganisation (e.g., at the beginning of the millennium, Enron, WorldCom, Parmalat, and the accounting firm Arthur Andersen; later in the same decade Lehman Brothers, Merrill Lynch, Chrysler, GM, and others). Insolvency law wears – much more than company law – the heavy burden of balancing the interests of creditors to their best satisfaction with the protection of all the other interests involved, such as those of workers, suppliers, and other related parties, as well as all debt or equity investors.

The complexity of balancing these varying interests is magnified in case the undertaking operates cross-border.

Recital 4 Regulation 2015/848/EU

The activities of undertakings have more and more cross-border effects and are therefore increasingly being regulated by Union law. The insolvency of such undertakings also affects the proper functioning of the internal market, and there is a need for a Union act requiring coordination of the measures to be taken regarding an insolvent debtor's assets.

This need has long been considered compelling by the Member States, but it was not until the very beginning of the 2000s that the Regulation dealing with cross-border insolvency saw the light of day.

In contrast to the CJEU case law allowing the primary, as well as the secondary, right of establishment despite the fact that this may lead to forum shopping (*see*, in particular, the *Segers*, *Centros*, *Inspire Art*, and *Polbud* cases, in Chapter 5, § 5.9, and Chapter 6, §§ 6.2–6.4), the ultimate aim of a regulation on cross-border insolvency is to prevent forum shopping by undertakings. Indeed, the European institutions have adopted a hostile approach to forum shopping in insolvency law, which is deemed fit to jeopardise the good functioning of the internal market.

Recital 5 Regulation 2015/848/EU

It is necessary for the proper functioning of the internal market to avoid incentives for parties to transfer assets or judicial proceedings from one Member State to another, seeking to obtain a more favourable legal position to the detriment of the general body of creditors (forum shopping).

The contrast between the general approach and that taken in the Regulation, as well as in the Recast Regulation, is not without reason. Indeed, it probably depends on the fact that forum shopping may be allowed only in cases where the various legislations are harmonised: in the absence of uniform conditions, insolvent debtors would find it useful to migrate abroad, in search of a forum that guarantees the interests of the debtor's management and owners, notwithstanding that this may harm the interests of creditors and other related parties.

Therefore, in the field of insolvency law, because of the deep differences existing amongst the several domestic insolvency regimes, and the usual reluctance of the Member States to relinquish portions of their sovereignty to the Union, the current state of EU law does not permit forum shopping. This is, however, only a stage in the development of EU law, which might later consider harmonising insolvency law. Only recently, the Parliament and the EU Commission have approved Directive 2019/1023/EU of 20 June 2019 on preventive restructuring frameworks, on discharge of debt and disqualifications, and on measures to increase the efficiency of procedures concerning restructuring, insolvency, and discharge of debt. Some detail will be given later at § 20.12.

For the time being, the Recast Regulation does not address substantive law matters, as Recital 22 Regulation 2015/848/EU clarifies.

Recital 22 Regulation 2015/848/EU

This Regulation acknowledges the fact that as a result of widely differing substantive laws it is not practical to introduce insolvency proceedings with universal scope throughout the Union. The application without exception of the law of the State of the opening of proceedings would, against this background, frequently lead to difficulties. This applies, for example, to the widely differing national laws on security interests to be found in the Member States. Furthermore, the preferential rights enjoyed by some creditors in insolvency proceedings are, in some cases, completely different. At the next review of this Regulation, it will be necessary to identify further measures in order to improve the preferential rights of employees at European level. This Regulation should take account of such differing national laws in two different ways. On the one hand, provision should be made for special rules on the applicable law in the case of particularly significant rights and legal relationships (e.g. rights in rem and contracts of employment). On the other hand, national proceedings covering only assets situated in the State of the opening of proceedings should also be allowed alongside main insolvency proceedings with universal scope. Consequently, neither the Regulation nor the Recast Regulation could provide uniform substantive law provisions for the Member States; rather, they confine themselves to the identification of the national court competent to open insolvency proceedings and the establishment of a mechanism for the automatic recognition of such proceedings (and their effects) throughout the Union.

Considering the above, the following paragraphs will only give a general overview of EU insolvency law, along with a focus on the main issues related to company law, such as the definition of the 'centre of main interests' (COMI) as a connecting factor for determining the jurisdiction to open an insolvency proceeding in a case where the insolvent debtor is a company or firm, and the problems arising when insolvency of a group of companies is at issue.

FURTHER READING

Alfried Heidbrink, Catia Tomasetti, Maurizio Schiliro, Joost Vrancken Peeters, Claudi Rossell, Alicia Videon, and Julia McCabe, 'Country Status Reports on EU Insolvency Regulation: Three Years in Force', 2 *ECL* 66–82 (2005).

Paul J. Omar, 'The Convergence of Company and Insolvency Initiatives within the European Union', 2 *ECL* 59–65 (2005).
Bob Wessels, 'The EC Insolvency Regulation: Three Years in Force', 2 *ECL* 50–58 (2005).
Michel Menjucq, 'EC-Regulation No 1346/2000 on Insolvency Proceedings and Groups of Companies', 5 *ECFR* 135–147 (2008).
Reinhard Bork and Renato Mangano, *European Cross-border Insolvency Law* (Oxford University Press, 2016).

20.3 Main and Secondary Proceedings

As mentioned earlier, the Regulation and the Recast Regulations do not set out an EU insolvency procedure as such; rather, they establish that there can be only one national court having jurisdiction to open the so-called main insolvency proceedings, governed by the law of the opening State, and that their effects be compulsorily recognised across the Union. In addition to these main proceedings, however, EU insolvency law also provides for the possibility to open one or more secondary proceedings. The rationale and the details of such two-fold structure are laid down as follows:

Recital 23 Regulation 2015/848/EU

This Regulation enables the main insolvency proceedings to be opened in the Member State where the debtor has the centre of its main interests. Those proceedings have universal scope and are aimed at encompassing all the debtor's assets. To protect the diversity of interests, this Regulation permits secondary insolvency proceedings to be opened to run in parallel with the main insolvency proceedings. Secondary insolvency proceedings may be opened in the Member State where the debtor has an establishment. The effects of secondary insolvency proceedings are limited to the assets located in that State. Mandatory rules of coordination with the main insolvency proceedings satisfy the need for unity in the Union.

Since it justifies the opening of secondary proceedings, the protection of the 'diversity of interest' turns out to be a delicate and important concept under the Recast Regulation. Therefore, it is specified under which circumstances it is convenient to open these proceedings.

Recital 40 Regulation 2015/848/EU

Secondary insolvency proceedings can serve different purposes, besides the protection of local interests. Cases may arise in which the insolvency estate of the debtor is too complex to administer as a unit, or the differences in the legal systems concerned are so great that difficulties may arise from the extension of effects deriving from the law of the State of the opening of proceedings to the other Member States where the assets are located. For that reason, the insolvency practitioner in the main insolvency proceedings may request the opening of secondary insolvency proceedings where the efficient administration of the insolvency estate so requires.

This dualistic system finds its detailed regulation in Article 3 as well as in Chapter III (Articles 34–52).

On the one hand, Article 3(2–4) Regulation 2015/848/EU provides the general features of the relationship between the two types of proceedings.

Article 3(2–4) Regulation 2015/848/EU

2. Where the centre of the debtor's main interests is situated within the territory of a Member State, the courts of another Member State shall have jurisdiction to open insolvency proceedings against that debtor only if it possesses an establishment within the territory of that other Member State. The effects of those proceedings shall be restricted to the assets of the debtor situated in the territory of the latter Member State.
3. Where insolvency proceedings have been opened in accordance with paragraph 1, any proceedings opened subsequently in accordance with paragraph 2 shall be secondary insolvency proceedings.
4. The territorial insolvency proceedings referred to in paragraph 2 may only be opened prior to the opening of main insolvency proceedings in accordance with paragraph 1 where
   (a) insolvency proceedings under paragraph 1 cannot be opened because of the conditions laid down by the law of the Member State within the territory of which the centre of the debtor's main interests is situated; or
   (b) the opening of territorial insolvency proceedings is requested by: (i) a creditor whose claim arises from or is in connection with the operation of an establishment situated within the territory of the Member State where the opening of territorial proceedings is requested; or (ii) a public authority which, under the law of the Member State within the territory of which the establishment is situated, has the right to request the opening of insolvency proceedings.

When main insolvency proceedings are opened, the territorial insolvency proceedings shall become secondary insolvency proceedings.

On the other hand, Chapter III sets out a detailed discipline that specifically concerns secondary proceedings. In particular, Article 34 deals with their opening.

Article 34 Regulation 2015/848/EU

Where main insolvency proceedings have been opened by a court of a Member State and recognised in another Member State, a court of that other Member State which has jurisdiction pursuant to Article 3(2) may open secondary insolvency proceedings in accordance with the provisions set out in this Chapter. Where the main insolvency proceedings required that the debtor be insolvent, the debtor's insolvency shall not be re-examined in the Member State in which secondary insolvency proceedings may be opened. The effects of secondary insolvency proceedings shall be restricted to the assets of the debtor situated within the territory of the Member State in which those proceedings have been opened.

Because the effects of such proceedings are restricted to the debtor's assets situated in the opening Member State, it is also provided that:

Article 35 Regulation 2015/848/EU

Save as otherwise provided for in this Regulation, the law applicable to secondary insolvency proceedings shall be that of the Member State within the territory of which the secondary insolvency proceedings are opened.

In this respect, the Recast Regulation better acknowledges than the Regulation that secondary proceedings can be potentially detrimental to the efficient administration of the debtor's estate, in that they can complicate and slow down the main proceedings. Therefore, it introduces three improvements to the previous regulation.

The first is laid under Article 36, which is expressly aimed at avoiding the opening of unnecessary secondary proceedings.

Article 36 Regulation 2015/848/EU

1. In order to avoid the opening of secondary insolvency proceedings, the insolvency practitioner in the main insolvency proceedings may give a unilateral undertaking (the 'undertaking') in respect of the assets located in the Member State in which secondary insolvency proceedings could be opened, that when distributing those assets or the proceeds received as a result of their realisation, it will comply with the distribution and priority rights under national law that creditors would have if secondary insolvency proceedings were opened in that Member State. The undertaking shall specify the factual assumptions on which it is based, in particular in respect of the value of the assets located in the Member State concerned and the options available to realise such assets.
2. Where an undertaking has been given in accordance with this Article, the law applicable to the distribution of proceeds from the realisation of assets referred to in paragraph 1, to the ranking of creditors' claims, and to the rights of creditors in relation to the assets referred to in paragraph 1 shall be the law of the Member State in which secondary insolvency proceedings could have been opened. The relevant point in time for

determining the assets referred to in paragraph 1 shall be the moment at which the undertaking is given ...

6. An undertaking given and approved in accordance with this Article shall be binding on the estate ...
7. Where the insolvency practitioner has given an undertaking, it shall inform local creditors about the intended distributions prior to distributing the assets and proceeds referred to in paragraph 1. If that information does not comply with the terms of the undertaking or the applicable law, any local creditor may challenge such distribution before the courts of the Member State in which main insolvency proceedings have been opened in order to obtain a distribution in accordance with the terms of the undertaking and the applicable law. In such cases, no distribution shall take place until the court has taken a decision on the challenge.
8. Local creditors may apply to the courts of the Member State in which [the] main insolvency proceedings have been opened, in order to require the insolvency practitioner in the main insolvency proceedings to take any suitable measures necessary to ensure compliance with the terms of the undertaking available under the law of the State of the opening of main insolvency proceedings.
9. Local creditors may also apply to the courts of the Member State in which secondary insolvency proceedings could have been opened in order to require the court to take provisional or protective measures to ensure compliance by the insolvency practitioner with the terms of the undertaking.
10. The insolvency practitioner shall be liable for any damage caused to local creditors as a result of its non-compliance with the obligations and requirements set out in this Article.

The second improvement is the judicial review of the decision to open secondary proceedings.

Article 39 Regulation 2015/848/EU

The insolvency practitioner in the main insolvency proceedings may challenge the decision to open secondary insolvency proceedings before the courts of the Member State in which secondary insolvency proceedings have been opened on the ground that the court did not comply with the conditions and requirements of Article 38.

The third improvement consists of strengthening the coordination between the two types of proceedings, by providing a cooperation and exchange of information between insolvency practitioners (Article 41), courts (Article 42), and insolvency practitioners and courts (Article 43).

In addition to these innovations, the Recast Regulation also improved the actual mechanism concerning the decision to open secondary proceedings. In fact, under the new regulation, courts are empowered to refuse the opening of secondary proceedings if this would not be necessary to protect the interest of local creditors.

Article 38 Regulation 2015/848/EU

1. A court seised of a request to open secondary insolvency proceedings shall immediately give notice to the insolvency practitioner or the debtor in possession in the main insolvency proceedings and give it an opportunity to be heard on the request.
2. Where the insolvency practitioner in the main insolvency proceedings has given an undertaking in accordance with Article 36, the court referred to in paragraph 1 of this Article shall, at the request of the insolvency practitioner, not open secondary insolvency proceedings if it is satisfied that the undertaking adequately protects the general interests of local creditors.
3. Where a temporary stay of individual enforcement proceedings has been granted in order to allow for negotiations between the debtor and its creditors, the court, at the request of the insolvency practitioner or the debtor in possession, may stay the opening of secondary insolvency proceedings for a period not exceeding 3 months, provided that suitable measures are in place to protect the interests of local creditors.

   The court referred to in paragraph 1 may order protective measures to protect the interests of local creditors by requiring the insolvency practitioner or the debtor in possession not to remove or dispose of any assets which are located in the Member State where its establishment is located unless this is done in the ordinary course of business. The court may also order other measures to protect the interest of local creditors during a stay, unless this is incompatible with the national rules on civil procedure.

   The stay of the opening of secondary insolvency proceedings shall be lifted by the court of its own motion or at the request of any creditor if, during the stay, an agreement in the negotiations referred to in the first subparagraph has been concluded.

   The stay may be lifted by the court of its own motion or at the request of any creditor if the continuation of the stay is detrimental to the creditor's rights, in particular if the negotiations have been disrupted or it has become evident that they are unlikely to be concluded, or if the insolvency practitioner or the debtor in possession has infringed the prohibition on disposal of its assets or on removal of them from the territory of the Member State where the establishment is located.
4. At the request of the insolvency practitioner in the main insolvency proceedings, the court referred to in paragraph 1 may open a type of insolvency proceedings as listed in Annex A other than the type initially requested, provided that the conditions for opening that type of proceedings under national law are fulfilled and that that type of proceedings is the most appropriate as regards the interests of the local creditors and coherence between the main and secondary insolvency proceedings ...

Last, but no less important, the Recast Regulation has repealed the requirement according to which secondary proceedings must necessarily be winding-up proceedings: rather these might also aim at reorganising the insolvent debtor. Such a requirement constituted a big hurdle to the successful rescue or restructuring of businesses, and is no longer in line with today's approach of national legislators to the issue of insolvency. Especially after the onset of the financial crisis in 2008, the protection of employment has been given much more importance under national laws, which in fact tend to avoid – where possible – the liquidation and shutting down of businesses. Safeguarding jobs and giving a second chance to honest entrepreneurs are the key elements of the new European approach to business failure that has inspired the Recast Regulation. Not by chance, following this path, Directive 2019/1023/EU was ultimately approved.

In light of all these innovations, arguably the secondary proceedings will no longer be a 'necessary evil', as some scholars defined them, but rather an opportunity.

John Anthony Edwards Pottow, 'A New Role for Secondary Proceedings in International Bankruptcies', 46 *Texas Int'l L.J.* 580–599, at 584 (2011)

In sum, the most accurate understanding (from the normative perspective of a universalist) of secondary proceedings is that they are a necessary evil. They are required to dampen territorialist and competitive impulses – perhaps tolerated due to the idiosyncrasies of local property law – but sit as an otherwise theoretical thorn in the side of universalists confronting a divergent array of priority rules. This begrudging tolerance explains why they are cut down through explicit scope restriction in universalist-animated legal documents like the UNCITRAL Model Law, Chapter 15, and so forth. The corollary observation to this characterization is that if one of the anchoring sticking points – divergence in priority rules – can be resolved, then secondary proceedings (at least in their current, stronger form) may no longer be needed.

FURTHER READING

John Anthony Edwards Pottow, 'A New Role for Secondary Proceedings in International Bankruptcies', 46 *Texas Int'l L.J.* 580–599 (2011).

20.4 The 'Centre of Main Interests' (COMI)

As mentioned earlier, in order to determine the jurisdiction in which to open insolvency proceedings, EU law refers to the concept of 'centre of main interests', or COMI, this being the place where the debtor conducts the administration of its interests on a regular basis and which is ascertainable by third parties. As regards companies, the COMI is presumed to be their registered office, provided that this has not moved to another Member State within the three months before the request for the opening of insolvency proceedings. As mentioned, this last rule aims at preventing forum shopping.

Article 3 Regulation 2015/848/EU

1. The courts of the Member State within the territory of which the centre of the debtor's main interests is situated shall have jurisdiction to open insolvency proceedings ('main insolvency proceedings'). The centre of main interests shall be the place where the debtor conducts the administration of its interests on a regular basis and which is ascertainable by third parties.

In the case of a company or legal person, the place of the registered office shall be presumed to be the centre of its main interests in the absence of proof to the contrary. That presumption shall only apply if the registered office has not been moved to another Member State within the 3-month period prior to the request for the opening of insolvency proceedings.

In the case of an individual exercising an independent business or professional activity, the centre of main interests shall be presumed to be that individual's principal place of business in the absence of proof to the contrary. That presumption shall only apply if the individual's principal place of business has not been moved to another Member State within the 3-month period prior to the request for the opening of insolvency proceedings.

In the case of any other individual, the centre of main interests shall be presumed to be the place of the individual's habitual residence in the absence of proof to the contrary. This presumption shall only apply if the habitual residence has not been moved to another Member State within the 6-month period prior to the request for the opening of insolvency proceedings.

The concept of a company's COMI has been better shaped by the CJEU in four landmark cases, *Eurofood*, *Interedil*, *Leonmobili*, and *Rastelli*, all examined in §§ 20.5–20.8.

As anticipated in Chapter 5, and more recently in *Kornhaas*, the CJEU returned to the point, this time being requested to shed some light on the relations between cross-border insolvency and freedom of establishment. This decision is examined in § 20.9.

FURTHER READING

Federico Maria Mucciarelli, 'The Transfer of the Registered Office and Forum-shopping in International Insolvency Cases: An Important Decision from Italy – Case Note on the Decision "B & C" of the Italian Corte di Cassazione', 2 *ECFR* 512–533 (2005).

Marek Szydło, 'The Notion of Comi in European Insolvency Law', 20 *EBLR* 747–766 (2009).

Dario Latella, 'The "COMI" Concept in the Revision of the European Insolvency Regulation', 11 *ECFR* 479–494 (2014).

Rolef J. de Weijs and Martijn S. Breeman, 'Comi-migration: Use or Abuse of European Insolvency Law?', 11 *ECFR* 495–530 (2014).

20.5 *Eurofood* Case

In *Eurofood* (C-341/04, Eurofood IFSC Ltd, [2006] ECR I-03813), the reference was made in the context of insolvency proceedings concerning the Irish company Eurofood IFSC Ltd ('*Eurofood*').

Eurofood IFSC Ltd was a subsidiary company of the Italian Parmalat SpA, with registered office in Dublin and whose principal objective was the provision of financing facilities for companies in the Parmalat group.

On 24 December 2003, Parmalat SpA was admitted to extraordinary administration proceedings in Italy and Mr Bondi was appointed as the extraordinary administrator of the company.

On 27 January 2004, the Bank of America NA applied to the High Court of Ireland for compulsory winding-up proceedings to be commenced against Eurofood and for the nomination of a provisional liquidator. That application was based on the contention that the company was insolvent. On the same day, the High Court complied with that request and appointed Mr Farrell as the provisional liquidator.

On 9 February 2004, the Italian Minister for Production Activities admitted Eurofood to the extraordinary administration proceedings and appointed Mr Bondi as the extraordinary administrator. After one day, an application was lodged before the *Tribunale Civile e Penale di Parma* (Italy) for a declaration that Eurofood was insolvent.

On 20 February 2004, the *Tribunale Civile e Penale di Parma*, taking the view that Eurofood's COMI was in Italy, held that it had international jurisdiction to determine whether Eurofood was in a state of insolvency.

On 23 March 2004 the High Court decided that, according to Irish law, the insolvency proceedings in respect of Eurofood had been opened in Ireland on the date on which the application was submitted by the Bank of America NA, namely 27 January 2004. Taking the view that the Eurofood's COMI was in Ireland, it held that the proceedings opened in Ireland were the main proceedings. It also held that the circumstances in which the proceedings were conducted before the *Tribunale Civile e Penale di Parma* were such as to justify, pursuant to Article 26 of the Regulation (Article 33 of the Recast Regulation), the refusal of the Irish courts to recognise the decision of that court. Finding that Eurofood was insolvent, the High Court made an order for winding-up and appointed Mr Farrell as the liquidator.

Mr Bondi having appealed against that judgment, the Supreme Court of Ireland considered it necessary to stay the proceedings and to refer to the CJEU for a preliminary ruling. Amongst other things, the CJEU was essentially asked the following, fundamental, question:

C-341/04, Eurofood IFSC Ltd, [2006] ECR I-03813, § 24

(4) Where,
  (a) the registered offices of a parent company and its subsidiary are in two different Member States,
  (b) the subsidiary conducts the administration of its interests on a regular basis in a manner ascertainable by third parties and in complete and regular respect for its own corporate identity in the Member State where its registered office is situated and
  (c) the parent company is in a position, by virtue of its shareholding and power to appoint directors, to control and does in fact control the policy of the subsidiary, in determining the 'centre of main interests', are the governing factors those referred to at (b) above or on the other hand those referred to at (c) above?

(5) Where it is manifestly contrary to the public policy of a Member State to permit a judicial or administrative decision to have legal effect in relation [to] persons or bodies whose right to fair procedures and a fair hearing has not been respected in reaching such a decision, is that Member State bound, by virtue of Article 17 of the said regulation, to give recognition to a decision of the courts of another Member State purporting to open insolvency proceedings in respect of a company, in a situation where the court of the first Member State is satisfied that the decision in question has been made in disregard of those principles and, in particular, where the applicant in the second Member State has refused, in spite of requests and contrary to the order of the court of the second Member State, to provide the provisional liquidator of the company, duly appointed in accordance with the law of the first Member State, with any copy of the essential papers grounding the application?

To this question, the CJEU answered as follows:

C-341/04, Eurofood IFSC Ltd, [2006] ECR I-03813, §§ 26–37

26 By its fourth question, which should be considered first since it concerns, in general, the system which the Regulation establishes for determining the competence of the courts of the Member States, the national court asks what the determining factor is for identifying the centre of main interests of a subsidiary company, where it and its parent have their respective registered offices in two different Member States.

27 The referring court asks how much relative weight should be given as between, on the one hand, the fact that the subsidiary regularly administers its interests, in a manner ascertainable by third parties and in respect for its own corporate identity, in the Member State where its registered office is situated and, on the other hand, the fact that the parent company is in a position, by virtue of its shareholding and power to appoint directors, to control the policy of the subsidiary.

28 Article 3 of the Regulation makes provision for two types of proceedings. The insolvency proceedings opened, in accordance with Article 3(1), by the competent court of the Member State within whose territory the centre of a debtor's main interests is situated, described as the 'main proceedings', produce universal effects in that they apply to the assets of the debtor situated in all the Member States in which the regulation applies. Although, subsequently, proceedings under Article 3(2) may be opened by the competent court of the Member State where the debtor has an establishment, those proceedings, described as 'secondary proceedings', are restricted to the assets of the debtor situated in the territory of the latter State.

29 Article 3(1) of the Regulation provides that, in the case of a company, the place of the registered office shall be presumed to be the centre of its main interests in the absence of proof to the contrary.

30 It follows that, in the system established by the Regulation for determining the competence of the courts of the Member States, each debtor constituting a distinct legal entity is subject to its own court jurisdiction.

31 The concept of the centre of main interests is peculiar to the Regulation. Therefore, it has an autonomous meaning and must therefore be interpreted in a uniform way, independently of national legislation.

32 The scope of that concept is highlighted by the 13th recital of the Regulation, which states that the 'centre of main interests' should correspond to the place where the debtor conducts the administration of his interests on a regular basis and is therefore ascertainable by third parties.

33 That definition shows that the centre of main interests must be identified by reference to criteria that are both objective and ascertainable by third parties. That objectivity and that possibility of ascertainment by third parties are necessary in order to ensure legal certainty and foreseeability concerning the determination of the court with jurisdiction to open main insolvency proceedings. That legal certainty and that foreseeability are all the more important in that, in accordance with Article 4(1) of the Regulation, determination of the court with jurisdiction entails determination of the law which is to apply.

34 It follows that, in determining the centre of the main interests of a debtor company, the simple presumption laid down by the Community legislature in favour of the registered office of that company can be rebutted only if factors which are both objective and ascertainable by third parties enable it to be established that an actual situation exists which is different from that which locating it at that registered office is deemed to reflect.

35 That could be so in particular in the case of a 'letterbox company' not carrying out any business in the territory of the Member State in which its registered office is situated.

36 By contrast, where a company carries on its business in the territory of the Member State where its registered office is situated, the mere fact that its economic choices are or can be controlled by a parent company in another Member State is not enough to rebut the presumption laid down by the Regulation.

37 In those circumstances, the answer to the fourth question must be that, where a debtor is a subsidiary company whose registered office and that of its parent company are situated in two different Member States, the presumption laid down in the second sentence of Article 3(1) of the Regulation, whereby the centre of main interests of that subsidiary is situated in the Member State where its registered office is situated, can be rebutted only if factors which are both objective and ascertainable by third parties enable it to be established that an actual situation exists which is different from that which locating it at that registered office is deemed to reflect. That could be so in particular in the case of a company not carrying out any business in the territory of the Member State in which its registered office is situated. By contrast, where a company carries on its business in the territory of the Member State where its registered office is situated, the mere fact that its economic choices are or can be controlled by a parent company in another Member State is not enough to rebut the presumption laid down by the Regulation.

FURTHER READING

Thomas Bachner, 'The Battle over Jurisdiction in European Insolvency Law – ECJ 2.5.2006, C-341/04 (Eurofood)', 3 *ECFR* 311–329 (2006).

Bob Wessels, 'The Place of the Registered Office of a Company: A Cornerstone in the Application of the EC Insolvency Regulation', 3 *ECL* 183–190 (2006).

20.6 *Interedil* Case

In *Interedil* (C-396/09, *Interedil srl*, [2011] ECR I-09915), the reference was made in proceedings between Interedil Srl, in liquidation ('*Interedil*'), on the one hand, and Fallimento Interedil Srl and Intesa Gestione Crediti SpA ('*Intesa*'), of which Italfondario SpA is the successor, on the other, concerning a petition for bankruptcy filed by Intesa against Interedil.

Interedil was constituted in the legal form of a '*società a responsabilità limitata*' under Italian law and had its registered office in Monopoli (Italy). On 18 July 2001, its registered office was transferred to London (United Kingdom). On the same date, it was removed from the register of companies of the Italian State. Following the transfer of its registered office, Interedil was registered with the United Kingdom register of companies and entered in the register as an 'FC' (Foreign Company).

On 28 October 2003, Intesa filed a petition with the *Tribunale di Bari* for the opening of bankruptcy ('*fallimento*') proceedings against Interedil. Interedil challenged the jurisdiction of that court on the ground that, as a result of the transfer of its registered office to the United Kingdom, only the courts of that Member State had jurisdiction to open insolvency proceedings. On 13 December 2003, Interedil requested that the Italian Supreme Court (*Corte Suprema di Cassazione*) give a ruling on the preliminary issue of jurisdiction.

On 20 May 2005, the *Corte Suprema di Cassazione* adjudicated by way of order on the preliminary issue of jurisdiction referred to it and held that the Italian courts had jurisdiction. It took the view that the presumption in the second sentence of Article 3(1) of the Regulation that the centre of main interests corresponded to the place of the registered office could be rebutted as a result of various circumstances, namely the presence of immovable property in Italy owned by Interedil, the existence of a lease agreement in respect of two hotel complexes and a contract concluded with a banking institution, and the fact that the Bari register of companies had not been notified of the transfer of Interedil's registered office. Doubting the validity of the *Corte Suprema di Cassazione*'s finding, in the light of the criteria established by the Court in Case C-341/04 *Eurofood IFSC*, [2006] ECR I-03813, the *Tribunale di Bari* decided to stay the proceedings and to refer the following questions to the Court for a preliminary ruling:

C-396/09, Interedil srl, [2011] ECR I-09915, § 17

1. Is the term 'the centre of a debtor's main interests' in Article 3(1) of [the] Regulation ... to be interpreted in accordance with Community law or national law, and, if the former, how is that term to be defined and what are the decisive factors or considerations for the purpose of identifying the 'centre of main interests'?
2. Can the presumption laid down in Article 3(1) of [the] Regulation ..., according to which '[i]n the case of a company ... the place of the registered office shall be presumed to be the centre of its main interests in the absence of proof to the contrary', be rebutted if it is established that the company carries on genuine business activity in a State other than that in which it has its registered office, or is it necessary, in order for the presumption to be deemed rebutted, to establish that the company has not carried on any business activity in the State in which it has its registered office?
3. If a company has, in a Member State other than that in which it has its registered office, immovable property, a lease agreement concluded by the debtor company with another company in respect of two hotel complexes, and a contract with a banking institution, are these sufficient factors or considerations to rebut the presumption laid down in Article 3(1) of [the] Regulation ... that the place of the company's 'registered office' is the centre of its main interests and are such circumstances sufficient for the company to be regarded as having an 'establishment' in that Member State within the meaning of Article 3(2) of [the] Regulation ... ?

4. If the ruling on jurisdiction by the Corte [suprema] di cassazione in the aforementioned Order ... is based on an interpretation of Article 3 of [the] Regulation ... which is at variance with that of the Court of Justice ..., is the application of that provision of Community law, as interpreted by the Court of Justice, precluded by Article 382 of the [Italian] Code of Civil Procedure, according to which rulings on jurisdiction by the Corte [suprema] di cassazione are final and binding?

Having examined the Case, the EJC ruled as follows:

C-396/09, Interedil srl, [2011] ECR I-09915, §§ 43–44, 59, 64 and Operative Parts 2–4

The term 'centre of a debtor's main interests' in Article 3(1) of Regulation No. 1346/2000 on insolvency proceedings must be interpreted by reference to European Union law.

That concept is peculiar to the Regulation and must therefore be interpreted in a uniform way, independently of national legislation.

For the purposes of determining a debtor company's main centre of interests, the second sentence of Article 3(1) of Regulation No. 1346/2000 on insolvency proceedings must be interpreted as meaning that a debtor company's main centre of interests must be determined by attaching greater importance to the place of the company's central administration, as it may be established by objective factors ascertainable by third parties. If the bodies responsible for the management and supervision of a company are to be found in the same place as its registered office and the management decisions of the company are taken, in a manner ascertainable by third parties, in that place, the presumption in that provision cannot be rebutted. If a company's central administration is not to be found in the same place as its registered office, the presence of company assets and the existence of contracts for the financial exploitation of those assets in a Member State other than that in which the registered office is situated cannot be regarded as sufficient factors to rebut the presumption unless a comprehensive assessment of all the relevant factors makes it possible to establish, in a manner ascertainable by third parties, that the company's actual centre of management and supervision and of the management of its interests is located in that other Member State.

When a debtor company's registered office is transferred before a request to open insolvency proceedings is lodged, the company's centre of main activities is presumed to be the place of its new registered office.

The term 'establishment' within the meaning of Article 3(2) of Regulation No 1346/2000 on insolvency proceedings must be interpreted as requiring the presence of a structure consisting of a minimum level of organisation and a degree of stability necessary for the purpose of pursuing an economic activity. The presence alone of goods in isolation or bank accounts does not, in principle, meet that definition.

FURTHER READING

Federico M. Mucciarelli, 'The Hidden Voyage of a Dying Italian Company, From the Mediterranean Sea to Albion – A Comment to the ECJ Decision "Interedil" on Cross-border Transfer of Registered Office before the Filing for Insolvency', 9 *ECFR* 571–579 (2012).

Renato Mangano, 'The Puzzle of the New European COMI Rules: Rethinking COMI in the Age of Multinational, Digital and Glocal Enterprises', 20 *EBOR* 779–800 (2019).

20.7 *Leonmobili* Case

A distinction of *Interedil* was later made in *Leonmobili* (C-353/15, *Leonmobili srl*, [2016] OJ C-326/4, 05-09-2016).

Leonmobili Srl ('*Leonmobili*') is a limited-liability company dealing with the wholesale and retail trade of furniture and furnishings, directed by Mr Leone and whose registered office was located in Modugno (Italy). On 18 July 2012, the shareholders' meeting decided to transfer the company to Bulgaria. Following this decision, the tax ID (VAT number) of said company was closed, its relations with various social bodies were resolved, and cancellation from the register of companies in Italy took place on 12 September 2012.

On the same day, *Leonmobili* was registered in the company register in Sofia (Bulgaria), and soon after, the shareholders' meeting appointed another director, of Bulgarian citizenship, who rented a property with machinery and equipment in Bulgaria to start a new phase of the activity with a new staff.

Homag Holzbearbeitungssysteme GmbH and seven other companies, holders of credits for a total amount of approximately €3 million, filed an application for the bankruptcy of *Leonmobili* before the *Tribunale di Bari* (Italy). The *Tribunale di Bari*, believing that the transfer of the *Leonmobili* headquarters to Bulgaria was fictitious and that the centre of main interest of the company remained in Italy, declared the bankruptcy of *Leonmobili*. Indeed, following the transfer of *Leonmobili* in Bulgaria, it was found that the Bulgarian director had conferred on Mr Leone a general power of attorney to act both in Italy and abroad in the name and on behalf of this company.

Mr Leone and *Leonmobili* lodged an appeal, claiming that the decision of *Tribunale di Bari* – confirmed meantime by the Italian *Corte di Cassazione* as concerns the Italian jurisdiction – infringed the principles that emerged in *Interedil*. The *Corte di Appello di Bari* stayed the proceedings and sought a preliminary ruling from the CJEU, on the question of whether, in the absence of an establishment in another Member State, the presumption referred to in paragraph 1, last part, and paragraph 2 of Article 3 of Regulation No 1346/2000, can be overcome by those who contest the jurisdiction, with proof that the centre of main interests is in a State other than that in which the company has placed the registered office.

The CJEU, although referring to both *Eurofood* and *Interedil*, distinguished the case and ruled on the stated question as follows:

C-353/15, *Leonmobili srl*, [2016] OJ C-326/4, 05-09-2016, Operative Part

Article 3(1) of Council regulation (EC) No 1346/2000 of 29 May 2000 on insolvency proceedings must be interpreted as meaning that, where a company's registered office has been transferred from one Member State to another Member State, the court seised, subsequent to that transfer, of an application to open insolvency proceedings in the Member State of origin may disregard the presumption that that company's centre of main interests is situated at the place of the new registered office and find that the centre of those interests remained, as at the date on which that application was brought before it, in that Member State of origin, although the company no longer had an establishment there, only if it is apparent from other objective evidence, ascertainable by third parties, that, nonetheless, the company's actual centre of management and supervision and of the management of its interests was still located there at that date.

20.8 *Rastelli* Case

In *Rastelli* (C-191/10, *Rastelli Davide e C. Snc* v. *Jean-Charles Hidoux*, [2011] ECR I-13209), the reference was made in the course of proceedings between the company Rastelli Davide e C. Snc ('*Rastelli*') and Mr Hidoux, in his capacity as liquidator appointed by the court for the company Médiasucre international ('*Médiasucre*'), concerning the joinder of Rastelli to insolvency proceedings opened in respect of Médiasucre.

By a judgment of 7 May 2007, the *Tribunal de commerce de Marseille* (Commercial Court, Marseille) put Médiasucre, which had its registered office in Marseille, into liquidation and appointed Mr Hidoux as liquidator.

Following that judgment, Mr Hidoux brought proceedings before that court against Rastelli, which had its registered office in Robbio (Italy). It requested that Rastelli be joined to the insolvency proceedings that had been opened against Médiasucre on the ground that the property of the two companies was intermixed.

By a judgment of 19 May 2008, the *Tribunal de commerce de Marseille* declined jurisdiction with regard to Article 3 of the Regulation, on the grounds that Rastelli's registered office was in Italy and that it had no establishment in France. Ruling on the procedural question raised by Mr Hidoux, the *Cour d'appel d'Aix-en-Provence* (Court of Appeal, Aix-en-Provence), by a judgment of 12 February 2009, set aside that judgment and held that the *Tribunal de commerce de Marseille* had jurisdiction. In that regard, the *Cour d'appel* held that the liquidator's application was not intended to open insolvency proceedings against Rastelli but to join it to the judicial liquidation already opened against Médiasucre and that, under Article L. 621–2 of the Commercial Code, the court which has jurisdiction to rule on the application for joinder is the court before which the proceedings were initially brought.

Ruling on an appeal brought against that judgment, the *Cour de cassation* decided to stay the proceedings and to refer the following questions to the Court of Justice for a preliminary ruling:

C-191/10, Rastelli Davide e C. Snc v. Jean-Charles Hidoux, [2011] ECR I-13209, § 12

1. Where a court in a Member State opens the main insolvency proceedings in respect of a debtor, on the view that the centre of the debtor's main interests is situated in the territory of that Member State, does [the Regulation] preclude the application, by that court, of a rule of national law conferring upon it jurisdiction to join to those proceedings a company whose registered office is in another Member State solely on the basis of a finding that the property of the debtor and the property of that company have been intermixed?
2. If the action for joinder falls to be categorised as the opening of new insolvency proceedings in respect of which the jurisdiction of the court of the Member State first seised is conditional on proof that the company to be joined has the centre of its main interests in that Member State, can such proof be inferred solely from the finding that the property of the two companies has been intermixed?

In examining the case, the CJEU largely referred to its previous rulings in *Eurofood* and *Interedil*. In particular, with regard to the first question, the Court ruled as follows:

C-191/10, Rastelli Davide e C. Snc v. Jean-Charles Hidoux, [2011] ECR I-13209, §§ 13–14, 19–29

13. By its first question, the national court is essentially asking whether the Regulation is to be interpreted as meaning that a court of a Member State that has opened main insolvency proceedings against a company, on the view that the centre of the debtor's main interests is situated in the territory of that Member State, can, under a rule of its national law, join to those proceedings a second company whose registered office is in another Member State solely on the basis that the property of the two companies has been intermixed.
14. It should be borne in mind at the outset that the Regulation does not contain a rule concerning judicial or legislative competence that expressly refers to the joinder to insolvency proceedings opened in one Member State of a company whose registered

office is in another Member State on the ground that the property of the two companies has been intermixed ...

19. It is, therefore, necessary to examine only whether jurisdiction to hear an action for the purposes of joinder of insolvency proceedings can be based on Article 3(1) of the Regulation.
20. In that context, it should be noted that the Court has held that Article 3(1) of the Regulation must be interpreted as meaning that it also confers international jurisdiction on the courts of the Member State within the territory of which insolvency proceedings were opened to hear an action which derives directly from the initial insolvency proceedings and which is closely connected with them, within the meaning of recital 6 in the preamble to the Regulation (Case C 339/07 Seagon [2009] ECR I 767, paragraphs 19 to 21). It must therefore be examined whether an application for joinder of insolvency proceedings on the ground that property has been intermixed can be deemed to be such an action.
21. Mr Hidoux and the French Government contend that the action for the purposes of joinder of insolvency proceedings on the ground that property has been intermixed must be considered as an action which derives directly from the initial insolvency proceedings and which is closely connected with them. In support of their contention, they argue that such a joinder does not have the consequence of instituting new proceedings, which would be independent in relation to the proceedings initially opened, but has the sole consequence of extending the initial proceedings to another entity (under French law, which is the law applicable to the initial proceedings under Article 4(1) of the Regulation). They infer from this that a French court that has opened main insolvency proceedings with regard to a company in France also has jurisdiction to join to the proceedings another company that has its registered office in another Member State.
22. That contention is based, essentially, on the argument that, in French law, extending the main insolvency proceedings does not institute new proceedings but simply joins an additional debtor, whose property is inseparable from that of the first debtor, to the proceedings that have already been opened.
23. That single procedure does not, however, alter the fact, referred to by the Netherlands and Austrian governments and by the European Commission, that joining to the initial proceedings an additional debtor, legally distinct from the debtor concerned by those proceedings, produces with regard to that additional debtor the same effects as the decision to open insolvency proceedings.
24. That analysis is supported by the fact, referred to by the national court, that although the single procedure is justified by the finding that the two debtors form a de facto unit because their property is intermixed, that finding has no bearing on the legal personality of the two debtors.
25. The Court has held that in the system established by the Regulation for determining the competence of the Member States, which is based on the centre of the debtor's main interests, each debtor constituting a distinct legal entity is subject to its own court jurisdiction (Eurofood IFSC, paragraph 30).

26. It follows that a decision producing, with regard to a legal entity, the same effects as the decision to open main insolvency proceedings can only be taken by the courts of the Member State that would have jurisdiction to open such proceedings ...
28. Therefore, the possibility that a court designated under that provision as having jurisdiction, with regard to a debtor, to join another legal entity to insolvency proceedings on the sole ground that their property has been intermixed, without considering where the centre of that entity's main interests is situated, would constitute a circumvention of the system established by the Regulation. This would result, inter alia, in a risk of conflicting claims to jurisdiction between courts of different Member States, which the Regulation specifically intended to prevent in order to ensure uniform treatment of insolvency proceedings within the European Union.
29. The answer to the first question is therefore that the Regulation is to be interpreted as meaning that a court of a Member State that has opened main insolvency proceedings against a company, on the view that the centre of the debtor's main interests is situated in the territory of that Member State, can, under a rule of its national law, join to those proceedings a second company whose registered office is in another Member State only if it is established that the centre of that second company's main interests is situated in the first Member State.

With respect to the second question, the CJEU's reasoning has been the following:

C-191/10, Rastelli Davide e C. Snc v. Jean-Charles Hidoux, [2011] ECR I-13209, §§ 30, 37–39

30. By its second question, the national court is essentially asking whether the Regulation is to be interpreted as meaning that, where a company, whose registered office is situated within the territory of a Member State, is subject to an action that seeks to extend to it the effects of insolvency proceedings opened in another Member State against another company established within the territory of that other Member State, the mere finding that the property of those companies has been intermixed is sufficient to establish that the centre of the main interests of the company concerned by the action is also situated in that other Member State ...
37. With regard to the situation, referred to in the second question, where the property of two companies is intermixed, it is apparent from the explanations provided by the French government that, to characterise such a situation, the national court uses two alternative criteria drawn, respectively, from the existence of intermingled accounts and from abnormal financial relations between the companies, such as the deliberate organisation of transfers of assets without consideration.
38. As has been submitted by the French, Netherlands and Austrian governments and by the European Commission, such factors are in general difficult to ascertain by third parties.

Furthermore, intermixing of property does not necessarily imply a single centre of interests. Indeed, it cannot be excluded that such intermixing may be organised from two management and supervision centres situated in two different Member States.

39. The answer to the question is, therefore, that the Regulation is to be interpreted as meaning that where a company, whose registered office is situated within the territory of a Member State, is subject to an action that seeks to extend to it the effects of insolvency proceedings opened in another Member State against another company established within the territory of that other Member State, the mere finding that the property of those companies has been intermixed is not sufficient to establish that the centre of the main interests of the company concerned by the action is also situated in that other Member State. In order to reverse the presumption that this centre is the place of the registered office, it is necessary that an overall assessment of all the relevant factors allows it to be established, in a manner ascertainable by third parties, that the actual centre of management and supervision of the company concerned by the joinder action is situated in the Member State where the initial insolvency proceedings were opened.

20.9 *Kornhaas* Case

In *Kornhaas* (C-594/14 *Simona Kornhaas* v. *Thomas Dithmar,* [2015] ECLI: EU:C:2015:806), the reference was made in the course of insolvency proceedings opened in Germany by the Local Court of Erfurt. The debtor company, of which Ms Kornhaas was the director, was registered in the Companies Register of Cardiff (United Kingdom) as a private limited company and a branch of it was established in Germany. On that basis, the branch was registered in the Companies Register administered by the Local Court of Jena and the insolvency proceedings were opened in Germany.

Contending that the debtor company had been insolvent at least since 1 November 2006 and that, between 11 December 2006 and 26 February 2007, Ms Kornhaas had made payments borne by that company totalling €110,151.66, Mr Dithmar, liquidator of the debtor company, sought reimbursement of that sum from Ms Kornhaas on the basis of the first sentence of Paragraph 64(2) of the GmbHG (Gesellschaft mit beschränkter Haftung Gesetz, Law on limited-liability companies). Pursuant to this provision, '*the managing directors must reimburse the company with any payments which they made after the company became insolvent or after it was established that the company was over-indebted …*'.

The action was upheld by the Regional Court of Erfurt. Hearing the appeal brought by Ms Kornhaas, the Higher Regional Court of Jena confirmed the judgment delivered by the Regional Court of Erfurt, whilst giving permission for an appeal to the Bundesgerichtshof (Federal Court of Justice).

The Federal Court of Justice took the view that the action brought by Mr Dithmar was well founded under German law, the purpose of the first sentence of Paragraph 64(2) of the GmbHG being to prevent the assets of the insolvent estate being reduced before the opening of the insolvency proceedings. In the Federal Court's view therefore, that provision, although formally integrated in legislation on company law, would fall within insolvency law and would be enforceable against a managing director of a limited company.

The Federal Court of Justice was uncertain, however, whether such a provision was consistent with EU law. In that regard, pursuant to Article 4 (1) of Regulation No 1346/2000, the law applicable to insolvency proceedings and their effects would be German law, as the law of the Member State within the territory of which such proceedings were opened. There was no agreement in German scholarship on the question whether the first sentence of Paragraph 64(2) of the GmbHG may be enforceable against managing directors of companies established in accordance with the law of other EU Member States, but having the centre of their main interests in Germany.

According to the Federal Court of Justice, the first sentence of Article 64(2) of the GmbHG contained no infringement of the freedom of establishment and, in any case, such an infringement would have been justified on the grounds that: (i) it would be applied without discrimination; (ii) it would correspond to an overriding reason in the public interest, namely to protect creditors; (iii) it would be suitable for preserving the assets of the insolvent estate or restoring them; and (iv) would not go beyond what is necessary in order to attain that objective.

The referring court observed, however, that the case law of the CJEU following from, *inter alia*, the judgments in *Überseering* (*see,* Chapter 5, § 5.4) and *Inspire Art* (*see,* Chapter 6, § 6.4) could also be interpreted as meaning that the internal affairs of companies established in one Member State but carrying out their main operations in another Member State were, in the context of freedom of establishment, governed by the company law of the Member State of formation. The application of the first sentence of Paragraph 64(2) GmbHG to managing directors of companies of another Member State could accordingly infringe freedom of establishment within the meaning of Article 49 TFEU and Article 54 TFEU.

In those circumstances, the Federal Court of Justice decided to stay the proceedings and to refer, *inter alia*, the following essential question to the Court of Justice for a preliminary ruling:

C-594/14, Simona Kornhaas v. Thomas Dithmar, [2015] ECLI:EU: C:2015:806, § 13

If a liquidator brings an action before a German court against a director of a private limited company under the law of England and Wales, in respect of whose assets in Germany insolvency proceedings have been opened pursuant to Article 3(1) of Regulation No 1346/2000, the purpose of the action being to seek reimbursement of payments which the director made before the opening of the insolvency proceedings but after the company had become insolvent, does this action infringe freedom of establishment under Articles 49 and 54 TFEU?

The CJEU ruled as follows:

C-594/14, Simona Kornhaas v. Thomas Dithmar, [2015] ECLI:EU:C:2015:806, §§ 22–29

22. ... the referring court asks, in essence, whether Article 49 TFEU and Article 54 TFEU preclude the application of a provision of national law, such as the first sentence of Paragraph 64(2) of the GmbHG, to a managing director of a company established under the law of England and Wales, which is the subject of insolvency proceedings opened in Germany.
23. In that regard, it follows from the case-law of the Court that, in some circumstances, the refusal by one Member State to recognise the legal capacity of a company formed in accordance with the law of another Member State in which it has its registered office on the ground, in particular, that the company has moved its actual centre of administration to its territory may constitute a restriction of freedom of establishment incompatible, in principle, with Article 49 TFEU and Article 54 TFEU (see, to that effect, judgment in Überseering, C-208/00, EU:C:2002:632, paragraph 82).
24. The Court has also found before that, to the extent that national provisions concerning minimum capital are incompatible with freedom of establishment, as guaranteed by the Treaty, the same must necessarily be true of the penalties attached to noncompliance with those obligations, such as the personal joint and several liability of directors where the amount of capital does not reach the minimum provided for by the national legislation or where during the company's activities it falls below that amount (see, to that effect, judgment in Inspire Art, C-167/01, EU:C:2003:512, paragraph 141).
25. However, as regards a provision of national law such as the first sentence of Paragraph 64(2) of the GmbHG, it is clear that the latter concerns neither the refusal by a host Member State to recognise the legal capacity of a company formed in accordance with the law of another Member State and having transferred its actual headquarters into the territory of that first Member State, nor the personal liability of administrators where the capital of that company has not reached the minimum amount laid down by the national legislation.
26. First, it follows from the order for reference that the legal capacity of the debtor company is in no way called into question in the context of the case in the main proceedings. The wording of the first sentence of Paragraph 64(2) of the GmbHG even seems to exclude such questioning as the application of that provision presupposes the existence of a 'company'.

27. Second, the personal liability of the managing directors of a company on the basis of the first sentence of Paragraph 64(2) of the GmbHG is related, not to the fact that the capital of that company does not reach the minimum amount laid down by the German legislation or by the legislation in accordance with which that company has been established, but only to the fact that, in essence, the managing directors of such a company have made payments at a stage when they would have been required, under Paragraph 64(1) of the GmbHG, to apply for the opening of insolvency proceedings.
28. In the light of the above, the application of a provision of national law such as the first sentence of Paragraph 64(2) of the GmbHG in no way concerns the formation of a company in a given Member State or its subsequent establishment in another Member State, to the extent that that provision of national law is applicable only after that company has been formed, in connection with its business, and more specifically, either from the time when it must be considered, pursuant to the national law applicable under Article 4 of Regulation No 1346/2000, to be insolvent, or from the time when its over-debtedness is recognised in accordance with that national law. A provision of national law such as the first sentence of Paragraph 64(2) of the GmbHG does not, therefore, affect freedom of establishment.
29. In those circumstances, the answer to the second question is that Article 49 TFEU and Article 54 TFEU do not preclude the application of a national provision, such as the first sentence of Paragraph 64(2) of the GmbHG, to a managing director of a company established under the law of England and Wales which is the subject of insolvency proceedings opened in Germany.

FURTHER READING

Aleksandra Krawczyk-Giehsmann, 'Shareholders' Liability for Ruining a Company in Light of the CJEU's Judgment in Kornhaas', 21 *EBOR* 475–504 (2020).

20.10 Summary

The foregoing case law preview permits a summary of the EU *acquis* on cross-border insolvency.

As seen, the regime set by Regulation 848/2015 confines itself to the identification of the national court competent to open proceedings, the applicable law, and a mechanism for the automatic recognition of decisions.

Given such a narrow scope of application (and given the ambiguities that resulted from the previous regime set forth by Regulation 1346/2000), the contribution of the CJEU has been of the utmost importance to identify the boundaries of the European insolvency framework as well as its main concepts.

In particular, as far as the concept of COMI is concerned,

(a) the presumption laid down in favour of the registered office of a debtor company can be rebutted only if an overall assessment of all relevant factors (which must be both objective and ascertainable by third parties) enables it to be established that an actual situation exists which is different from that which locating it at that registered office is deemed to reflect. This can be the case, for example, of a 'letterbox company' not carrying out any business in the territory of the Member State in which its registered office is situated (*see*, C-341/04, *Eurofood*, §§ 34–35; C-191/10, *Rastelli*, § 39);
(b) the same presumption can be rebutted also if it is apparent from other objective evidence, ascertainable by third parties, that the company's actual centre of management and supervision and of the management of its interests is still located in the place where the registered office was placed before it has been moved (*see*, C-353/15, *Leonmobili srl*, Operative Part);
(c) a court of a Member State that has opened main insolvency proceedings against a debtor company, on the view that its COMI is situated in the territory of that Member State, can, under a rule of its national law, join to those proceedings a second company whose registered office is in another Member State only if it is established that the COMI of this second company is situated in the first Member State (*see*, C-191/10, *Rastelli*, §29).

As far as the relations between the four fundamental freedoms of the EU and cross-border insolvency issues are concerned, the CJEU largely referred to its case law dealing with freedom of establishment in holding that an infringement of the freedom of establishment may only occur where:

(a) a Member State refuses to recognise the legal capacity of a company formed in accordance with the law of another Member State in which it has its registered office on the ground, in particular, that the company has moved its actual centre of administration to its territory (*see*, *Überseering*, C-208/00, § 82; *Kornhaas*, C-594/14, § 23);
(b) a Member State provides for personal liability of administrators in case the capital of a company formed in accordance with the law of another Member State has not reached the minimum amount laid down by the national legislation (*see*, *Inspire Art*, C-167/01, § 141; *Kornhaas*, C-594/14, § 24).

Therefore, a national provision allowing a liquidator to bring a reimbursement action *vis-à-vis* a director of a company registered in another Member State does not fall within these two circumstances and thus cannot be deemed to violate the freedom of establishment.

20.11 Members of a Group of Companies

As it is apparent from both the *Eurofood* and *Rastelli* cases, no provision concerning groups of companies was contained under the Regulation of 2000.

This considerable omission was mainly due to two reasons. The first one is that when the Regulation was negotiated between the 1980s and 1990s, the phenomenon of groups of companies was not as widespread as it is today. The second, and perhaps weightier reason, is that the subject raised complex problems, and the European institutions may have considered politically and practically prudent to postpone it to a later date.

In any case, the lack of such measures has in fact caused enormous problems, resulting in the need to open separate proceedings for each individual member of the group.

The Recast Regulation has therefore filled this loophole by introducing a new chapter (Chapter V) entirely dedicated to insolvency proceedings of members of a group of companies. The grounds for the new chapter are expressed in the new preamble.

Recital 51 Regulation 2015/848/EU

This Regulation should ensure the efficient administration of insolvency proceedings relating to different companies forming part of a group of companies.

Recital 53 Regulation 2015/848/EU

The introduction of rules on the insolvency proceedings of groups of companies should not limit the possibility for a court to open insolvency proceedings for several companies belonging to the same group in a single jurisdiction if the court finds that the centre of main interests of those companies is located in a single Member State. In such cases, the court should also be able to appoint, if appropriate, the same insolvency practitioner in all proceedings concerned, provided that this is not incompatible with the rules applicable to them.

Specifically, Chapter V tackles the problem of insolvency of groups' members by adopting a two-fold approach: on the one hand, it establishes a duty of cooperation and communication between the actors involved in these proceedings.

Recital 52 Regulation 2015/848/EU

Where insolvency proceedings have been opened for several companies of the same group, there should be proper cooperation between the actors involved in those proceedings. The various insolvency practitioners and the courts involved should therefore be under a similar obligation to cooperate and communicate with each other as those involved in [the] main and secondary insolvency proceedings relating to the same debtor. Cooperation between the insolvency practitioners should not run counter to the interests of the creditors in each of the proceedings, and such cooperation should be aimed at finding a solution that would leverage synergies across the group.

On the other hand, the new chapter creates the so-called group coordination proceedings.

Recital 57 Regulation 2015/848/EU

Group coordination proceedings should always strive to facilitate the effective administration of the insolvency proceedings of the group members, and to have a generally positive impact for the creditors. This Regulation should therefore ensure that the court with which a request for group coordination proceedings has been filed makes an assessment of those criteria prior to opening group coordination proceedings.

In more detail, the opening of such proceedings can be requested before any court having jurisdiction over the insolvency proceedings of a member of the group by an insolvency practitioner appointed in the context of a member's proceedings.

The court granting the opening shall then appoint an independent coordinator, whose tasks are set out under Article 72.

Article 72 Regulation 2015/848/EU

1. The coordinator shall:
   (a) identify and outline recommendations for the coordinated conduct of the insolvency proceedings;
   (b) propose a group coordination plan that identifies, describes and recommends a comprehensive set of measures appropriate to an integrated approach to the resolution of the group members' insolvencies. In particular, the plan may contain proposals for:
      (i) the measures to be taken in order to re-establish the economic performance and the financial soundness of the group or any part of it;
      (ii) the settlement of intra-group disputes as regards intra-group transactions and avoidance actions;
      (iii) agreements between the insolvency practitioners of the insolvent group members.

2. The coordinator may also:
   (a) be heard and participate, in particular by attending creditors' meetings, in any of the proceedings opened in respect of any member of the group;
   (b) mediate any dispute arising between two or more insolvency practitioners of group members;
   (c) present and explain his or her group coordination plan to the persons or bodies that he or she is to report to under his or her national law;
   (d) request information from any insolvency practitioner in respect of any member of the group where that information is or might be of use when identifying and outlining strategies and measures in order to coordinate the proceedings; and
   (e) request a stay for a period of up to 6 months of the proceedings opened in respect of any member of the group, provided that such a stay is necessary in order to ensure the proper implementation of the plan and would be to the benefit of the creditors in the proceedings for which the stay is requested; or request the lifting of any existing stay. Such a request shall be made to the court that opened the proceedings for which a stay is requested ...

FURTHER READING

Arie Van Hoe, 'Enterprise Groups and their Insolvency: It's the (Common) Interest, Stupid!', 11 *ECFR* 200–213 (2014).

20.12 Restructuring, Insolvency, and Discharge of Debt: An Overview

As anticipated, the Parliament and the EU Commission have approved Directive 2019/1023/EU of 20 June 2019 on preventive restructuring frameworks, on discharge of debt and disqualifications, and on measures to increase the efficiency of procedures concerning restructuring, insolvency, and discharge of debt ('Directive on Restructuring'). The issues addressed by this Directive are mostly beyond the scope of this book, as they refer to all debtors, not only and not specifically to companies. It is however useful to have a brief overview and to set out the implications of such a Directive as regards company law.

First of all, Recital 12 to Directive 2019/1023/EU acknowledges that Regulation 2015/848/EU deals with issues of jurisdiction, recognition, and enforcement, applicable law and cooperation in cross-border insolvency proceedings as well as with the interconnection of insolvency registers. Its scope covers preventive procedures which promote the rescue of economically viable debtors as well as discharge procedures for entrepreneurs and other natural persons. However, the Regulation does not tackle the disparities between national laws regulating those procedures. Furthermore, an instrument limited only to cross-border insolvencies would not remove all obstacles to free movement, nor would it be feasible for investors to determine in advance the cross-border or domestic nature of the potential financial difficulties of the debtor in the future. There is, therefore, a need to go beyond matters of judicial cooperation and to establish substantive minimum standards for preventive restructuring procedures as well as for procedures leading to a discharge of debt for entrepreneurs.

The directive sums up the actual state of the law of Member States as follows.

Recitals 4–6 Directive 2019/1023/EU

(4) There are differences between Member States as regards the range of the procedures available to debtors in financial difficulties in order to restructure their business. Some Member States have a limited range of procedures that allow the restructuring of businesses only at a relatively late stage, in the context of insolvency procedures. In other Member States, restructuring is possible at an earlier stage but the procedures available are not as effective as they could be, or they are very formal, in particular because they limit the use of out-of-court arrangements. Preventive solutions are a growing trend in insolvency law. The trend favours approaches that, unlike the traditional approach of liquidating a business in financial difficulties, have the aim of restoring it to a healthy state or, at least, saving those of its units which are still economically viable. That approach, among other benefits to the economy, often helps to maintain jobs or reduce job losses. Moreover, the degree of involvement of judicial or administrative authorities, or the persons appointed by them, varies from no involvement or minimal involvement in some Member States to full involvement in others. Similarly, national rules giving entrepreneurs a second chance, in particular by granting them discharge from the debts they have incurred in the course of their business, vary between Member States in respect of the length of the discharge period and the conditions for granting such a discharge.

(5) In many Member States, it takes more than three years for entrepreneurs who are insolvent but honest to be discharged from their debts and make a fresh start. Inefficient discharge of debt and disqualification frameworks result in entrepreneurs having to relocate to other jurisdictions in order to benefit from a fresh start in a reasonable period of time, at considerable additional cost to both their creditors and the entrepreneurs themselves. Long disqualification orders, which often accompany a procedure leading to discharge of debt, create obstacles to the freedom to take up and pursue a self-employed, entrepreneurial activity.

(6) The excessive length of procedures concerning restructuring, insolvency and discharge of debt in several Member States is an important factor triggering low recovery rates and deterring investors from carrying out business in jurisdictions where procedures risk taking too long and being unduly costly.

Having described this picture, Directive 2019/1023/EU pinpoints the importance of an early action which would ultimately enable a firm to avoid an insolvency from which recovery is impossible or, at least, too costly.

As already mentioned (§ 11.6), the company law of some European Member States (such as Italy and Sweden, and, for some aspects, France and Spain) requires that, in cases of serious losses of the stated capital and bringing the net assets below the value of the minimum capital requirement, a recapitalise or liquidate rule (ROL) shall operate. The ROL may be considered an early action tool required in the likelihood of insolvency, which is triggered by serious losses. The Directive on Restructuring does not recognise the ROL as a mandatory tool, rather it acknowledges the existence of other events triggering early warning tools, such as non-payment of taxes or social security contributions. Such events take the form of alert mechanisms urging immediate and appropriate restructuring measures to be taken.

Recitals 22–24 Directive 2019/1023/EU

(22) The earlier a debtor can detect its financial difficulties and can take appropriate action, the higher the probability of avoiding an impending insolvency or, in the case of a business the viability of which is permanently impaired, the more orderly and efficient the liquidation process would be. Clear, up-to-date, concise and user-friendly information on the available preventive restructuring procedures as well as one or more early warning tools should therefore be put in place to incentivise debtors that start to experience financial difficulties to take early action. Early warning tools which take the form of alert mechanisms that indicate when the debtor has not made certain types of payments could be triggered by, for example, non-payment of taxes or social security contributions. Such tools could be developed either by Member States or by private entities, provided that the objective is met. Member States should make information about early warning tools available online, for example on a dedicated website or webpage. Member States should be able to adapt the early warning tools depending on the size of the enterprise and to lay down specific provisions on early warning tools for large-sized enterprises and groups that take into account their peculiarities. This Directive should not impose any liability on Member States for potential damage incurred through restructuring procedures which are triggered by such early warning tools.

(...)

(24) A restructuring framework should be available to debtors, including legal entities and, where so provided under national law, natural persons and groups of companies, to enable them to address their financial difficulties at an early stage, when it appears likely that their insolvency can be prevented and the viability of the business can be ensured. A restructuring framework should be available before a debtor becomes insolvent under national law, namely before the debtor fulfils the conditions under

national law for entering collective insolvency proceedings, which normally entail a total divestment of the debtor and the appointment of a liquidator. In order to avoid restructuring frameworks being misused, the financial difficulties of the debtor should indicate a likelihood of insolvency and the restructuring plan should be capable of preventing the insolvency of the debtor and ensuring the viability of the business.

As specifically concerns companies, Article 19 Directive 2019/1023/EU specifies that Member States shall ensure that, where there is a likelihood of insolvency, directors of companies have due regard, as a minimum, to: (a) the interests of creditors, equity holders, and other stakeholders; (b) the need to take steps to avoid insolvency; and (c) the need to avoid deliberate or grossly negligent conduct that threatens the viability of the business.

Whether it is possible to acknowledge, in a timely manner, the likelihood of insolvency is a widely discussed issue amongst legal scholars and courts, especially in the US. US case law affirms that a corporation is in the zone of insolvency when it is close enough to insolvency that a reasonable person would know that its ability to pay creditors is significantly threatened (*Wooley* v. *Lucksinger*, 2008 WL 6457570 (So.2d) (La.App. 1 Cir., 2008)). In a famous case which occurred in the early 90s, the Delaware Chancery Court affirmed that at least where a corporation is operating in the zone or vicinity of insolvency, a board of directors is not merely the agent of the residue risk bearers, but owes its duty to the corporate enterprise, and so to all stakeholders including creditors (*Credit Lyonnais Bank Nederland, N.V.* v. *Pathe Communications Corp.*, No. Civ. A. 12150, 1991 WL 277613 (Del. Ch. Dec. 20, 1991)). This principle was later overruled in 2007 when the Supreme Court of Delaware affirmed that when a solvent corporation is navigating in the zone of insolvency, the focus for Delaware directors does not change: directors must continue to discharge their fiduciary duties to the corporation and its shareholders by exercising their business judgment in the best interests of the corporation for the benefit of its shareholder owners (*North American Catholic Educational Programming Foundation, Inc.* v. *Gheewalla*, 930 A.2d 92 (Del. 2007)).

The European approach to such issues, before the Directive on Restructuring will be implemented, is various although fundamentally converging. Some legislations care more about early warning tools and focus on directors' liability in cases where creditors or other stakeholders suffer prejudice from delayed actions: among these not only legislations requiring the ROL, but also those favouring alert measures (France) or implementing the so-called wrongful trading rule (*see*, UK's Section 214 Insolvency Act 1986); some other legislations (such as Germany and Spain), instead, focus more on a prompt filing for bankruptcy, within a predetermined time-frame – from three weeks to two months after insolvency has surfaced – and merely allow directors to stop operations in the likelihood of insolvency (so-called *drohende* Zahlungsunfähigkeit or *insolvencia inminente*). Italy has anticipated the implementation of the Directive on Restructuring: the new Italian bankruptcy code (leg. dec. n. 14/2019), considering the likelihood of insolvency ('business crisis or financial distress') as a relevant condition, provides for alert mechanisms (the application of which, however, is very controversial in practice and, thus, entry into force has been postponed to 2021) and for various restructuring tools; also, an amendment to the civil code adopts the wrongful trading rule in case directors delay to undertake the necessary actions (Article 2486(3) Italian Civil Code).

Article 214 Insolvency Act 1986 – Wrongful trading

(1) Subject to subsection (3) below, if in the course of the winding up of a company it appears that subsection (2) of this section applies in relation to a person who is or has been a director of the company, the court, on the application of the liquidator, may declare that that person is to be liable to make such contribution (if any) to the company's assets as the court thinks proper.

(2) This subsection applies in relation to a person if—

(a) the company has gone into insolvent liquidation,

(b) at some time before the commencement of the winding up of the company, that person knew or ought to have concluded that there was no reasonable prospect that the company would avoid going into insolvent liquidation, and

(c) that person was a director of the company at that time;

but the court shall not make a declaration under this section in any case where the time mentioned in paragraph (b) above was before 28th April 1986.

(3) The court shall not make a declaration under this section with respect to any person if it is satisfied that after the condition specified in subsection (2)(b) was first satisfied in relation to him that person took every step with a view to minimising the potential loss to the company's creditors as (on the assumption that he had knowledge of the matter mentioned in subsection (2)(b)) he ought to have taken.

(4) For the purposes of subsections (2) and (3), the facts which a director of a company ought to know or ascertain, the conclusions which he ought to reach and the steps which he ought to take are those which would be known or ascertained, or reached or taken, by a reasonably diligent person having both—

(a) the general knowledge, skill and experience that may reasonably be expected of a person carrying out the same functions as are carried out by that director in relation to the company, and

(b) the general knowledge, skill and experience that that director has.

(5) The reference in subsection (4) to the functions carried out in relation to a company by a director of the company includes any functions which he does not carry out but which have been entrusted to him.

(6) For the purposes of this section a company goes into insolvent liquidation if it goes into liquidation at a time when its assets are insufficient for the payment of its debts and other liabilities and the expenses of the winding up.
(6A) For the purposes of this section a company enters insolvent administration if it enters administration at a time when its assets are insufficient for the payment of its debts and other liabilities and the expenses of the administration.
(7) In this section 'director' includes a shadow director.
(8) This Section is without prejudice to section 213.

It is widely recognized that the Directive on Restructuring was largely inspired by the famous Chapter 11 of US Bankruptcy Code as regards reorganizations. Reorganizations are based on a free bargaining between the debtor and the creditors as a whole, deciding upon majority vote. Negotiations shall be conducted in a situation where single creditors are banned from bringing individual enforcement actions for the recovery of their credits ('automatic stay'). Also, similarly as in US Chapter 11, filing for 'bankruptcy protection' permits debtors to retain control over their businesses ('debtor in possession'), generally without even the need of an appointed practitioner ('trustee') to oversee the negotiations. As the Directive puts it,

Recitals 30–32 Directive 2019/1023/EU

(30) To avoid unnecessary costs, to reflect the early nature of preventive restructuring and to encourage debtors to apply for preventive restructuring at an early stage of their financial difficulties, they should, in principle, be left in control of their assets and the day-to-day operation of their business. The appointment of a practitioner in the field of restructuring, to supervise the activity of a debtor or to partially take over control of a debtor's daily operations, should not be mandatory in every case, but made on a case-by-case basis depending on the circumstances of the case or on the debtor's specific needs. Nevertheless, Member States should be able to determine that the appointment of a practitioner in the field of restructuring is always necessary in certain circumstances, such as where: the debtor benefits from a general stay of individual enforcement actions; the restructuring plan needs to be confirmed by means of a cross-class cram-down; the restructuring plan includes measures affecting the rights of workers; or the debtor or its management have acted in a criminal, fraudulent, or detrimental manner in business relations.
(31) For the purpose of assisting the parties with negotiating and drafting a restructuring plan, Member States should provide for the mandatory appointment of a practitioner in the field of restructuring where: a judicial or administrative authority grants the debtor a general stay of individual enforcement actions, provided that in such case a practitioner is needed to safeguard the interests of the parties; the restructuring plan needs to be confirmed by a judicial or administrative authority by means of a cross-class cram-down; it was requested by the debtor; or it is requested by a majority of creditors provided that the creditors cover the costs and fees of the practitioner.

(32) A debtor should be able to benefit from a temporary stay of individual enforcement actions, whether granted by a judicial or administrative authority or by operation of law, with the aim of supporting the negotiations on a restructuring plan, in order to be able to continue operating or at least to preserve the value of its estate during the negotiations. Where so provided by national law, it should also be possible for the stay to apply for the benefit of third-party security providers, including guarantors and collateral givers. However, Member States should be able to provide that judicial or administrative authorities can refuse to grant a stay of individual enforcement actions where such a stay is not necessary or where it would not fulfil the objective of supporting the negotiations. Grounds for refusal might include a lack of support by the required majorities of creditors or, where so provided under national law, the debtor's actual inability to pay debts as they fall due.

Article 5 Directive 2019/1023/EU

1. Member States shall ensure that debtors accessing preventive restructuring procedures remain totally, or at least partially, in control of their assets and the day-to-day operation of their business.
2. Where necessary, the appointment by a judicial or administrative authority of a practitioner in the field of restructuring shall be decided on a case-by-case basis, except in certain circumstances where Member States may require the mandatory appointment of such a practitioner in every case.
3. Member States shall provide for the appointment of a practitioner in the field of restructuring, to assist the debtor and creditors in negotiating and drafting the plan, at least in the following cases:
   (a) where a general stay of individual enforcement actions, in accordance with Article 6(3), is granted by a judicial or administrative authority, and the judicial or administrative authority decides that such a practitioner is necessary to safeguard the interest of the parties;
   (b) where the restructuring plan needs to be confirmed by a judicial or administrative authority by means of a cross-class cram-down, in accordance with Article 11; or
   (c) where it is requested by the debtor or by a majority of the creditors, provided that, in the latter case, the cost of the practitioner is borne by the creditors.

Article 6 Directive 2019/1023/EU

1. Member States shall ensure that debtors can benefit from a stay of individual enforcement actions to support the negotiations of a restructuring plan in a preventive restructuring framework.

Member States may provide that judicial or administrative authorities can refuse to grant a stay of individual enforcement actions where such a stay is not necessary or where it would not achieve the objective set out in the first subparagraph.

2. Without prejudice to paragraphs 4 and 5, Member States shall ensure that a stay of individual enforcement actions can cover all types of claims, including secured claims and preferential claims.
3. Member States may provide that a stay of individual enforcement actions can be general, covering all creditors, or can be limited, covering one or more individual creditors or categories of creditors.

Where a stay is limited, the stay shall only apply to creditors that have been informed, in accordance with national law, of negotiations as referred to in paragraph 1 on the restructuring plan or of the stay.

4. Member States may exclude certain claims or categories of claims from the scope of the stay of individual enforcement actions, in well-defined circumstances, where such an exclusion is duly justified and where:
   (a) enforcement is not likely to jeopardise the restructuring of the business; or
   (b) the stay would unfairly prejudice the creditors of those claims.
5. Paragraph 2 shall not apply to workers' claims.

By way of derogation from the first subparagraph, Member States may apply paragraph 2 to workers' claims if, and to the extent that, Member States ensure that the payment of such claims is guaranteed in preventive restructuring frameworks at a similar level of protection.

6. The initial duration of a stay of individual enforcement actions shall be limited to a maximum period of no more than four months.
7. Notwithstanding paragraph 6, Member States may enable judicial or administrative authorities to extend the duration of a stay of individual enforcement actions or to grant a new stay of individual enforcement actions, at the request of the debtor, a creditor or, where applicable, a practitioner in the field of restructuring. Such extension or new stay of individual enforcement actions shall be granted only if well-defined circumstances show that such extension or new stay is duly justified, such as:
   (a) relevant progress has been made in the negotiations on the restructuring plan;
   (b) the continuation of the stay of individual enforcement actions does not unfairly prejudice the rights or interests of any affected parties; or
   (c) insolvency proceedings which could end in the liquidation of the debtor under national law have not yet been opened in respect of the debtor.
8. The total duration of the stay of individual enforcement actions, including extensions and renewals, shall not exceed 12 months.

Where Member States choose to implement this Directive by means of one or more procedures or measures which do not fulfil the conditions for notification under Annex A to Regulation (EU) 2015/848, the total duration of the stay under such procedures shall be limited to no more than four months if the centre of main interests of the debtor has been transferred from another Member State within a three-month period prior to the filing of a request for the opening of preventive restructuring proceedings.

9. Member States shall ensure that judicial or administrative authorities can lift a stay of individual enforcement actions in the following cases:
   (a) the stay no longer fulfils the objective of supporting the negotiations on the restructuring plan, for example if it becomes apparent that a proportion of creditors which, under national law, could prevent the adoption of the restructuring plan do not support the continuation of the negotiations;
   (b) at the request of the debtor or the practitioner in the field of restructuring;
   (c) where so provided for in national law, if one or more creditors or one or more classes of creditors are, or would be, unfairly prejudiced by a stay of individual enforcement actions; or
   (d) where so provided for in national law, if the stay gives rise to the insolvency of a creditor.

Member States may limit the power, under the first subparagraph, to lift the stay of individual enforcement actions to situations where creditors had not had the opportunity to be heard before the stay came into force or before an extension of the period was granted by a judicial or administrative authority.

Member States may provide for a minimum period, which does not exceed the period referred to in paragraph 6, during which a stay of individual enforcement actions cannot be lifted.

As mentioned, negotiations on restructuring measures are aimed at finding an agreement on the implementation of a plan. The agreement is found when a restructuring plan proposed by the debtor is approved by creditors upon majority vote. Despite approval by majority vote, Member States shall ensure that restructuring plans are binding on the parties only if they are confirmed by a judicial or administrative authority. The same authority shall consider claims lodged by dissenting creditors. In cases where creditors are organised in classes and not all classes have favourably approved the plan, the authority shall carry a scrutiny of the plan and verify whether the dissenting class is negatively affected by the restructuring plan in a way which departs from the normal ranking of liquidation priorities to be applied under national law ('cram-down').

Article 10 Directive 2019/1023/EU

1. Member States shall ensure that at least the following restructuring plans are binding on the parties only if they are confirmed by a judicial or administrative authority:
   (a) restructuring plans which affect the claims or interests of dissenting affected parties;

(b) restructuring plans which provide for new financing;
(c) restructuring plans which involve the loss of more than 25 % of the workforce, if such loss is permitted under national law.

2. Member States shall ensure that the conditions under which a restructuring plan can be confirmed by a judicial or administrative authority are clearly specified and include at least the following:
   (a) the restructuring plan has been adopted in accordance with Article 9;
   (b) creditors with sufficient commonality of interest in the same class are treated equally, and in a manner proportionate to their claim;
   (c) notification of the restructuring plan has been given in accordance with national law to all affected parties;
   (d) where there are dissenting creditors, the restructuring plan satisfies the best-interest-of-creditors test;
   (e) where applicable, any new financing is necessary to implement the restructuring plan and does not unfairly prejudice the interests of creditors.

Compliance with point (d) of the first subparagraph shall be examined by a judicial or administrative authority only if the restructuring plan is challenged on that ground.

3. Member States shall ensure that judicial or administrative authorities are able to refuse to confirm a restructuring plan where that plan would not have a reasonable prospect of preventing the insolvency of the debtor or ensuring the viability of the business.
4. Member States shall ensure that where a judicial or administrative authority is required to confirm a restructuring plan in order for it to become binding, the decision is taken in an efficient manner with a view to expeditious treatment of the matter.

Article 11 Directive 2019/1023/EU

1. Member States shall ensure that a restructuring plan which is not approved by affected parties, as provided for in Article 9(6), in every voting class, may be confirmed by a judicial or administrative authority upon the proposal of a debtor or with the debtor's agreement, and become binding upon dissenting voting classes where the restructuring plan fulfils at least the following conditions:
   (a) it complies with Article 10(2) and (3);
   (b) it has been approved by:
      (i) a majority of the voting classes of affected parties, provided that at least one of those classes is a secured creditors class or is senior to the ordinary unsecured creditors class; or, failing that,
      (ii) at least one of the voting classes of affected parties or where so provided under national law, impaired parties, other than an equity-holders class or any other

class which, upon a valuation of the debtor as a going concern, would not receive any payment or keep any interest, or, where so provided under national law, which could be reasonably presumed not to receive any payment or keep any interest, if the normal ranking of liquidation priorities were applied under national law;

(c) it ensures that dissenting voting classes of affected creditors are treated at least as favourably as any other class of the same rank and more favourably than any junior class; and

(d) no class of affected parties can, under the restructuring plan, receive or keep more than the full amount of its claims or interests.

By way of derogation from the first subparagraph, Member States may limit the requirement to obtain the debtor's agreement to cases where debtors are SMEs.

Member States may increase the minimum number of classes of affected parties or, where so provided under national law, impaired parties, required to approve the plan as laid down in point (b)(ii) of the first subparagraph.

2. By way of derogation from point (c) of paragraph 1, Member States may provide that the claims of affected creditors in a dissenting voting class are satisfied in full by the same or equivalent means where a more junior class is to receive any payment or keep any interest under the restructuring plan.

Member States may maintain or introduce provisions derogating from the first subparagraph where they are necessary in order to achieve the aims of the restructuring plan and where the restructuring plan does not unfairly prejudice the rights or interests of any affected parties.

Article 14 Directive 2019/1023/EU

1. The judicial or administrative authority shall take a decision on the valuation of the debtor's business only where a restructuring plan is challenged by a dissenting affected party on the grounds of either:
   (a) an alleged failure to satisfy the best-interest-of-creditors test under point (6) of Article 2(1); or
   (b) an alleged breach of the conditions for a cross-class cram-down under point (ii) of Article 11(1)(b).
2. Member States shall ensure that, for the purpose of taking a decision on a valuation in accordance with paragraph 1, judicial or administrative authorities may appoint or hear properly qualified experts.
3. For the purposes of paragraph 1, Member States shall ensure that a dissenting affected party may lodge a challenge with the judicial or administrative authority called upon to confirm the restructuring plan.

Member States may provide that such a challenge can be lodged in the context of an appeal against a decision on the confirmation of a restructuring plan.

With respect to the restructuring of companies, the role of equity holders is also important. As there is a possible conflict of interest for equity holders, if they are not permitted to take advantage of the restructuring plan, Member States shall ensure by other means that those equity holders are not allowed to unreasonably prevent or create obstacles to the adoption and confirmation of a restructuring plan (Article 12 Directive 2019/1023/EU).

FURTHER READING

Federico Pernazza, 'The Legal Transplant in Italian Law of the Procédure d'Alerte. Duties and Responsibilities of the Companies' Bodies', 3 *Italian Law Journal*, 553–583 (2017).

Danilo Scarlino, 'Zone of Insolvency, Directors' Duties and Creditors' Protection in U.S.', 29 *EBLR* 1–31 (2018).

Sergio Coimbra Henriques, 'The Duties of Directors When There Is a Likelihood of Insolvency and the Proposal for a New Directive', 16 *ECL* 50–57 (2019).

Gaia Balp, 'Early Warning Tools at the Crossroads of Insolvency Law and Company Law', 19 *Global Jurist*, 1–22 (2019).

Index